"This commentary on Matthew is a welco͞r has developed a well-deserved reputation foɪ ᴄxᴄᴇɴᴄᴇ ɪɴ ɪɴɪ ᴊᴄɴᴏɪᴀɪɴɪpɪ ᴏᴜᴜ will only add to that reputation. It is a go-to-text for anyone who wishes to rightly interpret the first gospel."

—Daniel L. Akin, president, Southeastern Baptist Theological Seminary

"At a time when more and more people are bemoaning the state of teaching and preaching in our churches, it's refreshing to read one Greek teacher who is trying to make things right. Quarles will give you a thorough immersion into the Greek text of Matthew without being pedantic or overly technical. His superbly researched work is foundational for the study of the first Gospel. Here's a guide that shows you the right way to use your Greek in ministry. My favorite sections are the 'homiletical sugges- tions' that are based on the text itself. Quarles is fast acquiring master status on the Gospel of Matthew."

—David Alan Black, Dr. M. O. Owens Jr. Chair of New Testament Studies and professor of New Testament and Greek, Southeastern Baptist Theological Seminary

"Quarles continues to distinguish himself as one of today's leading Matthean schol- ars with this commentary. Unlike the other volumes in the EGGNT series thus far, this is not a survey of the best of previous commentators with assessment of inter- pretive debates, but a full-fledged grammatical and discourse analysis of Matthew itself. Quarles blends the best of the classic Mounce/Wallace approach with the best of the newer Levinson/Runge approach to create a work like the Baylor Handbook on the Greek New Testament on steroids. A wonderful gift to both the academy and the church."

—Craig L. Blomberg, Distinguished Professor of New Testament, Denver Seminary

"Quarles has provided exegetes of the Greek New Testament a model guide for the study and interpretation of the Gospel of Matthew. Readers will be impressed by the way this scholar and master teacher weighs the lexical and grammatical options judi- ciously and clearly. Quarles's commentary is learned yet very readable. All exegetes of the Greek text will benefit from this carefully written book. I highly recommend it."

—Craig A. Evans, John Bisagno Distinguished Professor of Christian Origins, Houston Baptist University

"These volumes aim to close the gap between the Greek text and the available tools: Greek language tools on the one side and commentaries and other studies on New Testament texts on the other. Quarles fills this gap admirably for Matthew. We get clear presentation, balanced judgments and a good sense of the value and limitations of language analysis for understanding this Gospel."

—John Nolland, tutor in New Testament, Trinity College, Bristol, UK

"Of all the recently published New Testament and Greek resources, the EGGNT series is the one that excites me the most. You can think of this volume as a seminary-level Greek exegesis course in paperback. Also, each EGGNT volume provides sermon outlines based on the structure of the Greek text—connecting meticulous exegetical analysis to the faithful preaching and teaching of God's Word.

Quarles's excellent new volume on Matthew will not disappoint. It is a faithful guide to the Greek text and will benefit students, pastors, and scholars for years to come."

—Robert L. Plummer, professor of New Testament interpretation, The Southern Baptist Theological Seminary and host, Daily Dose of Greek

The Exegetical Guide to the Greek New Testament

Volumes Available

Matthew	Charles L. Quarles
Luke	Alan J. Thompson
John	Murray J. Harris
Romans	John D. Harvey
Ephesians	Benjamin L. Merkle
Philippians	Joseph H. Hellerman
Colossians, Philemon	Murray J. Harris
James	Chris A. Vlachos
1 Peter	Greg W. Forbes

Forthcoming Volumes

Mark	Joel F. Williams
Acts	L. Scott Kellum
1 Corinthians	Jay E. Smith
2 Corinthians	Colin G. Kruse
Galatians	David A. Croteau
1–2 Thessalonians	David W. Chapman
1–2 Timothy, Titus	Ray Van Neste
Hebrews	Dana M. Harris
2 Peter, Jude	Terry L. Wilder
1–3 John	Robert L. Plummer
Revelation	Bruce N. Fisk

EXEGETICAL
GUIDE TO THE
GREEK
NEW
TESTAMENT

MATTHEW

Charles L. Quarles

EXEGETICAL
GUIDE TO THE **MATTHEW**
GREEK
NEW
TESTAMENT

Andreas J. Köstenberger
Robert W. Yarbrough
GENERAL EDITORS

ACADEMIC
Nashville, Tennessee

ISBN: 978-1-4336-7616-1

Dewey Decimal Classification: 226.2
Subject Heading: BIBLE N.T. MATTHEW-STUDY\BIBLE-CRITICISM

Printed in the United States of America
1 2 3 4 5 6 7 8 9 10 • 22 21 20 19 18 17

VP

To Richard R. Melick, Jr.
for his admirable fulfillment of
2 Timothy 2:2

Contents

MATTHEW

Preface

It is an honor to contribute this volume to the Exegetical Guide to the Greek New Testament series. As a student learning Greek, a pastor preparing sermons, and a professor teaching Greek exegesis, I found Murray Harris's volume on Colossians and Philemon to be enormously helpful. I was grieved when another publisher discontinued the original series. Over a decade ago I urged (practically begged) B&H Academic to revive it. Thus I was thrilled to see them undertake this much needed, but in some ways daunting, publication project.

I am grateful to Ray Clendenen for recognizing the need to encourage study of the biblical languages and for championing this project in its early stages. I commend Murray Harris for setting a high standard for the series with the revision of his initial work. His volume on the Gospel of John in this series provided a helpful model for my own work. Bob Yarbrough used his skill as a Greek scholar in carefully editing my particular volume. His eye for detail has strengthened the volume in a number of ways.

President Danny Akin, Provost Bruce Ashford, Dean Chuck Lawless, and the trustees of Southeastern Baptist Theological Seminary granted me two half sabbaticals, during which I wrote most of this volume. They graciously granted the first half sabbatical after I had taught at SEBTS for only one semester! This demonstrates the administration's commitment to the advancement of biblical scholarship and is but one example of many kindnesses shown to me.

Several of the New Testament students in the PhD program at Southeastern Baptist Theological Seminary proofread various chapters. Students in the spring 2015 Seminar on the Greek Text of Matthew worked through the first half of the book and made helpful suggestions. They include Levi Baker, Thomas Cribb, David Crowther, Michael Guyer, Chris Jones, Noah Kelley, Shane Koehler, Andrew Koetsier, Shane Kraeger, Greg Lamb, David Miller, Jon Morales, Daniel Roberts. My teaching assistant, David Flannery, proofread most of the book and spotted several additional careless mistakes. I am especially grateful to Christy Thornton for preparing the grammar index and to Robbie Booth for preparing the Greek index.

Director Jason Fowler and his excellent staff at the library at SEBTS aided my work in numerous ways. I thank them for tracking down some difficult-to-find resources and for scanning and emailing materials to me as I worked at my home office. Director

Fowler even offered tips to expedite my research in this digital world that later bene-fitted me greatly.

For several years I have looked forward to dedicating this volume to my mentor and friend, Richard R. Melick Jr. Several years ago, after I taught a Bible study in a local church, a participant complimented me with the words, "You remind me of Curtis Vaughn!" I explained that I had never personally met Dr. Vaughn but that I greatly respected him and felt like I knew him since he mentored the man who had mentored me, Rick Melick.

I hope that one day one of my students will teach or preach somewhere and a mem-ber of the audience will approach him afterward and say, "You remind me of Richard Melick." I trust that the student will express thanks for that high compliment and reply, "I have never met Dr. Melick, but I greatly respect him and feel like I know him because he mentored the man who mentored me." The expression of respect for Dr. Melick will be a tribute to one whose life is a remarkable fulfillment of Paul's admo-nition: "And what you have heard from me in the presence of many witnesses, commit to faithful men who will be able to teach others also" (2 Tim 2:2 CSB).

Charles L. Quarles
December 2015

Publisher's Preface

It is with great excitement that we publish this volume of the Exegetical Guide to the Greek New Testament series. When the founding editor, Dr. Murray J. Harris, came to us seeking a new publishing partner, we gratefully accepted the offer. With the help of the coeditor, Andreas J. Köstenberger, we spent several years working together to acquire all of the authors we needed to complete the series. By God's grace we succeeded and contracted the last author in 2011. Originally working with another publishing house, Murray's efforts spanned more than twenty years. As God would have it, shortly after the final author was contracted, Murray decided God wanted him to withdraw as coeditor of the series. God made clear to him that he must devote his full attention to taking care of his wife, who faces the daily challenges caused by multiple sclerosis.

Over the course of many years, God has used Murray to teach his students how to properly exegete the Scriptures. He is an exceptional scholar and professor. But even more importantly, Murray is a man dedicated to serving Christ. His greatest joy is to respond in faithful obedience when his master calls. "There can be no higher and more ennobling privilege than to have the Lord of the universe as one's Owner and Master and to be his accredited representative on earth."[1] Murray has once again heeded the call of his master.

It is our privilege to dedicate the Exegetical Guide to the Greek New Testament series to Dr. Murray J. Harris. We pray that our readers will continue the work he started.

B&H Academic

---

1. Murray J. Harris, *Slave of Christ: A New Testament Metaphor for Total Devotion to Christ* (Downers Grove: InterVarsity, 1999), 155.

General Introduction to the EGGNT Series

Studying the New Testament in the original Greek has become easier in recent years. Beginning students will work their way through an introductory grammar or other text, but then what? Grappling with difficult verb forms, rare vocabulary, and grammatical irregularities remains a formidable task for those who would advance beyond the initial stages of learning Greek to master the interpretive process. Intermediate grammars and grammatical analyses can help, but such tools, for all their value, still often operate at a distance from the Greek text itself, and analyses are often too brief to be genuinely helpful.

The Exegetical Guide to the Greek New Testament (EGGNT) aims to close the gap between the Greek text and the available tools. Each EGGNT volume aims to provide all the necessary information for understanding of the Greek text and, in addition, includes homiletical helps and suggestions for further study. The EGGNT is not a full-scale commentary. Nevertheless these guides will make interpreting a given New Testament book easier, in particular for those who are hard-pressed for time and yet want to preach or teach with accuracy and authority.

In terms of layout, each volume begins with a brief introduction to the particular book (including such matters as authorship, date, etc.), a basic outline, and a list of recommended commentaries. At the end of each volume, you will find a comprehensive exegetical outline of the book. The body of each volume is devoted to paragraph-by-paragraph exegesis of the text. The treatment of each paragraph includes:

1. The Greek text of the passage, phrase by phrase, from the fifth edition of the United Bible Societies' *Greek New Testament* (UBS[5]).
2. A structural analysis of the passage. Typically, verbal discussion of the structure of a given unit is followed by a diagram, whereby the verbal discussion serves to explain the diagram and the diagram serves to provide a visual aid illumining the structural discussion. While there is no one correct or standard way to diagram Greek sentences, the following format is typically followed in EGGNT volumes:
   a. The original Greek word order is maintained.
   b. When Greek words are omitted, this is indicated by ellipses (. . .).

c. The diagramming method, moving from left to right, is predicated upon the following. In clauses with a finite verb, the default order is typically verb-subject-object. In verbless clauses or clauses with nonfinite verb forms, the default order is typically subject-(verb)-object. Departures from these default orders are understood to be pragmatically motivated (e.g., contrast, emphasis, etc.).

d. Indents are used to indicate subordination (e.g., in the case of dependent clauses).

e. Retaining original word order, modifiers are centered above or below the word they modify (e.g., a prepositional phrase in relation to the verb).

f. Where a given sentence or clause spans multiple lines of text, drawn lines are used, such as where a relative pronoun introduces a relative clause (often shifting emphasis).

g. Underline is used to indicate imperatives; dotted underline is used to indicate repetition (the same word or cognate used multiple times in a given unit); the symbol ⋮ may be used where an article is separated from a noun or participle by interjected material (such as a prepositional phrase).

h. In shorter letters diagrams are normally provided for every unit; in longer letters and Revelation, ellipses may be used to show less detail in diagramming (keeping larger blocks together on the same line) in order to focus primarily on the larger structure of a given unit; in the Gospels and Acts, detailed diagrams will usually not be provided, though less detailed diagrams may be used to illustrate important or more complex structural aspects of a given passage.

3. A discussion of each phrase of the passage with discussion of relevant vocabulary, significant textual variants, and detailed grammatical analysis, including parsing. When more than one solution is given for a particular exegetical issue, the author's own preference, reflected in the translation and expanded paraphrase, is indicated by an asterisk (*). When no preference is expressed, the options are judged to be evenly balanced, or it is assumed that the text is intentionally ambiguous. When a particular verb form may be parsed in more than one way, only the parsing appropriate in the specific context is supplied; but where there is difference of opinion among grammarians or commentators, both possibilities are given and the matter is discussed.

Verbal forms traditionally labeled deponent (having their lexical form in the middle voice rather than active) are tagged with "dep." before the lexical form is given. This is not to overlook that some today argue that "deponent" is a label that needs to be dropped. It is simply to alert the user of this EGGNT volume to how verbs are still described in many grammars, reference works, and perhaps even their language-learning programs.

4. Various translations of significant words or phrases.

5. A list of suggested topics for further study with bibliography for each topic. An asterisk (*) in one of the "For Further Study" bibliographies draws attention to a discussion of the particular topic that is recommended as a useful introduction to the issues involved.

6. Homiletical suggestions designed to help the preacher or teacher move from the Greek text to a sermon outline that reflects careful exegesis. The first suggestion for a particular paragraph of the text is always more exegetical than homiletical and consists of an outline of the entire paragraph. These detailed outlines of each paragraph build on the general outline proposed for the whole book and, if placed side by side, form a comprehensive exegetical outline of the book. All outlines are intended to serve as a basis for sermon preparation and should be adapted to the needs of a particular audience.[1]

The EGGNT volumes will serve a variety of readers. Those reading the Greek text for the first time may be content with the assistance with vocabulary, parsing, and translation. Readers with some experience in Greek may want to skip or skim these sections and focus attention on the discussions of grammar. More advanced students may choose to pursue the topics and references to technical works under "For Further Study," while pastors may be more interested in the movement from grammatical analysis to sermon outline. Teachers may appreciate having a resource that frees them to focus on exegetical details and theological matters.

The editors are pleased to present you with the individual installments of the EGGNT. We are grateful for each of the contributors who has labored long and hard over each phrase in the Greek New Testament. Together we share the conviction that "all Scripture is inspired by God and is profitable for teaching, for rebuking, for correcting, for training in righteousness" (2 Tim 3:16 CSB) and echo Paul's words to Timothy: "Be diligent to present yourself approved to God, a worker who doesn't need to be ashamed, correctly teaching the word of truth" (2 Tim 2:15 CSB).

Thanks to David Croteau, who served as assistant editor for this volume.

Andreas J. Köstenberger
Robert W. Yarbrough

---

1. As a Bible publisher, B&H Publishing follows the "Colorado Springs Guidelines for Translation of Gender-Related Language in Scripture." As an academic book publisher, B&H Academic asks that authors conform their manuscripts (including EGGNT exegetical outlines in English) to the B&H Academic style guide, which affirms the use of singular "he/his/him" as generic examples encompassing both genders. However, in their discussion of the Greek text, EGGNT authors have the freedom to analyze the text and reach their own conclusions regarding whether specific Greek words are gender specific or gender inclusive.

Abbreviations

For abbreviations used in discussion of text-critical matters, the reader should refer to the abbreviations listed in the Introduction to the United Bible Societies' *Greek New Testament*.

*   indicates the reading of the original hand of a manuscript as opposed to subsequent correctors of the manuscript, *or*

indicates the writer's own preference when more than one solution is given for a particular exegetical problem, *or*

in the "For Further Study" bibliographies, indicates a discussion of the particular topic that is recommended as a useful introduction to the issues involved

§, §§   paragraph, paragraphs

Books of the Old Testament

Gen	Genesis	Song	Song of Songs (Canticles)
Exod	Exodus	Isa	Isaiah
Lev	Leviticus	Jer	Jeremiah
Num	Numbers	Lam	Lamentations
Deut	Deuteronomy	Ezek	Ezekiel
Josh	Joshua	Dan	Daniel
Judg	Judges	Hos	Hosea
Ruth	Ruth	Joel	Joel
1–2 Sam	1–2 Samuel	Amos	Amos
1–2 Kgs	1–2 Kings	Obad	Obadiah
1–2 Chr	1–2 Chronicles	Jonah	Jonah
Ezra	Ezra	Mic	Micah
Neh	Nehemiah	Nah	Nahum
Esth	Esther	Hab	Habakkuk
Job	Job	Zeph	Zephaniah
Ps(s)	Psalm(s)	Hag	Haggai
Prov	Proverbs	Zech	Zechariah
Eccl	Ecclesiastes	Mal	Malachi

Books of the New Testament

Matt	Matthew	1–2 Thess	1–2 Thessalonians
Mark	Mark	1–2 Tim	1–2 Timothy
Luke	Luke	Titus	Titus
John	John	Phlm	Philemon
Acts	Acts	Heb	Hebrews
Rom	Romans	Jas	James
1–2 Cor	1–2 Corinthians	1–2 Pet	1–2 Peter
Gal	Galatians	1–3 John	1–3 John
Eph	Ephesians	Jude	Jude
Phil	Philippians	Rev	Revelation
Col	Colossians		

Dead Sea Scrolls

1QM	War Scroll
1QS	Rule of the Community
CD	Damascus Document

General Abbreviations

ABD	*The Anchor Bible Dictionary*, 6 vols., ed. D. N. Freedman (New York: Doubleday, 1992)
abs.	absolute(ly)
acc.	accusative
act.	active (voice)
adj.	adjective, adjectival(ly)
adv.	adverb, adverbial(ly)
AsJT	*Asia Journal of Theology*
Albright-Mann	W. F. Albright and C. S. Mann, *Matthew*, Anchor Bible 26 (Garden City, NY: Doubleday, 1971).
Allen	W. C. Allen, *A Critical and Exegetical Commentary on the Gospel According to St. Matthew*, International Critical Commentary (New York: Charles Scribner's Sons, 1907).
anar.	anarthrous
aor.	aorist
apod.	apodosis
appos.	apposition, appositional
Aram.	Aramaic, Aramaism
art.	(definite) article, articular
attrib.	attributive (ly)
AUSS	*Andrews University Seminary Studies*
BBR	*Bulletin for Biblical Research*

BDAG	*A Greek-English Lexicon of the New Testament and Other Early Christian Literature*, rev. and ed. F. W. Danker (Chicago/London: University of Chicago, 2000), based on W. Bauer's *Griechisch-deutsches Wörterbuch* (6th ed.) and on previous English ed. W. F. Arndt, F. W. Gingrich, and F. W. Danker. References to BDAG are by page number and quadrant on the page, *a* indicating the upper half and *b* the lower half of the left-hand column, and *c* and *d* the upper and lower halves of the right-hand column. With the use of dark type, biblical references are now clearly visible within each subsection.
BDF	F. Blass and A. Debrunner, *A Greek Grammar of the New Testament and Other Early Christian Literature*, tr. and rev. by R. W. Funk (Chicago: University of Chicago Press, 1961)
Beale and Carson	G. K. Beale and D. A. Carson, eds., *Commentary on the New Testament Use of the Old Testament* (Grand Rapids: Baker, 2007)
BGk.	Biblical Greek (i.e., LXX and NT Greek)
Bib	*Biblica*
BibInt	*Biblical Interpretation*
BJRL	*Bulletin of the John Rylands University Library of Manchester*
BR	*Biblical Research*
Blomberg	C. L. Blomberg, *Matthew: An Exegetical and Theological Exposition of the Holy Scripture*. New American Commentary. Nashville: Holman Reference, 1992.
Brown	Raymond Edward Brown, *The Death of the Messiah: From Gethsemane to the Grave (A Commentary on the Passion Narratives in the Four Gospels)* (New York: Doubleday, 1994).
BSac	*Bibliotheca Sacra*
BT	*Bible Translator*
BTB	*Biblical Theology Bulletin*
Burton	E. de W. Burton, *Syntax of the Moods and Tenses in New Testament Greek* (3rd ed.) (Edinburgh: T&T Clark, 1898)
Campbell	C. R. Campbell, *Basics of Verbal Aspect in Biblical Greek* (Grand Rapids: Zondervan, 2008)
Carson	D. A. Carson, "Matthew," in *Expositor's Bible Commentary* (Grand Rapids: Zondervan, 2010)
CBQ	*Catholic Biblical Quarterly*
CEV	Contemporary English Version (1995)
cf.	*confer* (Lat.), compare
comp.	comparative, comparison
cond.	condition(al)
conj.	conjunctive, conjunction
contemp.	contemporaneous
Conybeare and Stock	E. C. Conybeare and G. Stock, *Grammar of Septuagint Greek* (Grand Rapids: Baker, 2001)
cstr.	construction, construe(d)

CSB	Christian Standard Bible
CTJ	*Calvin Theological Journal*
CTR	*Criswell Theological Review*
CurTM	*Currents in Theology and Missions*
D&A	W. D. Davies and D. C. Allison, *Matthew*, 3 vols.,International Critical Commentary (London: T& TClark, 2004)
dat.	dative
dbl.	double
def.	definite
dem.	demonstrative
delib.	deliberative
dep.	deponent
DJG	*Dictionary of Jesus and the Gospels*, 2nd ed, ed. J. B. Green, J. K. Brown, and N. Perrin (Downers Grove: InterVarsity, 2013)
DLNT	*Dictionary of the Later New Testament and Its Developments*, ed. R. P. Martin and P. H. Davids (Leicester / Downers Grove: InterVarsity, 1997)
DNTB	*Dictionary of New Testament Background*, ed. C. A. Evans and S. E. Porter (Leicester / Downers Grove: InterVarsity, 2000)
DPL	*Dictionary of Paul and His Letters*, ed. G. F. Hawthrone, R. P. Martin, and D. G. Reid (Downers Grove: InterVarsity, 1993)
dimin.	diminutive
dir.	direct
EDNT	*Exegetical Dictionary of the New Testament*, 3 vols., ed. H. Balz and G. Schneider (Grand Rapids: Eerdmans, 1990–93)
ed(s).	edited by, edition(s), editor(s)
e.g.	*exempli gratia* (Lat.), for example
Eng.	English
epex.	epexegetic, epexegetical(ly)
esp.	especially
ESV	English Standard Version (2011)
et al.	*et alii* (Lat.), and others
etym.	etymology (etymological)
Eusebius, *History*	Eusebius, *Ecclesiastical History*
Evans	C. A. Evans, *Matthew*, New Cambridge Bible Commentary (Cambridge: Cambridge University Press, 2012)
EvQ	*Evangelical Quarterly*
EVV	English versions of the Bible
ExpTim	*Expository Times*
f(f).	and the following (verse[s] or page[s])
F	R. T. France, *Matthew* (New International Commentary on the New Testament; Grand Rapids: Eerdmans, 2007)
Fanning	Buist Fanning, *Verbal Aspect in New Testament Greek* (Oxford: Oxford University Press, 1991)

fem.	feminine
fig.	figurative(ly)
Formula Quotations	George Soares Prabhu, *The Formula Quotations in the Infancy Narrative of Matthew: An Enquiry into the Tradition History of Mt. 1–2.* (Rome: Gregorian and Biblical Press, 1976)
fr.	from
fut.	future
gen.	genitive
Gk.	Greek
G	R. Gundry, *Matthew*, 2nd ed. (Grand Rapids: Eerdmans, 1995)
G. B. Winer	G. B. Winer, *A Greek Grammar of the New Testament* (Andover, MA: Codman, 1825)
Geneva	Geneva Bible (1599)
Gildersleeve	B. L. Gildersleeve, *A Syntax of Classical Greek from Homer to Demosthenes* (New York: American Book Company, 1900)
Gos. Pet.	Gospel of Peter
Greg.	*Gregorianum*
H	D. Hagner, *Matthew*, 2 vols. Word Biblical Commentary 33 (Dallas: Word, 1993–1995)
Harris	M. Harris, *Prepositions and Theology in the Greek New Testament* (Grand Rapids: Zondervan, 2012)
Heb.	Hebrew, Hebraism
Hill	D. Hill, *The Gospel of Matthew*, New Century Bible (London: Oliphants, 1978)
HTR	*Harvard Theological Review*
HUT	*Hermeneutische Untersuchungen zur Theologie*
IBS	*Irish Biblical Studies*
IDBSup	*Interpreter's Dictionary of the Bible (Supplement Volume)*
i.e.	*id est* (Lat.), that is
impers.	impersonal
impf.	imperfect (tense)
impv.	imperative (mood), imperatival(ly)
incl.	including
indecl.	indeclinable
indef.	indefinite
indic.	indicative (mood)
indir.	indirect
inf.	infinitive
ingr.	ingressive
instr.	instrument, instrumental(ly)
intrans.	intransitive(ly)
Int	*Interpretation*
interr.	interrogative

iter.	iterative
J. Pennington	J. Pennington, *Heaven and Earth in the Gospel of Matthew* (Grand Rapids: Baker, 2007)
JBL	*Journal of Biblical Literature*
JETS	*Journal of the Evangelical Theological Society*
JJS	*Journal of Jewish Studies*
Jos. *Ant.*	Josephus, *Jewish Antiquities*
JSNT	*Journal for the Study of the New Testament*
JSNTSup	*Journal for the Study of the New Testament Supplements*
JTS	*Journal of Theological Studies*
Kingsbury	J. D. Kingsbury, *Matthew: Structure, Christology, Kingdom* (Philadelphia: Fortress, 1975)
KJ21	21st Century King James Version
KJV	King James Version (= "Authorized Version") (1611)
LEB	Lexham English Bible
Levinsohn	S. Levinsohn, *Discourse Features of New Testament Greek*, 2nd ed. (Dallas: SIL International, 2000)
lit.	literal(ly)
LN	J. P. Louw and E. A. Nida, eds., *Introduction and Domains*, vol. 1 of *Greek-English Lexicon of the New Testament Based on Semantic Domains* (New York: United Bible Societies, 1988).
loc.	locative
LSJ	H. G. Liddell and R. Scott, *Greek-English Lexicon* (Oxford: Clarendon, 1996)
LTJ	*Lutheran Theological Journal*
Luz	U. Luz, *Matthew*, 3 vols. Hermeneia (Minneapolis: Fortress, 2001–2007)
LXX	Septuagint (= Greek Old Testament)
Macc	Maccabees
Marshall	I. H. Marshall, *The Gospel of Luke*, New International Greek Testament Commentary [Grand Rapids: Eerdmans, 1978], 468.
masc.	masculine
McKay	K. L. McKay, *A New Syntax of the Verb in New Testament Greek: An Aspectual Approach* (New York: Peter Lang, 1994)
Metzger	B. M. Metzger, *A Textual Commentary on the Greek New Testament* (Stuttgart: Deutsche Bibelgesellschaft / New York: United Bible Societies, 1994; original ed. of 1971 based on UBS³)
mg.	margin
MH	J. H. Moulton and W. F. Howard, *Accidence and Word-Formation*, vol. 2 of *A Grammar of New Testament Greek*, ed. J. H. Moulton (Edinburgh: T&T Clark, 1939)
mid.	middle
mng.	meaning
Morris	L. Morris, *The Gospel According to Matthew* (Pillar New Testament Commentary; Grand Rapids: Eerdmans, 1992)

Moule	C. F. D. Moule, *An Idiom Book of New Testament Greek*, 2nd ed. (Cambridge: CUP, 1960)
Moulton	J. H. Moulton, *A Grammar of New Testament Greek, Vol. I: Prolegomena* 3rd ed. (Edinburgh: Clark, 1908)
ms(s).	manuscript(s)
MSG	The Message
MT	Masoretic Text
N	J. Nolland, *Matthew* (New International Greek Testament Commentary; Grand Rapids: Eerdmans, 2005)
n.	note
NA28	*Novum Testamentum Graece*, Nestle-Aland, 28th edition.
NASB	New American Standard Bible (1995)
NDBT	*New Dictionary of Biblical Theology*, ed. T. D. Alexander and B. S. Rosner (Downers Grove: InterVarsity, 2000)
NEB	New English Bible (1970)
neg.	negative, negation
Neot	*Neotestamentica*
NET	New English Translation Bible (2005)
NETS	New English Translations of the Septuagint (2007)
neut.	neuter
NIDNTT	*The New International Dictionary of New Testament Theology*, 3 vols., ed. C. Brown (Grand Rapids: Zondervan, 1975–78)
NIDNTTE	*New International Dictionary of New Testament Theology and Exegesis*, 5 vols., ed. M. Silva (Grand Rapids: Zondervan, 2014)
NIV	New International Version (2011)
NJB	New Jerusalem Bible (1985)
NKJV	New King James Version
NLT	New Living Translation of the Bible (1996)
nom.	nominative
NovT	*Novum Testamentum*
NovTSup	Novum Testamentum Supplements
NRSV	New Revised Standard Version (1990)
NSBT	New Studies in Biblical Theology
NT	New Testament
NTS	*New Testament Studies*
obj.	object(ive)
orig.	origin, original(ly)
OT	Old Testament
p(p).	page(s)
pass.	passive
periph.	periphrastic
pers.	person(al)
pf.	perfect

pl.	plural
pluperf.	pluperfect, pluperfective
Porter, *Idioms*	S. E. Porter, *Idioms of the Greek New Testament* (Sheffield: JSOT, 1992)
Porter, *VA*	S. E. Porter, *Verbal Aspect in the Greek of the New Testament, with Reference to Tense and Mood*, Studies in Biblical Greek 1 (New York: Peter Lang, 1989)
poss.	possessive, possession
pred.	predicate, predicative
pref.	prefix
prep.	preposition(al)
pres.	present
prob.	probably
prog.	progressive
pron.	pronoun
prot.	protasis
PRS	*Perspectives in Religious Studies*
ptc.	participle, participial(ly)
Quarles, *Theology*	C. L. Quarles, *A Theology of Matthew* (Philipsburg: P&R, 2013)
Quarles, *Sermon*	C. L. Quarles, *Sermon on the Mount* NAC Studies in Bible and Theology (Nashville: B&H Academic, 2011)
R	A. T. Robertson, *A Grammar of the Greek New Testament in the Light of Historical Research*, 4th ed. (Nashville: Broadman, 1934)
rdg(s).	(textual) reading(s)
REB	Revised English Bible (1990)
ref.	reference
refl.	reflexive
rel.	relative
rev.	revised, revision
RevExp	*Review and Expositor*
ResQ	*Restoration Quarterly*
R-P	M. Robinson and W. Pierpont, *The New Testament in the Original Greek* (Southborough, MA: Chilton Book Publishing, 2005)
RSV	Revised Standard Version (1952)
RTR	*Reformed Theological Review*
Runge	S. E. Runge, *Discourse Grammar of the Greek New Testament: A Practical Introduction for Teaching and Exegesis* (Peabody, MA: Hendrickson, 2010)
SBLMS	*Society of Biblical Literature Monograph Series*
SBLSP	*Society of Biblical Literature Seminar Papers*
SBJT	*Southern Baptist Journal of Theology*
SBT	*Studies in Biblical Theology*
SE	*Studia Evangelica*

Sem.	Semitic, Semitism
sg.	singular
sim.	similar(ly)
Sir	Sirach/Ecclesiasticus
SJT	*Scottish Journal of Theology*
Smyth	H. W. Smyth, *Greek Grammar* (Boston: Harvard University Press, 1984)
SNTSMS	Society for New Testament Studies Monograph Series
ST	*Studia Theologica*
subj.	subject(ive)
subjunc.	subjunctive
subord.	subordinate, subordination
subst.	substantive, substantival(ly)
superl.	superlative
SwJT	*Southwestern Journal of Theology*
TDNT	*Theological Dictionary of the New Testament*, 9 vols., ed. G. Kittel and G. Friedrich, trans. G. W. Bromiley (Grand Rapids: Eerdmans, 1964–74)
temp.	temporal(ly)
Thayer	J. H. Thayer, *Greek-English Lexicon of the New Testament* (New York: American Book Company, 1889)
Thucydides	*Historicus History of the Peloponnesian War*
TJ	*Trinity Journal*
TLG	Thesaurus Linguae Graecae
tr.	translate(d), translator(s), translation(s)
TS	*Theological Studies*
Turner, *Matthew*	D. Turner, *Matthew*, Baker Exegetical Commentary on the New Testament (Grand Rapids: Baker, 2008)
Turner, *Style*	N. Turner, *Style*, vol. 4 of *A Grammar of New Testament Greek*, ed. J. H. Moulton (Edinburgh: T&T Clark, 1976)
Turner, *Syntax*	N. Turner, *Syntax*, vol. 3 of *A Grammar of New Testament Greek*, ed. J. H. Moulton (Edinburgh: T&T Clark, 1978)
Turner, *Grammatical Insights*	N. Turner, *Grammatical Insights into the New Testament* (Edinburgh: T&T Clark, 1965)
TynBul	*Tyndale Bulletin*
UBS[5]	*The Greek New Testament*, ed. B. Aland, K. Aland, J. Karavidopoulos, C. M. Martini, and B. M. Metzger, 5th rev. ed. (Stuttgart: Deutsche Bibelgesellschaft/New York: United Bible Societies, 2014)
UBS Journal	*Union Biblical Seminary Journal*
v(v).	verse(s)
var.	variant (form or reading)
vb(s).	verb(s)
VE	*Vox Evangelica*
voc.	vocative
vol(s).	volume(s)

W	Daniel B. Wallace, *Greek Grammar Beyond the Basics: An Exegetical Syntax of the New Testament* (Grand Rapids: Zondervan, 1996)
W. E. Jelf	W. E. Jelf, *A Grammar of the Greek Language* (London: Parker, 1881)
Wis	Wisdom of Solomon
WTJ	*Westminster Theological Journal*
WUNT	Wissenschaftliche Untersuchungen zum Neuen Testament
WW	*Word and World*
YLT	Young's Literal Translation
Z	M. Zerwick, *Biblical Greek Illustrated by Examples*, trans. J. Smith (Rome: Pontifical Biblical Institute, 1963)
ZNW	*Zeitschrift für die neutestamentliche Wissenschaft und die Kunde der älteren Kirche*

MATTHEW

Introduction

Those who are called to expound the Holy Scriptures should strive to "rightly handle the word of truth" (2 Tim 2:15). Correct biblical interpretation is almost always hard work. Since we are now separated from the human authors and original readers of the New Testament by nearly two millennia, interpreters must be good historians who recognize and appreciate the differences between then and now. They must develop the skill of stepping into the first-century world and reading the NT as the original readers might have read it.

Responsible interpreters must also be good linguists. Although the general truths of a passage are plain in any decent English translation, if a preacher or teacher wishes to expound the details of a NT text, he had best rely on his Greek Testament. Since the Greek language in which the NT was written does not share word-for-word equivalencies with modern English, no English translation is a perfect and exact representation of the divinely inspired Greek text. Translations are, by necessity, interpretations. Though modern translators exercise great care in their handling of the God-breathed Word, they cannot claim for themselves the inspiration that produced the Greek Gospels and Letters. If an exegete wishes to heed the call of the Renaissance and the Reformation (*ad fontes*—to the sources), he needs to dust off his Greek New Testament and look behind the translations to the Greek of Matthew, Paul, and Peter.

Studying the Greek text of the New Testament will help settle some interpretive questions. It does not settle all of them. Even after analysis of grammar and syntax, careful consideration of structure, and researching of vocabulary, legitimate questions often remain. Thus, analyzing the Greek text is an important—I would even argue crucial—step in responsible exegesis, but that is not the entirety of the task. Consequently, this volume does not fully interpret the Gospel of Matthew. It is not a commentary on Matthew. It is merely a first step toward the interpretation and exegesis of Matthew.

Although I have included homiletical suggestions in this volume at the publisher's request, readers will often wonder how the analysis in this volume led to particular exegetical insights. The apparent disconnect results from the fact that exegesis involves more than just linguistic analysis. Sometimes the exegetical insights in the suggested outlines were derived from other steps in the interpretive process (considerations of the literary and historical context, the development of theological themes in the book, etc.) that could not be discussed in this book due to space constraints. This only confirms that the study of Greek grammar and syntax is an important element of interpretation but is not sufficient by itself.

During my analysis of the Greek text, I regularly compared five English translations: New International Version, Christian Standard Bible, Lexham English Bible, English Standard Version, and New Living Translation. These translations were selected because they represent a variety of approaches to translation, including formal equivalence, optimal equivalence, and dynamic equivalence. When I indicate that a particular decision is supported by "most EVV," I am referring merely to the majority of these five selected translations, not to all versions in the history of the English translation of the Bible.

When I discuss the meaning of a particular word, form, or construction, it is important to note that I am referring to its sense in the specific context of that particular occurrence. Constant use of clarifications like "in this context" or "in this particular case" would have unnecessarily consumed too much valuable space. However, readers will often find that particular nuances in a specific context do not carry over to occurrences in a different context.

Other volumes in this series have had the luxury of detailed discussion of various interpretations, textual variants, and issues of translation. However, due to the relative length of this Gospel, discussions here had to be far briefer. Although I am keenly interested in textual criticism, a concern to reserve space for grammatical and syntactical analysis required me to refer students to Metzger on all but a few lengthy and important variants. I was also able to give only scant attention to discourse features of the Gospel. This volume also omits the full translation and structural diagrams contained in volumes on shorter New Testament books.

Similarly, I originally included more extensive discussions of the form of OT quotations in Matthew. These were ultimately replaced with references to the treatment of these quotations in Beale and Carson's *Commentary on the New Testament Use of the Old Testament*. This was necessary to ensure that adequate attention could be given to the grammar and syntax of the first Gospel.

About 30 percent of the sentences in Matthew begin with καί. I agree with S. Black that this is the default ("unmarked") sentence conjunction in Matthew used to express continuity of time, action, or actor (S. Black, *Sentence Conjunctions in the Gospel of Matthew:* καί, δέ, τότε, γάρ, οὖν *and Asyndeton in Narrative Discourse* [JSNTSup 122; Sheffield: Sheffield Academic Press, 2002], 112). Δέ, on the other hand, signals a new development in a narrative or dialogue. In dialogues, δέ often signals a shift in speaker. Initially I discussed each occurrence of δέ, but the treatment became repetitive. I ultimately decided to save space by treating only less common uses of the conjunctions, such as ascensive καί or adversative δέ.

The Gospel of Matthew was the favorite Gospel of the early church. R. T. France did not exaggerate when he wrote, "It is a fact that mainstream Christianity was, from the early second century on, to a great extent Matthean Christianity" (R. T. France, *Matthew: Evangelist and Teacher* [Downers Grove: InterVarsity, 1989], 16). Recognition of the significance of the Gospel of Matthew for the early church prompted E. Renan to describe Matthew's Gospel as the most important book ever written (Morris 1). This Gospel is a precious treasure for the disciples of Jesus and is worthy of our most diligent study. Those who open their Greek Testament to the Gospel of Matthew should do so with deep reverence, keenly aware that as they trudge through the grammar and syntax of this ancient testimony to Jesus, they are treading on holy ground.

Although this volume does not contain sufficient space for a detailed discussion of the background of the Gospel, a brief introduction is appropriate. For a more detailed presentation, see A. Köstenberger, S. Kellum, and C. Quarles, *The Cradle, the Cross, and the Crown: An Introduction to the New Testament, 2nd Edition* (Nashville: B&H, 2016), 222–76.

AUTHOR

Like the other canonical Gospels, Matthew is technically anonymous. The author does not explicitly identify himself in the pages of the Gospel. However, considerable evidence exists supporting the traditional view that this Gospel was written by the apostle Matthew.

- The earliest manuscripts that contain titles for the Gospel ascribe the Gospel to Matthew. These include the major uncials Vaticanus and Sinaiticus that date to the mid-300s and perhaps $\mathfrak{P}^4$, which dates to around AD 200. This manuscript is accompanied by a small fragment in another scribal hand that reads ευαγγελιον κατα μαθθαιον. Some scholars believe the fragment is part of the title sheet of the Matthew portion of this Gospel codex. The fragment is in a different scribal hand than the rest of $\mathfrak{P}^4$. See P. Comfort, "Exploring the Common Identification of Three New Testament Manuscripts: $\mathfrak{P}^4$, $\mathfrak{P}^{64}$ and $\mathfrak{P}^{67}$," *TynBul* 46 (1995): 43–54; S. Gathercole, "The Earliest Manuscript Title of Matthew's Gospel (BnF Suppl. gr. 1120 ii 3 / $\mathfrak{P}^4$)," *NovT* 54 (2012): 209–35; T. Wasserman, "The Early Text of Matthew," in *The Early Text of the New Testament,* ed. C. E. Hill and M. J. Kruger (Oxford: Oxford University Press, 2012), 95. Although the title appears in a number of different forms in the ancient manuscripts, they all share one thing in common: they ascribe the Gospel to Matthew.
- In the early second century, Papias, bishop of Hierapolis, discussed the composition of the Gospels in his *Expositions of the Lord's Sayings.* He wrote: "Therefore, on the one hand Matthew arranged in order the sayings in the Hebrew dialect; on the other hand, each translated these as he was able." Thereafter, the early church unanimously affirmed Matthew's authorship of the Gospel.
- A couple of features of this Gospel fit well with this early view of authorship. Only this Gospel identifies the tax collector Levi of Mark 2:14 and Luke 5:27 as "Matthew." This name, meaning "Gift of Yahweh" in Hebrew, may be the apostolic name given to the disciple by Jesus (like Simon's name "Cephas" or "Peter"). Use of this name may reflect the author's own personal touch.

Furthermore, this Gospel uses the more precise term νόμισμα ("state coin") in the discussion of the payment of the imperial tax in Matthew 22:15–22, which is just the kind of precision one might expect of a tax collector.

Although many scholars brushed aside any serious connection between the Gospel and Matthew in the skeptical environment of twentieth-century Gospels scholarship, scholars are now increasingly warning against casually dismissing or quietly ignoring the evidence for Matthean authorship. Some scholars who previously rejected Matthean authorship have reversed their opinion and are now inclined to affirm it (see *The Cradle, the Cross, and the Crown*, 2nd ed., 226 n. 14). Given the strength of the evidence supporting Matthew's authorship of the Gospel, this book will refer to the author of the Gospel as Matthew.

DATE

Most contemporary scholars date Matthew to the mid- to late 80s. This dating is based on two primary lines of evidence: (1) the reference to the destruction of the Jerusalem temple was possible only after the fall of Jerusalem had occurred (AD 70) and enough time had passed since the destruction of the city that the Gospel need not focus on it; and (2) the church consisting of Jesus's disciples had formally separated from the Jewish synagogues, an event related to the Council of Jamnia that many believe to have occurred in AD 85–90. The first argument is unpersuasive for those who affirm Jesus's identity as the Son of God and recognize that he was capable of predictive prophecy. The second argument is also unpersuasive since the Gospels, Acts, and Paul's Letters show that tensions between Jewish leaders and Jesus's followers can be traced to the earliest days of the church.

The earliest possible date is likely established by the date of composition of Mark. Most scholars believe the author of Matthew used Mark's Gospel in writing his own Gospel. Mark was probably written in the early to mid-50s.

The latest possible date is probably established by the fall of Jerusalem in AD 70. Matthew's decision to include Jesus's teaching about the procedure to use in offering temple sacrifice (5:23–24) makes the most sense if the temple was still standing and sacrifice was still being offered. The decision to include Jesus's prohibition about swearing by the temple (22:16–22) suggests that the temple was still standing when the Gospel was written. Swearing by the temple involved wishing the temple to be destroyed if one did not fulfill his vow. Such a vow would be meaningless if the temple had already been reduced to rubble. Furthermore, Matthew 17:24–27 affirms the payment of the temple tax. However, after the fall of Jerusalem, this tax went to support the pagan temple of Jupiter Capitolinus in Rome. It is unlikely that a Gospel that insisted that Yahweh alone is worthy of worship (4:10) would encourage Jesus's disciples to support idolatry financially.

Thus the Gospel of Matthew was probably written during the 60s.

PROVENANCE

Scholars have suggested a variety of places of origin for the Gospel of Matthew. Most modern scholars favor a Syrian provenance (prob. Antioch). Ignatius, bishop of Antioch (AD 35–100) is the first church father to quote from Matthew in his writings. This may suggest that the Gospel originated in Syria and only later spread elsewhere. On the other hand, Jerome (c. AD 345–420) stated that the Gospel was written in Palestine, and this is the earliest extant testimony to a place of composition. Ultimately, differences of opinion regarding the place of composition have little impact on the interpretation of the Gospel.

LANGUAGE OF COMPOSITION

The early church seems to have believed widely that the Gospel of Matthew was first written in Hebrew. This is attested by Papias (c. AD 110), Irenaeus (c. AD 130–200); Pantaenus (died c. AD 190); Origen (c. AD 185–254); Eusebius (c. AD 260–340); Cyril of Jerusalem (c. AD 315–87); Epiphanius (c. AD 315–403); Jerome (c. AD 345–420); and Augustine (AD 354–430). Some internal evidence supports this view. The gematria in 1:17 works only in Hebrew since the Greek transliteration of the name David has a different numerical value. Furthermore, the widely accepted interpretation of 2:23 assumes that both Matthew and his first readers were familiar with the OT in Hebrew.

Other portions of the Gospel seem to have been composed in Greek. The alliteration using the Greek letter π that marks the first four beatitudes probably implies Greek composition. The Greek Gospel reads so smoothly at most points that only the most accomplished translator would have been capable of producing it from a Hebrew or Aramaic original. Perhaps most importantly, the view that Matthew used Mark's Greek Gospel in composing his own Gospel poses a problem for the idea of a Semitic original.

At present, insufficient evidence exists to prove or disprove an original Semitic-language edition of Matthew (D. A. Carson and D. Moo, *Introduction to the New Testament* [Grand Rapids: Zondervan, 2005], 102). Fortunately, the question of the original language of the Gospel seldom affects interpretation.

STRUCTURE

Although some portions of the Gospel are arranged topically, Matthew follows a general chronological order, moving through the genealogy, birth, baptism, Galilean ministry, journey to and ministry in Jerusalem, trial, crucifixion, resurrection, and postresurrection appearances. In addition to this general chronological framework, Matthew gives some important clues to his structure. Given the nature of the present volume, a more extensive discussion of the structure of the Gospel is appropriate.

Five times Matthew uses the construction "and it happened that when Jesus finished" (Καὶ ἐγένετο ὅτε ἐτέλεσεν ὁ Ἰησοῦς) followed by a reference to Jesus's teachings (7:28–29; 11:1; 13:53; 19:1; 26:1). This formula marks the end of each of the five major discourses in this Gospel. Each major discourse is preceded and followed by a lengthy section of narrative. B. W. Bacon argued that the five occurrences of the structural formula divide the Gospel into five major sections, each consisting of a narrative section followed by a major discourse (Bacon, *Studies in Matthew* [New York: Holt, 1930]) and this view would exert significant influence in subsequent scholarship.

Some variety exists in each formula.

Καὶ ἐγένετο ὅτε ἐτέλεσεν ὁ Ἰησοῦς τοὺς λόγους τούτους (7:28–29)
Καὶ ἐγένετο ὅτε ἐτέλεσεν ὁ Ἰησοῦς διατάσσων τοῖς δώδεκα μαθηταῖς αὐτοῦ (11:1)
Καὶ ἐγένετο ὅτε ἐτέλεσεν ὁ Ἰησοῦς τὰς παραβολὰς ταύτας (13:53)
Καὶ ἐγένετο ὅτε ἐτέλεσεν ὁ Ἰησοῦς τοὺς λόγους τούτους (19:1)
Καὶ ἐγένετο ὅτε ἐτέλεσεν ὁ Ἰησοῦς πάντας τοὺς λόγους τούτους (26:1)

The first six words of all five occurrences of the formula match. The first, fourth, and fifth occurrences also have the matching words τοὺς λόγους τούτους. The fifth and final occurrence of the formula adds the adj. πάντας, which several scholars see as Matthew's indication that the last of the major discourses has come to its end. The five discourses seem also to fit a chiastic structure, at least as far as length is concerned. Discourses 1 (5–7) and 5 (23/24–25) are the two longest discourses. Discourses 2 (10) and 4 (18) are the shortest. Thus some scholars recognize the following structure to the discourses:

> Discourse 1
>> Discourse 2
>>> Discourse 3
>> Discourse 4
> Discourse 5

This structure would place the parables of the kingdom at the center of Jesus's discourses. This would seem appropriate given Matthew's summary of Jesus's teaching as the "gospel of the kingdom" (4:23).

The precise relationship of these discourses to the narratives that precede and follow them is more difficult to discern. Bacon suggested the discourses are closely connected to the narrative sections that immediately *precede* them, so that each of the five major sections of Matthew consist of narrative plus discourse in that order. H. Frankemölle, P. Rolland, and others have argued that each discourse is most closely connected to the narrative section that *follows* it. Scholars like P. Gaechter and D. L. Barr ("The Drama of Matthew's Gospel: A Reconsideration of Its Structure and Purpose," *Theology Digest* 24 [1978]: 352) have argued that the discourses are connectors that join the preceding and following narratives. U. Luz seems to be correct in arguing that the relationship of the discourses to the narratives does not follow a set and uniform pattern (Luz 1.3). For a brief introduction to the major views and a new solution, see W. J. C. Weren, "The Macrostructure of Matthew's Gospel: A New Proposal," *Bib* 87 (2006): 171–200.

The discourse formula is not the only structural marker for which the interpreter must account. Matthew 4:23 and 9:35, for example, are similar.

Καὶ περιῆγεν ἐν ὅλῃ τῇ Γαλιλαίᾳ διδάσκων ἐν ταῖς συναγωγαῖς αὐτῶν καὶ κηρύσσων τὸ εὐαγγέλιον τῆς βασιλείας καὶ θεραπεύων πᾶσαν νόσον καὶ πᾶσαν μαλακίαν ἐν τῷ λαῷ. (4:23)

Καὶ περιῆγεν ὁ Ἰησοῦς τὰς πόλεις πάσας καὶ τὰς κώμας διδάσκων ἐν ταῖς συναγωγαῖς αὐτῶν καὶ κηρύσσων τὸ εὐαγγέλιον τῆς βασιλείας καὶ θεραπεύων πᾶσαν νόσον καὶ πᾶσαν μαλακίαν. (9:35)

The matching words Καὶ περιῆγεν . . . διδάσκων ἐν ταῖς συναγωγαῖς αὐτῶν καὶ κηρύσσων τὸ εὐαγγέλιον τῆς βασιλείας καὶ θεραπεύων πᾶσαν νόσον καὶ πᾶσαν μαλακίαν seem to mark 4:23–9:35 as a unit. Yet this unit contains a brief narrative, followed by a major discourse, followed by a more extensive narrative with multiple pericopes. This inclusio casts doubt on Bacon's claim that 7:28 constitutes a major break.

On the other hand, 26:1 does seem to constitute a major break. It announces the formal end of Jesus's public teaching ministry and marks the beginning of the passion narrative. As Luz observed, "The relationship between the contents of the narrative sections and their corresponding discourses is varied; sometimes they are minimal. Therefore it is also possible to attach the narrative sections to different discourses. In my judgment a unified coordination of the discourses with their narrative context is not possible" (Luz 1.3).

The five major discourses of the Gospel of Matthew are clearly an important feature of the structure of the Gospel. However, other structural markers must be examined as well.

J. D. Kingsbury popularized the views of E. Lohmeyer and N. B. Stonehouse that the key to Matthew's structure was the construction Ἀπὸ τότε ἤρξατο ὁ Ἰησοῦς that appears in 4:17 and 16:21 (Kingsbury 7–9). This divided the Gospel into three major sections: 1:1–4:16 ("the Person of Jesus Messiah"); 4:17–16:20 ("the Proclamation of Jesus Messiah"); and 16:21–28:20 ("the Suffering, Death, and Resurrection of Jesus Messiah"). Not only do the captions of this outline fail to reflect the contents of the sections, the use of a brief construction that only appears twice as the key to structure is problematic as well. Luz has pointed out, for example, that 5:17 and 10:34 both contain the construction μὴ νομίσητε ὅτι ἦλθον followed by an infinitive. If a brief construction need appear only twice to constitute a major feature of the structure, this construction could as easily form the key to the structure as Kingsbury's proposal, at least on purely formal grounds.

The construction in 4:17 and 16:21 does seem to mark important transitions in the narrative. In 4:17, the construction functions chronologically to mark the beginning of Jesus's adult ministry. In 16:21, it marks both a chronological transition as Jesus's public ministry comes to a close and he anticipates his crucifixion as well as a geographical transition as Jesus directs his attention to Jerusalem.

Matthew's structure is complex and seems to involve a combination of several different strategies operating at once. The five major discourses are clearly important, but chronological arrangement and geographical movement are important features of the structure of the narrative too.

The outline below is an adaptation of the outline suggested in Quarles, *Theology*, 14–15. The minor revision is due to an increased emphasis on the inclusio in 4:23 and 9:35.

I. Introduction (1:1–4:16)
    A. Genealogy, Birth, and Childhood of Jesus (1:1–2:23)
    B. Preparation for Jesus's Ministry (3:1–4:16)[1]
II. Galilean Ministry (4:17–16:20)
    A. First Stage of Jesus's Galilean Ministry (4:17–25)
    B. First Discourse: Sermon on the Mount (5:1–7:29)[2]
    C. Continuation of First Stage of Jesus's Galilean Ministry (8:1–9:38)
    D. Second Discourse: Instruction of the Twelve (10:1–11:1)[3]
    E. Second Stage of Jesus's Galilean Ministry (11:2–12:50)
    F. Third Discourse: Parables on the Kingdom (13:1–53)[4]
    G. Rejection and Withdrawal to the North (13:54–16:20)[5]
III. Journey to Jerusalem (16:21–20:34)[6]
    A. Return to Galilee (16:21–17:27)
    B. Fourth Discourse: Instructions about Life in the Kingdom (18:1–35)
    C. Journey Through Judea (19:1–20:34)[7]
IV. Jerusalem Ministry (21:1–28:20)
    A. Final Ministry in Jerusalem (21:1–22:46)
    B. Rebuke of the Pharisees and Abandonment of the Temple (23:1–39)
    C. Fifth Discourse: The Fall of Jerusalem and the Coming Kingdom (24:1–25:46)
    D. Jesus's Passion (26:1–27:66)
    E. Jesus's Resurrection (28:1–20)

RECOMMENED COMMENTARIES

Blomberg, C. L. *Matthew: An Exegetical and Theological Exposition of Holy Scripture*. New American Commentary. Nashville: Holman Reference, 1992.

Carson D. A., W. W. Wessel, and M. L. Strauss. *Matthew and Mark*. Expositor's Bible Commentary. Edited by T. Longman III and D. E. Garland. Grand Rapids: Zondervan, 2010.

Davies, W. D. and D. C. Allison. *A Critical and Exegetical Commentary on the Gospel According to Saint Matthew*. 3 vols. International Critical Commentary. Edinburgh: T&T Clark, 1988–97.

Evans , C. A. *Matthew*. New Cambridge Bible Commentary. New York: Cambridge University Press, 2012.

---

1 "From that time Jesus began to . . ." (4:16).
2 "And when Jesus finished these sayings, . . ." (7:28).
3 "When Jesus had finished . . ." (11:1).
4 "And when Jesus had finished . . ." (13:53).
5 "Jesus withdrew" (14:13; 15:21). Jesus travels to Gennesaret (14:34), the district of Tyre and Sidon (15:21), and to the district of Caesarea Philippi (16:13).
6 "From that time Jesus began . . ." and "he must go to Jerusalem" (16:21).
7 "Now when Jesus had finished these sayings, he went away from Galilee and entered the region of Judea beyond the Jordan" (19:1).

France, R. T. *The Gospel of Matthew*. New International Commentary on the New Testament. Grand Rapids: Eerdmans, 2007.

Hagner, D. A. *Matthew*. 2 vols. Word Biblical Commentary 33. Dallas: Word, 1993.

Keener, C. S. *A Commentary on the Gospel of Matthew*. Grand Rapids: Eerdmans, 1999.

Luz, U. *Matthew: A Commentary*. 3 vols. Hermeneia. Minneapolis: Fortress, 1989–2001.

Nolland, J. *The Gospel of Matthew: A Commentary on the Greek Text*. New International Commentary on the New Testament. Grand Rapids: Eerdmans, 2005.

Osborne, G. R. *Matthew*. Zondervan Exegetical Commentary on the New Testament. Grand Rapids: Zondervan, 2010.

Turner, D. L. *Matthew*. Baker Exegetical Commentary on the New Testament. Grand Rapids: Baker, 2008.

Wilkins, M. J. *Matthew*. NIV Application Commentary. Grand Rapids: Zondervan, 2004.

I. Introduction (1:1–4:16)

A. GENEALOGY, BIRTH, AND CHILDHOOD OF JESUS (1:1–2:23)

1. Title (1:1)

1:1 The first verse of the Gospel (sometimes termed *incipit*, Latin for "it begins") serves as a title. Although most EVV regard the first phrase as the title of the genealogy of Jesus, scholars debate whether the verse serves as the title for merely the genealogy (H 1.5); the entire account of Jesus's birth (Carson 86–87); a larger section of the Gospel, such as 1:1–4:16 (Kingsbury 9); or the entire Gospel (Jerome; D&A 1.149–56). The three descriptors of Jesus show that Jesus's identity is the primary focus of the title.

Βίβλος, -ου, ὁ (or βύβλος) normally referred to an entire papyrus roll or a "book" in contrast to a brief document (LSJ 333a). The noun could refer to the major divisions of a work, such as the nine books of Herodotus. Greek writers used a distinct term, βιβλίον, to refer to a brief "paper" or "document" (though this noun was also occasionally used to refer to an entire book; 1 Macc 1:56; 12:9). Matthew used βιβλίον to refer to a "certificate of divorce" in 19:7. Elsewhere in the NT, the term βίβλος refers to Old Testament books, including the book (sg.) of Moses (Mark 12:26; referring to the Pentateuch), the book of Isaiah (Luke 3:4), the book of Psalms (Luke 20:42; Acts 1:20), and the book (sg.) of the Prophets (Acts 7:42; referring to the Book of the Twelve Prophets). The term also referred to books about magic (Acts 19:19) and the "book of life" (Phil 4:3; Rev 3:5; 20:15). Although βιβλίον sometimes also refers to lengthy literary works (BDAG 176b), the term βίβλος never refers to brief documents in the NT and refers to brief documents only rarely in the LXX (Gen 2:4; 5:1). Nolland (71 n. 4) claimed that the term frequently referred to less substantial pieces of writing in the LXX, but the examples he offered are actually uses of the form βιβλίον and thus do not prove his point. This poses problems for the popular view that 1:1 serves merely as a title for the genealogy, birth narrative, or first major section of the Gospel. Normal word usage suggests that 1:1 serves as the orig. title for the entire Gospel (Jerome; D&A 1.149–56).

The noun γένεσις, "origin," may refer to the birth of a human being (Matt 1:18). On this basis many commentators conclude that the phrase βίβλος γενέσεως refers to Jesus's genealogy or the account of his birth (e.g., Carson 86–87; H 1.5). However, the phrase βίβλος γενέσεως appears twice in the LXX (Gen 2:4; 5:1). In both instances, the phrase introduces an account of creation, first the creation of the heavens and earth and then the creation of humanity. If Matthew's use of this phrase is influenced by the LXX, the phrase may refer to a creation account here as well. Furthermore, the word γένεσις was used by Matthew's contemporaries as a title for the first book of the Bible in Greek, "Genesis" (Philo *Post.* 127; *Abr.* 1; *Aet.* 19). This title also appears in the oldest extant mss. of the Greek Bible. Thus the phrase βίβλος γενέσεως would prob. cause Matthew's readers to recall the book of Genesis and to recognize that Matthew's Gospel bore a title sim. to that of the first book of the Greek Bible (F 26; Evans 32).

If Matthew had merely intended 1:1 to serve as a title of the genealogy alone, he would likely have followed the LXX by introducing the genealogy with the phrase Αὗται αἱ γενέσεις (Gen 6:9; 10:1; 11:10, 27; 25:12, 19; 36:1, 9; 37:2; Exod 6:14; Num 3:1; Ruth 4:18; 1 Chr 1:29; 4:2). Thus either Matthew introduced his genealogy of Jesus in a unique way, or he purposefully gave his Gospel a title identical to that of the first book of the Bible, a book best known for its account of God's acts of creation.

An important feature of the structure of the Gospel may confirm the latter interpretation. It may be no accident that the Gospel begins with the noun γένεσις and ends with the phrase τῆς συντελείας τοῦ αἰῶνος ("end of the age"). These references stretch from the orig. of the world (by allusion to the Genesis creation account) to the consummation of the age and frame the entirety of the Gospel.

Matthew will explain the etym. significance of the name Ἰησοῦς in 1:21. One's view of the use of the gen. Ἰησοῦ is dependent on the interpretation of the phrase βίβλος γενέσεως. If the phrase merely introduces the genealogy or birth narrative of Jesus, the gen. is subj. and refers to Jesus's coming into being. If the phrase recalls the OT creation accounts, the gen. is likely a gen. of producer or source (W 104–6, though some also label this as a subj. gen.; D&A 1.156) and identifies Jesus as the author of a new creation, a new genesis. For an explicit ref. to the new creation brought about by the Messiah, see Matthew 19:28. For a discussion of the new creation theme in Matthew, see Quarles, *Theology,* 177–89. Some scholars (H 1.9; N 71) affirm that Matthew intended his readers to think of the Genesis creation accounts when they read the phrase "book of origin" but argue that he did not go so far as to present Jesus as the author of a new creation. Instead, Matthew alluded to Genesis to show his readers that he was recording events that were just as important as the creation of the world.

The title Χριστός (from the vb. χρίω, "anoint") means "anointed one" and is thus the equivalent to the Heb. "Messiah." The term referred to the long-awaited deliverer of God's people whose coming the prophets had foretold. The gen. is appos. and thus serves to identify Jesus.

The gen. υἱοῦ "son" is appos. Like many Heb. names transliterated into Gk., Δαυίδ is indecl. (BDF §53). Here it serves as a gen. of relationship (W 83–84). The phrase "son of David" is usually a messianic title in Matthew (9:27; 12:23; 15:22; 20:30, 31; 21:9,

15; cf., 22:42). The phrase identifies Jesus as the one through whom God's covenant with David (2 Sam 7:16) will be fulfilled, the promised king.

The gen. υἱοῦ (second occurrence) is appos. Like Δαυίδ, Ἀβραάμ is indecl. and serves as a gen. of relationship. The description identifies Jesus as a descendant of Abraham and thus the one through whom God's covenant with Abraham will be fulfilled (Gen 12:1–4).

FOR FURTHER STUDY

1. Matthew's Incipit

> Evans, C. A. "'The Book of the Genesis of Jesus Christ': The Purpose of Matthew in Light of the Incipit." Pages 61–72 in *The Gospel of Matthew.* Edited by T. R. Hatina. Vol. 2 of *Biblical Interpretation in Early Christian Gospels.* New York: T.&T. Clark, 2008.
>
> Huizenga, L. A. "Matt 1:1: 'Son of Abraham' as a Christological Category." *Horizons in Biblical Theology* 30 (2008): 103–13.
>
> Nolland, J. "What Kind of Genesis Do We Have in Matt 1.1?" *NTS* 42 (1996): 463–71.
>
> Tatum, W. B. "The Origin of Jesus Messiah (Matt 1:1, 18a): Matthew's Use of the Infancy Traditions." *JBL* 96 (1977): 523–35.

HOMILETICAL SUGGESTIONS

The Gospel at a Glance (1:1)

1. Jesus is the author of a new creation
2. Jesus is the fulfillment of God's covenant with David
3. Jesus is the fulfillment of God's covenant with Abraham

2. Genealogy (1:2–17)

These vv. record the genealogy of Jesus and follow a simple structure: (anar.) father + δὲ ἐγέννησεν + (art.) son. Several additional phrases disrupt this normal structure. These disruptions are likely of special importance to Matthew for various reasons. The first disruption shows that Jacob fathered Judah καὶ τοὺς ἀδελφοὺς αὐτοῦ. This addition is likely designed to remind readers that the son of Abraham fathered the twelve patriarchs, who fathered the twelve tribes. The allusion reminds readers that Jesus as the "son of Abraham" (1:1) founded a new Israel (10:1–4; 19:28). See Quarles, *Theology,* 97–130. The additional phrase in 1:3 καὶ τὸν Ζάρα reminds readers of the providence of God in determining which of Judah's twin sons would be the firstborn (Gen 38:27–30).

The ordinary structure is also disrupted by the addition of the title τὸν βασιλέα to describe David in v. 6. Although several other kings are named in the genealogy, only David is granted this title. This suggests that Jesus's identity as the "son of David" emphasizes his rightful kingship.

The additional phrase καὶ τοὺς ἀδελφοὺς αὐτοῦ ἐπὶ τῆς μετοικεσίας Βαβυλῶνος in 1:11 puzzles commentators. The Old Testament only mentions one brother of Jechoniah, but Matthew refers to brothers (pl.). Gundry suggested that the "brothers" referred to

Jechoniah's "fellow Jews" (G 17). Although such an interpretation is possible lexically, the grammar of the text precludes it. The noun τοὺς ἀδελφούς is a dir. obj. of the vb. ἐγέννησεν and indicates that Josiah fathered these brothers. Thus Matthew refers to Jeconiah and all other legitimate heirs to the throne. The prep. ἐπί with the gen. obj. is temp. and indicates that Josiah fathered his sons about the time of the Babylonian captivity. Μετοικεσία, -ας, ἡ, "deportation," removing someone from his home and native land to a foreign country (BDAG 643a). Although the head noun μετοικεσία is a verbal noun, the gen. Βαβυλῶνος does not fit in subj. or obj. categories since Babylon is the place to which Israel was deported, not the conquering people responsible for the deportation or the conquered people who suffered the deportation. Thus the gen. may be categorized as a gen. of direction (BDF §166). However, the noun Βαβυλῶνος may be an instance of metonymy in which a place name refers to the people that inhabit the place (e.g., 2:3; 8:34), "the Babylonians." If so, this is an example of the subj. gen.

In four instances the structure is slightly disrupted by an identification of the mother that uses ἐκ + (art.), "*mother,*" at the end of the clause. The absence of mention of mothers in the description of the large majority of the generations suggests that the mothers are of particular importance in these four cases. Although several theories attempting to explain these references to mothers have been posed, the most convincing explanation is that all four women (Tamar, Rahab, Ruth, and Bathsheba) were regarded as Gentiles. The presence of these Gentile women in Jesus's family tree demonstrates God's intention to include Gentiles in his redemptive plan (3:9; 8:5–13; 12:15–21; 28:19–20).

Most importantly, the last clause of the genealogy (16b) radically disrupts the structure. Until the last clause, the cadence of the genealogy is so regular that it is almost hypnotic. The disruption in v. 16 would have startled readers with an awareness that Jesus's birth was different from that of any of his ancestors and, in fact, different from the conception of any other person in all history. The phrase τὸν ἄνδρα is appos. and serves to identify Joseph. Although the noun ἀνήρ often means "husband" (BDAG 79b), the context suggests that it here refers to Mary's "man" in another sense, i.e., her betrothed. Μαρίας is a gen. of relationship. The prep. phrase ἐξ ἧς functions like the phrase ἐκ + (art.) mother which was used four times in the genealogy to identify the mothers by whom fathers conceived their children (BDAG 296c).

Although the genealogy consistently used act. forms of γεννάω, Matthew shifted to the pass. vb. ἐγεννήθη, a "divine pass." which refers to an activity of God. The grammar implies that God miraculously conceived Jesus by Mary, as the birth narrative will explicitly demonstrate. The primary purpose of the genealogy is expressed by the description of Ἰησοῦς as ὁ λεγόμενος χριστός. The art. ptc. is subst. and in appos. to the name Jesus. Although the ptc. could be another example of the divine pass., this phrase was commonly used to explain how one was generally recognized by others (BDAG 590b; BDF §412). In such situations the ptc. and the noun expressing the name or title appear in the same case as the noun being described (e.g., 4:18; 9:9; 10:2), hence Χριστός.

The textual var. in the genealogy are not exegetically significant. Some mss. have Ἀσά rather than Ἀσάφ (1:7–8) and Ἀμών rather than Ἀμώς (1:10), but these appear to simply be different transliterations of the same Heb. names. Gundry argued that Matthew's spellings are intended to introduce secondary allusions to the Asaph of the Psalms and Amos the prophet, but this cannot be confirmed since var. spellings are also found in mss. of the LXX and Josephus introduces still other var. spellings with even less likeness to the orig. Heb. On the var. spellings in 1:7–8 and 10, see Metzger, 1–2. On the more important var. in 1:11, 16, see Metzger, 2–6.

The primary sources for the genealogy are likely LXX 1 Chr 1:28, 34; 2:1–15; and Ruth 4:18–22.

1:17 The particle οὖν shows that the verse draws an inference from the preceding genealogy. The adj. Πᾶσαι does not necessarily indicate that Matthew has provided an exhaustive list of the generations from Abraham to David. In this context it merely refers to the sum of those in Matthew's list. Αἱ γενεαὶ . . . γενεαὶ δεκατέσσαρες requires no explicit vb. The vb. εἰσί is implied. The prep. phrases ἀπό + gen. and ἕως + gen. establish the beginning point and ending point of a time period (BDAG 105d; 423b). On the phrase μετοικεσία Βαβυλῶνος, see 1:11.

FOR FURTHER STUDY

2. *The Genealogy of Jesus*

Bockmuehl, M. N. A. "The Son of David and His Mother." *JTS* 62 (2011): 476–93.

Freed, E. D. "The Women in Matthew's Genealogy." *JSNT* 29 (1987): 3–19.

Hood, J. B. *The Messiah, His Brothers, and the Nations: Matthew 1:1–17*. Library of New Testament Studies 441. London: T.&T. Clark, 2011.

Hutchison, J. C. "Women, Gentiles, and the Messianic Mission in Matthew's Genealogy." *BSac* 158 (2001): 152–64.

Kennedy, R. J. *The Recapitulation of Israel: Use of Israel's History in Matthew 1:1–4:11*. WUNT 257. Tübingen: Mohr Siebeck, 2008.

Smit, P. "Something About Mary? Remarks About the Five Women in the Matthean Genealogy." *NTS* 56 (2010): 191–207.

Viviano, B. "Making Sense of the Matthean Genealogy: Matthew 1:17 and the Theology of History." Pages 91–109 in *New Perspectives on the Nativity*. Edited by J. Corley. New York: T.&T. Clark, 2009.

HOMILETICAL SUGGESTIONS

From Genealogy to Theology: Lessons from Jesus's Family Tree (1:2–17)

1. Jesus is the Davidic Messiah
2. Jesus is the Savior of the Gentiles
3. Jesus is the virgin-born Son of God

3. *Jesus's Birth (1:18–25)*

1:18 The noun γένεσις here means "origin, birth" (BDAG 192d) and is roughly equivalent to γέννησις, a factor which prompted a number of scribes to replace the former word with the latter in their mss. The gen. phrase τοῦ Ἰησοῦ Χριστοῦ is an obj. gen., Jesus is the one given birth. Gen. phrases normally follow the noun they modify. The placement of τοῦ Ἰησοῦ Χριστοῦ before ἡ γένεσις likely emphasizes the phrase "of Jesus Christ" and highlights the uniqueness of Jesus's birth (H 1.17). Jesus's conception and birth are unlike that of any of his ancestors mentioned in the preceding genealogy. The vb. ἦν is 3rd sg. impf. indic. of εἰμί.[8] The adverb οὕτως is common in Matthew and means "as follows." BDAG 741d–42d, 2 suggests it is the equivalent of τοιαύτη here.

Μνηστευθείσης gen. sg. fem. of aor. pass. ptc. of μνηστεύω, "become engaged for marriage." The phrase μνηστευθείσης τῆς μητρός is gen. abs., a cstr. common in Matthew. BDF §423 refers to this example as the "harshest and at the same time the rarest" exception to the principle in classical Greek that the antecedent of a gen. abs. does not appear as the subj. of the main clause. They note that the harshness is mitigated by the inf. clause that precedes the main vb. and admit that the phenomenon is paralleled in classical authors. Like most gen. abs., the ptc. is temp. (W 655). With an aor. vb., the aor. ptc. may describe antecedent or contemp. action (W 624–25). In this case the ptc. is contemp. Τῷ Ἰωσήφ is dat. of indir. obj. Πρὶν ἤ "before" was used in Ionic Greek instead of the Attic πρίν to mark temp. precedence, and this practice was adopted in Koine (BDAG 863b; 433c). Συνελθεῖν 2nd aor. act. inf. of dep. συνέρχομαι, "come together," refers to uniting in a sexual relationship or to the formal marriage which was followed by cohabitation and sexual relationships. Εὑρέθη 3rd sg. aor. pass. indic. of εὑρίσκω, "find." The phrase ἐν γαστρί (dat. sing. fem. of γαστήρ, -τρος, ἡ, "stomach, womb") with various vbs., incl. ἔχω, was used by ancient medical writers and in the LXX (18x, e.g., Exod 21:22) to describe pregnancy. Ἔχουσα nom. sing. fem. of pres. act. ptc. of ἔχω, is prob. concessive. The phrase πνεύματος ἁγίου refers to the Holy Spirit. The absence of the def. art. after preps. is common (BDF §255 [3]; R 791–92). The phrase ἐκ πνεύματος ἁγίου is causal and indicates that the Spirit accomplished Mary's pregnancy. However, the discovery of the pregnancy was not accompanied by knowledge of the cause of the pregnancy. Thus, the clause likely means "(Mary) was discovered (to be pregnant), although her pregnancy was produced by the Holy Spirit." This analysis is preferable to the claim that the prep. phrase is "a rather cryptic remark, not well integrated in the syntax of the sentence" (N 93). D&A suggest another alternative: the vb. εὑρίσκω means "it turned out to be" rather than "she was discovered" (D&A 1.200) and cite Acts 5:39; Romans 7:10; and Philippians 2:8 as examples.

On the textual var., see Metzger 6–7.

1:19 The particle δέ serves simply to connect lines of narrative. Although ὁ ἀνήρ followed by the gen. of rel. αὐτῆς could refer to Joseph as Mary's "husband," after the discussion of betrothal in the previous verse, the noun merely means "fiancée," a usage that appears in the LXX (Deut 22:23). The antecedent of αὐτῆς, the gen. sg. fem. 3rd per. pron. from αὐτός, is Μαρίας. Δίκαιος ὤν uses the nom. sg. masc. of the pres. ptc. of εἰμί with the adj. δίκαιος, "righteous" (BDAG 246b–47b) and describes one who

---

8 Although some sources parse forms of εἰμί as act., stative verbs technically do not have voice. Thus, this volume will not include voice when parsing forms of εἰμί.

"conforms to the laws of God and people." The ptc. clause may be adj. and offer a description of Joseph's character or may be adv. If adv., the clause may be *causal, explaining Joseph's motivation for breaking the engagement, or concessive, showing that despite Joseph's fidelity to the law he showed mercy on an allegedly immoral woman. Like ὤν, θέλων (nom. sg. masc. of pres. act. ptc. of θέλω) used anar. is likely adv. (here likely causal). Δειγματίσαι aor. act. inf. of δειγματίζω, "to publicly disgrace." The use of the conj. καί here is debated and one's view significantly affects the meaning of the passage.

The conj. may serve simply as a coordinating conj. mng. "and." In this view the two ptc. clauses are both causal. Both Joseph's righteousness and his desire not to publicly disgrace Mary motivated his decision to seek a quiet divorce. The conj. introduces the result of what precedes it (BDAG 494a–96c, esp. 495a 1.b.ζ) and indicates that Joseph's compassion toward Mary was prompted by his righteousness (NLT).

The conj. may be mildly adversative and emphasize a fact as "surprising or unexpected or noteworthy" and be tr. "and yet, and in spite of that, nevertheless" (BDAG 495b 1.b.η). Other examples of this usage in Matthew include 3:13; 6:26; 10:29; 12:43; 13:17; and 26:60. The first ptc. clause is concessive, and the second is causal: "although Joseph was righteous and yet because he did not desire to shame her publicly"). Thus, Joseph's fidelity to the law, which demanded a harsh penalty for adultery (Deut 22:20–24) was cast in tension with his compassion toward Mary (D&A 204; H 18).

Most of commentators appear to support option 2 based on the claim that "righteous" in Matthew consistently refers to right behavior in accordance with the law. However, on several occasions, "righteous" refers more to character than mere behavior (5:45; 23:28, 35) and includes compassion to others (25:37). Furthermore, Jesus taught that loving and forgiving others is a critical part of having true righteousness that exceeds that of the scribes and Pharisees (5:43–48).

Ἐβουλήθη 3rd sg. of aor. pass. indic. of dep. βούλομαι, "desire, plan." Note that deponents in the fut. and aor. prefer pass. forms (BDF §78–79). The adverb λάθρα means "secretly" and modifies ἀπολῦσαι (aor. act. inf. of ἀπολύω, "to release, divorce"). Matthew often places adv. before the verbals they modify (with the exception of imperatives; BDF §474).

1:20 The clause ταῦτα δὲ αὐτοῦ ἐνθυμηθέντος (gen. sg. masc. of aor. pass. ptc. of dep. ἐνθυμέομαι, "think") is a gen. abs., used temp. to show that Joseph's dilemma was on his mind when the angel appeared. The particle ἰδού draws attention to what follows. The phrase ἄγγελος κυρίου is drawn from the OT and often appears there without the def. art. (e.g., Gen 16:7; 22:11, 15; Exod 3:2; 4:24). The prep. κατά with ὄναρ (acc. sg. neut. of ὄναρ, "dream") appears again in 2:12, 13, 19, 22; and 27:19. The prep. is prob. temp. and means "during a dream" (BDAG 511a–13d, esp. 2a) although CSB, NLT, and ESV use "in a dream." Ἐφάνη 3rd sg. 2nd aor. pass. indic. of φαίνω, "appear." The pron. αὐτῷ serves as the indir. obj. Λέγων is nom. sg. masc. of pres. act. ptc. of λέγω. The adv. ptc. may express *purpose (2:2, the angel appeared in order to communicate what follows; D&A 1.207) or attendant circumstance (8:3).

Φοβηθῇς is 2nd sg. aor. pass. subj. of φοβέω, "fear." The neg. μή with the aor. subj. may prohibit starting an action or *may prohibit an action as a whole (W 723). Παραλαβεῖν is aor. act. inf. of παραλαμβάνω, "to take," and serves as a complementary inf. completing the idea of the prohibition. Μαρίαν and τὴν γυναῖκα (acc. sg. fem. of γυνή, "woman, wife") serve as a dbl. acc. of obj./complement (W 182–89) which BDF §157 refers to as an acc. of obj. and pred. acc. On the various forms of Semitic names, see BDF §53.

The conj. γάρ is causal, expressing the reason Joseph should abandon his fear. Τὸ γεννηθέν is nom. sg. neut. of aor. pass. ptc. of γεννάω, "conceive, give birth." The art. ptc. is subst. Although the ptc. refers to a person, the neut. gender was likely used due to an implied παιδίον, "little child" (see 1:11, 13 [2x], 14, 20 [2x]). Exodus 21:22 (LXX) shows that this noun was used of children still developing in the womb. The use of the neut. ptc. in no way implies that the conceived child was not yet viewed as a person. The phrase ἐν αὐτῇ is unexpected since the genealogy consistently used the prep. ἐκ to identify the role of the mother in conception (1:3, 5, 6), incl. even that of Mary (1:16). This followed the well-established pattern of the LXX. The LXX used the prep. ἐν with γεννάω to mark the place or time in which a child was conceived. Although the LXX sometimes uses the bare dat. to identify the parent to whom a child was born (2 Sam 5:14; 1 Chr 3:4; Jer 16:2), it does not appear to contain any examples of the use of the prep. ἐν to portray a person's involvement in the act of conception. This suggests that Matthew intended the prep. to be understood as loc. in order to emphasize the pass. role Mary played in the conception (H 1.19). The prep. presents Mary here more as the environ in which a conception occurred than a participant in the act of conception. Another unexpected twist is the use of ἐστίν (3rd sg. pres. indic. of εἰμί, "be") with an ἐκ phrase to describe the Spirit's role. Without the vb. ἐστίν, the use of the ἐκ phrase with γεννάω would likely have led readers to conclude that the Spirit fulfilled the male role in the act of conception. The insertion of the ἐστιν precludes this interpretation by portraying the Spirit as the source of Jesus's orig. rather than an agent in the act of conception itself. The placement of the vb. between the noun πνεύματος (gen. sg. neut. of πνεῦμα, "Spirit") and the adj. ἁγίου (gen. sg. neut. of ἅγιος, "holy") is unusual but not unprecedented (Prov 9:10; 13:15).

1:21 The implied subj. of τέξεται (3rd sg. fut. mid. indic. of τίκτω, "give birth") is Mary. The fut. tense is predictive (W 568). The υἱόν serves as the dir. obj. and specifies the gender of the child, which the cstr. in the previous verse left ambiguous. The καί simply joins the two clauses but has the sense "and then" rather than merely "and" since the formal naming followed birth. BDAG lists this use of καί as an example in which "more discriminating usage would call for other particles" (494a–96c 1.b.β). However, their suggested rev. is no improvement on Matthew's clear and more emphatic style. With καλέσεις (2nd sg. fut. act. indic. of καλέω, "call, name"), Matthew shifted from the predictive fut. to the impv. fut., Of the NT writers only Matthew frequently uses the impv. fut., and this is prob. due to the influence of the LXX on Matthew's style (BDF §362; W 569–70). The combination of καλέω with τὸ ὄνομα αὐτοῦ anticipates the quotation of Isaiah 7:14 in 1:23. Τὸ ὄνομα and Ἰησοῦν are dbl.

acc. of obj./complement. Notice that the cstr. breaks a principle recommended for distinguishing the obj. and complement: "If one of the two is a proper name, it will be the object" (W 184). However, it follows another principle: "If one of the two is articular, it will be the object" (W 184). Αὐτοῦ is a gen. of poss.

The Heb. name Yeshua, which is transliterated Ἰησοῦς, means "Yahweh saves." The clause introduced by γάρ shows why the name is appropriate. Pers. pron. were not used with the two previous vbs. in the verse. This suggests that the pers. pron. αὐτός is emphatic: *He* (and not another) will save. Σώσει (3rd sg. fut. act. indic. of σώζω, "save") is a predictive fut., though the fulfillment citation in the next verse shows that it expresses more of a promise about the fut. than a mere prediction. Esp. with the def. art., the noun λαός often referred to the people of Israel (BDAG 586c–87a, esp. 4) and was often used in opp. to "Gentiles." Matthew will later show that Jesus is the founder of a new people of God, and it is to this new Israel that the angel refers. The gen. sg. αὐτοῦ can be seen as a gen. of relationship or poss. Again, Matthew will later show that Jesus is the founder, and not just member, of this people. He has already implied this by presenting Jesus as the "son of Abraham" in 1:1 (see Quarles, *Theology*, 97–130). Although many interpreters treat the verse as if it said that Jesus will save his people from the punishment or wrath brought on by sin, Matthew wrote instead the stark phrase ἀπὸ τῶν ἁμαρτιῶν αὐτῶν. The ἀπό w. the gen. object ἁμαρτιῶν denotes separation "away from." The αὐτῶν is a subj. gen. identifying members of "his people" as those who committed the sins. The statement seems to personify "sins," portraying them as enemy combatants who have captured people and keep them as hostages or slaves until Jesus rescues them. The statement is likely an allusion to Ezekiel 36:28–29; 37:23 and is linked to the prophet's promise of a new Exodus and new covenant.

1:22 The antecedent of the near dem. pron. τοῦτο (nom. sg. neut. from οὗτος, "this") is the entire episode Matthew just narrated. Matthew makes that clear by adding the adj. ὅλον. The shift to the pf. tense with γέγονεν (3rd sg. pf. act. indic. of dep. γίνομαι, "come into being, happen") is unexpected and raises doubts that the verse contains an explanation inserted in the narrative by Matthew. "All this has happened . . ." sounds initially more like words spoken by the angel to Joseph (Carson 102). However, Matthew uses the pf. tense of γίνομαι in 21:4 and 26:56 to introduce his fulfillment citations with constructions sim. to the one here. Matthew 21:4 is clearly not a part of the preceding dir. discourse (which would require "this must happen" instead of "this has happened") and 26:56 is prob. not either (N 99). The pf. γέγονεν has been explained as a substitution for the aor. (BDF §343) or as indicating that the event "stands recorded" (Moule 15), but the pf. prob. has its common extensive or consummative nuance emphasizing the completion of the action (in this case, necessary to fulfill the OT prophecy). The conj. ἵνα with the subjunc. πληρωθῇ (3rd sg. aor. pass. subjunc. of πληρόω, "fulfill") introduces a purpose clause expressing the divine purpose for Jesus's miraculous conception and the angelic command to name him Jesus. The subst. ptc. τὸ ῥηθέν (nom. sg. neut. of aor. pass. ptc. of λέγω, "speak") is the subj. of the vb. The two prep. phrases carefully distinguish between the two kinds of agency involved in the production of inspired Scripture. Ὑπό with the gen. obj.

(κυρίου) expresses ultimate agency. The noun κύριος was commonly used in the LXX as the tr. of the divine name Yahweh and referred to the God of Israel. The application of this same title to Jesus later often bears the same sense. Διά with the gen. obj. (τοῦ προφήτου) expresses intermediate agency. The cstr. indicates that God spoke through OT writers and that he is ultimately responsible for the contents of the Scriptures. The cstr. recalls OT texts such as Ezekiel 38:17 and Daniel 9:10. Λέγοντος is gen. sg. masc. of pres. act. ptc. of λέγω, "speak." The ptc. prob. modifies the ptc. ῥηθέν and means: "what was spoken by the Lord through the prophet by saying." Consequently, the ptc. is pleonastic (redundant) and due to Semitic idiom (W 649–50). The gen. case of the ptc. looks to the Lord or the prophet (or both) as the speaker. Alternatively, the ptc. may be adj.: "the prophet who says . . ." (R 1123 [on 21:4]). For the text-critical issues, see Metzger 7–8.

1:23 On the use of Isa 7:14, see Beale and Carson 3c–5b. Ἰδού prompts attention. The noun παρθένος refers to a "virgin," one who has not engaged in intercourse (Quarles "Bethlehem," 188–95). For the mng. of the phrase combining ἐν γαστρί w. forms of ἔχω (ἕξει is 3rd sg. fut. act. indic.), see 1:18. The fut. tense is predictive. On τέξεται υἱόν, see 1:21. The conj. καί again has the sense "and then" since pregnancy obviously precedes giving birth. The second καί likely has this sense as well since the formal bestowal of a child's name normally followed birth. Καλέσουσιν is 3rd pl. fut. act. indic. of καλέω, "call, name."

Matthew recognized that some of his readers would not understand the etym. significance of the LXX's Gk. transliteration Ἐμμανουήλ (from the Heb. name in Isa 7:14) so he tr. the Heb. phrase Μεθ' ἡμῶν ὁ θεός. This statement appears to form an inclusio with the phrase ἐγὼ μεθ' ὑμῶν εἰμί in 28:20 (Kingsbury 96; D&A 1.217). The inclusio suggests that Jesus's identity as Immanuel is an important theme of the Gospel. Further, it identifies Jesus's disciples as his people to whom he promises his presence and equates Jesus with God. M introduces his tr. with ὅ ἐστιν μεθερμηνευόμενον. The combination of ἐστίν and μεθερμηνευόμενον (nom. sg. neut. of pres. pass. ptc. of μεθερμηνεύω, "tr., interpret") is pres. periph. In classical Gk., periph. cstr. emphasized the aspect of the ptc., but this is seldom the case in Hellenistic Gk. or the NT in particular (W 647–49).

1:24 Ἐγερθείς is nom. sg. masc. of aor. pass. ptc. of ἐγείρω, "raise." The voice is likely the "divine pass.;" God woke Joseph. The ptc. is prob. temp. and indicates that immediately upon wakening, Joseph obeyed the angel's instructions. The phrase ἀπό τοῦ ὕπνου expresses separation. In the LXX, the prep. ἐκ was more commonly used in sim. constructions. On the distinction between the prep. ἀπό and ἐκ, see R 574–78. In light of the emphasis on Joseph's obedience in the birth narrative, one would expect Matthew to use the intensive comp. particle καθώς rather than ὡς. However, he prefers ὡς (40x) over καθώς (only 3x). Matthew used καθώς only to describe the perfect obedience of Jesus's disciples to his command in 21:6, Jesus's perfect fulfillment of OT prophecy in 26:24, and Jesus's perfect fulfillment of his promise to rise again in 28:6. Nevertheless, he stresses Joseph's obedience by emphasizing the immediacy of the obedience, by stating that he did ὡς προσέταξεν (3rd sg. aor. act. indic. of προστάσσω, "command") αὐτῷ, and by listing each act by which Joseph fulfilled the angel's instructions. For example, παρέλαβεν τὴν γυναῖκα αὐτοῦ (1:24) matches παραλαβεῖν . . .τὴν γυναῖκα σοῦ (1:20), and καὶ ἐκάλεσεν τὸ ὄνομα αὐτοῦ Ἰησοῦν (1:25) matches καὶ καλέσεις τὸ ὄνομα αὐτοῦ Ἰησοῦν (1:21). A sim. feature will occur in 1:13-14 and 1:20-21.

1:25 The καί here seems to have the sense "and yet" (see on 1:19) since sexual priv-ileges were a marital right. Matthew clearly used ἐγίνωσκεν (3rd sg. impf. act. indic. of γινώσκω, "know") to speak of a sexual relationship since the vb. appears in a dis-cussion of marriage and childbearing. This nuance of the vb. was common in the LXX (e.g., Gen 4:1, 17; Judg 11:39; 21:12; 1 Sam 1:19). The impf. tense is prob. prog. and expresses Joseph's continuing resolve to abstain from sexual relationships with Mary. A great debate centers on the precise mng. of ἕως οὗ ἔτεκεν υἱόν. Many Roman Catholic scholars have argued that even after Jesus's birth, Joseph and Mary continued to abstain from sexual relationships. Protestant scholars often argue that ἕως οὗ implies that Joseph abstained from sexual relationship with Mary only "until" Jesus's birth and that they had sexual relationships thereafter. However, the grammar and vocabu-lary of this particular cstr. cannot settle the issue conclusively. Other NT data must be examined. The ἕως οὗ seems to *imply* fut. sexual relationships since if Matthew had wished to affirm Mary's perpetual virginity he would have best ended the statement with αὐτήν: Joseph did not have sexual relationships with her (ever). Most textual crit-ics suggest that some ancient scribes viewed the text as implying later sexual relations between Joseph and Mary and that this motivated the omission of the entire cstr. οὐκ ἐγίνωσκεν αὐτὴν ἕως οὗ in some texts (k and sy[s]). However, one cannot automatically assume this omission was intentional or exhume the possible theological motivations of an ancient scribe unless they are part of a clear tendency manifested elsewhere in the ms. or version. The most that can be said confidently based on the evidence of this cstr. is that Joseph did not have relations with Mary prior to Jesus's birth. Matthew does not explicitly state what happened afterward. For a discussion of the var., see Metzger, 8.

FOR FURTHER STUDY

3. *The Birth of Jesus*

Allison, C. C., Jr. "Divorce, Celibacy and Joseph (Matthew 1:18–25 and 19:1–12)." *JSNT* 49 (1993): 3–10.

Brown, R. E. "The Annunciation of Joseph (Matt 1:18–25)." *Worship* 61 (1987): 482–92.

_____. *The Birth of the Messiah: A Commentary on the Infancy Narratives in Matthew and Luke.* 1st ed. Garden City, NY: Doubleday, 1977.

Kingsbury, J. D. "The Birth Narrative of Matthew." Pages 154–65 in *The Gospel of Matthew in Current Study.* Edited by D. E. Aune. Grand Rapids: Eerdmans, 2001.

Klassen-Wiebe, S. "Matthew 1:18–25." *Int* 46 (1992): 392–95.

Lincoln, A. T. "Contested Paternity and Contested Readings: Jesus's Conception in Matthew 1.18–25." *JSNT* 34 (2012): 211–31.

Nolland, J. "No Son-of-God Christology in Matthew 1.18–25." *JSNT* 62 (1996): 3–12.

4. *Matthew's Use of Isaiah 7:14*

Compton, R. B. "The Immanuel Prophecy in Isaiah 7:14–16 and Its Use in Matthew 1:23: Harmonizing Historical Context and Single Meaning." *Detroit Baptist Seminary Journal* 12 (2007): 3–15.

Dennert, B. C. "A Note on Use of Isa 7:14 in Matt 1:23 Through the Interpretation of the Septuagint." *TJ* 30 (2009): 97–105.

Menken, M. J. J. "The Textual Form of the Quotation From Isaiah 7:14 in Matthew 1:23." *NovT* 43 (2001): 144–60.

Quarles, C. L. "Why Not 'Beginning from Bethlehem'?: A Critique of Dunn's Treatment of the Synoptic Birth Narratives." Pages 173–96 in *Memories of Jesus: A Critical Assessment of James D. G. Dunn's Quest of the Historical Jesus*. Edited by R. B. Stewart. Nashville: B&H, 2010.

HOMILETICAL SUGGESTIONS

The Birth of the Messiah (1:18–25)

1. Jesus is the virgin-born Immanuel
2. Jesus is the fulfillment of the divinely inspired Scriptures
3. Jesus is the Savior of sinners

4. *The Visit of the Magi (2:1–12)*

2:1 Τοῦ Ἰησοῦ γεννηθέντος is gen. abs. and temp., "after Jesus was born . . ." Γεννηθέντος gen. sg. masc. of aor. pass. ptc. of γεννάω "to conceive, give birth." Ἐν is loc. Τῆς Ἰουδαίας "of Judea" is either a partitive or poss. gen. Ἐν ἡμέραις is temp. and marks a period of time in which an event occurs (BDAG 326c–30b, esp. 10). The gen. Ἡρῴδου is difficult to classify. The cstr. refers to the days during which Herod reigned and thus may be regarded as a gen. of time. Τοῦ βασιλέως is simple appos. The phrase means "in the days during which Herod the king reigned" Ἰδού (1:20). On μάγοι, see G. Delling, *TDNT* 4.356–59. A μάγος was a member of the priestly caste from Persia or Babylonia who was an expert in astrology and the interpretation of dreams. The ἀπό expresses place of orig. Ἀνατολῶν (gen. pl. fem. of ἀνατολή) referred to the place of the rising of the sun, the east. Matthew used the sg. form of the noun to refer to an act of rising and the pl. form to refer to the east. Παρεγένοντο 3rd pl. 2nd aor. mid. indic. of dep. παραγίνομαι "come, arrive, be pres." Εἰς denotes entrance into the city. Greek writers referred to the holy city of the Jews as ἡ or τὰ Ἱεροσόλυμα or ἡ Ἱερουσαλήμ (BDAG 470c–471a; BDF §39, 56). Matthew always used the anar. form Ἱεροσόλυμα (sometimes regarded fem. sg. [2:3] and sometimes as neut. pl. [4:25 and 15:1]) except for the use of Ἱερουσαλήμ in 23:37 in a dir. quotation.

2:2 The ptc. λέγοντες may express purpose (the magi entered Jerusalem in order to pose their question) or attendant circumstance (NIV). The ptc. does not fit the pattern for attendant circumstance described in Wallace since (1) the ptc. is pres. rather than aor. tense, (2) it follows the main vb. in word order, and (3) it is not temp. antecedent to the main vb. (W 641–45). Furthermore, Matthew clearly used a ptc. of purpose (in the fut. tense) with a vb. referring to "coming" in Matthew 27:49. Given the rarity of fut.

ptcs. in the NT, it is not surprising that Matthew would use pres. ptc. in a sim. way. See also 19:3; 22:35; 27:55. However, 8:3 contains an apparent example of a ptc. of attendant circumstance that does not follow Wallace's pattern. Thus a decision is difficult. The ptc. does not merely introduce indirect discourse since the main vb. (παραγίνομαι) is not a vb. describing an act of speech (BDF §420). The use of the ptc. τεχθείς (nom. sg. masc. of aor. pass. ptc. of τίκτω "give birth") in the 1st attrib. position prob. refers to Jesus as the "born king," i.e., king by birthright, rather than merely a king who was born (D&A 1.233). The description may contrast Jesus, whose Davidic descent was demonstrated in the genealogy, with Herod, who had no claim to Davidic lineage. Τῶν Ἰουδαίων may be a *gen. of subord. ("king over the Jews") or partitive gen. ("king who is one of the Jews"; G 27), which contrasts Jesus's Jewishness as a descendant of Judah with Herod's Idumean descent. The gen. pron. αὐτοῦ ordinarily follows the noun it modifies. Its placement here is prob. emphatic: *his* star. The prep. ἐν is temp., and the sg. τῇ ἀνατολῇ refers to the star's rising (2:1). Προσκυνῆσαι is aor. act. inf. of προσκυνέω "worship" and expresses purpose.

2:3 Ἀκούσας (nom. sg. masc. of aor. act. ptc. of ἀκούω) is causal: "because the king Herod heard" (D&A 1.237). Ἡρῴδης refers to Herod the Great. The name is in simple appos. to ὁ βασιλεύς. Ἐταράχθη 3rd sg. aor. pass. indic. of ταράσσω "disturb, unsettle." The adj. πᾶσα shows that Ἱεροσόλυμα was regarded as fem. sg. in this context. Since the adj. πᾶς is sg. and the noun is anar., πᾶσα Ἱεροσόλυμα refers to "Jerusalem as a whole," i.e., the population of Jerusalem in general (BDAG 782b–84c, esp. 4a). The prep. μετά with the gen. αὐτοῦ expresses personal association and shows that most Jerusalemites shared Herod's emotional reaction to the appearance and questions of the magi. They were "implicit sympathizers" of Herod (D&A 1.238; N 112).

2:4 Συναγαγών (nom. sg. masc. of 2nd aor. act. ptc. of συνάγω "gather") is temp. Ἀρχιερεύς in the sg. refers to the high priest, but in the pl. refers to the current high priest along with his surviving predecessors and members of the Sanhedrin who belonged to the highest ranking priestly families (BDAG 139a–b). A γραμματεύς was an expert in matters related to the study of the Heb. Scriptures. The gen. τοῦ λαοῦ (of the [Jewish] people) prob. distinguishes these particular scribes from specialists in Roman law who advised Herod. Outside of Judaism a γραμματεύς was a clerk, secretary, or scholar (LSJ 358d–59a). Ἐπυνθάνετο 3rd sg. impf. mid. indic. of dep. πυνθάνομαι "seek to learn by inquiry." The use of the impf. tense with a vb. of asking indicates that the action of asking was complete but that the second action (giving birth) was presumed not to have yet occurred (BDF §328). The prep. phrase παρ' αὐτῶν (antecedent: chief priests and scribes) marks the source of information for the inquiry. The def. art. w. χριστός shows that the noun functions as a title rather than a name, i.e., the Messiah. The pres. tense of γεννᾶται (3rd sg. pres. pass. indic. of γεννάω, "give birth") is prob. futuristic and adds connotations of immediacy and certainty: "Where is the Messiah about to be born?"

2:5 The def. art. οἱ may be used as a dem. or pers. pron. and this is esp. common in combination with the use of δέ to mark progression in a narrative (BDAG 686a–89c, esp. 1). Ἐν Βηθλέεμ τῆς Ἰουδαίας (2:1). Γάρ is explanatory. The adv. οὕτως may pertain to what precedes or what follows. In combination with γέγραπται, it introduces a quotation and means "as follows." Διά with the gen. (τοῦ προφήτου) expresses intermediate agency and implies the ultimate divine agency explicitly stated in 1:22. On the var., see Metzger 8.

2:6 For a comparison of Matthew's quotation of Micah 5:1–3 with the MT and LXX, see D&A 1.242–44. For Matthew's use of the prophecy, see Beale and Carson 5d–7c. Οὐδαμῶς is a marker of emphatic negation (BDAG 734d) mng. "by no means." The prep. ἐν with τοῖς ἡγεμόσιν (dat. pl. masc. of ἡγεμών "governor, leader") marks Bethlehem's position within members of a group (BDAG 326c–30b, esp. 1d). Ἐκ σοῦ identifies Bethlehem as the place of orig. Ἐξελεύσεται (3rd sg. fut. mid. indic. of dep. ἐξέρχομαι, "come out." Ἡγούμενος (nom. sg. masc. of pres. mid. ptc. of dep. ἡγέομαι "lead, guide") is subst. Although subst. ptc. are most often articular, anar. subst. ptc. are amply attested in the NT. The anar. form is prob. qualitative. Ὅστις indicates that this figure belongs to a certain class: "a leader, one who will shepherd" (BDAG 729d–30b, esp. 2a). Ποιμανεῖ (3rd sg. fut. act. indic. of ποιμαίνω "shepherd") is a predictive fut. Μου is a gen. of relationship.

2:7 The temp. adv. τότε supports regarding the ptc. καλέσας as temp.: "then after Herod called." Λάθρᾳ (1:19). Ἠκρίβωσεν (3rd sg. aor. act. indic. of ἀκριβόω "ascertain precisely") emphasizes the importance of precision in assigning a date to the star's appearance (BDAG 39a). Although it is grammatically possible to view the ptc. φαινομένου as adj., it is prob. subst. and ἀστέρος is a subj. gen. Thus the phrase τὸν χρόνον τοῦ φαινομένου ἀστέρος means "the time of the appearance of the star," which presumably signaled the moment of the Messiah's birth.

2:8 Πέμψας (nom. sg. masc. of aor. act. ptc. of πέμπω "send") is temp.: "when he sent." Πορευθέντες (nom. pl. masc. of aor. pass. ptc. of dep. πορεύομαι "go") is a ptc. of attendant circumstance. Wallace (642) notes "in narrative literature, in almost all of the aor. ptc. + aor. impv. constructions, the ptc. is attendant circumstance." Used with an impv. vb., the ptc. assumes an impv. nuance. Ἐξετάσατε 2nd pl. aor. act. impv. of ἐξετάζω "scrutinize, examine, inquire." The aor. impv. expresses urgency (W 720). Although many EVV render the clause "search diligently for the child," the prep. περί prob. retains its normal sense "about, concerning" (BDAG 797c–97d, esp. 1b) and is used to identify the subj. about which an inquiry is made. Thus the LEB is prob. more accurate: "inquire carefully concerning the child." Ἐπάν is a temp. conj. used with the subjunc. and mng. "when, as soon as" (BDAG 358b–c). It stresses immediacy, and this suggests that the aor. impv. ἀπαγγείλατε (2nd pl. aor. act. impv. of ἀπαγγέλλω "give an account, report") expresses urgency.

When used with the subjunc. (προσκυνήσω 1st sg. aor. act. subjunc. of προσκυνέω, "worship"), the conj. ὅπως marks the purpose for an event (BDAG 718a–c). Herod attempted to hide his murderous intentions with pretensions of worship. Κἀγώ is a combination of καί and ἐγώ. The καί is likely adjunctive, "I too," and indicates that Herod desired to join the magi in their worship of the Messiah (2:2). Ἐλθών (nom. sg. masc. of 2nd aor. act. ptc. of dep. ἔρχομαι) is prob. a temp. ptc., "when I come." Αὐτῷ is dat. of dir. obj.

2:9 Although the οἱ may mark ἀκούσαντες as subst., the def. art. prob. functions as a dem. pron. (BDAG 686a–89c, esp. 1c). Ἀκούσαντες (nom. pl. masc. of aor. act. ptc. of ἀκούω, "hear" is prob. temp. "After they heard the king, they proceeded on their journey." Τοῦ βασιλέως is a gen. of dir. obj. (W 131–34). Ἐπορεύθησαν 3rd pl. aor. pass. indic. of dep. πορεύομαι, "go, travel." Ἰδού (1:20). ὁ ἀστήρ may refer to a number of different luminous astronomical phenomena (BDAG 145c–d). The prep. phrase ἐν τῇ ἀνατολῇ is temp., and the obj. refers to the star's rising or appearance (2:1, 2). Προῆγεν 3rd sg. impf. act. indic. of προάγω, "lead." Ἐλθών is prob. ptc. of attendant circumstance (W 640–45). Ἐστάθη 3rd sg. aor. pass. indic. of ἵστημι, "stand." Παιδίον is the dimin. form of παῖς and means "little child" or "infant."

2:10 Although most EVV treat ἰδόντες (nom. pl. masc. of 2nd aor. act. ptc. of ὁράω, "see") as temp., the ptc. prob. is causal. Matthew's point is not that sight of the star was antecedent or contemp. to the joy of the magi. Rather, sight of the star prompted that joy. Ἐχάρησαν (3rd pl. aor. pas. indic. of χαίρω, "rejoice"). Χαράν is a cognate acc. which emphasizes the magi's joy. This emphasis is amplified by the adj. μεγάλην (μέγας, μεγάλη, μέγα, "large, great") and even further by the adv. σφόδρα, "very."

2:11 Ἐλθόντες (nom. pl. masc. of 2nd aor. act. ptc. of dep. ἔρχομαι, "go, come") is temp., "when they went." Τῆς μητρός is gen. of simple appos. Αὐτοῦ is gen. of relationship. Πεσόντες (nom. pl. masc. of 2nd aor. act. ptc. of πίπτω, "fall") is a ptc. of attendant circumstance. Προσεκύνησαν 3rd pl. aor. act. indic. of προσκυνέω, "worship." Ἀνοίξαντες (nom. pl. masc. of aor. act. ptc. of ἀνοίγω, "open, unlock") is prob. a ptc. of attendant circumstance. The dir. obj. τοὺς θησαυρούς refers here to the repositories for one's valuables: "treasure boxes or chests." The three acc. nouns χρυσόν ("gold"), λίβανον ("incense"), and σμύρναν ("myrrh") are appos. to δῶρα ("gifts").

2:12 Although many EVV treat the ptc. χρηματισθέντες (nom. pl. masc. of aor. pass. ptc. of χρηματίζω, "warn") as temp., it is more likely causal. The divine warning did not merely precede the magi's taking an alternative route (NIV; NASB); it prompted the detour. The divine pass. reinforces the basic sense of the lexeme, which typically means "impart a divine message/warning." Κατ᾽ ὄναρ 1:20. Μὴ ἀνακάμψαι (aor. act. inf. of ἀνακάμπτω, "return") is inf. of indirect discourse (W 603–5). The warning suggests that the magi fell for Herod's deception and would have returned to him apart from divine intervention. The prep. διά w. the gen. ὁδοῦ ("road, highway") expresses extension through an area and means "via, through." Ἀνεχώρησαν 3rd pl. aor. act. indic. of ἀναχωρέω, "return, depart."

FOR FURTHER STUDY

5. *The Reign of Herod the Great*

Hoehner, H. W. *DNTB* 485–94.

_____. "The Date of the Death of Herod the Great." Pages 101–11 in *Chronos, Kairos, Christos*. Edited by J. Vardaman and E. Yamauchi. Winona Lake, IN: Eisenbrauns, 1989.

Steinmann, A. E. "When Did Herod the Great Reign?" *NovT* 51 (2009): 1–29.

6. The Visit of the Magi

Ferrari d'Occhieppo, K. "The Star of the Magi and Babylonian Astronomy." Pages 41–53 in *Chronos, Kairos, Christos*. Edited by J. Vardaman and E. Yamauchi. Winona Lake, IN: Eisenbrauns, 1989.

Molnar, M. R. *The Star of Bethlehem*. New Brunswick, NJ: Rutgers University Press, 2000.

Powell, M. A. "The Magi as Wise Men: Re-Examining a Basic Supposition." *NTS* 46 (2000): 1–20.

Yamauchi, E. "The Episode of the Magi." Pages 15–39 in *Chronos, Kairos, Christos*. Edited by J. Vardaman and E. Yamauchi. Winona Lake, IN: Eisenbrauns, 1989.

HOMILETICAL SUGGESTIONS

The Majesty of King Jesus (2:1–12)

1. A Majestic Birth
   a. Jesus's birth was announced by the star (natural revelation)
   b. Jesus's birth was announced by the Scriptures (special revelation)
2. A Majestic Baby
   a. Jesus is worthy of a lengthy journey
   b. Jesus is worthy of our sincere worship
   c. Jesus is worthy of our greatest treasures

5. The Flight to Egypt (2:13–15)

2:13 Ἀναχωρησάντων (gen. pl. masc. of aor. act. ptc. of ἀναχωρέω, "depart") is a gen. abs. and temp. The antecedent of αὐτῶν is μάγοι. Ἰδού (1:20). Κατ' ὄναρ (1:20). Φαίνεται is a historical pres. (comp. the use of the aor. in 1:20). Λέγων is prob. a ptc. of purpose; the angel (heavenly messenger) appeared in order to deliver a divine message (2:2). However, attendant circumstance is also possible (8:3; NIV). Ἐγερθείς (nom. sg. masc. of aor. pass. ptc. of ἐγείρω, "wake, rise") expresses attendant circumstance (W 641). Παράλαβε (2nd sg. aor. act. impv. of παραλαμβάνω, "take") expresses urgency. Φεῦγε (2nd sg. pres. act. impv. of φεύγω, "flee") and ἴσθι (2nd sg. pres. impv. of εἰμί, "be") emphasize duration, i.e., Joseph was to continue fleeing until he reached safety in Egypt (cf. 24:16–20) and then remain there. Ἕως with ἄν and the subjunc. (εἴπω) indicates that an event is contingent upon certain circumstances (BDAG 422d–24a). Μέλλει with the pres. inf. (ζητεῖν) may stress either *imminence or inevitability (BDAG 627b–28c). Ἀπολέσαι (aor. act. inf. of ἀπόλλυμι, "destroy") with the gen. art. τοῦ expresses purpose.

2:14 The def. art. ὁ here functions as a pers. or dem. pron., and the δέ marks a new development in the narrative. Ἐγερθείς (2:13). Παρέλαβεν 3rd sg. 2nd aor. act. indic. of παραλαμβάνω, "take." Νυκτός (gen. sg. fem. of νύξ, "night") is a gen. of time identifying the time during which an action occurred (W 122–24). The repetition of each element from the preceding command and the use of the gen. of time stress that Joseph's obedience was complete and immediate.

2:15 Ἦν (3rd sg. impf. indic. of εἰμί, "be"). Ἕως here serves as a prep. to indicate extent of time. The ἵνα with the subjunc. (πληρωθῇ) expresses purpose. Πληρωθῇ (3rd sg. aor. pass. subjunc. of πληρόω, "fulfill") is a divine pass., i.e., God fulfilled his prophecy through these events. Τὸ ῥηθέν nom. sg. neut. of aor. pass. ptc. of λέγω, "say." Ὑπό with the gen. (κυρίου) expresses ultimate agency and διά with the gen. (τοῦ προφήτου) expresses intermediate agency. The grammar attests to the divine inspiration of the words of the prophet. Λέγοντος 1:20. The quotation from Hosea 11:1 is identical to the LXX except that Matthew substituted ἐκάλεσα (1st sg. aor. act. indic. of καλέω, "call, summon") for the LXX's μετεκάλεσα, τὸν υἱόν for the LXX's τὰ τέκνα, and μου for the LXX's αὐτοῦ (referring to Israel). In its orig. context the statement described the Exodus. Matthew's adaptation indicates that Jesus's departure from Egypt signals the new Exodus. For Matthew's use of Hosea 11:1, see Beale and Carson 7b–8d.

6. The Slaughter of the Children of Bethlehem (2:16–18)

2:16 Τότε seems to imply that Herod's action occurred immediately after the flight of the holy family. It may mark a subsection of the narrative (Levinsohn 95). Thus they narrowly escaped. Ἰδών (nom. sg. masc. of aor. act. ptc. of ὁράω, "see, perceive") is prob. causal. Ἐνεπαίχθη 3rd sg. aor. pass. indic. of ἐμπαίζω, "trick." The phrase ὑπὸ τῶν μάγων expresses Herod's perception that the magi tricked him. He was not aware that he was actually tricked by God, who sent warning and instructions to the magi to evade Herod's snare. Ἐθυμώθη 3rd sg. aor. pass. indic. of θυμόω, "be angry." Ἀποστείλας (nom. sg. masc. of aor. act. ptc. of ἀποστέλλω, "send") expresses means. The ptc. helps clarify the vb. ἀνεῖλεν (3rd sg. aor. act. indic. of ἀναιρέω, "take away, destroy, execute"). Herod did not personally kill the children of Bethlehem but ordered their death. The dual use of πᾶς in the phrases πάντας τοὺς παῖδας and πᾶσι τοῖς ὁρίοις αὐτῆς emphasizes the horrific extent of the slaughter. Ἀπό with the gen. διετοῦς (gen. sg. masc. of διετής, "two years old") marks the starting point for a temp. range. The adv. κατωτέρω indicates the direction of the range, "lower, under." Κατά with the acc. (τὸν χρόνον) identifies the standard used to determine this time frame. Ἠκρίβωσεν 3rd sg. aor. act. indic. of ἀκριβόω, "ascertain precisely." Παρά with the gen. (τῶν μάγων) identifies the magi as the source of Herod's information (2:7).

2:17 Τότε may mean *"at that time" or introduce what follows in time (2:7, 16). See also Levinsohn 97. On ἐπληρώθη τὸ ῥηθὲν διὰ Ἰερεμίου τοῦ προφήτου λέγοντος, see 1:22 and 2:15. The divine pass. ῥηθέν implies divine inspiration, even without the stated ὑπὸ κυρίου.

2:18 This is a quotation of Jeremiah 31:15 (38:15 LXX). See Beale and Carson 8d–10d. The phrase ἐν Ῥαμά may modify the noun φωνή (thus the voice spoke in Ramah*; 1 Sam 10:2) or the vb. ἠκούσθη (3rd sg. aor. pass. indic. of ἀκούω, "hear"; thus the voice was heard in Ramah but did not necessarily originate there [which would be compatible with the theory that Rachel was buried in Bethlehem]). Κλαυθμός, "weeping." Ὀδυρμός, "mourning." The adj. πολύς expresses a high quantity or degree of intensity and describes the mourning as profuse and/or profound. Κλαίουσα (nom. sg. fem. of pres. act. ptc. of κλαίω, "weep") is prob. epex., i.e., it identifies the voice and explains the weeping in the previous lines. When used trans., the vb. means "weep for." Ἤθελεν 3rd sg. impf. act. indic. of θέλω, "want." Παρακληθῆναι (aor. pass. inf. of παρακαλέω, "comfort") is a complementary inf. On the var., see Metzger 8.

7. Herod's Death and the Return to Israel (2:19–23)

2:19 Τελευτήσαντος (gen. sg. masc. of aor. act. ptc. of τελευτάω, "die") is a gen. abs., temp., and likely expresses antecedence: "after Herod died." On the clause ἰδοὺ ἄγγελος κυρίου φαίνεται κατ᾽ ὄναρ τῷ Ἰωσήφ. . . , see 2:13.

2:20 On λέγων· ἐγερθεὶς παράλαβε τὸ παιδίον καὶ τὴν μητέρα αὐτοῦ, see 2:13. The vb. πορεύου (2nd sg. pres. mid. impv. of dep. πορεύομαι, "go, travel") replaced the vb. φεῦγε (2:13) because the flight to Egypt was an emergency evacuation but the return to Israel was not. The angel's words τεθνήκασιν γὰρ οἱ ζητοῦντες τὴν ψυχὴν τοῦ παιδίου clearly allude to Exodus 4:19: τεθνήκασιν γὰρ πάντες οἱ ζητοῦντές σου τὴν ψυχήν. Wallace (404) classifies the pl. number of the subst. ptc. as generalizing or categorical, but this overlooks the fact that Matthew adopted the pl. to heighten the parallel with Exodus 4:19. Τεθνήκασιν (3rd pl. pf. act. indic. of θνήσκω, "die") is prob. intensive. Those who would murder the child are now dead and no longer pose a threat. Ζητοῦντες (nom. pl. masc. of pres. act. ptc. of ζητέω, "seek") is contemp. with the pf. vb.: "those who were seeking." The prog. aspect of the ptc. in this context implies that Herod's search for Jesus continued until his death. The angel's application of a statement orig. made to and about Moses to Jesus identifies Jesus as the prophet like Moses promised in Deuteronomy 18:15–19.

2:21 The repetition of the elements of the command in 2:20 stresses Joseph's complete obedience. On ὁ δὲ ἐγερθεὶς παρέλαβεν τὸ παιδίον καὶ τὴν μητέρα αὐτοῦ, see 2:14. Εἰσῆλθεν 3rd sg. 2nd aor. act. indic. of dep. εἰσέρχομαι, "enter."

2:22 Ἀκούσας (nom. sg. masc. of aor. act. ptc. of ἀκούω, "hear") is causal: "Because he heard . . ., he was afraid." Ἀρχέλαος was a son of Herod the Great and ethnarch of Judea, Idumaea, and Samaria from Herod's death until he was deposed by Augustus in AD 6. He was notorious for his cruelty, and Joseph's fear was reasonable. The vb. βασιλεύει is a "pres. retained in indirect discourse" (W 537–39). Τῆς Ἰουδαίας is a gen. of dir. obj. (W 131–34). In this context the prep. ἀντί clearly expresses substitution: "instead of, in the place of" (Harris 50–51). Ἐκεῖ ("there") refers to Judea (2:22). Ἀπελθεῖν (2nd aor. act. inf. of dep. ἀπέρχομαι, "go"). Χρηματισθείς nom. sg. masc. of aor. pass. ptc. of χρηματίζω, "communicate a divine message/warning." Κατ᾽ ὄναρ 1:20. Ἀνεχώρησεν 3rd sg. aor. act. indic. of ἀναχωρέω, "depart." With τὰ μέρη ("parts"), the gen. τῆς Γαλιλαίας is clearly wholative (partitive).

2:23 Ἐλθών is prob. temp.: "when he came." Κατῴκησεν 3rd sg. aor. act. indic. of κατοικέω, "settle, make a home." The use of εἰς here seems to be an example of Matthew's substitution of εἰς for ἐν, a phenomenon more common in other NT writers (BDF §205). Λεγομένην (acc. sg. fem. of pres. pass. ptc. of λέγω) is adj. Ναζαρέτ was a small village in Galilee not mentioned in the OT or Josephus. The spelling of this place-name in Matthew is puzzling (2:23; 4:13; 21:11). Twice before, Matthew introduced his fulfillment citation using ἵνα with πληρωθῇ (1:22; 2:15), but he now shifts to ὅπως. Although ἵνα may express purpose or result, ὅπως clearly expresses purpose. The divine pass. πληρωθῇ suggests that the purpose was God's rather than Joseph's. The cstr. emphasizes that God was sovereignly orchestrating these events to fulfill his promises given through the prophets. Τὸ ῥηθέν 2:17. The shift from the sg. διὰ τοῦ προφήτου (1:22; 2:5, 15, 17) to the pl. διὰ τῶν προφητῶν suggests that the event fulfills a general theme attested by several prophets rather than a single specific text. Matthew is prob. referring to the OT prophecies that describe the Messiah as a "branch." The term used for "branch" in Isaiah 11:1 (*netser*) may be transliterated with the first three consonants (ν–ζ–ρ) that compose the nouns Ναζαρέτ and Ναζωραῖος. The Isaiah 11:1 prophecy is closely connected to other messianic prophecies such as Isaiah 4:2; Jeremiah 23:5; 33:15. Κληθήσεται 3rd sg. fut. pass. indic. of καλέω, "call." Beale and Carson 10d–11d.

FOR FURTHER STUDY

7. *The Slaughter of Innocents and the Flight to Egypt*

Cox, B. D., and S. Ackerman. "Rachel's Tomb." *JBL* 128 (2009): 135–48.
Hoehner, H. W. *DJG* 317–26.
Kalai, Z. "Rachel's Tomb: A Historiographical Review." Pages 215–23 in *Vielseitigkeit des Alten Testaments*. Edited by J. A. Loader and H. V. Kiewler. New York: P. Lang, 1999.
Park, E. C. "Rachel's Cry for Her Children: Matthew's Treatment of the Infanticide by Herod." *CBQ* 75 (2013): 473–85.
van Henten, J. W. "Matthew 2:16 and Josephus' Portrayal of Herod." Pages 101–22 in *Jesus, Paul, and Early Christianity*. Edited by R. Buitenwerf, H. W. Hollander, and J. Tromp. Boston: Brill, 2008.

HOMILETICAL SUGGESTIONS

Hints of Jesus's Future (2:13–23)

1. Jesus will lead his people on a new Exodus (2:13–15; Hos 11:1)
2. Jesus will turn his people's mourning into joy (2:16–18; Jeremiah 31)
3. Jesus will rule over and restore God's people (2:19–23; Isa 11:1–9)

B. PREPARATION FOR JESUS'S MINISTRY (3:1–4:16)

1. The Beginning of John's Ministry (3:1–6)

3:1 Ἐν with the dat. obj (ταῖς ἡμέραις) is used as a marker for a period of time during which something occurs (BDAG 326c–30b, esp. 10). The remote dem. ἐκείναις suggests that the days belonged to the period in which Jesus resided in Nazareth (2:23; N 135). Παραγίνεται 3rd sg. pres. mid. indic. of dep. παραγίνομαι, "come, make a public appearance." Ὁ βαπτιστής is nom. of simple appos. Κηρύσσων (nom. sg. masc. of pres. act. ptc. of κηρύσσω prob. expresses *purpose (2:2) or manner (YLT). See Luke 12:51, in which the vb. παραγίνομαι is followed by an inf. of purpose. See also Smyth §2065. Τῆς Ἰουδαίας is a partitive gen. Only a portion of Judea was wilderness. Jerusalem, for example, was located in this region.

3:2 After the ptc. κηρύσσων, λέγων is a pleonastic ptc. (W 649–50; BDF §420) that introduces the content of John's preaching. Μετανοεῖτε 2nd pl. pres. act. impv. of μετανοέω, "repent." The pres. impv. is prob. ingr.-prog.: begin and continue repenting (W 721; BDF §336). The γάρ is causal and marks the reason repentance is necessary. Ἤγγικεν 3rd sg. pf. act. indic. of ἐγγίζω, "draw near (in a temp. sense)." The pf. tense is prob. extensive (consummative), stressing completed action. This suggests the kingdom has completed its approach and is on the brink of arrival (G 43–44; H 47). The arrival of the kingdom will soon come with Jesus's performance of messianic signs (5:3, 10; 12:28). Ἡ βασιλεία τῶν οὐρανῶν is not merely a reverent circumlocution for the "kingdom of God" that avoids dir. ref. to God. Matthew's preferred description of the kingdom stresses the heavenly nature of this kingdom, thereby expressing that the Messiah's reign is not merely an earthly kingdom ruled by a political Messiah (John 18:36). The pl. τῶν οὐρανῶν refers to the abode of God. Matthew normally used the sg. form of the noun to refer to the sky and the pl. to refer to the realm in which God and the angels reside. However, a few exceptions to this general rule exist, so the interpreter must pay careful attention to the context when determining the referent of the noun. In Matthew 6:20 (comp. 19:21); 18:18 (2x); 21:25; 22:30; and possibly 5:34; 11:23; and 23:22, Matthew used the sg. form to refer to the abode of God. He possibly used the pl. form to refer to the sky (24:29). The exceptions may be explained as due to a heaven and earth pairing (explicit or implicit) or the use of different conventions for different audiences (J. Pennington, *Heaven and Earth in the Gospel of Matthew* [Grand Rapids: Baker, 2007], 125–61).

3:3 The dem. pron. οὗτος is retrospective and refers to the ministry and preaching of John in the wilderness just described. The γάρ may be causal; John's ministry occurred because Scripture had to be fulfilled (26:54). Alternatively, γάρ may be explanatory (marker of clarification; BDAG 189a–90a, esp. 2). Ἔστιν replaces ἵνα πληρωθῇ from the more common form of Matthew's fulfillment formula (D&A 1.292 n. 13). On ὁ ῥηθεὶς διὰ Ἠσαΐου τοῦ προφήτου λέγοντος, see 2:17. Βοῶντος (gen. sg. masc. of pres. act. ptc. of βοάω, "shout") is subst.: "The voice of one who shouts." Ἐν τῇ ἐρήμῳ (3:1). Ἑτοιμάσατε 2nd pl. aor. act. impv. of ἑτοιμάζω, "prepare." The aor. impv. expresses urgency. Κυρίου translates the divine name Yahweh (MT). The pres. impv. ποιεῖτε is ingr.-prog. Εὐθείας (acc. pl. fem. of εὐθύς, "straight") and τὰς τρίβους (τρίβος, "path") are dbl. acc. of complement-object. Matthew's quotation of Isaiah 40:3 is almost identical to the LXX. The one exception is that Matthew (like Mark and Luke) replaces the LXX's τοῦ θεοῦ ἡμῶν with αὐτοῦ. However, since the clear antecedent of the pron. is κυρίου (= Yahweh), the deity of the one for whom John prepares the way is by no means diminished.

3:4 The αὐτός is in the pred. position and functions as an intensive adj. (rather than a pron.): "John himself" or "this very John." The impf. vbs. εἶχεν may be customary or the impf. may simply mark background material (Levinsohn 172–75; Campbell 52). The prep. ἀπό with τριχῶν (θρίξ, τριχός, ἡ, "hair") identifies the material from which the garments were made. Καμήλου (gen. sg. masc. of κάμηλος, "camel") is gen. of source: "hair from a camel." Ζώνη, -ης, ἡ, "belt." Δερμάτινος, -α, -ον, "made of leather." Περί with the acc. means "around." Ὀσφῦς, -ύος, ἡ, "waist." Τροφή, -ῆς, ἡ, "food, nourishment." Ἀκρίς, -ίδος, ἡ, "locust." Μέλι, -ιτος, τό, "honey." Ἄγριος, -ία, -ον, "natural, wild."

3:5 Τότε prob. means "after John's initial preaching ministry as described in 3:1–4" and thus introduces the next sequence in the narrative. Ἐξεπορεύετο (3rd sg. impf. act. indic. of dep. ἐκπορεύομαι, "come out") is prob. ingr. (W 545). The place-names refer to the human inhabitants of the areas (metonymy). The repeated uses of πᾶσα with sg. articular nouns refer to the populations of those areas in general. The nuance of the gen. τοῦ Ἰορδάνου is influenced by the prep. περί in the pref. of περίχωρος. Thus the phrase means "the region surrounding the Jordan River."

3:6 Ἐβαπτίζοντο (3rd pl. impf. pass. indic. of βαπτίζω, "immerse") is prob. prog. Large numbers of people were being baptized one after another. The cstr. of ultimate pers. agency, ὑπ' αὐτοῦ, shows that the vb. is pass. rather than middle. Thus, this baptism was different from the self-administered washings that were common in ancient Judaism. Ἐξομολογούμενοι (nom. pl. masc. of pres. mid. ptc. of ἐξομολογέω, "confess") is either temp. (LEB) or a ptc. of purpose (MSG; H 1.49).

FOR FURTHER STUDY

8. *John the Baptist*

Bowens, L. M. "The Role of John the Baptist in Matthew's Gospel." *WW* 30 (2010): 311–18.

Evans, C. A. "The Baptism of John in Typological Context." Pages 45–71 in *Dimensions of Baptism: Biblical and Theological Studies*. Edited by S. E. Porter and A. R. Cross. New York: Sheffield Academic Press, 2002.

Hooker, M. D. "John's Baptism: A Prophetic Sign." Pages 22–40 in *The Holy Spirit and Christian Origins: Essays in Honor of James D. G. Dunn*. Edited by G. N. Stanton, B. W. Longenecker and S. C. Barton. Grand Rapids: Eerdmans, 2004.

Kelhoffer, J. A. "'Locusts and Wild Honey' (Mk 1.6c and Mt 3.4c): The *Status Quaestionis* Concerning the Diet of John the Baptist." *Currents in Biblical Research* 2 (2003): 104–27.

Meier, J. P. "John the Baptist in Matthew's Gospel." *JBL* 99 (1980): 383–405.

Witherington, B. *DJG* 383–91.

9. *The Kingdom of Heaven*
   Pennington, J. *Heaven and Earth in the Gospel of Matthew*. Grand Rapids: Baker, 2007.

HOMILETICAL SUGGESTIONS

John the Baptizer (3:1–6)
   1. John's message emphasized repentance
   2. John's ministry fulfilled prophecy (Isa 40:3)
   3. John's mission was to prepare for the coming of God
   4. John's manner associated him with Elijah (2 Kgs 1:8)
   5. John's mandate was the baptism of confessing sinners

2. *John's Message (3:7–12)*

3:7 Ἰδών (nom. sg. masc. of aor. act. ptc. of ὁράω, "see") is either temp. (most EVV) or causal. Πολλούς is subst. The gen. τῶν Φαρισαίων καὶ Σαδδουκαίων are wholative (partitive). Although the art. shared by the two nouns prob. suggests the unity of the two distinct groups (W 279), this is not an example of the Granville Sharp rule since it pertains only to sg. pers. nouns joined by καί and sharing a def. art. Ἐρχομένους (acc. pl. masc. of pres. mid. ptc. of dep. ἔρχομαι) is adj.: "who were coming." The prep. ἐπί with the acc. (τὸ βάπτισμα) may be *loc., hence "to the place of his baptism" (BDAG 363a–67c, 4; cf. NIV; N 142). However, vbs. of motion like ἔρχομαι with ἐπί with the acc. were often used to express opposition (Luke 14:31; Matt 23:35). Thus the cstr. here could mean "were coming against [opposing] his baptism" (BDAG 363a–67c, 12; D&A 1.304). Both of these options require John's question to be taken as sarcasm. Finally, the ἐπί could be a marker of purpose indicating that the two groups were coming to receive John's baptism (BDAG 363a–67c, 11; N 142). This baptism would be part of a precautionary effort to avoid God's wrath. Ὑπέδειξεν 3rd sg. aor. act. indic. of ὑποδείκνυμι, "warn." Φυγεῖν (aor. act. inf. of φεύγω, "flee") is complementary. Μελλούσης (gen. sg. fem. of pres. act. ptc. of μέλλω, "future, coming") is adj. The fut. wrath is God's eschatological wrath.

3:8 The οὖν is inferential and seems to imply that the only way to escape the divine wrath that is coming is through repentance. Ποιήσατε (2nd pl. aor. act. impv. of ποιέω, "do, produce") expresses urgency and intensity. Ἄξιον with the gen. τῆς μετανοίας means "correspondingly fitting or appropriate" (BDAG 93c–94b, 2).

3:9 Prohibitions using μή and the aor. subjunc. (δόξητε 2nd pl. aor. act. subjunc. of δοκέω, "think, presume") are "categorical prohibitions" (BDF §337) that forbid the action as a whole (W 723–24): "Do not presume at all to say." The prep. ἐν is loc. and describes the internal thoughts of each member of the group (BDAG 326c–30b, 1f). The nouns πατέρα and τὸν Ἀβραάμ are dbl. acc. of complement-obj. The γάρ introduces the reason one must not presume descent from Abraham ensures protection from the coming wrath. Δύναται 3rd sg. pres. mid. indic. of dep. δύναμαι, "be able." Ἐκ is a marker of orig. The God who made Adam from the dust, and brought forth Israel from Sarah's dead womb, could as easily have made Israel from stones. When serving as a dem. adj., τούτων is often in the first or second pred. position. Ἐγεῖραι (aor. act. inf. of ἐγείρω, "raise") here means "to cause to come into existence" (BDAG 271c–72c, 5). The dat. of advantage τῷ Ἀβραάμ is used rather than the expected gen. of relationship and possibly alludes to Genesis 21:2–3, in which this same dat. is used.

3:10 The placement of the adv. ἤδη at the beginning of the sentence and far from the vb. is prob. emphatic (D&A 1.309). The adv. ἤδη intensifies the temp. element of the pres. tense (κεῖται 3rd sg. pres. mid. indic. of dep. κεῖμαι, "lay, place on"): "is already placed (at this very moment)." BDAG notes that the vb. κεῖμαι may serve as the pass. form of τίθημι. D&A (309) thus see κεῖται as a divine pass. Ἡ ἀξίνη is an ax used for felling trees and chopping wood. After κεῖται, πρός w. the acc. (τὴν ῥίζαν) is loc. and means "at, against." The idea is prob. not that the ax rests against the root waiting for the divine axman to pick it up and begin his work but instead that the axman has gripped the ax and placed the blade against the root to ensure an accurate cut, readying himself to sever the root with a masterful swing (NLT; N 145). Because τὴν ῥίζαν is articular (*par excellence*) and sg., it likely refers to the taproot, which is the source of the tree's life and stability. Οὖν is inferential, introducing a conclusion drawn from the previous statement. Πᾶν with an anar. sg. noun (δένδρον) emphasizes the individual members of a class: "every single tree" and prob. implies no exceptions exist. Ποιοῦν (nom. sg. neut. of pres. act. ptc. of ποιέω, "make, produce") is adj. The pres. tense of the ptc. is prob. prog. Ἐκκόπτεται (3rd sg. pres. pass. indic. of ἐκκόπτω, "cut down") and βάλλεται (3rd sg. pres. pass. indic. of βάλλω, "throw") are either gnomic (N 145; LEB; ESV) or *futuristic, stressing immediacy and certainty (D&A 1.311; CSB; NIV).

3:11 Ἐγώ is mildly emphatic. The particle μέν marks a concessive clause and together with the particle δέ strongly contrasts two different baptisms performed by two differ-ent agents. With βαπτίζω the prep. ἐν may be loc. ("in water"; mg. of NIV, and NLT) or instr. ("with water"; most EVV). The prep. phrase εἰς μετάνοιαν denotes *purpose ("for repentance"; most EVV) or ref./respect ("with ref. to repentance;" H 1.51; BDAG 288c–91c, 5). The improper prep. ὀπίσω marks a position behind an entity in either space or time. Here the prep. has a temp. nuance (BDAG 716a–b, 2.b.). Ὀπίσω is one of only three prep. (also ἔμπροσθεν and sometimes ἐνώπιον) that use the enclitic form rather than the longer form of the 1st pers. pron. for its obj. (μου rather than ἐμοῦ; BDAG 275a–c). The Messiah appears after John. Ἰσχυρότερος is a comp. adj. (from ἰσχυρός, "strong"). Consequently, μου is clearly a gen. of comparison (W 110–12). The antecedent of the rel. pron. οὗ is "the coming One." The gen. is prob. poss. and mod-ifies τὰ ὑποδήματα ("sandals"). Βαστάσαι (aor. act. inf. of βαστάζω, "carry, remove") is epex. and modifies ἱκανός clarifying the nature of John's unworthiness. Αὐτός is mildly emphatic. Βαπτίσει is a predictive fut. The prep. ἐν has a compound obj. With πνεύματι ἁγίῳ, the prep. marks the (intermediate) pers. agent. With πυρί the prep. marks the instr. Some regard πνεύματι ἁγίῳ καὶ πυρί as an example of hendiadys, "fiery breath" (D&A 1.317). On hendiadys, see BDAG 494a–96c, 1.a.δ; BDF §442.16; T 335. Although Hagner rejects the view, he describes it as the view of the "majority of scholars" (1.51). Nevertheless, several factors raise doubts about this widely accepted view. First, the primary purpose of hendiadys was to avoid a series of genitives. Here, however, a single adj. gen. πυρός would have been sufficient and Matthew shows no aversion to this gen. elsewhere (5:22; 13:42, 50; 18:9). Furthermore, the interpretation of πνεύματι ἁγίῳ as "breath" is unsubstantiated in Matthew. Matthew consistently used πνεῦμα in combination with the adj. ἅγιος in ref. to the Holy Spirit (1:18, 20; 12:32; 28:19). Thus the interpretation expressed by most EVV ("with the Holy Spirit and fire") is preferable.

3:12 The antecedent of οὗ and αὐτοῦ is "the Coming One." The three fut. vbs. διακαθαριεῖ (3rd sg. fut. act. indic. of διακαθαρίζω, "clean out"), συνάξει (3rd sg. fut. act. indic. of συνάγω, "gather"), and κατακαύσει (3rd sg. fut. act. indic. of κατακαίω, "burn") are predictive and refer to eschatological punishment. Ἀποθήκη, -ης, ἡ, "barn, storehouse."

FOR FURTHER STUDY

10. The Preaching of John the Baptist

Beasley-Murray, G. R. *Baptism in the New Testament*. Grand Rapids: Eerdmans, 1994.
Charles, J. D. "The 'Coming One/Stronger One' and His Baptism: Matt 3:11–12, Mark 1:8, Luke 3:16–17." *Pneuma* 11 (1989): 37–49.
Dunn, J. D. G. "Spirit-and-Fire Baptism." *NovT* 14 (1972): 81–92.
Keener, C. S. "'Brood of Vipers' (Matthew 3.7; 12.34; 23.33)." *JSNT* 28 (2005): 3–11.
Lang, F. *TDNT* 6.928–48.
Schreiner, T. R., and S. D. Wright. *Believer's Baptism: Sign of the New Covenant in Christ*. NAC Studies in Bible & Theology 3. Nashville: B&H, 2006.
Stählin, G. *TDNT* 5.435–47.

HOMILETICAL SUGGESTIONS

The Coming Wrath (3:7–10)

1. God's wrath is his fierce rage against sinful rebellion that he will unleash after final judgment
2. Sinners often vainly attempt to escape God's wrath like snakes slithering away from a brush fire
   a. They rely on rituals to protect them from God's wrath
   b. They rely on heritage to protect them from God's wrath
3. God's destruction of unrepentant sinners is certain and imminent
4. Sinners can escape God's wrath by repenting and displaying the sincerity of their repentance through transformed living

One Greater than John (3:11–12)

1. Jesus performs a more glorious baptism than John the Baptist
   a. John baptized with water to display a sinner's repentance
   b. Jesus baptized with the Spirit to effect a sinner's transformation (Ezek 36:25–27)
2. Jesus displays a more awesome power than John the Baptist

    a. John warned about God's coming wrath in his role as a prophet
    b. Jesus brings about God's coming wrath in his role as eschatological judge
3. Jesus's Baptism by John (3:13–17)

3:13 Τότε prob. indicates that Jesus's arrival occurred after the event described in the preceding paragraph rather than concurrently. The preps. that indicate movement (ἀπό, πρός) suggest that παραγίνεται means "come" rather than "make an appearance" (see also 2:2; 3:1). The preps. ἀπό with the gen. (τῆς Γαλιλαίας) and ἐπί with the acc. (τὸν Ἰορδάνην) are both loc., showing the point of orig. ("from") and destination ("to") of Jesus's movement. Πρός serves as a marker of movement toward someone. The gen. art. τοῦ with the inf. (βαπτισθῆναι aor. pass. inf. of βαπτίζω, "immerse") expresses purpose. Ὑπ' with the gen. (αὐτοῦ; antecedent "John") expresses pers. agency: "by him."
3:14 Διεκώλυεν 3rd sg. impf. act. indic. of διακωλύω, "prevent, keep from happening." The impf. tense is conative: John attempted to prevent (unsuccessfully). See BDF §326; H 1.55. Λέγων is a ptc. of means. Ἐγώ is mildly emphatic and stresses the contrast with σοῦ and σύ. Ὑπό with the gen. (σοῦ) expresses ultimate agency. The inf. βαπτισθῆναι is epex., defining the nature of the χρείαν. The καί introduces a statement that is surprising, unexpected, or particularly noteworthy (BDAG 494a–96c1.b.η). This special use of καί suggests that the clause σὺ ἔρχῃ πρός με may be an exclamation rather than a question. The use of ἀποκρίνομαι to introduce Jesus's response does not settle the issue since the vb. may introduce answers to questions or simply mark the continuation of discourse (BDAG 113c–14a, 1; Morris 64). The prep. πρός takes the longer form ἐμέ as its obj. except after vbs. of motion in which case it takes the enclitic form με (11:28; 19:14).
3:15 Ἀποκριθείς (nom. sg. masc. of aor. pass. ptc. of dep. ἀποκρίνομαι, "answer") is pleonastic, and most modern EVV either leave the ptc. or main vb. untranslated. The prep. πρός with the acc. (αὐτόν; antecedent–John) indicates that Jesus directed his statement to John. Ἄφες 2nd sg. aor. act. impv. of ἀφίημι, "permit" (BDAG 156c–57b, 5b). Ἄρτι is a temp. adv. referring to the immediate pres. Γάρ is causal and introduces the reason John should comply. The dem. adv. οὕτως refers to an action in the preceding context as a means, i.e., by John's baptizing Jesus. Πρέπον (nom. sg. neut. of pres. act. ptc. of πρέπω, "be fitting, appropriate") with ἐστίν forms a pres. periph. cstr. Ἡμῖν is a pers. dat. of ref. rather than an ethical dat. After forms of πρέπω accompanied by an inf., the dat. of ref. is used in place of the normally expected acc. of ref. (acc. subj. of inf.). Πληρῶσαι (aor. act. inf. of πληρόω, "fulfill, accomplish [a goal]") is complementary. The goal for which Jesus aspires and which requires his submission to John's baptism is πᾶσαν δικαιοσύνην (δικαιοσύνη, -ης, ἡ, "righteousness"). The adj. πᾶς modifying a sg. anar. noun emphasizes the individual members of a class: "each and every act of righteousness (of which John's baptism is one)." Τότε means "immediately after." Ἀφίησιν (3rd sg. pres. act. indic. of ἀφίημι, "permit") is a historical pres. and likely highlights the vb. On the textual var., see Metzger 8–9.
3:16 Βαπτισθείς (nom. sg. masc. of aor. pass. ptc. of βαπτίζω, "immerse") is temp. This is suggested by the temp. adv. εὐθύς. Ἀνέβη (3rd sg. aor. act. indic. of ἀναβαίνω, "go up") with the prep. ἀπό with the gen. (τοῦ ὕδατος) may refer to John's raising Jesus

from beneath the surface of the water* or Jesus's climbing the bank of the Jordan (G 51). Some grammarians and commentators make much of Matthew's use of ἀπό rather than Mark's ἐκ (Mark 1:10) since ἐκ generally refers to motion from within and ἀπό refers to motion from the edge or surface of an object. G suggests that Matthew's prep. indicated Jesus clambered up the riverbank without first confessing his sins (since he had none; G 51). Allen and Turner think Matthew changed Mark's ἐκ to ἀπό due to an evolution in views of baptism from immersion in Mark to sprinkling or pouring in Matthew (Allen 29; Turner, *Grammatical Insights* 29 [Note that this is a reversal of Turner's earlier view expressed in *Syntax* 259. See below.]). Both views are unlikely. First, ἀνέβη plus ἀπό in no way implies sprinkling or pouring. Second, in Koine Gk., the sense of the two preps. often overlaps (R 577–78; Harris 57–58). Matthew often has ἀπό where Mark has ἐκ with no clear difference in sense between the two (D&A 1.327; Turner, *Syntax* 259). Ἰδού (1:20). Ἠνεῴχθησαν (3rd pl. aor. pass. indic. of ἀνοίγω, "open") is a divine pass (H 1.57). Εἶδεν 3rd sg. aor. act. indic. of ὁράω, "see." Καταβαῖνον (acc. sg. neut. of pres. act. ptc. of καταβαίνω, "descend") is adj. modifying πνεῦμα. Ὡσεί is a marker denoting comparison. Περιστεράν, "dove." Most EVV accept the presence of the conj. καί and regard ἐρχόμενον as modifying πνεῦμα. However, the oldest extant mss. do not contain the conj. LEB translates the passage as if ἐρχόμενον modifies περιστεράν, but this is unlikely since the noun is fem. and the ptc. is neut. On the var., see Metzger 9–10.

3:17 Ἰδού (1:20). No finite vb. is stated. This may be a pred. cstr.: "There was a voice." Alternatively, the subj. φωνή may imply a vb. of speech. The pl. τῶν οὐρανῶν refers to the abode of God rather than merely the sky (3:2). The prep. ἐκ marks the place from which the voice came. Λέγουσα is a pleonastic ptc. after the implied vb. of speech. The dem. pron. οὗτος refers to Jesus. The def. art. with υἱός is monadic. Ὁ ἀγαπητός is in the second attrib. position. Although the first attrib. position emphasizes the adj., the second attrib. position may place emphasis on both the noun and the adj. (R 776–77): "my Son, who is loved (by God)." See Genesis 22:2 (LXX), in which the phrase "whom you love" explains a sim. cstr. With the vb. εὐδόκησα (1st sg. aor. act. indic. of εὐδοκέω, "take pleasure"), ἐν with the dat. (ᾧ; antecedent: Jesus) marks the pers. object.

FOR FURTHER STUDY

11.The Baptism of Jesus

Gero, S. "Spirit as a Dove at the Baptism of Jesus." *NovT* 18 (1976): 17–35.
Keck, L. E. "Spirit and the Dove." *NTS* 17 (1970): 41–67.
Webb, R. L. "Jesus's Baptism: Its Historicity and Implications." *BBR* 10 (2000): 261–309.

HOMILETICAL SUGGESTIONS

God Said It and I Believe It! (3:13–17)

1. Jesus is superior to John
2. Jesus was perfectly obedient to the Father

3. Jesus bears the Spirit and has the power to baptize with the Spirit
4. Jesus is God's unique, loved, and pleasing Son

4. Jesus's Temptation in the Wilderness (4:1–11)

4:1 Τότε indicates that the events of 4:1–11 occurred after Jesus's baptism. Ἀνήχθη 3rd sg. aor. pass. indic. of ἀνάγω, "lead, bring up." The vb. is appropriate since the Judean wilderness was at a higher elevation than the Jordan valley. The prep. ὑπό with the gen. (τοῦ πνεύματος) marks the ultimate agent who led Jesus. Πειρασθῆναι (aor. pass. inf. of πειράζω, "tempt, test") is an inf. of purpose/result. Ὑπὸ τοῦ διαβόλου (ultimate agency) shows that the devil acts as the tempter. Διάβολος, "slanderer, accuser, devil."

4:2 Νηστεύσας (nom. sg. masc. of aor. act. ptc. of νηστεύω, "fast, go without food") is temp. and describes antecedent action as the ὕστερον ("afterward") with the main vb. implies. The phrase ἡμέρας τεσσεράκοντα καὶ νύκτας τεσσεράκοντα is an acc. of extent of time that indicates Jesus fasted without a break for the forty-day period (W 202). Ἐπείνασεν 3rd sg. aor. act. indic. of πεινάω, "be hungry."

4:3 Προσελθών (nom. sg. masc. of aor. act. ptc. of dep. προσέρχομαι, "approach") is prob. temp., expressing antecedent action. Ὁ πειράζων (nom. sg. masc. of pres. act. ptc. of πειράζω, "tempt") is subst. Εἰ with the indic. (2nd sg. pres. indic. of εἰμί, "be") marks the prot. of a first-class cond. statement that assumes the truthfulness of the prot. for the sake of argument. The position of υἱός may indicate emphasis. The anar. cstr. does not imply that υἱός is indef. Anar. pred. nominatives that stand before the vb. are "normally qualitative, sometimes definite, and only rarely indefinite" (W 262). The statement of the Father in 3:17 (in which the pred. nom. follows the vb.) strongly suggests that the noun is def. in the pres. cstr. Εἰπέ (2nd sg. 2nd aor. act. impv. of λέγω, "say, speak") does not seem to express any special urgency beyond what the impv. inherently conveys. All twelve impv. forms of λέγω in Matthew are in the aor. tense, so the aor. seems to be used by default. After some vbs. of speech, ἵνα may introduce a quotation (BDAG 475c–77b, 2.γ–δ; D&A 1.361): "Command that these stones become loaves of bread" (see LEB). Alternatively, ἵνα may introduce a purpose clause: "Speak, so that these stones become loaves of bread." The near dem. οὗτοι suggests that the devil pointed to particular stones scattered around him. Γένωνται 3rd pl. aor. mid. subjunc. of dep. γίνομαι, "become." By calling upon Jesus to transform stones into bread by his mere command, the devil is acknowledging Jesus's divine power.

4:4 The cstr. ὁ δὲ ἀποκριθεὶς εἶπεν appears eighteen times in Matthew (4:4; 12:39, 48; 13:11, 37; 15:3, 13, 24, 26; 16:2; 17:11; 19:4; 20:13; 21:29, 30; 24:2; 25:12; 26:23; cf. 26:66) and reflects a Hebraic expression (Z §366). The δέ marks a new development in the narrative (Runge 31–32), and this is esp. true when it is preceded by an independent use of the nom. masc. def. art. (BDAG 686a–89c, 1.c.; BDF §251). The def. art. ὁ serves as a substitute for the pers. pron. αὐτός or the dem. pron. οὗτος. One could view the def. art. as modifying the ptc. in which case the ptc. ἀποκριθείς (nom. sg. masc. of aor. pass. ptc. of dep. ἀποκρίνομαι, "answer") would be regarded as subst.: "the one who answered said." However, in light of Matthew's clear use of the def. art. as a pers. pron. with a vb. of speech in 2:5, the def. art. is more likely the subj. of εἶπεν and the ptc. is pleonastic. Γέγραπται (3rd sg. pf. pass. indic. of γράφω, "write") is likely a resultative pf. that stresses the pres. existence (and by implication, continuing authority) of the Scripture (W 575–76, esp. comments on Rom 3:10). Although Wallace labels this usage "intensive perfect," Robertson (895–96) and BDF (§342) label it "extensive" and place it in the subcategory "punctiliar-durative." These grammarians agree that the emphasis falls on the continuing effect on the subj. or object. Nevertheless, they define the categories "intensive" and "extensive" differently. Robertson and BDF equate the intensive pf. with the "perfect with a pres. force." Wallace appropriately distinguishes the two. The prep. phrases ἐπ' ἄρτῳ (dat. sg. masc. of ἄρτος, "bread, loaf") and ἐπὶ παντὶ ῥήματι (dat. sg. neut. of ῥῆμα, "word") express the basis for a state of being (BDAG 363a–67c, 6). The adj. μόνῳ ("only, alone") followed by the adversative conj. ἀλλ' clarifies that food is necessary for life, but not sufficient to sustain life. Life also requires obedience to God's precepts (H 1.65). Ζήσεται (3rd sg. fut. mid. indic. of ζάω, "live") is either *gnomic or predictive. Παντί (dat. sg. neut.) is adj., sg., and anar., thus emphasizing the individual components of a group: "every single word." Ἐκπορευομένῳ (dat. sg. neut. of pres. mid. ptc. of dep. ἐκπορεύομαι, "go out, proceed") is adj. The prep. διά with the gen. (στόματος) marks extension through an object. The gen. θεοῦ is partitive.

4:5 Τότε means "afterward." Παραλαμβάνει is a historical pres. Τήν with ἁγίαν πόλιν is the def. art. *par excellence* (W 222): Jerusalem is regarded as the holiest city on earth. Matthew will later show that this reputation is not consistent with the true character of most of the city's inhabitants. Ἔστησεν (3rd sg. aor. act. indic. of ἵστημι, "stand") is used intrans.: "cause to be in a place." Jesus did not voluntarily climb to the pinnacle. Τὸ πτερύγιον is difficult to identify precisely. It refers to the edge or tip of an object. The context suggests that it was a projection sticking out from the temple at a height from which a fall would normally be fatal (F 132).

4:6 Λέγει is a historical pres. Εἰ υἱὸς εἶ τοῦ θεοῦ (4:3). Βάλε (2nd sg. aor. act. impv. of βάλλω, "throw") may express urgency. Σεαυτόν (acc. sg. masc. of σεαυτοῦ, 2nd sg. reflex. pron.) Γάρ is causal, pointing to an alleged biblical justification for the command. Γέγραπται (4:4). The UBS⁵, NA²⁸, and R-P treat the ὅτι as a discourse marker introducing the biblical quotation. However, Matthew does not elsewhere introduce a quotation of Scripture using γέγραπται and ὅτι (cf. 2:5; 4:4, 7, 10; 11:10; 21:13; 26:24). The ὅτι is prob. part of the quotation itself, since Psalm 91:11 (90:11 LXX) begins with ὅτι. The quotation is identical to the LXX except for the omission of the second line of verse 11, which was likely part of Satan's attempt to distort the mng. of the passage. Ἐντελεῖται (3rd sg. fut. mid. indic. of ἐντέλλω, "give instructions, command") is predictive fut. Ἀροῦσίν (3rd pl. fut. act. indic. of αἴρω, "lift up") is predictive fut. Μήποτε is a marker of negated purpose ("lest, so . . . not") used with the subjunc. Προσκόψῃς (2nd sg. aor. act. subjunc. of προσκόπτω, "strike against"). Πρός is spatial but should be tr. "against" rather than merely "toward" since the vb. implies actual contact with the object (most EVV).

4:7 Ἔφη 3rd sg. aor. act. indic. of φημί, "state, say." The vb. normally introduces dir. discourse (BDAG 1053a–b). Πάλιν, "again." Γέγραπται (4:4). Ἐκπειράσεις (2nd sg.

fut. act. indic. of ἐκπειράζω, "test, tempt") is an impv. fut. Although κύριον is anar., it is def. The noun is prob. anar. because it functioned in the LXX as the tr. of the divine name Yahweh. Proper names are normally anar. (W 245–47). The def. art. in the appos. cstr. τὸν θεόν σου is monadic (W 223) and describes Yahweh as the only true God (Deut 6:4).

4:8 Πάλιν prob. expresses repetition of an event sim. in nature to a previous event. The repetition of παραλαμβάνει αὐτὸν ὁ διάβολος εἰς . . . from 4:5 suggests this. The τότε in 4:5 and πάλιν of 4:8 seem to imply that Matthew has arranged the three temptations in chronological order. Luke inverts the order of the second and third temptations (H 1.62; D. Bock, *Luke* [2 vols.; Baker Exegetical Commentary on the New Testament; Grand Rapids: Baker, 1994], 1:364–65). However, Luke used markers indicating narrative transitions that did not imply that the events were consecutive. Ὄρος ("mountain") refers to a relatively high elevation of land in contrast to a βοῦνος ("hill"). The adj. ὑψηλόν ("high"), esp. with the adv. λίαν ("very"), emphasizes the height of the mountain. Δείκνυσιν (3rd sg. pres. act. indic. of δείκνυμι, "show") is a historical pres. Δόξα, -ης, ἡ, "magnificence, splendor, or greatness."

4:9 Δώσω (1st sg. fut. act. indic. of δίδωμι, "give") is a predictive fut. expressing a promise. The 3rd-class cond. prot. ἐὰν πεσὼν προσκυνήσῃς μοι expresses a cond. for the promise. The cstr. makes no assumption regarding the fulfillment of the cond. Πεσών (nom. sg. masc. of aor. act. ptc. of πίπτω, "fall") is prob. ptc. of attendant circumstance (most EVV).

4:10 Τότε, "afterward." Λέγει is a historical pres. The pres. impv. ὕπαγε is prob. ingr.-prog.: "Get going and keep on going!" (W 721–22). Γέγραπται γάρ (4:6). Κύριον τὸν θεόν σου (4:7). Προσκυνήσεις (2nd sg. fut. act. indic. of προσκυνέω, "worship") and λατρεύσεις (2nd sg. fut. act. indic. of λατρεύω, "serve [by carrying out religious duties]") are impv. fut. Αὐτῷ is dat. of dir. obj. Μόνῳ (4:4).

4:11 Τότε, "afterward." Ἀφίησιν (3rd sg. pres. act. indic. of ἀφίημι, "leave") is a historical pres. Ἰδού (1:20). Προσῆλθον 3rd pl. aor. act. indic. of dep. προσέρχομαι, "approach." Διηκόνουν (3rd pl. impf. act. indic. of διακονέω, "serve") is prog. and prob. refers to providing food (N 169). Interestingly, two features of the temptations, angels protecting Jesus from harm (4:6) and supernatural provision of food (4:3), are granted to Jesus with divine approval (D&A 1.374).

FOR FURTHER STUDY

12. The Temptation of Jesus

Allison, D. C., Jr. "Behind the Temptations of Jesus: Q 4:1–13 and Mark 1:12–13." Pages 195–213 in *Authenticating the Activities of Jesus*. Edited by B. D. Chilton and C. A. Evans. Leiden: Brill, 1999.

Evans, C. A. "Jesus and Evil Spirits in the Light of Psalm 91." *Baptistic Theologies* 1 (2009): 43–58.

Gibson, J. B. *The Temptations of Jesus in Early Christianity*. JSNTSup 112. Sheffield: Sheffield Academic Press, 1995.

McKinley, J. E. "Jesus Christ's Temptation." *SBJT* 16 (2012): 56–71.

Roets, J. "The Victory of Christ over the Tempter as Help to the Believers' Fight Against Sin: A Reflection on Matthew 4:1–11." *Mid-America Journal of Theology* 22 (2011): 107–27.

Schaivo, L., and L. Milton. "The Temptation of Jesus: The Eschatological Battle and the New Ethic of the First Followers of Jesus in Q." *JSNT* 25 (2002): 141–64.

Slingerland, H. D. "The Transjordanian Origin of St. Matthew's Gospel." *JSNT* 3 (1979): 18–28.

Stegner, W. R. "The Use of Scripture in Two Narratives of Early Jewish Christianity (Matthew 4:1–11; Mark 9:2–8)." Pages 98–120 in *Early Christian Interpretation of the Scriptures of Israel*. Edited by C. A. Evans and J. A. Sanders. Sheffield: Sheffield Academic Press, 1997.

HOMILETICAL SUGGESTIONS

Facing Temptation (4:1–11)

1. Obedience is more important than our next meal
2. Faithfulness is more important than our personal safety
3. Worship is more important than wealth

5. The Beginning of Jesus's Galilean Ministry (4:12–16)

4:12 Ἀκούσας (nom. sg. masc. of aor. act. ptc. of ἀκούω, "hear") is either temp. (most EVV) or *causal (G 412; D&A 1.375; see the similarities in 2:22–23). Παρεδόθη 3rd sg. aor. pass. indic. of παραδίδωμι, "hand over, place in custody." Ἀνεχώρησεν (2:22). The vb. may connote withdrawal from a place due to concern's for one's safety. Of the ten occurrences in Matthew, most seem to have this connotation (2:12, 13, 14, 22; 12:15; 14:13). Although Γαλιλαία was part of the tetrarchy of Herod Antipas, who had imprisoned John, the region was likely safer than the Jordan Valley, where John had been apprehended.

4:13 Καταλιπών (nom. sg. masc. of aor. act. ptc. of καταλείπω, "leave") is temp. (most EVV). Ναζαρά (2:23). Ἐλθών is a ptc. of attendant circumstance and thus coordinates with the main vb. This explains the absence of a conj. joining the two participles. Κατῴκησεν 3rd sg. aor. act. indic. of κατοικέω, "reside." On εἰς with the vb. κατῴκησεν, see 2:23. Καφαρναούμ, "Capernaum." The cstr. τὴν παραθαλασσίαν (παραθαλάσσιος, -ία, "beside the sea, lake") is prob. subst. and appos. The fem. gender of the adj. is influenced by an implied fem. noun πόλις, "city" (2:23). Note that of the six occurrences in the LXX, most are associated with the noun πόλις (2 Chr 8:17; 1 Macc 7:1; 11:8; 2 Macc 8:11; Jer 29:7; Ezek 25:9). Although the cstr. could be an example of the second attrib. position of the adj. mng. "Capernaum, the one by the sea," this is unlikely since ancient sources do not mention two Capernaums in Galilee. Ὁρίοις (ὅριον, -ου, τό) refers to territories assigned to the tribes of Israel. Thus, Ζαβουλών and Νεφθαλίμ are poss.

4:14 On ἵνα πληρωθῇ τὸ ῥηθὲν διὰ Ἠσαΐου τοῦ προφήτου λέγοντος, see the identical cstr. (except for the change in the name of the prophet) in 2:17.

4:15 Γῆ Ζαβουλὼν καὶ γῆ Νεφθαλίμ refers to the land allotted to these two tribes (Josh 19:10–16, 32–39), thus the gen. express poss. The acc. case of ὁδόν is initially puzzling. However, the acc. is sometimes used in *appos. to indecl. nouns of other cases in the LXX (Conybeare and Stock §57). Alternatively, D&A (1:382) suggest that the "surprising accusative" is adv. The ὁδὸς θαλάσσης is the *Via Maris*, a major trade route connecting Egypt and Syria. The gen. θαλάσσης expresses direction or destination: "route to the sea" (BDAG 691a–92b, esp. 1). Πέραν with the gen. (τοῦ Ἰορδάνου) functions as a prep. mng. "across" and may refer to either the east (H 1.73) or west (N 173; D&A 1.382–83) side of the Jordan. The gen. τῶν ἐθνῶν indicates that Γαλιλαία belonged to the Gentiles (poss. gen.) in the sense that Gentiles composed the majority of the population (H 1.73).

4:16 ὁ λαός often refers in Matthew to the people of Israel. It prob. has that sense here despite the preceding ref. to the Gentiles (D&A 1.385). The ptc. phrase ὁ καθήμενος (nom. sg. masc. of pres. mid. ptc. of dep. κάθημαι, "sit") may be appos., but more likely the def. art. functions like a rel. pron. (BDAG 687a–89c, esp. 2.c.β.). Ἐν with σκότει (darkness) expresses state or cond. Εἶδεν 3rd sg. aor. act. indic. of ὁράω, "see." Despite its separation from φῶς by the vb., the adj. μέγα modifies φῶς. The position of φῶς prob. marks it as emphatic. Τοῖς καθημένοις (dat. pl. masc. of pres. mid. ptc.) individualizes the people viewed corporately in the first part of the verse. The phrase ἐν χώρᾳ ("region") καὶ σκιᾷ ("shadow") θανάτου is prob. a hendiadys mng. "in the land of death's shadow" (NIV; G 60). However, some tr. render it as a prep. sharing two objects: "in the region and the shadow of death" (ESV; sim. LEB). Ἀνέτειλεν 3rd sg. aor. act. indic. of ἀνατέλλω, "rise." Αὐτοῖς is a dat. of advantage.

HOMILETICAL SUGGESTIONS

Beginning the Work (4:12–16)

1. Jesus wisely avoided unnecessary danger (4:12–13)
2. Jesus fulfilled messianic prophecy (4:14–16)
3. Jesus summoned sinners to repentance (4:17)

II. Galilean Ministry (4:17–16:20)

A. FIRST STAGE OF JESUS'S GALILEAN MINISTRY (4:17–25)

1. The Calling of the First Disciples (4:17–22)

4:17 Ἀπὸ τότε uses the adv. τότε as a subst. The cstr. is common in Matthew (4:17; 16:21; 26:16) and appears in the LXX (4x) and once in Luke (16:16). It means "from that time on." Ἤρξατο 3rd sg. aor. mid. indic. of ἄρχω, "begin." The pres. act. inf. κηρύσσειν and λέγειν are complementary. On μετανοεῖτε· ἤγγικεν γὰρ ἡ βασιλεία τῶν οὐρανῶν, see 3:1.

4:18 Περιπατῶν (nom. sg. masc. of pres. act. ptc. of περιπατέω, "walk") is temp. and contemp.: "while he was walking" (most EVV). Παρά with the acc. (τὴν θάλασσαν) means "at the edge of the sea" (BDAG 756b–58b, esp. C.1.β.). Τῆς Γαλιλαίας is prob. wholative/partitive, "the sea that is part of Galilee" or perhaps a gen. of appos. that marks category-example, i.e., "Galilee" is an example of a lake/sea. Εἶδεν 3rd sg. aor. act. indic. of ὁράω, "see." Δύο, "two." Σίμωνα and Ἀνδρέαν are accusatives of simple appos. and modify ἀδελφούς. Although nouns in simple apposition normally agree with the head noun in case and number, the compound appos. cstr. matches the pl. The ptc. clause τὸν λεγόμενον Πέτρον is attrib. and modifies Σίμωνα. Αὐτοῦ modifies τὸν ἀδελφόν and is a gen. of relationship. Βάλλοντας (acc. pl. masc. of pres. act. ptc. of βάλλω, "throw") is *attrib. or pred. Εἰς with the acc. (τὴν θάλασσαν) is appropriate since the weighted casting net (ἀμφίβληστρον) sank "into" the water. Γάρ identifies the reason the brothers were casting their nets. Ἦσαν 3rd pl. impf. indic. of εἰμί, "be." Ἁλιεῖς (nom. pl. masc. of ἁλιεύς) refers to one who fishes as an occupation.

4:19 Λέγει is a historical pres. and emphasizes the statement it introduces. Δεῦτε is a hortatory particle used as the pl. of δεῦρο, mng. "come on." The particle was prob. regarded as more terse and forceful than the impv. form of ἀκολουθέω. Ὀπίσω functions as a prep. with the gen. (μου) and indicates that the brothers were to follow "behind" Jesus. For μου after ὀπίσω, see 3:11. The disciples of the rabbis walked behind the master to show respect and so the disciples could see and imitate the master's example (H 1.76–77). Ποιήσω (1st sg. fut. act. indic. of ποιέω, "make") is a predictive fut.

that expresses a promise. The dbl. accusatives ὑμᾶς and ἁλιεῖς are object/complement. Ἀνθρώπων is an obj. gen. identifying that for which the men will fish.

4:20 The def. art. οἱ serves as a dem. pron. and the ptc. ἀφέντες (nom. pl. masc. of aor. act. ptc. of ἀφίημι, "leave") is attendant circumstance (most EVV). The temp. adv. εὐθέως ("immediately") stresses that the obedience of the new disciples was instantaneous (8:22). Τὰ δίκτυα (acc. pl. neut. of δίκτυον) is a general term for "net" that is less specific than ἀμφίβληστον. Ἠκολούθησαν 3rd pl. aor. act. indic. of ἀκολουθέω, "follow."

4:21 Προβάς (nom. sg. masc. of aor. act. ptc. of προβαίνω, "go ahead, advance") is prob. temp. and antecedent: "after he went on." Ἐκεῖθεν is an adv. of place mng. "from there." The idea is that Jesus left the place along the shore where he issued the command to Peter and Andrew and then continued further along the shoreline. Εἶδεν (4:18). The adj. ἄλλους distinguishes the second set of two brothers from the previously mentioned set but does not emphasize the differences between the two sets like ἕτερος sometimes does. Ἰάκωβον and Ἰωάννην are appos., modifying ἀδελφούς. The def. art. τόν lacks a subst. However, the def. art. followed by a gen. cstr. (τοῦ Ζεβεδαίου) is often used to express a relationship of *kinship, ownership, or dependence (BDAG 686a–689c, 2.g.). Τὸν ἀδελφόν is acc. of simple appos., modifying Ἰωάννην. Αὐτοῦ is a gen. of relationship. Ἐν τῷ πλοίῳ, "in the boat." Μετά with the gen. (Ζεβεδαίου) expresses association. Τοῦ πατρός is gen. of simple appos. Αὐτῶν is gen. of relationship. Καταρτίζοντας (acc. pl. masc. of pres. act. ptc. of καταρτίζω, "mend") is attrib. Τὰ δίκτυα (4:20). Αὐτῶν is gen. of poss. Ἐκάλεσεν 3rd sg. aor. act. indic. of καλέω, "call."

4:22 On οἱ δὲ εὐθέως ἀφέντες . . . ἠκολούθησαν αὐτῷ, see 4:20. The objects of the disciples' abandonment are now τὸ πλοῖον καὶ τὸν πατέρα αὐτῶν rather than merely "nets."

FOR FURTHER STUDY

13. Fishers of Men

Mánek, J. "Fishers of Men." *NovT* 2 (1957): 138–41.
Neudecker, R. "Master-Disciple/Disciple-Master Relationship in Rabbinic Judaism and in the Gospels." *Gregorianum* 80 (1999): 245–61.
Smith, C. W. "Fishers of Men." *HTR* 52 (1959): 187–204.
Wuellner, W. H. *The Meaning of "Fishers of Men."* Philadelphia: Westminster, 1967.

HOMILETICAL SUGGESTIONS

The Call of the First Disciples (4:17–22)

1. Discipleship involves following Jesus's example
2. Discipleship involves prompting others to follow Jesus
3. Discipleship involves loving Jesus more than occupations, possessions, or family

2. Jesus's Teaching and Healing in Galilee (4:23–25)

4:23 Περιῆγεν (3rd sg. impf. act. indic. of περιάγω, "go around, wander") is prog. (9:35–36). Coupled with the adj. ὅλη (ὅλος, "whole, entire"), the prep. ἐν means "throughout." The three nom. sg. masc. pres. act. ptc. διδάσκων ("teaching"), κηρύσσων ("preaching"), and θεραπεύων ("healing") prob. express purpose. Jesus did not just happen to engage in these activities as he traveled. These aspects of his mission were the motivation for his travels. Although most EVV treat the ptc. as circumstance, the tense of the ptc. (pres. rather than aor.) and the word order (ptc. follows the vb. rather than preceding the vb.) suggest that the ptc. express purpose (W 640–44 [esp. note 67] and 635–37). The συναγωγή was a building where faithful Jews gathered for biblical instruction, worship, and judicial proceedings (BDAG 963a–d). The third pers. pl. pron. αὐτῶν is often interpreted as implying that Matthew desired to distinguish himself from those who attended synagogue in Galilee (D&A 1.413–14; H 1.80), but some dispute this (N 182–83). On the relationship between "teaching" and "preaching," see Luz 1.206–8. Τῆς βασιλείας may be a descriptive gen. mng. "about the kingdom." Alternatively, εὐαγγέλιον may be regarded as a verbal noun ("proclamation" rather than "good news") and τῆς βασιλείας as an obj. gen. (BDAG 402c–3b, 1.b.). The use of πᾶσαν with sg. anar. nouns emphasizes the individual members of a class: "every disease and every sickness." However, the focus on various kinds of diseases in 4:24 may suggest that Matthew stresses every kind of disease and every kind of sickness as well (NLT). The repetition of πᾶσαν marks the adj. as emphatic. Νόσος, -ου, ἡ, "disease." Μαλακία, -ας, ἡ, "sickness." These maladies illustrate the dark shadow of death that blankets the region (4:16; N 183). Ἐν with the dat. (τῷ λαῷ) means "among" and the art. form of λαός refers to Israel as God's people (H 1.80).

4:24 Ἀπῆλθεν 3rd sg. aor. act. indic. of dep. ἀπέρχομαι, "go." Αὐτοῦ modifying ἡ ἀκοή ("report, fame") is prob. an obj. gen. (D&A 1.416). Normally the prep. εἰς would merely indicate that the report penetrated the borders of Syria (NLT). However, in conjunction with the adj. ὅλην ("whole"), the prep. indicates that the message spread "throughout" the entirety of Syria (most EVV). Προσήνεγκαν 3rd pl. aor. act. indic. of προσφέρω, "carry toward." The def. art. τούς modifies all five of the acc. pl. ptc. subst. (four ptc. and one noun) that follow. Although the cstr. does not satisfy the criteria of the Granville Sharp rule, the shared def. art. does pres. the five subgroups as different categories of a larger group. Ἔχοντας acc. pl. masc. of pres. act. ptc. of ἔχω, "have." With the adv. κακῶς, the ptc. serves as an idiom for experiencing physical harm (BDAG 502b, 1.a.). Ποικίλαις (dat. pl. fem. of ποικίλος) means "different kinds of." Νόσοις, 4:23. Βασάνος, -ου, ἡ, "torture, severe pain." The dat. phrase expresses means and modifies the ptc. that follows. Συνεχομένους acc. pl. masc. of pres. pass. ptc. of συνέχω, "be afflicted." Δαιμονιζομένους acc. pl. masc. of pres. pass. ptc. of dep. δαιμονίζομαι, "be possessed by a demon." Σεληνιαζομένους acc. pl. masc. of pres. pass. ptc. of dep. σεληνιάζομαι, "suffer epileptic seizures." Παραλυτικός, -η, -ον, paralyzed. Ἐθεράπευσεν 3rd sg. aor. act. indic. of θεραπεύω, "heal."

4:25 Ἠκολούθησαν, 4:20. Ὄχλος, -ου, ὁ, refers to a large number of people gathered together. The adj. πολλοί ("many") stresses even more the large number of people following Jesus. The ἀπό with the three gen. obj. expresses point of orig. On πέραν τοῦ Ἰορδάνου, see 4:15.

FOR FURTHER STUDY

14. Demon Possession and Exorcism

Berends, W. "Biblical Criteria for Demon-Possession." *WTJ* 37 (1975): 342–65.
Loader, W. R. G. "Son of David, Blindness, Possession, and Duality in Matthew." *CBQ* 44 (1982): 570–85.
Parker, S. T. "Decapolis Reviewed." *JBL* 94 (1975): 437–41.
Ross, J. M. "Epileptic or Moonstruck?" *BT* 29 (1978): 121–28.

HOMILETICAL SUGGESTIONS

Jesus's Compassion for People (4:23–25)

1. Jesus was concerned about people's spiritual needs
   a. He taught in the synagogues
   b. He preached the gospel of the kingdom
2. Jesus was concerned about people's physical needs
   a. He healed the sick among the Jews
   b. He healed the sick from among the Syrians
3. Jesus's compassion and power attracted large numbers of people

B. FIRST DISCOURSE: SERMON ON THE MOUNT (5:1–7:29)

1. Structure

The Sermon on the Mount bears evidence of a carefully planned structure. The main body of the sermon is marked by references to the "Law and the Prophets" that serve as an inclusio (5:17; 7:12). Similarly, the Beatitudes are bracketed by an inclusio ("the kingdom of heaven is theirs;" 5:3, 10). The six antitheses share sim. structures and are bracketed by references to exceptional righteousness (5:20, 46–48). After an introduction in 6:1, Jesus's discussions of each of the three pillars of Judaism—almsgiving, prayer, and fasting—each share sim. structures. The main inclusio in 5:17 and 7:12 suggests that 5:3–16 forms the introduction to the sermon and 7:13–27 forms the conclusion of the sermon. The entirety of the sermon is bracketed by the ref. to the commencement of the sermon in 5:1–2 and the completion and reaction to the sermon in 7:28–29.

FOR FURTHER STUDY

15. The Sermon on the Mount

Allison, D. C. *The Sermon on the Mount: Inspiring the Moral Imagination*. New York: Crossroad, 1999.

Betz, H. D. *The Sermon on the Mount: A Commentary on the Sermon on the Mount, Including the Sermon on the Plain*. Hermeneia. Minneapolis: Fortress, 1995.

Greenman, J. P., T. Larsen, and S. R. Spencer. *The Sermon on the Mount Through the Centuries*. Grand Rapids: Brazos, 2007.

Guelich, R. A. *The Sermon on the Mount*. Waco, TX: Word, 1982.

Kissinger, W. S. *Sermon on the Mount: A History of Interpretation and Bibliography*. Metuchen, NJ: Scarecrow, 1975.

Lloyd-Jones, D. M. *Studies in the Sermon on the Mount*. Grand Rapids: Eerdmans, 1976.

Quarles, C. L. *Sermon on the Mount: Restoring Christ's Message to the Modern Church*. NAC Studies in Bible & Theology. Edited by E. Ray Clendenen. Nashville: B&H, 2011.

Stott, J. R. W. *The Message of the Sermon on the Mount (Matthew 5–7): Christian Counter-Culture*. The Bible Speaks Today. Edited by J. R. W. Stott. Downers Grove: InterVarsity, 1975.

2. Introduction (5:1–16)

a. Setting (5:1–2)

5:1 Ἰδών (nom. sg. masc. of aor. act. ptc. of ὁράω, "see") is prob. *temp. (NIV; CSB; LEB) or causal. The clause ἀνέβη εἰς τὸ ὄρος appears three times in the LXX and always describes Moses's ascent of Sinai (Exod 19:3; 24:18; 34:4; cf. Exod 24:15). Ἀνέβη 3rd sg. aor. act. indic. of ἀναβαίνω, "go up, ascend." The def. art. with ὄρος prob. identifies the mountain as "well-known" or the best of its class (*par excellence*, thus inviting comparison with Sinai; Quarles, *Sermon*, 35) or the generic use of the art. to refer to "mountainous country" (N 192). Καθίσαντος (gen. sg. masc. of aor. act.

ptc. of καθίζω, "sit") is gen. abs. and temp. Προσῆλθαν 3rd pl. aor. act. indic. of dep. προσέρχομαι, "approach."

5:2 Ἀνοίξας (nom. sg. masc. of aor. act. ptc. of ἀνοίγω, "open") is prob. attendant circumstance. With τὸ στόμα ("mouth"), αὐτοῦ is partitive. Ἐδίδασκεν (3rd sg. impf. act. indic. of διδάσκω, "teach") is ingr. Jesus "began teaching" them (NIV; LEB; CSB). On λέγων, see 3:2.

b. Beatitudes (5:3–12)

5:3 Μακάριος, -ία, -ιον, "blessed, favored (by God)" (Quarles, Sermon, 39–40, 42). The adj. is in the first pred. position, which may place slight emphasis on the adj. (W 307–8). Πτωχός, -ή, -όν, "poor." Τῷ πνεύματι is dat. of *ref. (BDF §197) or sphere (D&A 1.444). Wallace wrestled with these classifications (155) and concluded that the dat. was equivalent to the adv. "spiritually." Πνεύματι refers to the human spirit (BDAG 832c–36d, 3.b.). The def. art. is prob. either monadic (each person has only one spirit) or implies poss. ("his spirit;" Wallace 215). The conj. ὅτι is causal and identifies the reason the poor are blessed. The position of αὐτῶν is prob. emphatic (H. 1.92) and implies that this blessing belongs only to the poor in spirit. The pres. tense of ἔστιν contrasts with the fut. tense vbs. in the ὅτι clauses of the other beatitudes and implies that the kingdom is in some sense presently enjoyed. On ἡ βασιλεία τῶν οὐρανῶν, see 3:2. The clause ὅτι αὐτῶν ἐστιν ἡ βασιλεία τῶν οὐρανῶν is repeated verbatim in 5:10 and serves as an inclusio bracketing the beatitudes. Notice also that the recipients of the first four blessings are alliterated with the letter π (πτωχοί, πενθοῦντες, πραεῖς, πεινῶντες). This feature divides the beatitudes into two equal parts.

5:4 Μακάριοι, 5:3. Πενθοῦντες (nom. pl. masc. of pres. act. ptc. of πενθέω, "mourn") is subst., but the prog. aspect remains. Ὅτι, 5:3. Αὐτοί is emphatic and implies that this blessing belongs only to those who mourn. Παρακληθήσονται (3rd pl. fut. pass. indic. of παρακαλέω, "comfort, encourage") is a divine pass. and is predictive, stating an eschatological promise that awaits fut. fulfillment (D&A 1.448–49). On the var., see Metzger 10.

5:5 Μακάριοι, 5:3. Πραΰς, πραεῖα, πραΰ, "meek." For a definition of this adj. based on OT usage, see Quarles, Sermon, 55–56. Ὅτι αὐτοί, 5:3. Κληρονομήσουσιν 3rd pl. fut. act. indic. of κληρονομέω, "inherit." Although τὴν γῆν is correctly tr. "the earth" in most EVV, the clause was used in the OT to refer to Israel inheriting the land of promise (Ps 37:11; Isa 61:7). The use of the clause here suggests the transfer of OT promises made to Israel to the disciples of Jesus and thus portrays Jesus's disciples as the new Israel.

5:6 Μακάριοι, 5:3. Πεινῶντες (nom. pl. masc. of pres. act. ptc. of πεινάω, "hunger for") and διψῶντες (nom. pl. masc. of pres. act. ptc. of διψάω, "thirst for") are subst. but retain the prog. aspect of the pres. tense. Τὴν δικαιοσύνην (3:15) is the obj. of these intense longings. Ὅτι αὐτοί, 5:3. Χορτασθήσονται (3rd pl. fut. pass. indic. of χορτάζω, "satisfy, fill") is a divine pass. and predictive fut. expressing an eschatological promise.

5:7 Μακάριοι, 5:3. Ἐλεήμονες (nom. pl. masc. of ἐλεήμων, -ον, "merciful") is subst. Ὅτι αὐτοί, 5:3. Ἐλεηθήσονται (3rd pl. fut. pass. indic. of ἐλεέω, "express mercy") is a divine pass. and predictive fut., expressing a promise.

5:8 Μακάριοι, 5:3. Καθαροί (nom. pl. masc. of καθαρός, -α, -ον, "pure, clean") is subst. Τῇ καρδίᾳ is a dat. of *ref. or sphere (see 5:3 on τῷ πνεύματι). Ὅτι αὐτοὶ, 5:3. The position of τὸν θεόν may suggest it is mildly emphatic. Ὄψονται (3rd pl. fut. mid. indic. of ὁράω, "see") is a predictive fut., expressing a promise that awaits eschatological fulfillment.

5:9 Μακάριοι, 5:3. Εἰρηνοποιοί (nom. pl. masc. of εἰρηνοποιός, -ον, "reconciling, restoring peace") is subst. Ὅτι αὐτοί, 5:3. The position of υἱοὶ θεοῦ may suggest that it is mildly emphatic. Κληθήσονται (3rd pl. fut. pass. indic. of καλέω, "call") is a divine pass. and predictive fut.

5:10 Μακάριοι, 5:3. Δεδιωγμένοι (nom. pl. masc. of pf. pass. ptc. of διώκω, "persecute") is subst. The shift to the pf. ptc. following the use of pres. ptc. in 5:4 and 6 is unexpected. The pf. ptc. prob. refers to individuals who had already suffered persecution at the time Jesus pronounced his blessing (D&A 1.459). Hagner suggests that the pf. tense expresses the temp. perspective of Matthew and his community (1.95). Ἕνεκεν with the gen. (δικαιοσύνης) functions as a prep. expressing cause. On ὅτι αὐτῶν ἐστιν ἡ βασιλεία τῶν οὐρανῶν, see 5:3.

5:11 Μακάριοι, 5:3. The use of ἔστε (2nd pl. pres. indic. of εἰμί) suggests that the vb. implied in the previous eight beatitudes is likewise pres. tense. The shift from 3rd pers. to 2nd pers. indicates that the beatitudes are directly applicable to Jesus's disciples. The shift and other factors also suggests that vv. 11–12 function as a commentary on the final beatitude in 5:10 (Quarles, *Sermon*, 40–41). The temp. particle ὅταν ("whenever") with aor. subjunc. may indicate that the blessing follows the experience of persecution (BDAG 730d–31b, 1.a.β.). In Matthew's use of the cstr., the time of the action is contingent, but the action is assumed to occur (Quarles, *Sermon*, 71). Ὀνειδίσωσιν 3rd pl. aor. act. subjunc. of ὀνειδίζω, "reproach, insult." Διώξωσιν 3rd pl. aor. act. subjunc. of διώκω, "persecute." Εἴπωσιν 3rd pl. aor. act. subjunc. of λέγω. Πᾶν with the anar. sg. πονηρόν (πονηρός, -ά, -όν, "evil") stresses individual acts of evil speech. Πονηρόν may be in the neut. gender because of an implied ῥῆμα ("word"), which some later scribes inserted in the text. Thus, the persecutors exhaust their vocabulary in hurling insults and accusations against the disciple. Καθ' with the gen. ὑμῶν denotes hostile opposition: "against" (BDAG 511a–13d, 2.b.). Ψευδόμενοι nom. pl. masc. of pres. mid. ptc. of dep. ψεύδομαι, "lie, speak falsehoods." The ptc. is pres. in the oldest mss. but missing from many Western texts. An early scribe may have *omitted it because: (1) he wished to conform the text to the parallel in Luke 6:22, or (2) because he deemed the ptc. redundant, awkward, and unnecessary. Alternatively, a scribe may have added it early to clarify that the charges against the persecuted disciple were false. See Metzger 10–11. The ptc. is characteristic of Matthew's style since his Gospel uses terms with ψευδ- six times in texts in which Luke's parallel lacks them (Gundry 74). The ptc. is prob. epex. and simply clarifies the vb. εἴπωσιν (NIV; CSB). Ἕνεκεν, 5:10. The longer form of the pron. (ἐμοῦ) is prob. not emphatic (BDAG 275a–c).

5:12 Χαίρετε (2nd pl. pres. act. impv. of χαίρω, "rejoice") and ἀγαλλιᾶσθε (2nd pl. pres. mid. impv. of ἀγαλλιάω, "be overjoyed") are prob. ingr.-prog. Ὅτι is causal, expressing the reason for the joy. The pl. τοῖς οὐρανοῖς refers to the abode of God, where the persecuted disciple's reward is kept. Γάρ identifies the reason for the great reward. Οὕτως points to a similarity between the persecution of the prophets and that described in 5:11. Ἐδίωξαν 3rd pl. aor. act. indic. of διώκω. Τούς with πρὸ ὑμῶν functions like a rel. pron. "who came before you." Thē prep. πρό has a temp. rather than locat. sense here.

HOMILETICAL SUGGESTIONS

Blessings for the Coming Age (5:3–12)
1. The kingdom for those who recognize their spiritual poverty
2. Comfort for those who mourn for their sin
3. The renewed earth for those who submit to God
4. Righteousness for those who long to be holy
5. Mercy for those who show mercy to others
6. Unhindered fellowship with God for those whose hearts are pure
7. Acceptance in God's family for those who reconcile others
8. The kingdom for those who suffer persecution

c. Salt and Light (5:13–16)

5:13 Ὑμεῖς is emphatic. Ἔστε 2nd pl. pres. indic. of εἰμί. The def. art. with ἅλας is prob. monadic (Quarles, *Sermon*, 80; D&A 1.472). Γῆ is used in an associative sense to refer to humanity as the inhabitants of the earth (BDAG 196a–c, 2). The gen. τῆς γῆς is obj. Δέ prob. has a mild adversative sense. Ἐάν with the subjunc. (μωρανθῇ 3rd sg. aor. pass. subjunc. of μωραίνω, "be foolish, become insipid") marks the prot. of a third-class cond. sentence. The prep. ἐν with τίνι (dat. sg. neut. of the interr. pron. τίς, τί, "who, what") marks the instr. Ἁλισθήσεται (3rd sg. fut. pass. indic. of ἁλίζω, "salt") is a delib. fut. that implies some doubt about the response (W 570). The position of εἰς οὐδέν is prob. emphatic and offers an immediate reply to the preceding question. Ἰσχύω, "be able," is often followed by a complementary inf., which in this case is replaced by the εἰς phrase and means "it is not able to do/accomplish anything," i.e., it is useless. The temp. adv. ἔτι ("still") refers to the cond. of the salt after loss of its flavor or purity. Εἰ μή is equivalent to πλήν (when used as a prep.) and introduces an exception (BDAG 277b–79c, 6.i.). Βληθέν (acc. sg. neut. of aor. pass. ptc. of βάλλω, "throw") is temp. and antecedent, modifying καταπατεῖσθαι (pres. pass. inf. of καταπατέω, "trample"). The pres. tense of the inf. is iter. and suggests repeated instances of trampling. The phrase ὑπὸ τῶν ἀνθρώπων identifies the pers. agents of the pass. inf. The def. art. is generic ("humankind;" W 227–28).

5:14 On ὑμεῖς ἐστε, see 5:13. The def. art. with φῶς is prob. monadic (Quarles, *Sermon*, 85). The gen. τοῦ κόσμου is prob. obj. The anar. πόλις indicates that Jesus was referring to any city in general. This suggests that δύναται (3rd sg. pres. mid. indic. of dep. δύναμαι, "be able") is gnomic (D&A 1.475). Κρυβῆναι (aor. pass. inf. of κρύπτω, "hide") is complementary. Ἐπάνω with the gen. (ὄρους gen. sg. neut. of ὄρος, "mountain") means "on (the top of)." Although most EVV tr. κειμένη (nom. sg. fem. of pres.

mid. ptc. of dep. κεῖμαι, "lie on") as if it were adj., the word order suggests that it is adv. and prob. cond., "if it sits on top of a mountain."

5:15 Οὐδέ, "and not." The lack of a clear subj. suggests that καίουσιν (3rd pl. pres. act. indic. of καίω, "burn, light") and τιθέασιν (3rd pl. pres. act. indic. of τίθημι, "set, put") are gnomic pres. Λύχνος, -ου, ὁ, "lamp." Μόδιος, -ιου, ὁ, "basket for measuring grain." Λυχνία, -ας, ἡ, "lampstand." Λάμπει 3rd sg. pres. act. indic. of λάμπω, "shine." Πᾶσιν is prob. masc. (the neut. possesses an identical form) and a dat. of advantage. The light shines for the benefit of all the people who are in the house (5:16). The dat. does not mark the indirect obj. since the vb. λάμπω is intrans. (W 140–42). The def. art. τοῖς with the prep. phrase ἐν τῇ οἰκίᾳ functions like a rel. pron.

5:16 On οὕτως, see 5:12. The aor. λαμψάτω (3rd sg. aor. act. impv. of λαμπω) expresses urgency. Although the ὑμῶν modifying τὸ φῶς may be a gen. of source or producer, it is more likely a gen. of appos. The gen. of appos. is often used to identify the referent of a metaphor (W 95–100) and 5:14 identifies Jesus's disciples as the light. Ὅπως with subjunc. vbs. expresses purpose. Ἴδωσιν 3rd pl. aor. act. subjunc. of ὁράω. On τὰ καλὰ ἔργα, see 26:10. Δοξάσωσιν 3rd pl. aor. act. subjunc. of δοξάζω, "glorify." Πατέρα acc. sg. masc. of πατήρ, πατρός, ὁ, "father." The τόν with ἐν τοῖς οὐρανοῖς functions like a rel. pron. The clause distinguishes God from earthly fathers.

HOMILETICAL SUGGESTIONS

Salt of the Earth (5:13)

1. Jesus's disciples are to be purifying agents in a corrupt world
2. Jesus's disciples purify the world by living righteous lives and proclaiming the gospel
3. Jesus's disciples will lose their ability to be purifying agents if their lives are not pure
4. Jesus's disciples will face frightening consequences if their lives are not pure
   a. Hypocrisy will permanently damage their testimony
   b. Hypocrisy will make their testimony counterproductive
   c. Hypocrisy invites the disgust of unbelievers

Shining the Light (5:14–16)

1. Jesus's disciples are to live righteous lives that draw others to God
2. Jesus's disciples share his mission of bringing salvation to the ends of the earth
3. Righteous living and bold witness are essential traits of true disciples
4. The righteous character of the disciple is a gift from God that results from his new relationship to the heavenly Father

3. The Body of the Sermon (5:17–7:12)

a. Teaching About the Law (5:17–20)

5:17 Μή with the aor. subjunc. νομίσητε (νομίζω, "think") prohibits the action as a whole. The vb. refers to forming an idea with some suggestion of tentativeness or uncertainty (BDAG 675c–76a, 2), thus: "Do not even entertain the thought that. . . ." Καταλῦσαι (aor. act. inf. of καταλύω, "destroy") expresses purpose. Matthew normally used the conj. καί when referring to the various parts that compose Holy Scripture (7:12; 11:13; 22:40). Thus the disjunctive particle ἤ is unusual. It prob. implies that Jesus was primarily charged with destroying the law but that he denied destroying the law or any other portion of Scripture (Quarles, *Sermon*, 89). Alternatively, the disjunctive particle may have been prompted by the neg. (D&A 1.484). Πληρῶσαι aor. act. inf. of πληρόω, "fulfill" (Quarles, *Sermon*, 90–91).

5:18 Ἀμήν is an asseverative particle that introduces a solemn declaration and strong affirmation (BDAG 53c–54a). Ἕως ἄν with the subjunc. (παρέλθῃ) marks circumstances necessary for the commencement of an action or event. Ὁ οὐρανὸς καὶ ἡ γῆ is a merism denoting the entire created universe (Gen 1:1). Ἰῶτα, τό (indeclin.) "letter iota." Κεραία, -ας, ἡ, "horn, serif." Οὐ μή with the subjunc. (παρέλθῃ) expresses emphatic negation. Ἕως ἄν πάντα γένηται identifies the nature of Jesus's fulfillment of the law and prophets (5:17).

5:19 Οὖν marks an inference drawn from the abiding authority of the Scriptures. Ὅς ἐάν (= ὃς ἄν) with the subjunc. (λύσῃ and διδάξῃ) causes the rel. clause to function like the prot. of a cond. sentence (third class): "if someone breaks . . ." The contingency is not primarily the identity of the subj. but the performance of the action. The dem. adj. τούτων may be prospective (looking forward to Jesus's commands later in the sermon) or *retrospective (referring to the commandments of the Law and the Prophets). Τῶν ἐλαχίστων (ἐλάχιστος) serves as the superl. of μίκρος ("small") and is in the second attrib. position, which places emphasis on both the noun and the adj. and presents the adj. as a "sort of climax" (R 777). The coordinating conj. καί introduces a second necessary cond. The dem. adv. οὕτως refers to the preceding action. Thus the cond. involves both breaking commandments and teaching others to break commandments. Κληθήσεται is a divine pass. and predictive fut., referring to the verdict in eschatological judgment. Δέ is adversative, contrasting different individuals performing different actions with different consequences. The dem. pron. οὗτος strengthens the contrast. The prep. ἐν with the dat. τῇ βασιλείᾳ is prob. loc. and indicates that both parties will gain entrance into the kingdom despite their different statuses there (H 1.109). Alternatively, the prep. may be temp. and refer to the occasion of final judgment (Chrysostom, *Homilies on Matthew* 16.5).

5:20 Ἐὰν μή, "if not, unless." Περισσεύσῃ 3rd sg. aor. act. subjunc. of περισσεύω, "abound." The position of the pron. ὑμῶν (subj. gen.) prob. expresses emphasis and strengthens the contrast between the disciple's righteousness and that of the scribes and Pharisees. Δικαιοσύνη, ἡ, "righteousness." Πλεῖον is the acc. sg. neut. comp. form of πολύς used adv.: "more than." The shared def. art. τῶν groups γραμματέων and Φαρισαίων since both have the same inferior righteousness. Both nouns are gen. of comparison. Οὐ μή with the subjunc. (εἰσέλθητε) expresses emphatic negation and asserts the absolute impossibility of entering the kingdom without the righteousness Jesus demands.

HOMILETICAL SUGGESTIONS

Jesus's View of the Old Testament (5:17–20)
1. Jesus affirmed the authority of the OT
2. Jesus fulfilled the prophecies of the OT
3. Jesus affirmed the inspiration and infallibility of the OT
4. Jesus urged his disciples to teach and obey the OT

b. Six Antitheses (5:21–48)

Jesus's teaching in 5:21–48 is structured around six occurrences of the formula Ἠκούσατε ὅτι ἐρρέθη τοῖς ἀρχαίοις (or abbreviated expressions) contrasted with ἐγὼ δὲ λέγω ὑμῖν ὅτι. The formula contrasts Jesus's interpretation of the Scriptures with popular rabbinic interpretations. Matthew divided the six major sections (called antitheses) into two major triads (sets consisting of three each). The first set begins with the full introductory formula (5:21) and contains three antitheses containing moral principles expressed using πᾶς with a subst. ptc. in the pres. tense (5:22, 28, 31). The second set begins with the complete introductory formula (5:33) and contains three antitheses using infs. of indir. discourse expressing commands (5:34, 39) or impv. (5:44).

i. First Antithesis: Murder (5:21–26)

5:21 Ἠκούσατε reminds Jesus's hearers that most of them had not read the Scriptures personally but were informed of their contents by readers in the synagogue. Ἐρρέθη (3rd sg. aor. pass. indic. of λέγω) is a divine pass. referring to the divine inspiration of the Scriptures. Ἀρχαῖος, -αία, -αῖον, "ancient." Φονεύσεις (2nd sg. fut. act. indic. of φονεύω, "murder") is impv. fut. used in a prohibition. Ὃς δ᾿ ἄν, 5:19. Φονεύσῃ 3rd sg. aor. act. subjunc. Ἔνοχος, -ον, "liable, guilty." Ἔσται is prob. gnomic rather than predictive and expresses a legal principle. In the LXX both the pres. and fut. tenses of εἰμί are used with ἔνοχος with no discernible difference in mng. (e.g., Lev 20:12, 13). The dat. τῇ κρίσει identifies the tribunal to which one is liable (BDAG 338d–39a, 2.a.).
5:22 Ἐγώ is emphatic, contrasting Jesus with synagogue readers and rabbinic interpreters. Δέ is adversative, contrasting different speakers (Jesus vs. synagogue readers and rabbinic interpreters) and different recipients (you [ὑμῖν] vs. the ancients). Πᾶς with the art. sg. ptc. (ὀργιζόμενος nom. sg. masc. of pres. pass. ptc. of ὀργίζω, "be angry" pass.) means "everyone who is angry." The pres. ptc. is prog. Τῷ ἀδελφῷ is dat. of dir. obj. Ἔνοχος ἔσται τῇ κρίσει, 5:21. Ὃς δ᾿ ἄν, 5:19. Ῥακά, an indecl. term of insult, mng. "empty head." Ἔνοχος ἔσται with the dat., 5:21. Συνέδριον, -ου, τό, "Sanhedrin," high council in Jerusalem. Μωρέ, voc. sg. masc. of μωρός, -ά, -όν, "fool, rebel." The dat. that followed ἔνοχος ἔσται previously now is replaced by an εἰς phrase, which refers to the penalty assigned by the tribunal. Γέεννα, -ης, ἡ, "Gehenna, hell"

(place of eschatological punishment). Πυρός (gen. sg. neut. of πῦρ, τό, "fire") is either *attrib. gen. ("fiery Gehenna;" LEB) or attributed gen. ("fire of hell" or "hell-fire;" most EVV). On the var., see Metzger 11.

5:23 Οὖν is inferential and introduces an application in the form of a command. Ἐάν with the subjunc. (προσφέρῃς 2nd sg. pres. act. subjunc. of προσφέρω, "pres.") marks the prot. of a third-class condition. The shift from the 2nd pers. pl. (5:21–22) and 3rd. pers. sg. (5:22) now to the 2nd pers. sg. (5:23–26) makes the instruction more intensely pers. and dir. Τὸ δῶρον, "gift," sometimes serves in Matthew as a synonym for "offering (to God)" or "sacrifice" (8:4; 23:18–19). This usage is common in the LXX (e.g., Lev 1:2, 14; 2:1, 4). Τὸ θυσιαστήριον, "place of sacrifice, altar." Κἀκεῖ is a combination (crasis) of the conj. καί and adv. of place ἐκεῖ, "there." Μνησθῇς 2nd sg. aor. pass. subjunc. of dep. μιμνήσκομαι, "remember." The shift from pres. to aor. tense portrays the act of sacrifice as a process and the recollection of the memory as punctiliar, as in the Eng. idiom "it suddenly occurred to me." The τι is enclitic and thus the indef. pron., "something." Κατά with the gen. (σοῦ) denotes hostile opposition.

5:24 The aor. impv. ἄφες (2nd sg. aor. act. impv. of ἀφίημι, "leave") and διαλλάγηθι (2nd sg. aor. pass. impv. of dep. διαλλάσσομαι, "reconcile") express urgency. Ἐκεῖ, "there," is clarified by ἔμπροσθεν τοῦ θυσιαστηρίου, "in front of the altar." The pres. impv. ὕπαγε is ingr.-prog. When a second impv. follows ὑπάγω in the NT, a conj. between the two is almost always absent (BDAG 1028a–c, 2.a.). This may imply that the two impv. were not intended to refer to two separate and distinct actions but that the impv. form of ὑπάγω merely emphasized the urgency of fulfilling the second impv. Thus ὕπαγε functions much like the interjection δεῦρο. The acc. sg. neut. adj. πρῶτον functions as an adv. of time expressing priority: "first." This temp. priority is reinforced by the τότε in the next clause for the effect: "then and only then." Ἐλθών is attendant circumstance. The pres. impv. πρόσφερε commands continuation of an action previously began but halted, thus: "finish offering."

5:25 Despite the use of the pres. impv. (ἴσθι 2nd sg. pres. impv. of εἰμί), the adv. ταχύ shows that the command expresses urgency. Matthew likely used the pres. tense merely because no aor. form existed. Εὐνοῶν (nom. sg. masc. of pres. act. ptc. of εὐνοέω, "make friends") is periph. Ἀντιδίκος, -ου, ὁ, "accuser, plaintiff." Σου is an obj. gen. Ἕως ὅτου w. the pres. indic. (εἶ), "while" (BDAG 422d–24a, 2.c.). Μήποτε is a marker of negated purpose, "lest, so that . . . not." Παραδῷ 3rd sg. aor. act. subj. of παραδίδωμι, "hand over." Κριτής, -οῦ, ὁ, "judge." Ὑπηρέτης, -ου, ὁ, "officer of the court." Φυλακή, -ῆς, ἡ, "prison." Βληθήσῃ 2nd. sg. fut. pass. indic. of βάλλω, "throw." Note that Matthew also used μήποτε with the fut. indic. in 7:6.

5:26 Ἀμὴν λέγω σοι, cf. 5:18. Οὐ μή with the subj. (ἐξέλθῃς 2nd sg. aor. act. subjunc. of dep. ἐξέρχομαι) is emphatic negation. Ἐκεῖθεν, 4:21. Ἕως ἄν with the subjunc., 5:18. Ἀποδῷς 2nd sg. aor. act. subjunc. of ἀποδίδωμι, "repay." Ἔσχατος, -η, -ον, "last." Κοδράντης, -ου, ὁ, "Quadrans, smallest Roman coin = 1/64 of a denarius."

HOMILETICAL SUGGESTIONS

Dealing with Anger (5:21–26)

1. Understand your anger (5:21–22)
   a. The anger Jesus prohibited is intense
   b. The anger Jesus prohibited is enduring
   c. The anger Jesus prohibited is unreasonable
   d. The anger Jesus prohibited is escalating
   e. The anger Jesus prohibited is directed at a spiritual brother or sister
2. Understand the importance of dealing with your anger (5:23–24)
3. Understand the urgency of dealing with your anger (5:25–26)

ii. Second Antithesis: Adultery (5:27–30)

5:27 Ἠκούσατε ὅτι ἐρρέθη, 5:21. Μοιχεύσεις (2nd sg. fut. act. indic. of μοιχεύω, "commit adultery") is an impv. fut. used in a prohibition.

5:28 Ἐγὼ δὲ λέγω ὑμῖν ὅτι, 5:21. Πᾶς, 5:22. The pres. ptc. βλέπων is prob. prog.: "keeps on looking." Since γυναῖκα (γύνη, -ης, ἡ, "woman, wife") is indef. and is not modified by a gen. of relationship, it prob. means "woman" rather than "wife" (H 1.120). Πρός with the art. inf. (τὸ ἐπιθυμῆσαι aor. act. inf. of ἐπιθυμέω, "desire someone sexually") expresses purpose. Scholars debate whether the acc. αὐτήν is an acc. of ref. (acc. of subj. of the inf.) or the *dir. obj. of the inf. If the former, the look is flirtatious and intended to stir the desire of the woman. If the latter, the look is lustful and intended to fuel the man's own passions. See the discussion with bibliography in Quarles, *Sermon*, 117–18. The adv. ἤδη may mark the completion of an action prior to another point in time ("already"; most EVV) or indicate logical proximity and immediateness ("in fact, thereby"; BDAG 434c–d, 3). Ἐν with the dat. τῇ καρδίᾳ may be *spherical or instr.

5:29 Εἰ with the pres. indic. (σκανδαλίζει 3rd sg. pres. act. indic. of σκανδαλίζω, "cause to sin") marks the prot. of a first-class cond. statement that assumes the reality of the prot. for the sake of argument. In Koine Gk., the cstr. is sometimes a virtual equivalent to ἐάν with the subjunc. (third-class condition) and refers to a purely hypothetical situation (BDF §372.3). Here the context indicates that the prot. is merely hypothetical (Quarles, *Sermon*, 119–23). The adj. δεξιός ("right") is in the second attrib. position (5:19). The aor. impv. ἔξελε (2nd. sg. aor. act. impv. of ἐξαιρέω, "take out") and βάλε (2nd. sg. aor. act. impv. of βάλλω) express urgency. The prep. ἀπό with the gen. (σοῦ) expresses separation: "away from you." Γάρ introduces the reason that such a drastic action is advantageous. Συμφέρει (3rd sg. pres. act. indic. of συμφέρω, "be advantageous"). Σοι is a dat. of advantage. After impers. expressions, ἵνα with the subjunc. (ἀπόληται 3rd sg. 2nd aor. mid. subjunc. of ἀπόλλυμι, "be ruined, destroyed") functions as a substitute for a complementary inf. (BDAG 475c–77b, 2.b.) Μέλος, -ους, τό, "member or limb of the body." Ὅλος, 1:22. Βληθῇ 3rd. sg. aor. pass. subjunc. of βάλλω. Γέενναν, 5:22.

5:30 See 5:29. Ἔκκοψον 2nd. sg. aor. act. impv. of ἐκκόπτω, "cut off." Ἀπέλθῃ 3rd. sg. aor. act. subjunc. of dep. ἀπέρχομαι, "go away."

HOMILETICAL SUGGESTIONS

Sexual Purity (5:27–30)

1. Jesus commands his disciples to strive for sexual purity
2. Jesus denounced double standards for sexual ethics
3. Jesus taught that sexual purity is worth enormous sacrifice

iii. Third Antithesis: Divorce (5:31–32)

5:31 Ἐρρέθη δέ, 5:21. Ὅς ἄν, 5:19. Ἀπολύσῃ 3rd sg. aor. act. subjunc. of ἀπολύω, "divorce." Since γυναῖκα is def. and modified by a gen. of relationship (αὐτοῦ), it clearly means "wife" (cf. 5:28). Δότω 3rd. sg. aor. act. impv. of δίδωμι, "give." Ἀποστάσιον, -ου, τό, "certificate of divorce" (Deut 24:1, 3).

5:32 Ἐγὼ δὲ λέγω ὑμῖν ὅτι, 5:22. Πᾶς, 5:22. Ἀπολύων nom. sg. masc. of pres. act. ptc. of ἀπολύω, "divorce." Τὴν γυναῖκα αὐτοῦ, 5:31. The prep. παρεκτός with the gen. (λόγου) clearly expresses an exception ("except for, apart from") and is not inclusive. Λόγος here may mean "reason, cause" or "subj. under discussion, matter" (BDAG 598d–601d, 2.d. or 1.a.ε.). Πορνεία, -ας, ἡ, "unlawful sexual intercourse." Ποιεῖ (3rd sg. pres. act. indic. of ποιέω, "make, cause" [BDAG 839b–42a, 2.h.]) is prob. gnomic. Αὐτήν is the acc. of ref. (subj. of inf.). The pass. form of the vb. μοιχεύω was used to describe the female role (μοιχευθῆναι aor. pass. inf.) and the act. form was used to describe the male role (5:27–28). Ὅς ἐάν, 5:19. Ἀπολελυμένην (acc. sg. fem. of pf. pass. ptc. of ἀπολύω) is subst. Γαμήσῃ 3rd sg. aor. act. subjunc. of γαμέω, "marry." Μοιχᾶται 3rd sg. pres. pass. indic. of μοιχάω, "to cause to commit adultery."

HOMILETICAL SUGGESTIONS

The Sanctity of Marriage (5:31–32)

1. Jesus championed the sanctity of marriage against powerful cultural forces
2. Jesus prohibited divorce except in the most extenuating circumstances
3. Jesus taught that remarriage after unjustified divorce constitutes adultery

iv. Fourth Antithesis: Oaths (5:33–37)

5:33 Πάλιν functions as a discourse marker indicating a shift to a new but related topic based on a different OT text (BDAG 752b–53a, 3). Ἠκούσατε ὅτι ἐρρέθη τοῖς ἀρχαίοις, 5:21. Ἐπιορκήσεις (2nd sg. fut. act. indic. of ἐπιορκέω, "swear falsely, commit perjury") and ἀποδώσεις (2nd sg. fut. act. indic. of ἀποδίδωμι, "fulfill [an oath]") are impv. fut. The Δέ is adversative and contrasts the prohibition with the positive command. The position of τῷ κυρίῳ prob. marks it as mildly emphatic. The cstr. prob. serves as the indir. obj. (NIV; ESV). Ὅρκος, -ου, ὁ, "oath." Σου is subj. gen.

5:34 Ἐγὼ δὲ λέγω ὑμῖν, 5:22. Ὀμόσαι (aor. act. inf. of ὀμνύω, "swear") is inf. of indir. discourse used to express a prohibition. Ὅλως, "at all." Μήτε is a neg. copula that divides a series of items into separate parts: "neither . . . nor." In oath formulas in the LXX, the prep. ἐν was used to mark that by which one swore. The resulting oath means "may such and such be destroyed if I failed to keep my word." Οὐρανός, 3:2. All uses of ὅτι in the series are causal, expressing the reason the oath is prohibited. Θρόνος, -ου, ὁ, "throne." Τοῦ θεοῦ is prob. poss.

5:35 Μήτε, 5:34. Ἐν, 5:34. Ὑποπόδιον, -ου, τό, "footstool." Πούς, πόδος, ὁ, "foot." The shift from the consistent use of ἐν in the oath formulas to εἰς Ἱεροσόλυμα is intentional and likely refers to an oath taken while facing toward the city of Jerusalem. Ὅτι, 5:34. Πόλις, 2:23. The τοῦ with μεγάλου βασιλέως is the def. art. *par excellence*, which gives the adj. μέγας (2:10) a superl. force (W 298).

5:36 Μήτε, 5:34. Ἐν, 5:34. The neg. with ὀμόσῃς (2nd sg. aor. act. subjunc. of ὀμνύω, "swear") prohibits the action as a whole. Ὅτι, 5:34. Δύνασαι (2nd sg. pres. mid. indic. of dep. δύναμαι, "be able") is prob. gnomic. Μίαν, 5:18. Θρίξ, 3:4. Λευκός, -ή, -όν, "white." Ποιῆσαι (aor. act. inf. of ποιέω) is a complementary inf. The disjunctive ἤ ("or") establishes two alternatives, each viewed as the opposite of the other. Μέλας, μέλαινα, μέλον, "black." The series of acc. is the equivalent of the dbl. acc. of object-complement.

5:37 Ἔστω 3rd sg. pres. impv. of εἰμί. The use of the sg. ὁ λόγος modified by the pl. subj. gen. ὑμῶν suggests that λόγος means "speech" rather than "word" (BDAG 598d–601d, 1.a.β.; most EVV). Ναί, "yes." The subst. περισσός, -ή, -όν, is used in a comp. sense ("more") with the gen. of comp. τούτων for the sense "anything that exceeds these things (simple affirmations or denials)." Ἐκ marks the source of speech that defies Jesus's instruction. The art. πονηροῦ (5:11) is subst. In this case the art. also serves as the def. art. *par excellence,* referring to Satan as the epitome of evil (BDAG 851b–52a, 1.b.β.).

HOMILETICAL SUGGESTIONS

True Integrity (5:33–37)

1. Oaths are often attempts to mask deception
2. Oaths are often irreverent and blasphemous
3. Oaths in everyday life are unnecessary for those who are consistently honest
4. Attempts to deceive others are a result of Satanic influence

v. Fifth Antithesis: Retaliation (5:38–42)

5:38 Ἠκούσατε ὅτι ἐρρέθη, 5:21. The prep. ἀντί with the gen. in both occurrences is used to identify one thing as the equivalent (appropriate compensation) to another (Harris 49, B). Ὀδούς, ὀδόντος, ὁ, "tooth."

5:39 Ἐγὼ δὲ λέγω ὑμῖν, 5:22. Ἀντιστῆναι (aor. act. inf. of ἀνθίστημι, "oppose, retaliate against") is an inf. of indir. discourse expressing a prohibition. The art. πονηρῷ (5:11) is subst. and possibly *masc. (thus pers.: "the evil person"; most EVV) or neut. (thus impers.: "evil, the evil thing"; H 1.130–31; Luz 1.276). Ὅστις ("any person, who-ever") is the pendant nom., which expresses emphasis. The pres. tense ῥαπίζει (3rd sg. pres. act. indic. of ῥαπίζω, "slap") seems to refer in context to a single slap. Thus, the pres. tense is prob. gnomic rather than prog. or iter. Adj. and pron. such as πᾶς and ὅστις are often followed by gnomic verbals. Εἰς expresses movement directed at the surface of an area (BDAG 288d–91c, 1.a.γ.). Δεξιός, 5:29. Σιαγών, -ονος, ἡ, "cheek, jaw." Στρέψον (2nd sg. aor. act. impv. of στρέφω, "turn") expresses urgency.

5:40 Τῷ θέλοντί (dat. sg. masc. of pres. act. ptc. of θέλω, "desire") is subst. and the indir. obj. in an emphatic position. Σοι is prob. a dat. of association used with κριθῆναι (aor. pass. inf. of κρίνω, "go to court, enter into a legal dispute") to identify a legal opponent (BDAG 567d–69a, 5.a.β.). Χιτών, -ῶνος, ὁ, "tunic, shirt." Λαβεῖν (aor. act. inf. of λαμβάνω, "take") and κριθῆναι are complementary infs. Ἄφες (2nd sg. aor. act. impv. of ἀφίημι, "leave, relinquish") expresses urgency.

5:41 Ὅστις, 5:39. Ἀγγαρεύσει (3rd sg. fut. act. indic. of ἀγγαρεύω, "compel, force into service") is prob. gnomic (5:39). Μίλιον, -ου, τό, "Roman miles (1000 paces)." Ἕν, 5:18. Ὕπαγε (2nd sg. pres. act. impv. of ὑπάγω, "go, proceed") is prog.: "continue going." Μετά with the gen. (αὐτοῦ) marks accompaniment. Δύο, "two."

5:42 The dat. of indir. obj (τῷ αἰτοῦντί) is in an emphatic position. Δός (2nd sg. aor. act. impv. of δίδωμι, "give") expresses urgency. The subst. ptc. τὸν θέλοντα is in an emphatic position. Ἀπό with the gen. (σοῦ) expresses source. The inf. δανίσασθαι (aor. mid. inf. of δανείζω, "lend" [act.], "borrow" [mid.]) is complementary. Ἀποστραφῇς 2nd sg. aor. pass. subjunc. of ἀποστρέφω, "turn away" (mid./pass.). The use of the aorist subjunc. in a prohibition forbids the action as a whole.

HOMILETICAL SUGGESTIONS

Vengeance (5:38–42)

1. The OT does not justify vengeance (v. 38)
2. Jesus prohibited acts of vengeance (vv. 39–42)
   a. Vengeance through acts of violence (v. 39)
   b. Vengeance through legal battles (v. 40)
   c. Vengeance through withholding acts of kindness (vv. 41–42)

vi. Sixth Antithesis: Hate (5:43–48)

5:43 Ἠκούσατε ὅτι ἐρρέθη, 5:21. Ἀγαπήσεις (2nd sg. fut. act. indic. of ἀγαπάω, "love") and μισήσεις (2nd sg. fut. act. indic. of μισέω, "hate") are impv. Πλησίος, -α, -ον, "close by," used subst. "neighbor." Ἐχθρός, -ά, -όν, "hostile," used subst. "enemy." Although the first portion of the statement is a quotation of OT texts such as Lev 19:18, the sec-ond portion ("hate your enemy") does not appear anywhere in the OT.

5:44 Ἐγὼ δὲ λέγω ὑμῖν, 5:22. Ἀγαπᾶτε 2nd pl. pres. act. impv. "love." Τοὺς ἐχθρούς, 5:43. Προσεύχεσθε 2nd pl. pres. mid. impv. of dep. προσεύχομαι, "pray." Both pres. impvs. are prog.: "continue loving and continue praying." Ὑπέρ with the gen. (τῶν διωκόντων) expresses interest or advantage: "for the sake of, on behalf of." Τῶν διωκόντων (gen. pl. masc. of pres. act. ptc. of διώκω, "persecute") is subst. and the pres. tense is prog.

5:45 Ὅπως with the aor. subjunc. (γένησθε) expresses purpose. In this context γίνομαι prob. has connotations of a change in nature (BDAG 196d–99d, 5). On υἱοὶ τοῦ πατρὸς ὑμῶν τοῦ ἐν οὐρανοῖς, see 5:16. The ὅτι is causal, expressing the reason expressions of love demonstrate resemblance of God's children to the heavenly Father. Ἥλιος, -ου, ὁ, "sun." Αὐτοῦ is poss. All creation, incl. the sun, belongs to God. The vbs. ἀνατέλλει (3rd sg. pres. act. indic. of ἀνατέλλω, "cause to rise") and βρέχει (3rd sg. pres. act. indic. of βρέχω, "send rain") emphasize divine causation of weather phenomena. The adjs. πονηρούς ("evil"), ἀγαθούς ("good"), δικαίους ("righteous"), and ἀδίκους ("unrighteous") are subst. and arranged to form a chiasm.

5:46 Ἐάν with the subjunc. (ἀγαπήσητε 2nd pl. aor. act. subjunc. of ἀγαπάω) forms the prot. of a third-class cond. sentence that makes no assumption regarding the fulfillment of the prot. Γάρ is prob. causal and introduces a reason for loving others (BDAG 189a–90a) Τοὺς ἀγαπῶντας (acc. pl. masc. of pres. act. ptc. of ἀγαπάω) is subst. The interr. pron. τίνα here functions as an adj. mng. "what sort of." Μισθός, -ου, ὁ, "reward." The neg. οὐχί prompts an affirmative response to the question. The καί is either *ascensive ("even") or adjunctive ("also"). Τελώνης, -ου, ὁ, "tax collector." In the subst. cstr. τὸ αὐτό, αὐτός serves as the identical adj. mng. "the same (thing)." Ποιοῦσιν (3rd pl. pres. act. indic. of ποιέω) is prob. customary and describes the habitual action of the tax collectors.

5:47 On ἐάν with the subjunc. (ἀσπάσησθε 2nd pl. aor. mid. subjunc. of dep. ἀσπάζομαι, "greet"), see 5:46. τοὺς ὑμῶν The lack of concord of μόνον with ἀδελφοὺς shows that the neut. adj. is functioning as an adv. mng. "only." The interr. pron. τί means "what?" (cf. 5:46). Περισσός, -ή, -όν, "extraordinary, remarkable" (5:20). Ποιεῖτε 2nd pl. pres. act. indic. of ποιέω. The neg. οὐχὶ implies a positive response to the question. The καί is either *ascensive or adjunctive (5:46). Ἐθνικός, -ή, -όν, "gentile, pagan." Τὸ αὐτὸ ποιοῦσιν, 5:46.

5:48 Οὖν is inferential and with a command has an "intensive force" (BDAG 736b–37b, 1.b.). Ἔσεσθε (2nd pl. fut. indic. of εἰμί) is impv. The ὑμεῖς is emphatic. Τέλειος, -α, -ον, "perfect (in a moral sense)." Ὡς is a comp. particle mng. "like, as." Οὐράνιος, -ον, "heavenly," is apparently equivalent to the cstr. in 5:16.

HOMILETICAL SUGGESTIONS

Christian Love (5:43–48)

1. Loving others is the essence of God's will
2. Loving others demonstrates resemblance to God's character
3. Loving others is essential to the extraordinary righteousness that should characterize Jesus's disciples

c. The Disciple's Avoidance of Hypocrisy in Religious Practices (6:1–18)

i. Structure

Each subsection begins with ὅταν plus the pres. subjunc. (6:2, 5, 16) and ends with the clause καὶ ὁ πατήρ σου ὁ βλέπων ἐν τῷ κρυπτῷ ἀποδώσει σοι (6:4, 6, 18). This structure is disrupted by the extensive discussion of prayer in 6:7–15. However, the placement of this subsection in the center of the sermon shows that it should not be regarded as a mere excursus.

ii. Introduction (6:1)

6:1 Προσέχετε (2nd pl. pres. act. impv. of προσέχω, "be in a state of alert") is prob. customary. The disciples should make this their habit. Followed by μή with the inf. (ποιεῖν pres. act. inf. of ποιέω), the vb. means "beware of, take effort to avoid." Δικαιοσύνην is dir. obj. of the inf. and refers to specific acts of righteousness that were prized in Judaism (almsgiving, prayer, fasting). Ἔμπροσθεν, orig. an adv. of place, here functions as a prep. with the gen. (τῶν ἀνθρώπων) to describe the action as occurring "in front of" people. Πρός with the art. inf. (τὸ θεαθῆναι aor. pass. inf. of dep. θεάομαι, "view [with implication that one is impressed by what he sees]") expresses purpose. Thus it is not the public location of the action but the desire for attention that prompted the choice of the location that concerned Jesus. Αὐτοῖς is dat. of agency. Εἰ μή "if not, otherwise." Δέ is adversative. The particle γε served to focus attention on an idea. The cstr. εἰ δὲ μή γε ("otherwise;" BDAG 190 b–d, b.β) marks this sentence as a stern warning regarding the consequences of failing to follow Jesus's command. Μισθός, -οῦ, ὁ, "reward." The pres. tense of ἔχετε is prob. gnomic. Despite the tr. in most EVV, παρά with the dat. (τῷ πατρί does not express source 1). Instead, the prep. may either express local proximity ("nearby the Father;" BDAG 756b–58b, b.1.γ.) or *identify one whose viewpoint is relevant ("in the Father's sight;" Quarles, *Sermon*, 173). On τῷ ἐν τοῖς οὐρανοῖς, see 5:16, 45.

iii. Giving to the Poor (6:2–4)

6:2 Οὖν is inferential. Ὅταν with the pres. subjunc. (ποιῇς 2nd sg. act. of ποιέω) means "whenever, anytime" and the subjunc. marks an indef. temp. clause (W 479). The cstr. emphasizes the need for complete consistency in conduct and allows no exceptions. Ἐλεημοσύνη, -ης, ἡ, "alms, offerings for the poor." Μή with the aor. subjunc. (σαλπίσῃς 2nd sg. act. of τχλπίζω, "blow a trumpet") prohibits an action as a whole. Ἔμπροσθεν 6:1. Ὥσπερ is a marker of similarity: "just like." Ὑποκριτής, -οῦ ὁ, "actor, performer, hypocrite." The def. art. is prob. the "well-known" or "familiar" art. (W 225). Such hypocrites were notorious. The pres. tense of ποιοῦσιν is customary. Ῥύμη, -ης, ἡ, "narrow street." Ὅπως with the aor. subjunc. (δοξασθῶσιν 3rd pl. aor. pass. subjunc. of δοξάζω, "glorify, praise") expresses purpose. Ὑπό with the gen. (τῶν ἀνθρώπων) identifies the agent of the pass. vb. Ἀμὴν λέγω ὑμῖν 5:18. Ἀπέχουσιν 3rd pl. pres. act. indic. of ἀπέχω, "receive in full." The pres. tense of the vb. is prob. prog., but the emphasis is on pres. time, i.e., the reward is being paid in full in the pres. life and no eschatological reward awaits. Μισθόν 6:1.

6:3 Σοῦ ποιοῦντος ἐλεημοσύνην (6:2) is a gen. abs. and temp. Μή with the aor. impv. (γνώτω 3rd sg. aor. act. impv. of γινώσκω, "know") is rare in the NT but occurs three times in Matthew (see 24:17, 18). The cstr. expresses urgency and prohibits the action as a whole. Ἀριστερός, -ά, -όν, "left." The fem. is used because the noun χείρ ("hand" [fem.]) is implied. Τί acc. sg. neut. of interr. pron. Ποιεῖ 3rd sg. pres. act. indic. of ποιέω. Δεξιά 5:39.

6:4 Ὅπως 6:2. The vb. ᾖ is 3rd sg. pres. subjunc. of εἰμί. Ἐλεημοσύνη 6:2. Κρυπτός, -ή, -όν, "hidden." Ἐν τῷ κρυπτῷ is loc. and means "in a hidden location." Καί here introduces a result. Βλέπων nom. sg. masc. of pres. act. ptc. of βλέπω, "see." Ἀποδώσει (3rd sg. fut. act. indic. of ἀποδίδωμι, "reward") is a predictive fut., expressing a promise. Σοι is dat. of indir. obj. See Metzger 12.

iv. Prayer (6:5–15)

6:5 Ὅταν with pres. subj. 6:2. Προσεύχησθε 2nd pl. pres. mid. subjunc. of dep. προσεύχομαι, "pray." Ἔσεσθε (2nd pl. fut. indic. of εἰμί) is impv. fut. used in a prohibition. The form gives Jesus's prohibition the ring of OT prohibitions. Ὡς "like, as." Ὑποκριταί 6:2. Ὅτι is causal. Φιλοῦσιν (3rd pl. pres. act. indic. of φιλέω, "love") is gnomic. Συναγωγαῖς 4:23. Γωνία, -ας, ἡ, "corner." Πλατεῖα, -ας, ἡ, "wide street." Ἑστῶτες (nom. pl. masc. of pf. act. ptc. of ἵστημι, "stand") is either *temp. (antecedent time) or cond. The pf. tense indicates that they enjoy praying only after they position themselves in a location where they will be observed. Προσεύχεσθαι pres. mid. inf. of dep. προσεύχομαι. Ὅπως 6:2. Φανῶσιν 3rd pl. aor. pass. subjunc. of φαίνω, "make an appearance." Ἀμὴν λέγω ὑμῖν, ἀπέχουσιν τὸν μισθὸν αὐτῶν 6:2.

6:6 Σύ is emphatic and δέ adversative, contrasting the disciple with hypocrites. Ὅταν with pres. subjunc. 6:2. Προσεύχῃ 2nd sg. pres. mid. subjunc. of dep. προσεύχομαι. The aor. impv. εἴσελθε (2nd sg. aor. act. impv. of dep. εἰσέρχομαι, "enter") and πρόσευξαι (2nd sg. aor. mid. impv.) may express urgency. Ταμεῖον, -ου, τό, "storeroom, inner room." Κλείσας (nom. sg. masc. of aor. act. ptc. of κλείω, "shut") is prob. temp. (antecedent): "after you close . . ." Θύρα, -ας, ἡ, "door." Καὶ ὁ πατήρ σου ὁ βλέπων ἐν τῷ κρυπτῷ ἀποδώσει σοι 6:4. See Metzger 12.

6:7 Προσευχόμενοι (nom. pl. masc. of pres. mid. ptc. of dep. προσεύχομαι) is temp. and roughly equivalent to the ὅταν προσεύχησθε cstr. in 6:5. Μή with the aor. subjunc. (βατταλογήσητε 2nd pl. aor. act. subjunc. of βατταλογέω, "stammer, mutter mindlessly") prohibits the action as a whole. On the mng. of the vb. "mumble gibberish believed to have magical powers," see Quarles, *Sermon*, 183–84. Ὥσπερ 6:2. Ἐθνικοί 5:47. Γάρ introduces the reason for the pagan practice. Δοκοῦσιν (3rd pl. pres. act. indic. of δοκέω, "suppose") refers to a false presumption (3:9). Ὅτι introduces the content of the pagan's thought. The prep. ἐν expresses cause (BDAG 326c–30b, 9.a.). Πολυλογία, -ας, ἡ, "verbosity." Εἰσακουσθήσονται 3rd pl. fut. pass. subjunc. of εἰσακούω, "listen (and respond)."

6:8 Οὖν is inferential. Μὴ with the aor. subjunc. (ὁμοιωθῆτε 2nd pl. aor. pass. subjunc. of ὁμοιόω, "be like" [pass.]) prohibits the action as a whole. With this vb., the dat. αὐτοῖς identifies the pattern to which one is conformed. Γάρ is causal. Οἶδεν (3rd sg. pf. act. indic. of οἶδα, "know") although the pf. form functions as a pres. (gnomic). The gen. pl. neut. rel. pron. ὧν means "of what, of that which." Χρεία, -ας, ἡ, "need." Πρό with the art. inf. (τοῦ αἰτῆσαι aor. act. inf. of αἰτέω, "ask") expresses subsequent time of the controlling vb. and is tr. "before" (W 596). The acc. ὑμᾶς is the subj. of the inf. and the acc. αὐτόν is the dir. obj. of the inf. See Metzger 12–13.

STRUCTURE

The model prayer consists of six petitions followed by a brief commentary on the fifth petition. Matthew divided the model prayer into two major sections. The first three petitions use 3rd sg. aor. impv. The last three petitions use the 2nd sg. aor. impv. or subjunc.

6:9 Οὕτως is a comp. adv. mng. "like this, in this way." Οὖν is inferential. Προσεύχεσθε 2nd pl. pres. mid. impv. of dep. προσεύχομαι, "pray." The pres. envisions customary or ongoing prayers. Ὑμεῖς is emphatic. Πάτερ is voc. sg. masc. of πατήρ, "father." Ἡμῶν is gen. of relationship. Ὁ ἐν τοῖς οὐρανοῖς 5:16. The aor. impv. is the normal tense and mood for prayer petitions and all the positive petitions in the prayer take this form (W 719–20). The tense prob. expresses the urgency of the appeal. Ἁγιασθήτω 3rd sg. aor. pass. impv. of ἁγιάζω, "treat as holy."

6:10 On the tense of the petitions, see 6:9. Ἐλθέτω 3rd sg. aor. act. impv. of dep. ἔρχομαι, "come." Βασιλεία 3:2. The gen. σου may be poss. or *subj. (referring to God reigning). Γενηθήτω 3rd sg. aor. pass. impv. of dep. γίνομαι, "perform" (BDAG 196d–99c, 2.a.). Θέλημα, -ατος, τό, "what is willed." Ὡς is the comp. particle mng. "like, as." Although οὐρανῷ is sg., it refers to the abode of God. This is apparently possible because of the merism. See 3:2. The shift in prep. from ἐν to ἐπί was necessary since heaven is a sphere of activity but has no material surface. Ἐπί is appropriate for γῆς since it "marks a position on a surface" (BDAG 363a–65c, 1.a.). Ephesians 1:10 is the only NT text that uses ἐπί with "heaven" or "heavens." Cf. Col 1:16.

6:11 Ἐπιούσιος, -ον, means "necessary for existence," "for today," or *"for the coming day" (Quarles, *Sermon*, 206). Δός 2nd sg. aor. act. impv. of δίδωμι, "give." On the tense, see 6:9. The temp. adv. σήμερον, "today, this very day," seems to preclude the eschatological interpretation that views the petition as a plea for the messianic feast.

6:12 On the tense of the petitions, see 6:9. Ἄφες 2nd sg. aor. act. impv. of ἀφίημι, "forgive." Ἡμῖν is emphatic and prob. dat. of advantage. Ὀφείλημα, -ατος, τό, "debt, sin." Ὡς, "like, as." Καί is adjunctive. Ἡμεῖς is emphatic. Ἀφήκαμεν 1st pl. aor. act. indic. of ἀφίημι. Most EVV render the vb. as a pf. tense in Eng.: "we have forgiven" (NIV; CSB; LEB; NRSV; ESV). However, a tr. like "forgive us like we forgave" is prob. more appropriate. Some commentators suggest that the aor. translates the Aram. *perfectum praesens*, which could be tr. with a pres. vb.: "as we are also forgiving" (H 1.150; Hill 138). Several later copyists and correctors used the Gk. pres. here. See Metzger 13. Ὀφειλέτης, -ου, ὁ, "debtor, sinner."

6:13 Μή with the aor. subjunc. 6:8. Εἰσενέγκῃς 2nd sg. aor. act. subjunc. of εἰσφέρω, "bring in, lead in." Πειρασμός, -οῦ, ὁ, "temptation, testing." Ῥῦσαι 2nd sg. aor. mid. impv. of dep. ῥύομαι, "rescue (from danger)." Ἀπό expresses separation (BDF §180). Τοῦ πονηροῦ is prob. masc. The def. art. marks the adj. as subst. and serves as the art. *par excellence*, thus "the evil one," i.e., Satan (CSB; NIV; LEB; NRSV; ESV mg.). Alternatively, the adj. may be neut. and refer to "evil" (ESV; CSB mg.; NIV mg.; LEB mg.; NRSV mg.). The doxology mentioned in the margin of most EVV appears in the majority of mss. but is absent from the earliest mss. and versions. It is prob. a later scribal addition. See Metzger 13–14.

6:14 Γάρ points back to 6:12 and shows the reason for the petition. Ἐάν with the subjunc. marks the prot. of a third-class cond. statement that makes no assumption about the fulfillment of the prot. Ἀφῆτε 2nd pl. aor. act. subjunc. of ἀφίημι, "forgive." On the dat. (τοῖς ἀνθρώποις) with ἀφίημι, see 6:12. Παράπτωμα, -ατος, τό, "moral wrongdoing, sin," demonstrates that ὀφείλημα in 6:12 was used in a moral rather than financial sense. Αὐτῶν is a subj. gen: "the wrongs they commit." Ἀφήσει (3rd sg. fut. act. indic. of ἀφίημι) may be gnomic or *predictive, referring to forgiveness granted in eschatological judgment (H 1.150; D&A 1.612). On the dat. (ὑμῖν), see 6:12. Ὁ πατὴρ ὑμῶν ὁ οὐράνιος 5:48.

6:15 Ἐάν with the subjunc. 6:14. Δέ is adversative, contrasting forgiveness and the refusal to forgive. Ἀφῆτε 6:14. Τοῖς ἀνθρώποις, οὐδὲ ὁ πατὴρ ὑμῶν ἀφήσει τὰ παραπτώματα ὑμῶν 6:14. The neg. conj. οὐδέ means "neither." Although the grammar presents forgiving others as a necessary condition for receiving eschatological forgiveness from God, a condition should not be confused with a cause. Forgiving others is necessary but not meritorious. See Metzger 14.

v. Fasting (6:16–18)

6:16 Ὅταν 6:2. Νηστεύητε 2nd pl. pres. act. subjunc. of νηστεύω, "fast." Μή with the pres. impv. (γίνεσθε 2nd pl. pres. mid. impv.) may express a *general precept or call for the cessation of an action already in progress (W 724–25). Ὡς οἱ ὑποκριταί 6:5. Σκυθρωπός, -ή, -όν, "sullen, gloomy." The adj. is pred.: "Do not be sullen." Ἀφανίζουσιν 3rd pl. pres. act. indic. of ἀφανίζω, "change the appearance of." The vb. is prob. part of the theatrical imagery associated with the ὑποκριταί, who wore different masks for each role (BDAG 154d–55a, 2.; Quarles, *Sermon*, 229). Πρόσωπον, -ου, τό, "face." Ὅπως 6:2. Φανῶσιν 3rd pl. aor. pass. subjunc. of φαίνω, "appear, be seen." Νηστεύοντες (nom. pl. masc. of pres. act. ptc. of νηστεύω, "fast") is prob. temp. and contemp.: "while they are fasting" (cf. LEB). Most EVV tr. the ptc. as if the performers wanted observers to watch the fasting (NIV; CSB; ESV). The Gk. is more poignant. The hypocrites want to be seen themselves. The attention is on the performer rather than the performance. Ἀμὴν λέγω ὑμῖν, ἀπέχουσιν τὸν μισθὸν αὐτῶν 6:2.

6:17 Σύ is emphatic. Δέ is adversative. Νηστεύων (nom. sg. masc. of pres. act. ptc. of νηστεύω, "fast") is temp. (most EVV) and this supports the analysis of the pl. form of the ptc. in the preceding verse. Ἄλειψαί (2nd sg. aor. mid. impv. of ἀλείφω, "anoint")

and νίψαι (2nd sg. aor. mid. impv. of νίπτω, "wash with water") express urgency. Πρόσωπον 6:16.
6:18 Ὅπως 6:2. Φανῇς 2nd sg. aor. pass. subjunc. of φαίνω, "appear, be seen." Νηστεύων is prob. temp. (6:16). Τοῖς ἀνθρώποις and τῷ πατρί are either dat. of pers. agency or indir. obj. Κρυφαῖος, -αία, -αῖον, "private, hidden." Thus τῷ ἐν τῷ κρυφαίῳ = ἐν τῷ κρυπτῷ (6:4, 6). Καὶ ὁ πατήρ σου ὁ βλέπων ἐν τῷ κρυφαίῳ ἀποδώσει σοι 6:4. See Metzger 14.

HOMILETICAL SUGGESTIONS

Doing the Right Thing the Right Way (6:1–8, 16–18)
1. Give, but not to boast (6:1–4)
2. Pray, but not to impress (6:5–8)
3. Fast, but not for show (6:16–18)

The Model Prayer (6:9–15)
1. Pray that God will get the glory he deserves
2. Pray that Jesus will reign over all
3. Pray that God's plan will be perfectly fulfilled
4. Pray for life's physical necessities
5. Pray for personal forgiveness
6. Pray for protection from temptation and sin

d. The Disciple's Priorities (6:19–34)

i. Two Kinds of Treasure (6:19–21)

6:19 Μή with the pres. impv. either expresses a general precept or calls for the cessation of an action already in progress. Θησαυρίζετε 2nd pl. pres. act impv. of θησαυρίζω, "store up treasure." Ὑμῖν is dat. of advantage. Θησαυρός, -οῦ, ὁ, "treasure." Θησαυρούς is a cognate acc. (W 189–90). Ἐπὶ τῆς γῆς 6:10. Ὅπου is a marker of place: "where." Σής, σητός, ὁ, "moth larvae." Βρῶσις, -εως, ἡ, "eating (poss. by vermin)" (BDAG 184d–85a; Quarles, *Sermon*, 236–37). Ἀφανίζει 3rd sg. pres. act. indic. of ἀφανίζω, "cause to disappear, ruin." Κλέπτης, -ου, ὁ, "thief." Διορύσσουσιν 3rd pl. pres. act. indic. of διορύσσω, "break in." Κλέπτουσιν 3rd pl. pres. act. indic. of κλέπτω, "steal."
6:20 θησαυρίζετε δὲ ὑμῖν θησαυροὺς ἐν οὐρανῷ, ὅπου οὔτε σὴς οὔτε βρῶσις ἀφανίζει καὶ ὅπου κλέπται οὐ διορύσσουσιν οὐδὲ κλέπτουσιν· 6:19. On ἐν οὐρανῷ, see 6:10.
6:21 Ὅπου 6:19. Θησαυρός 6:19. Ἐκεῖ, adv. of place, "there." Ἔσται (3rd sg. fut. indic. of εἰμί) is gnomic. Καί is adjunctive: "also, too." Καρδία, -ας, ἡ, "heart (as center of emotions and affections)."

ii. Two Conditions of the Eye (6:22–23)

6:22 Λύχνος, -ου, ὁ, "lamp." Ἐστίν is gnomic pres. Ὀφθαλμός 5:38. Ἐάν with the subjunc. forms the prot. of a third-class cond. statement that makes no assumption about the fulfillment of the condition. Οὖν is inferential. The ᾖ is 3rd sg. pres. subjunc. of εἰμί. Ἁπλοῦς, -ῆ, -οῦν, "single." Φωτεινός, -ή, -όν, "radiant, full of light." Ἔσται 3rd sg. fut. indic. of εἰμί, is a gnomic fut.

6:23 Δέ is adversative and introduces a contrasting statement. Ἐὰν ὁ ὀφθαλμός σου πονηρὸς ᾖ, ὅλον τὸ σῶμά σου σκοτεινὸν ἔσται 6:22. Πονηρός, -ά, -όν, "evil, sick," but when describing the eye, the adj. may mean "miserly, selfish" (Quarles, *Sermon*, 247–54). Εἰ with the indic. (ἐστίν) forms the prot. of a first-class cond. statement that assumes the fulfillment of the condition for the sake of argument. Οὖν is inferential. Ἐν σοί is loc.: "inside you." Πόσος, -η, -ον, is a correlative pron. used in questions (dir. or indir.) and exclamations in ref. to degree, magnitude, or quantity: "how much" or "how great." This sentence is prob. an exclamation (most EVV): "how great!" (BDAG 855d–56a).

iii. Two Masters (6:24)

6:24 Δύναται 5:14 (gnomic). Although in the sg. κύριος often serves as the tr. of Yahweh, here in the pl. (κυρίοις) it is obviously a ref. to "masters." Δουλεύειν (pres. act. inf. of δουλεύω, "serve, be a slave to") is a complementary inf. The ἤ . . . ἤ cstr. means "either . . . or." The four fut. vbs. are gnomic. These four vbs. form a chiasm. Μισήσει 3rd sg. fut. act. indic. of μισέω, "hate." Ἕτερος, -α, -ον, "other." Ἀγαπήσει 3rd sg. fut. act. indic. of ἀγαπάω, "love." Ἀνθέξεται 3rd sg. fut. mid. indic. of ἀντέχω, "be devoted to." Ἑνός and ἑτέρου are gen. of dir. obj. Καταφρονήσει 3rd sg. fut. act. indic. of καταφρονέω, "despise." Μαμωνᾶς, -ᾶ, ὁ, "wealth, property."

HOMILETICAL SUGGESTIONS

The Christian Perspective on Stuff (6:19–24)

1. Stuff does not last long (6:19–20)
2. Stuff can captivate your heart (6:21)
3. Stuff can corrupt you (6:22–23)
4. Stuff can push God away (6:24)

iv. The Result of Proper Priorities (6:25–34)

6:25 Διὰ τοῦτο indicates that the truths articulated in the preceding discussion are the basis for the following application. Λέγω ὑμῖν 5:18. Μή with the pres. impv. (μεριμνᾶτε 2nd pl. pres. act. impv. of μεριμνάω, "worry, be anxious") either issues a general prohibition or *calls for the cessation of an action already in progress. Τῇ ψυχῇ and τῷ σώματι are dat. of *ref. or advantage (BDF §188). Τί 5:13. Φάγητε (2nd pl. 2nd aor. act. subjunc. of ἐσθίω, "eat") and ἐνδύσησθε (2nd pl. aor. mid. subjunc. of ἐνδύω, "wear") are delib. subjunc. that express doubt about the availability of food and clothing (W 466–67). The position of the neg. and the context suggest that the sentence is a question rather than an affirmation. The neg. οὐχί in a question implies an affirmative response. Πλεῖον 5:20. Τῆς τροφῆς (τροφή, -ῆς, ἡ, "food, nourishment") and τοῦ ἐνδύματος (ἔνδυμα, -ατος, τό, "clothing") are gen. of comp. See Metzger 15.

6:26 Ἐμβλέψατε 2nd pl. aor. act. impv. of ἐμβλέπω, "examine, consider." Πετεινόν, -οῦ, τό, "bird." Τοῦ οὐρανοῦ 3:2. Σπείρουσιν (3rd pl. pres. act. indic. of σπείρω, "plant seeds"), θερίζουσιν (3rd pl. pres. act. indic. of θερίζω, "harvest crops"), and συνάγουσιν (3rd pl. pres. act. indic. of συνάγω, "gather") are gnomic pres. Οὐδέ "nor." Ἀποθήκας 3:12. Ὁ πατὴρ ὑμῶν ὁ οὐράνιος 5:48. Τρέφει (3rd sg. pres. act. indic. of τρέφω, "feed") is gnomic. The position of the neg. οὐχ and the context suggest that this sentence is a question with an implied affirmative response. Ὑμεῖς is mildly emphatic. Μᾶλλον ("more") with the vb. διαφέρετε (2nd pl. pres. act. indic. of διαφέρω, "be worth more, be superior to") is pleonastic. Αὐτῶν is gen. of comp.

6:27 Μεριμνῶν (nom. sg. masc. of pres. act. ptc. of μεριμνάω, "worry") is ptc. of means. Δύναται 5:14. Προσθεῖναι (aor. act. inf. of προστίθημι, "add to") is complementary. If the ἐπί with the acc. (τὴν ἡλικίαν) was loc. ("on, on top of"), this would suggest that Jesus's ref. was to stature rather than longevity. However, this prep. is often used to describe something "added to" something else with no ref. to location intended (BDAG 885b–d, 7.). Ἡλικία, -ας, ἡ, "length of life, bodily stature." Πῆχυς, -εως, ἡ, "cubit, distance from elbow to tip of middle finger (used of distance or time)."

6:28 Περί with the gen. (ἐνδύματος 6:25) expresses ref.: "about." The neut. sg. form of the interr. pron. (τί) means "why." Μεριμνᾶτε 2nd pl. pres. act. indic. of μεριμνάω (cf. 6:25). The question implies that the listeners are worrying and thus suggests that the prohibition in 6:25 means "stop worrying!" Καταμάθετε 2nd pl. 2nd aor. act. impv. of καταμανθάνω, "observe." The aor. impv. expresses urgency. Κρίνον, -ου τό, "flower, bloom." Ἀγρός, -οῦ, ὁ, "field." Πῶς prob. has its normal sense "how" but might mean "that" (= ὅτι) in this context (BDAG 900, 1.b.α.). Αὐξάνουσιν 3rd pl. pres. act. indic. of αὐξάνω, "grow." Κοπιῶσιν 3rd pl. pres. act. indic. of κοπιάω, "work, toil." Οὐδέ "and not, nor." Νήθουσιν 3rd pl. pres. act. indic. of νήθω, "spin (to make thread for cloth making)." See Metzger 15.

6:29 Λέγω δὲ ὑμῖν ὅτι 5:22. Οὐδέ "not even" (BDAG 734d–35a, 3; cf. 6:28). Although most EVV tr. πάσῃ "all," it prob. functions here not as a ref. to totality but to express the highest degree of something (BDAG 782b–84c, 3.b.): "his greatest glory." Δόξῃ 4:8. Περιεβάλετο 3rd sg. 2nd aor. mid. indic. of περιβάλλω, "put on (clothing)." Ὡς "like, as."

6:30 Εἰ with the indic. (ἀμφιέννυσιν 3rd sg. pres. act. indic. of ἀμφιέννυμι, "clothe") forms the prot. of a first-class cond. statement that assumes the fulfillment of the prot. The context establishes that God does indeed clothe the fields. Χόρτος, -ου, ὁ "grass." Ἀγροῦ 6:28. Σήμερον 6:11. Ὄντα (acc. sg. masc. of pres. ptc. of εἰμί) is adj.: "which exists today." Αὔριον, temp. adv.: "the next day, tomorrow." Κλίβανος, -ου, ὁ, "oven (made of pottery)." Βαλλόμενον (acc. sg. masc. of pres. pass. ptc. of βάλλω) is adj. Οὕτως, "in this way, thusly." The neg. οὐ poses a question that assumes an affirmative response. The last clause of the verse is an ellipsis. The vb. "clothe" from the prot. is assumed. The dat. πολλῷ combined with μᾶλλον is an idiom mng. "much more surely" (BDAG 613d–14c, 2.b.). Ὀλιγόπιστος, -ον, "little faith."

6:31 Οὖν is inferential. Matthew often uses οὖν to introduce a command that is the consequence of preceding discussion, and some grammarians refer to this as the "paraenetic use." Μή with the aor. subjunc. (μεριμνήσητε 2nd pl. aor. act. subjunc. of μεριμνάω, "worry") prohibits the action as a whole: "Do not worry at all!" The ptc. λέγοντες could be pleonastic, if one conceives of worry as thinking particular statements. However, it is more likely a ptc. of result or means. These kinds of statements are the result of anxiety. The three 1st pl. 2nd aor. subjunc. vbs. φάγωμεν (ἐσθίω, "eat"), πίωμεν (πίνω, "drink"), and περιβαλώμεθα (περιβάλλω, "wear [mid.]") are delib. and express doubt about the availability of food, drink, and clothing. The conj. ἤ means "or."

6:32 Γάρ introduces the reason for the prohibition. ἔθνος, -ους, τό, "gentile, pagan." Ἐπιζητοῦσιν (3rd pl. pres. act. indic. of ἐπιζητέω, "seek after, wish for") is prob. gnomic. The second γάρ introduces a second reason for the prohibition in 6:31 (rather than the immediately preceding clause). Most EVV attempt to express this by translating the γάρ "and." Οἶδεν (3rd sg. pf. act. indic. of οἶδα, "know") functions as a pres., prob. gnomic. Ὁ πατὴρ ὑμῶν ὁ οὐράνιος 5:48. Ὅτι is used as a marker of content. Χρῄζετε (2nd. pl. pres. act. indic. of χρῄζω, "have need of [w. gen.]") is either gnomic or prog. The near dem. pron. ταῦτα and τούτων refer to food, drink, and clothing. The adj. ἅπας may serve as an intensive form of πᾶς (BDAG 98c; BDF §275; R 771). In Attic Gk. the form πᾶς was used after vowels and ἅπας after consonants. NT authors, incl. Matthew (e.g., 2:4, 16), abandoned this practice. All three occurrences of ἅπας in Matthew can be described as emphatic (6:32; 24:39; 28:11). However, the shift from πᾶς to ἅπας could be merely stylistic since throughout this section Matthew has often used synonyms to avoid redundancy in word choice.

6:33 Δέ is adversative, contrasting Jesus's command with pagan behavior. Ζητεῖτε (2nd pl. pres. act. impv. of ζητέω, "seek") is either ingr.-prog. or customary. Πρῶτον functions as an adv. either of time or *degree ("above all"). Τὴν βασιλείαν [τοῦ θεοῦ] 3:2. Τὴν δικαιοσύνην 3:15. The pers. pron. αὐτοῦ presents the interpreter with an array of possibilities, and the situation is further complicated by a number of textual var. (Quarles, *Sermon*, 280 n. 570). If the text of the UBS⁵ is correct (see Metzger 15–16), the antecedent of αὐτοῦ is πατήρ (6:32), and the gen. is gen of poss. (the righteousness that characterizes God himself; 5:48), *producer/source (produced by God/that comes from God; Quarles, *Sermon*, 279–80), or ref. (righteousness that God requires; H 1.166; D&A 1.661; N 315). Three factors support the gen. of source:

1. "Seek righteousness" is synonymous with "hunger and thirst for righteousness" (5:6) The divine pass. in 5:6 assures the disciples that God will satisfy this hunger/thirst
2. 7:7 likely alludes to 6:33 and promises that this righteousness will be given by God
3. The phrase ταῦτα πάντα may include righteousness along with food, drink, and clothing as God's provisions.

Προστεθήσεται (3rd sg. fut. pass. indic. of προστίθημι, "add to, provide") is a divine pass. and predictive, expressing a promise for the fut. The two slightly different mngs. of the vb. may suggest two different interpretations. "Add to" would suggest that disciples attain the kingdom and righteousness they seek and that God adds food, drink, and clothing to these more precious possessions (D&A 1.662; N 315). "Provide" (BDAG 885b–d) may suggest that God grants the kingdom and righteousness as well as food, drink, and clothing to the disciples.

6:34 μὴ οὖν μεριμνήσητε 6:31. The prep. εἰς serves as a marker for a specific point of ref. (BDAG 288d–91c, 5) and is equivalent to περί in 6:28. Τὴν αὔριον (6:30) functions as a subst. and is an example of synecdoche, a figure of speech in which a part of something represents the whole, thus "tomorrow" = "the future." Μεριμνήσει (3rd sg. fut. act. indic. of Μεριμνάω) is prob. gnomic. Ἑαυτῆς, "itself" refers to "tomorrow" and is prob. a gen. of ref. and thus also equivalent to the use of περί in 6:28. Ἀρκετός, -ή, -όν, "sufficient, enough for." Τῇ ἡμέρᾳ is dat. of advantage. Κακία, -ας, ἡ, "evil, trouble, misfortune." The antecedent of αὐτῆς is prob. ἡμέρα, thus "A day's trouble is enough for a day" or "Each day has enough trouble of its own" (CSB; NIV; LEB).

HOMILETICAL SUGGESTIONS

Wringing Hands or Folded Hands? (6:25b–34)
1. Worry underestimates the power of God to provide (v. 25b)
2. Worry underestimates God's care for his children (vv. 26, 28–30)
3. Worry is both ineffective and counterproductive (v. 27)
4. Worry is often a result of misplaced priorities (vv. 25a, 32–33)
5. Worry underestimates God's knowledge of our situation (v. 32b)
6. Worry results from focusing on the future rather than the pres. (v. 34)

e. The Disciple's Relationships (7:1–11)

i. Relating to Brothers (7:1–5)

7:1 Μὴ κρίνετε (2nd pl. pres. act. impv. κρίνω) of expresses a general prohibition or *commands cessation of an action already in progress (7:3). Ἵνα with μή and the subjunc. (κριθῆτε) identifies a consequence that one seeks to avoid by fulfilling the command. The context shows that Jesus was referring specifically to hypocritical judgment.

7:2 Ἐν ᾧ in both occurrences identifies the instr. by which the action is performed. The ὅς functions as both a dem. and rel. pron. (BDAG 725d–27d, 1.b.) thus: "by that judgment by which . . ." (N 319 n. 435). Γάρ marks the reason for the prohibition. Κρίμα, -ατος, τό, "judgment" prob. refers to a standard of judgment, just as μέτρον, -ου, τό "measure, instrument for measuring" in the parallel statement refers to an object that serves as a standard for measurement. Κριθήσεσθε (2nd pl. fut. pass. indic. of κρίνω) and μετρηθήσεται (3rd sg. fut. pass. indic. of μετρέω, "give out in a measured amount") are divine pass. and either *predictive fut., likely referring to eschatological judgment, or gnomic fut., expressing a general principle. Μετρεῖτε 2nd pl. pres. act. indic.

7:3 Τί "why" modifies both clauses. Βλέπεις is prob. customary pres. (most EVV). Κάρφος, -ους, τό, "splinter, chip, speck." The τό with ἐν τῷ ὀφθαλμῷ functions like a rel. pron. Δέ is adversative. Σός, σή, σόν, is the 2nd. pers. poss. pron. that serves to emphasize or *contrast. Δοκός, -οῦ, ἡ, "beam, piece of heavy timber." Κατανοεῖς (2nd sg. pres. act. indic. of κατανοέω, "notice, consider") is prob. customary (most EVV). The Gk. word order forms a detailed chiasm (N 319).

7:4 Πῶς is used in this question to express *disapproval ("how dare you . . .;" BDAG 900d–901c, 1.a.γ.) or surprise ("how is it possible;" 1.a.β.). Ἐρεῖς (2nd. sg. fut. act. indic. of λέγω) is prob. delib. Impv. forms of ἀφίημι (ἄφες 2nd sg. aor. act. impv.) are used with the subjunc. (ἐκβάλω) in requests for permission: "let me cast out." When used with a noun without a finite vb., ἰδού is a marker of strong emphasis: "what do you know" or "of all things!" Κάρφος 7:3. Δοκός 7:3.

7:5 Ὑποκριτά is voc. of emphatic address (W 68–69, esp. n. 9). Ἔκβαλε (2nd sg. aor. act. impv. of ἐκβάλλω, "take out, remove") expresses urgency (rather than degree), and the urgent tone is reinforced by the πρῶτον, which serves as a temp. adv.: "first" (rather than an adv. of degree). Δοκόν 7:3. Τότε introduces what follows in time and confirms that πρῶτον is temp. Διαβλέψεις 2nd sg. fut. act. indic. of διαβλέπω, "see clearly," Ἐκβαλεῖν (aor. act. inf.) expresses purpose. Κάρφος 7:3.

HOMILETICAL SUGGESTIONS

The Most Popular Verse in the Bible (7:1–5)
1. Jesus forbade harsh and hypocritical judgment
2. Jesus warned that those who judge others harshly will be harshly judged by God
3. Jesus condemned minute attention to the faults of others that overlooks one's own more heinous sins

ii. Relating to Aggressive Opponents of the Gospel (7:6)

7:6 Μή with the aor. subjunc. (δῶτε) prohibits an action as a whole: "Do not ever give." Κύων, κυνός, ὁ, "dog." Μηδέ "nor." Βάλητε 2nd pl. 2nd aor. act. subjunc. of βάλλω. Μαργαρίτης, -ου, ὁ, "pearl." Χοίρος, -ου, ὁ, "pig." Μήποτε is a marker of neg. purpose: "lest, so that . . . not." Καταπατήσουσιν 3rd pl. fut. act. indic. of καταπατέω, "trample." Ἐν marks the instr. Στραφέντες nom. pl. masc. of 2nd aor. pass. ptc. of στρέφω, "turn" is pass. with act. force and prob. expresses attendant circumstance (most EVV). Ῥήξωσιν 3rd pl. aor. act. subjunc. of ῥήσσω (byword of ῥήγνυμι), "tear, rip up (with teeth, tusks)."

HOMILETICAL SUGGESTIONS

Handling the Gospel Wisely (7:6)
1. Believers should not push the gospel on the wicked who reject and oppose it
2. Pushing the gospel on the wicked often exposes the gospel to ridicule
3. Pushing the gospel on the wicked often invites persecution

iii. Relating to the Father (7:7–11)

7:7 The pres. impv. vbs. αἰτεῖτε, ζητεῖτε, and κρούετε (2nd pl. pres. act. impv. of κρούω, "knock") are prob. ingr.-prog., e.g., "Ask and keep on asking." The three impv. are prob. cond. impv. but still retain an injunctive force: "Ask and keep on asking and, if you do, . . ."). Καί (all three occurrences) introduces a result. Δοθήσεται (3rd sg. fut. pass. indic. of δίδωμι) is a divine pass. and predictive, expressing a promise. Εὑρήσετε (2nd pl. fut. act. indic. of εὑρίσκω) is predictive. Ἀνοιγήσεται (3rd sg. fut. pass. indic. of ἀνοίγω, "open") is a divine pass. and predictive fut. Ὑμῖν is prob. dat. of advantage. **7:8** Γάρ is causal. Πᾶς ὁ with the pres. ptc. (αἰτῶν) introduces a general truth that suggests that the vb. λαμβάνει is a gnomic pres. Despite the absence of the πᾶς, the next two clauses likewise express general truths. Thus εὑρίσκει and ἀνοιγήσεται (3rd sg. fut. pass. indic. of ἀνοίγω; divine pass.) are also gnomic. Κρούοντι dat. sg. masc. of pres. act. ptc. of κρούω, "open." The pres. ptc. are prob. prog. (e.g., "the one who keeps on asking") because they carry forward the prog. aspect of the impv. in the preceding verse.

7:9 Τίς is an interr. pron. but functions here as an adj. modifying ἄνθρωπος (BDAG 1006d–7d, 1.b.). The prep. ἐξ with ὑμῶν serves as a substitute for the partitive/wholative gen. The vb. αἰτήσει takes dbl. acc. (ὅν and ἄρτον) of pers./thing. The clause is prob. implicitly cond. (most EVV). This appears to be an example of the substitution of a question (thus delib. fut.) for condition (BDF §494). The rel. clause here is likely parenthetical (BDF §465, 2). The question using μή implies a neg. response. Ἐπιδώσει (3rd. sg. fut. act. indic. of ἐπιδίδωμι, "deliver, hand over") is delib. and cognitive (W 570–71). If parenthetical clauses disrupt the structure of a sentence, then the parenthesis is considered anacolouthon (BDF §469). Anacolouthon is "the failure to carry through the structure of the sentence as orig. conceived" (BDF §458). That is the case here. One expects the last clause to be a rel. clause, but Matthew used an interr. clause instead. Grammarians view the substitution of an interr. clause for a rel. clause as an indication of the influence of Semitic thought (BDF §469). Marshall noted that Matthew's formulation "reflects a Semitic cond. sentence expressed paratactically with the apodosis in the form of a question" (Luke 468). The last clause is necessary to complete the thought of the sentence, but this results in two questions with finite vbs. that are not joined by a conj. forming a single sentence. Despite the awkward structure, the point of the sentence is clear.

7:10 After ἤ, the καί is prob. adjunctive ("also"; LEB; cf. N 327), but most EVV choose to omit the conj. in tr. Ἰχθύς, -ύος, ὁ, "fish." Αἰτήσει is prob. delib. and involves the substitution of a question for a condition (7:9). The use of μή in a question implies a neg. response. Ὄφις, -εως, ὁ, "snake." Ἐπιδώσει 7:9.

7:11 Εἰ with the indic. (οἴδατε) marks the prot. of a first-class cond. sentence that assumes the reality of the prot. for the sake of argument. The cond. sentence belongs to the semantic category of evidence-inference (W 682–83). Οὖν is inferential and makes a deduction based on the preceding illustrations. Ὑμεῖς is emphatic. The ptc. clause πονηροὶ ὄντες is either attrib. (CSB; ESV) or *concessive (NIV; LEB): "even though you are evil." The evil nature of human fathers would lead readers to expect

less generous treatment of their children. Δόμα, -ατος, τό, "gift." Διδόναι is a complementary inf. Πόσῳ μᾶλλον is an exclamation expressing greater degree or magnitude:
"how much more." It is an example of argument from lesser to greater (*qal wahomer*).
Ὁ πατὴρ ὑμῶν ὁ ἐν τοῖς οὐρανοῖς 5:16. The fut. indic. δώσει (δίδωμι) may be gnomic
(due to the lesser to greater argument) or predictive, expressing a promise for fut.
provisions by God. The adj. ἀγαθά is clearly subst. The anar. form prevents the subst.
from being interpreted merely as the good things mentioned in the preceding examples
(bread and eggs) and allows the subst. to be interpreted as a ref. to spiritual blessings
(Luke 11:13; Quarles, *Sermon*, 299–302). In light of the preceding context, the pres.
ptc. τοῖς αἰτοῦσιν is prob. prog.

HOMILETICAL SUGGESTIONS

The Father's Generosity (7:7–11)

1. The Father grants spiritual blessings to those who keep asking
2. The Father gives the kingdom and righteousness to those who keep seeking
3. The Father permits entrance through the gate of life to those who keep
   knocking
4. The Father's generosity to his children far exceeds the generosity of any
   father on earth

4.　*The Conclusion of the Sermon (7:12–29)*

a. Summary of the Sermon (7:12)

7:12 Οὖν is inferential but draws a conclusion from the entire body of the sermon
and not merely from the preceding context since (1) the verse does not seem to be an
appropriate application of the preceding verse, and (2) the ref. to the "Law and the
Prophets" forms an inclusio with 5:17. Πάντα with ὅσα means "everything that" and
ἐάν makes the expression more general (BDAG 729a–c, 2). After θέλητε (2nd pl. pres.
act. subjunc.), the ἵνα clause serves as a marker of obj. that functions like a complementary inf. Ποιῶσιν 3rd pl. pres. act. subjunc. Οὕτως is an adv. normally mng. "in this
way." However, it sometimes functions as a summary of the immediately preceding
context and approximates the dem. pron. οὗτος in sense. Thus the command "to do
thusly" means to do what you wish for others to do to you. Καί is prob. adjunctive.
Ὑμεῖς is mildly emphatic. The pres. impv. ποιεῖτε is ingr.-prog. The antecedent of οὗτος
is the entire preceding sentence. On ὁ νόμος καὶ οἱ προφῆται, see 5:17.

b. Two Roads and Gates (7:13–14)

7:13 The aor. impv. εἰσέλθατε expresses urgency. Διά with the gen. serves as a marker
of extension through an object. Στενός, -ή, -όν, "narrow." Πύλη, -ης, ἡ, "gate, door."
Ὅτι is causal, introducing the reason for the command. Πλατύς, -εῖα, -ύ, "wide, broad."
Εὐρύχωρος, -ον, "spacious." Ἀπάγουσα (nom. sg. fem. of pres. act. ptc. of ἀπάγω, "lead
[in the sense of being extended along a route toward a particular destination]") is

attrib. Εἰς marks extension toward a specific place. Ἀπώλεια, -ας, ἡ, "destruction." The antecedent of αὐτῆς is πύλη. See Metzger 16.

7:14 The interr. pron. τί here functions as an exclamatory expression of extent or degree (BDAG 1006d–7d, 3), a Sem. Στενή 7:13. Πύλη 7:13. Τεθλιμμένη nom. sg. fem. of. pf. mid. ptc. of θλίβω, "constrict, make narrow." The ptc. is in the pred. position and functions as a pred. adj. On ἡ ὁδὸς ἡ ἀπάγουσα εἰς . . ., see 7:13. Ὀλίγος, -η, -ον, "few."

HOMILETICAL SUGGESTIONS

The Road Not Taken (7:13–14)

1. The road to destruction is easy and traveled by many
2. The road to life is difficult and traveled by few

c. Two Trees and Fruits (7:15–20)

7:15 Προσέχετε (2nd pl. pres. act. impv. of προσέχω, "beware, stay away from" [when followed by ἀπό with the gen.]) is ingr.-prog. Ψευδοπροφήτης, -ου, ὁ, "false prophet." Ὅστις is used to emphasize a characteristic that confirms one's identity (BDAG 729d–30b, 2.b.). Ἐν is a marker of state or condition. Ἐνδύμα, -ατος, τό, "clothing." Πρόβατον, -ου, τό, "sheep." The gen. προβάτων may express poss. or source (clothing derived from sheep, i.e., sheepskins or wool). The Δέ is adversative and contrasts the true character of the prophets with their outer appearance. Ἔσωθεν is an adv. of place: "inside, within." Λύκος, -ου, ὁ, "wolf." Ἅρπαξ, -αγος, "ravenous, bloodthirsty." The adj. ἅρπαγες is attrib. (W 312).

7:16 Ἀπό with a vb. expressing knowledge identifies the source of perception. Αὐτῶν is prob. gen. of producer: "fruits they produce." Ἐπιγνώσεσθε (2nd pl. fut. mid. indic. of ἐπιγινώσκω, "know, recognize") is prob. gnomic (H 1.183) though it could be predictive (Guelich 395) or even impv. Μήτι is a neg. particle that prompts a neg. response to a question more emphatically than the more common μή. Συλλέγουσιν (3rd pl. pres. act. indic. of συλλέγω, "gather") is prob. gnomic. Ἀπό expresses source. Ἄκανθα, -ης, ἡ, "thorn plant." Σταφυλή, -ῆς, ἡ, "(bunch of) grapes." Τρίβολος, -ου, ὁ, "thistle." Σῦκον, -ου, τό, "fig."

7:17 Οὕτως has its normal adv. sense: "in the same way." Δένδρον, -ου, τό, "tree." Ποιεῖ is gnomic. Σαπρός, -ά, -όν, "bad, poor quality."

7:18 Δύναται is gnomic. Δένδρον 7:17. Ποιεῖν is a complementary inf. Οὐδέ "and not." Δένδρον 7:17. Σαπρόν 7:17.

7:19 Πᾶν with the anar. noun (δένδρον) emphasizes the individual elements of a group: "every single tree." Ποιοῦν is an attrib. ptc. Ἐκκόπτεται (3rd sg. pres. pass. indic. of ἐκκόπτω, "cut off") and βάλλεται are gnomic.

7:20 Ἄρα is an inferential particle introducing the implication of the immediately preceding discussion. Γέ is an emphatic particle that stresses the preceding inferential particle. On ἀπὸ τῶν καρπῶν αὐτῶν ἐπιγνώσεσθε αὐτούς, see 7:16.

HOMILETICAL SUGGESTIONS

False Prophets (7:15–20)

1. Stay away from false prophets
2. False prophets are masters of disguise
3. False prophets show their true nature by their disobedience to Christ
4. False prophets will be judged and punished for their disobedience
5. (Again) stay away from false prophets

d. Two Confessions (7:21–23)

7:21 The placement of the neg. οὐ shows that it negates the πᾶς rather than the vb. Πᾶς with the art. ptc. (ὁ λέγων) means "everyone who . . ." The indir. obj. μοι is significant. The sinner addresses Jesus in his appeal for entrance into the kingdom. The dbl. voc. κύριε κύριε appears to be a confession of Jesus's deity. The dbl. voc. appears eighteen times in the LXX always in ref. to Yahweh and normally as a tr. for the divine name and title Adonai Yahweh. Εἰσελεύσεται is a predictive fut. referring to entrance into the kingdom in association with eschatological judgment. Βασιλείαν τῶν οὐρανῶν 3:2. Ἀλλά is adversative and introduces a clarification to the preceding clause. The pres. ptc. ποιῶν is prob. prog. or customary: ("keeps on doing" or "habitually does"). Τὸ θέλημα refers not to God's secret plan for the individual's life but to God's desire expressed through his commands as interpreted by Jesus in this sermon. Τοῦ πατρός is a subj. gen. The 1st pers. pron. μου (gen. of relationship) stands in stark contrast to the common Matthean phrase "your Father who is in heaven" (e.g., 5:45).

7:22 Ἐροῦσίν is a predictive fut. This is confirmed by the phrase ἐν ἐκείνη τῇ ἡμέρα, which refers to the time of eschatological judgment. The ἐν is temp. "during, on." Κύριε κύριε 7:21. The neg. οὐ governs all three clauses and implies an affirmative response to all three questions. Σός, σή, σόν, is the 2nd pers. poss. pron. and emphatic. The repetition of the phrase τῷ σῷ ὀνόματι and its placement at the beginning of each clause make it emphatic. The dat. τῷ σῷ ὀνόματι is prob. instr. and indicates that the claimants had invoked the power and authority of Jesus to perform their supernatural feats: "by your name" (Quarles, *Sermon*, 341; H. Bietenhard, *TDNT* 5.242–83, esp. 271; D&A 1.715–16). Ἐπροφητεύσαμεν, ἐξεβάλομεν, and ἐποιήσαμεν are constative. Δύναμις, -εως, ἡ, normally means "power" but sometimes refers to amazing expressions of power: "miracles."

7:23 Τότε prob. means "after the preceding" rather than "at that moment." Ὁμολογήσω (1st sg. fut. act. indic. of ὁμολογέω, "profess, proclaim publicly") is predictive, describing the announcement of the verdict in eschatological judgment. The indir. obj. αὐτοῖς makes clear that the words are directed to the claimants, but the nature of the vb. emphasizes the public nature of the proclamation. Ὅτι introduces dir. discourse. Οὐδέποτε "never." Ἔγνων 1st sg. aor. act. indic. of γινώσκω, "know (as a personal acquaintance)." Ἀποχωρεῖτε (2nd pl. pres. act. impv. of ἀποχωρέω, "depart, leave"). Ἀπό expresses separation. The NT always uses the form ἐμοῦ rather than the enclitic μοῦ with this prep. (BDAG 275a–c). The subst. ptc. οἱ ἐργαζόμενοι (nom. sg. masc.

of pres. mid. ptc. of dep. ἐργάζομαι, "work, accomplish") is prob. prog. or customary pres. Such activity was a way of life for the claimants. Ἀνομία, -ας, ἡ, "deeds contrary to the law, transgressions." See Psalm 6:9 (LXX).

HOMILETICAL SUGGESTIONS

More Than a Password (7:21–23)

1. Entering the kingdom requires more than orthodoxy
2. Entering the kingdom requires more than evidence of supernatural power
3. Entering the kingdom requires a commitment to obey Jesus's teaching

e. Two Hearers and Builders (7:24–27)

7:24 Οὖν is inferential and draws a conclusion from the immediately preceding discussion of the importance of obedience in eschatological judgment. The parallels between 7:24 and 7:26 suggest that πᾶς ὅστις with the indic. (ἀκούει) is equivalent to πᾶς with the subst. ptc. Both cstr. mean "everyone who. . . ." Both cstr. tend to introduce general statements containing gnomic vbs. The position of μου is prob. emphatic. The use of the near dem. τούτους suggests that Jesus was referring to the Sermon on the Mount. Both ἀκούει and ποιεῖ are prob. prog. or customary. Ὁμοιωθήσεται (3rd sg. fut. pass. indic. of ὁμοιόω, "compare") is prob. gnomic (25:1). Φρόνιμος, -ον, "wise, prudent." Ὅστις is used to introduce an action that is characteristic of a person. The vb. ᾠκοδόμησεν (3rd sg. aor. act. indic. of οἰκοδομέω, "build, construct [a house]") is constative. Πέτρα, -ας, ἡ, refers to "bedrock," a stratum of rock just beneath the surface of the soil rather than a large boulder. See Metzger 17.

7:25 Κατέβη 3rd sg. 2nd aor. act. indic. of καταβαίνω. Βροχή, -ης, ἡ, "rain." Ποταμός, -οῦ, ὁ, "river, stream, torrent." Ἔπνευσαν 3rd pl. aor. act. indic. of πνέω, "blow." Ἄνεμος, -ου, ὁ, "wind." The use of the pl. "winds" with the aor. vb. suggests that Jesus was not speaking of winds that blew consecutively but of several powerful winds converging at once. Προσέπεσαν 3rd pl. 2nd aor. act. indic. of προσπίπτω, "strike against (with great force)." Οἰκίᾳ is dat. of dir. obj. Ἔπεσεν 3rd sg. 2nd aor. act. indic. of πίπτω. Γάρ is causal. Τεθεμελίωτο 3rd. sg. pluperf. pass. indic. of θεμελιόω, "lay a foundation."

7:26 See 7:24. Μωρός, -ά, -όν, "foolish, stupid." Ἄμμος, -ου, ἡ, "sand, sandy subsoil."

7:27 See 7:25. Προσέκοψαν 3rd pl. aor. act. indic. of προσκόπτω, "beat, strike against." Ἦν 3rd. sg. impf. indic. of εἰμί. Πτῶσις, -εως, ἡ, "downfall, destruction." Αὐτῆς is subj. gen. Μεγάλη expresses intensity.

HOMILETICAL SUGGESTIONS

Wise Up! (7:24–27)

1. Ignoring Jesus's teaching is foolish
2. Ignoring Jesus's teaching leads to destruction
3. Obeying Jesus's teaching is wise
4. Obeying Jesus's teaching leads to eternal blessing

f. The Response to the Sermon (7:28–29)

7:28 The expression καὶ ἐγένετο ὅτε ἐτέλεσεν ὁ Ἰησοῦς followed by some ref. to his instruction (e.g., τοὺς λόγους τούτους) is an important structural marker in the Gospel. See Introduction. Ἐτέλεσεν 3rd sg. aor. act. indic. of τελέω, "finish, complete." Ἐξεπλήσσοντο 3rd pl. impf. pass. indic. of ἐκπλήσσω, "amaze, astound." After vbs. that express feeling, the prep. ἐπί is normally causal.

7:29 Γάρ is causal. The impf. form of εἰμί (ἦν) with the pres. ptc. (διδάσκων) forms the impf. periph. The pres. ptc. ἔχων is subst. "one who has." Ὡς is comp. Like the gen. τοῦ λαοῦ describing the scribes in 2:4, αὐτῶν is prob. partitive. In this context it prob. distinguishes Jewish scribes from Christian scribes (Matt 13:52).

C. CONTINUATION OF THE FIRST STAGE OF JESUS'S
GALILEAN MINISTRY (8:1–9:38)

1. The Cleansing of the Leper (8:1–4)

8:1 Καταβάντος (gen. sg. masc. of 2nd aor. act. ptc. of καταβαίνω) αὐτοῦ is gen. abs., temp., and antecedent: "after he came down." Cf. Exodus 34:29. The prep. ἀπό denotes separation from a place (τοῦ ὄρους). Ἠκολούθησαν 3rd pl. aor. act. indic. of ἀκολουθέω. Αὐτῷ is dat. of dir. obj. With ὄχλοι, the adj. πολλοί is ambiguous. It may refer either to a large number of crowds or to the *great size of the crowds (most EVV; BDAG 847c–50a, 2.a.α.). Cf. 4:25.

8:2 Ἰδού 1:20. Λεπρός, -ά, -όν, "having a serious skin disorder or disease." Προσελθών (nom. sg. masc. of 2nd aor. act. ptc. of dep. προσέρχομαι) is attendant circumstance (most EVV). Προσεκύνει (3rd sg. impf. act. indic. of προσκυνέω) is prob. ingr. with the implication that he continued his worship for some time (W 544). Αὐτῷ is dat. of dir. obj. The ptc. λέγων is somewhat difficult. Although the NIV translates it as a finite vb., the word order, temp. order, and tense do not fit the normal pattern for attendant circumstance (W 640–45). Remaining possibilities are pleonastic (if Matthew conceived of worship as involving verbal expression), temp., means, or result. Regardless of one's classification, the worship of the leper involved more than mere prostration. It also involved the following confession. Κύριε is the simple voc. The connection of the title with the vb. προσκυνέω suggests that the title means far more than merely "sir." Ἐάν with the subjunc. (θέλῃς) forms the prot. of a third-class cond. statement that makes no assumption about the fulfillment of the prot. Since the vb. in the apod. is pres. indic. (δύνασαι), the cstr. may be either third- or fifth-class condition (W 696–97). Καθαρίσαι (aor. act. inf.) is complementary.

8:3 Ἐκτείνας (nom. sg. masc. of aor. act. ptc. of ἐκτείνω, "stretch out") is attendant circumstance or ptc. of means. Ἥψατο 3rd sg. aor. mid. indic. of ἅπτω, "touch" (mid.). Αὐτοῦ is gen. of dir. obj. (common after vbs. of sensation). Although it does not fit the pattern described in Wallace, λέγων is attendant circumstance. Both Matthew and Luke used the ptc. λέγων after ἥψατο, but Mark uses the finite vb.: καὶ λέγει αὐτῷ. The vb. θέλω resolves the doubts implied in the cond. sentence in the preceding verse. Καθαρίσθητι (2nd sg. aor. pass. impv. of καθαρίζω, "cleanse, make clean") expresses urgency. The pass. impv. is "performative" (W 492–93). Καί introduces a result. Εὐθέως "immediately." Ἐκαθαρίσθη 3rd sg. aor. pass. indic. of καθαρίζω. Αὐτοῦ is difficult to classify, but the cstr. means "the skin condition that he suffered." Λέπρα, -ας, ἡ, "leprosy, serious skin disease."

8:4 Λέγει is historical pres. and emphasizes the statement it introduces. When ὅρα (2nd sg. pres. act. impv. of ὁράω) is followed by a neg. (μηδενί) and the subjunc. (εἴπῃς), it means "watch out, make sure that you do not. . . ." Ἀλλά is adversative, contrasting the prohibition with the positive command. Ὕπαγε (2nd sg. pres. act. impv. of ὑπάγω) is ingr.-prog. When a second impv. follows ὑπάγω in the NT, a conj. between the two is almost always absent (BDAG 1028a–c, 2.a.). This may imply that the two impv. were not intended to refer to two separate and distinct actions but that the impv. form of ὑπάγω merely emphasized the urgency of fulfilling the second impv. Σεαυτόν "yourself." Δεῖξον (2nd sg. aor. act. impv. of δείκνυμι, "show") expresses urgency. Ἱερεύς, -έως, ὁ, "priest." Προσένεγκον (2nd sg. 2nd aor. act. impv. of προσφέρω, "present") expresses urgency. Προσέταξεν 3rd sg. aor. act. indic. of προστάσσω, "command." The subj. Μωϋσῆς implies Moses's authorship of Leviticus. The prep. εἰς with the acc. (μαρτύριον) expresses purpose. Μαρτύριον, -ίου, τό, "witness, testimony." The RSV tr. αὐτοῖς "to the people" (apparently referring to members of the large crowds in 8:1) since the pl. number does not agree with the potential antecedent "priest" (τῷ ἱερεῖ; indir. obj.). The dat. αὐτοῖς may express *advantage or disadvantage.

FOR FURTHER STUDY

16. Leprosy

Browne, S. G. "Leprosy: The Christian Attitude." *ExpTim* 73 (1961/2): 243–45.
Ellingsworth, P. *DJG* 463–64.
Michaelis, W. *TDNT* 4.233–34.

HOMILETICAL SUGGESTIONS

Willing and Able! (8:2–4)

1. Sometimes people acknowledge Jesus's power but doubt his compassion
2. Jesus showed compassion to those society despised
3. Jesus displayed power that the OT attributed to God alone (2 Kgs 5:7)
4. Jesus urged his followers to bear testimony to others

2. The Healing of the Paralyzed Servant (8:5–13)

8:5 Εἰσελθόντος αὐτοῦ is gen. abs., temp. and prob. antecedent (NIV; ESV) though possibly contemp. (CSB; LEB). Καφαρναούμ 4:13. Προσῆλθεν 3rd sg. 2nd aor. act. indic. of dep. προσέρχομαι. Ἑκατοντάρχος, -ου, ὁ, "centurion, Roman officer commanding one hundred soldiers." Παρακαλῶν (nom. sg. masc. of pres. act. ptc.) may be adj. or adv. If adv., the ptc. prob. expresses purpose, i.e., the centurion approached Jesus in order to make this appeal.

8:6 Λέγων is pleonastic. Κύριε is the simple voc. Παῖς, παιδός, ὁ or ἡ, *"servant, child (son)." Βέβληται (3rd sg. pf. pass. indic. of βάλλω) is a resultative pf. All three instances in which Matthew used this vb. to describe the sick use the pf. tense (cf. 8:14; 9:2). Although most EVV view the vb. as having a weakened sense ("lying"), the pf. tense suggests the strong sense in which illness forced the patient to become bedridden. Thus the pass. voice of βάλλω was used to portray someone as "struck down" (N 354) or incapacitated by illness. Παραλυτικός, -ή, -όν, "paralyzed, disabled, lame." BDAG claims that the adj. is always subst. in the NT (768d). However, most EVV treat παραλυτικός as if it were a pred. adj.: "lying at home paralyzed" (CSB). However, such a function for the adj. is improbable with the vb. βάλλω, and neither Matthew nor other NT writers use pred. adj. with βάλλω in the medical sense (cf. 8:14; 9:2). Perhaps the best solution is to reconsider the punctuation of the text: "My servant is lying at home. (He is) paralyzed, suffering terribly"; or "My servant is lying at home. (He is) a paralytic who is suffering terribly." Δεινῶς is an adv. pointing to an extreme neg. on a scale: "terribly, in the worst sort of way." Βασανιζόμενος nom. sg. masc. of pres. pass. ptc. of βασανίζω, "torture." Nolland tr. the ptc. as attendant circumstance (351), but the word order and tense do not fit the common pattern for attendant circumstance. The ptc. may be adj. and describing the nom. of appos. or pred. nom. παραλυτικός. If adv., the ptc. is prob. temp. and contemp.: "He has been laid up my house while he has suffered greatly."

8:7 Λέγει is historical pres. and places emphasis on Jesus's statement. Ἐγώ is mildly emphatic. Ἐλθών is prob. temp. and antecedent: "after I come." Most EVV treat the ptc. as attendant circumstance, but this is unlikely for an aor. ptc. with a fut. vb. Θεραπεύσω (1st sg. fut. act. indic. of θεραπεύω, "heal") is predictive and expresses a promise (most EVV). However, the NIV treats the vb. as a delib. fut.

8:8 Ἀποκριθείς (nom. sg. masc. of aor. pass. ptc. of dep. ἀποκρίνομαι, "answer") is pleonastic. Ὁ ἑκατόνταρχος 8:5. Ἔφη 3rd sg. aor. act. indic. of φημί "say." Κύριε is the simple voc. Ἱκανός, -ή, -όν, "good enough." After the adj. ἱκανός, the ἵνα with the subjunc. (εἰσέλθῃς) functions like an explanatory inf. (BDF §379). BDAG considers the adj. with ἵνα to be a fixed expression (475c–77b , 2.b.β.). The position of μου is emphatic. Ὑπό with the acc. (τὴν στέγην), "under." Στέγη, -ης, ἡ, "roof." Εἰσέλθῃς 2nd sg. 2nd aor. act. subjunc. of dep. εἰσέρχομαι. The neut. μόνον is used as an adv.: "only." Εἰπέ (2nd sg. 2nd aor. act. impv. of λέγω), see 4:3. Although most EVV treat the dat. λόγῳ as a dir. obj., it prob. expresses instr.: "with a (single) word" (see H 1.204; cf. 8:16). In this context λόγος prob. means "utterance" rather than "word." Καί introduces a result of the preceding clause. Ἰαθήσεται (3rd sg. fut. pass. indic. of dep. ἰάομαι, "heal, cure, restore"). Ὁ παῖς μου 8:5.

8:9 Ὑπό with the acc. (ἐξουσίαν) serves as a marker of controlling position "under obligation to" (BDAG 1035d–36d, 2). The ptc. ἔχων is prob. adj. (LEB). Ἐμαυτόν "myself." Στρατιώτης, -ου, ὁ, "soldier." Πορεύθητι (2nd sg. aor. pass. impv. of dep. πορεύομαι) expresses urgency. Καί introduces the result. Πορεύεται is prob. gnomic, expressing the general truth about how a soldier relates to his superior. Ἔρχου (2nd sg. pres. mid. impv. of dep. ἔρχομαι) is ingr.-prog. Καί introduces the result. Ἔρχεται is prob. gnomic. Ποίησον (2nd sg. aor. act. impv. of ποιέω) expresses urgency.

8:10 Ἀκούσας (nom. sg. masc. of aor. act. ptc. of ἀκούω) is temp. and contemp.: "when Jesus heard." Ἐθαύμασεν 3rd sg. aor. act. indic. of θαυμάζω, "marvel, wonder." Εἶπεν 3rd sg. aor. act. indic. of λέγω. Τοῖς ἀκολουθοῦσιν (dat. pl. masc. of pres. act. ptc. of ἀκολουθέω) is subst. On ἀμὴν λέγω ὑμῖν, see 5:18. Παρά with the dat. (οὐδενί) is used to connect a quality or characteristic with a person (BDAG 756b–58b, 4). The position of the prep. phrase is prob. emphatic. Τοσοῦτος, -αύτη, -οῦτον, "so great, so strong" (high degree of quality; BDAG 1012a–c, 3). Ἐν τῷ Ἰσραήλ involves substitution of a place for its people, i.e., "among Israelites." Εὗρον 1st sg. 2nd aor. act. indic. of εὑρίσκω. See Metzger 17.

8:11 Λέγω δὲ ὑμῖν ὅτι introduces an important pronouncement. Πολλοί emphasizes the large numbers of Gentiles who will enter the kingdom. Ἀπό with the gen. (ἀνατολῶν καὶ δυσμῶν) expresses separation with vbs. of motion like ἥξουσιν. The pl. ἀνατολῶν (see 2:2) clearly refers to the east, since it is combined with ref. to δυσμή, -ῆς, ἡ, which is consistently used in the pl. to refer to the west. Ἥξουσιν (3rd pl. fut. act. indic. of ἥκω, "come") is predictive and expresses a promise. Ἀνακλιθήσονται (3rd pl. fut. pass. indic. of ἀνακλίνω, "seated as guests" [pass.]) is predictive. Μετά with the gen. (Ἀβραὰμ καὶ Ἰσαὰκ καὶ Ἰακώβ) identifies the company with whom an experience is shared. On ἐν τῇ βασιλείᾳ τῶν οὐρανῶν, see 3:2.

8:12 Δέ is adversative and contrasts those of the east and west with the sons of the kingdom. The gen. τῆς βασιλείας may be partitive ("the sons who are a part of the kingdom"). More likely, in this context "sons" is equivalent to "heirs" and the gen. is obj. ("the heirs of the kingdom"). However, the immediate and remote context clearly shows that these sons are the putative heirs, not the actual heirs (see 3:9; 25:34). Ἐκβληθήσονται (3rd pl. fut. pass. indic. of ἐκβάλλω, "throw out") is predictive. Σκότος, -ους, τό, "darkness." Ἐξώτερος, -α, -ον, "outer." The adj. is in the second attrib. position, which places emphasis on both the noun and adj. and presents the adj. as climactic. This is an example of the use of the comp. as a superl. (BDAG 355b, 2; BDF §62): "the darkness farthest out." Ἐκεῖ is an adv. of place that refers to the "outer darkness" just mentioned. Ἔσται is a predictive fut. Κλαυθμός, -οῦ, ὁ, "weeping." Βρυγμός, -οῦ, ὁ, "gnashing, grinding, chattering." Τῶν ὀδόντων (5:38) is subj. gen. The def. art. with κλαυθμός and βρυγμός is prob. *par excellence* and thus describes weeping and gnash-ing of the worst sort. BDAG notes that the art. with κλαυθμός "indicates the unique and extreme character of the action" (546). Although the noun βρυγμός is particularly associated with anger in the LXX (D&A 2.31), it may express pain (1 Enoch 108:3, 5; 2 Enoch 40:9–10), horror, severe distress (N 358), or "despairing remorse" (H. Schlier, TDNT 1.639–40). Note bodily expressions of terror in Dan 5:6 and Nah 2:10.

8:13 Τῷ ἑκατοντάρχῃ 8:5. Ὕπαγε (2nd sg. pres. act. impv. of ὑπάγω) is ingr.-prog. Ὡς introduces the subj. of the vb. γενηθήτω and is practically equivalent to the rel. pron. ὅ (BDAG 1103d–6c, 1.b.β.): "May what you believed (healing of child by Jesus's command) be done." Ἐπίστευσας 2nd sg. aor. act. indic. of πιστεύω. The aor. impv. γενηθήτω expresses urgency: "Be done (now)." The 3rd pers. impv. is difficult to tr. since using "let" (most EVV) makes the tr. sound like granting permission, using the fut. tense (LEB) sounds like a prediction, and using "must" (W) sounds like a state-ment of necessity rather than a command. Like the impv. in 8:3, this impv. is "perfor-mative." Καί introduces a result. Ἰάθη 3rd sg. aor. pass. indic. of dep. ἰάομαι, "heal." Παῖς 8:6. With an obj. that expresses time (τῇ ὥρᾳ), the prep. ἐν is clearly temp. The temp. ἐν may mark a period of time during which an event occurs ("during") or a specific point in time at which an action occurs ("on, at"). Since the "hour" was the smallest unit by which most reckoned time in the first century, ὥρα often refers to a specific moment of time, and that is prob. the sense here (CSB; NIV; ESV).

FOR FURTHER STUDY

17. The Messianic Banquet

Bird, M. F. "Who Comes from the East and the West? Luke 13.28–29/Matt 8.11–12 and the Historical Jesus." *NTS* 52 (2006): 441–57.

Priest, J. "A Note on the Messianic Banquet." Pages 222–38 in *The Messiah: Developments in Earliest Judaism and Christianity.* Edited by J. H. Charlesworth. Minneapolis: Fortress, 1992.

Smith, D. E. "The Messianic Banquet Reconsidered." Pages 64–73 in *The Future of Early Christianity: Essays in Honor of Helmut Koester.* Edited by B. A. Pearson, A. T. Kraabel, and G. W. A. Nickelsburg. Minneapolis: Fortress, 1991.

HOMILETICAL SUGGESTIONS

A Greater Faith (8:5–13)

1. Our sense of unworthiness should not prevent us from seeking Jesus's help
2. Jesus commends faith that trusts in his absolute authority
3. Jesus graciously includes outcasts in his kingdom
4. Jesus will exclude many who feel entitled to his kingdom

3. The Healing of Peter's Mother-in-Law and Others (8:14–17)

8:14 Matthew carefully arranged the narrative with a chiastic structure (H 1.208–9). Ἐλθών (nom. sg. masc. of 2nd aor. act. ptc. of dep. ἔρχομαι) is temp. and contemp. Πέτρου is gen. of poss. Εἶδεν 3rd sg. aor. act. indic. of ὁράω. Πενθερά, -ᾶς, ἡ, "mother-in-law." Βεβλημένην (acc. sg. fem. of pf. pass. ptc. of βάλλω) 8:6. Πυρέσσουσαν acc. sg. fem. of pres. act. ptc. of πυρέσσω, "have a fever." Both ptc. are pred. ptc. in the second pred. position. Thus the idea is not that he saw the mother-in-law *who* was laid up and had a fever, but that he saw *that* the mother-in-law was laid up and had a fever. The attrib. ptc. places the emphasis on the noun, but the pred. ptc. places more emphasis on the action or state of the noun.

8:15 Ἥψατο 8:3. Τῆς χειρός is gen. of dir. obj. (8:3). Αὐτῆς is partitive/wholative. Ἀφῆκεν 3rd sg. aor. act. indic. of ἀφίημι, "leave." Πυρετός, -οῦ, ὁ, "fever." Ἠγέρθη 3rd sg. aor. pass. indic. of ἐγείρω, "rise" (pass.). Διηκόνει 3rd sg. impf. act. indic. of διακονέω, "serve." The impf. is prob. ingr. (most EVV). Αὐτῷ is dat. of dir. obj.

8:16 Ὀψία, -ας, ἡ, "evening." Γενομένης (gen. sg. fem. of aor. mid. ptc. of dep. γίνομαι, "come" [BDAG 196d–99d, 3.c.]) is gen. abs. and obviously temp.: "when evening came." The gen. abs. ὀψίας δὲ γενομένης is used seven times in Matthew (8:16; 14:15, 23; 16:2 [without δέ]; 20:8; 26:20; 27:57). Προσήνεγκαν 3rd pl. aor. act. indic. of προσφέρω, "carry, bring." Δαιμονιζομένους (acc. pl. masc. of pres. pass. ptc. of dep. δαιμονίζομαι, "be possessed by a demon") with the adj. πολλούς is subst.: "many who were demon possessed." Ἐξέβαλεν 3rd sg. aor. act. indic. of ἐκβάλλω. The dat. λόγῳ is instr. (8:8). Again, it likely means "utterance" rather than "word," since Jesus's statements that effected healing in 8:3, 13 consisted of more than one word. Ἔχοντας (acc.

pl. masc. of pres. act. ptc. of ἔχω) is subst. Used with κακῶς, it meant "those who were sick." Ἐθεράπευσεν 3rd sg. aor. act. indic. of θεραπεύω, "heal."

8:17 Ὅπως is a conj. marker expressing purpose, in this case, the divine purpose. Πληρωθῇ (3rd sg. aor. pass. subjunc. of πληρόω, "fulfill") is a divine pass. Τὸ ῥηθέν is also a divine pass., in which the cstr. of agency explicit in 1:22 and 2:15 (ὑπὸ κυρίου) is implied. Διά with the gen. (Ἡσαΐου) expresses intermediate agency. Τοῦ προφήτου is simple appos. The ptc. λέγοντος is pleonastic (1:22) and introduces dir. discourse (Isa 53:4). Αὐτός is emphatic. Ἀσθένεια, -ας, ἡ, "(debilitating) disease." Ἔλαβεν 3rd sg. aor. act. indic. of λαμβάνω. Νόσος, -ου, ἡ, "illness, disease." Ἐβάστασεν 3rd sg. aor. act. indic. of βαστάζω, "bear, carry."

FOR FURTHER STUDY

18. The Healing of Peter's Mother-in-Law

> Strange, J. F., H. Shanks, and L. Milton. "Has the House Where Jesus Stayed in Capernaum Been Found?" *Biblical Archaeology Review* 8 (1982): 26–37.
> Twelftree, G. H. *DJG* 163–72.

HOMILETICAL SUGGESTIONS

He Has the Power! (8:14–17)

1. Jesus heals with his powerful touch
2. Jesus casts out demons with his powerful command
3. Jesus saves sinners with his powerful sacrifice

4. The Demands of Discipleship (8:18–22)

8:18 Ἰδών (nom. sg. masc. of aor. act. ptc. of ὁράω) is temp. Περί with the acc. (αὐτόν) means "around, surrounding him." Ἐκέλευσεν 3rd sg. aor. act. indic. of κελεύω, "command." Ἀπελθεῖν (aor. act. inf. of dep. ἀπέρχομαι, "move away, depart") is inf. of indir. discourse (W 603–5). With the art. (τό), the adv. πέραν functions as a subst. mng. "the shore or land on the other side" (opposite side of the river or lake). See Metzger 17.

8:19 Προσελθών (nom. sg. masc. of aor. act. ptc. of dep. προσέρχομαι) is attendant circumstance. Εἷς prob. emphasizes the uniqueness of a scribe's willingness to follow Jesus. Γραμματεύς "scribe" (2:4). Διδάσκαλε is the simple voc. Ἀκολουθήσω is a predictive fut. that expresses a promise. Σοι is dat. of dir. obj. Ὅπου ("where") following by the particle of contingency (ἐάν) means "wherever" or "anywhere." The particle of contingency requires the subjunc. (ἀπέρχῃ 2nd sg. pres. mid. subjunc. of dep. ἀπέρχομαι, "go").

8:20 Λέγει is historical pres. and emphasizes the statement it introduces. Ἀλώπηξ, -εκος, ἡ, "fox." Φωλεός, -οῦ, ὁ, "den, lair, hole (in which an animal lives)." Ἔχουσιν is gnomic pres. Τὰ πετεινὰ τοῦ οὐρανοῦ 6:26. Κατασκήνωσις, -εως, ἡ, "dwelling, place to live, nest (of a bird)." The gnomic pres. ἔχουσιν is implied. Δέ is adversative, contrasting the comfort enjoyed by animals with the homelessness of Jesus. The mng. of the phrase ὁ υἱὸς τοῦ ἀνθρώπου is one of the most hotly debated topics in NT studies.

Yet the phrase is one of the most important in the Gospels. Limited space allows only these observations.

1. The grammar does not support the view that the phrase is the equivalent of *bar enash*, an Aram. phrase mng. "a person," "one," or "I." One cannot equate the consistently def. Gk. phrase with the consistently indef. Aram. phrase.
2. Several descriptions of the phrase "son of man" in Matthew allude to the Son of Man vision of Dan 7:13–14 (e.g., Matt 24:30; 26:64). This suggests that the def. art. used in the phrase is the art. of previous ref. Thus "the son of man" means the son of man figure described in Daniel 7.
3. In its orig. context, the phrase "one like a son of man" emphasized the human characteristics of this figure. The gen. τοῦ ἀνθρώπου was a gen. of relationship, indicating that the figure was the son of a human parent. This emphasis was necessary because other features of the vision suggested that the figure was divine. His appearance was described as theophanic. He was enthroned beside the Ancient of Days and ruled over a vast eternal kingdom. He received the worship of all the peoples of the earth. These features would have suggested that the figure was divine and thus not human. The title "son of man" affirmed the human characteristics of the figure.
4. With the art. of previous ref., the use of "the son of man" by Jesus affirms both his humanity (as implied by the orig. mng. of the phrase in Daniel) and his deity (as implied by the orig. context of the phrase in Daniel).

Ποῦ is an interr. particle. Thus BDAG treats this sentence as an "indirect question" (857d–58b, 1.b.) Although the structure of the sentence suggests that it is a statement rather than a question (most EVV), the subjunc. κλίνῃ (3rd sg. pres. act. subjunc. of κλίνω, "lay") is likely delib., and this supports classifying the sentence as an indir. question (W 478).

8:21 Ἕτερος is often the equivalent of ἄλλος, so the adj. does not imply any more than that this speaker is distinct from the first. Τῶν μαθητῶν is prob. partitive. Several commentators doubt that the scribe of 8:19 is a disciple (N 367; D&A 2.54; REB). However, this cstr. seems to imply that both the scribe of 8:19 and the speaker in 8:21 were disciples in some sense (H 1.217; F 328; most EVV). Albright-Mann (without justification) amend the δέ to οὐδέ to avoid this implication. Matthew could have easily avoided the implication by a rel. clause or by using an appos. cstr. Κύριε is the simple voc. Ἐπίτρεψον (2nd sg. aor. act. impv. of ἐπιτρέπω, "allow, permit") expresses urgency. Μοι is the dat. of dir. obj. Πρῶτον is temp. Ἀπελθεῖν (2nd aor. act. inf. of dep. ἀπέρχομαι) and θάψαι (aor. act. inf. of θάπτω, "bury") are complementary. See Metzger 17.

8:22 Λέγει is historical pres. and emphasizes the statement it introduces. Ἀκολούθει (2nd sg. pres. act. impv.) is customary, since Matthew specifically identified the man as a disciple: "keep on following." Μοι is dat. of dir. obj. Ἄφες (2nd sg. aor. act. impv. of ἀφίημι) expresses urgency. Τοὺς νεκρούς ("the dead ones") is acc. of ref. (subj. of inf.). Θάψαι 8:21.

FOR FURTHER STUDY

19. The Son of Man

Boccaccini, G. *Enoch and the Messiah Son of Man: Revisiting the Book of Parables.* Grand Rapids: Eerdmans, 2007.

Burkett, D. *The Son of Man Debate: A History and Evaluation.* SNTSMS 107. Cambridge: Cambridge University Press, 1999.

Charlesworth, J. H. *The Messiah: Developments in Earliest Judaism and Christianity.* Minneapolis: Fortress, 1992.

Green, J. B. *DJG* 88–92.

Quarles, C. L. "Lord or Legend? Jesus as the Messianic Son of Man." Pages XXX–XX in *The Reliability of the Gospel Tradition: Bart Ehrman and Craig Evans in Debate.* Edited by R. Stewart. Minneapolis: Fortress, forthcoming.

20. Jewish Burial Practices

Evans, C. A. *Jesus and the Ossuaries: What Jewish Burial Practices Reveal About the Beginning of Christianity.* Waco, TX: Baylor University Press, 2003.

HOMILETICAL SUGGESTIONS

The Demands of Discipleship (8:18–22)

1. Following Jesus must be a higher priority than personal comfort
2. Following Jesus must be a higher priority than family obligations

5. Controlling the Weather (8:23–27)

8:23 Ἐμβάντι (dat. sg. masc. of aor. act. ptc. of ἐμβαίνω, "board, embark") with αὐτῷ is one of four instances in Matthew (9:27, 28; 14:6) in which the dat. ptc. and pron. (or noun) are used in place of a gen. abs., which Matthew often uses even when the referent in the main clause is in the dat. (e.g., 1:20; 8:1, 5, 28; 9:18). The cstr. does not appear to be different in sense from the gen. abs. and might be labeled a "dative absolute" (T 243; G. B. Winer, *A Greek Grammar of the New Testament* [Andover, MA: Codman, 1825], 80; W. E. Jelf, *A Grammar of the Greek Language* [London: Parker & Co., 1881] §699). The cstr. may be influenced by the dat. of time. Most gen. abs. are also temp., but the dat. of time may focus on the point of time at which an action occurred, while the gen. focuses on the period during which the action took place (W 155–56). The use of this cstr. in Matthew deserves more attention than it has received. It is sometimes complicated by textual var. (e.g., 8:1). Πλοῖον, -ου, τό, "ship, relatively small fishing vessel." The prep. phrase εἰς (τὸ) πλοῖον normally accompanies usage of the vb. ἐμβαίνω, and it always does so in Matthew (8:23; 9:1; 13:2; 14:22; 15:39). The prep. phrase confirms the nautical sense of the vb. Ἡκολούθησαν 3rd pl. aor. pass. indic. of ἀκολουθέω.

8:24 Ἰδού draws attention to what follows. Σεισμός, -οῦ, ὁ, "earthquake, storm (possibly)." Μέγας expresses intensity or, in contexts describing dangerous situations, severity. Ἐγένετο 3rd sg. aor. mid. indic. of dep. γίνομαι. The prep. ἐν with τῇ θαλάσσῃ does not imply that the quaking was beneath the surface. Greek speakers used ἐν in ref. to the sea in situations in which Eng. usage might lead one to expect ἐπί. Ὥστε with the inf. (καλύπτεσθαι pres. pass. inf. of καλύπτω, "cover") expresses result. Τὸ πλοῖον is acc. of ref. (subj. of acc.). Ὑπό with the gen. (τῶν κυμάτων) marks the impers. cause of the action of the pass. inf. Κῦμα, -ατος, τό, "wave." Αὐτός is emphatic. Δέ is adversative and introduces an unexpected statement. Ἐκάθευδεν 3rd sg. impf. act. indic. of καθεύδω, "sleep." The impf. tense is prog., with an emphasis on simultaneity (W 543–44): "He was still (while the storm raged and the ship capsized) sleeping."

8:25 Προσελθόντες (nom. pl. masc. of 2nd aor. act. ptc. of dep. προσέρχομαι) is attendant circumstance. Ἤγειραν 3rd pl. aor. act. indic. of ἐγείρω, "wake." Although λέγοντες does not meet the criteria for attendant circumstance suggested by W (640–43), the parallel in Mark 4:38 uses the finite vb. and this may support attendant circumstance (cf. Matt 8:3). However, like Matthew, Luke used the ptc. (8:24) and his dbl. voc. "Master, Master" gives the impression that the disciples were trying to wake Jesus. Thus, the ptc. in Luke and Matthew may express means: "by saying." Κύριε is prob. emphatic use of the voc. Σῶσον (2nd sg. aor. act. impv. of σώζω) expresses urgency. Ἀπολλύμεθα (1st pl. pres. mid. indic. of ἀπόλλυμι, "perish, die" (mid.) is prob. prog. or tendential (without intention of the subjects expressed). Thus the idea may be "we are in the process of dying this very moment" or "we are about to die." See Metzger 18.

8:26 Λέγει is historical pres. The neut. interr. pron. τί means "why." Δειλός, -ή, -όν, "cowardly, afraid." Ὀλιγόπιστος, -ον, "possessing little faith." Τότε introduces the next in a succession of events or actions. Ἐγερθείς (nom. sg. masc. of aor. pass. ptc. of ἐγείρω, "stand up (from a reclining position)" is attendant circumstance (most EVV). Ἐπετίμησεν 3rd sg. aor. act. indic. of ἐπιτιμάω, "rebuke." Τοῖς ἀνέμοις (dat. pl. masc. of ἄνεμος, -ου, ὁ, "wind") and τῇ θαλάσσῃ are dat. of dir. obj. Ἐγένετο means "came into being" and is often used of phenomena of nature (BDAG 196d–99c, 3.a.). Γαλήνη, -ης, ἡ, "smooth surface on a body of water, calm." Μεγάλη expresses intensity: "great calm" (CSB; LEB; ESV), "completely calm" (NIV), and "dead calm" (NRSV). The combined noun and adj. suggest the Eng. expression "the lake was as smooth as glass."

8:27 Ἐθαύμασαν 3rd pl. aor. act. indic. of θαυμάζω, "wonder, be astonished." The ptc. λέγοντες may be attendant circumstance (cf. Mark 4:41). However, BDAG (444c–445a, 1.a.α.) suggests that the ptc. marks the expression of astonishment (means): "They expressed astonishment by saying. . . ." Ποταπός, -ή, -όν, "what kind of (person; masc.)" (interr. adj. posing a query regarding class or kind). Ὅτι may be explanatory or *causal (BDAG 731d–32d, 2.b. and 4). Οἱ ἄνεμοι 8:26. Ὑπακούουσιν (3rd pl. pres. act. indic. of ὑπακούω, "obey") is prob. gnomic, describing what normally happens due to the kind of person Jesus is.

HOMILETICAL SUGGESTIONS

Who Can This Be? (8:23–27)

1. Jesus displayed his trust through peaceful sleep
2. Jesus controlled the weather by his powerful command
3. Jesus inspired awe by his power over nature

6. The Exorcism of Two Demon-Possessed Men (8:28–34)

8:28 Ἐλθόντος αὐτοῦ is gen. abs., temp. and either antecedent or contemp. Εἰς τὸ πέραν 8:18. Χώρα, -ας, ἡ, "region, district." Τῶν Γαδαρηνῶν (Γαδαρηνός, -ή, -όν, "of Gadara") is subst.: "of the Gadarenes." Ὑπήντησαν 3rd pl. aor. act. indic. of ὑπαντάω, "meet." Αὐτῷ is dat. of dir. obj. Δαιμονιζόμενοι (nom. pl. masc. of pres. pass. ptc. of δαιμονίζω, "be demon-possessed") is adj., modifying δύο: "two demon-possessed men." Μνημεῖον, -ου, τό, "tomb, grave." Ἐξερχόμενοι is either *adj. (like the preceding ptc.) or temp., "as they were coming out of (from among) the tombs." Note that Mark 5:2 uses the pl. "tombs" even though he mentions only one demon-possessed man. This suggests the ἐκ means "out from among" rather than "out of." Χαλεπός, -ή, -όν, "difficult, violent." The adj. is prob. attrib. (fourth position), which suggests a series of three adj.: two adj. ptc. and one adj. proper. Λίαν "very," expressing high degree. Ὥστε with the inf. (μὴ ἰσχύειν) expresses result. The indef. pron. τινά means "a (any) person" and is subj. of the inf. ἰσχύειν. Παρελθεῖν is a complementary inf. ("to pass"). Διά with the obj. τῆς ὁδοῦ ἐκείνης expresses extension through an area. See Metzger 18–19.

8:29 Ἰδού calls attention to what follows. Ἔκραξαν 3rd pl. aor. act. indic. of κράζω, "scream, shriek." After a vb. of speech, λέγοντες is pleonastic. The interr. τί means "what?" rather than "why?" in this context. Ἡμῖν and σοί are prob. dat. of association. The cstr. τί ἡμῖν καί σοί is an idiom of the LXX (2 Sam 16:10; 1 Kgs 17:18; 2 Kgs 3:13), denying that the parties have anything in common (N 375). The CSB translates the Heb. text behind the LXX idiom "Do we agree on anything?" (2 Sam 16:10). Υἱέ is simple voc. Ἦλθες 2nd sg. 2nd aor. act. indic. of dep. ἔρχομαι. Ὧδε is adv. of place "here." Πρό may be a marker of location or of priority in time. With obj. καιροῦ, the prep. is clearly temp.: "before." Καιρός refers to the end time and its accompanying judgment (BDAG 497c–98d, 3.b.). Βασανίσαι (aor. act. inf. of βασανίζω, "torture") expresses purpose.

8:30 Ἦν 3rd sg. impf. indic. of εἰμί. Μακράν is an adv. of place "far away, in the distance." Ἀπό expresses separation. Ἀγέλη, -ης, ἡ, "herd." Χοῖρος, -ου, ὁ, "swine, pig." Despite its distance from ἦν, Βοσκομένη (nom. sg. fem. of pres. pass. ptc. of βόσκω, "graze" [pass.]) is periph.

8:31 Δαίμων, -ονος, ὁ, "demon." Παρεκάλουν (3rd pl. impf. act. indic. of παρακαλέω, "urge strongly") is either prog. ("they kept on urging") or ingr. ("they started urging"). Since παρακαλέω is a vb. of speech, λέγοντες is pleonastic. Εἰ with the indic. (ἐκβάλλεις 2nd sg. pres. act. indic.) forms the prot. of a first-class cond. sentence. The apod. is an appeal. Ἀπόστειλον (2nd sg. 2nd aor. act. impv. of ἀποστέλλω) expresses urgency. However, after παρακαλέω, the impv. surely expresses an appeal rather than a command. The context clearly shows that Jesus is the one giving the orders. Ἀγέλην τῶν χοίρων 8:30.

8:32 The pres. impv. ὑπάγετε is prob. ingr.-prog. The use of the pres. rather than the aor. (which would imply urgency) is prob. due to the distance the demons had to travel rather than to hesitation or delay on the part of the demons. The subst. ptc. οἱ ἐξελθόντες (nom. pl. masc. of 2nd aor. act. ptc. of dep. ἐξέρχομαι) does not imply that only some demons exited the men but rather the opposite. By combining forms of ἐξέρχομαι ("go

out") and ἀπέρχομαι ("go away," ἀπῆλθον 3rd pl. 2nd aor. act. indic.) Matthew emphasizes the complete nature of the exorcism. Εἰς τοὺς χοίρους 8:30. Ἰδού 8:29. Ὥρμησεν
3rd sg. aor. act. indic. of ὁρμάω, "rush, stampede." The adj. πᾶσα with ἡ ἀγέλη (8:30)
implies that there was a sufficient number of demons to fill the herd. Κατά with the
gen. expresses descent: "down." Κρημνός, -οῦ, ὁ, "steep bank, cliff, bluff." Ἀπέθανον
3rd pl. aor. act. indic. of ἀποθνῄσκω, "die." A few commentators (e.g., G 160; Luz 2.25)
suggest that the shift from the sg. to the pl. indicates that δαίμονες is the subj. of the
second vb.: "the demons died." This is highly unlikely. The antecedent χοίρους is much
nearer and a more suitable subj. for the vb. Ὕδωρ, -ατος, τό, "water." Matthew uses the
noun seven times, three of which are pl. (8:32; 14:28, 29). All instances of the pl. refer
to the waters of the Sea of Galilee. All instances of the sg. refer to smaller quantities
of water (e.g., Jordan River, basin).

8:33 Οἱ βόσκοντες (nom. pl. masc. of pres. act. ptc. of βόσκω, "tend, herd") is subst.
Ἔφυγον 3rd pl. aor. act. indic. of φεύγω, "flee." Ἀπελθόντες (nom. pl. masc. of aor.
act. ptc. of dep. ἀπέρχομαι, "go away") is prob. attendant circumstance (most EVV)
but possibly temp. (NRSV). Ἀπήγγειλαν 3rd pl. aor. act. indic. of ἀπαγγέλλω, "report,
announce." After πάντα, the conj. καί is prob. ascensive: "everything, even the things
related to the demon-possessed men." The ascensive conj. may suggest that the herders
would ordinarily have been hesitant to discuss such matters. Skepticism regarding the
supernatural is not peculiar to the twenty-first century. The art. τά serves in place of
the dem. pron.: "those things, matters." Τῶν δαιμονιζομένων (gen. pl. masc. of pres.
pass. ptc. of δαιμονίζω) is subst. and prob. a gen. of ref. (H 1.33; D&A 2.84; LEB).
The rendering in most EVV (e.g., "what had happened to the demon-possessed men"
NIV) suggests obj. gen.

8:34 Ἰδού 8:32. Ἐξῆλθεν 3rd sg. aor. act. indic. of dep. ἐξέρχομαι, "go out." Εἰς the
acc. (ὑπάντησιν) expresses purpose. Ὑπάντασις, -εως, ἡ, "meeting." Τῷ Ἰησοῦ is dat. of
association. The terminology thus far in the sentence is sim. to that used to describe
the demon-possessed in 8:28a and may hint at a comp. (so also N 378). Ἰδόντες (nom.
pl. masc. of 2nd aor. act. ptc. of ὁράω, "see") is attendant circumstance. Παρεκάλεσαν
3rd pl. aor. act. indic. of παρακαλέω, "urge, exhort." Ὅπως with the subjunc. μεταβῇ
(3rd sg. 2nd aor. act. subjunc. of μεταβαίνω) "pass by." Ἀπό expresses separation.
Ὁρίον, -ου, τό, "regions, district (pl.)." The pl. of ὁρίον is apparently equivalent to the
sg. χώρα (8:28).

FOR FURTHER STUDY

21. Jesus's Exorcisms

Montgomery, J. W. *Demon Possession: A Medical, Historical, Anthropological and
    Theological Symposium.* Minneapolis: Bethany Fellowship, 1976.
Twelftree, G. *Jesus the Exorcist: A Contribution to the Study of the Historical Jesus.*
    WUNT 54. Tübingen: Mohr Siebeck, 1993.

HOMILETICAL SUGGESTIONS

This World with Devils Filled (8:28–34)

1. The characteristics of the demon-possessed
2. Jesus's authority to free the demon-possessed
3. Jesus's power to destroy the demons

7. The Healing of the Paralyzed Man (9:1–8)

9:1 Ἐμβάς nom. sg. masc. of aor. act. ptc. of ἐμβαίνω, "board (a ship)." Εἰς πλοῖον 8:23. The ptc. clause is prob. attendant circumstance (NIV; CSB), but potentially temp. (NRSV). Διεπέρασεν 3rd sg. aor. act. indic. of διαπεράω, "traverse, cross over." The context shows that he crossed over the Sea of Galilee. The adj. ἰδίαν ("one's own") indicates that the πόλιν refers to Capernaum as Jesus's hometown and ministry head-quarters (4:13).

9:2 Ἰδού 1:20. Προσέφερον 3rd pl. impf. act. indic. of προσφέρω, "bring, carry." Of the twelve occurrences of this vb. in the indic. mood in Matthew, all are aor. except this one. The impf. is prob. prog. and serves to summarize the lengthy effort detailed in Mark 2:3–4 (par. Luke 5:18–19). The antecedent of αὐτῷ is Jesus (8:34). Παραλυτικός 4:24. Παραλυτικόν is subst., "a lame or paralyzed person." This is the third ref. to Jesus's healing victims of paralysis in Matthew (cf. 4:24; 8:6). Κλίνη, -ης, ἡ, "bed, pallet." Thus ἐπὶ κλίνης, "on a bed." Βεβλημένον acc. sg. masc. of pf. pass. ptc. of βάλλω (8:6). The pf. tense makes the weakened sense of the vb. assumed by most EVV unlikely. Ἰδών (nom. sg. masc. of aor. act. ptc. of ὁράω, "see") is prob. temp. (most EVV). Εἶπεν 3rd sg. aor. act. indic. of λέγω. Τῷ παραλυτικῷ is subst. Θάρσει 2nd sg. pres. act. impv. of θαρσέω, "have courage." The pres. tense is prob. ingr.-prog. Τέκνον is voc. of simple address. Ἀφίενται 3rd pl. pres. pass. indic. of ἀφίημι, "for-give." The pres. tense is prob. instantaneous/aoristic (W 517–18; BDF §320; most EVV). Σου is subj. gen.

9:3 Ἰδού 1:20. Τινες nom. pl. masc. of τις, τι, "some (pl.)." Τῶν γραμματέων (2:4) is partitive gen. With the vb. of speech εἶπαν, the prep. phrase ἐν ἑαυτοῖς may mean "among themselves" (refl. pron. serving as a substitute for the reciprocal pron.; BDAG 268b–69c 2) or "in(side) themselves" (BDAG 1.a.γ.). Since Mark 2:6 has "in their hearts" and Matthew 9:4 refers to "their thoughts," the latter interpretation is clearly intended (N 380). The dem. pron. οὗτος is sometimes used with connotations of con-tempt (BDAG 740b–41d 1.a.α.). The charge that immediately follows supports this. Βλασφημεῖ 3rd sg. pres. act. indic. of βλασφημέω, "speak irreverently (about God)."

9:4 Ἰδών (nom. sg. masc. of aor. act. ptc. of ὁράω) may be *causal or temp. Most EVV tr. the ptc. clause in a way that leaves these options open. Ἐνθύμησις, -εως, ἡ, "thought, reflection." Αὐτῶν is sub. gen. Ἱνατί is an interr. particle that means "why; for what reason?" and is an abbreviation of the question ἵνα τί γένηται. Ἐνθυμεῖσθε 2nd pl. pres. mid. indic. of dep. ἐνθυμέομαι, "think." Πονηρά is subst., "wicked things." Καρδία here refers to the heart as the organ of thought and thus may be tr. "mind" (CSB mg.).

However, this may disrupt the association of the heart with evil that will be later taught in 15:19. Ὑμῶν is partitive/wholative.

9:5 Γάρ is often used in questions in which Eng. idiom requires that the particle remain untranslated (BDAG 189a–90a 1.f.). Although the interr. pron. τίς, τί in the neut. gender may mean "why," "what," or "which," since this question presents two options, it must be tr. "which?" Εὔκοπος, -ον, "easy." Matthew used the comp. form of the adj. since the question compares two possible statements. Εἰπεῖν (aor. act. inf. of λέγω) is epex. inf. On ἀφίενταί σου αἱ ἁμαρτίαι, see 9:2. Ἤ is the disjunctive particle ("or"), which serves to contrast two possible statements. The pres. impv. ἔγειρε and περιπάτει are ingr.-prog. and performative (9:2).

9:6 Δέ is prob. adversative. The action Jesus performed is not the one that the rhetorical question might have led the audience to expect. Ἵνα with the subjunc. (εἰδῆτε 2nd pl. pf. act. subjunc. of οἶδα; pf. with pres. force [W 579–80]) expresses purpose. Ὅτι serves as a marker of discourse content, showing the content of knowledge. Ἔχει is prob. gnomic pres. The pres. inf. ἀφιέναι is epex. and defines the nature of Jesus's ἐξουσίαν. Ὁ υἱὸς τοῦ ἀνθρώπου 8:20. Ἐπί with τῆς γῆς is loc. (6:10). The dash in the text indicates that the editors view the purpose clause as an example of brachylogy (BDF §483) in which the main clause ("I say this" or "I do this") is omitted. It is also possible to view the statement τότε λέγει τῷ παραλυτικῷ as parenthetical and Jesus's command as the main clause. Although the parenthetical clause disrupts the connection between the purpose clause and Jesus's commands, the Gospel writers evidently felt that it was helpful to specify that although Jesus was addressing the scribes (or the reader; N 382) in the purpose clause in the 2nd pers. pl., he shifted to addressing the paralytic in the 2nd pers. sg. Ἐγερθείς (nom. sg. masc. of aor. pass. ptc. of ἐγείρω) is prob. attendant circumstance (most EVV). Ἆρόν (2nd sg. aor. act. impv. of αἴρω, "take up") expresses urgency. Τὴν κλίνην 9:2. Ὕπαγε (2nd sg. pres. act. impv. of ὑπάγω, "go") is ingr.-prog.

9:7 Ἐγερθείς (nom. sg. masc. of aor. pass. ptc. of ἐγείρω) is attendant circumstance (most EVV). Ἀπῆλθεν 3rd sg. aor. act. indic. of dep. ἀπέρχομαι.

9:8 Ἰδόντες (nom. pl. masc. of aor. act. ptc. of ὁράω) is temp. and contemp.: "when they saw" (most EVV). Ἐφοβήθησαν 3rd pl. aor. pass. indic. of φοβέω. Ἐδόξασαν 3rd pl. aor. act. indic. of δοξάζω. Τὸν δόντα (acc. sg. masc. of pres. act. ptc. of δίδωμι) is attrib.: "the God who gives." Τοιοῦτος, -αύτη, -οῦτον, is a correlative adj. that highlights a person or thing in the immediate context. Thus ἐξουσίαν τοιαύτην means "such authority" or "authority like this."

FOR FURTHER STUDY

22. Jesus's Healing of the Paralyzed Man

Branscomb, H. "Mk 2.5: Son Thy Sins Are Forgiven." *JBL* 53 (1934): 53–60.
Cabaniss, A. "A Fresh Exegesis of Mk 2.1–12." *Int* 11 (1957): 324–27.
Luther, M. "'Take Your Bed and Go': Sermon on Matthew 9:2–8." *WW* 16 (1996): 281–83.

Reicke, B. "The Synoptic Reports on the Healing of the Paralytic: Matthew 9,1–8 with Parallels." Pages 319–29 in *Studies in New Testament Language and Text*. Edited by J. K. Elliott. Leiden: Brill, 1976.

HOMILETICAL SUGGESTIONS

Mighty to Save (9:1–7)

1. Jesus as Son of Man has authority to forgive sinners
2. Jesus grants forgiveness to those who believe
3. Jesus proved his authority to forgive through supernatural healing
4. Evil people respond to Jesus's claims by calling him a blasphemer
5. People should respond by fearing and glorifying God

8. The Calling of Matthew (9:9–13)

9:9 Παράγων (nom. sg. masc. of pres. act. ptc. of παράγω, "leave, go away") is temp. and contemp. (most EVV): "As/while Jesus was leaving." Ἐκεῖθεν, "from there." Εἶδεν 3rd sg. 2nd aor. act. indic. of ὁράω. Καθήμενον (acc. sg. masc. of pres. mid. ptc. of dep. κάθημαι, "sit") is either *attrib. ("a man who was sitting"), temp. ("while he was sitting"), or pred. ("a man is sitting"). Τελώνιον, -ου, τό, "place where tolls were collected, tax collecting station." This was prob. not an "office" or "booth," since Matthew would likely have used the prep. ἐν rather than ἐπί if Matthew occupied a shelter of some kind. However, the prep. would still have been appropriate if Matthew were sitting outside the shelter. Μαθθαῖος, -ου, ὁ, "Matthew." Λεγόμενον (acc. sg. masc. of pres. pass. ptc. of λέγω, "name") is attrib. (BDAG 588a–90c 4). Matthew normally introduces names without using the ptc. He used the ptc. to identify Simon's nickname given to him by Jesus (4:18; 10:2). This may suggest that Matthew was a nickname and Levi was the name given to him by his parents. Λέγει is historical pres. Ἀκολούθει (2nd sg. pres. act. impv. of ἀκολουθέω) is ingr.-prog. Μοι is dat. of dir. obj. Ἀναστάς (nom. sg. masc. of aor. act. ptc. of ἀνίστημι, "stand up") is attendant circumstance (most EVV). Ἠκολούθησεν (3rd sg. aor. act. indic. of ἀκολουθέω). Αὐτῷ is dat. of dir. obj.

9:10 Ἀνακειμένου (gen. sg. masc. of pres. mid. ptc. of ἀνάκειμαι, "recline [to eat]") is gen. abs. and temp.: "while he was reclining." The use of καί is an example of parataxis in place of hypotaxis (BDF §458; BDAG 494a–96c 1.b.β.). Ἰδού 1:20. Τελῶναι 5:46. Ἁμαρτωλός, -όν, "sinful" (subst.). Ἐλθόντες (nom. sg. masc. of 2nd aor. act. ptc. of dep. ἔρχομαι) is attendant circumstance (most EVV). Συνανέκειντο (3rd pl. impf. mid. indic. of dep. συνανάκειμαι, "recline [to eat] together with") is either prog. or ingr. After a συν-compound, the dat. τῷ Ἰησοῦ καὶ τοῖς μαθηταῖς express association.

9:11 Ἰδόντες 9:8. Ἔλεγον is either prog. ("they kept saying") or inceptive ("they began to say;" LEB) impf. Διὰ τί "why." Μετά with the gen. obj. τῶν τελωνῶν καὶ ἁμαρτωλῶν expresses association. Ἐσθίει may be *prog., gnomic, or customary.

9:12 The def. art. functions like the dem. or pers. pron. (cf. 2:9). Ἀκούσας (nom. sg. masc. of aor. act. ptc. of ἀκούω) is temp. (most EVV). Εἶπεν 9:2. Χρεία, -ας, ἡ, "need." Ἔχουσιν is gnomic pres. Οἱ ἰσχύοντες (nom. pl. masc. of pres. act. ptc. of ἰσχύω, "be in good health, be strong") is subst. Ἰατρός, -οῦ, ὁ, "healer, physician." Ἀλλά is strongly adversative and introduces an opposing statement. Οἱ κακῶς ἔχοντες (nom. pl. masc. of pres. act. ptc. of ἔχω) is subst. On the idiom, see 4:24. The second clause assumes the vb. and dir. obj. from the preceding clause.

9:13 Πορευθέντες (nom. pl. masc. of aor. pass. ptc. of dep. πορεύομαι, "go") is attendant circumstance. Μάθετε (2nd pl. aor. act. impv. of μανθάνω, "learn") expresses urgency. Τί "what" (interr. pron.). Ἐστίν "it means" (BDAG 282d–86b 2.c.α.). Ἔλεος, -ους, τό, "mercy." Θυσία, -ας, ἡ, "sacrifice, offering." See Beale and Carson 33d–35a. Γάρ introduces the reason it is important to learn the mng. of Hosea 6:6. Ἦλθον 1st sg. aor. act. indic. of dep. ἔρχομαι. The aor. act. inf. καλέσαι (καλέω) expresses purpose. Δικαίους is subst. Ἀλλά introduces a strong contrast. The second clause assumes the vb. and purpose inf. from the preceding clause. Ἁμαρτωλούς (9:10) is subst.

FOR FURTHER STUDY

23. Matthew's Call to Discipleship

Hill, D. "The Use and Meaning of Hosea 6,6 in Matthew's Gospel." *NTS* 24 (1977): 107–19.

Kiley, M. "Why 'Matthew' in Matt 9.9–13." *Bib* 65 (1984): 347–51.

Lee, G. M. "They That Are Whole Need Not a Physician." *ExpTim* 76 (1965): 254.

HOMILETICAL SUGGESTIONS

Jesus, Friend of Sinners (9:9–13)

1. Jesus called a despised sinner to be his disciple
2. The gift of salvation is celebrated in Matthew's name, "Gift of God"
3. Disciples abandon sinful lifestyles and follow Jesus's example
4. Disciples introduce other sinners to Jesus
5. Disciples express the character of God by showing mercy to other sinners

9. A Question Regarding Fasting (9:14–17)

9:14 Τότε "after that (preceding episode)." Προσέρχονται is historical pres. Λέγοντες is either *purpose (2:2) or attendant circumstance (8:3; NIV). Διὰ τί "why?" Νηστεύομεν (1st pl. pres. act. indic. of νηστεύω, "fast") and νηστεύουσιν (3rd pl. pres. act. indic.) are *customary or gnomic pres. The customary pres. is more likely because the gnomic pres. would imply that Jesus and his disciples did not fast at all.

9:15 Εἶπεν 9:2. The neg. μή with the indic. (δύνανται) is used to pose a question whose implied answer is no. Οἱ υἱοί does not refer to lit. "sons" but refers to those who stand in close relation to an object (BDAG 1024c–27c 2.c.β.). Νυμφῶν, -ῶνος, ὁ, "wedding hall, bridal chamber." Πενθεῖν (pres. act. inf. of πενθέω, "mourn") is a complementary inf. Ἐφ' ὅσον is temp. and means "as long as" (BDAG 18.c.β.). Μετά with the gen. (αὐτῶν) expresses association/accompaniment. Νυμφίος, -ου, ὁ, "groom (in a wedding)." Ἐλεύσονται (3rd pl. fut. mid. indic. of dep. ἔρχομαι) is predictive. Δέ is mildly adversative. Ὅταν "whenever." Ἀπαρθῇ 3rd sg. aor. pass. subjunc. of ἀπαίρω, "take away." Subjunc. was required by the ὅταν (which contains a particle of contingency). Ἀπό with αὐτῶν expresses separation. Τότε "then," in the sense of "at that moment." Νηστεύσουσιν is a predictive fut.

9:16 Ἐπιβάλλει 3rd sg. pres. act. indic. of ἐπιβάλλω, "put on." Ἐπίβλημα, -ατος, τό, "a patch (for repairing clothing)." Ῥάκος, -ους, τό, "piece of cloth." The gen. ῥάκους is gen. of material. Ἄγναφος, -ον, "unshrunken." Ἐπί with the dat. (ἱματίῳ) means "on (top of)" and implies contact with the object. Παλαιός, -ή, -όν, "old" with the connotation of being worn out. Αἴρει (3rd sg. pres. act. indic. of αἴρω, "take away." Γάρ is causal. Πλήρωμα, -ατος, το, "that which makes something complete," hence, "repair" (BDAG 829c–30a 1.b.). Αὐτοῦ is obj. gen. Ἀπό with the gen. (τοῦ ἱματίου) expresses separation. Σχίσμα, -τος, τό, "tear." Χείρων, -ον, "worse," comp. adj. from κάκος. Γίνεται is gnomic pres.

9:17 Βάλλουσιν is gnomic pres. Οἶνος, -ου, ὁ, "wine." Νέος, -α, -ον, "new, or recent origin." The adj. denotes wine that is still fermenting. Ἀσκός, -οῦ, ὁ, "leather bag (sometimes used to store and transport liquids)." Παλαιούς 9:16. Εἰ δὲ μή γε "otherwise" (BDAG 644d–46d 1.a.α.). Ῥήγνυνται (3rd pl. pres. mid. indic. of ῥήγνυμι, "burst, rupture") is gnomic. Ἐχεῖται (3rd sg. pres. mid. indic. of ἐκχέω, "pour out") is gnomic. Ἀπόλλυνται (3rd pl. pres. mid. indic. of ἀπόλλυμι), "perish, be ruined or destroyed." Ἀλλά is a strong adversative. Βάλλουσιν is gnomic pres. Καινός, -ή, -όν, "new, fresh." Καί introduces a result. Ἀμφότεροι, -αι, -α, "both." Συντηροῦνται (3rd pl. pres. pass. indic. of συντηρέω, "be preserved, saved from ruin") is a gnomic pres.

FOR FURTHER STUDY

24. Jesus's View of Fasting

Beckwith, R. T. "The Feast of New Wine and the Question of Fasting." *ExpTim* 95 (1984): 334–35.

Brooke, G. J. "The Feast of New Wine and the Question of Fasting." *ExpTim* 95 (1984): 175–76.

Kee, H. C. "The Old Coat and the New Wine." *NovT* 12 (1970): 13–21.

_____. "The Question About Fasting." *NovT* 11 (1969): 161–73.

Steinhauser, M. G. "The Patch of Unshrunk Cloth." *ExpTim* 97 (1976): 312–13.

HOMILETICAL SUGGESTIONS

Fast or Feast (9:14–17)

1. Jesus's disciples are not obligated to keep traditional Jewish customs
2. The joy of Christianity is inconsistent with the somber nature of some Jewish customs
3. Attempting to impose Jewish customs on Christianity leads to the destruction of both

10. The Healing of the Ruler's Daughter and of the Hemorrhaging Woman (9:18–26)

9:18 Λαλοῦντος (gen. sg. masc. of pres. act. ptc. of λαλέω) is gen. abs. and temp. (contemp.; most EVV). On the chronological issues, see H 1.248. The antecedent of αὐτοῦ (subj. of the ptc. clause) is Jesus. The ταῦτα (dir. obj. of ptc.) refers to the content of Jesus's discourse in vv. 15–17. The antecedent of αὐτοῖς is the disciples of John (9:14). Ἰδού 1:20. Ἄρχων, -οντος, ὁ, "ruler (of synagogue)." Ἐλθών (nom. sg. masc. of aor. act. ptc. of dep. ἔρχομαι) is attendant circumstance (most EVV). Προσεκύνει (3rd sg. impf. act. indic. of προσκυνέω) is ingr. or prog. The pres. ptc. (λέγων) may be attendant circumstance (most EVV) or means (8:2). The ὅτι introduces dir. discourse. Θυγάτηρ, -τρός, ἡ, "daughter." Ἄρτι is a temp. adv. that refers to the immediate past: "just now." Ἐτελεύτησεν 3rd sg. aor. act. indic. of τελευτάω, "die." Ἐλθών (nom. sg. masc. of aor. act. ptc. of dep. ἔρχομαι) is attendant circumstance but assumes an impv. force since it is coupled with an impv. Ἐπίθες (2nd sg. aor. act. impv. of ἐπιτίθημι) expresses urgency. Καί introduces a result. Ζήσεται (3rd. sg. fut. mid. indic. of ζάω) is predictive.

9:19 Ἐγερθείς (2:13) is attendant circumstance. Jesus stood from reclining at the table (9:10). Ἠκολούθησεν (3rd sg. aor. act. indic. of ἀκολουθέω) is sg. because Matthew is focused on Jesus as the primary subj. Thus οἱ μαθηταὶ αὐτοῦ is treated as parenthetical (H 1.248).

9:20 Ἰδού 1:20. Some EVV view the particle as temp.: "just then" (NIV; CSB; cf. NRSV). Γυνή without further qualification means "woman" rather than "wife." Αἱμορροοῦσα (nom. sg. fem. of pres. act. ptc. of αἱμορροέω, "bleed, hemorrhage") is attrib. Δώδεκα "twelve" (indecl.). Ἔτος, -ους, τό, "year." Προσελθοῦσα (nom. sg. fem. of aor. act. ptc. of dep. προσέρχομαι) is attendant circumstance. Ὄπισθεν (adv.) "from behind." Ἥψατο 3rd sg. aor. mid. indic. of ἅπτω, "touch (mid.)." Κράσπεδον, -ου, τό, "hem, tassel" (cf. Deut 22:12; Matt 23:5). Κρασπέδου is gen. of dir. obj. Τοῦ ἱματίου is partitive.

9:21 Γάρ is causal. Ἔλεγεν is prog. impf. Ἐν ἑαυτῇ (cf. 9:3). Ἐάν with the subjunc. (ἅψωμαι) forms the prot. of a third-class cond. statement. The context shows the woman wishes for and attempts the fulfillment of the prot. Ἅψωμαι 1st sg. aor. mid. subjunc. of ἅπτω, "touch." The neut. μόνον is adv., "only," and marks the vb. as the sole condition. Τοῦ ἱματίου is gen. of dir. obj. Σωθήσομαι (1st sg. fut. pass. indic. of σώζω) is predictive. Although most EVV tr. the vb. as "heal," it is preferable to tr. it "save" to avoid obscuring possible allusion to Matthew 1:21 (cf. 8:25). See H 1.250–51. The cond. sentence expresses cause and effect.

9:22 Στραφείς (nom. sg. masc. of aor. pass. ptc. of στρέφω, "turn around" [pass. with act. force]) and ἰδών (nom. sg. masc. of aor. act. ptc. of ὁράω) are either temp. or attendant circumstance (NIV; CSB place the two ptc. in a separate sentence). Εἶπεν 9:2. Θάρσει 9:2. Θύγατερ (9:18) is voc. of simple address. Πίστις here refers to belief or faith, not faithfulness. Σου is subj. gen. Σέσωκεν (3rd sg. pf. act. indic. of σώζω) is resultative or perhaps aoristic. Ἐσώθη 3rd sg. aor. pass. indic. of σώζω. Ἀπό marks a temp. starting point (BDAG 105a–7b 2.b.α.; cf. 27:45). With a vb. of prog. aspect, the prep. would indicate the beginning of a process. However, with the aorist, the prep. means "she was healed from this time on" and thus suggests a permanent healing. Ὥρα means "hour," but since the hour was the smallest increment by which time was reckoned, the tr. "moment" or "instant" is appropriate (cf. NIV; CSB). However, the

CSB's "from that moment" is superior to the NIV's "at that moment" (which would be appropriate for ἐπί with the dat.).

9:23 Ἐλθών (nom. sg. masc. of aor. act. ptc. of dep. ἔρχομαι) and ἰδών (nom. sg. masc. of aor. act. ptc. of ὁράω) are prob. temp. (most EVV). Ἄρχοντος 9:18. Αὐλητής, -οῦ, ὁ, "flute player." Θορυβούμενον (acc. sg. masc. of pres. pass. ptc. of θορυβέω, "be distressed" [pass. for intrans.]) is attrib.

9:24 Ἔλεγεν is prob. the instantaneous impf. (most EVV; W 542–43) but may be ingr. or prog. (either "he began saying" or "he kept saying"). Ἀναχωρεῖτε (2nd pl. pres. act. impv. of ἀναχωρέω, "leave") is ingr.-prog. Γάρ is causal. Ἀπέθανεν 3rd sg. aor. act. indic. of ἀποθνήσκω, "die." Κοράσιον, -ου, τό, "little girl" (dimin.). Καθεύδει 3rd sg. pres. act. indic. of καθεύδω, "sleep." This is a euphemism for death that emphasizes its temporary nature. Καί introduces a result. Κατεγέλων (3rd pl. impf. act. indic. of καταγελάω, "laugh [at]") is prob. ingr. impf. Αὐτοῦ is gen. of dir. obj.

9:25 Ὅτε "when." Δέ is adversative. Ἐξεβλήθη 3rd sg. aor. pass. indic. of ἐκβάλλω, "expel, throw out." Εἰσελθών (nom. sg. masc. of 2nd aor. act. ptc. of dep. εἰσέρχομαι) is prob. temp.: "after he entered." Ἐκράτησεν 3rd sg. aor. act. indic. of κρατέω, "grasp, hold." Χειρός is gen. of dir. obj. Καί prob. introduces a result. Ἠγέρθη 3rd sg. aor. pass. indic. of ἐγείρω, "wake up, raise (from the dead)." The pass. form of the vb. can mean merely to "get up" (8:15; 9:6, 7, 19), and most EVV assume that sense here (BDAG 271c–72c 4 also assumes this sense, although, oddly, it describes the girl as called back from the dead). However, the context strongly suggests that the pass. vb. means "to be raised from the dead" (BDAG cf. 14:2; 16:21; 17:9, 23; 27:52; 28:6, 7; D&A 2.133). Τὸ κοράσιον 9:24.

9:26 Ἐξῆλθεν 3rd sg. aor. act. indic. of dep. ἐξέρχομαι. Φήμη, -ης, ἡ, "news, report." The remote dem. pron. ἐκείνην shows that the noun γῆν refers to a "region" rather than the entire earth.

FOR FURTHER STUDY

25. The Resurrection of Jairus's Daughter

Harris, M. J. "'The Dead Are Restored to Life': Miracles or Revivification in the Gospels." Pages 295–326 in *The Miracles of Jesus*. Edited by D. Wenham and C. L. Blomberg. Sheffield: JSOT, 1986.

26. The Healing of the Hemorrhaging Woman

Cummings, J. T. "The Tassel of His Cloak: Mark, Luke, Matthew and Zechariah." Pages 47–61 in *Studia Biblica 1978: II. Papers on the Gospels*. Edited by E. A. Livingstone. Sheffield: JSOT, 1980.

Kalin, E. R. "Matthew 9:18–26: An Exercise in Redaction Criticism." *CurTM* 15 (1988): 39–47.

Robbins, V. K. "The Woman Who Touched Jesus's Garment: Socio-Rhetorical Analysis of the Synoptic Accounts." *NTS* 33 (1987): 502–15.

HOMILETICAL SUGGESTIONS

Overcoming Death and Defilement (9:18–26)
1. Jesus shows compassion to desperate people who seek his help
2. Jesus accepted believing women as his beloved daughters
3. Jesus's touch transformed people from a state of defilement to a state of purity

11. The Healing of Two Blind Men (9:27–31)

9:27 Παράγοντι (dat. sg. masc. of pres. act. ptc. of παράγω, "pass on") with τῷ Ἰησοῦ is another example of the dat. abs. (8:23). Ἐκεῖθεν "from there." Ἠκολούθησαν 3rd pl. aor. act. indic. of ἀκολουθέω. Τυφλός, -ή, -όν, "blind." Κράζοντες (nom. pl. masc. of pres. act. ptc. of κράζω, "shout") and λέγοντες (nom. pl. masc. of pres. act. ptc.) are attrib. Ἐλέησον (2nd sg. aor. act. impv. of ἐλεέω, "show mercy") expresses urgency. Υἱὸς Δαυίδ 1:1.

9:28 Ἐλθόντι (dat. sg. masc. of aor. act. ptc. of dep. ἔρχομαι) is another example of the dat. abs. (see 8:23). Προσῆλθον 3rd pl. aor. act. indic. of dep. προσέρχομαι. Τυφλοί 9:27. Λέγει is historical pres. Πιστεύετε 2nd pl. pres. act. indic. of πιστεύω. Ὅτι introduces the content of their faith. Δύναμαι may be gnomic pres. Ποιῆσαι (aor. act. inf. of ποιέω) is complementary. Λέγουσιν is historical pres. Ναί "yes." Κύριε is simple voc.

9:29 Τότε "after that." Ἥψατο 9:20. Τῶν ὀφθαλμῶν is gen. of dir. obj. Λέγων (nom. sg. masc. of pres. act. ptc.) may be *temp. or attendant circumstance. Κατά with the acc. (τὴν πίστιν) may indicate standard ("according to"; most EVV) or cause ("because of"). Γενηθήτω (3rd sg. aor. pass. impv.) expresses urgency and is performative. Ὑμῖν is dat. of advantage.

9:30 Ἠνεῴχθησαν 3rd pl. aor. pass. indic. of ἀνοίγω, "open" (cf. Isa 35:5). Ἐνεβριμήθη 3rd sg. aor. pass. indic. of dep. ἐμβριμάομαι, "warn sternly." Λέγων after the vb. of speech is pleonastic. Ὁρᾶτε (2nd pl. pres. act. impv. of ὁράω, "pay attention" [BDAG 719b–20b 2]) is ingr.-prog. Γινωσκέτω 3rd sg. pres. act. impv. of γινώσκω.

9:31 The def. art. οἱ functions like a dem. or pers. pron. Ἐξελθόντες (nom. pl. masc. of aor. act. ptc. of dep. ἐξέρχομαι) is prob. attendant circumstance (most EVV). Διεφήμισαν 3rd pl. aor. act. indic. of διαφημίζω, "spread, make known." On ἐν ὅλῃ τῇ γῇ ἐκείνῃ, see 9:26.

FOR FURTHER STUDY

27. The Son of David as Healer

Baxter, W. S. "Healing and the 'Son of David': Matthew's Warrant." *NovT* 48 (2006): 36–50.

Duling, D. C. "Therapeutic Son of David: An Element in Matthew's Christological Apologetic." *NTS* 24 (1978): 392–410.

Novakovic, L. *Messiah, the Healer of the Sick: A Study of Jesus as the Son of David in the Gospel of Matthew.* WUNT 170. Tübingen: Mohr Siebeck, 2003.

Paffenroth, K. "Jesus as Anointed and Healing Son of David in the Gospel of Matthew." *Bib* 80 (1999): 547–54.

12. The Healing of the Speechless Demon-Possessed Man (9:32–34)

9:32 Αὐτῶν ἐξερχομένων (gen. pl. masc. of pres. mid. ptc. of dep. ἐξέρχομαι) is gen. abs. and temp. (contemp.): "while they were going away." Ἰδού 1:20. Προσήνεγκαν 3rd pl. aor. act. indic. of προσφέρω, "bring to." Κωφός, -ή, -όν, "mute, unable to speak." Δαιμονιζόμενον (acc. sg. masc. of pres. mid./pass. ptc. of dep. δαιμονίζομαι, "be demon-possessed."

9:33 Ἐκβληθέντος (gen. sg. neut. of aor. pass. ptc. of ἐκβάλλω) is gen. abs. and temp. (antecedent). Τοῦ δαιμονίου 7:22. Ἐλάλησεν 3rd sg. aor. act. indic. of λαλέω. Ὁ κωφός 9:32. Ἐθαύμασαν 3rd pl. aor. act. indic. of θαυμάζω, "marvel, be astonished." Λέγοντες (nom. pl. masc. of pres. act. ptc. of λέγω) may be attendant circumstance (NIV; NRSV) or *result (see 2:2). Οὐδέποτε "never." Ἐφάνη 3rd sg. aor. pass. indic. of φαίνω, "become visible, be seen" (BDAG 1046d–47d 2.a.). Οὕτως "like this."

9:34 Ἔλεγον (3rd pl. impf. act. indic. of λέγω) is aoristic ("they said;" NIV; CSB), ingr. ("they started saying;" LEB mg.), or prog. ("they kept saying;" LEB). Ἐν with the dat. (τῷ ἄρχοντι) marks pers. agency. Ἄρχων, -οντος, ὁ, "ruler." Δαιμονίων 7:22. Ἐκβάλλει (3rd sg. pres. act. indic. of ἐκβάλλω) is prob. gnomic. Τὰ δαιμόνια 7:22.

FOR FURTHER STUDY

28. *Matthew 9:34 as a Scribal Addition*

> Birdsall, J. N. "A Note on the Textual Evidence for the Omission of Matthew 9:34." Pages 117–22 in *Jews and Christians: The Parting of the Ways AD 70–135*. Edited by J. D. G. Dunn. Tübingen: Mohr Siebeck, 1992.

29. *Pharisees' Charges Against Jesus*

> Sheets, D. D. "Jesus as Demon-Possessed." Pages 27–49 in *Who Do My Opponents Say I Am? An Investigation of the Accusations Against Jesus*. Edited by S. McKnight and J. B. Modica. London: T&T Clark, 2008.
>
> Stanton, G. N. "Jesus of Nazareth: A Magician and a False Prophet Who Deceived God's People?" Pages 164–80 in *Jesus of Nazareth Lord and Christ: Essays on the Historical Jesus and New Testament Christology*. Edited by J. B. Green and M. Turner. Grand Rapids: Eerdmans, 1994.

HOMILETICAL SUGGESTIONS

Jesus, Son of David (9:27–34)

1. The blind men confessed that Jesus is the Son of David
2. The opening of blind eyes proved that Jesus is the Son of David (Isa 35:5)
3. The loosening of the tongue of the mute proved that Jesus is the Son of David (Isa 35:6)
4. Hardened sinners dismiss Jesus's claims with unreasonable explanations
5. Repentant sinners affirm Jesus's mercy and his power

13. The Extension of Jesus's Ministry (9:35–38)

9:35 Περιῆγεν 3rd sg. impf. act. indic. of περιάγω, "go around." Κώμη, -ης, ἡ, "village." Διδάσκων (nom. sg. masc. of pres. act. ptc. of διδάσκω), κηρύσσων (nom. sg. masc. of pres. act. ptc. of κηρύσσω), and θεραπεύων (nom. sg. masc. of pres. act. ptc. of θεραπεύω) are either purpose ptc. or ptc. of attendant circumstance (most EVV). With the anar. nouns, the sg. πᾶσαν means "every (single)." Νόσος, -ου, ἡ, "disease." Μαλακία, -ας, ἡ, "sickness, weakness."

9:36 Ἰδών (nom. sg. masc. of aor. act. ptc. of ὁράω) is either *temp. (contemp.; most EVV) or causal. Ἐσπλαγχνίσθη 3rd sg. aor. pass. indic. of dep. σπλαγχνίζομαι, "have pity, compassion." Περί with the gen. (αὐτῶν) expresses ref.: "concerning" (BDF §229). Ὅτι is causal. Ἦσαν 3rd pl. impf. indic. of εἰμί. Ἐσκυλμένοι (nom. pl. masc. of pf. pass. ptc. of σκύλλω, "be harassed, dejected" [pass.]) and ἐρριμμένοι (nom. pl. masc. of pf. pass. ptc. of ῥίπτω, "be thrown down, cast aside" [pass.]) are part of a pluperf. periph. cstr. (W 647–49). Ὡσεί is a marker of comp.: "like, as." Πρόβατον, -ου, τό, "sheep." Ἔχοντα (acc. pl. neut. of pres. act. ptc. of ἔχω) is attrib. Ποιμήν, -ένος, ὁ, "shepherd." See Numbers 27:17; 2 Chronicles 18:16.

9:37 Τότε "after that." Λέγει is historical pres. Μὲν . . . δέ forms a strong contrast: "on one hand, . . . on the other hand." Θερισμός, -οῦ, ὁ, "crop to be harvested (fig.)." Ἐργάτης, -ου, ὁ, "(agricultural) worker." Ὀλίγος, -η, -ον, "few, lacking in number."

9:38 Δεήθητε (2nd pl. aor. pass. impv. of dep. δέομαι, "ask, request") expresses urgency. Οὖν is inferential. Τοῦ κυρίου is gen. of dir. obj. Τοῦ θερισμοῦ (9:37) is gen. of subord. Ὅπως with the subjunc. replaced the inf. after vbs. of asking in the Koine period (BDAG 718a–c 2.b.; BDF §392). Ἐκβάλῃ 3rd sg. aor. act. subjunc. of ἐκβάλλω. Ἐργάτας 9:37. Θερισμόν 9:37. Αὐτοῦ identifies the supervisor of the harvest. The cstr. is the opposite of κυρίου τοῦ θερισμοῦ in 9:38a.

FOR FURTHER STUDY

30. *Fields Ready for Harvest*

Charette, B. "A Harvest for the People: An Interpretation of Matthew 9:37f." *JSNT* 38 (1990): 29–35.

31. *Sheep Without a Shepherd*

Heil, J. P. "Ezekiel 34 and the Narrative Strategy of the Shepherd and Sheep Metaphor in Matthew." *CBQ* 55 (1993): 698–708.

HOMILETICAL SUGGESTIONS

Proclaiming the Gospel (9:35–38)

1. Jesus wanted everyone to hear the gospel
2. Jesus's compassion for the people showed that he was the Davidic Shepherd (Ezekiel 34)
3. Jesus recognized that many were eager to hear the gospel
4. Jesus urged his disciples to pray for new workers to share the gospel

D. SECOND DISCOURSE: INSTRUCTION OF THE TWELVE (10:1–11:1)

1. Authority Given to the Twelve (10:1–4)

10:1 Προσκαλεσάμενος (nom. sg. masc. of aor. mid. ptc. of προσκαλέω, "summon [to oneself]") is prob. either attendant circumstance (NIV; NRSV; ESV) or temp.: "after he summoned." Ἔδωκεν 3rd sg. aor. act. indic. of δίδωμι. With the head noun ἐξουσίαν, πνευμάτων is a gen. of subord.: "authority over spirits." Ἀκάθαρτος, -ον, "unclean, evil." Ὥστε with the inf. ἐκβάλλειν (pres. act. inf. of ἐκβάλλω) and θεραπεύειν (pres. act. inf. of θεραπεύω, "heal") expresses intended result or purpose. The antecedent of αὐτά is πνευμάτων. On the phrase πᾶσαν νόσον καὶ πᾶσαν μαλακίαν, see 9:35.

10:2 The phrase τῶν δώδεκα ἀποστόλων is in a position of emphasis. Although the dem. pron. is often retrospective (pointing back to antecedents in the preceding context), in this case ταῦτα is prospective (pointing forward to the names in the list that follows). Matthew arranged the names of the twelve apostles in groups of two. The first two sets are paired by identifying them as brothers. The remaining four sets are demarcated by the use of the conj. καί within the sets and asyndeton (absence of a conj.) between the sets. Σίμων (Simon) is always named first in lists of the Twelve. Matthew emphasized his primacy by adding the adj. πρῶτος ("first"). Ὁ λεγόμενος (nom. sg. masc. of pres. pass. ptc. of λέγω) is subst. and appos. Πέτρος ("Peter") is the pred. nom. of the ptc. Ἀνδρέας ("Andrew;" 4:18) is identified using the appos. cstr. ὁ ἀδελφὸς αὐτοῦ. Ἰάκωβος ("Jacob, James;" 4:21; 17:1) is identified using the appos. cstr. ὁ τοῦ Ζεβεδαίου. Τοῦ Ζεβεδαίου is a gen. of relationship that identifies Zebedee as the father of James (and consequently of his brother John). Thus ὁ τοῦ Ζεβεδαίου is a brachylogy, a shortened form of ὁ υἱός τοῦ Ζεβεδαίου. Ἰωάννης ("John;" 4:21; 17:1).

10:3 Φίλιππος ("Philip") is mentioned by name only here in Matthew. Βαρθολομαῖος ("Bartholomew") is a transliteration from Aram. mng. "son of Tolmay." Θωμᾶς ("Thomas") is a common name in Gk., but it may be a Grecised form of the Aram. word for "twin" (John 11:16). Bartholomew and Thomas are mentioned only here in Matthew. Μαθθαῖος ("Matthew;" 9:9). Τελώνης, -ου, ὁ, "tax collector." Ἰάκωβος ("James"). On the cstr. ὁ τοῦ Ἀλφαίου ("Alphaeus"), see 10:2. Θαδδαῖος ("Thaddaeus") is mentioned by name only here in Matthew. See Metzger 21.

10:4 Σίμων ("Simon") is distinguished from Peter by the appos. ὁ Καναναῖος which is a Gk. tr. of an Aram. term mng. "zealot" (cf. Luke 6:15). The name Ἰούδας ("Judas") is always placed last in lists of the apostles, and this indicates his rank among the Twelve due to his sin of betrayal. Judas is further identified with two appos. cstr. Ἰσκαριώτης, -ου, ὁ, prob. means "from Kerioth (a village in southern Judea)." See Metzger 21–22. Ὁ παραδούς (nom. sg. masc. of aor. act. ptc. of παραδίδωμι, "betray") is subst. and appos.: "the one who betrayed" (26:25; 27:3). The καί is adjunctive: "also."

FOR FURTHER STUDY

32. The Authority of the Twelve

Horbury, W. "The Twelve and the Phylarchs." *NTS* 32 (1986): 503–27.

Luz, U. "The Disciples in the Gospel According to Matthew." Pages 98–128 in *The Interpretation of Matthew*. Edited by G. N. Stanton. Philadelphia: Fortress, 1983.

McKnight, S. "Jesus and the Twelve." *BBR* 11 (2001): 203–31.

Williams, D. J. "Judas Iscariot." *DJG* (1992): 406–8.

2. Instructions to the Twelve Regarding Itinerant Ministry (10:5–15)

10:5 Τούτους τοὺς δώδεκα is prob. placed at the beginning of the sentence for emphasis. Ἀπέστειλεν 3rd sg. aor. act. indic. of ἀποστέλλω, "send (with a message/on a mission)." Παραγγείλας (nom. sg. masc. of aor. act. ptc. of παραγγέλλω, "command, give instructions") is prob. a ptc. of means (NIV; NRSV) but possibly temp. (CSB). After the ptc. of speech, λέγων is pleonastic. The position of the phrase εἰς ὁδὸν ἐθνῶν may indicate that it is emphatic. Ἐθνῶν is prob. a gen. of destination (W 100–101). Thus the phrase means: "a road that leads to Gentiles." BDAG (3.a.) suggests the tr.: "Do not turn to the Gentiles." The prohibitions using μή with the aor. subjunc. ἀπέλθητε (2nd pl. aor. act. subjunc. of dep. ἀπέρχομαι) and εἰσέλθητε (2nd pl. aor. act. subjunc. of dep. εἰσέρχομαι) forbid the action as a whole. Σαμαρίτης, -ου, ὁ, "Samaritan."

10:6 Δέ is adversative, and this nuance is reinforced by the adv. μᾶλλον which serves as a marker of an alternative ("instead;" BDAG 613d–14c 3.a.α.). Πορεύεσθε (2nd pl. pres. mid. impv. of dep. πορεύομαι) is ingr.-prog. Τὰ πρόβατα 9:36. Ἀπολωλότα (acc. pl. neut. of pf. act. ptc. of ἀπόλλυμι, "be lost") is attrib. The pf. tense is intensive (resultative). The gen. οἴκου may be partitive (N 416) or epex. (D&A 2.167; H 1.270). The gen. Ἰσραήλ is prob. relationship, so "house of Israel" refers to the clan or tribe that descended from the patriarch (BDAG 698c–699c 3).

10:7 Πορευόμενοι (nom. pl. masc. of pres. mid. ptc. of dep. πορεύομαι) is prob. temp. (most EVV). Grammatically, attendant circumstance is a possibility. Most attendant circumstance ptc. are aor. tense with an aor. main vb. Here both the ptc. and main vb. are pres. tense. However, Matthew frequently uses ptc. forms of πορεύομαι to express attendant circumstance. Every instance of the aor. ptc. of πορεύομαι followed by an aor. main vb. in Matthew is attendant circumstance (W 644; cf. 9:13, 18 [2x]; 28:7, 19–20). Perhaps Matthew used the pres. impv. and ptc. here because he wanted to stress the prog. nature of the action. However, treating the ptc. as attendant circumstance would introduce a redundancy into the passage since Jesus issued the command "go" using πορεύομαι in 10:6. Κηρύσσετε (2nd pl. pres. act. impv. of κηρύσσω, "preach") is ingr.-prog. Λέγοντες (nom. pl. masc. of pres. act. ptc. of λέγω) is pleonastic since it follows a vb. of speech. The ὅτι is recitative (introduces dir. quotation). On ἤγγικεν ἡ βασιλεία τῶν οὐρανῶν, see 3:2.

10:8 Ἀσθενοῦντας (acc. pl. masc. of pres. act. ptc. of ἀσθενέω, "be weak or sick") is subst.: "those who are sick." Θεραπεύετε 2nd pl. pres. act. impv. of θεραπεύω, "heal." Νεκρούς is subst. Ἐγείρετε 2nd pl. pres. act. impv. of ἐγείρω. See Metzger 22. Λεπρούς (8:2) is subst. Καθαρίζετε 2nd pl. pres. act. impv. of καθαρίζω, "cleanse." Ἐκβάλλετε 2nd pl. pres. act. indic. of ἐκβάλλω. Each of the pres. impv. vbs. in this series is ingr.-prog. Despite the parataxis, the two clauses in the sentence δωρεὰν ἐλάβετε, δωρεὰν δότε have a clear logical connection of cause and effect. Δωρεάν is the acc. of δωρέα,

-ας, ἡ ("gift") used as an adv. "freely." Ἐλάβετε 2nd pl. aor. act. indic. of λαμβάνω. Δότε (2nd pl. aor. act. impv. of δίδωμι) expresses urgency.

10:9 Μή with the aor. subjunc. (κτήσησθε 2nd pl. aor. mid. subjunc. of dep. κτάομαι, "procure, acquire") prohibits the action as a whole. Χρυσός, -οῦ, ὁ, "gold." Μηδέ is the disjunctive "nor." Ἄργυρος, -ου, ὁ, "silver." Χαλκός, -οῦ, ὁ, "copper coin." BDAG lists this use of εἰς as an example of a "pregnant" cstr. in which εἰς means "to place into." Ζώνη, -ης, ἡ, "belt, girdle."

10:10 Πήρα, -ας, ἡ, "knapsack, traveler's pack." Εἰς ὁδόν (lit. "for the road") is an idiom mng. "for use on the journey" (BDAG 691a–92b 2). Μηδέ "nor." Χιτών, -ῶνος, ὁ, "tunic." Ὑπόδημα, -ατος, τό, "sandal." It is possible that the adj. δύο modifies both χιτῶνας and ὑποδήματα. Ῥάβδος, -ου, ἡ, "staff, walking stick." Ἄξιος, -ία, -ον, "worthy." Γάρ is causal. Ἐργάτης, -ου, ὁ, "worker (esp. agricultural)." After the adj. ἄξιος, the gen. (τῆς τροφῆς) identifies what is deserved. Τροφή, -ῆς, ἡ, "food, nourishment."

10:11 Εἰς ἣν δ᾽ ἂν πόλιν is a combination of the prep. εἰς, the rel. pron. ἥν, the conj. δέ, the particle of contingency ἄν, and the obj. of the prep. πόλιν. With the particle of contingency, the rel. pron. means "whichever." The disjunctive particle ἤ (or) causes the rel. pron. to modify both πόλιν and κώμην (9:35). The particle of contingency combined with the rel. pron. requires the use of the subjunc. (εἰσέλθητε 2nd pl. aor. act. subjunc. of dep. εἰσέρχομαι). Ἐξετάσατε (2nd pl. aor. act. impv. of ἐξετάζω, "try to find out") expresses urgency. This should be the disciple's first step after entering a new city or village. The nom. interr. pron. τίς ("who") shows that the clause that follows the impv. is an indir. question. The antecedent of αὐτῇ is "city" or "village." Κἀκεῖ is an adv. formed by crasis from καὶ ἐκεῖ mng. "and there." Despite the tense of the command μείνατε (2nd pl. aor. act. impv. of μένω), the command is prog. due to the lexical idea. Ἕως with the particle of contingency ἄν means "as long as." The particle of contingency required the use of the subjunc. (ἐξέλθητε 2nd pl. aor act. indic. of dep. ἐξέρχομαι).

10:12 Εἰσερχόμενοι (nom. pl. masc. of pres. mid. ptc. of dep. εἰσέρχομαι) is temp. (most EVV). With a vb. and prep. denoting entrance, τὴν οἰκίαν appears to refer to a building ("house"). However, in the main clause, the command ἀσπάσασθε (2nd pl. aor. mid. impv. of dep. ἀσπάζομαι, "greet") with the obj. αὐτήν (antecedent: οἰκίαν) suggests that the noun refers to persons in the sense of "household, family." Thus BDAG (695b–d 3) suggests that this passage is an example of a "kind of middle position" between the local and pers. senses of the noun.

10:13 Ἐάν with the subjunc. (ᾖ 3rd sg. pres. subjunc. of εἰμί) is the prot. of a third-class cond. statement. It makes no assumption about the fulfillment of the prot. in this context. The two conditions contrasted by the μὲν . . . δέ cstr. seem to be equally valid possibilities. The description of ἡ οἰκία as ἀξία implies that the noun refers to the "household" rather than the "house." Ἐλθάτω 3rd sg. aor. act. impv. of dep. ἔρχομαι. The phrase ἡ εἰρήνη ὑμῶν is a brachylogy for "the blessing of peace that you pronounce." Thus ὑμῶν is subj. gen. Ἐπί with the acc. (αὐτήν) means "on, over." Ἐπιστραφήτω 3rd sg. aor. pass. impv. of ἐπιστρέφω, "return."

10:14 This sentence appears to be an example of anacolouthon. The rel. clause that begins the sentence apparently offers a description of "that household or city." Robertson refers to the rel. clause as an example of the "suspended subj." (R 437). However this does not fit since the tension is not created by the nom. case of ὅς (which serves as the subj. in its rel. clause and thus requires the nom.) but by the gender and number of the pron. The gender and number of the rel. pron. normally agree with that of the referent in the main clause. Yet ὅς is masc. and both οἰκίας and πόλεως (the referents) are fem. This may be explained by the consideration that οἰκία and πόλις refer to the inhabitants of the house and city by metonymy. However, in this case, one would have expected the rel. pron. to be pl. (cf. Luke 9:5) and Matthew prob. did not mean that rejection by a single inhabitant of the house or city was sufficient cause to abandon the house or city. More likely the rel. pron. constitutes a personification of the household or city. This would explain both the masc. gender (which indicates that the ref. is pers.) and the sg. number (which views the inhabitants of the house/city as a whole). See 23:37–39, in which the personification of Jerusalem results in an awkward shift from a 3rd sg. fem. pron. to a 2nd sg. pron. and then to a series of 2nd pl. pron. Despite the grammatical difficulties apparently arising from the personification, the sentence is clear. The particle of contingency ἄν broadens the rel. pron. ὅς to "who-ever." The particle ἄν required the subjunc. (δέξηται 3rd sg. aor. mid. subjunc. of dep. δέχομαι, "receive, welcome"). Μηδέ "and not" or "nor." The particle ἄν (with the rel. pron.) serves as the subj. of ἀκούσῃ too and this requires the subjunc. form (3rd sg. aor. act. subjunc. of ἀκούω). Ἐξερχόμενοι (nom. pl. masc. of pres. mid. ptc.) is prob. temp. (most EVV), although the NIV treats it as attendant circumstance. The adv. ἔξω here functions as a prep. with the gen. (τῆς οἰκίας ἢ τῆς πόλεως). The remote dem. pron. ἐκείνης modifies both gen. nouns and prob. expresses contempt. Ἐκτινάξατε 2nd pl. aor. act. impv. of ἐκτινάσσω, "shake off." Κονιορτός, -οῦ, ὁ, "dust." The gen. τῶν ποδῶν expresses separation: "off of your feet." Ὑμῶν is partitive.

10:15 Ἀμὴν λέγω ὑμῖν 5:18. Ἀνεκτός, -όν, "bearable, endurable." Ἀνεκτότερον is the nom. sg. neut. comp. form of the adj. Ἔσται (3rd sg. fut. indic. of εἰμί). The dat. γῇ and πόλει are dat. of ref. Σοδόμων ("Sodom") and Γομόρρων ("Gomorrah") are prob. epex. (appos.). With the obj. ἡμέρᾳ, the prep. ἐν is temp. Although Wallace labels κρίσεως as a descriptive gen., he notes that it expresses a temp. idea: "the day when judg-ment occurs" (W 81 n. 26). After the comp. adj. ἀνεκτότερον, the particle ἤ is comp. ("than"). The remote dem. pron. ἐκείνη prob. expresses contempt.

FOR FURTHER STUDY

33. Jesus's Missionary Discourse

Caird, J. B. "Uncomfortable Words: II. 'Shake Off the Dust from Your Feet.'" *ExpTim* 81 (1969): 40–43.

Hooker, M. D. "Uncomfortable Words: X. The Prohibition of Foreign Missions (Mt 10.5–6)." *ExpTim* 82 (1971): 361–65.

Scott, J. J., and L. Milton. "Gentiles and the Ministry of Jesus: Further Observations on Matt 10:5–6; 15:21–28." *JETS* 33 (1990): 161–69.

HOMILETICAL SUGGESTIONS

The Messiah's Undershepherds (10:5–15)

1. The apostles extend the Messiah's ministry (10:5–8)
   a. The Messiah is a Shepherd-King who gathers Israel's lost sheep (Ezek 34:23–24)
   b. The Messiah is a shepherd who heals Israel's sick and wounded sheep (Ezek 34:4, 16)
   c. The apostles announce the coming of the Shepherd-King (10:5–7)
   d. The apostles heal Israel's sick and wounded sheep (10:8)
2. The apostles depend on the Messiah's provision (10:9–10)
3. The apostles offer the Messiah's message and blessing (10:11–13)
4. The apostles proclaim the Messiah's judgment (10:14–15)

3. Warnings and Instructions Regarding Coming Persecution (10:16–31)

10:16 Ἰδού 1:20. Ἐγώ is emphatic. The comp. particle ὡς modifies the pron. ὑμᾶς. Πρόβατα 7:15. Μέσος, -η, -ον, "middle." Λύκων 7:15. Γίνεσθε 2nd pl. pres. mid. impv. of dep. γίνομαι. Οὖν is inferential. Φρόνιμος, -ον, "wise, shrewd." The comp. ὡς may compare the nature or degree of wisdom. BDAG 1103d–6b suggests the tr.: "Be as wise as serpents are" (2.b.). Ὄφις, -εως, ὁ, "serpent." The use of the pl. ὄφεις prevents confusion with the serpent of Genesis 3:1. Ἀκέραιος, -ον, "innocent." Ὡς is comp.: "like, as." Αἱ περιστεραί 3:16.

10:17 Προσέχετε (2nd pl. pres. act. indic. of προσέχω, "beware of" [when followed by ἀπό]) is prob. customary. Jesus was urging constant vigilance. Γάρ is causal. Παραδώσουσιν (3rd pl. fut. act. indic. of παραδίδωμι, "hand over") is predictive. Συνέδριον, -ου, τό, "local judicial council (when pl.)." The position of the two prep. phrases appears to give the sentence a chiastic structure, or the phrase ἐν ταῖς συναγωγαῖς αὐτῶν is in an emphatic position. Μαστιγώσουσιν (3rd pl. fut. act. indic. of μαστιγόω, "beat with a whip, flog") is predictive.

10:18 Ἐπί with the acc. here serves as a "marker of legal proceedings" with the sense "before" (BDAG 363a–67c 10). Ἡγεμών, -όνας, ὁ, "governor." Ἀχθήσεσθε (2nd pl. fut. pass. indic. of ἄγω, "lead") is predictive. Ἕνεκεν with the gen. (ἐμοῦ) means "because of." Εἰς with the acc. obj. (μαρτύριον) expresses purpose. Μαρτύριον, -ου, τό, "testimony." After the verbal noun, the dat. αὐτοῖς and τοῖς ἔθνεσιν function like indir. obj., identifying those to or for whom the action is performed: "to them and to the nations/Gentiles."

10:19 Ὅταν (5:11) "whenever." The particle of contingency requires use of the subjunc. (παραδῶσιν 3rd pl. aor. act. subjunc. of παραδίδωμι, "hand over"). The prohibition using μή with the aor. subjunc. (μεριμνήσητε 2nd pl. aor. act. subjunc. of μεριμνάω, "worry, be anxious") prohibits the action as a whole. The interr. particle πῶς ("how") and the interr. pron. τί ("what") introduce two indir. questions that are the focus of the anxiety. The particle ἤ is disjunctive. Λαλήσητε (2nd pl. aor. act. subjunc. of λαλέω) is delib. Γάρ is causal. Δοθήσεται (3rd sg. fut. pass. indic. of δίδωμι) is predictive and a divine pass. Ἐν with the obj. ἐκείνη τῇ ὥρα is clearly temp. On ὥρα, see 8:13; 9:22. The interr. τί followed by the delib. subjunc. λαλήσητε forms another indir. question. The point of the sentence is that the anxiety-inducing question will be answered at the moment of trial as the Spirit speaks through the disciple.

10:20 Γάρ is causal. Ὑμεῖς is mildly emphatic. Ἐστέ 2nd pl. pres. indic. of εἰμί. Οἱ λαλοῦντες (nom. pl. masc. of pres. act. ptc. of λαλέω) is subst.: "the ones who are speaking." Ἀλλά introduces a strong contrast between a neg. and pos. statement. Τοῦ πατρός is prob. gen. of source: "the Spirit sent by your Father" with ref. to Matthew 3:16–17. Τὸ λαλοῦν (nom. sg. neut. of pres. act. ptc. of λαλέω) is subst.: "the one who is speaking." Ἐν with the obj. ὑμῖν expresses pers. agency (most EVV): "through you."

10:21 Παραδώσει (3rd sg. fut. act. indic. of παραδίδωμι) is predictive fut. The anar. nouns ἀδελφός and ἀδελφόν are prob. qualitative. The relationship between the individuals makes the betrayal all the more shocking and grievous. Εἰς with the obj. θάνατον prob. expresses purpose rather than mere result. The clause καὶ πατὴρ τέκνον (in which the anar. nouns are also qualitative) assumes the vb. and prep. phrase that immediately precede. Ἐπαναστήσονται (3rd pl. fut. mid. indic. of ἐπανίστημι, "rise up in rebellion") is predictive fut. Ἐπί with the acc. (γονεῖς) expresses opposition (BDAG 363a–67c, 12.b.): "against." Γονεύς, -έως, ὁ, "parent." Θανατώσουσιν (3rd pl. fut. act. indic. of θανατόω, "put to death") is predictive. The antecedent of αὐτούς is γονεῖς.

10:22 Ἔσεσθε (2nd pl. fut. indic. of εἰμί) with μισούμενοι (nom. pl. masc. of pres. pass. ptc. of μισέω, "hate") is a fut. periph. cstr. It prob. emphasizes the prog. nature of the fut. action. After the pass. ptc., ὑπὸ πάντων expresses pers. agency: "by all people." Διὰ τὸ ὄνομά μου expresses cause. Ὁ ὑπομείνας (nom. sg. masc. of aor. act. ptc. of ὑπομένω, "endure") is subst. Εἰς τέλος expresses extension in time up to a goal: "until the end." Τέλος, -ους, τό, "end." The οὗτος is grammatically unnecessary. Its use immediately after its antecedent suggests that it is emphatic (BDAG 740b–41d, 1.a.ε.): "this very one." Σωθήσεται (3rd sg. fut. pass. indic. of σώζω) is predictive (used to express a promise) and poss. a divine pass.

10:23 Ὅταν 5:11. Διώκωσιν 3rd pl. pres. act. subjunc. of διώκω, "persecute, pursue." The subjunc. was required by the particle of contingency in ὅταν. Φεύγετε (2nd pl. pres. act. impv. of φεύγω, "flee, escape.") is ingr.-prog. Although writers in the Koine period often used ἄλλος and ἕτερος interchangeably and without distinction to simply mean "another," the use of τὴν ἑτέραν to describe the city to which the persecuted disciple flees may imply that the city is presumed to be of a different kind, which will treat the disciple differently than the previous city did (cf. definitions 1.b.γ. and 2 in BDAG 301d–2c). However, the dem. pron. may simply mean "the next (city)" on the road that the disciple is traveling (N 426). See Metzger 23. On ἀμὴν γὰρ λέγω ὑμῖν, see 5:18. Οὐ μή with the subjunc. (τελέσητε 2nd pl. aor. act. subjunc. of τελέω, "complete, finish") expresses emphatic negation (W 468–69). The vb. τελέω is normally followed by a verbal noun or ptc. describing the activity that the subj. completed. No such activity is identified here. Thus the sentence is considered "elliptical" (N 427). Most likely the activity that will not be completed is "fleeing." Τοῦ Ἰσραήλ is prob. a partitive gen. The cities are the individual parts that make up the nation of Israel. Ἕως combined with ἄν and the aor. subjunc. (ἔλθῃ 3rd sg. aor. act. subjunc. of dep. ἔρχομαι) identifies the circumstance that is a necessary prelude to an event. Thus the disciples will always have another city to which to flee and will not have exhausted the list of cities at the time the Son of Man comes. On ὁ υἱὸς τοῦ ἀνθρώπου, see 8:20.

10:24 Ἐστίν is gnomic pres. Ὑπέρ with the acc. (τὸν διδάσκαλον) often serves as a marker of degree to express excelling or surpassing. Here it takes on the sense "to be superior or more exalted" (BDAG 1030b–31c, B.). Οὐδέ "and not" or "nor." After τὸν κύριον, αὐτοῦ is a gen. of subord.

10:25 Ἀρκετός, -ή, -όν, "enough, sufficient, adequate." The nom. sg. neut. form ἀρκετόν shows that an impers. vb. (ἐστί) is implied and ἀρκετόν is a pred. adj. Τῷ μαθητῇ is prob. an *ethical dat. ("in the disciple's view of things;" see LEB) or a dat. of ref. ("regarding the disciple;" see D&A 2.194, who sees the perspective as God's). The ἵνα with the subjunc. (γένηται 3rd sg. aor. mid. subjunc. of dep. γίνομαι) has a weakened sense that replaces a complementary inf. Ὡς is comp. mng. "like." In the cstr. ὁ διδάσκαλος αὐτοῦ, the αὐτοῦ is prob. objective, i.e., "his teacher" is "the one who teaches him." In the expression ὁ κύριος αὐτοῦ, the αὐτοῦ is a gen. of subord. However, in light of 10:24, both may be gen. of subord. Εἰ with the indic. (ἐπεκάλεσαν 3rd pl. aor. act. indic. of ἐπικαλέω, "call [a name]") forms the prot. of a first-class cond. sentence that assumes the fulfillment of the prot. for the sake of argument. Τὸν οἰκοδεσπότην is a position of emphasis. Οἰκοδεσπότης, -ου, ὁ, "master of the house." Βεελζεβούλ, ὁ, "Beelzebul, a false god later equated with Satan." The dbl. acc. is object-complement. Πόσῳ μᾶλλον means "how much more!" and is exclamatory (rather than interr.). Πόσος, -η, -ον, expressing degree or magnitude. Μᾶλλον, comp. adv. "more." The expression was used in the argument from the lesser to the greater, which was common among the rabbis. The point is that if the highly esteemed person is subjected to horrible name-calling, the person of lowly esteem is far more likely to be so subjected. Οἰκιακός, -οῦ, ὁ, "member of a household."

10:26 The particle οὖν draws an application from the immediately preceding discussion. Μή with the aor. subjunc. (φοβηθῆτε 2nd pl. aor. pass. subjunc. of φοβέω, "be afraid of" [mid./pass.]) prohibits the action as a whole. Γάρ is causal. The sentence οὐδὲν . . . ἐστιν κεκαλυμμένον may be viewed as a periph. pf. with οὐδέν as subj. (LEB; NRSV; ESV) or as an impers. use of ἐστίν ("there is") with οὐδέν serving as pred. nom. and κεκαλυμμένον (nom. sg. neut. of pf. pass. ptc. of καλύπτω, "hide") as an attrib. ptc. (NIV; CSB). The antecedent of the rel. pron. ὅ is οὐδέν. Ἀποκαλυφθήσεται (3rd sg. fut. pass. indic. of ἀποκαλύπτω, "uncover") is predictive. The clause following καί is elliptical and assumes the οὐδὲν . . . ἐστιν from the previous clause. Κρυπτός, -ή, -όν, "hidden, secret." Γνωσθήσεται (3rd sg. fut. pass. indic. of γινώσκω) is predictive. Hagner (1.285) suggests that the two pass. vbs. are divine pass. indicating that God is the agent uncovering and making known truth through his disciples. However, this is based in part on his mistranslation of γνωσθήσεται ("will be known") as "will be *made* known," which appears to confuse γινώσκω with γνωρίζω (compare NIV and CSB with LEB; NRSV; and ESV).

10:27 Σκοτία, -ας, ἡ, "darkness." Εἴπατε (2nd pl. aor. act. impv. of λέγω), see 4:3. The disciples were to begin their bold proclamation of Jesus's teaching immediately during their missionary travels. Οὖς, ὠτός, τό, "ear." The prep. phrase εἰς τὸ οὖς (lit. "in [one] ear") was an idiom referring to a message whispered privately (BDAG 739c–40a; LN 24.067 B). Ἀκούετε 2nd pl. pres. act. indic. of ἀκούω. Κηρύξατε (2nd pl. aor. act. impv. of κηρύσσω, "preach") expresses urgency. Ἐπί with the gen. (τῶν δωμάτων) is a marker of position on a surface: "on." Δῶμα, -ατος, τό, "roof, housetop." The housetop is to serve as the disciple's platform from which he preaches.

10:28 Μή with the pres. impv. (φοβεῖσθε 2nd pl. pres. mid. impv. of φοβέω, "be afraid" [mid.]) prob. calls for the cessation of an action already in progress: "Stop being afraid." Although the cstr. can be used to express a general prohibition, the shift from the use of μή with the aor. subjunc. in 10:26 suggests that Matthew wishes to communicate something other than a general prohibition. The prep. ἀπό serves to identify the persons who are the source of the fear. Τῶν ἀποκτεννόντων (gen. pl. masc. of pres. act. ptc. of ἀποκτέννω, "kill") is subst. Δέ is adversative and introduces a contrast. Δυναμένων (gen. pl. masc. of pres. mid. ptc. of dep. δύναμαι) is attrib. Ἀποκτεῖναι (aor. act. inf. of ἀποκτείνω, "kill") is complementary. Φοβεῖσθε is either ingr.-prog. or *customary. Δέ is adversative. Although μᾶλλον often means "more," after an adversative conj. that contrasts a prohibition with a positive command, it serves as the marker of an alternative: "instead." Τὸν δυνάμενον (acc. sg. masc. of pres. mid. ptc. of dep. δύναμαι) is subst. The shift to the sg. is required since the ref. of the ptc. is no longer "people" but God. Ἀπολέσαι (aor. act. inf. of ἀπόλλυμι, "destroy") is complementary. The καί . . . καί cstr. means "both . . . and," and ψυχήν appears in the position of greater emphasis. On ἐν γεέννῃ, see 5:22.

10:29 The neg. οὐχί introduces a question that prompts an affirmative response. Στρουθίον, -ου, τό, "sparrow." Ἀσσαρίον, -ου, τό, "Roman copper coin." The gen. ἀσσαρίου is the gen. of price (W 122). Πωλεῖται (3rd sg. pres. pass. indic. of πωλέω, "sell") is gnomic pres. The καί possesses a concessive nuance and is used to introduce a surprising and unexpected statement: "and yet" (BDAG 494a–96c 1.b.η.). In the cstr. ἓν ἐξ αὐτῶν, the prep. phrase serves as a substitute for the partitive gen. identifying one belonging to a larger group. Πεσεῖται (3rd sg. fut. mid. indic. of πίπτω, "fall") is gnomic. Ἄνευ is a prep. mng. "without." When the obj. of the prep. is pers. (τοῦ πατρὸς ὑμῶν), the prep. means "without the knowledge and consent of."

10:30 The ὑμῶν is in a position that prob. expresses emphasis related to the contrast between sparrows and Jesus's disciples. Δέ is likely adversative. Καί is ascensive. Θρίξ, τριχός, ἡ, "hair." Ἠριθμημέναι (nom. pl. fem. of pf. pass. ptc. of ἀριθμέω, "count") with εἰσίν is pf. periph.

10:31 Οὖν is inferential. On μὴ φοβεῖσθε, see 10:28. The gen. phrase πολλῶν στρουθίων (10:29) is gen. of dir. obj. Διαφέρετε 2nd pl. pres. act. indic. of διαφέρω, "be worth more than, be superior to." Ὑμεῖς is mildly emphatic.

FOR FURTHER STUDY

34. The Coming Persecution of Jesus's Disciples

Allison, D. C. "The Hairs of Your Head Are All Numbered." *ExpTim* 101 (1990): 334–36.

Cook, J. G. "The Sparrow's Fall in Mt 10:29b." *ZNW* 79 (1988): 138–44.

Marshall, I. H. "Uncomfortable Words: VI. 'Fear Him Who Can Destroy Both Soul and Body in Hell' (Mt 10.28 RSV)." *ExpTim* 81 (1970): 276–80.

McKnight, S. "Jesus and the End-Time: Matthew 10:23." *SBLSP* 25 (1986): 501–20.

Wedderburn, A. J. M. "Matthew 10,23b and the Eschatology of Jesus." Pages 165–81 in *Ende der Tage und die Gegenwart des Heils*. Edited by M. Becker and W. Fenske. Leiden: Brill, 1999.

Zell, P. E. "Exegetical Brief: Matthew 10:23—Which Coming of the Son of Man?" *Wisconsin Lutheran Quarterly* 102 (2005): 210–12.

HOMILETICAL SUGGESTIONS

Clear and Present Danger (10:16–31)

1. How should we view persecution?
   a. The horrors of persecution
      i. Persecution is dangerous (10:16)
      ii. Persecution is heartbreaking (10:21, 34–35)
      iii. Persecution is lonely (10:22a)
   b. The blessings of persecution
      i. Persecution helps spread the gospel (10:17–20)
      ii. Persecution is the prelude to indescribable joy (10:22b)
      iii. Persecution shows that we are like Jesus (10:24–25)
2. How should we respond to persecution?
   a. Exercise wisdom (10:16b)
   b. Refrain from sin (10:16c)
   c. Avoid worry (10:19–20)
   d. Flee to safety (10:23)
   e. Refuse to be silent (10:26–27)
   f. Fear the heavenly Judge more than earthly persecutors (10:28)
   g. Realize that God knows about your suffering (10:29–30)
   h. Believe that God cares about your suffering (10:31)

4. The Consequences of Confessing or Denying Jesus (10:32–33)

10:32 The particle οὖν does not seem to introduce an inference developed from what immediately precedes. The preceding statement was about the value of Jesus's disciples to God, not eschatological judgment. Davies and Allison see the particle as intensive (2:215 n. 7). However, the particle occasionally marks the resumption of a previous topic, and this is likely the significance of the particle here. The particle prob. indicates that the topic of eschatological judgment addressed in 10:28 (but interrupted in 10:29–31) is being resumed (BDAG 736b–37b 2.a.; cf. N 439). Πᾶς ὅστις is the equivalent of πᾶς ὅς (BDAG 782b–84c 1.b.α.): "everyone who." Ὁμολογήσει (3rd sg. fut. act. indic. of ὁμολογέω, "confess") is an example of the substitution of the fut. indic. for the aor. subjunc. that often occurs with indef. rel. clauses (W 871; BDF §380 [2]). The parallelism between 10:32 and 33 suggests that πᾶς ὅστις with the fut. indic. is the equivalent of ὅστις with ἄν and the aor. subj. The phrase ἐν ἐμοί is a substitute for the acc. of pers., which shows the influence of Aram. grammar on Matthew's Gk. (BDF §220). The prep. ἔμπροσθεν is common in judicial settings (BDAG 325a–c 1.b.β.), in which it means "before (the judge[s])." The vbs. ὁμολογέω and ἀρνέομαι are also common in judicial settings, and this suggests that Jesus was referring to testimony before a court (D&A 2.214–15). Τῶν ἀνθρώπων are prob. human judges. Ὁμολογήσω (1st sg. fut. act. indic. of ὁμολογέω) is a pred. fut. used to express a promise. Κἀγώ is formed by crasis of καί and ἐγώ and here means, "I, in turn" (BDAG 487a–c 3.b.). Ἐν αὐτῷ is an Aram. in which the prep. phrase serves as a substitute for the acc. of pers. On τοῦ πατρός μου τοῦ ἐν [τοῖς] οὐρανοῖς, see 5:16. Up to this point in Matthew, Jesus referred to "your/our father in the heavens" (see 5:16, 45, 48; 6:1, 9). The shift to the 1st pers. sg. pron. suggests that Jesus did not intend to make assumptions about his disciples being sons of the heavenly Father. Their identity as God's children would be indicated by their testimony before people.

10:33 The δέ is adversative and introduces a statement that is the opposite of the previous one. Ὅστις ("one who") combined with ἄν and the aor. subjunc. (ἀρνήσηταί 3rd sg. aor. mid. subjunc. of dep. ἀρνέομαι, "deny") constitutes a cond. rel. clause that is equivalent to the prot. of a third-class cond. statement (BDF §380). The acc. of pers. με replaced ἐν with the dat. of pers. in the first element of the parallelism, confirming the interpretation suggested in 10:32. Ἔμπροσθεν τῶν ἀνθρώπων 10:32. Ἀρνήσομαι (1st. sg. fut. mid. indic. of dep. ἀρνέομαι) is predictive fut. and expresses a warning regarding eschatological judgment. Κἀγώ 10:32. Ἔμπροσθεν τοῦ πατρός μου τοῦ ἐν [τοῖς] οὐρανοῖς 10:32.

FOR FURTHER STUDY

35. Confessing and Denying Jesus

Fleddermann, H. "The Q Saying on Confessing and Denying." *SBLSP* 26 (1987): 606–16.
Jonge, H. J. de. "The Sayings on Confessing and Denying Jesus in Q 12:8–9 and Mark 8:38." Pages 105–21 in *Sayings of Jesus: Canonical and Non-Canonical: Essays in Honor of Tjitze Baarda*. Edited by W. L. Peterson, J. S. Vos and H. J. de Jonge. Leiden: Brill, 1997.

5. Choosing Jesus over Family or Safety (10:34–39)

10:34 Μὴ νομίσητε ὅτι ἦλθον 5:17. Βάλλω may indicate bringing about "a change in state or condition" (BDAG 163b–64a 4). Βαλεῖν aor. act. inf. of βάλλω. Ἐπὶ τὴν γῆν 6:10. Μάχαιρα, -ης, ἡ, "dagger, short sword."

10:35 Ἦλθον 1st sg. aor. act. indic. of dep. ἔρχομαι. Γάρ is causal. Διχάσαι (aor. act. inf. of διχάζω, "divide, separate") expresses purpose. Κατά with the gen. (τοῦ πατρός) expresses hostile opposition (BDAG 511a–13d 2.b.α.). Θυγάτηρ, -τρός, ἡ, "daughter." Νύμφη, -ης, ἡ, "bride, daughter-in-law." Πενθερά, -ᾶς, ἡ, "mother-in-law." See Beale and Carson 35d–37d.

10:36 Ἐχθρός, -ά, -όν, "hostile, enemy" (subst.). Τοῦ ἀνθρώπου appears to refer to the male leader of a household (NIV; CSB) rather than a generic person (ESV). Οἰκιακοί 10:25.

10:37 Ὁ φιλῶν (nom. sg. masc. of pres. act. ptc. of φιλέω, "love") is subst. Ὑπέρ with the acc. (ἐμέ) is a marker of degree with the sense "more than." Ἐστίν 3rd sg. pres. indic. of εἰμί. Μου is the use of the gen. with certain adj. (ἄξιος; W 134–35). Θυγατέρα 10:35.

10:38 The rel. pron. ὅς often functions like a combination of the dem. pron. and rel. pron. (BDAG 725d–27d 1.b.α.): "the one who." Λαμβάνει 3rd sg. pres. act. indic. of λαμβάνω. Σταυρός, -οῦ, ὁ, "cross." BDAG suggests that the cross is a figure for the "suffering/death which believers endure in following the crucified Lord" (941a–c 3). The antecedent of αὐτοῦ is ὅς. Ἀκολουθεῖ 3rd sg. pres. act. indic. of ἀκολουθέω. Ὀπίσω with μου functions as a prep. marking a position behind a preceding entity: "behind." For μου after ὀπίσω, see 3:11. Οὐκ ἔστιν μου ἄξιος 10:37.

10:39 Ὁ εὑρών (nom. sg. masc. of pres. act. ptc. of εὑρίσκω, "find") is subst. The vb. sometimes means "to attain a state or condition" (BDAG 411b–12c 3). Nolland suggests that "obtain life" is an idiom for being successful in life (442). Davies and Allison suggest that the idiom means "preserve life." Ψυχή, -ῆς, ἡ, "soul, life." Ἀπολέσει (3rd sg. fut. act. indic. of ἀπόλλυμι, "destroy, lose"). Ὁ ἀπολέσας (nom. sg. masc. of aor. act. ptc. of ἀπόλλυμι) is subst. The prep. ἔνεκεν with the gen. (ἐμοῦ) means "because of, for the sake of." Εὑρήσει (3rd sg. fut. act. indic. of εὑρίσκω) is predictive and issues a warning.

FOR FURTHER STUDY

36. Disciples' Rejection by Family

> Black, M. "'Not Peace but a Sword': Matt 10:34ff; Lk 12:51ff." Pages 287–94 in *Jesus and the Politics of His Day*. Edited by E. Bammel and C. F. D. Moule. Cambridge: Cambridge University Press, 1984.
>
> Roberts, T. A. "Some Comments on Matthew 10:34–36 and Luke 12:51–53." *ExpTim* 69 (1958): 304–6.
>
> Sim, D. C. "The Sword Motif in Matthew 10:34." *Hervormde Teologiese Studies* 56 (2000): 84–104.

6. Rewards for Kind Treatment of Jesus's Followers (10:40–42)

10:40 Ὁ δεχόμενος (nom. sg. masc. of pres. mid. ptc. of dep. δέχομαι, "receive, welcome") is subst. Both the position of ἐμέ as well as the use of the longer form rather than the enclitic form express emphasis. Δέχεται 3rd sg. pres. mid. indic. of dep. δέχομαι. Τὸν ἀποστείλαντα (acc. sg. masc. of aor. act. ptc. of ἀποστέλλω, "send") is subst.

10:41 Ὁ δεχόμενος 10:40. Εἰς ὄνομα followed by the gen. (προφήτου) prob. means "for the sake of" with the sense "because of his identity as a prophet" (BDAG 711c–14c 3). Μισθός, -οῦ, ὁ, "reward." The gen. προφήτου could be a gen. of destination: "reserved for a prophet" (D&A 2.227). Alternatively, the gen. may be subj. or a gen. of orig./ source, implying that the prophet grants a reward to the one who shows kindness to him (1 Kgs 17:9–24; 2 Kgs 4:9–37; H 1.296; D&A 2.227). Λήμψεται (3rd sg. fut. mid. indic. of λαμβάνω) is predictive and expresses a promise. Δίκαιον is subst. The grammar and syntax of the second sentence mirrors that of the first.

10:42 Ὅς ἄν with the aor. subjunc. (ποτίσῃ 3rd sg. aor. act. subjunc. of ποτίζω, "give a drink") forms a rel. cond. clause comparable to the prot. of a third-class cond. statement (BDF §380). Ἕνα and ποτήριον are the dbl. acc. of pers.-thing. Τῶν μικρῶν (μικρός, -ά, -όν, "small, little") is subst. and the gen. is partitive. Ποτήριον, -ου, τό, "cup." Ψυχρός, -ά, -όν, "cold." The omission of the noun ὕδωρ ("water") is considered an ellipsis (BDF §241 [7]), but the use of the subst. adj. is common. The subst. adj. ψυχροῦ is a gen. of content. Μόνος, -η, -ον, "only" may function as an adj. modifying ποτήριον (most EVV): "only (one) cup" or "just a cup." Since the adj. is acc. sg., it may function as an adv. and modify the prep. phrase that follows: "only because he is a disciple." On the mng. of εἰς ὄνομα followed by a pers. gen. (μαθητοῦ), see 10:41. CSB and ESV tr. it: "because he is a disciple." On ἀμὴν λέγω ὑμῖν, see 5:18. Οὐ μή with the aor. subjunc. (ἀπολέσῃ 3rd sg. aor. act. subjunc. of ἀπόλλυμι, "lose") expresses emphatic negation. On τὸν μισθὸν αὐτοῦ, see 10:41.

FOR FURTHER STUDY

37. Rewards for Disciples

de Ru, G. "The Conception of Reward in the Teaching of Jesus." *NovT* 8 (1966): 202–22.
Hill, D. "Δίκαιοι as a Quasi-Technical Term." *NTS* 11 (1965): 296–302.

HOMILETICAL SUGGESTIONS

The Priorities of a Sacrificial Faith (10:32–42)

1. Be more concerned about the verdict of the heavenly court than human courts (10:32–33)
2. Be more loyal to the heavenly Father than your earthly family (10:34–37)
3. Be willing to sacrifice your physical life for the sake of eternal life (10:38–39)
4. Be willing to take risks in order to secure rewards (10:40–42)

7. Conclusion of the Missionary Discourse (11:1)

11:1 On καὶ ἐγένετο ὅτε ἐτέλεσεν . . ., see 7:28. Διατάσσων (nom. sg. masc. of pres. act. ptc. of διατάσσω, "give instructions, command") is complementary. Τοῖς δώδεκα μαθηταῖς is dat. of indir. obj. Μετέβη 3rd sg. aor. act. indic. of μεταβαίνω, "go away, depart." Ἐκεῖθεν is an adv. of place, identifying the location from which one departed: "from there." The gen. def. art. (τοῦ) with the inf. (διδάσκειν pres. act. inf. of διδάσκω and κηρύσσειν pres. act. inf. of κηρύσσω) expresses purpose. Ἐν ταῖς πόλεσιν shows the location in which Jesus performed his teaching and preaching ministry. The most natural antecedent of αὐτῶν is τοῖς δώδεκα μαθηταῖς, which would indicate that Jesus focuses his ministry at this time on the disciples' hometowns. However, Matthew frequently used 3rd pers. pl. pron. to refer to the Jews or the inhabitants of the cities of Israel (4:23; 7:29; 9:35; 10:17), and this is prob. what Matthew intended here as well (H 1.297; D&A 2.239). Thus the pron. indicates that Jesus's ministry was currently conducted according to the instructions he gave his disciples in 10:5–6.

E. SECOND STAGE OF JESUS'S GALILEAN MINISTRY (11:2–12:50)

1. Jesus and John the Baptist (11:2–19)

a. John's Question About the Messiah (11:2–6)

11:2 Ὁ Ἰωάννης is John the Baptist (3:1, 13). Ἀκούσας (nom. sg. masc. of aor. act. ptc. of ἀκούω) is prob. temp. (most EVV). Ἐν with the dat. (τῷ δεσμωτηρίῳ) shows the location in which John heard the reports. Δεσμωτήριον, -ου, τό, "prison." The gen. τοῦ Χριστοῦ modifying τὰ ἔργα is subj.: "the works performed by the Messiah." Πέμψας (nom. sg. masc. of aor. act. ptc. of πέμπω, "send") is prob. attendant circumstance (most EVV). Διὰ τῶν μαθητῶν αὐτοῦ clearly expresses agency: "through his disciples." Although the NIV translates the sentence as if the prep. phrase marked the dir. obj., most EVV supply the dir. obj. "message" or "word." Since the disciples posed a question on John's behalf, the dir. obj. "question" better fits the context. See Metzger 23.

11:3 Εἶπεν 3rd sg. 2nd aor. act. indic. of λέγω. The antecedent of αὐτῷ is Χριστοῦ. The position of the pron. σύ suggests that it is emphatic (D&A 2.241). Εἶ 2nd sg. pres. indic. of εἰμί. Ὁ ἐρχόμενος (nom. sg. masc. of pres. mid. ptc. of dep. ἔρχομαι) is subst.: "the coming one" (3:1; Ps 118:26; Dan 7:13; Mal 3:1). The disjunctive particle ἤ marks an alternative. Ἕτερον is subst. Προσδοκῶμεν (1st pl. pres. act. subjunc. of προσδοκάω, "wait for, expect") may be either indic. or subjunc. morphologically. However, the grammatical context suggests that the form is a delib. subjunc.: "shall we wait?"

11:4 Ἀποκριθείς (nom. sg. masc. of aor. pass. ptc. of dep. ἀποκρίνομαι) is attendant circumstance (most EVV). Εἶπεν 11:3. Πορευθέντες (nom. pl. masc. of aor. pass. ptc. of dep. πορεύομαι) is attendant circumstance. Ἀπαγγείλατε (2nd pl. aor. act. impv. of ἀπαγγέλλω, "announce") expresses urgency. The rel. pron. ἅ is acc. and serves as the dir. obj. of the 2nd pl. pres. act. indic. vbs. ἀκούετε and βλέπετε.

11:5 Τυφλοί is subst. and qualitative, as are the five other adj. in this v. These qualitative adj. emphasize the "class traits" of the individuals (W 244). Hence, these individuals are identified by their maladies. Ἀναβλέπουσιν 3rd pl. pres. act. indic. of ἀναβλέπω, "see again, regain sight." Χωλός, -ή, -όν, "crippled, lame." Περιπατοῦσιν 3rd pl. pres. act. indic. of περιπατέω. The absence of the conj. καί between the second and third clauses suggests that Matthew was pairing the clauses. This would result in a triadic structure of paired clauses. Λεπρός, -ά, -όν, "leprous." Καθαρίζονται 3rd pl. pres. pass. indic. of καθαρίζω. Κωφός, -ή, -όν, "deaf." Ἀκούουσιν 3rd pl. pres. act. indic. of ἀκούω. Ἐγείρονται 3rd pl. pres. pass. indic. of ἐγείρω. Πτωχός, -ή, -όν, "poor." Εὐαγγελίζονται 3rd pl. pres. pass. indic. of εὐαγγελίζω.

11:6 Μακάριος, -ία, -ιον, "blessed (by God)." Ἐστίν 3rd sg. pres. indic. of εἰμί. Ὅς ἐάν is equivalent to ὅς ἄν (BDAG 725d–27d 1.j.a.), which gives the cstr. the sense of the prot. of a third-class cond. statement: "Blessed is he if he is not offended" (5:19, 32). Σκανδαλισθῇ 3rd sg. aor. pass. subjunc. of σκανδαλίζω, "offend, cause to stumble." Ἐν with the dat. (ἐμοί) may express cause (NIV) or pers. agency (LEB; CSB; ESV; H 1.301; N 452).

HOMILETICAL SUGGESTIONS

Doubts in the Dungeon (11:2–6)

1. Doubts come when Jesus does not seem to fulfill God's promises (11:2–3; Isa 42:7)
2. Jesus fulfills God's promises, but his people often misinterpret them
   a. John may have misinterpreted the nature of the promise (literal prison rather than spiritual bondage)
   b. John may have misunderstood the time of fulfillment (present rather than eschatological)
3. Faith is renewed by confirmation that Jesus fulfills God's promises (11:4–5; Isa 29:18; 35:5–6; 26:19; 61:1

b. Jesus's Description of John (11:7–15)

11:7 Τούτων πορευομένων (gen. pl. masc. of pres. mid. ptc. of dep. πορεύομαι) is gen. abs. and temp. (contemp.). The antecedent of τούτων is "his (John's) disciples" (11:2). Ἤρξατο 3rd sg. aor. mid. indic. of ἄρχω, "begin mid." Λέγειν (pres. act. inf. of λέγω) is a complementary inf. Τοῖς ὄχλοις is dat. of indir. obj. Περί with the gen. (Ἰωάννου) expresses ref. or concern: "about John." The neut. interr. pron. τί could mean either "why?" or "what?" However, the absence of another obj. for the inf. θεάσασθαι indicates that τί serves as that obj. and thus means "what?" Ἐξήλθατε 2nd pl. aor. act. indic. of dep. ἐξέρχομαι, "come/go out." Ἔρημος, -ον, "wilderness" (subst.). Θεάσασθαι aor. mid. inf. of dep. θεάομαι, "look at." Κάλαμος, -ου, ὁ, "reed." The acc. κάλαμον poses a potential (but incorrect) reply to the rhetorical question. Ὑπό with the gen. (ἀνέμου) identifies the impers. cause of the action of the pass. ptc. (σαλευόμενον acc. sg. masc. of pres. pass. ptc. of σαλεύω, "shake"). The ptc. is attrib.

11:8 The adversative conj. ἀλλά prob. implies a neg. response to the preceding question. Τί ἐξήλθατε ἰδεῖν 11:7. Ἰδεῖν (aor. act. inf. of ὁράω). Ἐν with the dat. (μαλακοῖς) serves as a marker of a state or condition (BDAG 326c–30c 2.a.). The acc. ἄνθρωπον poses a potential (but incorrect) answer to the rhetorical question. Μαλακός, -ή, -όν, "soft." Μαλακοῖς is subst. and refers to "soft things/garments." Ἠμφιεσμένον (acc. sg. masc. of pf. pass. ptc. of ἀμφιέννυμι, "clothe") is attrib. Ἰδού 1:20. Οἱ φοροῦντες (nom. pl. masc. of pres. act. ptc. of φορέω, "wear") is subst. Τὰ μαλακά is subst. Ἐν with the dat. (τοῖς οἴκοις) identifies location. Τῶν βασιλέων is poss. "Houses of kings" are palaces. Εἰσίν (3rd sg. pres. indic. of εἰμί) is gnomic.

11:9 Ἀλλὰ τί ἐξήλθατε ἰδεῖν 11:8. The acc. προφήτην poses a partially correct but ultimately insufficient answer to the rhetorical question. See Metzger 23. Ναί is a particle of affirmation: "yes." The expression λέγω ὑμῖν appears to be used to express emphasis (5:18). The καί may serve as a coordinating conj. (most EVV) or an *ascensive marker (LEB; BDAG 494a–96c 2.b.). Περισσότερον is the acc. sg. comp. form of περισσός, -ή, -όν, "great, extraordinary." Προφήτου is the gen. of comp. (W 110–12).

11:10 The antecedent of οὗτος is Ἰωάννης (11:2). Ἐστίν 10:37. Περί with the gen. (οὗ) expresses ref. or concern: "about whom." Γέγραπται (3rd sg. pf. pass. indic. of γράφω) is intensive pf. (most EVV). See Beale and Carson 38d–40c. Ἰδού 1:20. Ἐγώ is mildly emphatic. Ἀποστέλλω 1st sg. pres. act. indic. of ἀποστέλλω, "send." The pres. tense is prob. completely futuristic (W 536). Ἄγγελος here means "messenger" rather than "angel." The pron. μου that modifies τὸν ἄγγελον is prob. subj. gen. and identifies the one sending the messenger. Πρό with the gen. (προσώπου) is clearly loc. The idiom "before the face/presence" means "ahead of." The antecedent of the rel. pron. ὅς is ἄγγελον. Κατασκευάσει (3rd sg. fut. act. indic. of κατασκευάζω, "prepare") is predictive fut., expressing a promise. The gen. prep. σου identifies the one who will travel τὴν ὁδόν. Ἔμπροσθέν with the gen. (σου) marks position in front of a pers. or obj. and is roughly equivalent to πρὸ προσώπου.

11:11 Ἀμὴν λέγω ὑμῖν 5:18. Ἐγήγερται (3rd sg. pf. pass. indic. of ἐγείρω, "raise up") is intensive pf. If the vb. means "raise up" in the sense of bringing into existence (Matt 3:9), the voice is an example of the divine pass. However, since the pass. voice of the vb. is also used to speak of the appearance of false prophets and false Messiahs in Matt 24:11, 24, most EVV view the pass. as intrans.: "appear" (BDAG 271c–72c, cf. definitions 5 and 12). Ἐν with the pl. pers. obj. (γεννητοῖς) identifies position within a group: "among." Γεννητός, -ή, -όν, "born." Γεννητοῖς is substant.: "those who have been born." Γυναικῶν is subj. gen. The women gave birth to these human beings. Μείζων is the nom. sg. masc. comp. form of μέγας. The adj. is subst. and serves as the subj. of the sentence. Ἰωάννου is a gen. of comp. Βαπτιστής, -οῦ, ὁ, "baptist, baptizer." Τοῦ βαπτιστοῦ is subst. and gen. of simple appos. Δέ is adversative and serves to contrast the high standing of John with the even higher standing of Jesus's disciples. Μικρότερος is the nom. sg. masc. comp. form of μικρός, -ά, -όν, "small." The adj. is subst. and an example of the substitution of the comp. for the superl. (W 299–300). Ἐν τῇ βασιλείᾳ τῶν οὐρανῶν 3:2. In contrast with the subst. use of the adj. μείζων earlier in the verse, it serves as a pred. adj. in its second usage. Αὐτοῦ is gen. of comp. Ἐστίν is prob. a gnomic pres.

11:12 The ἀπὸ . . . ἕως cstr. expresses a temp. range, with the ἀπό marking the beginning of the range and ἕως marking the end. Ἰωάννου is a descriptive gen., and the temp. phrase means "from the days in which John lived or preached." Τοῦ βαπτιστοῦ 11:11. Ἕως with the gen. (ἄρτι [adv. of time] = τοῦ νῦν [Matt 24:21]) functions as a temp. prep., marking the end of a period. Ἡ βασιλεία τῶν οὐρανῶν 3:2. Βιάζεται 3rd sg. pres. mid./pass. indic. of βιάζω, "use force, violence." Scholars debate whether the vb. is pass. ("the kingdom of God suffers violence") or mid. ("the kingdom forces its way"). Most EVV assume the pass., but most also give the tr. of the mid. voice in the margin. The next clause suggests the pass. voice; violent people are acting against the kingdom. Βιαστής, -οῦ, ὁ, "violent person." The anar. subst. βιασταί is prob. qualitative. Ἀρπάζουσιν 3rd pl. pres. act. indic. of ἁρπάζω, "snatch, plunder." The antecedent of αὐτήν is βασιλεία.

11:13 Γάρ introduces the reason for the violent response to the kingdom. Οἱ προφῆται καὶ ὁ νόμος refers to the OT but reverses the normal order used when referring to the OT's two major sections (cf. 5:17). The order prob. places emphasis on the prophets, who most clearly predicted the coming of the kingdom. Ἕως 11:12. Ἕως Ἰωάννου prob. means "until John began his ministry." John's ministry marked the transition from prophecy to fulfillment. Ἐπροφήτευσαν 3rd pl. aor. act. indic. of προφητεύω, "prophesy."

11:14 Εἰ with the indic. (θέλετε 2nd pl. pres. act. indic. of θέλω) forms the prot. of a first-class cond. statement. The cstr. assumes the fulfillment of the prot. for the sake of argument. Δέξασθαι (aor. mid. inf. of dep. δέχομαι, "receive") is complementary. Αὐτός is emphatic. Ἐστίν 10:37. Ἡλίας "Elijah." The art. ptc. ὁ μέλλων (nom. sg. masc. of pres. act. ptc. of μέλλω) is subst. and appos. Ἔρχεσθαι (pres. mid. inf. of dep. ἔρχομαι) is complementary. As it stands, the cond. statement does not belong to the category of cause and effect, evidence inference, equivalence, or principle. The apod. is prob. an example of ellipsis that omits the words "I say to you." If so, the category is likely cause and effect. Because of the audience's willingness to receive Jesus's testimony about John, he offers that testimony. This suggestion is strengthened by the next verse.

11:15 The art. ptc. ὁ ἔχων (nom. sg. masc. of pres. act. ptc. of ἔχω) is subst. Οὖς, ὠτός, τό, "ear." See Metzger 24. Ἀκουέτω (3rd sg. pres. act. impv. of ἀκούω) is ingr.-prog. Although most EVV tr. this 3rd pers. impv. using "let," it is better to use "must" or "should" since "let" is largely used in granting permission.

FOR FURTHER STUDY

38. The Doubts of John the Baptist

Collins, J. J. "The Works of the Messiah." *Dead Sea Discoveries* 1 (1994): 98–112.

Falcetta, A. "The Logion of Matthew 11:5–6 Par: From Qumran to Abgar." *Revue Biblique* 110 (2003): 222–48.

Kvalbein, H. "The Wonders of the End-Time: Metaphoric Language in 4Q521 and the Interpretation of Matthew 11.5 Par." *Journal for the Study of the Pseudepigrapha* 18 (1998): 87–110.

Wold, B. "Agency and Raising the Dead in 4QPseudo-Ezekiel and 4Q521 2 ii." *ZNW* 103 (2012): 1–19.

39. The Dress of John the Baptist

LaVerdiere, E. "A Garment of Camel's Hair." *Emmanuel* 92 (1986): 545–51.

40. The Structure of Matthew 11–12

Boerman, D. "The Chiastic Structure of Matthew 11–12." *CTJ* 40 (2005): 313–25.

41. Least in the Kingdom

Viviano, B. T. "The Least in the Kingdom: Matthew 11:11, Its Parallel in Luke 7:28 (Q), and Daniel 4:14." *CBQ* 62 (2000): 41–54.

42. Violence and the Kingdom

Weaver, D. J. "'Suffering Violence' and the Kingdom of Heaven (Mt 11:12): A Matthean Manual for Life in a Time of War." *Hervormde Teologiese Studies* 67 (2011): 1011.

HOMILETICAL SUGGESTIONS

God's Herald (11:7–10)

1. John did not bow to pressure but courageously confronted crowds and kings
2. John did not pursue personal comfort but faithfully embraced a life of sacrifice
3. John did not merely serve as a prophet but gladly announced the coming of Yahweh

Thy Kingdom Come (11:11–15)

1. The greatness of the kingdom and its subjects (11:11)
2. The violence against the kingdom (11:12)
3. The promise of the kingdom (11:13)
4. The arrival of the kingdom (11:14; Mal 3:1; 4:5)

c. Dissatisfaction with John and Jesus (11:16–19)

11:16 The interr. pron. τίνι is a dat. of comp. Ὁμοιώσω (1st sg. fut. act. indic. of ὁμοιόω, "compare") after the interr. pron. is clearly a delib. fut. Γενέα, -ας, ἡ, "generation" in the sense of a group of people who all live at a certain time. The use of the near dem. ταύτην with τὴν γενεάν shows Jesus was referring to the generation of his contemporaries. Ὅμοιος, -οία, -οιον, "like, similar." Παιδίοις is dat. of comp. Καθημένοις (dat. pl. neut. of pres. mid. ptc. of dep. κάθημαι, "sit") is attrib. Ἀγορά, -ᾶς, ἡ, "market." Although the NIV, CSB, and LEB connect the rel. pron. with the ptc. that immediately follows, the rel. pron. (ἅ) does not likely function together with the ptc. (προσφωνοῦντα nom. pl. neut. of pres. act. ptc. of προσφωνέω, "call out") since this does not occur elsewhere in Matthew The rel. pron. more likely serves as the subj. of the vb. λέγουσιν. The connection between the pron. and the vb. is disrupted by the verse division. The ptc. is prob. temp.: "while they are calling out." For a sim. cstr., see 25:1. Τοῖς ἑτέροις is subst.: "to the other children."

11:17 Although it is morphologically possible for λέγουσιν to be dat. sg. neut. of the pres. act. ptc. of λέγω and thus serve as an attrib. ptc. modifying τοῖς ἑτέροις, Matthean style suggests that λέγουσιν is 3rd pl. pres. act. indic. of λέγω and that the rel. pron. ἅ serves as its subj. (11:16). Ηὐλήσαμεν 1st pl. aor. act. indic. of αὐλέω, "play the flute." The καί introduces a concession and thus has the sense "and yet." Ὠρχήσασθε 2nd pl. aor. mid. indic. of dep. ὀρχέομαι, "dance." Ἐθρηνήσαμεν 1st sg. aor. act. ptc. of θρηνέω, "sing a funeral hymn." See Metzger 24. Ἐκόψασθε 2nd pl. aor. mid. indic. of κόπτω, "beat oneself as an act of mourning" (mid.). The first line refers to the somber tone of John's ministry. The second line refers to the celebrative nature of Jesus's ministry.

11:18 The γάρ introduces an explanation of the appropriateness of the previous analogy. Ἦλθεν 3rd sg. aor. act. indic. of dep. ἔρχομαι, "make a public appearance" (BDAG 393c–95b 1.b.β.). The μήτε . . . μήτε cstr. means "neither . . . nor." Ἐσθίων (nom. sg. masc. of pres. act. ptc. of ἐσθίω, "eat") and πίνων (nom. sg. masc. of pres. act. ptc. of πίνω, "drink") are prob. ptc. of manner, since refraining from food and drink are indicative of the somber tone of ministry equated with the refusal to dance in the previous analogy. Καί introduces a result. Λέγουσιν 11:17. Ἔχει 3rd sg. pres. act. indic. of ἔχω.

11:19 Ἦλθεν 11:18. Ὁ υἱὸς τοῦ ἀνθρώπου 9:6. Ἐσθίων καὶ πίνων 11:18. Καὶ λέγουσιν 11:18. Ἰδού 1:20. Φάγος, -ου, ὁ, "glutton." Οἰνοπότης, -ου, ὁ, "heavy wine drinker, drunkard." Τελώνης, -ου, ὁ, "tax-collector." Φίλος, -ου, ὁ, "friend." Ἁμαρτολός, -όν, "sinner." The gen. τελωνῶν and ἁμαρτωλῶν are either subj. gen. (BDAG 1058d–59b 2.a.α.) or obj. gen. The obj. gen. seems more likely since 9:9 indicates that Jesus befriended tax collectors. Καί is again concessive or adversative—"and yet"—since the vindication described in the clause contrasts with the accusations leveled in the previous clause (D&A 2.264). Ἐδικαιώθη (3rd sg. aor. pass. indic. of δικαιόω, "vindicate, declare the innocence of the accused") is prob. gnomic. The def. art. (ἡ) is common with abstract nouns such as σοφία. Ἀπό with the gen. (τῶν ἔργων) is causal. Αὐτῆς is subj. gen. and the antecedent is σοφία. Reference to the "deeds performed by wisdom" implies personification of wisdom. See Metzger 24.

FOR FURTHER STUDY

43. Games of the Children in the Market

Cotter, W. J. "The Parable of the Children in the Marketplace, Q (Lk) 7:31–35: An Examination of the Parable's Image and Significance." *NovT* 29 (1987): 289–304.

44. Jesus as Wisdom

Shantz, C. "Wisdom Is as Wisdom Does: The Use of Folk Proverbs in Q 7:31–35." *Toronto Journal of Theology* 17 (2001): 249–62.

2. Divine Retribution and Revelation (11:20–27)

a. Personal Responsibility for Rejecting Jesus (11:20–24)

11:20 Τότε in this context means "after that." Ἤρξατο 3rd sg. aor. act. indic. of ἄρχω, "begin" (mid.). Ὀνειδίζειν (pres. act. inf. of ὀνειδίζω, "reprimand, scold") is a complementary inf. The antecedent of the rel. pron. αἷς is πόλεις. Ἐγένοντο 3rd pl. aor. mid. indic. of dep. γίνομαι, "happen, occur." Δύναμις, -εως, ἡ, "miracle." Πλεῖσται is the nom. pl. fem. superl. form of the adj. πολύς, which is used attrib. to refer to the majority or most of his miracles. The gen. αὐτοῦ is subj. and identifies the miracles as those that "he" (Jesus) performed. The ὅτι introduces the reason for Jesus's rebuke. Μετενόησαν 3rd pl. aor. act. indic. of μετανοέω.

11:21 Οὐαί is an interjection that, when used with a 2nd pers. pron., expresses intense displeasure: "Woe!" Σοι is prob. dat. of disadvantage. Χοραζίν ("Chorazin") and Βηθσαϊδά ("Bethsaida") were cities located to the northeast of the Sea of Galilee and not far from Capernaum. Ὅτι identifies the reason for the pronouncement of woe. The particle εἰ with the indic. in a secondary tense (ἐγένοντο 3rd pl. aor. mid. indic. of dep. γίνομαι, "happen") in the prot. and ἄν with a secondary tense in the apod. (μετενόησαν 3rd pl. aor. act. indic. of μετανοέω, "repent") form a second-class cond. statement.

Second-class condition is presumed contrary to fact (W 694–96). Since both clauses use the aor. (rather than the impf.), they express a past contrary to fact cond. statement: "If this had happened (but it did not), this would have happened (but it did not)." Τύρος ("Tyre") and Σιδῶν ("Sidon") were two ancient Phoenician cities that were denounced by the prophets and came under divine judgment due to their sin. Αἱ δυνάμεις 11:20. The art. ptc. γενόμεναι (nom. pl. fem. of aor. mid. ptc. of dep. γίνομαι) is attrib. Ἐν with ὑμῖν is loc., and the antecedent of the pron. is the cities of Chorazin and Bethsaida. Πάλαι is a temp. adv. mng. "long ago." Σάκκος, -ου, ὁ, "sackcloth." Σποδός, -οῦ, ἡ, "ashes." Since the prep. ἐν was used to identify one's clothing, BDAG suggests the interpretation "clothed in sackcloth and ashes" (326c–30b 2.a.).

11:22 Πλήν is an adv. that serves as a conj. marking contrast: "nevertheless." The statement contrasts the more favorable standing of Chorazin and Bethsaida in final judgment with their failure to repent that was assumed in the preceding second-class cond. statement. Λέγω ὑμῖν introduces an important pronouncement. Τύρῳ καὶ Σιδῶνι (11:21) may be dat. of ref. or advantage. Ἀνεκτός, -όν, "bearable, endurable." Ἀνεκτότερον is the nom. sg. neut. form of the comp. adj.: "more bearable." Ἔσται (3rd sg. fut. act. indic. of εἰμί) is predictive. With the obj. ἡμέρᾳ, the prep. ἐν is clearly temp. and may mark either a period or *point of time during or at which an event occurs. The gen. κρίσεως may be an attrib. gen. ("judgment day"). It refers to the day on which eschatological judgment occurs. After the comp. adj., the particle ἤ denotes comp.: "than." The dat. ὑμῖν expresses ref. or advantage.

11:23 Καὶ σύ before the noun of dir. address expresses emphasis. Καφαρναούμ 4:13. The use of the neg. μή in a question assumes a neg. response. The use of the neg. μή with a vb. in the indic. mood indicates that the sentence is interr. Otherwise, a nonindic. form would normally have been used (with rare exceptions). Ἕως with a gen. of place (οὐρανοῦ) serves as the "marker of a limit reached" (BDAG 422d–24c 3): "as far as." Ὑψωθήσῃ 2nd sg. fut. pass. indic. of ὑψόω, "lift up." With this vb. and the obj. οὐρανοῦ, the ἕως assumes the nuance "as high as." The use of the sg. of οὐρανός to refer to heaven is unusual for Matthew, but that appears to be the sense here since the noun is opposed with Hades. The grammar is likely influenced by Isaiah 14:13–15 LXX (which also used the sg.) to which 11:23a apparently alludes. With the vb. καταβήσῃ and the obj. ᾅδου, ἕως assumes the nuance "as low as." Ἅδης, -ου, ὁ, "Hades, place of the dead." Καταβήσῃ 2nd sg. fut. mid. indic. of καταβαίνω, "descend." On the second-class cond. sentence ὅτι εἰ ἐν Σοδόμοις ἐγενήθησαν αἱ δυνάμεις αἱ γενόμεναι ἐν σοί, ἔμεινεν ἂν μέχρι τῆς σήμερον, see 11:21. Σόδομα, -ων, τά, "Sodom," a notoriously wicked city destroyed by God (Gen 19:1–29). Ἔμεινεν 3rd sg. aor. act. indic. of μένω. Μέχρι with the gen. (τῆς σήμερον) functions as a prep. showing continuance of an action through time up to a particular point: "until." Matthew prefers to use ἕως in this capacity but may have avoided it here to prevent confusion arising from different uses of ἕως in a relatively brief context. Matthew's only other usage of μέχρι is 28:15. Both usages of μέχρι are in the phrase μέχρι τῆς σήμερον, which suggests the expression was standardized. However, compare the expression ἕως τῆς σήμερον in 27:8 and note the textual var. in 28:15. For the two variation units, see Metzger 24–25.

11:24 On πλὴν λέγω ὑμῖν ὅτι γῇ Σοδόμων ἀνεκτότερον ἔσται ἐν ἡμέρᾳ κρίσεως ἢ σοί, see 11:22.

FOR FURTHER STUDY

45. Punishment for Rejecting Jesus

Comber, J. A. "Composition and Literary Characteristics of Matt 11:20–24." *CBQ* 39 (1977): 497–504.

Strickert, F. "2 Esdras 1.11 and the Destruction of Bethsaida." *JSP* 16 (1997): 111–22.

HOMILETICAL SUGGESTIONS

When Miracles Don't Matter (11:20–24)

1. Jesus's miraculous power confirms his claims and calls for sinners to repent
2. Sinners' refusal to repent shows they are more wicked than the most notorious sinners of OT times
3. Those who do not respond to Jesus's miracles with repentance will face terrifying punishment because greater revelation results in greater accountability

b. Divine Sovereignty in Revelation (11:25–27)

11:25 Ἐν with the obj. ἐκείνῳ τῷ καιρῷ is used temp. to identify the period of time during which an action occurred. The use of the ptc. ἀποκριθείς (nom. sg. masc. of aor. pass. ptc. of dep. ἀποκρίνομαι, "reply, answer") is surprising since no question has been posed to Jesus in the preceding context. Two explanations are possible. First, the cstr. may simply mean "he said" and indicate the continuation of discourse, perhaps adding a touch of solemnity to the utterance (D&A 2.273; BDF §420). Second, and more likely, this section may constitute Jesus's response to the disbelief that he described in the preceding context (H 1.318). Nolland observed that in Gk. influenced by Sem. languages the ptc. was used broadly "to indicate response to a situation either indicated or implied in the context" (470). The ptc. is prob. epex. and clarifies the vb. εἶπεν (3rd sg. aor. act. indic. of λέγω) thus: "he said in reply." LEB regards the ptc. as attendant circumstance. Most EVV do not tr. the ptc., apparently because they accept option 1 above. Ἐξομολογοῦμαί 1st sg. pres. mid. indic. of ἐξομολογέω, "praise." Σοι is dat. of dir. obj. Πάτερ is the voc. of simple address. Κύριε is the voc. of simple appos. The gen. phrases τοῦ οὐρανοῦ καὶ τῆς γῆς are gen. of subord. The phrases constitute a merism that refers to the entire created world. Ὅτι introduces the reason for Jesus's praise. Ἔκρυψας 2nd sg. aor. act. indic. of κρύπτω, "hide." The antecedent of ταῦτα is difficult to identify precisely. If retrospective, the dem. pron. prob. refers to the works and words of Jesus detailed in 11:5, which confirmed Jesus's identity as the Coming One and the presence of the kingdom in the time of fulfillment (H 1.318; N 470). The dem. pron. could be prospective and refer to the knowledge of the Father and the Son described in 11:27. Ἀπό with the gen. expresses separation. These things were hidden away from the view of the wise and understanding. Σοφός, -ή, -όν, "wise." Συνετός, -ή, -όν, "intelligent, insightful." Both adj. are subst. The absence of the art. is common with the obj. of prep. Those who failed to understand these things prob. are those of Jesus's generation (11:16–19) and in particular the inhabitants of Chorazin, Bethsaida, and Capernaum who witnessed much of Jesus's ministry but refused to repent and believe. Ἀπεκάλυψας 2nd sg. aor. act. indic. of ἀποκαλύπτω, "reveal." The antecedent of the pron. αὐτά is ταῦτα. Νήπιος, -ια, -ιον, "child (ranging in age from before birth to puberty)."

11:26 The affirmative particle ναί ("yes") adds emphasis. Ὁ πατήρ is an example of the substitution of the nom. for the voc. The presence of the def. art. with the nom. of address suggest a Sem. background for the saying (W 56–59). The ὅτι could introduce a second expression of praise (cf. 11:25). The ὅτι introduces the reason the Father hides and reveals, as explained in the previous verse. Οὕτως summarizes a preceding thought: "You doing this, acting in this way." Εὐδοκία, -ας, ἡ, "something that brings pleasure." Ἐγένετο 3rd sg. aor. mid. indic. of dep. γίνομαι, "be" (equivalent to εἰμί). Ἔμπροσθεν with the gen. (σου) indicates the immediate presence of the obj. of the prep: "in front of, before." The prep. may be used in reverent expressions to avoid directly associating a subj., particularly God, with an action (BDAG 325b–c 1.b.δ.). The cstr. is roughly equivalent to the ethical dat. The cstr. should be tr. "for doing so was pleasing to you."

11:27 Πάντα ("all things") appears to be limited in this context to all things related to the knowledge and revelation of the Father. Μοι is dat. of indir. obj. Παρεδόθη (3rd sg. aor. pass. indic. of παραδίδωμι, "hand over, give") is a divine pass., as the phrase expressing agency immediately shows. Ὑπό with the gen. (τοῦ πατρός) is used to express ultimate pers. agency. Μου is gen. of relationship. Ἐπιγινώσκει (3rd sg. pres. act. indic. of ἐπιγινώσκω, "know [personally]") is gnomic. The combination εἰ μή means "except." Οὐδέ joins neg. clauses (οὐδείς in the preceding clause) and means "nor." The indef. pron. τις means "anyone" rather than "a certain one." Thus the beginning of the clause should be tr.: "nor does anyone know." The rel. pron. ᾧ identifies a second exception to the claim that no one knows the Father. The rel. pron. is dat. since it serves as the indir. obj. of the inf. ἀποκαλύψαι in the rel. clause. The particle ἐάν imposes contingency on the rel. pron.: "whomever, anyone to whom." The particle justifies translating the rel. clause as the prot. of a cond. sentence: "and to anyone else if . . ." Βούληται 3rd sg. pres. mid. subjunc. of dep. βούλομαι, "desire, want." Ἀποκαλύψαι (aor. act. inf. of ἀποκαλύπτω, "reveal") is a complementary inf. See Metzger 25–26.

FOR FURTHER STUDY

46. The Text of Matthew 11:25

Klijn, A. F. J. "Matthew 11:25/Luke 10:21." Pages 3–14 in *New Testament Textual Criticism: Its Significance for Exegesis*. Edited by E. J. Epp and G. D. Fee. Oxford: Clarendon, 1981.

47. Similarities Between the Gospels of Matthew and John

Sabbe, M. "Can Mt 11:25–27 and Lc 10:22 Be Called a Johannine Logion?" Pages 363–71 in *Logia: Les Paroles de Jesus*. Edited by J. Delobel. Leuven, Belgium: Leuven University Press, 1982.

48. The Saying on Revelation and Concealment

Allison, D. C., Jr. "Two Notes on a Key Text: Matthew 11:25–30." *JTS* 39 (1988): 477–85.
Minear, P. S. "Two Secrets, Two Disclosures." *Horizons in Biblical Theology* 29 (2007): 75–85.

HOMILETICAL SUGGESTIONS

Father and Son (11:25–27)

1. Jesus's praise of the Father (11:25–26)
   a. The Father created and sustains the universe in display of his mighty power
   b. The Father reveals and conceals truth in display of his sovereign grace
2. Jesus's authority from the Father (11:27a)
3. Jesus's relationship with the Father (11:27b–c)
4. Jesus's revelation of the Father (11:27d)

3. Relief from the Burdens of the Rabbis (11:28–12:14)

a. The Promise of Rest (11:28–30)

11:28 The emphasis on rest for the weary and burdened seems more closely related to the discussions of Sabbath law in the next chapter than to the preceding discussions. However, the theme of this paragraph is related to the description of Jesus as the friend of sinners (11:19) and the celebratory nature of his ministry (11:17). Δεῦτε is a hortatory particle mng. "Come here!" The prep. phrase πρός με specifies that the audience is to come "toward/to me." The prep. πρός takes the longer form ἐμέ as its obj. except after vbs. of motion, in which case it takes the enclitic form με (3:14; 19:14). Πάντες is subst. and pers. (implied by the masc. gender). The form is the voc. of simple address (which overlaps with the nom. form in the pl.). The art. prevents the ptc. from being misread as adv., which would pervert the mng. The ptc. are either attrib. (most EVV) or subst. and appos. Κοπιῶντες nom. pl. masc. of pres. act. ptc. of κοπιάω, "be weary." Πεφορτισμένοι nom. sg. masc. of pf. pass. ptc. of φορτίζω, "load down, burden." Κἀγώ is a result of crasis of καί and ἐγώ: "and I." Ἀναπαύσω (1st sg. fut. act. indic. of ἀναπαύω, "give rest, give relief.")

11:29 Ἄρατε (2nd pl. aor. act. impv. of αἴρω, "pick up") expresses urgency. Ζυγός, -οῦ, ὁ, "yoke." Μου is prob. either a gen. of poss. or *subj. gen. By adding the prep. phrase ἐφ᾽ ὑμᾶς, the image is made more vivid, since animals wore the yoke on their shoulders. Μάθετε 2nd pl. aor. act. impv. of μανθάνω, "learn." Ἀπό with the gen. (ἐμοῦ) identifies the pers. source of instruction. Ὅτι could introduce the content of instruction: "learn that I am gentle." However, it more likely is causal (most EVV). Πραΰς, πραεῖα, πραΰ, "gentle." Ταπεινός, -ή, -όν, "humble, lowly." Τῇ καρδίᾳ may be classified as a dat. of *ref. or sphere (W 145–46; Matt 5:8). Καί introduces a result. Εὑρήσετε (2nd pl. fut. act. indic. of εὑρίσκω, "find") is predictive and expresses a promise. Ἀνάπαυσις, -εως, ἡ, "rest, relief." Ταῖς ψυχαῖς is a dat. of advantage: "for your souls." BDAG (1098d–1100a 2.d. and g.) notes that ψυχή in this passage may refer to "the seat and center of life that transcends the earthly" (most EVV) or may reflect Sem. influence and simply be refl. ("rest for yourselves"). Since the ref. is a dir. quotation of Jer 6:16 (which follows the MT rather than the LXX that reflects Sem. idiom, the latter interpretation is likely correct.

11:30 Γάρ introduces the reason Jesus's disciples enjoy rest. Ὁ ζυγός μου 11:29. Χρηστός, -ή, -όν, "comfortable, easy to wear." Φορτίον, -ου, τό, "load, burden." Ἐλαφρός, -ά, -όν, "light." Ἐστίν is prob. gnomic. Compare this verse to Matt 23:4.

FOR FURTHER STUDY

49. The Promise of Rest

> Betz, H. D. "Logion of the Easy Yoke and of Rest (Matt 11:28–30)." *JBL* 86 (1967): 10–24.
>
> Charette, B. "'To Proclaim Liberty to the Captives': Matthew 11:28–30 in the Light of OT Prophetic Expectation." *NTS* 38 (1992): 290–97.
>
> Deutsch, C. *Hidden Wisdom and the Easy Yoke: Wisdom, Torah and Discipleship in Matthew 11:25–30. JSNTSup* 18. Sheffield: JSOT, 1987.
>
> Janzen, J. G. "The Yoke That Gives Rest." *Int* 41 (1987): 256–68.
>
> Stanton, G. N. "Salvation Proclaimed, 10: Matthew 11:28–30: Comfortable Words?" *ExpTim* 94 (1982): 3–9.

HOMILETICAL SUGGESTIONS

The Christian's Rest (11:28–30)

1. Legalism wearies the sinner with work (11:28)
2. Legalism burdens the sinner with impossible demands (11:28; 23:4)
3. Jesus grants sinners rest from their efforts to please God by their actions (11:29)
4. Jesus produces righteousness in his disciples with a result that is not burdensome (11:30)

b. Rest from Oppressive Traditions: Two Sabbath Controversies (12:1–14)

i. First Sabbath Controversy (12:1–8)

12:1 The prep. ἐν with the obj. τῷ καιρῷ is clearly temp. Although καιρός may refer generically to a period of time, in this agricultural setting the noun may refer to an agricultural season (13:30; 21:34). The remote dem. ἐκείνῳ would apparently refer to the harvest season in the same year as the events described in the previous chapter. Ἐπορεύθη 3rd sg. aor. pass. indic. of dep. πορεύομαι, "go, proceed." The pl. of the noun σάββατον is often used to refer to a single Sabbath in NT Gk. (BDAG 909b–10a 1.b.β.). Δία marks extension through an area. Σπόριμος, -ον, "grain field" (subst.). Δέ may simply mark the continuation of narrative or may be slightly adversative since such conduct was deemed improper on the Sabbath. Ἐπείνασαν 3rd pl. aor. act. indic. of πεινάω, "be hungry." Καί introduces a result: "and so." Ἤρξαντο 3rd pl. aor. mid. indic. of ἄρχω, "begin" (mid.). Τίλλειν (pres. act. inf. of τίλλω, "pick") and ἐσθίειν (pres. act. inf. of ἐσθίω, "eat") are complementary. Στάχυς, -υος, ὁ, "head of grain." Στάχυας is the dir. obj. of τίλλειν and the implied dir. obj. of ἐσθίειν.

12:2 Οἱ Φαρισαῖοι 3:7. Ἰδόντες (nom. pl. masc. of aor. act. ptc. of ὁράω, "see") is prob. temp. (most EVV), but the context also implies a cause-effect relationship between the observation and protest of the disciples' behavior. Εἶπαν 3rd pl. aor. act. indic. of λέγω. Ἰδού 1:20. Ποιοῦσιν 3rd pl. pres. act indic. of ποιέω. The rel. pron. ὅ functions as both a dem. and rel. pron.: "that which." The rel. clause serves as the dir. obj. of ποιοῦσιν, and the rel. pron. serves as the dir. obj. of the inf. ποιεῖν. Ἔξεστιν 3rd sg. (impers.) pres. indic. of ἔξειμι, "it is right, permissible." Ποιεῖν (pres. act. inf. of ποιέω) is complementary. Ἐν with the obj. σαββάτῳ (12:1) is clearly temp.: "on/during the Sabbath." Note that Matthew uses the pl. and the sg. interchangeably to refer to a single Sabbath day.

12:3 The def. art. ὁ functions as a substitute for the dem. pron. This is common, esp. in combination with δέ, showing continuation in a narrative. Εἶπεν 3rd sg. aor. act. indic. of λέγω. The use of the neg. οὐκ in a question implies an affirmative response. Ἀνέγνωτε 2nd pl. aor. act. indic. of ἀναγινώσκω, "read." The interr. pron. τί verifies that Jesus was posing a question. The pron. serves as both the dir. obj. of ἀνέγνωτε and ἐποίησεν (3rd sg. aor. act. indic. of ποιέω). Δαυίδ 1:1. Ἐπείνασεν 3rd sg. aor. act. indic. of πεινάω, "be hungry." Οἱ μετ᾽ αὐτοῦ serves as a secondary subj. of the vb. However, since Matthew's emphasis was on the actions of David, he employed a sg. vb. The combination of the def. art. and the prep. phrase is an ellipsis mng. "the men who were with him" (BDAG 686a–89c 2.e.).

12:4 Although the interr. particle πῶς normally means "how," in this case the particle functions as the equivalent of ὅτι "that" and focuses on what David did (see the τί in 12:3) rather than how he did it (BDAG 900d 1.b.α.). Εἰσῆλθεν 3rd sg. aor. act. indic. of dep. εἰσέρχομαι. The def. art. modifying οἶκον τοῦ θεοῦ is monadic, i.e., only one house of God existed. The placement of the dir. obj. τοὺς ἄρτους τῆς προθέσεως before the vb. (ἔφαγον 3rd pl. aor. act. indic. of ἐσθίω, "eat") is prob. emphatic. The rel. clause that follows the vb. will explain the emphasis. The gen. τῆς προθέσεως (πρόθεσις, -εως, ἡ, "presentation") is prob. epex. and refers to the bread presented to God (Lev 24:5–9). Despite the shift from the pl. to the sg. and from the masc. to the neut., the antecedent of ὅ is ἄρτους. The lack of agreement in gender and number (cf. Mark 2:26) is prob. due to the influence of Lev 24:5–9 (LXX), which has a sim. shift in number from "loaves" (pl.) to clauses in which "loaves" is the implied subj., but the vbs. are sg. See Metzger 26. Ἐξόν (nom. sg. neut. of pres. ptc. of ἔξειμι "be permissible") with ἦν (3rd sg. impf. indic. of εἰμί) forms the impf. periph. The dat. αὐτῷ, τοῖς μετ᾽ αὐτοῦ, and τοῖς ἱερεῦσιν are dat. of ref. Ἱερεύς, -έως, ὁ, "priest." The dat. of ref. often accompanies ἔξεστιν. These dat. of ref. assume the function of the acc. of ref. (acc. of subj. of the inf.) in terms of their relationship to φαγεῖν (aor. act. inf. of ἐσθίω). Οὐδέ "nor." Εἰ μή "except." Μόνος, -η, -ον, "alone."

12:5 The conj. ἤ introduces an alternative. Οὐκ ἀνέγνωτε 12:3. Ἐν with τῷ νόμῳ is loc. Τῷ νόμῳ refers not to a specific law regarding conduct on the Sabbath (for which Matthew would likely have used the acc. rather than this prep. phrase) but to the first major section of the Heb. Bible, the five books of Moses. The ὅτι introduces indir. discourse content, a brief summary of the teaching regarding responsibilities of the priests on the Sabbath. Τοῖς σάββασιν 12:1. Οἱ ἱερεῖς 12:4. Τὸ σάββατον 12:2. Βεβηλοῦσιν (3rd pl. pres. act. indic. of βεβηλόω, "profane, desecrate") is prob. gnomic. Καί is adversative and introduces a surprising and unexpected fact: "and yet." Ἀναίτιος, -ον, "innocent." Εἰσίν is prob. gnomic.

12:6 Λέγω δὲ ὑμῖν introduces a solemn and important announcement (5:18). Ὅτι introduces dir. discourse. Μεῖζον is the nom. sg. neut. comp. form of the adj. μέγας, μεγάλη, μέγα, "great." Despite the anar. form (which prob. stresses quality), the adj. is subst. The gender of the adj. is initially puzzling. In context Jesus seems to be saying he is greater than the temple and thus qualified to act in ways normally prohibited on the Sabbath. However, the neut. gender may be interpreted as referring to "something greater." Although some commentators suggest Jesus was extolling the greatness of the kingdom, Jesus's ministry, or God's mercy (H 1.330), the subst. adj. is most naturally a ref. to Jesus personally (D&A 2.314; G 223; N 484). If the subst. adj. refers to Jesus directly, the neut. gender may be explained as due to emphasis on the quality of Jesus's greatness rather than pers. identity (Turner, *Syntax* 21; BDF §131; G; D&A). Although this phenomenon occurs with the positive adj. (6:34), it is particularly common in Matthew in pred. cstr. using the comp. adj. (cf. 6:25; 12:41, 42). Although most EVV tr. the adj. "something greater" (NIV; CSB; LEB; NRSV; ESV), such tr. may treat the grammar too woodenly and without the sensitivity to the use of neut. adj. in classical and Koine Gk. discussed in standard grammars. The tr. "someone greater" is justifiable, and prob. preferable (cf. Geneva; KJV; NLT). Ἐστίν 3rd sg. pres. indic. of εἰμί. Ὧδε most often functions as an adv. of place ("here, in this place") but may also function as an adv. of time ("here, at this moment"). In this context the sense is loc. and refers to Jesus's pres. location.

12:7 Δέ is adversative and contrasts Jesus's greatness with the unjust condemnation he received. Εἰ with the indic. in a secondary tense (ἐγνώκειτε 2nd pl. pluperf. act. indic. of γινώσκω) in the prot., and ἄν with the indic. in a secondary tense (κατεδικάσατε 2nd pl. aor. act. indic. of καταδικάζω, "condemn") in the apod. forms a second-class cond. statement that presents both the prot. and apod. as past contrary to fact. The Pharisees did not know the mng. of Hosea 6:6 and did condemn the innocent. On τί ἐστιν· ἔλεος θέλω καὶ οὐ θυσίαν, see 9:13. Τοὺς ἀναιτίους 12:5. The art. adj. is subst.

12:8 Γάρ introduces the reason for Jesus's innocence in his conduct on the Sabbath. Κύριος may serve in some instances as a mere title of authority but used in connection with the Sabbath prob. serves as the Gk. substitute for the divine name Yahweh (Exod 20:8–11; Lev 26:2 [in which Yahweh refers to "my Sabbaths"]). Ἐστίν (12:6) is gnomic pres. Given the connotations of authority in Κύριος, τοῦ σαββάτου is prob. gen. of subord., expressing that the Son of Man has authority over the Sabbath. Ὁ υἱὸς τοῦ ἀνθρώπου 9:6.

FOR FURTHER STUDY

50. Matthew's Use of Hosea 6:6

Hill, D. "On the Use and Meaning of Hosea 6:6 in Matthew's Gospel." *NTS* 24 (1977): 107–19.

Lybæk, L. "Matthew's Use of Hosea 6:6 in the Context of the Sabbath Controversies." Pages 491–99 in *The Scriptures in the Gospels*. Edited by C. M. Tuckett. Leuven, Belgium: Peeters, 1997.

51. Sabbath Controversies

See the Shabbath tractate of the Mishnah.

Doering, L. "Sabbath Laws in the New Testament Gospels." Pages 207–53 in *The New Testament and Rabbinic Literature*. Edited by R. Bieringer, F. G. Martínez, D. Pollefeyt and P. J. Tomson. Leiden: Brill, 2010.

Eskenazi, T. C., and D. J. Harrington. *The Sabbath in Jewish and Christian Traditions*. New York: Crossroad, 1991.

Viljoen, F. P. "Sabbath Controversy in Matthew." *Verbum et Ecclesia* 32 (2011): 1–8.

HOMILETICAL SUGGESTIONS

Jesus's Authority over the Sabbath (12:1–8)

1. Jesus has authority over the Sabbath because he is the new David
2. Jesus has authority over the Sabbath because he is the new temple
3. Jesus has authority over the Sabbath because he is the Lord of the Sabbath

ii. Second Sabbath Controversy (12:9–14)

12:9 Μεταβάς (nom. sg. masc. of aor. act. ptc. of μεταβαίνω, "go away") is prob. temp. and antecedent (CSB; NIV; LEB), but some tr. regard it as attendant circumstance (NRSV; ESV). Ἐκεῖθεν ("from there") refers to the environ of the grain fields mentioned in 12:1. Ἦλθεν 3rd sg. aor. act. indic. of dep. ἔρχομαι. Εἰς with the obj. τὴν συναγωγήν (4:23) is prob. loc. and refers to entrance into a synagogue building rather than merely a synagogue gathering. Matthew often uses αὐτῶν in ref. to the synagogues (4:23; 9:35; 10:17; 13:54; cf. 23:34). The gen. is prob. poss. Some commentators suggest that the pron. indicates that Matthew writes to a Christian audience that had separated from the synagogue (D&A 1.413–14).

12:10 Ἰδού 1:20. Although the sentence lacks an explicit copula, one is implied, and several ancient mss. supply it. Χείρ, χειρός, ἡ, "hand." Ἔχων (nom. sg. masc. of pres. act. ptc. of ἔχω) is attrib.: "a man who had." Ξηρός, -ά, -όν, "dried up, withered, atrophied." Ἐπηρώτησαν 3rd pl. aor. act. indic. of ἐπερωτάω, "question." After a vb. of speech, λέγοντες is pleonastic. The εἰ serves to introduce an indir. question (BDAG 277b–79c 2): "they asked if it is permissible." Ἔξεστιν 12:2. Τοῖς σάββασιν 12:1. Θεραπεῦσαι (aor. act. inf. of θεραπεύω, "heal") is complementary. Ἵνα with the subjunc. (κατηγορήσωσιν 3rd pl. aor. act. subjunc. of κατηγορέω, "accuse, bring charges against") is a purpose clause expressing the motive of their question. Αὐτοῦ is gen. of dir. obj.

12:11 Ὁ δὲ εἶπεν αὐτοῖς 12:3. The interr. pron. τίς ("who") introduces a question. Ἔσται (3rd sg. fut. indic. of εἰμί) is delib. Ἐκ with the obj. ὑμῶν may identify the group from which one dissociates himself or the group from which one originated (BDAG 295d–98b 1.b; 3.b. and c.). Ἕξει (3rd sg. fut. act. indic. of ἔχω) is prob. delib. Πρόβατον, -ου, τό, "sheep." Ἐάν with the subjunc. (ἐμπέσῃ 3rd sg. aor. act. subjunc. of ἐμπίπτω, "fall") forms the prot. of a third-class cond. statement that presents a hypothetical situation. The adj. ἕν may indicate that the man owns only one sheep or may be a Sem. simply mng. "a sheep" (N 488). The antecedent of τοῦτο is πρόβατον. Τοῖς σάββασιν 12:1. Βόθυνος, -ου, ὁ, "pit." The apod. of the cond. statement is a question. The neg. οὐχί implies a positive response to the question. Κρατήσει (3rd sg. fut. act. indic. of κρατέω) and ἐγερεῖ (3rd sg. fut. act. indic. of ἐγείρω) are delib. fut.

12:12 Πόσος, -η, -ον, is a pron. expressing degree or magnitude. It may introduce a question (LEB; BDAG 736b–37b 1.c.γ.) or mark an exclamation (most EVV). Πόσῳ is dat. of measure (W 166–67). Οὖν does not seem to have an inferential sense here since the affirmation is this clause goes well beyond the implications of the preceding statement. It prob. functions merely as a transitional particle marking the second premise of a logical argument. Διαφέρει (3rd sg. pres. act. indic. of διαφέρω, "be worth more than") is gnomic. Προβάτου (12:11) is a gen. of comp. Ὥστε marks the inference of the syllogism: "therefore." Ἔξεστιν τοῖς σάββασιν 12:10. The adv. καλῶς ("well, rightly [in accord with a standard]") in combination with ποιεῖν (pres. act. inf. of ποιέω) means "to do what is right." Ποιεῖν is a complementary inf.

12:13 Τότε "immediately afterward." Λέγει is historical pres. Ἔκτεινον (2nd sg. aor. act. impv. of ἐκτείνω, "extend, stretch out") demands an immediate response. Τὴν χεῖρα 12:10. Σου is partitive. Ἐξέτεινεν 3rd sg. aor. act. indic. of ἐκτείνω. Ἀπεκατεστάθη 3rd sg. aor. pass. indic. of ἀποκαθίστημι, "restore." Ὑγιής, -ές, "healthy, normal." Ὡς marks a comp.: "like." Ἡ ἄλλη is subst. and refers to the other hand.

12:14 Ἐξελθόντες (nom. pl. masc. of aor. act. ptc. of dep. ἐξέρχομαι) is either temp. ("after they went out") or attendant circumstance (most EVV). Οἱ Φαρισαῖοι 3:7. Συμβούλιον, -ου, τό, "plan." Ἔλαβον 3rd pl. aor. act. indic. of λαμβάνω. BDAG notes that the combination of λαμβάνω and συμβούλιον is a Latinism mng. "form a plan" (957b–c 3). Κατ᾽ αὐτοῦ has a hostile sense: "against him." Ὅπως with the subjunc. (ἀπολέσωσιν 3rd pl. aor. act. subjunc. of ἀπόλλυμι, "destroy") expresses purpose (LEB). Several EVV interpret the ὅπως as a marker of how an event develops: "how." However, the indic. mood of the vb. would have been expected if Matthew intended that sense (BDAG 718a–c).

FOR FURTHER STUDY

See For Further Study 49 and 50

HOMILETICAL SUGGESTIONS

Righteousness Is More Important than Ritual (12:9–14)

1. Acts of mercy are more important than ritual acts (12:7)

2. Compassion to those in crisis is more important than religious observance (12:11–12)
3. Doing good is better than refusing to help others for the sake of ritual (12:13)

4. The Servant of the Lord (12:15–21)

12:15 Γνούς (nom. sg. masc. of aor. act. ptc. of γινώσκω) is prob. causal (cf. NIV; ESV), but several versions treat it as temp. (LEB; NRSV). If temp., γινώσκω must refer to the acquisition of knowledge rather than the poss. of knowledge: "became aware" rather than "knew." Ἀνεχώρησεν 3rd sg. aor. act. indic. of ἀναχωρέω, "departed, leave." Ἐκεῖθεν "from there." Ἠκολούθησαν 3rd pl. aor. act. indic. of ἀκολουθέω, "follow." Αὐτῷ is dat. of dir. obj. If ὄχλοι is not orig., πολλοί would function as a subst. (cf. 7:13, 22). Ἐθεράπευσεν 3rd sg. aor. act. indic. of θεραπεύω, "heal." This is one of several occasions on which the adj. πᾶς modifies a pers. pron. in Matthew (cf. 23:8; 26:31). See Metzger 26.

12:16 Ἐπετίμησεν 3rd sg. aor. act. indic. of ἐπιτιμάω, "warn (to stop an action from happening)." Αὐτοῖς is dat. of dir. obj. Ἵνα is a marker of an obj. that introduces a clause that functions like a complementary inf. Φανερός, -ά, -όν, "known (for what one really is)." Ποιήσωσιν 3rd pl. aor. act. subjunc. of ποιέω. On the mng. of φανερός in combination with ποιέω, see BDAG 1047d–48a.

12:17 Although ἵνα with the subjunc. marked the content of Jesus's warning in the previous clause, here ἵνα with πληρωθῇ (3rd sg. aor. pass. subjunc. of πληρόω) expresses purpose. The vb. is prob. a divine pass. Τὸ ῥηθέν (nom. sg. neut. of aor. pass. ptc. of λέγω) is subst. and a divine pass. (1:22). Διὰ Ἡσαΐου identifies the intermediate agent through whom God spoke. Τοῦ προφήτου is gen. of simple appos. After a verbal referring to speech (or writing), λέγοντος (gen. sg. masc. of pres. act. ptc. of λέγω) is pleonastic. The ptc. introduces a dir. quotation.

12:18 Matthew 12:17–20 contains a quotation of Isaiah 42:1–4, the longest OT quotation in the Gospel. Matthew provides his own tr. of the Heb. text rather than following the LXX (which interpreted the text as a ref. to Jacob/Israel, evidently due to Isa 41:8). See Beale and Carson 42a–44b. Ἰδού 1:20. Παῖς, παιδός, ὁ, "son, servant." In the context of Isaiah, the antecedent of μου is Yahweh (Isa 42:1–7). The antecedent of the rel. pron. ὅν is παῖς. Ἡρέτισα 1st sg. aor. act. indic. of αἱρετίζω, "choose." Ἀγαπητός, -ή, -όν, "loved." The adj. is subst. The gen. μου could be a gen. of relationship but is more likely a subj. gen.: "the one loved by me" (cf. NIV). Εἰς functions as a substitute for ἐν, and not surprisingly a number of later mss. replace εἰς with ἐν. The antecedent of the rel. pron. ὅν is again παῖς. Εὐδόκησεν 3rd sg. aor. act. indic. of εὐδοκέω, "be pleased, take delight." Ἡ ψυχή here refers to the seat of feelings and emotions: "soul." Μου is thus a partitive gen. Θήσω (1st sg. fut. act. indic. of τίθημι, "put, place") is predictive fut., expressing a promise. In context the antecedent of μου is Yahweh. Ἐπί with the acc. (αὐτόν) marks the individual to or for whom something is done and in this context marks the recipient of the Spirit (BDAG 363a–67c 14.b.β.). Κρίσις, -εως, ἡ, "judgment," in this context refers to "justice," in the sense of the administration of what is right (BDAG 569a–d3). Τοῖς ἔθνεσιν may be either dat. of indir. obj. (most

EVV), dat. of advantage, or dat. of disadvantage. Since the passage later refers to the Gentiles' hope, the dat. of disadvantage is unlikely. Ἀπαγγελεῖ (3rd sg. fut. act. indic. of ἀπαγγέλλω, "announce, proclaim") is another predictive fut.

12:19 Ἐρίσει 3rd sg. fut. act. indic. of ἐρίζω, "quarrel" (predictive). Οὐδέ "nor." Κραυγάσει 3rd sg. fut. act. indic. of κραυγάζω, "cry out" (predictive). Ἀκούσει 3rd sg. fut. act. indic. of ἀκούω (predictive). The indef. pron. τις means "anyone" rather than "a certain one." Πλατεία, -ας, ἡ, "wide road or street." Τὴν φωνήν here refers to an "utterance" or one's "speech." The gen. αὐτοῦ is prob. subj.

12:20 Κάλαμος, -ου, ὁ, "reed." Here the noun stands for that which is fragile. Συντετριμμένον (acc. sg. masc. of pf. mid. ptc. of συντρίβω, "damage") is attrib. Κατεάξει 3rd sg. fut. act. indic. of κατάγνυμι, "break" (predictive). Λίνον, -ου, τό, "lamp wick (made from flax)." Τυφόμενον (acc. sg. neut. of pres. pass. ptc. of τύφω, "smolder") is attrib. Σβέσει 3rd sg. fut. act. indic. of σβέννυμι, "put out, quench" (predictive). Ἕως with ἄν and the subjunc. (ἐκβάλῃ 3rd sg. aor. act. subjunc. of ἐκβάλλω) indicates that commencement of an action is dependent on this particular circumstance. Thus the events of the preceding clause will not occur before the time described in the ἕως clause but will occur after it. Ἐκβάλλω here means "to bring about" (BDAG 299b–d 5). Εἰς with the obj. νῖκος (νῖκος, -ου, τό, "victory") may identify a goal: "leads justice to victory." However, the phrase may be an idiom mng. "successfully" (N 495; NASB mg.). Τὴν κρίσιν (12:18).

12:21 With the fut. vb. ἐλπιοῦσιν, the dat. (τῷ ὀνόματι) identifies the thing on which hope is based. Thus the usage resembles the dat. of cause. Ἔθνη 12:18.

FOR FURTHER STUDY

52. Jesus as Isaiah's Servant

Beaton, R. *Isaiah's Christ in Matthew's Gospel*. SNTSMS 123. Cambridge: Cambridge University Press, 2002.

_____. "Messiah and Justice: A Key to Matthew's Use of Isaiah 42.1–4?" *JSNT* 75 (1999): 5–23.

Byrne, B. "The Messiah in Whose Name 'the Gentiles Will Hope' (Matt 12:21): Gentile Inclusion as an Essential Element of Matthew's Christology." *Australian Biblical Review* 50 (2002): 55–73.

Crowe, B. D. "Fulfillment in Matthew as Eschatological Reversal." *WTJ* 75 (2013): 111–27.

Menken, M. J. J. "The Quotation from Isaiah 42:1–4 in Matthew 12:18–21." *Bijdragen* 59 (1998): 251–66.

Myers, A. D. "Isaiah 42 and the Characterization of Jesus in Matthew 12:17–21." Pages 70–89 in *The Synoptic Gospels: Studies in the Function of Scripture in Early Judaism and Christianity*. Edited by C. A. Evans and H. D. Zacharias. London: T&T Clark, 2012.

Neyrey, J. H. "The Thematic Use of Isaiah 42:1–4 in Matthew 12." *Bib* 63 (1982): 457–73.

HOMILETICAL SUGGESTIONS

Jesus Is the Isaianic Servant (12:15–21)

1. He is God's chosen servant

2. He is loved by God
3. He is the Father's delight
4. He is the bearer of God's Spirit
5. He brings justice to the nations
6. His ministry is temporally characterized by quietness and peacefulness
7. The nature of his ministry will change when he executes judgment and restores justice
8. He is the hope for all the nations of the world

5. Jesus's Exorcisms (12:22–30)

12:22 Τότε "afterward." Προσηνέχθη 3rd sg. aor. pass. indic. of προσφέρω, "bring, offer." Αὐτῷ is dat. of indir. obj. Δαιμονιζόμενος nom. sg. masc. of pres. pass. ptc. of dep. δαιμονίζομαι, "be possessed by an evil spirit." The ptc. is subst. Τυφλός, -ή, -όν, "blind." Κωφός, -ή, -όν, "mute, unable to speak." The two adj. are attrib.: "a demon-possessed man who was blind and mute." Ἐθεράπευσεν 3rd sg. aor. act. indic. of θεραπεύω, "heal." Ὥστε with the inf. expresses result. The subst. τὸν κωφόν omits ref. to blindness and demon possession for the sake of brevity. This creates some tension with the inf. phrases since λαλεῖν (pres. act. inf. of λαλέω) reverses the inability to speak and βλέπειν reverses blindness specifically. Some scribes removed the tension by adding καὶ τυφλόν.

12:23 Καί introduces a result. Ἐξίσταντο 3rd pl. impf. mid. indic. of ἐξίστημι, "be amazed" (mid.). Πάντες with an art. pl. noun simply means "all." Ἔλεγον 3rd pl. impf. act. indic. of λέγω. The two impf. vbs. are prog. The neg. interr. particle μήτι either implies a neg. response to the question (more emphatically than the simple neg. μή) or *expresses doubt or uncertainty about the statement ("perhaps;" BDAG 649a–b): "Could this be the Son of David" (CSB; cf. LEB). Ἐστίν 3rd sg. pres. indic. of εἰμί. Ὁ υἱὸς Δαυίδ 1:1.

12:24 Δέ is prob. mildly adversative, contrasting the crowds' affirmation of Jesus's possible messianic identity with the Pharisees' emphatic denial. Ἀκούσαντες (nom. pl. masc. of aor. act. ptc. of ἀκούω) is either *temp. (most EVV) or attendant circumstance. Εἶπον 3rd pl. aor. act. indic. of λέγω. The οὗτος prob. expresses contempt (D&A 2.335) or is dismissive (N 498). Ἐκβάλλει (3rd sg. pres. act. indic. of ἐκβάλλω) may be gnomic so that the Pharisees deny that Jesus performed any exorcism by divine power. Εἰ μή functions as the equivalent of πλήν and means "except (only)." Ἐν with the dat. (τῷ Βεελζεβούλ; 10:25) marks the pers. agent (BDF §219.1; D&A 2.335; contrary to W 373–74): Jesus casts out demons through or by Beelzebul. The cstr. reflects the notion that one can control spirits by calling on the power of higher ranking spirits. Ἄρχοντι (dat. sg. masc. of ἄρχων, "ruler") is dat. of simple appos. Τῶν δαιμονίων is gen. of subord.: "the ruler over the demons."

12:25 Εἰδώς (nom. sg. masc. of pf. act. ptc. of οἶδα) may be temp., *causal, or attendant circumstance (NIV; NRSV). Δέ is mildly adversative and introduces Jesus's rebuttal to the Pharisees' claim. See Metzger 26. Ἐνθύμησις, -εως, ἡ, "thought" (9:4). Αὐτῶν is subj. gen. The use of πᾶς with a sg. anar. noun (βασιλεία) emphasizes the individual members of the class: "every single kingdom." Μερισθεῖσα (nom. sg. fem. of aor. pass. ptc. of μερίζω, "divide") is attrib. The prep. κατά with the gen. (ἑαυτῆς) expresses hostile opposition: "against itself." Ἐρημοῦται (3rd sg. pres. pass. indic. of ἐρημόω, "make desolate, make uninhabited") is prob. gnomic pres. καὶ Σταθήσεται (3rd sg. fut. pass. indic. of ἵστημι, "stand firm" [intrans.]) is prob. gnomic fut.

12:26 Εἰ with the indic. (ἐκβάλλει 3rd sg. pres. act. indic. of ἐκβάλλω) forms the prot. of a first-class cond. sentence that assumes the fulfillment of the prot. for the sake of argument, even though the context makes clear that Satan is not responsible for the exorcisms. Σατανᾶς, -ᾶ, ὁ, "Satan." Ἐπί with the acc. (ἑαυτόν) is a marker of hostile opposition (BDAG 363a–67c 12.b) and is equivalent in sense to the use of κατά with the gen. in 12:25. Ἐμερίσθη 3rd sg. aor. pass. indic. of μερίζω, "divide." Πῶς is an interr. particle that may be used to challenge or reject an assumption (BDAG 900d–901c 1.a.δ.): "by no means; it is impossible." Σταθήσεται 12:25.

12:27 Εἰ with the indic. (ἐκβάλλω) 12:26. Ἐγώ is emphatic and anticipates the comp. between Jesus's exorcisms and the exorcisms of the disciples of the Pharisees. Ἐν with the dat. (Βεελζεβούλ) expresses pers. agency (12:24). Although υἱός normally refers to a son, the term is sometimes used to refer to disciples or pupils to whom the teacher related as a father relates to a son (BDAG 1024c–27a 2.a.). Ἐν with the dat. marks pers. agency and with the interr. pron. τίνι (dat. sg. masc.) means "by whom?" Ἐκβάλλουσιν 3rd pl. pres. act. indic. of ἐκβάλλω. Διά with the acc. (τοῦτο) is causal and thus introduces a result of the previous ref. to exorcisms performed by the disciples of the Pharisees. Αὐτοί is emphatic. Κριτής, -οῦ, ὁ, "judge." Ἔσονται 3rd pl. fut. mid. indic. of εἰμί. The fut. is pred. and may refer to upcoming criticisms from their own students in rabbinic debates (H 1.342; cf. N 499) or eschatological judgment in which the disciples of the Pharisees would assist in condemning their teachers for their irrational rejection of Jesus (D&A 2.339). Ὑμῶν is obj. gen.

12:28 Δέ is prob. adversative and contrasts the true implications of Jesus's exorcisms with the explanations of the Pharisees. Εἰ with the indic. (ἐκβάλλω) marks the prot. of a first-class cond. statement and assumes the fulfillment of the prot. for the sake of argument. However, the context demonstrates that both the prot. and its resulting apod. are true. Ἐν with the dat. πνεύματι clearly expresses pers. agency. The gen. θεοῦ may express source ("Spirit sent by God") or be attrib. ("divine Spirit"). Ἐγώ is emphatic and implies that Jesus's exorcisms were unique manifestations of the power of the Spirit. Ἄρα marks an inference. Since it is unnecessary in the apod. of a cond. statement, it should be considered emphatic (BDAG 127b–d 2.a.). Ἔφθασεν (3rd sg. aor. act. indic. of φθάνω, "arrive, overtake") is a constative aor. and describes an event that has already occurred. Although some scholars have argued that the aor. tense is futuristic, the context does not support this classification (N 501; D&A 2.340; H 1.343). Ἐπί with the acc. (ὑμᾶς) is used to describe divine blessings that come upon someone (BDAG 363a–67d 14.b.β.). The gen. τοῦ θεοῦ following ἡ βασιλεία is relatively rare in Matthew (21:31, 43). This phrase forms a better contrast with "kingdom of Satan" (12:26) and a better parallel to "Spirit of God" than the phrase "kingdom of heaven," which Matthew normally preferred (H 1.343; N 501; D&A 2.339).

12:29 The particle ἤ is used simply to introduce a rhetorical question that is part of a series of such questions (NIV: "or again;" see 12:26, 27), and its normal disjunctive sense is significantly weakened. The particle suggests that Jesus is adding a new point to his earlier argument. The interr. particle πῶς often questions the manner or way in which an objective is achieved, but here it questions the possibility of an action apart from the step identified in the prot. introduced by ἐάν. Δύναται 3rd sg. pres. mid. indic. of dep. δύναμαι. The indef. pron. τις means "anyone." Thus the cstr. means: "or how could anyone possibly be able to . . ." Εἰσελθεῖν (aor. act. inf. of dep. εἰσέρχομαι) is complementary. Ἰσχυρός, -ά, -όν, "strong." Τοῦ ἰσχυροῦ is subst. (the gen. is poss.) and may refer specifically to Satan or to a human being who serves as a ref. to Satan in a human analogy (BDAG 483d–84a 1.a. and b.). Σκεῦος, -ους, τό, "property, possessions." The pl. with a gen. of poss. (αὐτοῦ) is sometimes uses to refer to all of a person's possessions (BDAG 927c–28a 1.). Ἁρπάσαι aor. act. inf. of ἁρπάζω, "snatch, steal." Ἐάν with the neg. μή is used to introduce a necessary condition: "unless." The neut. sg. form of the adj. πρῶτος (πρῶτον) is used as an adv. of time ("first") and indicates that the necessary condition must precede the actions in the previous clause. Δήσῃ 3rd sg. aor. act. subjunc. of δέω, "bind, tie up." Καί introduces the result of the preceding clause. The temp. particle τότε means "after that" and confirms what was already implied by the πρῶτον: the binding must precede the plundering. Διαρπάσει 3rd sg. fut. act. indic. of διαρπάζω, "plunder." The fut. may be gnomic or predictive (in which case the choice of the fut. tense was influenced by the "first/then afterward" contrast).

12:30 This verse may begin a new paragraph (N 503) and relate more closely to the discussion that follows than to that which precedes. However, "the one who is not with me" may refer to the Jewish exorcists mentioned in 12:27 and thus relate more closely to the preceding context, thereby supporting the paragraph division in the UBS[5] (H 1.344). The use of the art. with the ptc. ὤν (nom. sg. masc. of pres. ptc. of εἰμί) marks it as subst. The prep. μετά with the gen. (ἐμοῦ) expresses close association, in which someone is an ally of another (BDAG 636b–38b 2.a.γ.). The prep. κατά with the gen. (ἐμοῦ) expresses hostile opposition. Ἐστίν 3rd sg. pres. indic. of εἰμί. The art. ptc. συνάγων (nom. sg. masc. of pres. act. ptc. of συνάγω, "gather") is also subst. Σκορπίζει (3rd sg. pres. act. indic. of σκορπίζω, "scatter"). The pres. tense may be gnomic since the statement sounds proverbial.

FOR FURTHER STUDY

53. Jesus's Exorcisms

See For Further Study 21

Caragounis, C. C. "Kingdom of God, Son of Man and Jesus's Self-Understanding, 2 Pts." *TynBul* 40 (1989): 223–38.

Dunn, J. D. G. "Matthew 12:28/Luke 11:20—a Word of Jesus." Pages 29–49 in *Eschatology and the New Testament: Essays in Honor of George Raymond Beasley-Murray*. Edited by H. Gloer. Peabody, MA: Hendrickson, 1988.

54. The Pharisees as Exorcists

Shirock, R. J., Jr. "Whose Exorcists Are They? The Referents of Οἱ Υἱοὶ Ὑμῶν at Matthew 12:27/Luke 11:19." *JSNT* 46 (1992): 41–51.

55. The Pharisees' Charges Against Jesus

MacLaurin, E. C. B. "Beelzeboul." *NovT* 20 (1978): 156–60.

Sheets, D. D. "Jesus as Demon-Possessed." Pages 27–49 in *Who Do My Opponents Say That I Am? An Investigation of the Accusations Against Jesus*. Edited by S. McKnight and J. B. Modica. New York: T&T Clark, 2008.

HOMILETICAL SUGGESTIONS

Davidic or Demonic? Jesus's Power over Demons (12:22–30)

1. Demonic?
   a. Satan is too smart to use his own power against his own kingdom (12:25–26)
   b. It is inconsistent to ascribe Jewish exorcisms to the power of God and Jesus's exorcisms to the power of Satan (12:27)
   c. Failure to defend Jesus against such ridiculous charges is tantamount to opposing him (12:27, 30)
   d. The need to ascribe Jesus's exorcisms to Satan rather than claiming that they simply did not occur shows that the exorcisms were undeniable
2. Davidic!
   a. David (1 Sam 16:23) was known for his power over demons
   b. Jesus's authority over demons shows he is the "son of David" (12:23)
   c. This "son of David" has inaugurated the kingdom of God (12:28)
   d. This "son of David" is plundering Satan's kingdom (12:29)

6. Blaspheming the Holy Spirit (12:31–32)

12:31 Διὰ τοῦτο ("because of this") marks this paragraph as an inference of the preceding discussion. The antecedent of τοῦτο is prob. the entire preceding discussion (12:25–30) and not merely 12:30. Λέγω ὑμῖν 5:18. The use of πᾶς with a sg. anar. noun (ἁμαρτία καὶ βλασφημία) normally focuses on the individual members of the class: "every single sin . . ." However, this is likely an example of the use of πᾶς to designate every kind belonging to a class (BDAG 782b–84c 5). Since Matthew sometimes repeats the adj. πᾶς when he intends it to modify more than one noun in a series (4:23; 9:35; 10:1), the single πᾶς may be regarded as modifying only the noun ἁμαρτία. This could suggest that the noun βλασφημία is a subcategory of "sin." Thus the καί may be ascensive: "every (kind of) sin, even blasphemy." This interpretation avoids the apparent contradiction between the two clauses that results if πᾶς modifies βλασφημία (every blasphemy will be forgiven, but blasphemy of the Spirit will not). However, Matthew 2:4 and 12:25 are examples in which Matthew appears to have intended a single πᾶς to modify two nouns joined by a conj. (and 12:25 uses a sg. vb. like 12:31), and this is likely so here as well. If the πᾶς modifies both nouns (most EVV), the apparent contradiction may be removed by the insertion of "other" ("every [other] sin and blasphemy will be forgiven . . .") or by transforming the next clause into an exception clause (NLT). This is preferable to adding the phrase "against God" to describe the blasphemy in the first clause (NIRV; cf. CEV) since stating that blasphemy against God will be forgiven but blasphemy of the Spirit will not could be taken as casting doubt on the deity of the Spirit. Βλασφημία, ας, ἡ, "blasphemy." Ἀφεθήσεται (3rd sg. fut. pass. indic. of ἀφίημι, "forgive") is predictive and refers to final forgiveness in eschatological judgment. Δέ is adversative and prob. introduces the single exception to the previous clause. Τοῦ πνεύματος is an obj. gen.

12:32 The combination of the rel. pron. ὅς and the particle of contingency ἐάν means "whoever" or "anyone who." The ἐάν required the use of the subjunc. (εἴπῃ 3rd sg. aor. act. subjunc. of λέγω). Κατά with the gen. (τοῦ υἱοῦ τοῦ ἀνθρώπου, 9:6) expresses hostile opposition: "against." Ἀφεθήσεται 12:31. The combination of ὅς with ἄν is equivalent to the ὅς ἐάν cstr. Κατά with the gen. (τοῦ πνεύματος τοῦ ἁγίου) expresses hostile opposition. Although Matthew normally used the fourth attrib. position to describe the Holy Spirit (1:18, 20; 3:11), the cstr. τοῦ πνεύματος τοῦ ἁγίου is in the second attrib. position, in which both the noun and the adj. are emphasized and the adj. is climactic (W 306–7; R 777). For the first attrib. position, see Matt 28:19. The οὔτε . . . οὔτε cstr. means "neither . . . nor." The prep. ἐν serves as a temp. marker mng. "during." The dem. pron. τούτῳ is functioning as an adj.: "this age." The art. ptc. μέλλοντι (dat. sg. masc. of pres. act. ptc. of μέλλω) is subst. and after ref. to "this age" refers to the "future or coming age."

FOR FURTHER STUDY

56. The Unforgiveable Sin

Boring, M. E. "Unforgiveable Sin Logion Mark 3:28–29/Matt 12:31–32/Luke 12:10: Formal Analysis and History of the Tradition." *NovT* 18 (1976): 258–79.
O'Neill, J. C. "The Unforgivable Sin." *JSNT* 19 (1983): 37–42.
Williams, J. G. "Note on the Unforgivable Sin Logion." *NTS* 12 (1965): 75–77.

7. Words Reveal One's True Character (12:33–37)

12:33 The ἤ . . . ἤ cstr. means "either . . . or." Ποιήσατε (2nd pl. aor. act. impv. of ποιέω) expresses urgency. Several scholars regard the impv. as cond. Δένδρον, -ου, τό, "tree." The clause καὶ τὸν καρπὸν αὐτοῦ καλόν is either a second object (with its pred.) of the vb. ποιήσατε (ESV) or is elliptical and implies a fut. form of the vb. εἰμί, in which case the impv. is cond.: "Make the tree good and its fruit will be good" (NIV; CSB; H 1.348; D&A 2.349; see W 489–90). Although the latter view better suits the context, the absence of an explicit fut. indic. vb. in the clause that would function as the prot. and Matthew's use of the acc. (rather than nom.) forms of κάρπος and κάλος pose insurmountable difficulties for it. BDAG (839a–42a 5.b.) notes that ποιέω may mean "assume" or "suppose" but gives only the pres. text as a possible example from the NT (though Herodotus and Plato apparently used the term in this way). Perhaps the best solution is that of Nolland (506) who suggests an implied vb. in the second clause: "Make the tree good, and it will make the fruit good." The wise farmer knows that he improves the quality of his fruit by applying fertilizer to the tree since the tree determines the quality of the fruit. Σαπρός, -ά, -όν, "bad, of poor quality." The γάρ is causal. The prep. ἐκ identifies a source of information or insight (BDAG 295d–98b 3.g.β.). Γινώσκεται (3rd sg. pres. pass. indic. of γινώσκω) is gnomic.

12:34 Γεννήματα ἐχιδνῶν 3:7. Although the interr. particle πῶς may question the manner or way in which an action is performed, esp. in combination with δύναμαι (12:29), the particle introduces rhetorical questions that challenge the possibility of an action (see also 23:33). Thus Jesus is not questioning how his opponents succeed in speaking good things despite their evil natures (most EVV) but is emphatically denying that his opponents are capable of speaking good things because of these evil natures (NIV). Thus the idea seems to be "how can you possibly be able to speak good things . . .?" Δύνασθε 2nd pl. pres. mid. indic. of dep. δύναμαι. Ἀγαθά is subst. and refers not to polite pleasantries but to confessing Jesus's identity as Immanuel and Savior. Λαλεῖν (pres. act. inf. of λαλέω) is complementary. The ptc. ὄντες (nom. pl. masc. of pres. ptc. of εἰμί) may be temp. (most EVV), attrib. (NIV), causal ("since you are evil"), cond. ("if you are evil"), or concessive ("even though you are evil"). Despite the popularity of the temp. classification, the concessive view should be seriously considered (7:11). Πονηρός, -ά, -όν, "evil." Γάρ introduces the reason it is impossible for the evil to speak good things. The prep. ἐκ with the gen. (τοῦ περισσεύματος) indicates source (15:19). Περίσσευμα, -ατος, τό, "abundance, fullness." The gen. τῆς καρδίας is difficult to classify. The phrase τοῦ περισσεύματος τῆς καρδίας appears to mean "what the heart is full of" (BDAG 805a). Thus the gen. may be conceived of as the opposite of the gen. of content (W 92–94) and might be called the gen. of container. Alternatively, the gen. could be considered objective and the phrase tr.: "the things that fill the heart." Λαλεῖ 3rd sg. pres. act. indic. of λαλέω. The pres. is gnomic.

12:35 Ἐκ with the gen. (τοῦ ἀγαθοῦ θησαυροῦ) expresses source. Θησαυρός, -οῦ, ὁ, "treasure, treasure chest." Ἐκβάλλει 3rd sg. pres. act. indic. of ἐκβάλλω. The pres. tense is gnomic. Ἀγαθά and πονηρά are subst. and due to the neut. gender mean "good/evil things."

12:36 Λέγω δὲ ὑμῖν 5:18. The ὅτι introduces dir. discourse. Πᾶν with an anar. sg. noun (ῥῆμα) focuses on the individual members of a class: "every single word." Ῥῆμα is a pendent nom., a nom. placed at the beginning of the sentence that serves as the logical rather than the syntactical subj. of the sentence and is replaced by a pron. (αὐτοῦ) in the main clause. Ἀργός, -ή, -όν, "worthless, useless." The rel. clause ὃ λαλήσουσιν (3rd pl. pres. act. indic. of λαλέω) offers a description of the worthless words. Ἀποδώσουσιν (3rd pl. fut. act. indic. of ἀποδίδωμι, "give an account (with λόγον)" is predictive, and the prep. phrase at the end of the sentence shows that it is eschatological. Περί with the gen. (αὐτοῦ; antecedent = ῥῆμα) identifies the offense for which one must give an account (BDAG 797c–98d 1.b.). The prep ἐν with the obj. ἡμέρᾳ is clearly temp.: "on/during the day of judgment." The gen. κρίσεως is attrib. and refers to the occasion on which eschatological divine judgment occurs.

12:37 Γάρ introduces the reason people must give account for their speech on judgment day. BDAG categorizes the use of ἐκ in this verse as identifying "the underlying rule or principle." However, this is mistaken. The words are the basis for the judgment, but the principles that determine the judgment are: (1) whether the Spirit is blasphemed (12:32), and (2) whether the words are worthless (12:36). Although λόγος in 12:36 referred to an accounting for one's actions, here λόγος means "word." The gen. σου is subj. and refers to the words that "you" speak. Δικαιωθήσῃ 2nd sg. fut. pass. indic. of δικαιόω, "pronounce innocent, justify." Καταδικασθήσῃ 2nd sg. fut. pass. indic. of καταδικάζω, "pronounce guilty, condemn."

FOR FURTHER STUDY

57. False Prophecy

> Minear, P. S. "False Prophecy and Hypocrisy in the Gospel of Matthew." Pages 76–93 in *Neues Testament und Kirche: Für Rudolph Schnackenburg*. Edited by J. Gnilka. Freiburg: Herder, 1974.

HOMILETICAL SUGGESTIONS

The Unforgivable Sin (12:31–37)

1. The unforgivable sin is ascribing the miraculous works of Jesus to the power of Satan
2. One's words show the true condition of the heart and will be used as evidence in final judgment
3. Ascribing Jesus's miracles to the power of Satan shows that a person is the offspring of vipers rather than a child of God

8. The Demand for a Sign (12:38–42)

12:38 Τότε means "(immediately/soon) after that." Ἀπεκρίθησαν 3rd pl. aor. pass. indic. of dep. ἀποκρίνομαι. Αὐτῷ is dat. of dir. obj. After τινες, the gen. γραμματέων and Φαρισαίων are partitive. Although the phrase τῶν γραμματέων καὶ Φαρισαίων does not satisfy one important criterion of the Granville Sharp rule since the nouns are pl., the shared def. art. presents the scribes and Pharisees as unified in their requests. This is prob. an example in which the first group should be viewed as a subset of the second (N 509). Λέγοντες (nom. pl. masc. of pres. act. ptc. of λέγω) is pleonastic. Διδάσκαλε is simple voc. Θέλομεν 1st pl. pres. act. indic. of θέλω. The prep. ἀπό with the gen. (σοῦ) marks the originator of an action: "from/by you." Σημεῖον, -ου, τό, "sign, miracle." Ἰδεῖν (aor. act. inf. of ὁράω) is complementary.

12:39 The def. art. ὁ functions as a substitute for the pers. pron. αὐτός. Ἀποκριθείς (nom. sg. masc. of aor. pass. ptc. of dep. ἀποκρίνομαι) is pleonastic. Εἶπεν 3rd sg. aor. act. indic. of λέγω. The antecedent of αὐτοῖς is the scribes and Pharisees of 12:38. Γενεά, -ᾶς, ἡ, "generation." Πονηρά 9:4. Μοιχαλίς, -ίδος, ἡ, "adultery" (sometimes used as an adj.: "adulterous, who commits adultery"). Σημεῖον 12:38. Ἐπιζητεῖ (3rd sg. pres. act. indic. of ἐπιζητέω, "seek") is prob. gnomic, thus the quest for a sign indicates the generation's true character. Καί introduces a concession: "and yet." Δοθήσεται (3rd sg. fut. pass. indic. of δίδωμι) is predictive. The εἰ μή combination introduces an exception. The gen. Ἰωνᾶ ("of Jonah") is difficult to classify. Scholars have suggested: (1) a sign performed by Jonah (subj. gen.); (2) a sign given to Jonah (obj. gen.); or (3) Jonah functioning as a sign (gen. of appos.). See N 510–11. The third category comes closest since 12:40 shows that the experience of Jonah functioned as a sign. In the gen. of appos., the head noun identifies a broader category of which the gen. is an example. Τοῦ προφήτου is gen. of simple appos.

12:40 Γάρ is explanatory and clarifies the promise of the sign of Jonah. Ὥσπερ (in the prot.) and οὕτως in the apod. marks a close comp. between the experience of Jonah and that of the Son of Man. Ἦν 3rd sg. impf. indic. of εἰμί. Ἐν with the dat. (τῇ κοιλίᾳ) identifies a location. Κοιλία, -ας, ἡ, "belly, stomach." Κῆτος, -ους, τό, "sea monster, huge fish." The gen. τοῦ κήτους is partitive. Τρεῖς ἡμέρας καὶ τρεῖς νύκτας is an idiom that may refer to an entire day and any portion of the preceding and following day. Ἔσται (3rd sg. fut. mid. indic. of εἰμί) is predictive. Ὁ υἱὸς τοῦ ἀνθρώπου 9:6. Ἐν with the dat. (τῇ καρδίᾳ) identifies a location. Τῆς γῆς is partitive.

12:41 Νινευίτης, -ου, ὁ, "Ninevite, inhabitant of Nineveh." Νινευῖται is appos. to ἄνδρες. Ἀναστήσονται 3rd pl. fut. mid. indic. of ἀνίστημι, "rise up." Although the vb. may mean to appear in order to carry out a particular function (BDAG 83a–85a 9), the vb. may also mean "rise from the dead" and the use of the vb. ἐγείρω in 12:42 suggests that is the sense here (D&A 2.357–8; H 1.354). The fut. is predictive and eschatological. Ἐν with the dat. (τῇ κρίσει) is temp.: "during the (final) judgment." Μετά with the gen. (τῆς γενεᾶς) may be a marker of placement ("among") or association ("with;" most EVV). The near dem. pron. ταύτης shows that the phrase refers to the evil and adulterous generation of 12:39. Κατακρινοῦσιν 3rd pl. fut. act. indic. of κατακρίνω, "condemn." The antecedent of αὐτήν is γενεᾶς. Ὅτι is causal. Μετενόησαν 3rd pl. aor. act. indic. of μετανοέω, "repent." The use of the prep. εἰς does not fit in the common categories. It prob. means "at, in the face of" with the sense "in response to" (BDAG 288d–93c 10.a.), but Mantey argued that the sense is causal: "because of" (H. E. Dana and J. R. Mantey, *A Manual Grammar of the Greek New Testament* [New York: Macmillan, 1955], 104). Κήρυγμα, -ατος, τό, "preaching, proclamation." Ἰωνᾶ 12:39. Καί introduces a concessive clause: "and yet." Ἰδού 1:20. Πλεῖον is the nom. sg. neut. comp. form of the adj. πολύς, πολλή, πολύ, which here refers to being higher on a scale: "greater." The adj. is subst.: "something greater." Ἰωνᾶ is gen. of comp. On the gender of the adj. and the possibility of translating it "someone greater," see 12:6. Note also that 12:40 clearly compared Jonah to Jesus. The adv. of place ὧδε means "here, in this place."

12:42 Βασίλισσα, -ης, ἡ, "queen." Νότος, -ου, ὁ, "south." Ἐγερθήσεται 3rd sg. fut. pass. indic. of ἐγείρω, "raise (from the dead)." Ἐν τῇ κρίσει μετὰ τῆς γενεᾶς ταύτης καὶ κατακρινεῖ αὐτήν, ὅτι 12:42. Ἦλθεν 3rd sg. aor. act. indic. of dep. ἔρχομαι. The prep. ἐκ marks the direction from which one comes (BDAG 295c–98b). Πέρας, -ατος, τό, "ends, limits." The gen. τῆς γῆς is partitive. Ἀκοῦσαι (aor. act. inf. of ἀκούω) expresses purpose. Καὶ ἰδοὺ πλεῖον Σολομῶνος ὧδε 12:41.

FOR FURTHER STUDY

58. The Demand for a Sign

Chow, S. "The Sign of Jonah Reconsidered: Matthew 12:38–42 and Luke 11:29–32."
Theology & Life 15–16 (1993): 53–60.

Hutchinson, A. M. "Christian Prophecy and Matthew 12:38–42, a Test Exegesis." *SBLSP*
11 (1977): 379–85.

Linton, O. "Demand for a Sign from Heaven (Mk 8:11–12 and Parallels)." *ST* 19 (1965):
112–29.

HOMILETICAL SUGGESTIONS

Prove It! (12:38–42)

1. The demand for a sign was hypocritical since the people had just rejected such a sign (12:22–37)
2. The hypocritical demand for a sign exposed the wickedness of these people (12:39)
3. Jesus offered the supreme sign of his identity by his resurrection from the dead (12:40)
4. The scribes and Pharisees were more wicked than notorious Gentiles who ultimately repented (12:41–42)
5. Jesus is greater than Jonah since he is the God of the prophets rather than a mere prophet of God
6. Jesus is greater than Solomon because he is a perfect and eternal king

9. The Parable of Demonic Habitation (12:43–45)

12:43 Ὅταν with the subjunc. (ἐξέλθῃ 3rd sg. aor. act. subjunc. of dep. ἐξέρχομαι) has some similarities to a third-class cond. cstr. because the prot. is a condition for the apod. However, with third-class condition the contingency is whether the action of the prot. occurs. With ὅταν and the subjunc., the action is assumed to occur and often to occur repeatedly. The contingency is the time in which the action occurs. Thus the cstr. is best tr. "whenever . . ." Ἀκάθαρτος, -ον, "unclean." The prep. ἐκ prefixed to the vb. makes the prep. ἀπό somewhat redundant and emphasizes the separation of the demon from the person he formerly inhabited. Διέρχεται 3rd sg. pres. mid. indic. of dep. διέρχομαι, "travel around (from place to place)." The pres. tense is gnomic; this is the manner in which demons typically behave. Διά with the gen. (τόπων: "places") marks extension through an area. Ἄνυδρος, -ον, "waterless, dry." Ζητοῦν (nom. sg. neut. of pres. act. ptc. of ζητέω) may be attendant circumstance or purpose. Ἀνάπαυσις, -εως, ἡ, "rest, resting place." Καί is concessive: "and yet." Εὑρίσκει 3rd sg. pres. act. indic. of εὑρίσκω, "find." The pres. tense is gnomic.

12:44 Τότε "after that." Λέγει (3rd sg. pres. act. indic. of λέγω) is gnomic. The prep. εἰς with τὸν οἶκον indicates that the demon reenters the house/person. Μου is a gen. of poss. and shows that the demon never relinquished ownership of the person he formally inhabited. Ἐπιστρέψω (1st sg. fut. act. indic. of ἐπιστρέφω, "return"). The fut.

tense here is voluntative (Smyth §1912) and thus expresses the decision of the demon to return to his home rather than merely making a prediction that he will return home. The adv. ὅθεν marks the place from which one came: "from whence." Ἐξῆλθον 1st sg. aor. act. indic. of dep. ἐξέρχομαι. Ἐλθόν (nom. sg. neut. of aor. act. ptc. of dep. ἔρχομαι) is prob. temp. (most EVV). Εὑρίσκει 3rd sg. pres. act. indic. of εὑρίσκω, "find." The three ptc. are prob. attrib. (most EVV) although it is possible that the last two ptc. are concessive: "unoccupied, even though it was swept and decorated." Although the noun τὸν οἶκον that appears in D is not orig., the scribe was correct that it is implied. Σχολάζοντα acc. sg. masc. of pres. act. ptc. of σχολάζω, "be unoccupied." Σεσαρωμένον acc. sg. masc. of pf. pass. ptc. of σαρόω, "sweep." Κεκοσμημένον acc. sg. masc. of pf. pass. ptc. of κοσμέω, "decorate, organize."

12:45 Τότε "after that." Πορεύεται 3rd sg. pres. mid. indic. of dep. πορεύομαι. Παραλαμβάνει 3rd sg. pres. act. indic. of παραλαμβάνω, "take along (as company)." The pres. tense of both vbs. is prob. gnomic. Jesus is describing typical demonic behavior. The prep. μετά with the gen. (ἑαυτοῦ) expresses accompaniment: "together with himself." Πονηρότερα is the comp. form (acc. pl. neut.) of the adj. πονηρός: "more evil, wicked." After the comp. adj., ἑαυτοῦ is clearly a gen. of comp. Εἰσελθόντα (nom. pl. neut. of aor. act. ptc. of dep. εἰσέρχομαι) is prob. temp. or *attendant circumstance (most EVV). Note that although neut. pl. nouns take sg. vbs., they use pl. ptc. Κατοικεῖ 3rd sg. pres. act. indic. of κατοικέω, "take up residence." The implied subj. of the vb. is πνεύματα. Ἐκεῖ "there" (adv. of place). Γίνεται 3rd sg. pres. mid. indic. of dep. γίνομαι. The art. adj. ἔσχατα and πρώτων are subst. BDAG (397c–98a 2.a.) suggests that the adj. should be tr. "the last state," and most EVV follow this advice. The pl. number may suggest that the adj. refers to multiple experiences. However, the use of the pl. adj. in a sim. comp. in 2 Peter 2:20 suggests that the use of the pl. may be idiomatic. Χείρονα is the comp. form (nom. pl. neut.) of the adj. κακός: "worse." After the comp. adj., τῶν πρώτων is clearly gen. of comp. The comp. adv. οὕτως is used to introduce the moral of a parable (BDAG 741d–42c 1.b.). Ἔσται (3rd sg. pres. indic. of εἰμί) is predictive. Καί is prob. adjunctive: "also, too." Γενεᾷ (γενεά, -ᾶς, ἡ, "generation") is prob. dat. of ref. The near dem. pron. αὕτη suggests that Jesus was referring to the pres. generation (12:38–39).

FOR FURTHER STUDY

59. *The Parable About the Wandering Demon*

Gould, E. P. "Matt. xii. 43–45." *JBL* 3 (1883): 62–62.
Plummer, A. "The Parable of the Demon's Return." *ExpTim* 3 (1892): 349–51.

HOMILETICAL SUGGESTIONS

From Bad to Worse (12:43–45)

1. The exorcisms of the Pharisees left victims vulnerable to worse possession since they did not impart the Holy Spirit

2. Those who reject Jesus will also become more and more wicked and suffer worse and worse consequences for that wickedness

10. Jesus's Spiritual Family (12:46–50)

12:46 Ἔτι is an adv. expressing continuance and indicating that Jesus's speech was still in progress when his family appeared. Λαλοῦντος (gen. sg. masc. of pres. act. ptc. of λαλέω) is gen. abs., temp., and contemp. Ἰδού 1:20. Εἱστήκεισαν 3rd pl. pluperf. act. indic. of ἵστημι. With this particular lexeme, the pf. is often the equivalent in sense to the pres. and the pluperf. to the aorist ("pluperf. with simple past force;" W 586). Ἔξω is an adv. of place: "outside." Ζητοῦντες (nom. pl. masc. of pres. act. ptc. of ζητέω) is prob. attrib.: "who were seeking." Λαλῆσαι (aor. act. inf. of λαλέω) is complementary.

12:47 This verse is absent from several early mss. Nevertheless, the authenticity of the verse is supported by the context, since 12:48 has Jesus reply to a speaker who is only mentioned in this verse. The verse could have been accidentally omitted due to homoeoteleuton since both verses 46 and 47 end with λαλῆσαι (in addition to other similarities which would facilitate such an error). See Metzger 26–27. Εἶπεν 3rd sg. aor. act. indic. of λέγω. Ἰδού 1:20. Ἑστήκασιν 3rd pl. pf. act. indic. of ἵστημι. See 12:46.

12:48 The def. art. ὁ serves as a substitute for the 3rd pers. pron. αὐτός. Ἀποκριθείς (nom. sg. masc. of aor. pass. ptc. of dep. ἀποκρίνομαι) is pleonastic and means "in reply." Εἶπεν 12:47. Λέγοντι (dat. sg. masc. of pres. act. ptc. of λέγω) is subst. Τίς and τίνες are interr. and introduce a rhetorical question that Jesus will answer himself.

12:49 Ἐκτείνας (nom. sg. masc. of aor. act. ptc. of ἐκτείνω, "stretch, extend") is attendant circumstance. Ἐπί with the acc. (τοὺς μαθητάς) may mean "over," but it more likely refers to movement in a particular direction: "toward." Thus the gesture points directly at Jesus's disciples. Εἶπεν 12:47. Ἰδού 1:20. The gen. μου is gen. of relationship.

12:50 The γάρ introduces the reason Jesus identified his disciples as his family. The pron. ὅστις ("anyone") is already indef. (due to the suffixed indef. pron.), but the use of ἄν with the subjunc. (ποιήσῃ 3rd sg. aor. act. subjunc. of ποιέω) serves to heighten the indefiniteness: "whoever" (BDAG 729d–30b 1.e.β.). For the combination of ποιέω with τὸ θέλημα τοῦ πατρός μου τοῦ ἐν οὐρανοῖς, see 7:21. The masc. pron. αὐτός is the generic use of the masc. Some tr. seek to preserve the generic sense by eliminating the pron. (NIV; ESV; NRSV). However, the pron. is emphatic and omitting the pron. in tr. results in the loss of this emphasis. The LEB retains the pron., but translates it "he," which may confuse modern readers. Thus the rendering of the CSB is to be preferred: "that person." Μου is gen. of relationship. The use of the conj. καί rather than the disjunctive ἤ ("or") indicates that the obedient disciple is not brother or sister or mother to Jesus (depending on age and gender) but enjoys all three of these family roles at once (regardless of age and gender). Jesus's affection for his disciples is like the affection one has for all of one's beloved family members combined (N 519). The pres. ἐστίν is gnomic.

FOR FURTHER STUDY

60. Jesus's Spiritual Family

Evans, C. A. "Context, Family, and Formation." Pages 11–24 in *The Cambridge Companion to Jesus*. Edited by M. Bockmuehl. Cambridge: Cambridge University Press, 2001.

Strickert, F. M. "Jesus's True Family: The Synoptic Tradition and Thomas." Pages 246–57 in *For a Later Generation: The Transformation of Tradition in Israel, Early Judaism, and Early Christianity*. Edited by R. A. Argall, B. A. Bow, and R. A. Werline. Harrisburg, PA: Trinity Press, 2000.

Yeo, K. "The Mother and Brothers of Jesus (Lk 8:19–21, Mk 3:31–35, Mt 12:46–50)." *AsJT* 6 (1992): 311–17.

HOMILETICAL SUGGESTIONS

Our New Family (12:46–50)

1. Jesus's disciples form his spiritual family
2. Obedience to Jesus is an essential characteristic of Jesus's family members
3. Jesus's love for his disciples is like the love of all family relationships combined

F. THIRD DISCOURSE: PARABLES ON THE KINGDOM (13:1–53)

1. Teaching on the Shores of Galilee (13:1–2)

13:1 Ἐν with the dat. (τῇ ἡμέρᾳ ἐκείνῃ) is clearly temp.: "on that day." However, the noun ἡμέρα prob. refers to a general time period rather than a day consisting of twenty-four hours (BDAG 436c–38c 4.a.). Ἐξελθών (nom. sg. masc. of aor. act. ptc. of dep. ἐξέρχομαι) may be temp. or attendant circumstance (most EVV). Τῆς οἰκίας is gen. of separation. Ἐκάθητο (3rd sg. impf. mid. indic. of dep. κάθημαι, "sit") is either prog. (most EVV) or *conative. The context shows that Jesus was unable to remain sitting beside the sea, despite his desire. Παρά with the acc. (τὴν θάλασσαν) is a marker of position that extends along a line: "at the edge of the sea" or "at the shoreline."

13:2 Συνήχθησαν 3rd pl. aor. pass. indic. of συνάγω. Since ὄχλοι already refers to a large number of people, the adj. πολλοί and the pl. number of the noun and adj. emphasize even more the great numbers. Ὥστε with an inf. (καθῆσθαι pres. mid. inf. of dep. κάθημαι, "sit") expresses result. Αὐτόν is acc. subj. of the inf. Ἐμβάντα (acc. sg. masc. of aor. act. ptc. of ἐμβαίνω, "embark, board [a ship]") is temp. The adj. πᾶς with the sg. art. noun (ὁ ὄχλος) views the group as a whole: "the entire crowd." Ἐπί with the acc. (τὸν αἰγιαλόν) serves as a marker of place: "at, on." Αἰγιαλός, -οῦ, ὁ, "shore." Εἰστήκει (3rd sg. pluperf. act. indic. of ἵστημι, "stand") is pluperf. with a simple past force (W 586).

2. The Parable of the Sower (13:3–9)

13:3 Ἐλάλησεν 3rd sg. aor. act. indic. of λαλέω, "speak." Πολλά is subst. and because it is neut. pl. means "many things." Ἐν with the dat. (παραβολαῖς) marks the instr. Λέγων (nom. sg. masc. of pres. act. ptc. of λέγω) is pleonastic. Ἰδού 1:20. Ἐξῆλθεν 3rd sg. aor. act. indic. of dep. ἐξέρχομαι. The art. ptc. σπείρων (nom. sg. masc. of pres. act. ptc. of σπείρω, "plant or scatter seeds") is subst.: "sower" (most EVV) or "farmer" (NIV). The inf. σπείρειν (pres. act. inf. of σπείρω) with the gen. art. (τοῦ) expresses purpose.

13:4 Ἐν with the art. inf. (τῷ σπείρειν; 13:3) is temp. and contemp.: "While he was scattering seeds." Αὐτόν is the acc. of the subj. of the inf. The rel. pron. ἅ here functions as a dem. pron.: "these" (BDAG 725d–27d 2.b.). Although μέν has a number of uses, here it functions together with the ἄλλα δέ in vv. 5, 7, and 8 to separate one thought from another in a series (BDAG 629d–30c 1.c.). The sense may be expressed in tr. by "on one hand . . . on the other hand" or by enumerating the sequence: "first, second, third, fourth." In combination with the rel. pron., the cstr. may be tr. "some . . . others." Ἔπεσεν 3rd pl. aor. act. indic. of πίπτω. Παρά with the acc. (τὴν ὁδόν) 13:1. Ἐλθόντα (nom. pl. neut. of aor. act. ptc. of dep. ἔρχομαι) is *attendant circumstance (most EVV) or temp. Note that although neut. pl. nouns take sg. vbs., they use pl. ptc. Πετεινόν, -οῦ, τό, "bird." Κατέφαγεν 3rd sg. 2nd aor. act. indic. of κατεσθίω, "eat up, devour." The antecedent of αὐτά is ἅ, which refers to seeds.

13:5 The adj. ἄλλα is used subst.: "others (other seeds)." The δέ is adversative and contrasts the second group of seeds from the first. The subj. of ἔπεσεν (3rd sg. aor. act. indic. of πίπτω) is an implied ἅ, which refers to "that which was sown" (13:19).

Ἐπί with the acc. (τὰ πετρώδη) is a marker of location: "on, upon." Πετρώδης, -ες, "rocky, stony." The art. pl. adj. is used subst.: "rocky areas." The particle ὅπου identifies a place: "where." Εἶχεν (3rd sg. impf. act. indic. of ἔχω) is either prog. or general ("where it does not generally have"). The noun γῆ refers to topsoil and the adj. πολλήν could refer either to the small area of soil on the surface of the rocky ground or, as the next clause demands, the shallow depth of that soil. Εὐθέως is an adv. of time: "immediately." Ἐξανέτειλεν 3rd. sg. aor. act. indic. of ἐξανατέλλω, "spring up, shoot up." Διά with the art. inf. (ἔχειν pres. act. inf. of ἔχω) expresses cause. Βάθος, -ους, τό, "depth." Γῆς is attrib. gen.: "deep soil."

13:6 Ἥλιος, -ου, ὁ, "sun." Δέ is adversative and contrasts the ultimate demise of the plant with its initial promise. Ἀνατείλαντος (gen. sg. masc. of aor. act. ptc. of ἀνατέλλω, "rise, dawn, appear on the horizon") is gen. abs. and expresses contemp. time. Ἐκαυματίσθη 3rd sg. aor. pass. indic. of καυματίζω, "burn up, scorch." Διὰ τὸ μὴ ἔχειν 13:5. Ῥίζα, -ης, ἡ, "root (system)." BDAG (905d–6a 1.b.) suggests that the phrase means "no firm root" and thus the danger of falling. But the main vb. that immediately follows shows the lack of root causing withering rather than falling. The shallow soil prevented the root system from penetrating deeply, and the roots spread just below the surface, the portion of the soil that dries out most quickly. Ἐξηράνθη 3rd sg. aor. pass. indic. of ξηραίνω, "dry up, wither."

13:7 Ἄλλα δὲ ἔπεσεν ἐπί (with the acc.) 13:5. Ἄκανθα, -ης, ἡ, "thorn plant." Ἀνέβησαν 3rd pl. 2nd aor. act. indic. of ἀναβαίνω, "come up." Ἔπνιξαν 3rd pl. aor. act. indic. of πνίγω, "choke." The antecedent of αὐτά is ἄλλα ("other seeds").

13:8 Ἄλλα δὲ ἔπεσεν ἐπί (with the acc.) 13:5. Although most EVV tr. ἐδίδου (3rd sg. impf. act. indic. of δίδωμι, "produce") as an aoristic impf., Matthew's preference for the aor. form of the vb. elsewhere (thirty-six occurrences; impf. only here and 15:36) makes this unlikely. Furthermore, the aoristic impf. is rare except for the use of the vb. λέγω in narrative literature. The impf. is prob. ingr. ("and they started bearing fruit") or *prog. ("they kept producing fruit;" H 1.369; cf. Mark 4:8). The nom. sg. neut. rel. pron. ὅ shifts the focus from a handful of seeds to three different single seeds that each produces a different yield. In a series using μὲν δέ (cf. 13:4), the rel. pron. functions like a dem. pron. and means "one . . . the other." Ἑκατόν, "one hundred." Ἑξήκοντα, "sixty." Τριάκοντα, "thirty."

13:9 The art. ptc. ἔχων (nom. sg. masc. of pres. act. ptc. of ἔχω) is subst.: "the one who has." Οὖς, ὠτός, τό, "ear." Ἀκουέτω (3rd sg. pres. act. impv. of ἀκούω) is ingr.-prog. On the expression, see 11:15.

FOR FURTHER STUDY

61. The Parable of the Sower

Evans, C. A. "On the Isaianic Background of the Sower Parable." *CBQ* 47 (1985): 464–68.

Kagarise, R. J. "Divine Sovereignty, Human Responsibility, and Jesus's Parables: The Structure and Meaning of Matthew 13:10–17." *Evangelical Journal* 19 (2001): 29–41.

Payne, P. B. "The Authenticity of the Parable of the Sower and Its Interpretation." Pages 162–207 in *Gospel Perspectives: Studies of History and Tradition in the Four Gospels.* Edited by R. T. France and D. Wenham. Sheffield: JSOT, 1980.

Wellum, K. "The Parable of the Sower." *SBJT* 13 (2009): 52–57.

Wenham, D. "Interpretation of the Parable of the Sower." *NTS* 20 (1974): 299–319.

3. Jesus's Use of Parables (13:10–17)

13:10 Προσελθόντες (nom. pl. masc. of aor. act. ptc. of dep. προσέρχομαι, "approach") is *attendant circumstance (most EVV) or temp. The def. art. with μαθηταί is the art. of previous ref. (cf. 10:1). Εἶπαν 3rd pl. aor. act. indic. of λέγω. Διά with the interr. pron. τί queries the reason for something and means "why?" Ἐν with the dat. (παραβολαῖς) identifies parables as the means by which Jesus spoke. Λαλεῖς (2nd sg. pres. act. indic. of λαλέω) may be prog. or customary pres. Use of the 3rd pers. pron. αὐτοῖς (anteced-ent: ὄχλοι; 13:2) rather than a 1st pers. pron. indicates that Jesus used parables pri-marily as an instr. of instruction to the crowds but more dir. forms of instruction when speaking exclusively to his disciples.

13:11 The def. art. ὁ functions as a pers. pron. (3rd sg.). Ἀποκριθείς (nom. sg. masc. of aor. pass. ptc. of dep. ἀποκρίνομαι) is either *pleonastic (most EVV) or attendant circumstance (LEB). Εἶπεν 3rd sg. aor. act. indic. of λέγω. The antecedent of αὐτοῖς is μαθηταί (13:10). Although one may challenge the punctuation of the UBS[5] and view ὅτι as introducing discourse, the ὅτι is prob. causal and provides an answer to the ques-tion introduced with διὰ τί (most EVV). Thus the response implies a clause like the first clause in 13:13. The placement of the ὑμῖν and ἐκείνοις in each clause appears to indicate emphasis and strongly contrasts the situation of the disciples and the crowds. Δέδοται (3rd sg. pf. pass. indic. of δίδωμι) is prob. a divine pass. and indicates that this privilege was granted by God himself. The pf. tense may be resultative, and thus emphasize the pres. benefits of the divine gift, or consummative, and thus emphasize that the gift was bestowed at some time in the past. Γνῶναι (aor. act. inf. of γινώσκω) is prob. subst. and serves as the subj. of the clause, while τὰ μυστήρια serves as the dir. obj. of the inf. (W 600–601; NIV). Alternatively, τὰ μυστήρια (μυστήριον, -ου, τό, "mystery") may be the subj. of the vb. δέδοται (since neut. pl. subj. take sg. vbs.), and the inf. may express purpose (CSB). The gen. τῆς βασιλείας is prob. an example of the rare gen. of ref. Τῆς βασιλείας τῶν οὐρανῶν 3:2. The use of the remote dem. pron. ἐκείνοις rather than the near dem. may merely indicate the physical distance between Jesus and the crowds, if one assumes that Jesus had ended his teaching session and the crowds had dispersed (13:10). However, the remote dem. may denote the spiritual distance between Jesus and the crowds that resulted from the spiritual state described in 13:14–15. Δέ is adversative and marks a contrast.

13:12 The causal γάρ closely relates this verse to the statement in 13:11. This suggests that the obj. of the vb. ἔχει and subj. of the vb. δοθήσεται is the subj. of the vb. δοθήσεται in 13:11 (thus knowledge or mystery). Ἔχει (3rd sg. pres. act. indic. of ἔχω) The use of ὅστις ("anyone") suggests that the statement is proverbial. Thus δοθήσεται (3rd sg. fut. pass. indic. of δίδωμι) and περισσευθήσεται (3rd sg. fut. pass. indic. of περισσεύω, "cause to abound") are prob. gnomic. However, the shift from the pres. to the fut.

indicates that the action expressed by the pres. tense precedes the action expressed by the fut. tense. Thus the classification of the fut. as gnomic does not preclude the action from being futuristic. The καί in the last clause is prob. ascensive: "even." The antecedent of the rel. pron. ὅ is more likely knowledge (γνῶναι) than mysteries (μυστήρια), and this suggests that γνῶναι is the subj. in Jesus's statement in 13:11. Ἔχει 3rd sg. pres. act. indic. of ἔχω. Ἀρθήσεται (3rd sg. fut. pass. indic. of αἴρω, "take away") may be *gnomic or predictive. Ἀπ' αὐτοῦ expresses separation and intensifies the mng. of the vb.

13:13 Διά with the acc. (τοῦτο) is causal: "because of this." The dem. pron. may be retrospective (pointing to something in the preceding context) or prospective (pointing to something in the following context). In this instance τοῦτο points to the causal clause introduced by ὅτι. Ἐν παραβολαῖς identifies a means. The antecedent of αὐτοῖς is ὄχλοι (13:2). Λαλῶ (1st sg. pres. act. indic. of λαλέω) may be prog. or customary. Ὅτι is causal (13:11). The ptc. βλέποντες (nom. pl. masc. of pres. act. ptc. of βλέπω) and ἀκούντες (nom. pl. masc. of pres. act. ptc. of ἀκούω) are both concessive: "even though they see/hear" (cf. NIV). Since the negated vbs. βλέπουσιν (3rd pl. pres. act. indic. of βλέπω) and ἀκούσιν (3rd pl. pres. act. indic. of ἀκούσιν) lexically match the concessive ptc., the clauses initially appear to be contradictory. The contradiction is removed however if:

1. the pres. ptcs. are conative ("even though they are trying to see/hear"),
2. Jesus was referring to two different kinds of sight and hearing, first physical and then spiritual,
3. Jesus was contrasting partial and full sight/hearing (NRSV; CSB?). Since 13:12 seems to refer to partial knowledge, which is insufficient and ultimately removed, in contrast to true knowledge, which God continues to increase, view 3 seems best supported by the context. The use of the concessive ptc. and the indic. form of the same lexeme in 13:14 (see also Isa 6:9) also supports this.

Οὐδέ "and not, nor." Συνίουσιν 3rd pl. pres. act. indic. of συνίημι, "understand, comprehend."

13:14 D&A (2:393–94) suggest that 13:14–15 is an early post-Matthean scribal interpolation. However, the fact that all extant mss. contain these verses convincingly supports their authenticity. The καί implies that this verse is a continuation of Jesus's response that began in 13:11. Thus the differences between this fulfillment citation and those added by Matthew may be that this citation preserves Jesus's own preferred vocabulary and diction. Ἀναπληροῦται (3rd sg. pres. pass. indic. of ἀναπληρόω, "fulfill") is prog. pres. The vb. may be a divine pass., in which case αὐτοῖς is a dat. of ref. (most EVV, particularly LEB; ESV; D used the cstr. ἐπ' αὐτοῖς, which expresses ref.). Alternatively, αὐτοῖς may be a dat. of agency and emphasize the people's responsibility for their spiritual state, but this usage is rare. Although most tr. and commentators view ἀναπληρόω as identical in sense to πληρόω, the vb. is not used elsewhere in Matthew. The prefixed ἀνα sometimes means "again" and is equivalent to the Eng. pref. "re-." LS note that in the pass. this vb. meant "to be restored to its former size or state" (116d; Thucydides Historicus 2. [5th cent.]). Matthew may have intended an etym. sense here in which the vb. meant "fulfill again" or "refulfill" (cf. ἀναβλαστάνω, ἀναβιόω, ἀναγεννάω; LS 98b F.; F 514). The unusual form would thus indicate Jesus's and Matthew's awareness that Isaiah's text was orig. about Isaiah's contemporaries but now received a second fulfillment in ref. to Jesus's contemporaries. Although ἀναπληρόω often uses the directional sense of ἀνα ("fill up"), this would not preclude the pref. from sometimes expressing repetition, since in some instances ἀναβλέπω may mean "look up" (Matt 14:19), but in other instances "see again" (11:5; 20:34). Προφητεία, -ας, ἡ, "prophesy." Ἡσαΐου ("Isaiah") is a subj. gen. Ἡ λέγουσα is attrib.: "(the prophecy of Isaiah) that says." Verses 14–15 contain a quotation of Isaiah 6:9–10 that fairly closely follows the LXX. Ἀκοή, -ῆς, ἡ, "hearing." In combination with a form of ἀκούω, ἀκοῇ is a cognate dat. that emphasizes the action of the vb. The emphasis may fall on the continuous nature of the hearing (CSB; NIV) or the quality of the hearing (LEB ["carefully"]; ESV and NRSV ["indeed"]). Ἀκούσετε (2nd pl. fut. act. indic. of ἀκούω) may be predictive (most EVV) or impv. (MT). If impv., the command is prob. concessive (Gildersleeve 1.116 §269; Smyth §1917): "Even if you carefully listen, nevertheless . . ." The concessive sense may be expressed in Eng. idiom, "Go ahead and try your best to listen, and yet you will never understand!" Καί is concessive: "and yet." The dbl. neg. οὐ μή with the subjunc. (συνῆτε 2nd pl. aor. act. subjunc. of συνίημι, "understand") expresses emphatic negation: "you absolutely will not understand/you will never understand." Βλέποντες (nom. pl. masc. of pres. act. ptc. of βλέπω) is difficult to classify syntactically because it does not appear to fit normal categories of usage. However, Matthew is quoting the LXX. The LXX uses the ptc. in a way almost completely absent from the NT (except in OT quotations) called the "intensive participle." The intensive ptc. is used in place of a cognate dat. "to convey the intensive force that is accomplished in Hebrew by the addition of the infinitive to the finite verb" (Conybeare and Stock §81; cf. Gen 22:17). The parallelism with the cognate dat. at the beginning of the verse strongly supports this analysis, and most EVV adopt it. Βλέψετε (2nd pl. fut. act. indic. of βλέπω) may be predictive (most EVV) or impv. (MT). If impv., the command is concessive (see above). Καί is concessive: "and yet." The dbl. neg. οὐ μή with the subjunc. (ἴδητε 2nd pl. aor. act. subjunc. of ὁράω, "perceive") expresses emphatic negation.

13:15 Isaiah's text forms a chiasm: heart, ears, eyes, eyes, ears, heart. Γάρ presents the cause of the spiritual ignorance described in the preceding verse. Ἐπαχύνθη (3rd sg. aor. pass. indic. of παχύνω, "make dull, become dull") could be a divine pass but is more likely an example of the use of the pass. for the intrans.: "became dull." Since the sg. ἡ καρδία is modified by the gen. τοῦ λαοῦ τούτου, which refers to a group of people, the noun clearly does not refer to a physical heart but rather to the collective spiritual insight and sensitivity of the people. Τοῖς ὠσὶν (οὖς, ὠτός, τό, "ear") is dat. of instr. The adv. βαρέως normally means "with difficulty" and with the vb. ἤκουσαν (3rd pl. aor. act. indic. of ἀκούω) means "became hard of hearing." The antecedent of αὐτῶν (partitive gen.) is λαοῦ, but Matthew used the pl. number of the pron. since the antecedent referred to a group of multiple persons even though the noun itself is sg. Ἐκάμμυσαν

(3rd pl. aor. act. indic. of καμμύω, "close, shut") portrays the spiritual condition of the people as the result of their own deliberate refusal to see the truth. This supports the view that ἐπαχύνθη is intrans. and has an active sense. Μήποτε (with subjunc. vbs.) is a marker of negated purpose that introduces outcomes that the people seek to avoid. Ἴδωσιν 3rd pl. aor. act. subjunc. of ὁράω. Τοῖς ὀφθαλμοῖς, τοῖς ὠσὶν, and τῇ καρδίᾳ are dat. of instr. Ἀκούσωσιν 3rd pl. aor. act. subjunc. of ἀκούω. Συνῶσιν 3rd pl. aor. act. subjunc. of συνίημι. Ἐπιστρέψωσιν 3rd pl. aor. act. indic. of ἐπιστρέφω, "return, repent." Καί appears to introduce a result. Ἰάσομαι 1st sg. fut. mid. indic. of dep. ἰάομαι, "heal." The shift from the aor. subjunc. to the fut. indic. may suggest that divine healing would have been the def. result if the three preceding conditions had been met.

13:16 Ὑμῶν modifies οἱ ὀφθαλμοί and is in a position of emphasis. Δέ is adversative and contrasts the spiritual condition of the disciples with that of the people. Μακάριος, -ία, -ιον, "blessed, enjoying God's favor." Ὅτι is causal. However, the causal conj. prob. marks the second clause as the evidence demonstrating the truthfulness of the first clause (inference-evidence) rather than the cause of the effect described in the first clause. Thus the sense is: "Your eyes are evidently/obviously blessed, since they are truly seeing" and logically implies that spiritual sight is actually the result of divine blessing. If the ὅτι marked the actual cause of divine blessing, the second clause would likely be temp. antecedent to the first. Furthermore, the next verse supports this interpretation. Βλέπουσιν 3rd pl. pres. act. indic. of βλέπω. Τὰ ὦτα (13:15) is a second subj. modified by the pred. adj. μακάριοι. Ὅτι again introduces the evidence for the preceding inference. Ἀκούουσιν 3rd pl. pres. act. indic. of ἀκούω.

13:17 Ἀμὴν γὰρ λέγω ὑμῖν 5:18. Ὅτι introduces dir. discourse. Δίκαιοι is subst. Ἐπεθύμησαν 3rd pl. aor. act. indic. of ἐπιθυμέω, "strongly desire, long for." Ἰδεῖν (aor. act. inf. of ὁράω) is complementary. The neut. pl. rel. pron. ἅ means "the things." Βλέπετε 2nd pl. pres. act. indic. of βλέπω. Καί is concessive: "and yet." Εἶδαν 3rd pl. aor. act. indic. of ὁράω. Ἀκοῦσαι (aor. act. inf. of ἀκούω) is also a complement to ἐπεθύμησαν. Ἀκούετε 2nd sg. pres. act. indic. of ἀκούω. Καί is concessive. Ἤκουσαν 3rd pl. aor. act. indic. of ἀκούω.

FOR FURTHER STUDY

62. The Purpose of the Parables

McComiskey, D S. "Exile and the Purpose of Jesus's Parables (Mark 4:10–12; Matt 13:10–17; Luke 8:9–10)." *JETS* 51 (2008): 59–85.

Nel, M. "The Mysteries of the Kingdom of Heaven According to Matthew 13:10–17." *Neot* 43 (2009): 271–88.

Van Elderen, B. "The Purpose of the Parables According to Matthew 13:10–17." Pages 180–90 in *New Dimensions in New Testament Study*. Edited by R. N. Longenecker and M. C. Tenney. Grand Rapids: Zondervan, 1974.

HOMILETICAL SUGGESTIONS

His Grace and Our Responsibility (13:10–17)

1. God's grace enables hearers to understand the message of the kingdom (13:11, 16)
2. Sinners' hardness prevents them from understanding the message of the kingdom (13:13–15)
3. Those who hear the message and reject it often lose their opportunity (13:12; cf. 13:19)
4. Witnessing the ministry of Jesus and hearing the teaching of Jesus is a privilege coveted by prophets and saints (13:17)

4. The Explanation of the Parable of the Sower (13:18–23)

13:18 Ὑμεῖς is emphatic. Οὖν may be inferential and thus present the command as appropriate in light of the disciples' ability to hear what others cannot. Alternatively, it may be resumptive and mark a return to the discussion of the parable of the sower after an interruption. Ἀκούσατε (2nd pl. aor. act. impv. of ἀκούω) expresses urgency. Τὴν παραβολήν 13:3. The art. σπείραντος (gen. sg. masc. of aor. act. ptc. of σπείρω, "sow") is subst. and a gen. of ref.: the parable "about the sower."

13:19 Παντὸς ἀκούοντος (gen. sg. masc. of pres. act. ptc. of ἀκούω) . . . καὶ μὴ συνιέντος (gen. sg. masc. of pres. act. ptc. of συνίημι, "understand") is gen. abs., temp. and contemp.: "when anyone hears . . ." Τὸν λόγον "the message." Τῆς βασιλείας is gen. of ref. Ἔρχεται (3rd sg. pres. act. indic. of dep. ἔρχομαι) is gnomic. Ὁ πονηρός is subst.: "the evil one." Ἁρπάζει (3rd sg. pres. act. indic. of ἁρπάζω, "seize, snatch") is gnomic. The art. ἐσπαρμένον (acc. sg. neut. of pf. pass. ptc. of σπείρω, "sow") is subst.: "the message that was sown." The use of the loc. ἐν τῇ καρδίᾳ shows that the soils represent conditions of the heart. The antecedent of οὗτος is the entire preceding clause. Ἐστίν 3rd sg. pres. indic. of εἰμί, "represent, symbolize" (BDAG 282d–86b 2.c.α.). The gender of the art. σπαρείς (nom. sg. masc. of aor. pass. ptc. of σπείρω) is initially puzzling since the neut. was used in 13:3–9 prob. due to the neut. gender of the noun σπέρμα ("seed"). Hagner (1.380) suggests that the masc. gender indicates that Matthew is now describing persons as those who are sown and thus mixing his images. More likely the referent of "seed" in the parable, "the message" (λόγος), influenced Matthew to use the masc.: "the message that was sown." Παρά with the acc. (τὴν ὁδόν) means "along."

13:20 Ὁ σπαρείς 13:19. Ἐπὶ τὰ πετρώδη 13:5. Οὗτός ἐστιν 13:19. The art. ἀκούων (nom. sg. masc. of pres. act. ptc. of ἀκούω) is subst. Εὐθύς "immediately." Μετά with the gen. (χαρᾶς) expresses manner (emotion): "with joy, joyfully." Λαμβάνων (nom. sg. masc. of pres. act. ptc. of λαμβάνω) is also subst. since it is joined by καί to an art. ptc. that is subst.

13:21 Ἔχει 3rd sg. pres. act. indic. of ἔχω. Ῥίζαν 13:6. The phrase ἐν ἑαυτῷ ("in himself") is prob. equivalent to ἐν τῇ καρδίᾳ in 13:19 and implies that, although the message is welcomed, it never takes root in the heart (N 540). Πρόσκαιρος, -ον, "temporary." Γενομένης (gen. sg. fem. of aor. mid. ptc. of dep. γίνομαι) is gen. abs. Θλῖψις, -εως, ἡ, "tribulation, oppression." Διωγμός, -οῦ, ὁ, "persecution." Διά with the acc. (τὸν λόγον) expresses cause. Εὐθύς 13:20. Σκανδαλίζεται (3rd sg. pres. pass. indic. of σκανδαλίζω, "be led into sin/apostasy" [pass.]) is gnomic.

13:22 Ὁ σπαρείς 13:19. Εἰς expresses "presence in an area determined by other objects" (BDAG 288d–91c 1.a.ε.): "among." Ἀκάνθας 13:7. Οὗτός ἐστιν 13:19. The art. ἀκούων (nom. sg. masc. of pres. act. ptc. of ἀκούω) is subst. Ὁ ἀκούων 13:20. Μέριμνα, -ης, ἡ, "worry, anxiety." Τοῦ αἰῶνος is prob. obj. gen. ("worry about this [present] age/life") and refers to the anxiety described in 6:25–34. Ἀπάτη, -ης, ἡ, "deception, pleasure." Πλοῦτος, -ου, ὁ, "wealth." If ἀπάτη means "deception," πλούτου is prob. subj., expressing the idea that wealth deceives those who believe that it brings permanent happiness (most EVV). If ἀπάτη means "pleasure," πλούτου is prob. gen. of source ("the pleasure derived from wealth"). Συμπνίγει (3rd sg. pres. act. indic. of συμπνίγω, "choke") and γίνεται (3rd sg. pres. mid. indic. of dep. γίνομαι) are gnomic. Ἄκαρπος, -ον, "fruitless, unproductive."

13:23 ὁ σπαρείς and οὗτός ἐστιν 13:19. Ὁ ἀκούων 13:20. Συνιείς (nom. sg. masc. of pres. act. ptc. of συνίημι, "understand") is subst. and is modified by the def. art. before ἀκούων. Δή emphasizes that a statement is definitely established: "of course, indeed, certainly." Καρποφορεῖ (3rd sg. pres. act. indic. of καρποφορέω, "bear fruit") and ποιεῖ (3rd sg. pres. act. indic. of ποιέω) are gnomic. The combination μὲν . . . δὲ . . . δέ separates the various elements in a series. The rel. pron. ὅ (nom./acc., sg. neut.) prob. refers to individual seeds that each represents true disciples. As part of the μὲν δέ cstr., the pron. means "one . . . , another . . . , still another . . . ." Note that the NIV seems to imply that a single individual produces the various amounts of fruit during different seasons. Most EVV clearly indicate that the different yields are produced by different disciples. Ἑκατόν, "one hundred." Ἑξήκοντα, "sixty." Τριάκοντα, "thirty."

FOR FURTHER STUDY

See For Further Study § 59

HOMILETICAL SUGGESTIONS

Ears to Hear (13:1–9, 18–23)

1. Some people respond to Jesus's teaching with confusion and quickly forget the message
2. Some people respond to Jesus's teaching with superficial excitement but do not survive persecution
3. Some people respond to Jesus's teaching with partial commitment but attempt to give Christ second place
4. Some people respond to Jesus's teaching with understanding and are transformed to live a righteous life

5. The Parable of the Weeds (13:24–30)

13:24 Ἄλλην παραβολήν simply means "another parable" rather than "another similar parable." The distinction between ἄλλος and ἐκεῖνος even in the classical period was not strictly maintained. Παρέθηκεν 3rd sg. aor. act. indic. of παρατίθημι, "present, set before." Λέγων (nom. sg. masc. of pres. act. ptc. of λέγω) is prob. ptc. of means (LEB; ESV) but may be viewed as pleonastic instead (CSB; NIV). Ὡμοιώθη (3rd sg. aor. pass. indic. of ὁμοιόω, "be like" [pass.]) is gnomic and is thus tr. as a simple pres. Ἡ βασιλεία τῶν οὐρανῶν 3:2. Ἀνθρώπῳ is dat. of dir. obj. (BDAG 707b–c 1.). Σπείραντι (dat. sg. masc. of aor. act. ptc. of σπείρω, "sow") is attrib. Σπέρμα, -ατος, τό, "seed." Ἀγρός, -οῦ, ὁ, "field."

13:25 Δέ is adversative and contrasts the hopeful labors of the farmer with the malicious efforts of the enemy. Ἐν with the art. inf. καθεύδειν (pres. act. inf. of καθεύδω, "sleep") expresses contemp. time: "while the men slept." Τοὺς ἀνθρώπους is acc. subj. of the inf. Ἦλθεν 3rd sg. aor. act. indic. of dep. ἔρχομαι. Ἐχθρός, -ά, -όν, "hostile, enemy" (subst.). Αὐτοῦ is prob. a gen. of relationship, but in this case it describes a neg. and nonfamilial relationship. Ἐπέσπειρεν 3rd sg. aor. act. indic. of ἐπισπείρω, "sow on top of a previously planted field, resow." Note that due to the lack of a stem change in the aor., this form is indistinguishable from the impf. Ζιζάνιον, -ου, τό, "weed (that resembles wheat but is inedible)." Ἀνὰ μέσον is an idiom mng. "in the middle of, among" that functions like a prep. with a gen. obj. (BDAG 57d–58a). Σῖτος, -ου, ὁ, "wheat, grain." Ἀπῆλθεν 3rd sg. aor. act. indic. of dep. ἀπέρχομαι.

13:26 Ἐβλάστησεν 3rd sg. aor. act. indic. of βλαστάνω, "sprout." Χόρτος, -ου, ὁ, "stalk, blade." Ἐποίησεν 3rd sg. aor. act. indic. of ποιέω. In combination with ὅτε in the previous clause, τότε means "at that (the same) time" rather than "afterward" (most EVV; contrary to BDAG 1012d–13a 2.; cf. 21:1). Ἐφάνη 3rd sg. aor. pass. indic. of φαίνω, "appear" (pass.). Καί is adjunctive.

13:27 Προσελθόντες (nom. pl. masc. of aor. act. ptc. of dep. προσέρχομαι) is attendant circumstance (most EVV). Οἰκοδεσπότης, -ου, ὁ, "master of the house." Εἶπον 3rd pl. aor. act. indic. of λέγω. Κύριε is simple voc. The neg. οὐχί implies a positive response to the question (e.g., "yes, of course I sowed good seed"). Σπέρμα 13:24. Ἔσπειρας 2nd sg. aor. act. indic. of σπείρω, "sow." Ἀγρῷ 13:24. Πόθεν is an interr. adv. questioning source: "from where?" Οὖν shows that the current question arose in light of the assumed response to the previous question: "so." Ἔχει 3rd sg. pres. act. indic. of ἔχω. Ζιζάνια 13:25.

13:28 The def. art. ὁ functions as a pers. pron. (αὐτός). Ἔφη 3rd sg. aor. act. indic. of φημί, "say." Ἐχθρός 13:25 is used as an attrib. adj. modifying ἄνθρωπος: "a hostile person." Ἐποίησεν 3rd sg. aor. act. indic. of ποιέω. Λέγουσιν (3rd pl. pres. act. indic. of λέγω) is historical pres. Θέλεις 2nd sg. pres. act. indic. of θέλω. Οὖν indicates that the current question was prompted by the previous statement. Ἀπελθόντες (nom. pl. masc. of aor. act. ptc. of dep. ἀπέρχομαι, "depart") is prob. attendant circumstance (most EVV). Συλλέξωμεν (1st pl. aor. act. subjunc. of συλλέγω, "gather") is delib. subjunc. The antecedent of αὐτά is ζιζάνια.

13:29 Ὁ δέ φησιν 13:28. The neg. οὐ offers a neg. response to the question in the previous verse. Μήποτε marks a potential outcome that the speaker seeks to avoid: "lest, otherwise." Συλλέγοντες (nom. pl. masc. of pres. act. ptc. of συλλέγω, "gather") may be temp. (CSB; NIV) or a ptc. of means (LEB; ESV; NET). Τὰ ζιζάνια 13:25. Ἐκριζώσητε (2nd pl. aor. act. subjunc. of ἐκριζόω, "uproot") expresses a probability or possibility: "you risk uprooting. . . ." Ἅμα is used as a prep. expressing association with the dat. (αὐτοῖς): "together with them." Τὸν σῖτον 13:25.

13:30 Ἄφετε (2nd pl. aor. act. impv. of ἀφίημι, "leave, permit") expresses urgency. Συναυξάνεσθαι (pres. mid. inf. of συναυξάνω, "grow together") may be complementary (if the preceding vb. grants permission) or express *purpose (if the vb. means to leave in place). Thus the cstr. may mean: "leave in place both (the weeds and wheat) so they may grow together" or *"permit both to grow together" (most EVV). Ἀμφότεροι, -αι, -α, "both." Ἕως functions as a prep. (with the gen.) mng. "until." Θερισμός, -οῦ, ὁ, "harvest." Ἐν with the obj. καιρῷ is clearly temp. Ἐρῶ 1st sg. fut. act. indic. of λέγω. Θεριστής, -οῦ, ὁ, "harvester, reaper." Συλλέξατε (2nd pl. aor. act. impv. of συλλέγω, "gather") expresses urgency. The adv. πρῶτον here means "first (in temp. order)." Τὰ ζιζάνια 13:25. Δήσατε 2nd pl. aor. act. impv. of δέω, "bind, tie up." Δέσμη, -ης, ἡ, "bundle." Πρός with the art. inf. (κατακαῦσαι aor. act. inf. of κατακαίω, "burn up") expresses purpose. Τὸν σῖτον 13:25. Δέ is adversative and contrasts the destiny of the wheat with that of the weeds. Συναγάγετε (2nd pl. aor. act. impv. of συνάγω, "gather") expresses urgency. Ἀποθήκη, -ης, ἡ, "barn, large storage area."

FOR FURTHER STUDY

63. The Parable of the Weeds

   Bailey, M. "The Kingdom in the Parables of Matthew 13, Part 3: The Parable of the Tares." *BSac* 155 (1998): 266–79.

   Catchpole, D. R. "John the Baptist, Jesus and the Parable of the Tares." *SJT* 31 (1978): 557–70.

   Doty, W. G. "Interpretation: Parable of the Weeds and Wheat." *Int* 25 (1971): 185–93.

   Luomanen, P. "Corpus Mixtum—an Appropriate Description of Matthew's Community?" *JBL* 117 (1998): 469–80.

   McIver, R. K. "The Parable of the Weeds Among the Wheat (Matt 13:24–30, 36–43) and the Relationship Between the Kingdom and the Church as Portrayed in the Gospel of Matthew." *JBL* 114 (1995): 643–59.

6. The Parable of the Mustard Seed (13:31–32)

13:31 Ἄλλην παραβολὴν παρέθηκεν αὐτοῖς λέγων 13:24. Ὅμοιος, -οία, -οιον, "like, similar." The combination of the adj. with ἐστίν is identical in sense to ὁμοιόω. Ἡ βασιλεία τῶν οὐρανῶν 3:2. Κόκκος, -ου, ὁ, "grain, seed, kernel." Κόκκῳ is dat. of comp. Σίναπι, -εως, ὁ, "mustard plant." Σινάπεως is either a gen. of source ("grain that comes from the mustard") or attrib. (most EVV). Λαβών (nom. sg. masc. of aor. act. ptc. of λαμβάνω) is attendant circumstance (most EVV). Ἔσπειρεν 3rd sg. aor. act. indic. of σπείρω, "sow." Ἐν τῷ ἀγρῷ αὐτοῦ 13:24.

13:32 Μικρότερον is the nom. sg. neut. comp. form of the adj. μικρός, -ά, -όν, ("small"). Since the adj. compares the mustard seed to all other seeds, this is an example of the substitution of the comp. for the superl. (Turner, *Syntax* 2–3; W 299–300; most EVV). In the μὲν . . . δέ cstr., μέν marks a concessive clause and δέ is adversative: "even though . . ., nevertheless . . ." Σπερμάτων (13:24) is gen. of comp. Ὅταν (with the subjunc.) means "whenever." Αὐξηθῇ 3rd sg. aor. pass. subjunc. of αὐξάνω, "grow" (pass.). Μεῖζον is the nom. sg. neut. comp. form of the adj. μέγας, μεγάλη, μέγα ("great, large") and is another example of the substitution of the comp. for the superl. Λάχονον, -ου, τό, "herb, vegetable." Τῶν λαχάνων is gen. of comp. Ἐστίν 3rd sg. pres. indic. of εἰμί (gnomic). Γίνεται (3rd sg. pres. mid. indic. of dep. γίνομαι) is also gnomic. Δένδρον, -ου, τό, "tree." Ὥστε with the inf. ἐλθεῖν (aor. act. inf. of dep. ἔρχομαι) and κατασκηνοῦν (pres. act. inf. of κατασκηνόω, "nest") indicates a result. Τὰ πετεινὰ τοῦ οὐρανοῦ 6:26. Ἐν with the dat. (τοῖς κλάδοις) here means "among." Κλάδος, -ου, ὁ, "branch."

FOR FURTHER STUDY

64. The Parable of the Mustard Seed

Carter, W. "Matthew's Gospel, Rome's Empire, and the Parable of the Mustard Seed (Matt 13:31–32)." Pages 181–201 in *Hermeneutik der Gleichnisse Jesu*. Edited by R. Zimmermann and G. Kern. Tübingen: Mohr Siebeck, 2008.

Crook, Z. A. "The Synoptic Parables of the Mustard Seed and the Leaven: A Test-Case for the Two-Document, Two-Gospel, and Farrer-Goulder Hypotheses." *JSNT* 78 (2000): 23–48.

Garroway, J. "The Invasion of a Mustard Seed: A Reading of Mark 5.1–20." *JSNT* 32 (2009): 57–75.

McArthur, H. K. "Parable of the Mustard Seed." *CBQ* 33 (1971): 198–210.

HOMILETICAL SUGGESTIONS

No Small Kingdom (13:31–33)

1. The kingdom has modest beginnings (13:31–32a; 13:33a)
2. The kingdom will grow dramatically (13:32b; 13:33b)
3. The kingdom will extend throughout the earth (13:32c; Dan 4:20–22)

7. The Parable of the Leaven and the Fulfillment of Prophecy (13:33–35)

13:33 Ἄλλην παραβολήν 13:24. Ἐλάλησεν 3rd sg. aor. act. indic. of λαλέω. Ὁμοία ἐστὶν ἡ βασιλεία τῶν οὐρανῶν 13:31. Ζύμη, -ης, ἡ, "leaven." Ζύμῃ is a dat. of comp. Λαβοῦσα (nom. sg. fem. of aor. act. ptc. of λαμβάνω) is attendant circumstance (most EVV). Ἐνέκρυψεν 3rd sg. aor. act. indic. of ἐγκρύπτω, "hide, put inside." Ἄλευρον, -ου, τό, "wheat flour." Ἀλεύρου is either partitive gen. or gen. of content. Σάτον, -ου, τό, "seah (Heb. dry measure equal to about thirteen liters)." Τρεῖς, τρία, "three." Ἕως οὗ "until" (BDAG 422d–24a 1.b.β.). Ἐζυμώθη 3rd sg. aor. pass. indic. of ζυμόω, "ferment, leaven." Ὅλον is subst.: "the whole thing."

13:34 The antecedent of ταῦτα is the instruction in parables in 13:3–8, 24–33. Ἐλάλησεν 3rd sg. aor. act. indic. of λαλέω. Ἐν with the obj. παραβολαῖς identifies means. Χωρίς with the gen. (παραβολῆς) expresses absence: "without, apart from." Ἐλάλει (3rd sg. impf. act. indic. of λαλέω) is customary.

13:35 Ὅπως with the subjunc. (πληρωθῇ 3rd sg. aor. pass. indic. of πληρόω, "fulfill") expresses purpose. Thus Jesus adopted this form of instruction with the intention of fulfilling prophecy. The art. ptc. τὸ ῥηθέν (nom. sg. neut. of aor. pass. ptc. of λέγω) is subst. and a divine pass. Διά with the gen. of pers. (τοῦ προφήτου) in combination with a pass. verbal clearly expresses intermediate agency. In the prophecy God was speaking through the prophet (1:22). Λέγοντος (gen. sg. masc. of pres. act. ptc. of λέγω) may be pleonastic or attrib. (1:22). The quotation is from Psalm 78:2. The first line is identical to the LXX, but the second seems to be an independent tr. from the Heb. text. Ἀνοίξω 1st sg. fut. act. indic. of ἀνοίγω, "open." Unlike preceding uses of the phrase ἐν παραβολαῖς, the phrase here expresses attendant circumstance ("as I speak parables") or means "by speaking parables" rather than instr. Ἐρεύξομαι 1st sg. fut. mid. indic. of dep. ἐρεύγομαι, "blurt out, proclaim." Κεκρυμμένα (acc. pl. neut. of pf. pass. ptc. of κρύπτω, "hide") is subst. and may be an example of the divine pass.: "things that have been hidden (by God?)." Ἀπό with the gen. (καταβολῆς) is used to mark the beginning point in time and in this context means: "from the creation of the world until now." Καταβολή, -ῆς, ἡ, "foundation (in the sense of the act of laying a foundation)." Κόσμου (obj. gen.) is absent from some early mss. and is prob. a scribal addition intended to clarify the mng. of the text.

FOR FURTHER STUDY

65. The Parable of the Leaven

Bailey, M. "The Kingdom in the Parables of Matthew 13, Part 5: The Parable of the Leavening Process." *BSac* 156 (1999): 61–71.

Campbell, D. "The Leaven." *ExpTim* 104 (1993): 307–8.

Crook, Z. A. "The Synoptic Parables of the Mustard Seed and the Leaven: A Test-Case for the Two-Document, Two-Gospel, and Farrer-Goulder Hypotheses." *JSNTS* 78 (2000): 23–48.

Seccombe, D. "Incongruity in the Gospel Parables." *TynBul* 62 (2011): 161–72.

8. The Meaning of the Parable of the Weeds (13:36–43)

13:36 Τότε means "after that." Ἀφείς (nom. sg. masc. of aor. act. ptc. of ἀφίημι) is prob. attendant circumstance (most EVV). In this context the vb. may mean "dismiss," in the sense of sending others back to their homes (BDAG 156b–57b), or "leave" (most EVV). Ἦλθεν 3rd sg. aor. act. indic. of dep. ἔρχομαι. The def. art. with οἰκίαν is prob. the art. of previous ref. and refers to the home mentioned in 13:1 that was serving as Jesus's ministry headquarters. Προσῆλθον 3rd pl. aor. act. indic. of dep. προσέρχομαι. Although most EVV see λέγοντες (nom. sg. masc. of pres. act. ptc. of λέγω) as attendant circumstance, the ptc. lacks several of the common characteristics and may be a ptc. of purpose: "They approached so they could ask." Διασάφησον 2nd sg. aor. act.

impv. of διασαφέω, "explain." Τῶν ζιζανίων (13:25) is gen. of ref. Τοῦ ἀγροῦ (13:27) is gen. of place and the phrase refers to "the weeds sown in the field" (cf. 13:25).

13:37 The def. art. ὁ functions as a pers. pron. (αὐτός). Ἀποκριθείς (nom. sg. masc. of aor. pass. ptc. of dep. ἀποκρίνομαι, "answer") is pleonastic but clarifies that Jesus's statement was given in response to the disciples' request. Εἶπεν 3rd sg. aor. act. indic. of λέγω. The art. ptc. σπείρων (nom. sg. masc. of pres. act. ptc. of σπείρω, "sow") is subst. Σπέρμα 13:24. As is common in the interpretation of parables, ἐστίν (3rd sg. pres. indic. of εἰμί) means "symbolizes, represents." Ὁ υἱὸς τοῦ ἀνθρώπου 9:6.

13:38 Ἀγρός 13:24. Ἐστίν 13:37. Since both ἀγρός (subj.) and κόσμος (pred. nom.) are art., the identity of the subj. and pred. nom. must be inferred from word order and context. Τὸ καλὸν σπέρμα (13:24) is the logical subj. of the sentence, and the οὗτοι was not grammatically necessary. Matthew either used the dem. pron. for emphasis or to diminish the awkwardness of a neut. sg. subj. and a masc. pl. pred. nom. Although the antecedent of οὗτοι is σπέρμα and normally the pron. would match the gender and num. of the antecedent, in this case the gender and number of the pron. were attracted to that of the pred. nom. (οἱ υἱοί) instead. Εἰσίν 3rd sg. pres. indic. of εἰμί, "represent." With the gen. τῆς βασιλείας, the noun clearly does not refer to physical descendants. The noun has the rarer but well-represented mng. "one who shares in or is closely related to something" (BDAG 1024c–27b 2.c.β.) and thus means "the heirs of the kingdom." Ζιζάνια 13:25. Εἰσίν, see above. Πονηρός, -ά, -όν, "evil." The art. τοῦ πονηροῦ is subst. and the art. is *par excellence* ("the evil one") and refers to Satan as the epitome of evil. Since the gen. sg. forms of the masc. and neut. adj. are identical, it is possible that the adj. is neut. and simply means "of evil" (N 559). However, the explicit ref. to the devil in the next verse suggests that the adj. is masc. and pers. With the gen. τοῦ πονηροῦ, the noun υἱοί refers to a relationship that defines one's character (BDAG 1024c–27b 2.c.α.). Thus these individuals were not conceived by Satan, but they exhibit his character as surely as a son resembles his father.

13:39 Ἐχθρός 13:25. Ὁ σπείρας (nom. sg. masc. of aor. act. ptc. of σπείρω, "sow") is attrib. Ἐστίν 13:37. Διάβολος, -ου, ὁ, "the devil." Θερισμός 13:30. Συντέλεια, -ας, ἡ, "completion, end." Αἰῶνός is subj. gen. Θεριστής 13:30.

13:40 Ὥσπερ marks the prot. and οὕτως marks the apod. of a comp. sentence: "just as . . . so also." Οὖν introduces the interpretation of the parable based on the identification of the referents in 13:37–39. Συλλέγεται (3rd sg. pres. pass. indic. of συλλέγω, "gather") is gnomic. Τὰ ζιζάνια 13:25. Πυρί is instr.: "with fire." Κατακαίεται 3rd sg. pres. pass. indic. of κατακαίω, "burn up, consume." Ἔσται (3rd sg. pres. indic. of εἰμί) is predictive. Ἐν is temp.: "at, during." Τῇ συντελείᾳ τοῦ αἰῶνος 13:39.

13:41 Ἀποστελεῖ (3rd sg. fut. act. indic. of ἀποστέλλω, "send") is predictive. Ὁ υἱὸς τοῦ ἀνθρώπου 9:6. Αὐτοῦ is prob. a gen. of authority, the inverse of the gen. of subord. Just as this cstr. refers to the evil angels over which Satan rules in 25:41, it here refers to the holy angels over which the Son of Man wields authority. Since Matthew has frequently described angels as under the authority of the Lord (1:20, 24; 2:13, 19; 28:2), the current description hints at Jesus's deity. Συλλέξουσιν (3rd pl. fut. act. indic. of συλλέγω, "gather") is predictive. Ἐκ with τῆς βασιλείας expresses separation.

BDAG suggests that βασιλεία here refers to a group of people from which others are removed (295d–298b 1.b.). However, verse 43 uses the category οἱ δίκαιοι to refer to this group, suggesting that βασιλεία here refers to the realm of the Son of Man—heaven and earth—from which the wicked are removed (H 1.394). Σκάνδαλον, -ου, τό, "offense, enticement to sin, person who causes an offense" (BDAG 926b–c 2, 3). The coordination of τὰ σκάνδαλα with τοὺς ποιοῦντας τὴν ἀνομίαν may suggest that both categories refer to persons (H 1.394), but most EVV view the noun as impers.: "everything that causes sin." The impers. view is supported by the possibility of an allusion to Zephaniah 1:3 (LXX, W). The art. ποιοῦντας (acc. pl. masc. of pres. act. ptc. of ποιέω) is subst.: "those who do, commit." Ἀνομία, -ας, ἡ, "lawless act."

13:42 Βαλοῦσιν (3rd pl. fut. act. indic. of βάλλω) is predictive. Κάμινος, -ου, ἡ, "furnace, oven." Τοῦ πυρός is attrib. gen.: "fiery/blazing furnace" (most EVV). Ἐκεῖ ἔσται ὁ κλαυθμὸς καὶ ὁ βρυγμὸς τῶν ὀδόντων 8:12.

13:43 Τότε may mean "at that time" or "after that time." The later sense is probable here since the preceding context refers to the removal of sinners and the causes of sin, which will result in the glorious state of Jesus's disciples described here. The description of the fut. state of God's people is influenced by Daniel 12:3 (Θ) and is sim. to Matthew 17:2. The art. adj. δίκαιοι is subst.: "righteous ones." Ἐκλάμψουσιν (3rd pl. fut. act. indic. of ἐκλάμπω, "shine") is predictive. Ὡς "like." Ἥλιος, -ου, ὁ, "sun." Ἐν could be temp. or *local. The gen. τοῦ πατρός modifying βασιλείᾳ may be subj. ("the Father's reign") or poss. ("the realm that belongs to the Father"). Αὐτῶν is a gen. of relationship and confirms that Jesus's disciples are children of God and thus of the King. Ὁ ἔχων ὦτα ἀκουέτω 11:15.

FOR FURTHER STUDY

See For Further Study § 61

HOMILETICAL SUGGESTIONS

Good and Evil (13:24–30, 36–43)
1. God is the source of good (through the gospel), and Satan is the source of evil (through temptation)
2. Good and evil people will coexist until Jesus returns
3. Jesus will separate and judge the good and the evil and assign them to two different destinies

9. The Parables of the Hidden Treasure and Valuable Pearl (13:44–46)

13:44 Ὁμοία ἐστὶν ἡ βασιλεία τῶν οὐρανῶν 13:31. Θησαυρός, -οῦ, ὁ, "treasure." Θησαυρῷ is dat. of comp. Κεκρυμμένῳ (dat. sg. masc. of pf. pass. ptc. of κρύπτω, "hide") is attrib. Ἐν τῷ ἀγρῷ 13:24. The antecedent of ὅν is θησαυρῷ. Εὑρών (nom. sg. masc. of aor. act. ptc. of εὑρίσκω, "find, discover") is either temp. (NIV) or *attendant circumstance (most EVV). Ἔκρυψεν 3rd sg. aor. act. indic. of κρύπτω. Ἀπό with the obj. τῆς χαρᾶς expresses the cause or motive (BDAG; NET) or manner (most EVV).

Cause is more likely since this usage has parallels elsewhere in Matthew (10:28; 14:26; 18:7; 28:4), but the use of the prep. to express manner does not. Ὑπάγει 3rd sg. pres. act. indic. of ὑπάγω. Πωλεῖ 3rd sg. pres. act. indic. of πωλέω, "sell." Πάντα is subst.: "everything." The correlative ὅσα stresses the quantity of the objects sold and clarifies the πάντα. Ἔχει 3rd sg. pres. act. indic. of ἔχω. Ἀγοράζει 3rd sg. pres. act. indic. of ἀγοράζω, "buy." The def. art. modifying ἀγρόν (13:24) is the art. of previous ref., and this is confirmed by the dem. pron. ἐκεῖνον. The four pres. tense vbs. are historical pres. that express the growing excitement of the story.

13:45 Πάλιν ὁμοία ἐστὶν ἡ βασιλεία τῶν οὐρανῶν 13:31. Ἀνθρώπῳ is dat. of comp. Ἔμπορος, -ου, ὁ, "merchant." Ἐμπόρῳ is dat. of simple appos. Ζητοῦντι (dat. sg. masc. of pres. act. ptc. of ζητέω, "seeking." Μαργαρίτης, -ου, ὁ, "pearl."

13:46 Εὑρών (nom. sg. masc. of aor. act. ptc. of εὑρίσκω, "find") is prob. temp. (most EVV). Πολύτιμος, -η, -ον, "extremely valuable." Μαργαρίτην 13:45. Ἀπελθών (nom. sg. masc. of aor. act. ptc. of dep. ἀπέρχομαι, "go away") is attendant circumstance (most EVV). Πέπρακεν (3rd sg. pf. act. indic. of πιπράσκω, "sell") is an example of the pf. for the aor. (BDF §343.1). Πάντα ὅσα 13:44. Εἶχεν 3rd sg. impf. act. indic. of ἔχω. Ἠγόρασεν 3rd sg. aor. act. indic. of ἀγοράζω, "buy." The antecedent of αὐτόν is μαργαρίτην, a 1st declension masculine noun.

FOR FURTHER STUDY

66. *The Historic Present in Matthew*

Wilmshurst, S. M. B. "The Historic Present in Matthew's Gospel: A Survey and Analysis Focused on Matthew 13.44." *JSNT* 25 (2003): 269–87.

67. *The Parables of the Hidden Treasure and Valuable Pearl*

Bailey, M. "The Kingdom in the Parables of Matthew 13, Part 6: The Parables of the Hidden Treasure and the Pearl Merchant." *BSac* 156 (1999): 175–89.

Carson, D. A. "The Homoios Word-Group as Introduction to Some Matthean Parables." *NTS* 31 (1985): 277–82.

Fenton, J. C. "Expounding the Parables: The Parables of the Treasure and the Pearl (Matt 13:44–46)." *ExpTim* 77 (1966): 178–80.

Gibbs, J. A. "Parables of Atonement and Assurance: Matthew 13:44–46." *CTQ* 51 (1987): 19–43.

10. The Parable of the Dragnet (13:47–50)

13:47 Πάλιν ὁμοία ἐστὶν ἡ βασιλεία τῶν οὐρανῶν 13:31. Σαγήνη, -ης, ἡ, "dragnet." Σαγήνη is dat. of comp. Βληθείσῃ (dat. sg. fem. of aor. pass. ptc. of βάλλω) is attrib. Ἐκ identifies a group from which a separation takes place: "from among." Γένος, -ους, τό, "kind, species." Συναγαγούσῃ (dat. sg. fem. of aor. act. ptc. of συνάγω, "gather") is attrib.

13:48 The antecedent of the rel. pron. ἥν is σαγήνη. The clause ὅτε ἐπληρώθη is parenthetical, since the rel. pron. of the obj. of the ptc. ἀναβιβάσαντες and the logical (but not grammatical) subj. of ἐπληρώθη. Ἐπί with the acc. (τὸν αἰγιαλόν) means "on the surface of." Αἰγιαλός, -οῦ, ὁ, "shore, beach." Καθίσαντες (nom. pl. masc. of aor. act.

ptc. of καθίζω, "sit") is attendant circumstance (most EVV). Συνέλεξαν 3rd pl. aor. act. indic. of συλλέγω, "gather, collect." The art. adj. καλά is subst. and means "the good things (fish)." Ἄγγος, -ους, τό, "container." Δέ is prob. adversative. Σαπρός, -ά, -όν, "worthless, bad." The adj. likely describes fish too bony to dress or fish that were prohibited by dietary laws. Ἔξω "out." Ἔβαλον 3rd pl. 2nd aor. act. indic. of βάλλω.

13:49 Οὕτως ἔσται ἐν τῇ συντελείᾳ τοῦ αἰῶνος 13:40. Ἐξελεύσονται (3rd pl. fut. mid. indic. of dep. ἐξέρχομαι, "go out") is predictive. Ἀφοριοῦσιν (3rd pl. fut. act. indic. of ἀφορίζω, "separate") is predictive. The art. adj. πονηρούς is subst.: "the evil/wicked ones." Ἐκ μέσου "from among" (BDAG 634d–35c 2.b.). The art. adj. δικαίων is subst.: "the righteous (ones)."

13:50 καὶ βαλοῦσιν αὐτοὺς εἰς τὴν κάμινον τοῦ πυρός· ἐκεῖ ἔσται ὁ κλαυθμὸς καὶ ὁ βρυγμὸς τῶν ὀδόντων 13:42.

FOR FURTHER STUDY

68. The Parable of the Dragnet

Bailey, M. "The Kingdom in the Parables of Matthew 13, Part 7: The Parables of the Dragnet and the Householder." *BSac* 156 (1999): 282–96.

Morrice, W. G. "The Parable of the Dragnet." *ExpTim* 95 (1984): 281–82.

_____. "The Parable of the Dragnet and the Gospel of Thomas." *ExpTim* 95 (1984): 269–73.

HOMILETICAL SUGGESTIONS

The Great Judgment (13:47–50)

1. The world contains all kinds of people, both evil and righteous
2. On the day of judgment, Jesus will send his angels to separate the evil from the righteous
3. The wicked will suffer eternally as a punishment for their sins

11. Kingdom Scribes (13:51–52)

13:51 Συνήκατε 2nd pl. aor. act. indic. of συνίημι, "understand." The antecedent of ταῦτα is evidently the truths about the kingdom taught in the preceding parables. Λέγουσιν (3rd pl. pres. act. indic. of λέγω) is historical pres. The antecedent of αὐτῷ is Ἰησοῦς (13:1). Ναί "yes."

13:52 The def. art. ὁ functions as a pers. pron. (αὐτός). Εἶπεν 3rd sg. aor. act. indic. of λέγω. The antecedent of αὐτοῖς is μαθηταί (13:36). Διὰ τοῦτο is clearly causal, but determining the antecedent of τοῦτο is difficult. One might conclude from the shift in number from ταῦτα (13:51) to τοῦτο (13:52) that the two pron. must have different antecedents. Thus τοῦτο does not refer to the kingdom parables or the truths taught in them. This would suggest that the antecedent of τοῦτο is the understanding expressed in 13:51. However, Matthew never uses the pl. ταῦτα as the obj. of διά (cf. 6:25; 12:27, 31; 13:13; 14:2; 18:23; 21:43; 23:34; 24:44). Thus the shift in number may be simply stylistic. The antecedent is prob. the same as that of ταῦτα, the truths of the parables (H 1.401; N 570). Alternatively, D&A suggest that the phrase διὰ τοῦτο has a weakened sense and serves merely to mark a transition: "so then, well." The adj. πᾶς with a sg. anar. noun (γραμματεύς) emphasizes the individual members of a class: "every single scribe." Γραμματεύς, -έως, ὁ, "scribe, expert in biblical interpretation." Μαθητευθείς (nom. sg. masc. of aor. pass. ptc. of μαθητεύω, "teach") is attrib. The dat. τῇ βασιλείᾳ τῶν οὐρανῶν (3:2) is dat. of ref. Ὅμοιος, -οία, -οιον, "like." Ἐστίν (3rd sg. pres. indic. of εἰμί) is gnomic. Ἀνθρώπῳ is dat. of ref. Οἰκοδεσπότης, -ου, ὁ, "householder." Οἰκοδεσπότῃ is dat. of simple appos. Ὅστις here serves as a substitute for the rel. pron. ὅς. Ἐκβάλλει 3rd sg. pres. act. indic. of ἐκβάλλω, "bring out." Ἐκ with the gen. identifies the source. Θησαυρός, -οῦ, ὁ, "treasure (chest)." Αὐτοῦ is gen. of poss. Καινός, -ή, -όν, "new." Καινά is subst.: "new things." Παλαιός, -ά, -όν, "old." Παλαιά is subst.: "old things."

FOR FURTHER STUDY

69. Scribe of the Kingdom

Hagner, D. A. "New Things from the Scribe's Treasure Box (Mt 13:52)." *ExpTim* 109 (1998): 329–34.

Hultgren, A. J. "Things New and Old at Matthew 13:52." *WW* 1 (1992): 109–17.

Phillips, P. M. "Casting Out the Treasure: A New Reading of Matthew 13.52." *JSNT* 31 (2008): 3–24.

Syiemlieh, B. J. "Portrait of a Christian Scribe (Matthew 13:52)." *AsJT* 20 (2006): 57–66.

HOMILETICAL SUGGESTIONS

All Bible Students Are Wealthy! (13:51–52)

1. The Christian who carefully studies the Bible has a wealth of treasures
2. The Old Testament is like an old treasure
3. Jesus's teaching is like a new treasure
4. Both treasures are to be valued and shared

12. Reaction to Jesus's Teaching and Miracles (13:53–58)

This section forms the conclusion to the collection of Jesus's kingdom parables. However, it also serves as a transition from chapter 13 to chapter 14. Both this paragraph (13:54) and 14:2 refer to Jesus's miracles (αἱ δυνάμεις) and different reactions to those miracles.

13:53 Καὶ ἐγένετο ὅτε ἐτέλεσεν ὁ Ἰησοῦς 7:28. Παραβολάς 13:3. Μετῆρεν 3rd sg. aor. act. indic. of μεταίρω, "go away." Ἐκεῖθεν is an adv. of place, marking a starting point for movement: "from there."

G. REJECTION AND WITHDRAWAL TO THE NORTH (13:54–16:20)

1. Jesus Rejected at Nazareth (13:54–58)

13:54 Ἐλθών (nom. sg. masc. of aor. act. ptc. of dep. ἔρχομαι) is either attendant circumstance (most EVV) or temp. (NIV). Πατρίς, -ίδος, ἡ, "homeland, hometown." Ἐδίδασκεν (3rd sg. impf. act. indic. of διδάσκω) is ingr. (most EVV). Αὐτούς has no clear antecedent in the preceding context. However, the following context shows that the referent is synagogue attendees in Jesus's hometown (Nazareth and its vicinity). The use of the gen. αὐτῶν to modify συναγωγῇ may suggest that Matthew knew of Christian assemblies that met in Nazareth at the time that he wrote and that he wished to distinguish these Jewish assemblies from those. Ὥστε with the inf. (ἐκπλήσσεσθαι pres. pass. inf. of ἐκπλήσσω, "be amazed" [pass.] and λέγειν pres. act. inf. of λέγω) expresses result. Αὐτούς is the acc. subj. of the inf. The interr. adv. πόθεν seeks to know the source of something: "from whence." The antecedent of the subst. τούτῳ is Ἰησοῦς. Since the cstr. is verbless, the dat. is dat. of recipient (W 148–49). The pl. form of δύναμις (αἱ δυνάμεις) refers to remarkable displays of supernatural power or "miracles" (CSB).

13:55 In a question, the neg. οὐχ implies a positive response: "This is—, right?" The antecedent of οὗτος is Ἰησοῦς. Ἐστίν 3rd sg. pres. indic. of εἰμί. Τέκτων, -ονος, ὁ, "carpenter, builder, craftsman" (BDAG 995b–c). Οὐχ implies a positive response to both elements of the compound question. Λέγεται 3rd sg. pres. pass. indic. of λέγω, "be called by a name" (pass.). Μαριάμ, ἡ, "Miriam, Mary." Ἰάκωβος, -ου, ὁ, "Jacob, James." Ἰωσήφ, ὁ, "Joseph." Σίμων, -ωνος, ὁ, "Simon." Ἰούδας, -α, ὁ, "Judah, Judas."

13:56 Ἀδελφή, -ῆς, ἡ, "sister." Οὐχί implies a positive response to the question. Πρός with the acc. (ἡμᾶς) means "be with (in the company of) someone" (BDAG 874 3.g.). Εἰσιν 3rd pl. pres. indic. of εἰμί. Πόθεν, 13:54. Οὖν is inferential, showing that the preceding questions lead logically to the pres. question. Τούτῳ 13:54. Ταῦτα refers to the wisdom and miracles mentioned in the parallel question in 13:54 but is intensified by the adj. πάντα and prob. includes all of Jesus's actions and words they found to be inexplicable.

13:57 Ἐσκανδαλίζοντο 3rd pl. impf. pass. indic. of σκανδαλίζω, "offend." BDAG (926a–b) states that the pass. voice of σκανδαλίζω followed by ἐν with the pers. dat. (ἐν αὐτῷ) means: "be led into sin or repelled." D&A (2:459–60) affirm this interpretation here and conclude that the cstr. refers to a denial of faith that results in eschatological judgment. However, in this context the cstr. more likely means "take offense at him" (N 576) or "were scandalized by him" (H 1.301, 406). If so, the prep. ἐν with the dat. expresses cause. Ἄτιμος, -ον, "dishonored, despised." Εἰ μή "except." Πατρίδι 13:54.

13:58 Ἐποίησεν 3rd sg. aor. act. indic. of ποιέω. Ἐκεῖ is adv. of place: "there." Δυνάμεις 13:54. Διά with the acc. (τὴν ἀπιστίαν) expresses cause. Ἀπιστία, -ας, ἡ, "disbelief, refusal to believe." Αὐτῶν is subj. gen.

FOR FURTHER STUDY

70. Jesus's Trade

Batey, R. A. "Is Not This the Carpenter?" *NTS* 30 (1984): 249–58.

Campbell, K. M. "What Was Jesus's Occupation?" *JETS* 48 (2005): 501–19.

Furfey, P. H. "Christ as Tekton." *CBQ* 17 (1955): 324–35.

71. Jesus's Family

Bauckham, R. "The Brothers and Sisters of Jesus: An Epiphanian Response to John P. Meier." *CBQ* 56 (1994): 686–700.

————. *Jude and the Relatives of Jesus in the Early Church*. Edinburgh: T&T Clark, 1990.

Meier, J. P. "The Brothers and Sisters of Jesus in Ecumenical Perspective." *CBQ* 54 (1992): 1–28.

Miller, S M. "What Happened to Jesus's 'Brothers?'" *Christian History* 17 (1998): 35.

Van Aarde, A. G. "The Carpenter's Son (Mt 13:55): Joseph and Jesus in the Gospel of Matthew and Other Texts." *Neot* 34 (2000): 173–90.

Yeo, K. "The Mother and Brothers of Jesus (Lk 8:19–21, Mk 3:31–35, Mt 12:46–50)." *AsJT* 6 (1992): 311–17.

HOMILETICAL SUGGESTIONS

Too Close to See (13:53–57)

1. Jesus's wisdom and miracles astonished many who knew him
2. Their supposed familiarity with Jesus blinded them to his true identity
3. Their refusal to believe guaranteed that they would not be given further incentive to believe

2. Herod Antipas's View of Jesus (14:1–5)

14:1 Ἐν with the obj. ἐκείνῳ τῷ καιρῷ is clearly temp. and means "during." Ἤκουσεν 3rd sg. aor. act. indic. of ἀκούω. Ἡρῴδης, -ου, ὁ, Herod (Antipas). Τετραάρχης, -ου, ὁ, "tetrarch" (title of a prince who ruled over a small region by the courtesy of Rome). Ἀκοή, -ῆς, ἡ, "report." Ἰησοῦ is gen. of ref. See Metzger 28.

14:2 Εἶπεν 3rd sg. aor. act. indic. of λέγω. Παῖς, παιδός, ὁ, "slave, servant." Παισίν is dat. of indir. obj. Αὐτοῦ is gen. of poss. or authority. The dem. pron. οὗτος is being used as a subst. and means "this man." Ἐστίν 3rd sg. pres. indic. of εἰμί. Ἰωάννης ὁ βαπτιστής 3:1. Αὐτός is emphatic and reaffirms Jesus's alleged identity as John. Ἠγέρθη (3rd sg. aor. pass. indic. of ἐγείρω, "raise, resurrect") is prob. a divine pass. Ἀπό expresses separation: "out from among." Τῶν νεκρῶν is subst.: "the dead (ones)." Διά with the acc. (τοῦτο) is causal: "because of this." The antecedent of the neut. pron. is the entire preceding clause. Δύναμις, -εως, ἡ, "miraculous power." The noun has a slightly different sense than its occurrence in 13:54, in which it meant "deed that displays supernatural power" or "miracle." Ἐνεργοῦσιν 3rd pl. pres. act. indic. of ἐνεργέω, "be at work." Ἐν with the pers. dat. (αὐτῷ) expresses agency: "Miraculous powers are at work through him" (most EVV).

14:3 Ὁ Ἡρῴδης 14:1. Γάρ introduces the reason for Herod's paranoid suspicion. Κρατήσας (nom. sg. masc. of aor. act. ptc. of κρατέω, "arrest, apprehend") may be *attendant circumstance (most EVV) or temp. (LEB). Τὸν Ἰωάννην 14:2. Ἔδησεν 3rd sg. aor. act. indic. of δέω, *"bind (with chains)" or "tie up (with rope)." Ἐν with the obj. φυλακῇ marks a location. Φυλακή, -ῆς, ἡ, "prison." Ἀπέθετο 3rd sg. aor. mid. indic. of ἀποτίθημι, "put away." Διά with the acc. of pers. (Ἡρῳδιάδα) identifies the person who serves as the cause or motivation for an action. Ἡρῳδιάς, -άδος, ἡ, "Herodias." Φίλιππος, -ου, ὁ, "Philip." Φιλίππου is a gen. of relationship. Thus τὴν γυναῖκα (acc. of simple appos. identifying Herodias) means "wife" rather than merely "woman." Τοῦ ἀδελφοῦ is a gen. of simple appos. that further identifies Philip. Αὐτοῦ is gen. of relationship. See Metzger 28–29.

14:4 Ἔλεγεν (3rd sg. impf. act. indic. of λέγω) may be pluperf. ("had been saying;" most EVV; cf. W 549) or *iter. ("repeatedly said;" NET; H 2.412; N 583). In this context the vb. seems to be both pluperf. and iter.. It describes events that occurred prior to the arrest documented in the preceding context. However, Matthew (who uses pluperf. vbs. eight times in his Gospel) chose to use the imperf. because he wished to emphasize John's relentlessness in boldly condemning the sins of the tetrarch. Γάρ introduces the reason for Herodias's animosity toward John. ὁ Ἰωάννης 3:1. The antecedent of αὐτῷ is Ἡρῴδης (14:1). Ἔξεστιν 3rd sg. pres. indic. of the impers. vb. ἔξειμι "it is permissible, right." Σοι is dat. of ref. and indicates that John's prohibition of marriage to Herodias pertained particularly to Herod. Ἔχειν (aor. act. inf. of ἔχω) is complementary. The antecedent of αὐτήν is Ἡρῳδιάς (14:3).

14:5 Θέλων (nom. sg. masc. of pres. act. ptc. of θέλω) is concessive: "Although he wanted . . ." The antecedent of αὐτόν is Ἰωάννην (14:3). Ἀποκτεῖναι (pres. act. inf. of ἀποκτείνω, "kill, put to death") is complementary. Ἐφοβήθη 3rd sg. aor. pass. indic. of φοβέω, "be afraid" (pass.). Ὅτι is causal and shows the reason for Herod's fear. The cstr. that combines ὡς with the dbl. acc. (προφήτην and αὐτόν) and the vb. ἔχω means "consider (someone) to be (something)." Εἶχον (3rd pl. impf. act. indic. of ἔχω) is prob. the prog. impf. The vb. expresses the ongoing opinion of the members of the crowd regarding John. Although the implied subj. of the vb. is "crowd," Matthew shifted to the pl. number because he was thinking of the crowd as composed of many individuals.

3. The Execution of John (14:6–12)

14:6 Γενέσια, -ίων, τά, "birthday celebration." The cstr. γενεσίοις γενομένοις (dat. pl. masc. of aor. mid. ptc. of dep. γίνομαι) is prob. a dat. abs. (see 8:23). Although other potential dat. abs. in Matthew (8:23; 9:27–28) are not truly abs., since they correspond to another dat. in the sentence, here the dat. pl. noun and ptc. do not correspond to any word in the rest of the sentence. The cstr. is temp. and contemp. (most EVV): "when Herod's birthday celebration occurred." Τοῦ Ἡρῴδου (14:1) is prob. a subj. gen. since Herod's birthday is the date on which he was born. Ὠρχήσατο 3rd sg. aor. mid. indic. of dep. ὀρχέομαι, "dance." Θυγάτηρ, -τρος, ἡ, "daughter." Τῆς Ἡρῳδιάδος (14:3) is gen. of relationship. Ἐν τῷ μέσῳ without a gen. modifier is apparently idiomatic and means "in public" (BDAG 634d–35c 1.b.). Καί here introduces the result of the preceding action. Ἤρεσεν 3rd sg. aor. act. indic. of ἀρέσκω, "please." Τῷ Ἡρῴδῃ (14:1) is dat. of dir. obj.

14:7 Ὅθεν is an adv. that marks the basis or reason for an action: "for this reason, therefore, hence." Μετά with the gen. (ὅρκου) marks an accompanying circumstance. The position of the prep. phrase is prob. emphatic. Ὅρκος, -ου, ὁ, "oath." Ὡμολόγησεν 3rd sg. aor. act. indic. of ὁμολογέω, "promise." The word order initially seems to suggest that αὐτῇ is the dat. of dir. obj. of ὡμολόγησεν. However, it is prob. the indir. obj. of the inf. δοῦναι (aor. act. inf. of δίδωμι), as affirmed by most EVV. The combination of the rel. pron. ὅ with the particle of contingency ἐάν is equivalent to the neut. sg. of ὅστις with ἄν or ἐάν ("whatever"). Αἰτήσηται 3rd sg. aor. mid. subjunc. of αἰτέω, "ask, request." The mid. voice of αἰτέω was used interchangeably with the act. in the Koine period. The subjunc. was required by the presence of ἐάν.

14:8 Although the def. art. ἡ may mark the ptc. προβιβασθεῖσα as subst. so the ptc. serves as the subj. of the sentence, the def. art. prob. functions as a substitute for the subst. use of the dem. pron.: "this daughter." If so, προβιβασθεῖσα (nom. sg. fem. of aor. pass. ptc. of προβιβάζω, "coach, prompt") is prob. causal. After the pass. ptc., the prep. ὑπό with the gen. of pers. (τῆς μητρός) expresses pers. agency. Αὐτῆς is gen. of relationship and the antecedent is θυγάτηρ (14:6). Δός (2nd sg. aor. act. impv. of δίδωμι) expresses urgency. Μοι is dat. of indir. obj. Φησίν (3rd sg. pres. act. indic. of φημί, "say") is historical pres. Ὧδε "here" suggests that the daughter was either holding or pointing to a platter. Ἐπί with the dat. means "on." Πίναξ, -ακος, ὁ, "platter." Ἰωάννου is a partitive gen. Τοῦ βαπτιστοῦ is simple appos. (3:1).

14:9 Λυπηθείς (nom. sg. masc. of aor. pass. ptc. of λυπέω, "be grieved, sad, distressed") is concessive: "although he was grieved (by the situation)." Διά with the acc. is causal. See Metzger 29. Τοὺς ὅρκους 14:7. The pl. form of the noun implies that Herod repeated his oath, perhaps intensifying it until he received the desired response. Συνανακειμένους (acc. pl. masc. of pres. mid. ptc. of dep. συνανάκειμαι, "recline together for a meal") is subst. The ptc. is the second obj. of the prep. Thus two factors prompted Herod's decision, the oaths and the many witnesses to those oaths. Ἐκέλευσεν 3rd sg. aor. act. indic. of κελεύω, "command." Δοθῆναι (aor. pass. inf. of δίδωμι) is complementary. The statement is elliptical and means "he ordered that it (the head) be given to her."

14:10 Πέμψας (nom. sg. masc. of aor. act. ptc. of πέμπω, "send") is often treated as attendant circumstance (most EVV). However, the ptc. is more likely a ptc. of means and serves to demonstrate that Herod did not personally behead John but ordered his subordinates to do so. See 2:16 in which a ptc. form of the synonym ἀποστέλλω functions in an identical way. This is necessary since the vb. means "behead" rather than "cause someone to behead." Ἀπεκεφάλισεν 3rd sg. aor. act. indic. of ἀποκεφαλίζω, "behead." Ἰωάννην 14:2. Ἐν τῇ φυλακῇ 14:3. The def. art. is due to previous ref. (14:3).

14:11 Ἠνέχθη 3rd sg. aor. pass. indic. of φέρω. Ἐπὶ πίνακι 14:8. Ἐδόθη 3rd sg. aor. pass. indic. of δίδωμι. Κοράσιον, -ου, τό, "(little) girl." The noun is the dimin. form of the noun κόρη ("girl") and may indicate that the girl was relatively young. Ἤνεγκεν 3rd sg. aor. act. indic. of φέρω.

14:12 Προσελθόντες (nom. pl. masc. of aor. act. ptc. of dep. προσέρχομαι, "come forward, approach") may be *attendant circumstance (most EVV) or temp. The antecedent of αὐτοῦ is Ἰωάννης. Ἦραν 3rd pl. aor. act. indic. of αἴρω, "pick up." Πτῶμα, -ατος, τό, "corpse." Ἔθαψαν 3rd pl. aor. act. indic. of θάπτω, "bury." See Metzger 29. Ἐλθόντες (nom. pl. masc. of aor. act. ptc. of dep. ἔρχομαι) is prob. attendant circumstance (most EVV). Ἀπήγγειλαν 3rd pl. aor. act. indic. of ἀπαγγέλλω, "announce, report."

FOR FURTHER STUDY

72. The Death of John the Baptist

Bach, A. "Calling the Shots: Directing Salome's Dance of Death." *Semeia* 74 (1996): 103–26.

Janes, R. "Why the Daughter of Herodias Must Dance (Mark 6.14–29)." *JSNT* 28 (2006): 443–67.

Kraemer, R. S. "Implicating Herodias and Her Daughter in the Death of John the Baptizer: A (Christian) Theological Strategy?" *JBL* 125 (2006): 321–49.

Lillie, W. "Salome or Herodias?" *ExpTim* 65 (1954): 251.

Vander Stichele, C. "Herodias Goes Headhunting." Pages 164–75 in *Women of the New Testament and Their Afterlives*. Edited by C. E. Joynes and C. Rowland. Sheffield: Sheffield Phoenix, 2009.

HOMILETICAL SUGGESTIONS

Better to Lose Your Head Than to Lose Your Mind (14:1–12)

1. Unrepentant sinners are often haunted by a guilty conscience (14:1–2)
2. Unrepentant sinners may go to any extreme to silence those that condemn their sins (14:3–5)
3. Unrepentant sinners sometimes value vengeance against their critics more than earthly treasures (14:6–8)
4. Unrepentant sinners often care more about their reputation than about their true character (14:9–12)

4. Jesus's Temporary Withdrawal (14:13–14)

14:13 Ἀκούσας (nom. sg. masc. of aor. act. ptc. of ἀκούω) is prob. temp. (most EVV) but has some causal overtones. The report about John's death prompted Jesus's pursuit of solitude. Ἀνεχώρησεν 3rd sg. aor. act. indic. of ἀναχωρέω, "depart." Ἐκεῖθεν "from there." Ἔρημος, -ον "remote, uninhabited." The adj. is attrib. The prep. κατά with the obj. ἰδίαν (acc. sg. fem. of ἴδιος, -α, -ον, "one's own") is an idiom mng. "by himself, privately" and is synonymous with the adv. use of μόνος. Κατά with the acc. is sometimes used to express isolation or separateness (BDAG 511a–13d B.1.c.; BDAG 466c–68a 5). Κατ' ἰδίαν is a stereotypical cstr. used even when the subj. is pl., masc., or neut. Ἀκούσαντες (nom. pl. masc. of aor. act. ptc. of ἀκούω) is prob. temp. (most EVV) with causal overtones and is best tr. "since (they) heard. . . ." Ἠκολούθησαν 3rd pl. aor. act indic. of ἀκολουθέω. Αὐτῷ is dat. of dir. obj. Πεζῇ is an adv. mng. "on foot" and serves as a contrast to ἐν πλοίῳ ("by ship"). Ἀπό with the gen. (τῶν πόλεων) denotes a beginning point for the travels rather than separation specifically.

14:14 Ἐξελθών (nom. sg. masc. of aor. act. ptc. of dep. ἐξέρχομαι) is temp. (most EVV). Matthew does not specify what Jesus exited. If Jesus had already arrived and spent time at the remote location, he may have exited a shelter. However, the parallel in Mark 6:32–44 shows that the crowd arrived at the shore before Jesus did and was waiting when he arrived. Thus most EVV supply "the boat" as the dir. obj. of the ptc. Εἶδεν 3rd sg. aor. act. indic. of ὁράω. Ἐσπλαγχνίσθη 3rd sg. aor. pass. indic. of dep. σπλαγχνίζομαι, "feel compassion." With a vb. expressing feeling, ἐπί with the dat. (αὐτοῖς) is causal: "because of them" (BDAG 363a–67c 6.c.). Ἐθεράπευσεν 3rd sg. aor. act. indic. of θεραπεύω, "heal." Ἄρρωστος, -ον, "sick, ill" is subst.: "the sick." Αὐτῶν may be gen. of relationship ("their sick family members") or a *partitive gen. ("the sick people that were part of the crowds").

5. The Miraculous Feeding of the Crowds (14:15–21)

14:15 Ὀψιός, ά, όν, "late, evening (subst.)." Ὀψίας γενομένης (gen. sg. fem. of aor. mid. ptc. of dep. γίνομαι) is gen. abs., temp. and contemp.: "when evening came." Προσῆλθον 3rd pl. aor. act. indic. of dep. προσέρχομαι, "come to." The antecedent of αὐτῷ is Jesus (14:13). Λέγοντες (nom. pl. masc. of pres. act. ptc. of λέγω) may be attendant circumstance (most EVV), but the word order and tense suggest that it is a purpose ptc.: "they approached Jesus to say. . . ." Ἔρημος, -ον, "deserted." Ἐστίν 3rd sg. pres. indic. of εἰμί. Ἤδη "already." Παρῆλθεν 3rd sg. aor. act. indic. of dep. παρέρχομαι, "pass by." Matthew's expression is abbreviated. The phrase ἡ ὥρα refers to an undefined period of time in the day. The ESV tr. the clause "and the day is now over." However, ὥρα is not to be equated with ἡμέρα. The phrase may refer to the evening mealtime. Ἀπόλυσον (2nd sg. aor. act. impv. of ἀπολύω, "dismiss") expresses urgency. Ἵνα with the subjunc. (ἀγοράσωσιν 3rd pl. aor. act. subjunc. of ἀγοράζω, "buy") expresses purpose. Ἀπελθόντες (nom. pl. masc. of aor. act. ptc. of dep. ἀπέρχομαι, "depart") is either temp., means, or *attendant circumstance (most EVV). Κώμη, -ης, ἡ, "village." Ἑαυτοῖς is a dat. of advantage: "for themselves." Βρῶμα, -ατος, τά, "food." The mng. of the pl. is not clearly differentiated from that of the sg.

14:16 If the noun Ἰησοῦς is a scribal addition, the def. art. ὁ functions like the subst. use of the dem. pron. and serves as the subj. of the vb. Since Jesus is countering the disciples' suggestion, δέ is prob. adversative. Εἶπεν 3rd sg. aor. act. indic. of λέγω. The antecedent of αὐτοῖς is οἱ μαθηταί (14:15). Χρεία, -ας, ἡ, "need." Ἔχουσιν 3rd pl. pres. act. indic. of ἔχω. Ἀπελθεῖν (aor. act. inf. of dep. ἀπέρχομαι, "go away") may be viewed as a complementary inf. (if χρείαν ἔχουσιν is viewed as a single verbal idea mng. simply "need") or an *exegetical inf. that defines the nature of the need (W 607). Δότε (2nd pl. aor. act. impv. of δίδωμι) expresses urgency. The antecedent of αὐτοῖς is τοὺς ὄχλους. Ὑμεῖς is emphatic. Φαγεῖν is aor. act. inf. of ἐσθίω, "eat."

14:17 The def. art. οἱ functions as a subst. dem. pron. and serves as the subj. Δέ is adversative and introduces the disciples' counterresponse to Jesus's command. Λέγουσιν 3rd pl. pres. act. indic. of λέγω. The antecedent of αὐτῷ is Ἰησοῦς (cf. 14:16). Ἔχομεν 1st pl. pres. act. indic. of ἔχω. The statement is elliptical and the implied obj. of the vb. is either the indef. pron. τι or βρώματα. Ὧδε "here." The εἰ μή cstr. means "except" and introduces an important qualification to the statement. Πέντε "five." Ἰχθύς, -ύας, ὁ, "fish."

14:18 The def. art. ὁ functions as a subst. dem. pron. and serves as the subj. Δέ is adversative, since Jesus's response challenges the disciples' implication that they did not have adequate resources to feed the crowds. Εἶπεν 3rd sg. aor. act. indic. of λέγω. Φέρετε (2nd pl. pres. act. impv. of φέρω, "bring") is ingr.-prog. Μοι is dat. of indir. obj. Ὧδε 14:17. The antecedent of αὐτούς is ἄρτους and ἰχθύας.

14:19 The four ptc. in this verse create some difficulties for the interpreter. Most EVV break the lengthy sentence up into several sentences for the sake of Eng. style. Unfortunately, this may obscure the intended syntactical function of the ptc. Some EVV (e.g., CSB; ESV; NET) tr. three of the four ptc. as finite vbs. which suggests that the ptc. are viewed as expressing attendant circumstance. Κελεύσας (nom. sg. masc. of aor. act. ptc. of κελεύω, "command") is prob. attendant circumstance and is used to avoid a string of indic. vbs. joined by καί. Ἀνακλιθῆναι (aor. pass. inf. of ἀνακλίνω, "recline") is complementary. Ἐπί with the gen. (τοῦ χόρτου) means "on." Χόρτος, -ου, ὁ, "grass." Λαβών (nom. sg. masc. of aor. act. ptc. of λαμβάνω) may be attendant circumstance (CSB; NET) or temp. (NIV; LEB; ESV). The temp. function seems awkward since this aor. ptc. would be antecedent and the next aor. ptc. would apparently be contemp. Πέντε "five." Ἰχθύας 14:17. Ἀναβλέψας (nom. sg. masc. of aor. act. ptc. of ἀναβλέπω, "look up") is prob. temp. and contemp. (most EVV), but some treat it as attendant circumstance (ESV). The sg. τὸν οὐρανόν refers to the sky rather than the abode of God. Εὐλόγησεν 3rd sg. aor. act. indic. of εὐλογέω, "bless." Κλάσας (nom. sg. masc. of aor. act. ptc. of κλάω, "break") is either attendant circumstance (most EVV) or *temp., in which case the action is antecedent to the main vb. (LEB). Ἔδωκεν 3rd sg. aor. act. indic. of δίδωμι. Τοῖς μαθηταῖς is dat. of indir. obj. The clause οἱ δὲ μαθηταὶ τοῖς ὄχλοις is elliptical and implies the vb. ἔδωκαν.

14:20 Ἔφαγον 3rd pl. aor. act. indic. of ἐσθίω, "eat." Πάντες is subst.: "everyone." Καί introduces a result. Ἐχορτάσθησαν 3rd pl. aor. pass. indic. of χορτάζω, "fill with food." Ἦραν 3rd pl. aor. act. indic. of αἴρω, "take up." Περισσεῦον (acc. sg. neut. of pres. act. ptc. of περισσεύω, "be left over") is subst.: "what was leftover." Κλάσμα, -ατος, τό, "fragments." Δώδεκα, "twelve." Κόφινος, -ου, ὁ, "basket." Κοφίνους is acc. of simple appos. Πλήρης, -ες, "full." The adj. πλήρεις is attrib.: "twelve full baskets."

14:21 Ἐσθίοντες (nom. pl. masc. of pres. act. ptc. of ἐσθίω, "eat") is subst. Ἦσαν 3rd pl. impf. indic. of εἰμί. Ἄνδρες refers specifically to "adult males" in this context. Ὡσεί is used to mark an approximation: "about, approximately" (BDAG 1106c–d 2). Πεντακισχίλιοι, -ια, -α, "five thousand." Although χωρίς is used as a prep. (with the gen.) to express separation, exception, or exclusion, in a context discussing numbers the prep. is equivalent to the Eng. expression "not counting" (NET). Most EVV use the tr. "besides" and this tr. is supported by BDAG (1095b–d 2.a.γ.). However, the tr. "besides" suggests addition to rather than exclusion from the women and children and this nuance is not well substantiated.

FOR FURTHER STUDY

73. The Feeding of the Five Thousand

Cousins, P. E. "Feeding of the Five Thousand." *EvQ* 39 (1967): 152–54.
Fryer, N. S. L. "Matthew 14:14–21: The Feeding of the Five Thousand: A Grammatico-Historical Exegesis." *In die Skriflig/In Luce Verbi* 21 (1987): 27–42.
Hurst, A. "Feeding the Five Thousand." *ExpTim* 101 (1989): 80–81.

6. The Miraculous Crossing of the Sea (14:22–33)

14:22 Εὐθέως "immediately" indicates that the events of the paragraph occurred as soon as the miraculous feeding was over. Ἠνάγκασεν 3rd pl. aor. act. indic. of ἀναγκάζω, "compel, strongly urge." Ἐμβῆναι (aor. act. inf. of ἐμβαίνω, "board, embark") is complementary. Πλοῖον is the dir. obj. of the preceding inf. Προάγειν (pres. act. inf. of προάγω, "go before, go ahead") is complementary, and the pres. tense is ingr.-prog. Αὐτόν is dir. obj. of the preceding inf. The adv. of place πέραν is functioning as a subst. mng. "the other side, the opposite side (of the lake)." Ἕως with the neut. gen. rel. pron. οὗ means "until" (BDAG 422 1.b.β.) and normally functions in conjunction with an aor. subjunc. vb. Ἀπολύσῃ 3rd sg. aor. act. subjunc. of ἀπολύω, "release, dismiss."

14:23 Ἀπολύσας (nom. sg. masc. of aor. act. ptc. of ἀπολύω, "dismiss") is either *temp. and antecedent to the action of the main vb. (most EVV) or attendant circumstance. Ἀνέβη εἰς τὸ ὄρος 5:1. Κατά with the acc. (ἰδίαν) marks isolation so that the phrase means "by himself, alone" (14:13). Προσεύξασθαι (aor. mid. inf. of dep. προσεύχομαι) expresses purpose. Ὀψίας γενομένης 14:15. Μόνος, -η, -ον, "alone." Ἦν 3rd sg. impf. indic. of εἰμί. Ἐκεῖ "there."

14:24 The temp. adv. ἤδη ("already") combined with the adj. πολλούς and a measure of distance implies that the ship had traveled a surprisingly long distance in a surprisingly brief amount of time. However, this seems to be in tension with the later statement about the condition of the sea and the direction of the wind. The verse is complicated by several textual var. and the rdg. in the text of the UBS[5] is not widely supported. If the rdg. in the UBS[5] is correct, this suggests that the ship initially made good time, but suddenly stopped making progress. See Metzger 30. Alternatively, ἤδη may be tr. "by this time" (ESV) or "meanwhile" (NET). Ἀπεῖχεν 3rd. sg. impf. act. indic. of ἀπέχω, "be at a distance from." With the vb. ἀπέχω, the acc. of measure (σταδίους πολλούς) is used to indicate distance and ἀπό with the gen. (τῆς γῆς) is used to mark the starting point of the measurement (BDAG 102c–3b 4). Στάδιον, -ου, τό, "one eighth of a mile (602 Eng. feet or 192 meters)." Since the preceding context seems to stress the rapid progress of the ship, βασανιζόμενον (nom. sg. neut. of pres. pass. ptc. of βασανίζω, "harass") is prob. concessive: "even though the ship was being harassed by the waves." However, most EVV seem to view the ptc. as attendant circumstance. Ὑπό with the gen. τῶν κυμάτων (κῦμα, -ατος, τό, "wave") expresses agency/cause. If the ptc. is concessive, the particle γάρ prob. modifies the preceding ptc. (NIV; NET). Thus the nature of the wind caused the condition of the sea. Ἦν 3rd sg. impf. indic. of εἰμί. Ἄνεμος, -ου, ὁ, "wind." Ἐναντίος, -α, -ον, "opposite, in opposition." The adj.

indicates that the wind was blowing from the direction in which they desired to go and was driving the waves in the same contrary direction.

14:25 Τέταρτος, -η, -ον, "fourth." Φυλακή, -ῆς, ἡ, "watch (three-hour period used for reckoning time at night)." The fourth watch was from 3 a.m. to 6 a.m. Τετάρτῃ φυλακῇ is dat. of time: "during the fourth watch." Τῆς νυκτός is partitive gen. Ἦλθεν 3rd sg. aor. act. indic. of dep. ἔρχομαι. Περιπατῶν (nom. sg. masc. of pres. act. ptc. of περιπατέω) is prob. ptc. of means: "he came to them by walking. . . ." Ἐπί with the acc. (τὴν θάλασσαν) may mean "on, on top of" (most EVV) but with vbs. of movement normally means "across" (compare BDAG 363a–67c 1.c.α. and 4.b.β.).

14:26 Ἰδόντες (nom. pl. masc. of aor. act. ptc. of ὁράω) is prob. temp. (most EVV), but could instead be causal (since the sight prompted the reaction of the main vb.) or attendant circumstance. Ἐπί with the gen. (τῆς θαλάσσης) has a slightly different nuance from the cstr. with the acc. in 14:25. This cstr. indicates that Jesus walked on the surface of the sea (BDAG 363a–67c 1.a.). Περιπατοῦντα (acc. sg. masc. of pres. act. ptc. of περιπατέω) may be pred. or temp. Ἐταράχθησαν 3rd pl. aor. pass. indic. of ταράσσω, "shake, disturb (emotionally)." Λέγοντες (nom. pl. masc. of pres. act. ptc. of λέγω) may be attendant circumstance (most EVV), but the tense shift and word order suggest that it expresses result. Their superstitious statement was an expression of their emotional state. Ὅτι is a marker of dir. discourse. Φάντασμα, -ατος, τό, "apparition." Although the noun often means "ghost" and most EVV tr. the term "ghost," in Jewish literature the term could speak of an angel of God (Jos. *Ant.* 1 §331, 333). The term refers to any visual manifestation that inspires fear. Ἐστίν 3rd sg. pres. indic. of εἰμί. Ἀπό with the gen. (τοῦ φόβου) expresses cause: "as a result of their fear." Most EVV tr. the phrase "in fear" but such a tr. seems to express manner rather than cause. Ἔκραξαν 3rd pl. aor. act. indic. of κράζω, "cry out, scream."

14:27 Ἐλάλησεν 3rd sg. aor. act. indic. of λαλέω. Αὐτοῖς (antecedent: οἱ μαθηταί). Λέγων (nom. sg. masc. of pres. act. ptc. of λέγω) is pleonastic. Θαρσεῖτε (2nd pl. pres. act. impv. of θαρσέω, "have courage") is ingr.-prog. Ἐγώ is emphatic. Εἰμί (1st sg. pres. indic. of εἰμί). The ἐγώ εἰμι recalls 1:23 and anticipates 28:20. Jesus is speaking as Yahweh spoke (Quarles, *Theology*, 152–54). Μή with the pres. impv. (φοβεῖσθε 2nd pl. pres. mid. impv. of φοβέω, "be afraid") calls for the cessation of an action already in progress (14:26).

14:28 Ἀποκριθείς (nom. sg. masc. of aor. pass. ptc. of dep. ἀποκρίνομαι, "answer") is pleonastic, and most modern EVV either leave the ptc. or main vb. untranslated. The LEB treats the ptc. as attendant circumstance. Εἶπεν 3rd sg. aor. act. indic. of λέγω. Κύριε is simple voc. Εἰ with the indic. (εἶ 2nd sg. pres. indic. of εἰμί) marks the prot. of a first-class cond. statement that assumes the fulfillment of the prot. for the sake of argument. Σύ is emphatic. Κέλευσον (2nd sg. aor. act. impv. of κελεύω, "command") expresses urgency. Μέ is acc. subj. of the inf. Ἐλθεῖν (aor. act. inf. of dep. ἔρχομαι) is a complementary inf. Πρός with the acc. (σε) marks the direction of movement: "toward." Ἐπί with the acc. (τὰ ὕδατα) means "across" (14:25). Matthew used the pl. of ὕδωρ when referring to the content of the Sea of Galilee, but the sg. when referring to smaller amounts of water incl. that of the Jordan River.

14:29 The def. art. ὁ functions as a subst. dem. pron. and serves as the subj. of the vb. Εἶπεν 3rd sg. aor. act. indic. of λέγω. Ἐλθέ (2nd sg. aor. act. impv. of dep. ἔρχομαι) expresses urgency. Καταβάς (nom. sg. masc. of aor. act. ptc. of καταβαίνω, "come down") may be attendant circumstance (NIV; ESV; NET) or temp. Ἀπό with the gen. (τοῦ πλοίου) denotes the starting place for movement: "from." Περιεπάτησεν 3rd sg. aor. act. indic. of περιπατέω. Ἐπὶ τὰ ὕδατα 14:28. Ἦλθεν 14:25. Πρός with the acc. 14:28.

14:30 Βλέπων (nom. sg. masc. of pres. act. ptc. of βλέπω) is temp. (most EVV). Δέ is prob. adversative and contrasts Peter's initial faith with his later fear. Ἐφοβήθη 3rd sg. aor. pass. indic. of φοβέω). Ἀρξάμενος (nom. sg. masc. of aor. mid. ptc. of ἄρχω, "begin to" [mid.]) is prob. causal, but could be temp. or attendant circumstance. Καταποντίζεσθαι (pres. pass. inf. of καταποντίζω, "drown") is complementary. Ἔκραξεν 3rd sg. aor. act. indic. of κράζω, "scream." Λέγων (nom. sg. masc. of pres. act. ptc. of λέγω) is pleonastic. Although it lacks the interjection ὦ, Κύριε is voc. of emotional address as suggested that the vb. κράζω and the context. Σῶσόν (2nd sg. aor. act. impv. of σώζω) expresses urgency.

14:31 Εὐθέως "immediately." Ἐκτείνας (nom. sg. masc. of aor. act. ptc. of ἐκτείνω, "stretch out, extend") is either temp., means, or attendant circumstance. Ἐπελάβετο 3rd sg. aor. mid. indic. of dep. ἐπιλαμβάνομαι, "grasp, take hold of." Αὐτοῦ is gen. of dir. obj. Λέγει (3rd sg. pres. act. indic. of λέγω) is historical pres. Ὀλιγόπιστε (ὀλιγόπιστος, -ον, "of little faith") is subst. and simple voc. Εἰς with the acc. (τί) expresses purpose. With the interr. pron., the phrase means "for what purpose" or "why?" (BDAG 288d–93c 4.f.). Ἐδίστασας 2nd sg. aor. act. indic. of διστάζω, "doubt."

14:32 Ἀναβάντων (gen. pl. masc. of aor. act. ptc. of ἀναβαίνω, "go up") is gen. abs., temp. and prob. contemp. (most EVV). Αὐτῶν refers to both Jesus and Peter. Ἐκόπασεν 3rd sg. aor. act. indic. of κοπάζω, "stop, cease."

14:33 The def. art. οἱ functions as a subst. dem. pron. that serves as the subj. Προσεκύνησαν 3rd pl. aor. act. indic. of προσκυνέω, "worship." Αὐτῷ (antecedent: Jesus) is dat. of dir. obj. Although some EVV (cf. CSB) treat λέγοντες (nom. pl. masc. of pres. act. ptc. of λέγω) as attendant circumstance, the ptc. may express means. Ἀληθῶς "truly, really." The position of θεοῦ is prob. emphatic. Υἱός is pred. nom. Εἶ 2nd sg. pres. indic. of εἰμί.

7. Jesus Heals the Sick in Gennesaret (14:34–36)

14:34 Διαπεράσαντες (nom. pl. masc. of aor. act. ptc. of διαπεράζω, "cross over, traverse") is temp. and antecedent (most EVV). Ἦλθον 3rd pl. aor. act. indic. of dep. ἔρχομαι. Ἐπί with the acc. (τὴν γῆν) here means "onto" and indicates that the boat landed. Εἰς with the acc. place name (Γεννησαρέτ, Gennesaret) means "at" (288d–91c 1.a.δ.).

14:35 Ἐπιγνόντες (nom. pl. masc. of aor. act. ptc. of ἐπιγινώσκω, "recognize") is either temp. (most EVV) or causal. The gen. τοῦ τόπου ἐκείνου is gen. of source and indicates the place of orig. Ἀπέστειλαν 3rd pl. aor. act. indic. of ἀποστέλλω, "send a message or messenger." Περίχωρος, -ον, "surrounding, neighboring." The adj. is subst.:

"surrounding region." Προσήνεγκαν 3rd pl. aor. act. indic. of προσφέρω, "bring." The art. ptc. τοὺς ἔχοντας (acc. pl. masc. of pres. act. ptc. of ἔχω) is subst. With the adv. κακῶς ("badly"), the cstr. is an idiom referring to the "sick."

14:36 Παρεκάλουν (3rd pl. impf. act. indic. of παρακαλέω, "urge") is prog. Ἵνα with the subjunc. (ἄψωνται 3rd pl. aor. mid. subjunc. of ἅπτω, "touch" [mid.]) expresses purpose. The acc. μόνον (from the adj. μόνος, -η, -ον) is adv. and limits the action to that expressed by the vb.: "only" or "merely." Τοῦ κρασπέδου (κράσπεδον, -ου, τό, "edge, border, hem") is gen. of dir. obj. Τοῦ ἱματίου is partitive gen. Αὐτοῦ is gen. of poss. Καί introduces a result. Ὅσοι ("as many as") indicates that all, without exception, who touched the hem of the garment were healed. Ἥψαντο 3rd pl. aor. mid. indic. of ἅπτω, "touch" (mid.). Διεσώθησαν 3rd pl. aor. pass. indic. of διασῴζω, "delivered, save." In the pass. voice, the vb. may mean "escape death" (BDAG 237b–c).

8. Human Tradition and Divine Commands (15:1–11)

15:1 Τότε introduces the next major segment of narrative and means "after this." Προσέρχονται is historical pres. Τῷ Ἰησοῦ is. dat. of pers. The prep. ἀπό marks the place from which the group came. Ἱεροσολύμων, 2:1. The order Φαρισαῖοι καὶ γραμματεῖς is unusual. Elsewhere Matthew preferred the order "scribes and Pharisees" (5:20; 12:38; 23:2, 13, 15, 23, 25, 27, 29), and the normal order is found in several ancient mss. (C L W). Λέγοντες (nom. pl. masc. of pres. act. ptc. of λέγω) is either a ptc. of attendant circumstance (most EVV) or a ptc. of purpose (H 2.430).

15:2 Διὰ τί, "why?" The pron. σου that modifies οἱ μαθηταί identifies the master whom the disciples follow. Παραβαίνουσιν (3rd pl. pres. act. indic. of παραβαίνω, "transgress, break") is prob. a customary pres. The disciples of Jesus habitually break the tradition. Παράδοσιν acc. sg. fem. of παράδοσις, -εως, ἡ, "tradition, instruction handed down by another." Τῶν πρεσβυτέρων is substant. and a gen. of source. Γάρ introduces the basis for the earlier accusation. Νίπτονται (3rd pl. pres. mid. indic. of νίπτω, "wash") is customary pres. This is confirmed by the rel. temp. clause introduced by ὅταν. Ἐσθίωσιν 3rd pl. pres. act. subjunc. of ἐσθίω, "eat." The subjunc. mood is required by the ὅταν. The pres. tense is prob. iter. and assumes the disciples ate many meals.

15:3 For the cstr. ὁ δὲ ἀποκριθεὶς εἶπεν, see 4:4. Διὰ τί expresses the question "why?" Although some EVV (NIV; ESV) treat καί as marking continuity with the preceding discussion, the position of the καί makes this doubtful. It is prob. an example of the adjunctive use ("also"; LEB). The ὑμεῖς is slightly emphatic (H 2.431). Παραβαίνετε (2nd pl. pres. act. indic. of παραβαίνω, "transgress, break") is prob. customary, indicting the Pharisees and scribes for an offense sim. (though worse) to that of which they accused Jesus's disciples. Τοῦ θεοῦ is a subj. gen. indicating that God issued the command (τὴν ἐντολήν). The acc. case of τὴν παράδοσιν (παράδοσις, -εως, ἡ, "tradition") shows that the prep. διά introduces the reason for which the Pharisees and scribes transgress God's command. The gen. pron. ὑμῶν may be subj. ("the tradition that you developed") but is more likely obj. ("the tradition handed down to you").

15:4 Γάρ introduces the basis for Jesus's preceding indictment. The def. art. ὁ modifying θεός is monadic and refers to the one and only God worshipped by faithful Jews

(BDF §254). By introducing a quotation of the Decalogue (Exod 20:12) and Exod 21:16 with the phrase ὁ θεὸς εἶπεν, Jesus affirmed the divine orig. of the OT law. See Metzger 31. Τίμα (2nd sg. pres. act. impv. of τιμάω, "honor") is prob. ingr.-prog.: "begin and continue to honor." The def. art. with πατέρα and μητέρα could be monadic (since most people have only one father and one mother), but more likely imply a gen. of relationship "your father and your mother" (W 215–16). Note that Exod 20:12 (LXX) used the pron. σου and Exod 21:16 (LXX) used the pron. αὐτοῦ. Καί is functioning as a coordinating conj. introducing a second divine quotation. The def. art. ὁ shows that the independent ptc. κακολογῶν (nom. sg. masc. of pres. act. ptc. of κακολογέω, "insult, curse") is subst.: "the one who curses." The use of the disjunctive ἤ rather than a coordinating conj. shows that the cursing of either parent is sufficient grounds for the penalty that follows. Θανάτῳ is a conceptual cognate dat. that emphasizes the action of the vb. (W168–69). The cstr. is a Sem. influenced by the Heb. inf. abs. (H 2.431). Τελευτάτω 3rd. sg. pres. act. impv. of τελευτάω, "die" (with the cognate dat. "surely die"). See Beale and Carson 50d–52d.

15:5 Δέ is adversative and Ὑμεῖς is emphatic. The two elements serve to contrast the divine command with the opinion of the religious leaders. The shift from the aor. form εἶπεν to the pres. form λέγετε implies that the opinion of the Pharisees and scribes amounts to a transgression of the orig. command. The combination of the rel. pron. ὅς with the particle of contingency ἄν may form the prot. of a cond. sentence: "if someone says" (BDAG 56b–57c 1.b.; BDF §380, 1). However, many commentators and EVV interpret the cstr. as *equivalent to an indef. pron.: "anyone, whoever" (G 304; N 616; CSB; LEB). The subjunc. vb. (εἴπῃ 3rd sg. aor. act. subjunc. of λέγω) is required by the particle of contingency. Τῷ πατρί and τῇ μητρί are dat. of indir. obj. Δῶρον, -ου, τό in this context means "gift to God." The noun serves as a predic. nom.: "it is a gift." The cstr. ὃ ἐάν may be equivalent to ὃ ἄν (BDAG 267b–68a 3.; BDF §107, 377) and functions with the subjunc. vb. (ὠφεληθῇς 2nd sg. aor. pass. subjunc. of ὠφελέω, "provide assistance, help, benefit;" pass. "be benefitted") to mark the prot. of a cond. statement (BDAG 56b–57c 1.b.; BDF §380, 1): "if something may have benefitted you. . . ." However, the cstr. ὃ ἐάν may be a *substitute for the indef. pron.: "anything, whatever" (CSB; LEB; cf. ESV). Ἐξ ἐμοῦ expresses source: "from me." The longer form of the pron. (ἐμοῦ rather than μου) is prob. not emphatic since the enclitic form is rare with prep. (BDAG 275a–c).

15:6 The first clause is the apod. of the cond. sentence begun with the prot. "if someone says . . ." in 15:5. Οὐ μή with the fut. indic. (τιμήσει 3rd sg. fut. act. indic. of τιμάω, "honor") expresses emphatic negation (BDAG 644d–46d 4.b.; BDF §365). Τὸν πατέρα αὐτοῦ implicitly includes the mother mentioned in the prot. Καί introduces a result from the preceding statement (BDAG 494a–96c 1.b.ζ.). Ἠκυρώσατε 2nd pl. aor. act. indic. of ἀκυρόω, "void." Τοῦ θεοῦ is subj. gen.: God spoke the message. Διὰ τὴν παράδοσιν ὑμῶν, 15:3. See Metzger 31.

15:7 Ὑποκριταί (voc. pl. masc. of ὑποκριτής, -ου, ὁ, "hypocrite, pretender") is voc. of simple dir. address. Καλῶς, "rightly, correctly, accurately" (with vb. of speech) (BDAG 505c–6a 4.b.). Ἐπροφήτευσεν 3rd. sg. aor. act. (constative) indic. of προφητεύω. Περί with the gen. (ὑμῶν) expresses ref. Ἡσαΐας, -ου, ὁ, "Isaiah (the OT prophet)." Λέγων is pleonastic (W 649–50).

15:8 Verses 8 and 9 quote Isaiah 29:13 with only slight deviation from the LXX. See Beale and Carson 52d–54c. Τιμᾷ 3rd sg. pres. act. indic. of τιμάω, "honor." The dem. pron. οὗτος is serving as a dem. adj. modifying the noun that it follows (BDAG 740b–741d 2.b.). The position of τοῖς χείλεσίν (dat. pl. neut. of χεῖλος, -ου, τό, "lip") is prob. emphatic and implies that the honor given does not extend beyond the lips. The def. art. implies a partitive gen.: "their lips." Δέ is adversative and contrasts the lip service with the apathy of the heart. Αὐτῶν is partitive gen. Πόρρω is an adv., expressing great distance: "far away." Ἀπέχει 3rd sg. pres. act. indic. of ἀπέχω, "to be distant" (BDAG 102c–3b, 4). Ἀπ' (from ἀπό) expresses separation. On ἐμοῦ, see 15:5.

15:9 Δέ prob. marks a new development in the discourse. Μάτην (acc. sg. fem. of μάτη, -ης, ἡ, "fault") is an adv. acc. mng. "in vain, in futility" (BDAG 621d; W 199–201). Σέβονται 3rd pl. pres. mid. indic. of σέβω, "worship (through gestures, ceremonies, or ritual acts)." Διδάσκοντες (nom. pl. masc. of pres. act. ptc. of διδάσκω) is prob. causal (NLT) showing the reason for the futility of the worship. Alternatively, the ptc. could express means. Διδασκαλίας (acc. pl. fem. of διδασκαλία, -ας, ἡ, "teaching, instruction") initially appears to be a cognate acc. However, the presence of two acc. nouns suggests that the cstr. is a dbl. acc. of obj. complement. Διδασκαλίας is the complement and ἐντάλματα (acc. pl. neut. of ἔνταλμα, -ατος, τό, "commandment") is the obj.: "teaching as doctrines human commands" (CSB). Ἀνθρώπων is subj. gen.: "commandments issued by men."

15:10 Καί links this sentence to the previous narrative and suggests that Jesus's address to the crowd occurred on the same occasion as his debate with the Pharisees and scribes. Προσκαλεσάμενος (nom. sg. masc. of aor. mid. ptc. of προσκαλέω, "call, summon" [exclusively mid. in NT]) is either attendant circumstance (most EVV) or temp. and antecedent: "after he summoned." Εἶπεν 3rd. sg. aor. act. indic. of λέγω. The shift from the sg. collective τὸν ὄχλον to the pl. αὐτοῖς is an example of *constructio ad sensum* (BDF §134). Ἀκούετε 2nd pl. pres. act. impv. of ἀκούω. Συνίετε 2nd pl. pres. act. impv. of συνίημι, "understand." The pres. tense of both impv. vbs. is likely ingr.-prog. (W 721). However, the NLT treats the second impv. as a conative pres.: "try to understand" (W 534).

15:11 Τὸ εἰσερχόμενον (nom. sg. neut. of pres. mid. ptc. of dep. εἰσέρχομαι) is subst.: "The thing that enters." Κοινοῖ (3rd. sg. pres. act. indic. of κοινόω, "defile, make impure") in both clauses is a gnomic pres. Ἀλλά is adversative and reinforces the contrast between what defiles and what does not. Τὸ ἐκπορευόμενον (nom. sg. neut. of pres. mid. ptc. of dep. ἐκπορεύομαι, "come out") is subst. Ἐκ introduces the source. Τοῦτο appears to be functioning as a subst. (BDAG 740b–41c 1.a.ε.) and expresses emphasis (G 306; perhaps tinged with contempt [BDF §290]). This may be a Sem. (T 37).

FOR FURTHER STUDY

74. Human Traditions

Carlston, C. E. "Things That Defile (Mark 7:14) and the Law in Matthew and Mark." *NTS* 15 (1968): 75–96.

Fitzmyer, J. A. "Aramaic Qorban Inscription from Jebel Hallet Et-Turi and Mark 7:11, Matt 15:5." *JBL* 78 (1959): 60–65.

HOMILETICAL SUGGESTIONS

Traditions or Transgressions (15:1–11)

1. Traditions become transgressions when they are valued above Scripture
2. Traditions become transgressions when they make worship hollow
3. Traditions become transgressions when they focus on what is on the outside rather than what is on the inside

9. Tares and Blind Guides (15:12–14)

15:12 Τότε introduces the next section of narrative. It prob. means "at that time" and shows that the disciples' concern was expressed soon after Jesus's dialogue with the Pharisees. Προσελθόντες (nom. pl. masc. of aor. act. ptc. of dep. προσέρχομαι) is either temp. and antecedent or a *ptc. of attendant circumstance (most EVV). Λέγουσιν is historical pres. Οἶδας 2nd sg. pf. (used as pres.) act. indic. of οἶδα, "know." Ὅτι marks the content of the knowledge. Ἀκούσαντες (nom. pl. masc. of aor. act. ptc. of ἀκούω) may be temp. and contemp. (most EVV) or *causal. Ἐσκανδαλίσθησαν 3rd pl. aor. pass. indic. of σκανδαλίζω, "shock, offend, anger."

15:13 On ὁ δὲ ἀποκριθεὶς εἶπεν, see 4:4. Since πᾶσα is sg. and modifies an anar. noun, it emphasizes the individual members of a class: "every single" (BDAG 782b–84c 1.a.α.). Φυτεία, -ας, ἡ, "plant, something that is planted." This metaphor is likely drawn from texts like Isa 60:21 and 61:3, in which God's people are described as seedlings that he planted. The referent of the rel. pron. ἥν is φυτεία and agrees with the referent in gender and number. The pron. is acc. since it serves as dir. obj. in the rel. clause. Ἐφύτευσεν 3rd sg. aor. (constative) act. indic. of φυτεύω, "plant." Μου is gen. of relationship and indicates that Jesus is the Son of the Father. Ὁ οὐράνιος is in the 2nd attrib. position and gives equal emphasis to God's fatherly and heavenly nature (W 306; R 777). The ref. to plants that were not planted by the Father prob. alludes to the parable of the wheat and tares (13:24–30, 36–43; N 623). Ἐκριζωθήσεται (3rd sg. fut. pass. indic. of ἐκριζόω, "uproot, destroy") is divine pass. and pred. fut., referring to eschatological judgment.

15:14 Ἄφετε 2nd pl. aor. act. impv. of ἀφίημι, "leave, separate oneself from." The aor. tense of the impv. may express urgency. Τυφλός, -ή, -όν, "blind." The first use of the adj. in this verse is attrib. and modifies the pred. nom. ὁδηγοί (ὁδηγός, -οῦ, ὁ, "guide, leader"). Εἰσιν 3rd pl. pres. indic. of εἰμί. The uses of the adj. in the third clause of the verse are subst. but anar. since they are indef.: "a blind person." Ἐάν with the subjunc. (ὁδηγῇ 3rd sg. pres. act. subjunc. of ὁδηγέω, "lead, guide") forms the prot. of a third-class cond. statement. Third-class cond. statements have a broad range of mngs. (W 696). Since Jesus had already identified the Pharisees and scribes as blind guides, the fulfillment of the prot. here is certain. Ἀμφότεροι (ἀμφότεροι, -αι, -α, "both") is substant.: "both (the leader and the follower)." Βόθυνος, -ου, ὁ, "pit." Although some commentators suspect that the pit is an allusion to Sheol (D&A 2.533), it is more likely a general image for disaster (N 623). Πεσοῦνται (3rd pl. fut. mid. indic. of πίπτω, "fall") is prob. gnomic.

HOMILETICAL SUGGESTIONS

Jesus's Warning About False Teachers (15:12–14)
1. False teachers will be offended by Jesus's teaching
2. False teachers are tares among wheat and will be destroyed
3. False teachers are spiritually blind
4. False teachers are leading others to destruction

10. Jesus's Explanation of Spiritual Defilement (15:15–20)

15:15 Ἀποκριθείς (nom. sg. masc. of aor. pass. ptc. of dep. ἀποκρίνομαι, "answer") is pleonastic. Δέ signals a new development in the narrative. Εἶπεν 3rd sg. aor. act. indic. of λέγω. The antecedent of αὐτῷ is Ἰησοῦ (15:1). The aor. impv. φράσον (2nd sg. aor. act. impv. of φράζω, "explain, interpret") prob. expresses urgency. Ἡμῖν may be slightly emphatic due to its position and thus imply that the disciples will receive an explanation not shared with the crowd (15:10). Although τὴν παραβολήν (esp. if it is modified by ταύτην) might be taken as referring to the parable of 15:14 or 15:13, which are in closer proximity, the context (15:18–20) shows conclusively that it refers to the parable of 15:10. The distance of the ref. from the referent makes it difficult to explain why latter scribes would have added the near (proximate) dem. pron. ταύτην rather than the remote dem. pron. ἐκείνην.

15:16 The def. art. ὁ functions as a substitute for the dem. or pers. pron. (BDAG 686a–689c 1.c.). Δέ marks development, the transition in speakers and from question to response. Εἶπεν, 15:15. Ἀκμήν is an adv. that expresses extension of time up to a point: "even now, still." Καί may be adjunctive (ESV) or ascensive. Ὑμεῖς is emphatic. Ἀσύνετος, -ον, "lacking understanding, foolish." Ἐστέ 2nd pl. pres. indic. of εἰμί. Although modern editors punctuate the sentence as a question, it could be declarative and thus an even more forceful indictment of the disciples. The next verse is clearly a question, but this does not decide the issue. The parallel in Mark 7:18 shares the same ambiguity. In 16:11, Jesus used a question to challenge the disciples for their lack of understanding, but he questioned how (πῶς) the disciples could fail to understand rather than if they failed to understand. On the difficulty of sometimes distinguishing the declarative indic. from the interr. indic. when interr. pron. and adverbs are absent, see R 915–16; BDF §440.

15:17 Οὐ with the indic. (νοεῖτε 2nd pl. pres. act. indic. of νοέω, "understand") poses a question that anticipates an affirmative response (R 917; BDF §440). The basic functions of the digestive system are obvious to all. Ὅτι introduces the content of knowledge. Πᾶν with the subst. ptc. means "everything, whatever" (BDAG 782 1.b.α.). The def. art. and the absence of a head noun (independent position) shows that εἰσπορευόμενον (nom. sg. neut. of pres. mid. ptc. of dep. εἰσπορεύομαι, "enter") is subst. The phrase εἰς τὸ στόμα modifies the ptc. that precedes it but the phrase εἰς τὴν κοιλίαν modifies the vb. that follows it. Κοιλία, -ας, ἡ, "belly, stomach." Χωρεῖ (3rd sg. pres. act. indic. of χωρέω, "move") is gnomic pres. Ἀφεδρῶν, -ῶνος, ὁ, "latrine." Ἐκβάλλεται (3rd sg. pres. pass. indic. of ἐκβάλλω) is gnomic pres.

15:18 Δέ is adversative and contrasts the significance of one's diet and one's words. The def. art. τά and the independent position of ἐκπορευόμενα (nom. pl. neut. of pres. mid. ptc. of dep. ἐκπορεύομαι, "exit, come out") show that it is subst. The shift from the sg. subst. ptc. in 15:17 with πᾶν to the pl. subst. ptc. in 15:18 is prob. for purely stylistic purposes. Both constructions mean "whatever, everything. . . ." The prep. ἐκ is used twice to express source. However, the context shows that with the obj. τοῦ στόματος it expresses dir. source and with the obj. τῆς καρδίας it expresses ultimate source. Ἐξέρχεται 3rd sg. pres. mid. indic. of dep. ἐξέρχομαι. Κἀκεῖνος, -η, -ο was formed by crasis of καί and ἐκεῖνος. Here the καί is ascensive and places emphasis on the remote dem. pron. (BDAG 500a 2.a.). The pron. has an unfavorable connotation (BDAG 301d–2c 1.γ.). Κοινοῖ (3rd. sg. pres. act. indic. of κοινόω, "defile") is prob. gnomic. The def. art. τόν with ἄνθρωπον is prob. anaphoric and refers to the person whose heart is the source of defiling things. However, the def. art. may be generic and refer to an individual who is representative of humanity as a whole (Gildersleeve 2.255).

15:19 Γάρ introduces the reason that things that issue from the heart are defiling. Ἐκ marks the source of defilement (τῆς καρδίας). Ἐξέρχονται (3rd pl. pres. mid. indic. of dep. ἐξέρχομαι) is gnomic pres. Διαλογισμός, -οῦ, ὁ, "thoughts, opinions." Πονηροί is attrib.: "evil thoughts." Φόνος, -ου, ὁ, "murder, homicide." Μοιχεία, -ας, ἡ, "adultery." Πορνεία, -ας, ἡ, "forbidden sexual act." Κλοπή, -ῆς, ἡ, "theft, stealing." Ψευδομαρτυρία, -ας, ἡ, "false testimony." Βλασφημία, -ας, ἡ, "slander, blasphemy." The pl. number of the nouns refers to multiple acts in each category.

15:20 Ταῦτα is retrospective and refers to the sinful thoughts, actions, and words listed in v. 19. Ἐστίν (3rd sg. pres. indic. of εἰμί) is prob. gnomic pres. The def. art. τά and the independent position of the ptc. κοινοῦντα (nom. pl. neut. of pres. act. ptc. of κοινόω, "defile") show that the ptc. is substant. On the art. use of ἄνθρωπον in both clauses, see 15:18. Δέ is adversative and contrasts what does and does not defile. The def. art. τό modifies the inf. φαγεῖν (aor. act. inf. of ἐσθίω, "eat") and marks it as the subj. of the clause. Ἄνιπτος, -ον, "unwashed." Χερσίν (dat. pl. fem. of χείρ, χειρός, ἡ, "hand") is instr. dat. Κοινοῖ (3rd sg. pres. act. indic. of κοινόω) is gnomic pres.

FOR FURTHER STUDY

75. Purity and Defilement

Booth, R. P. *Jesus and the Laws of Purity: Tradition History and Legal History in Mark 7.* *JSNTSup* 13. Sheffield: JSOT, 1986.

Lie, T. G. "Analysis of Jesus's Teaching Episode Within the Framework of the Seven Components of Teaching: Conflict over the Tradition of Ceremonial Defilement (Matt 15:1–20; Mark 7:1–23)." *Stulos* 3 (1995): 83–94.

HOMILETICAL SUGGESTIONS

Unclean! (15:15–20)

1. What a person eats will not defile a person spiritually
   a. Eating without practicing hand-washing rituals will not defile
   b. Eating nonkosher foods will not defile
2. The sins that issue from a depraved heart do defile a person
   a. Sinful thoughts defile ("evil thoughts")
   b. Sinful deeds defile ("acts of murder, adultery, sexual immorality, and thievery")
   c. Sinful words defile ("false testimonies, blasphemies")

11. Jesus's Exorcism of the Daughter of the Canaanite Woman (15:21–28)

15:21 Καί introduces a new paragraph that has only a loose connection to what precedes (BDAG 494a–96c 1.e.). Ἐξελθών (nom. sg. masc. of aor. act. ptc. of dep. ἐξέρχομαι, "go out, exit") is prob. temp. and contemp. (CSB) since ἐξέρχομαι and ἀναχωρέω are synonyms. Ἐκεῖθεν, "from there." Ἀνεχώρησεν 3rd sg. aor. act. indic. of ἀναχωρέω, "depart, withdraw." Εἰς introduces destination. In the pl., μέρος, -ους, τό may refer to a geographical region or district (BDAG 633a–34a 1.b.γ.). The gen. Τύρου and Σιδῶνος are appos. and examples of the category μέρη (W 95–97).

15:22 Καὶ ἰδού prompts attention to what follows (BDAG 468, 1.b.β.). Χαναναῖος, -α, -ον, "Canaanite." The prep. phrase ἀπὸ τῶν ὁρίων ἐκείνων prob. modifies γύνη and indicates that the Canaanite woman originated in that area (most EVV), but it could modify the ptc. ἐξελθοῦσα (nom. sg. fem. of 2nd aor. act. ptc. of dep. ἐξέρχομαι; prob. attendant circumstance [CSB; ESV; LEB]) and indicate that the woman met Jesus at the borders of the district (KJV; BDAG 347 1.a.α.). The vb. is often modified by ἐκ or ἀπό phrases that indicate the place from which one departed. However, the word order supports the adj. view. See the discussion in Luz 2.338–39. Ὅριον, -ου, τό, "boundary," but in the pl. "region, district." Ἔκραζεν (3rd sg. impf. act. indic. of κράζω, "cry out") is prob. iter. impf. ("she cried out again and again"; H 2.441) or prog. impf. ("she cried out constantly;" Luz 2.339). Λέγουσα (nom. sg. fem. of pres. act. ptc. of λέγω) is pleonastic. The aor. impv. ἐλέησον (2nd sg. aor. act. impv. of ἐλεέω, "show mercy, have mercy") expresses urgency. The pron. με rather than the expected 3rd pers. pron. αὐτήν shows the degree to which the mother empathized with her daughter. To heal the daughter was to show mercy to the mother. Κύριε (voc. sg. masc. of κύριος) is often regarded as a mere title of respect: "Sir." However, the appeal ἐλέησον με in combination with the voc. κύριε was consistently used in appeals to God in the LXX (Pss 6:3; 9:14; 30:10; 40:5, 11; 55:2; 85:3; 122:3; Ode 14:40). Thus the woman addresses Jesus in the same way in which OT saints pled to God. On υἱὸς Δαυίδ, see 1:1. Θυγάτηρ, -τρός, ἡ, "daughter." Μου is gen. of relationship. The adv. κακῶς ("badly, severely") expresses intensity or severity (BDAG 502b 1.b.). Δαιμονίζεται (3rd sg. pres. pass. indic. of dep. δαιμονίζομαι, "be demon-possessed"). The CSB ("is severely tormented by a demon") closely follows the suggested tr. of the vb. and adverb in BDAG 209d–10a.

15:23 Δέ is adversative. The desperate plea anticipates a response but none is offered. The def. art. ὁ serves as a substitute for the dem. or pers. pron. (BDAG 686a–89d 1.c.). Ἀπεκρίθη 3rd sg. aor. pass. indic. of dep. ἀποκρίνομαι. Αὐτῇ is dat. of indir. obj. Since the vb. ἀποκρίνομαι is often intrans. in Matthew, the dir. obj. λόγον emphasizes Jesus's complete silence (NLT) and is thus sim. to the cstr. in 26:62; 27:12, 14. Καί marks the continuation of the narrative and may imply that the disciples' request is a response to Jesus's silence. Προσελθόντες (nom. pl. masc. of 2nd aor. act. ptc. of dep. προσέρχομαι) expresses attendant circumstance (most EVV). Ἠρώτουν (3rd pl. impf. act. indic. of ἐρωτάω, "ask, request") may be ingr. or *iter. (H 2.441). Λέγοντες (nom. sg. masc. of pres. act. ptc. of λέγω) is pleonastic. The aor. impv. ἀπόλυσον (2nd sg. aor. act. impv. of ἀπολύω, "send away" [BDAG 117c–18b 3]) expresses urgency: "send her away immediately." Ὅτι is causal. Κράζει (3rd sg. pres. act. indic. of κράζω, "cry out") is prog. ("she keeps crying out [incessantly]") or iter. ("she cried out again and again"; G 311)." Ὄπισθεν is an adv. that here functions as a prep. with the gen. (ἡμῶν): "behind us" (BDAG 715d–16a 1.b.).

15:24 Ὁ δὲ ἀποκριθεὶς εἶπεν, 4:4. Ἀπεστάλην (1st sg. aor. pass. indic. of ἀποστέλλω, "send") is a divine pass. Εἰ μή, "except" (BDAG 277b–79b 6.i.α.). Εἰς with the acc. of pers. (τὰ πρόβατα) serves as a substitute for the dat. of advantage (BDAG 288d–93c 4.g.). Πρόβατον, -ου, τό, "sheep," used here figuratively for persons, the people of God (BDAG 866a–b 2). Ἀπολωλότα (acc. pl. neut. of pf. act. ptc. of ἀπόλλυμι, "loose, be lost" [BDAG 116 3]) is in the second attrib. position. Thus emphasis is placed on both the noun and the attrib. ptc. (W 306; R 777). Οἴκου may be partitive gen. (G 313), gen. of separation, gen. of source, or *gen. of appos. (NLT; Luz 3.339 n. 45: "the lost sheep are . . . the entire people of God"; D&A 2.551). Ἰσραήλ may be *gen. of relationship or gen. of appos. (NIV).

15:25 The def. art. functions as a dem. or pers. pron. (BDAG 686a–89d 1.c.). Δέ is adversative. The woman repeated her plea despite Jesus's discouraging reply. Ἐλθοῦσα (nom. sg. fem. of aor. act. ptc. of dep. ἔρχομαι) is ptc. of attendant circumstance. Προσεκύνει (3rd sg. impf. act. indic. of προσκυνέω, "worship, kneel before") is ingr. impf. (H 2.442). Αὐτῷ is dat. of dir. obj. Λέγουσα (nom. sg. fem. of pres. act. ptc. of λέγω) may be a ptc. of attendant circumstance (NIV; CSB) or ptc. of means in which the appeal was an act of worship by addressing Jesus as Yahweh was normally addressed. See 15:22 and Esther 4:17; Psalm 43:27; 78:9; 108:26 (LXX). Use of the voc. κύριε in combination with an appeal for help using impv. forms of βοηθέω is consistently addressed to Yahweh in the OT. Βοήθει (2nd sg. pres. act. impv. of βοηθέω, "help") is prob. ingr.-prog. Impv. forms of βοηθέω are consistently aor. in the LXX, but vary in tense in the NT. Μοι is dat. of dir. obj. and demonstrates the empathy of the mother with the daughter (15:22).

15:26 Ὁ δὲ ἀποκριθεὶς εἶπεν, 4:4. Ἐστίν is gnomic pres. Λαβεῖν (aor. act. inf. of λαμβάνω) and βαλεῖν (aor. act. inf. of βάλλω) are subst. and the compound subj. of the sentence. Τῶν τέκνων is gen. of poss. Κυναρίοις is dat. pl. neut. of κυνάριον, -ου, τό, "(house or pet) dog." The addition of the adj. "little" is appropriate since κυνάριον is the dimin. form of κύων and expresses endearment.

15:27 Ἡ δέ, 15:25. Εἶπεν 3rd sg. aor. act. indic. of λέγω. Ναί prob. expresses agreement with the statement of another (BDAG 665b–d b; most EVV). Oddly, the NIV takes the ναί as expressing correction rather than agreement: "Yes it is, Lord" (explicitly rejected in D&A 2.555). Some interpreters view the ναί as an emphatic repetition of the woman's previous request (BDF §441; BDAG 665b–d b). Κύριε, 7:22. Since the clause introduced by καί qualifies Jesus's statement, it may be mildly adversative: "yet." However, in the parallel in Mark 7:28, the καί is clearly ascensive, and that fits better with the causal γάρ here also. However, Nolland sees the καί as "linking" and the γάρ as introducing an implication from Jesus's statement (N 635). Gundry sees the καί as adjunctive and the γάρ as explanatory. The def. art. τά with κυνάρια (15:26) is generic. Ἐσθίει (3rd sg. pres. act. indic. of ἐσθίω, "eat") is gnomic pres. Ἀπό marks the source (τῶν ψιχίων) from which the pet dogs eat. Ψιχίον, -ου, τό, "morsel, crumb." Τῶν πιπτόντων (gen. pl. neut. of pres. act. ptc. of πίπτω, "fall") is attrib., so the def. art. is tr. like a rel. pron. Ἀπό expresses separation and in combination with πίπτω means "down from." Τράπεζα, -ης, ἡ, "table." Κυρίων is gen. of poss. Αὐτῶν is gen. of subord.

15:28 Τότε ("then") introduces that which follows in time (BDAG 1012d–13a 2). Ἀποκριθείς (nom. sg. masc. of aor. pass. ptc. of dep. ἀποκρίνομαι) is ptc. of attendant circumstance. Εἶπεν 3rd sg. aor. act. indic. of λέγω. With the interjection ὦ (BDAG 1101a–b 1), the voc. γύναι (voc. sg. fem. of γυνή) expresses emphatic or emotional address (W 68). The adj. μεγάλη (μέγας, μεγάλη, μέγα, "great") is in the 1st pred. position and the adj. is slightly emphatic (W 307–8). Σου is subj. gen. The aor. impv. γενηθήτω (3rd sg. aor. pass. impv. of dep. γίνομαι) expresses urgency. The context shows that the expression is a command that effects what it orders and is thus comparable to the use of γενηθήτω in Gen 1:3, 6; Exod 9:9; 10:21). Σοι is dat. of advantage. The comp. particle ὡς introduces a clause that serves as the subj. (BDAG 1103d–6b 1.b.β.): "as you wish (for it to be), it will be." Θέλεις 2nd sg. pres. act. indic. of θέλω, "want, wish." Καί introduces the result of Jesus's command (BDAG 494a–96c 1.b.ζ.). Ἰάθη 3rd sg. aor. pass. indic. of dep. ἰάομαι, "heal." Ἡ θυγάτηρ, 15:22. Αὐτῆς is gen. of relationship. Ἀπό marks a starting point in time (BDAG 105a–107b 2.b.). Ὥρα was the smallest unit by which time was normally reckoned and thus sometimes means "moment" (BDAG 1102c–3c 2.b.). The remote dem. pron. ἐκείνης indicates that Matthew was referring to the precise moment at which Jesus issued his command.

FOR FURTHER STUDY

76. The Exorcism of the Daughter of the Canaanite Woman

Derrett, J. D. M. "Law in the New Testament: The Syro-Phoenician Woman and the Centurion of Capernaum." *NovT* 15 (1973): 161–86.

Harrisville, R. A. "The Woman of Canaan: A Chapter in the History of Exegesis." *Int* 20 (1966): 274–87.

Hart, L. "The Canaanite Woman: Meeting Jesus as Sage and Lord: Matthew 15:21–28 & Mark 7:24–30." *ExpTim* 122 (2010): 20–25.

Jackson, G. S. *"Have Mercy on Me": The Story of the Canaanite Woman in Matthew 15.21–28. JSNTSup* 228. London: Sheffield Academic Press, 2002.

Russell, E. A. "The Canaanite Woman and the Gospels (Mt 15:21–28; Cf Mk 7:24–30)." Pages 263–300 in *Studia Biblica 1978 II. Papers on the Gospels*. Edited by E. A. Livingstone. *JSNTSup* 2. Sheffield: JSOT, 1980.

Ryan, T. J. "Matthew 15:29–31: An Overlooked Summary." *Horizons* 5 (1978): 31–42.

Senior, D. "Between Two Worlds: Gentiles and Jewish Christians in Matthew's Gospel." *CBQ* 61 (1999): 1–23.

HOMILETICAL SUGGESTIONS

Great Faith in a Great Savior (15:21–28)

1. A great faith
   a. She petitioned Jesus as one prays to God
   b. She addressed Jesus as Lord, a title of deity
   c. She recognized Jesus as the Davidic Messiah
   d. She worshipped Jesus as only God deserves
   e. She persisted in her appeals to Jesus even when his only response was silence
2. A great Savior
   a. Jesus showed compassion to the archenemy of Israel
   b. Jesus conquered the powerful demon that tormented her loved one

12. Jesus's Miracles of Healing (15:29–31)

15:29 Μεταβάς (nom. sg. masc. of aor. act. ptc. of μεταβαίνω, "go, pass over") is either temp. (antecedent) or attendant circumstance (NIV; ESV). Ἐκεῖθεν, "from there" (adv. of place), referring to Tyre and Sidon (15:21). For the combination of μεταβαίνω and ἐκεῖθεν, see 11:1 and 12:9. Ἦλθεν 3rd sg. aor. act. indic. of ἔρχομαι. Παρά with the acc. (τὴν θάλασσαν) means "along the edge of, beside" (BDAG 756a–58b C.1.b.α–β.). Τῆς Γαλιλαίας is gen. of appos. of the type category-example (W 95–100). Ἀναβάς (nom. sg. masc. of aor. act. ptc. of ἀναβαίνω) is either temp. (antecedent) or attendant circumstance (most EVV). Luz regards the def. art. with ὄρος as anaphoric, referring to the same mountain as 14:23 or 5:1. See 5:1 for the role of this description in the new Moses typology of Matthew. Ἐκάθητο 3rd sg. impf. mid. indic. of dep. κάθημαι. Although the impf. tense as aorist might be prog. here (LEB), it is prob. identical in sense to the aor. since the use of the aor. tense of κάθημαι is rare (only Jer 43:12 in biblical Gk., compared to fifty-seven uses of the impf.).

15:30 Προσῆλθον 3rd pl. aor. act. indic. of dep. προσέρχομαι. The adj. πολύς is attrib. and describes the crowds (ὄχλοι) as large or great in the sense that they consisted of many people (BDAG 847c–50a 2.a.α.). Ἔχοντες (nom. pl. masc. of pres. act. ptc. of ἔχω) is attrib.: "large crowds that had." Matthew uses the prep. μετά with the pl. refl. pron. ἑαυτῶν three times (25:3; 26:11) in which the refl. sense of the pron. is diminished.

The pron. serves as a simple substitute for the pers. pron.: "with them." Χωλός, -ή, -όν, "lame, crippled." Τυφλός, -ή, -όν, "blind." Κυλλός, -ή, -όν, "having a deformed hand or foot" (BDAG 575a). Κωφός, -ή, -όν, "unable to speak, mute" (BDAG 580d). In the series of five subst. adj., only the last is preceded by the conj. καί. Ἑτέρους is subst. and πολλούς is attrib.: "many others." Ἔρριψαν 3rd pl. aor. act. indic. of ῥίπτω, "throw, lay down." Παρά with the acc. (τοὺς πόδας) means "at, near." Αὐτοῦ is partitive gen. Ἐθεράπευσεν 3rd sg. aor. act. indic. of θεραπεύω, "heal."

15:31 Ὥστε with the inf. (θαυμάσαι aor. act. inf. of θαυμάζω, "marvel, be amazed") expresses the result of the action in the preceding clause (Jesus's healing of the crowds). Τὸν ὄχλον is acc. of ref. (acc. subj. of the inf.). The cause-and-effect relationship between Jesus's healing of the crowds and their amazement suggests that βλέποντας (acc. pl. masc. of pres. act. ptc. of βλέπω) is causal, in which case the pres. tense is likely prog. ("because they kept seeing" as Jesus healed one person after another). For κωφούς, κυλλούς, χωλούς, and τυφλούς, see 15:30. The ptc. λαλοῦντας, περιπατοῦντας, and βλέποντας (acc. pl. masc. of pres. act. ptc. of λαλέω, περιπατέω, and βλέπω respectively) are pred. ptc., and each is in the second pred. position (W 617–19). Ὑγιής, -ές, "healthy, physically normal." The last καί introduces a result from what precedes (BDAG 494a–96c 1.b.ζ.). Ἐδόξασαν 3rd pl. aor. act. indic. of δοξάζω, "glorify." Ἰσραήλ, like many Sem. names, is indecl. but the context shows that the noun is gen. The gen. could be construed as gen. of subord. ("God over Israel") or poss. in a broad sense, referring to the God worshiped by Israel. The use of the gen. Ἰσραήλ rather than αὐτῶν suggests to several commentators that Matthew is referring to Gentile crowds worshipping Yahweh (G 319; Carson 407; F 597). However, the phrase was frequently, perhaps esp., used by Jews themselves (N 641; D&A 2.569; H 2.446).

FOR FURTHER STUDY

77. Healings Beside the Sea of Galilee

Baxter, W. S. "Healing and the 'Son of David': Matthew's Warrant." *NovT* 48 (2006): 36–50.

Opatrný, D. "The Figure of a Blind Man in the Light of the Papyrological Evidence." *Bib* 91 (2010): 583–94.

Scott, J. M. C. "Matthew 15:21–28: A Test-Case for Jesus's Manners." *JSNT* 63 (1996): 21–44.

HOMILETICAL SUGGESTIONS

At Jesus's Feet (15:29–31)

1. Jesus is the new Moses, our Savior and Redeemer
   a. He sets us free from our slavery to sin
   b. He leads us to the Promised Land
2. Jesus is the glory of the Lord (Isa 35:1–6)
   a. Jesus performed the miracles described by Isaiah

b. Jesus is the glory of the Lord promised by Isaiah
3. Jesus inspires awe and praise

13. Jesus's Miraculous Feeding of the Four Thousand (15:32–38)

15:32 Δέ marks the beginning of a new narrative segment and links it to the preceding segment (BDAG 213a–d 2.). Προσκαλεσάμενος (nom. sg. masc. of aor. mid. ptc. of προσκαλέω, "summon") is either a temp. ptc. or *ptc. of attendant circumstance (most EVV). Although the vb. is always in the mid. voice in the NT, it is a true (indir. refl.) mid., indicating that the subj. called others to himself (W 419–23, 430). Σπλαγχνίζομαι (1st sg. pres. mid. indic. of dep. σπλαγχνίζομαι, "feel pity, have compassion") is prog. pres. Ἐπί with the acc. (τὸν ὄχλον) serves as a marker of those to whom feelings are directed (BDAG 363a–67c 15). Ὅτι is clearly causal (most EVV). Ἤδη, "already." Ἡμέραι τρεῖς is a parenthetical nom. (BDF §144). Προσμένουσιν (3rd pl. pres. act. indic. of προσμένω, "stay or remain with") is pres. of past action still in progress (W 519–20). Μοι is dat. of accompaniment (W 159–60). Ἔχουσιν may be pres. of past action still in progress: "they have not had and still do not have." Although the reader may expect the indef. pron (τὶ [enclitic]), the interr. pron. appears instead. This is likely an example of the substitution of the interr. pron. for the rel. (BDAG 1006d–7d; BDF §298 [4]). Φάγωσιν (3rd pl. aor. act. subjunc. of ἐσθίω, "eat") uses the subjunc. to express possibility rather than mere probability and encroaches on the sense of the optative (W 462): "anything they could possibly eat." Ἀπολῦσαι (aor. act. inf. of ἀπολύω, "release, send away") is a complementary inf. Αὐτούς is acc. of dir. obj. Νῆστις, ὁ, ἡ, "fasting, hungry." The adj. νήστεις may be subst. and thus appos. ("them, the ones who are fasting") or attrib. ("them [who are] hungry"). Θέλω (1st sg. pres. act. indic. of θέλω) is prog. pres. Μήποτε marks negated purpose, that which the subj. of the main clause wishes to avoid. Ἐκλυθῶσιν (3rd pl. aor. pass. subjunc. of ἐκλύω, "become exhausted, give out" [pass. used intrans.]) expresses (negated) purpose. The prep. ἐν has the sense "on" (BDAG 326c–30b 1.b.). The def. art. τῇ modifying ὁδῷ is used for simple identification and points to the road that each traveler must take to make his way home.

15:33 Λέγουσιν is historical pres. (W 526–32; Runge 126–43). Πόθεν is an interr. adv. that raises the question of the local source: "from where, whence?" Ἡμῖν is dat. of advantage: "for us." The prep. phrase ἐν ἐρημίᾳ modifies the adv. πόθεν: "From where in this desolate place?" The correlative adj. τοσοῦτοι (nom. pl. masc. of τοσοῦτος, -αύτη, -οῦτον, "so much, many") refers to an indefinitely high number of objects (BDAG 1012a–c 1.a.). Ὥστε with the inf. (χορτάσαι aor. act. inf. of χορτάζω, "feed") expresses an intended result or purpose (BDAG 1107a–c 2.b.). Τοσοῦτον refers to a high degree of quantity: "such a large, so great" (BDAG 1012a–c 2.a.).

15:34 Λέγει is historical pres. (W 526–32; Runge 126–43). Πόσος, -η, -ον, "how many, how much." Ἔχετε 2nd pl. pres. act. indic. of ἔχω. The def. art. (οἱ) functions like a dem. or pers. pron. and serves with δέ to mark the progress of a narrative (BDAG 686a–89c, 1.c.). Εἶπαν 3rd pl. aor. act. indic. of λέγω. The reply of the disciples is truncated and omits both the vb. (ἔχομεν) and the subst. ἄρτους. Ὀλίγος, -η, -ον, "few (in number)." Ἰχθύδιον, -ου, τό, is the dimin. form of ἰχθύς ("fish") and means "little fish."

15:35 Παραγγείλας (nom. sg. masc. of aor. act. ptc. of παραγγέλλω, "announce, give orders") is either temp. (antecedent) ptc. (CSB) or *ptc. of attendant circumstance (NIV). Ἀναπεσεῖν (aor. act. inf. of ἀναπίπτω, "recline [in order to eat]") is inf. of indir. discourse (W 603–5). Ἐπί with the acc. marks a position on the surface of an object. Γῆ refers to the earth in the sense of the ground (BDAG 196a–c 6.a.).

15:36 Ἔλαβεν 3rd sg. aor. act. indic. of λαμβάνω. Ἰχθύς, -ύος, ὁ, "fish." Εὐχαριστήσας (nom. sg. masc. of aor. act. ptc. of εὐχαριστέω, "give thanks") is either a temp. (antecedent) ptc. (LEB) or *ptc. of attendant circumstance (NIV; CSB). Ἔκλασεν 3rd sg. aor. act. indic. of κλάω, "break (bread)." Ἐδίδου (3rd sg. impf. act. indic. of δίδωμι, "give") is prob. ingr.: "he began distributing . . ." (LEB). Δέ marks continuation. The clause οἱ δὲ μαθηταὶ τοῖς ὄχλοις is elliptical and implies the 3rd pl. impf. act. indic. form of δίδωμι.

15:37 Ἔφαγον 3rd pl. 2nd aor. act. indic. of ἐσθίω, "eat." Πάντες is subst.: "everyone." Ἐχορτάσθησαν 3rd pl. aor. pass. indic. of χορτάζω, "be satisfied" (pass.). Περισσεῦον (acc. sg. neut. of pres. act. ptc. of περισσεύω, "be left over") is subst.: "what was left over." Κλασμάτων (gen. pl. neut. of κλάσμα, -ατος, τό, "crumb, fragment") is partitive. Ἦραν 3rd pl. aor. act. indic. of αἴρω, "take up." Σπυρίς, -ίδος, ἡ, "basket." Σπυρίδας is acc. of simple appos. and modifies περισσεῦον (LEB; CSB). Πλήρεις (acc. pl. fem. of πλήρης, -ες, "full") is in the 4th attrib. position: "seven full baskets."

15:38 Ἐσθίοντες (nom. pl. masc. of pres. act. ptc. of ἐσθίω, "eat") is subst. and prob. prog.: "those who were eating." Ἦσαν 3rd pl. impf. indic. of εἰμί. Τετρακισχίλιοι, -αι, -α, "four thousand." Ἄνδρες nom. pl. masc. of ἀνήρ, ἀνδρός, ὁ, "man (adult male)." Χωρίς is used as a prep. with the gen. and means "besides, in addition to" (BDAG 1095b–d 2.a.γ.). Γυναικῶν gen. pl. fem. of γύνη, -αικός, ἡ, "woman." Παιδίων gen. pl. fem. of παιδίον, -ου, τό, "child."

FOR FURTHER STUDY

78. The Feeding of the Four Thousand

Carter, W. "The Crowds in Matthew's Gospel." *CBQ* 55 (1993): 54–67.
Cousland, J. R. C. "The Feeding of the Four Thousand Gentiles in Matthew? Matthew 15:29–39 as a Test Case." *NovT* 41 (1999): 1–23.

HOMILETICAL SUGGESTIONS

The Great Provider (15:32–38)

1. Jesus cares about the needs of those who follow him
2. Jesus fully satisfies the needs of those who follow him
3. Jesus exceeds the needs of those who follow him

14. The Request for a Miraculous Sign (15:39–16:4)

15:39 Ἀπολύσας (nom. sg. masc. of aor. act. ptc. of ἀπολύω, "release, send away") is prob. temp. (antecedent) ptc. (most EVV): "after (Jesus) had sent away." Ἐνέβη 3rd sg. aor. act. indic. of ἐμβαίνω, "embark, board (a boat or ship)." Ἦλθεν 3rd sg. aor.

act. indic. of dep. ἔρχομαι. Ὅριον, -ου, τό, "border, region (when pl.)." Μαγαδάν is gen. (appos.), but like many other Sem. names is indecl. This was a region located on the shores of the Sea of Galilee but cannot be more specifically located based on currently available evidence.

16:1 Προσελθόντες (nom. pl. masc. of aor. act. ptc. of dep. προσέρχομαι, "approach") is prob. temp., expressing antecedent action (LEB), or ptc. of attendant circumstance (most EVV). Most tr. treat πειράζοντες (nom. pl. masc. of pres. act. ptc. of πειράζω, "test") as expressing purpose. However, they disagree over which verbal the ptc. modifies. LEB treats the ptc. as modifying προσελθόντες, but most EVV treat the ptc. as modifying ἐπηρώτησαν (3rd pl. aor. act. indic. of ἐπερωτάω, "make a request;" BDAG 362a–b 2). NIV translates the clause as if the ptc. πειράζοντες were an indic. vb. and the vb. ἐπηρώτησαν were a ptc. of means. This suggests that the tr. viewed πειράζοντες as a ptc. of purpose but adjusted the structure of the sentence so that it would read more smoothly in Eng. Αὐτόν serves as both the dir. obj. of ἐπηρώτησαν and the acc. subj. of the inf. ἐπιδεῖξαι (aor. act. inf. of ἐπιδείκνυμι, "show, perform in someone's presence;" BDAG 370a–b 1). Σημεῖον is dir. obj. of the inf. Ἐκ τοῦ οὐρανοῦ identifies the place from which the group sought a sign. Although Hagner sees οὐρανός as a circumlocution for the divine name, Luz's view is more likely: the sign was a cosmic sign displayed in the skies (2.348).

16:2a The cstr. ὁ δὲ ἀποκριθεὶς εἶπεν is common in Matthew (see 4:4). The δέ marks a new development in the narrative (Runge 31–32), and this is esp. true when it is preceded by an independent use of the nom. masc. def. art. (BDAG 686a–89c 1.c.; BDF §251). The def. art. ὁ serves as a substitute for the pers. pron. αὐτός or the dem. pron. οὗτος. Ἀποκριθείς is pleonastic.

16:2b–3 These verses contain the longest significant textual var. in Matthew. The verses are absent from an impressive group of witnesses incl. the earliest uncials (ℵ B), later uncials (Χ Γ), minuscles (*f*¹³ 157 579), early versions (syrᶜˑ ˢ copˢᵃˑ ᵇᵒᵐˢˢ mae arm), and the text of Matthew known to the early church fathers Origen and Jerome. Unfortunately, the papyri are too fragmentary to assist in assessing the var.

Some scholars suggest a scribal omission; the verses are orig. to Matthew but early texts and versions omitted the verses. Several motivations for such an omission have been suggested. The most popular suggestion is that the text was omitted because the description of meteorological indicators was not accurate in climates like that of Egypt. The text was excised to prevent readers who were unfamiliar with the climate of Palestine from assuming that the text was in error (N 646; G 323; D&A 2.580–81 n. 12). However, this explanation is not entirely satisfactory. First, the description was widely affirmed by writers from various parts of the world (Luz 2.349). Second, the description of meteorological indicators in Luke 12:54–56 was particularly suited to Palestine and yet no mss. excise that text. This is particularly striking since the weather prediction in Matthew merely refers to the opinion of others but the version in Luke adds Jesus's own affirmation ("and so it is . . . and it is"). Nolland (646) has suggested that the omission may be due to haplography resulting from parablepsis. The scribe was confused by the γεν in γενομένης (2b) and γενεά (4a). This explanation would be more convincing if ὀψίας did not precede γενομένης. One would have to argue that the ὀψίας was orig. left dangling and then erased by the scribe or omitted by those who used his text as an exemplar.

Others suggest a scribal interpolation. Later scribes adapted Luke 12:54–56 (or a related source) and inserted this description into the text of Matthew (F 604–5 n. 1; Hill 256–57; Luz 2.347; Hirunuma). However, Matthew 16:2b–3 has too little in common with Luke (λέγετε, τὸ . . . πρόσωπον, τοῦ οὐρανοῦ, τῶν καιρῶν/τὸν καιρόν) to demonstrate that Luke was the source. Furthermore, the Lukan saying appears in a different context (Jesus's teaching to the crowds rather than a debate with Jewish sects). Metzger claimed that the scribal interpolation view was the view of the majority of scholars (33), but this is prob. no longer correct.

Internal evidence is also ambiguous. The text has remarkable traces of Matthew's vocabulary and style (G 323–24). Elements not found elsewhere in Matthew appear in the LXX and were thus available to him. The only internal feature that raises serious questions is the vb. πυρράζω, which does not appear prior to Matthew nor thereafter (except in sources referring to Matthew) until the Byzantine era. However, it is just as plausible that Matthew coined this term as that a second-, third-, or fourth-century scribe did so, and the appearance of the term in C D W requires an orig. no later than that. Hellenistic Gk. writers commonly transformed adj. into intrans. vbs. by adding the -αζω suffix (BDF §108, 4). Note that Matthew apparently coined the term παρομοιάζω used in 23:27 (first usage in the TLG database), and it also has the -αζω suffix.

The editors of the UBS[5] assigned a C rating to the text, indicating that the committee had difficulty in deciding between the var. This difficulty is understandable since the evidence is not sufficient to lead to hard and fast conclusions. The most extensive analysis of this textual question to date (Hirunuma) admitted that the evidence was ambiguous. It noted that the Pharisees and Sadducees asked for a sign from heaven (evidently as proof of Jesus's messiahship) but that 16:2b–13 discussed the "signs of the times" instead. It suggested that the awkwardness of 16:2b–13 as a response to the group's request cast doubt on the authenticity of the passage. In light of the difficulties, including the text but marking it with brackets that indicate the difficulties is wise. The absence of the text in our earliest mss. and several versions from both Egypt and Syria, the lack of a good explanation for its omission, and the awkwardness of the passage in its context make it ever so slightly more probable that the passage was absent from the orig. Matthew. But the prevalence of Matthean diction and style in the passage counterbalances the other evidence (G 323–24). It is difficult to imagine that a later scribe could have mimicked Matthew so well. It is prob. only a matter of time before a second- or third-century papyrus is discovered that will help settle the question. In the meantime, we can take comfort that no doctrine is affected by the question. Several modern tr. mention the var., incl. the CSB, NIV, and NLT.

Ὀψία, -ας, ἡ, "evening." Γενομένης (gen. sg. fem. of aor. mid. ptc. of dep. γίνομαι) is a gen. abs. and temp. Although the aor. ptc. normally expresses antecedent action when temp. and modifying a vb. in a tense other than aor., most EVV treat the ptc.

as contemp. Λέγετε 2nd pl. pres. act. indic. of λέγω. The gen. abs. ὀψίας γενομένης is common in Matthew (8:16; 14:15, 23; 16:2; 20:8 [with pres. of λέγω]; 26:20; 27:57). Εὐδία, -ας, ἡ, "clear weather" (pred. nom. with a fut. form of εἰμί implied). Πυρράζει 3rd sg. pres. act. indic. of πυρράζω, "be red." Γάρ introduces the reason for the expectation of clear weather. Ὁ οὐρανός refers to the sky rather than to the abode of God, a mng. common for the sg. form in Matthew.

16:3 Πρωΐ is an adv. of time mng. "in the (early) morning" and normally refers to the fourth watch of the night, from 3 a.m. to 6 a.m. Σήμερον, "today." Χειμών, -ῶνος, ὁ, "bad weather" (pred. nom. with a fut. form of εἰμί implied). Πυρράζει γὰρ . . . ὁ οὐρανός, 16:2. Στυγνάζων (nom. sg. masc. of pres. act. ptc. of στυγνάζω, "be gloomy, overcast") poses a problem for some interpreters who argue that the sky cannot be red and overcast/gloomy at the same time. This tension may suggest that the ptc. is concessive: "The sky is red, though it is becoming overcast." Most EVV treat the ptc. as attendant circumstance. Μέν . . . δέ marks two contrasting statements: "On one hand . . . , but on the other hand. . . ." Γινώσκετε 2nd pl. pres. act. indic. of γινώσκω. Διακρίνειν (pres. act. inf. of διακρίνω, "evaluate;" BDAG 231b–d 3.a.) The combination of forms of γινώσκω with an inf. is unusual (Hirinuma). It does not occur elsewhere in the NT and only rarely in the LXX (Isa 7:15). The cstr. prob. means "you know how to interpret/evaluate" (most EVV). This interpretation is supported by the use of δύναμαι in the next clause, which suggests that the μέν-δέ contrast involves ability and inability. Τὸ πρόσωπον in this context means "appearance" (BDAG 887c–88c 4). Τὰ σημεῖα τῶν καιρῶν (obj. gen.) refers to signs that identify the various epochs in God's plan for history. Hagner suggests that the phrase refers specifically to "signs in the ministry of Jesus marking the dawn of the messianic age" (2.455). Several times in Matthew καιρός refers to the time of divine judgment on demons (8:29) or the season of eschatological harvest, in which God demands the fruits of repentance and judges those that lack them (13:30; 21:34, 41). Thus the phrase prob. refers to events that foreshadow judgment on the unrepentant. Δύνασθε 2nd pl. pres. mid. indic. of dep. δύναμαι. The absence of a complementary inf. is unusual, esp. since τὰ σημεῖα serves as the dir. obj. of this unstated inf. The implied inf. is διακρίνειν from the previous clause.

16:4 Although 16:3 was expressed in the 2nd pers., 16:4 shifts to the 3rd pers. and some commentators see this as evidence that 16:2b–3 is an early interpolation (N 604). Γενεά refers to those living at a particular time who are marked by specific characteristics (BDAG 191d–92b 2). Μοιχαλίς, -ίδος, ἡ, "adulteress," here used as an adj. "adulterous" (BDAG 656c 2.b.; so most EVV). Ἐπιζητεῖ (3rd sg. pres. act. indic. of ἐπιζητέω, "desire, want;" BDAG 371c 2.b.) is gnomic pres. The longing for a sign is endemic to spiritual adulterers. Δοθήσεται (3rd sg. fut. pass. indic. of δίδωμι) is prob. divine pass. The antecedent of αὐτῇ is γενεά and the sg. number of the pron. confirms that μοιχαλίς is functioning as an attrib. adj. modifying γενεά rather than as an independent subst. The combination εἰ μή means "except" and is equivalent to πλήν (BDAG 277b–79b 6.i.). Τὸ σημεῖον Ἰωνᾶ refers to the death, burial, and resurrection of the greater Jonah, Jesus. These events were analagous to Jonah's three days in the belly of the great fish (12:40). Καταλιπών (nom. sg. masc. of 2nd aor. act. ptc. of καταλείπω, "leave") is ptc. of attendant circumstance (most EVV). The referent of αὐτούς is "Pharisees and Sadducees" (16:1). Ἀπῆλθεν 3rd sg. 2nd aor. act. indic. of dep. ἀπέρχομαι.

FOR FURTHER STUDY

79. Meteorological Signs

Hirunuma, T. "Matthew 16:2b–3." Pages 35–45 in *New Testament Textual Criticism: Its Significance for Exegesis—Essays in Honor of Bruce M. Metzger*. Edited by G. D. Fee and E. J. Epp. Oxford: Clarendon, 1981.

80. The Sign of Jonah

Merrill, E. H. "The Sign of Jonah." *JETS* 23 (1980): 23–30.
Powell, M. A. "Echoes of Jonah in the New Testament." *WW* 27 (2007): 157–64.

HOMILETICAL SUGGESTIONS

Blind to the Signs (15:39–16:4)

1. Asking Jesus to prove himself is a result of our wickedness and spiritual adultery
2. Jesus's signs are misinterpreted and rejected by the wicked
3. Jesus's resurrection from the dead should be sufficient to prove his claims

15. The Dangerous Doctrine of the Pharisees and Sadducees (16:5–12)

16:5 Ἐλθόντες (nom. pl. masc. of aor. 2nd act. ptc. of dep. ἔρχομαι) is either ptc. of attendant circumstance (CSB) or temp. (NIV; ESV; LEB), expressing antecedent action. Πέραν is an adv. of place but with the def. art. functions as a subst.: "the shore on the other side (of the lake)." Ἐπελάθοντο 3rd pl. 2nd aor. mid. indic. of dep. ἐπιλανθάνομαι, "forget" (BDAG 374d 1.). Λαβεῖν (2nd aor. act. inf. of λαμβάνω) is complementary.

16:6 Δέ simply marks a line of narrative closely related to what precedes (BDAG 213a–d 1.; Runge 31–36). The antecedent of αὐτοῖς is μαθηταί (16:5). Ὁρᾶτε (2nd pl. pres. act. impv. of ὁράω) and προσέχετε (2nd pl. pres. act. impv. of προσέχω, "beware, be on guard against [when followed by ἀπό];" BDAG 879d–80b 1.) are ingr.-prog. (W 721–22). The ἀπό expressing separation is often used to mark that which one should avoid (BDF §149). Ζύμη, -ης, ἡ, "leaven, fermented dough," sometimes used to symbolize something that permeates that which it touches (often affecting it negatively). Φαρισαίων and Σαδδουκαίων are prob. gen. of source or subj. gen. (since ζυμή is related to the vb. ζυμόω).

16:7 The def. art. οἱ functions like a dem. or pers. pron. serving as the subj. Δέ, 16:6. Διελογίζοντο (3rd pl. impf. mid. indic. of dep. διαλογίζομαι, "think, reason" or "discuss, argue;" BDAG (232d 1.) suggests the former mng. here but most EVV assume the later mng.). The impf. tense is either ingr. (ESV; NLT) or *prog. (LEB). The use of the pres. tense of the vb. in the next verse suggests that it is prog. here. BDAG assumes that the vb. refers to thought rather than speech due to the phrase ἐν ἑαυτοῖς. However, with pl. obj. the prep. ἐν may mean "among," describing an action as internal to a group, rather than internal to the individuals of the group and the use of this cstr. in 21:25 implies interaction within the group (N 652). The ptc. λέγοντες (nom. pl. masc. of pres. act. ptc. of λέγω) is prob. pleonastic and suggests that the EVV are correct that the vb. διαλογίζομαι here refers to speech and not merely thought (N 652). Ὅτι may be *recitative (G 326), that is, mark the content of discourse (or thought). However, it may instead be causal (F 610) and part of an elliptical cstr.: "(He said that) because we did not take loaves." Ἐλάβομεν 1st pl. 2nd aor. act. indic. of λαμβάνω.

16:8 Γνούς (nom. sg. masc. of 2nd aor. act. ptc. of γινώσκω) is prob. causal (NLT). Matthew's word choice ("knowing" rather than "hearing") and other contextual features suggest that Jesus's knowledge was supernatural (cf. sim. usage of the ptc. in 12:15; 22:18; 26:10). Δέ marks the next sequence of the narrative. The interr. pron. τί introduces a question. Διαλογίζεσθε (2nd pl. pres. mid. indic. of dep. διαλογίζομαι, "think" or "discuss") is prob. prog. pres. Ἐν ἑαυτοῖς, 16:7. Ὀλιγόπιστοι (voc. pl. masc. of ὀλιγόπιστος, -ον, "having little faith") is subst. and expresses dir. address. Ὅτι is recitative (16:7). Ἔχετε 2nd pl. pres. act. indic. of ἔχω.

16:9 Οὔπω, "not yet." Νοεῖτε (2nd pl. pres. act. indic. of νοέω, "understand") is (negated) extending-from-past pres. (W 519–20). The οὔπω shows that they have not previously understood and still do not. The neg. particle οὐ normally anticipates a positive response to a question. Since οὐδέ is merely a combination of οὐ and δέ one would assume anticipation of a positive response here also (CSB; NIV; NLT). However, οὐδέ both in affirmations and questions may bear the sense "not even" (BDAG 734d–35a, 3.) and intensify an implied indictment: "Do you not even remember . . . ?" (H 2.459). Such intensification is possible even for the οὐδέ . . . οὐδέ cstr. (which often means "neither . . . nor") that appears here. Μνημονεύετε (2nd pl. pres. act. indic. of μνημονεύω, "remember") is prog. pres.: "still remember." Πέντε, "five." Πεντακισχιλίων (πεντακισχίλιοι, -αι, -α, "five thousand") may be a gen. of poss. or destination, referring to the loaves distributed to and consumed by the five thousand. Πόσος, -η, -ον, "how many?" Κόφινος, -ου, ὁ, "(large, heavy) basket" (BDAG 563b–c). Ἐλάβετε 2nd pl. 2nd aor. act. indic. of λαμβάνω.

16:10 Οὐδέ, 16:9. Ἑπτά, "seven." Τετρακισχιλίων (τετρακισχίλιοι,-αι,-α, "four thousand") may be a gen. of poss. or destination referring to the loaves distributed to and consumed by the four thousand. Πόσας, 16:9. Σπυρίς, -ίδος, ἡ, "basket, hamper (used to transport food)." Ἐλάβετε, 16:9.

16:11 The interr. particle πῶς is used to express surprise at someone's failure: "How is it possible that . . . ?" (BDAG 900d–1c 1.a.β.). Although οὐ is often used in questions to imply a positive response, after πῶς the particle οὐ negates the vb. νοεῖτε (2nd pl. pres. act. indic. of νοέω, "understand"): "how is it possible that you do not understand?" Ὅτι is recitative marking the content of understanding that the disciples lacked. Προσέχετε (2nd pl. pres. act. indic. of προσέχω, "beware, avoid [when accompanied by ἀπό]" [BDAG 879d–80b 1]) is ingr.-prog. (W 721–22). Δέ is adversative. The ἀπό expressing separation is often used to mark that which one should avoid (BDF §149). Ζύμη, -ης, ἡ, "leaven, fermented dough," sometimes used to symbolize something that permeates that which it touches (often affecting it negatively). Φαρισαίων and Σαδδουκαίων are prob. gen. of source or subj. gen. (since ζυμή is related to the vb. ζυμόω).

16:12 Τότε prob. means "then" in the sense "at that moment" (BDAG 1012c–13a 1.a.). Jesus's correction resulted in immediate understanding of his warning. Συνῆκαν 3rd pl. aor. act. indic. of συνίημι, "understand" (BDAG 972b–d). Ὅτι is recitative and introduces the content understood. After εἶπεν, προσέχειν (pres. act. inf. of προσέχω, 16:11) is inf. of indir. discourse and represents a command. On the use of ἀπό with προσέχω, see 16:11. Ζύμης, 16:11. The gen. τῶν ἄρτων is prob. gen of product: the leaven is used in the production of loaves (W 106–7). See Metzger 33. Ἀλλά is adversative and contrasts the incorrect and correct interpretations of Jesus's warning. Διδαχή, -ῆς, ἡ, "teaching (focusing on content)" (BDAG 241c–d 2). Φαρισαίων and Σαδδουκαίων are subj. gen. The use of a single def. art. may imply their unity, at least in regard to the dangers of their teaching. However, this is not a true example of the Granville Sharp rule, since the nouns are pl. (W 270–90, esp. 279).

FOR FURTHER STUDY

81. The Leaven of the Pharisees and Sadducees

Mitton, C. L. "Leaven." *ExpTim* 84 (1973): 339–43.
Newman, R. C. "Breadmaking with Jesus." *JETS* 40 (1997): 1–11.

HOMILETICAL SUGGESTIONS

Watch Out! (16:5–12)

1. The failure of the disciples to save loaves from his last miracle suggests they expected Jesus to provide miraculously for them again and again
2. This expectation was dangerously close to the demand for another sign by the Pharisees and Sadducees
3. Jesus warned that the teaching of the Pharisees and Sadducees was like leaven that corrupted everything it touches

16. Peter's Confession at Caesarea Philippi (16:13–20)

16:13 Ἐλθών (nom. sg. masc. of aor. act. ptc. of dep. ἔρχομαι) is either temp.* (most EVV) or attendant circumstance. Δέ marks the transition to a new section of narrative (BDAG 213a–d 2.; LEB; ESV). The pl. τὰ μέρη (acc. pl. neut. of μέρος, -ους, τό, "part") refers to a region or district (BDAG 633b–34a 1.b.γ.). Καισαρείας is an appos. gen. (W 95–100; category-example). Τῆς Φιλίππου is gen. of poss.: "Philip's Caesarea" or gen. of authority (inverse of the gen. of subord.), referring to the Caesarea in Philip's domain. Philip was a son of Herod the Great and was tetrarch of a large region, incl. Panias, which Philip rebuilt and named Caesarea. The gen. distinguishes this Caesarea from Caesarea Maritima, located on the coast of the Mediterranean Sea. Ἠρώτα (3rd sg. impf. act. indic. of ἐρωτάω, "question, ask") is prob. ingr. impf. (LEB). The antecedent of αὐτοῦ is Ἰησοῦς and the gen. identifies Jesus as the one whom the disciples followed. Λέγων (nom. sg. masc. of pres. act. ptc. of λέγω) is pleonastic and introduces the content of Jesus's question. Τίνα (acc. sg. masc. of interr. pron. τίς, τί, "who?," "what?") introduces a question regarding identity. Λέγουσιν (3rd pl. pres. act. indic. of λέγω) is prob. prog. pres. The def. art. οἱ modifying ἄνθρωποι is the generic (categorical) art. (W 227–31). For this reason most EVV tr. the phrase simply as "people." Εἶναι (pres. inf. of εἰμί) is inf. of indir. discourse (W 603–5). The def. art. τόν modifying υἱόν is anaphoric or the well-known art., referring to the Son of Man described in Dan 7:13. On the title "Son of Man," see 8:20. See also Metzger 34.

16:14 The def. art. οἱ functions as a dem. or pers. pron. and serves as the subj. of the sentence. The combination of the nom. art. and δέ marks development within a narrative (BDAG 686a–89c 1.c.). Εἶπαν 3rd pl. aor. act. indic. of λέγω. Οἱ serves as subj. again, but this time its referent is not the disciples but the "people" mentioned in Jesus's question. Μέν followed by δέ (2x) establishes a strong contrast between the differing opinions regarding Jesus's identity. The contrast is strengthened still more but the shift from οἱ to ἄλλοι (from ἄλλος, -η, -ο) which distinguishes these individuals from the former individuals and then again to ἕτεροι (from ἕτερος, -α, -ον). The shift from ἄλλος to ἕτερος does not imply that the third view is more drastically different than the second is from the first. The transition is common in lists of more than two (BDAG 399b–400a 1.b.δ.) and the contrast simply means "Some . . . ; others . . . ; still others. . . ." The three clauses are elliptical and imply the vb. λέγουσιν from Jesus's question in 16:13. Ἰωάννην is acc. of dir. obj. of this implied vb. Τὸν βαπτιστήν (acc. sg. masc. of βαπτιστής, -οῦ, ὁ, "Baptizer") is acc. of simple appos. Ἠλίαν, Ἰερεμίαν and ἕνα (εἷς, μία, ἕν, "one") are acc. of dir. obj. (of the implied vb. λέγετε). Τῶν προφητῶν is partitive gen. The particle ἤ is disjunctive and separates the final alternative view of Jesus from the preceding alternatives.

16:15 Λέγει is historical pres. Ὑμεῖς is mildly emphatic. Δέ is adversative and serves to contrast the disciples' view of Jesus with the views of other people described in 16:14. Τίνα, 16:13. Με (acc. sg. of ἐγώ) is acc. subj. of the inf. Εἶναι (pres. inf. of εἰμί) is inf. of indir. discourse.

16:16 Ἀποκριθείς (nom. sg. masc. of aor. pass. ptc. of dep. ἀποκρίνομαι, "answer") is either pleonastic (most EVV) or attendant circumstance (LEB). Δέ introduces the next movement within the narrative. Σίμων Πέτρος is apparently a shortened form of Σίμων ὁ λεγόμενος Πέτρος (4:18; 10:2), and Πέτρος is nom. of simple appos. Σύ is emphatic. Εἶ 2nd sg. pres. indic. of εἰμί. The def. art. ὁ is monadic. Jesus is the one and only Messiah. Ὁ υἱός is nom. of simple appos. and describes χριστός. Τοῦ θεοῦ is gen. of relationship. God is the Father of Jesus, the Son. The def. art. τοῦ shows that the ptc. ζῶντος (gen. sg. masc. of pres. act. ptc. of ζάω, "live, be alive") is adj. and attrib. This is the second attrib. position, which places emphasis on both the noun and the adj. (W 306–7). The description appears only here in Matthew and contrasts the true God with the "dead" idol gods that were worshipped in ancient Caesarea.

16:17 ἀποκριθεὶς δὲ . . . εἶπεν αὐτῷ, 16:16. Μακάριος, -ία, -ιον, "blessed." Εἶ 2nd sg. pres. indic. of εἰμί. Σίμων, 16:16. Βαριωνᾶ is a Gk. transliteration of an Aram. phrase mng. "son of Jonah." Ὅτι is causal and presents the proof that Simon enjoys God's favor. Σάρξ, σαρκός, ἡ, "flesh." Αἷμα, -ατος, τό, "blood." "Flesh and blood" refers to human beings in contrast with God (BDAG 914d–16b 3.a.). Ἀπεκάλυψεν 3rd sg. aor. act. indic. of ἀποκαλύπτω, "reveal." Σοι is dat. of indir. obj. Ἀλλά is a strong adversative and contrasts the current affirmation with the previous denial. The form ἀλλ᾽ is a product of elision. When followed by a word beginning with a vowel, the final α drops off in approximately two-thirds of the instances in the NT. Μου is a gen. of relationship and confirms Simon's confession that Jesus is the Son of God. The phrase ὁ ἐν τοῖς οὐρανοῖς demonstrates that Jesus is referring to God and not a human father. The def. art. here functions like a rel. pron. to introduce a rel. clause. The pl. οὐρανοῖς is Matthew's preferred way of referring to the abode of God.

16:18 Κἀγώ is a crasis of καί and ἐγώ. Ἐγώ is mildly emphatic. Ἐγώ σοι λέγω seems to emphasize the statement that follows, much like the Eng. "Mark my words. . . ." Ὅτι introduces the content of Jesus's statement. Σύ is emphatic. Εἶ (2nd sg. pres. indic. of εἰμί) is not merely a declaration of what is true, but an announcement that effects a new identity for Simon. Πέτρος, -ου, ὁ is the Gk. equivalent of the Aram. name "Cephas" (rock). Καί connects the sequence of clauses in Jesus's statement. Ἐπί with the dat. means "on top of and in contact with," i.e., "upon." Due to the cstr. term that follows, the ἐπί marks the foundation. The use of the proximate dem. pron. ταύτῃ suggests that Peter is the foundation of which Jesus speaks. If attention were being shifted from Simon as the rock to another rock, one would have expected the remote dem. pron. (ἐκείνῃ). This is sometimes disputed since τῇ πέτρᾳ (dat. sg. fem. of πέτρα, -ας, ἡ, "rock") is fem., but Πέτρος is masc. It is further claimed that the fem. form referred to an enormous boulder that was suitable as a foundation, but the masc. form referred merely to a small stone. However, although the fem. form was more suitable to describe a foundation, Matthew could not use the fem. form as a name for an adult male. Nor would it have been prudent to use the masc. form to describe the foundation of the church. Although πέτρος could be used interchangeably with πέτρα, the masc. form had fallen into disuse in the NT era. Although the masc. form appears 156 times in the NT, every example is as a name for Simon. The term for a smaller stone in the NT is λίθος, -ου, ὁ. Thus the alternation between the masc. and fem. form was the best way in the Gk. of Matthew's day to communicate what Jesus expressed orig. in Aram. (F 621; H 2.470; Luz 2.362; Turner, *Matthew* 404–5). Although Peter is identified as the foundation of the church, this in no way undermines the supremacy of Christ. Apostles and prophets composed the church's foundation, but Jesus is the chief cornerstone (Eph 2.20). Οἰκοδομήσω (1st sg. fut. act. indic. of οἰκοδομέω, "construct, build") is a predictive fut., but prob. expresses more of a promise than a mere prediction. Ἐκκλησία, -ας, ἡ, "community, congregation." All three occurrences of this term in the Gospels appear in Matthew (16:18; 18:17). The term was used frequently in the OT to describe "the congregation of Israel/God." Jesus's use of the pers. pron. μου to describe this congregation suggests that Jesus will form a new, or renewed, congregation. Μου is prob. a subj. gen. (ἐκκλησία is related to ἐκ + καλέω) and indicates that Jesus will gather this new people for God.

Πύλη, -ης, ἡ, "gate." The noun ᾅδης, -ου, ὁ, "Hades" refers to the place where the souls of the dead reside. The primary purpose of the gates of Hades is to keep the dead from escaping. Ancient texts often describe these gates as locked (cf. Rev 1:18), evidently to prevent the dead from returning to life. Κατισχύσουσιν (3rd pl. fut. act. indic. of κατισχύω, "prevail, defeat") is predictive fut. and prob. expresses an eschatological promise. In conjunction with the vb. κατισχύω, the gen. identifies the obj. of defeat. Thus αὐτῆς is gen. of dir. obj. The antecedent is ἐκκλησία. Although the promise could refer to the community of Jesus storming the gates of Hades in order to deliver its captives (N 675–76) or resisting the gates of Hades as these gates seek to swallow up the church (F 625), it more likely refers to the disciples of Jesus breaking out of Hades at the time of their resurrection (H 2.471–72). Jesus has already warned that his disciples will die. He now promises that their death will not be permanent (G 335).

16:19 Δώσω (1st sg. fut. act. indic. of δίδωμι) is pred. fut. The antecedent of σοι is Σίμων. Κλείς, κειδός, ἡ, "key." Τῆς βασιλείας is prob. a gen. of destination. The idea may be that the keys grant entrance *into* the kingdom of heaven (W 100–101). For the phrase βασιλεία τῶν οὐρανῶν, see 3:2. The combination of the rel. pron. ὅ and the particle of contingency ἐάν means "whatever, anything." The rel. clause functions like the prot. of a cond. sentence: "if you bind anything . . ." (BDAG 56b–57c 1.b.; BDF §380, 1). Δήσῃς (2nd sg. aor. act. subjunc. of δέω, "bind, forbid") is a use of the subjunc. to express condition. Ἔσται (3rd sg. fut. indic. of εἰμί) δεδεμένον (nom. sg. neut. of pf. pass. ptc. of δέω) is a fut. pf. periph. cstr.: "will (already) have been bound or forbidden" (BDF §352). On the mng. of δέω when contrasted with λύω, see BDAG 221c–22a 4; H 2.472–73. The cstr. implies that Peter will merely pronounce decisions already made by God. God is the legislator. Peter is the herald. The pl. τοῖς οὐρανοῖς refers to the abode of God. Λύσῃς (2nd sg. aor. act. subjunc. of λύω, "loose, permit") is cond. Ἔσται (3rd sg. fut. indic. of εἰμί) λελυμένον (nom. sg. neut. of pf. pass. ptc. of λύω) is a fut. pf. periph. cstr.: "will (already) have been permitted."

16:20 Τότε prob. introduces that which follows in time (but only briefly). Jesus's command was given at the end of the conversation focusing on his identity. Διεστείλατο 3rd sg. aor. mid. indic. of διαστέλλω, "command, give orders." Ἵνα is a marker of obj. After vbs. denoting requests, demands, or commands, the ἵνα clause serves as a substitute for the complementary inf. Μηδενί is indir. obj. of the vb. εἴπωσιν (3rd pl. aor. act. subjunc. of λέγω). Ὅτι is recitative and introduces the content of prohibited speech. The referent of αὐτός is Jesus. The use of the 3rd pers. pron. rather than the 1st shows that this is indir. discourse. The def. art. ὁ with χριστός is monadic. See Metzger 34.

FOR FURTHER STUDY

82. Binding and Loosing

Powell, M. A. "Binding and Loosing: A Paradigm for Ethical Discernment from the Gospel of Matthew." *CurTM* 30 (2003): 438–45.

83. The Gates of Hades

Basser, H. W. "Marcus's 'Gates': A Response." *CBQ* 52 (1990): 307–8.
Gero, S. "The Gates or the Bars of Hades? A Note on Matthew 16:18." *NTS* 27 (1981): 411–14.

Lewis, J. P. "'The Gates of Hell Shall Not Prevail against It' (Matt 16:18): A Study of the History of Interpretation." *JETS* 38 (1995): 349–67.

Marcus, J. "The Gates of Hades and the Keys of the Kingdom (Matt 16:18–19)." *CBQ* 50 (1988): 443–55.

84. *Peter's Confession at Caesarea Philippi*

Barber, M. P. "Jesus as the Davidic Temple Builder and Peter's Priestly Role in Matthew 16:16–19." *JBL* 132 (2013): 935–53.

Berge, P. S. "Exposition of Matthew 16:13–20." *Int* 29 (1975): 283–88.

Ferda, T. S. "The Seventy Faces of Peter's Confession: Matt. 16:16–17 in the History of Interpretation." *BibInt* 20 (2012): 421–57.

Suggs, M. J. "Matthew 16:13–20." *Int* 39 (1985): 291–95.

Wilcox, M. "Peter and the Rock: A Fresh Look at Matthew 16:17–19." *NTS* 22 (1975): 73–88.

85. *Peter's Name*

Fitzmyer, J. A. "'Aramaic Kepha' and Peter's Name in the New Testament." Pages 121–32 in *Text and Interpretation: Studies in the New Testament Presented to Matthew Black.* Edited by E. Best and R. McL. Wilson. Cambridge: Cambridge University Press, 1979.

HOMILETICAL SUGGESTIONS

The True Church (16:13–20)

1. The church's confession: Jesus's identity as Messiah and Son of God is the church's essential confession
2. The church's founder: Jesus builds the new people of God
3. The church's foundation: Peter, as representative and leader of the apostles, is the foundation of this new people of God
   a. The apostles proclaim the requirements for entering the kingdom
   b. The apostles pronounce God's decrees regarding right and wrong
4. The church's victory: the true church cannot be destroyed by persecution or martyrdom

III. Journey to Jerusalem (16:21–20:34)

A. RETURN TO GALILEE (16:21–17:27)

1. Simon's Protest to Jesus's Prophecy (16:21–23)

16:21 Ἀπὸ τότε ἤρξατο ὁ Ἰησοῦς, 4:17. Δεικνύειν (pres. act. inf. of alternate form of δείκνυμι, "explain") is a complementary inf. Τοῖς μαθηταῖς is indir. obj. of the inf. Ὅτι introduces indir. discourse. Δεῖ (3rd sg. pres. act. indic.) is an impers. vb. derived from δέω and means "it is necessary." It is an example of the "present retained in indirect discourse" (W 537). Αὐτόν is acc. subj. of the inf. ἀπελθεῖν (2nd aor. act. inf. of dep. ἀπέρχομαι; complementary inf.). Καί is used to connect three additional complementary inf. to the first (παθεῖν, ἀποκτανθῆναι, ἐγερθῆναι). Πολλά is dir. obj. of παθεῖν (aor. act. inf. of πάσχω, "suffer"). Ἀπό with the gen. (τῶν πρεσβυτέρων gen. pl. masc. of πρεσβύτερος, -α, -ον, "elder" [subst.]) identifies the agents who are indirectly responsible for the action (BDAG 105a–7b 5.e.β.). Three groups of indirect agents are named: τῶν πρεσβυτέρων; ἀρχιερέων (gen. pl. masc. of ἀρχιερεύς, -έως, ὁ, "chief priests"); γραμματέων (gen. pl. masc. of γραμματεύς, -έως, ὁ, "scribe (expert in the law of Moses)." One def. art. τῶν modifies all three nouns and this prob. presents them as unified in their role in Jesus's death (H 2.479). Ἀποκτανθῆναι aor. pass. inf. of ἀποκτείνω, "kill." The phrase τῇ τρίτῃ ἡμέρᾳ is dat. of time (W 155–57) and modifies ἐγερθῆναι (aor. pass. [divine] inf. of ἐγείρω, "raise (from the dead)."

16:22 Προσλαβόμενος (nom. sg. masc. of 2nd aor. mid. ptc. of προσλαμβάνω, "to take aside") is prob. ptc. of attendant circumstance (most EVV). The referent of αὐτόν is Jesus. Ἤρξατο 3rd sg. aor. mid. indic. of ἄρχω, "begin" (mid.). Ἐπιτιμᾶν (pres. act. inf. of ἐπιτιμάω, "rebuke, scold") is a complementary inf. Αὐτῷ is dat. of dir. obj. Λέγων (nom. sg. masc. of pres. act. ptc. of λέγω) is pleonastic. Ἵλεώς, -ων, "merciful, gracious." The expression ἵλεώς σοι may be a shortened form of the wish ἵλεώς ὁ θεὸς εἴη σοι ("May God be merciful to you!"; BDAG 474c–d). However, in the LXX ἵλεώς σοι sometimes translates a Heb. expression often tr. μὴ γένοιτο ("May it never be!") and that is prob. the sense here (BDF §128.5; H 2.480; Turner, *Matthew* 410). Ἵλεώς is the only NT example of the so-called Attic second declension, which used ω rather than ο as the stem vowel (BDF §44). Κύριε is simple voc. The dbl. neg. οὐ μή with the fut. indic. (ἔσται 3rd sg. fut. indic. of εἰμί) is one form of emphatic negation (BDAG 644d–46d 4.b.). Σοι is dat. of ref. The dem. pron. τοῦτο refers to the suffering and death of Jesus (16:21).

16:23 On ὁ δέ with a ptc., see 16:2. Στραφείς (nom. sg. masc. of 2nd aor. pass. ptc. of στρέφω, "turn [around]") is attendant circumstance (BDAG 948c–49a 1.b.a.). Ὕπαγε (2nd sg. pres. act. impv. of ὑπάγω, "go away") should not be classified in terms of the ordinary categories of pres. impv. vbs. (such as ingr.-prog.). All thirty-eight occurrences of the impv. forms of this vb. are pres. tense. The context suggests the same urgency that an aor. impv. normally expresses. The prep. phrase ὀπίσω ("behind") μου intensifies the command and makes it equivalent to the Eng. "Get out of my sight!" (BDAG 716a–b 1.b.). For μου after ὀπίσω, see 3:11. Σατανᾶ (voc. sg. masc. of σατανᾶς, "Satan" [transliteration of Heb.]) is voc. of simple address. Σκάνδαλον, -ου, τό, "temptation (to sin), *cause of offense or revulsion" (BDAG 926b–c). Although BDAG and most EVV affirm the former sense here, CSB affirms the latter (revised to "hindrance in the CSB). Εἶ 2nd sg. pres. indic. of εἰμί. Although the longer form ἐμοῦ is used, this is common with prep. and thus prob. not emphatic (BDAG 275a–c). Ὅτι is causal. Φρονεῖς 2nd sg. pres. act. indic. of φρονέω "think." When followed by τά modified by a gen. (τοῦ θεοῦ), the vb. may mean "take someone's side, espouse someone's cause" (BDAG 1065c–66a 2.b.). Nevertheless, most EVV tr. the vb. as focusing on thoughts or priorities more than allegiance. Ἀλλά is strongly adversative and introduces the affirmation that is opposite of the denial: "You are not . . . , but (you are). . . ."

FOR FURTHER STUDY

86. Peter's Rebuke of Jesus
> Osborne, B. A. E. "Peter: Stumbling-Block and Satan." *NovT* 15 (1973): 187–90.
> Stoutenburg, D. C. "Out of My Sight!', 'Get Behind Me!,' or 'Follow after Me!': There Is No Choice in God's Kingdom." *JETS* 36 (1993): 173–78.

HOMILETICAL SUGGESTIONS

"I Told You So" (16:21–23)
1. Jesus declared that his death and resurrection had been ordained by God
2. Peter refused to accept Jesus's prophecy
3. Jesus sternly rebuked Peter for his worldly priorities

2. The Demands of Discipleship (16:24–28)

16:24 Τότε prob. means "after that" and introduces an event that followed the event previously described (BDAG 1012c–13a 2). Εἰ with the indic. θέλει (3rd sg. pres. act. indic. of θέλω, "desire, want") forms the prot. of a 1st-class cond. sentence that assumes the fulfillment of the condition for the sake of argument. The indef. pron. τις ("anyone") implies that there are no exceptions. Ὀπίσω (adv.) serves as a prep., "behind, after" (BDAG 716a–b 2.a.). For μου after ὀπίσω, see 3:11. Ἐλθεῖν (aor. act. inf. of dep. ἔρχομαι) is a complementary inf. Ἀπαρνησάσθω (3rd sg. aor. mid. impv. of dep. ἀπαρνέομαι, "deny") prob. expresses urgency. The refl. pron. ἑαυτόν ("himself") makes the subj. also the obj. of his own action. Ἀράτω (3rd sg. aor. act. impv. of αἴρω, "lift, carry") prob. expresses urgency. Σταυρός, -οῦ, ὁ, "cross." Αὐτοῦ is prob. obj. gen. or gen. of destination and means: "the cross on which he will be crucified." Bearing this cross entails willingness to die as a martyr. Ἀκολουθείτω (3rd sg. pres. act. impv. of ἀκολουθέω, "follow"). The series of commands shifts from the aor. to the pres. tense because following Jesus is an ongoing process (prog. pres.). Μοι is dat. of dir. obj.

16:25 Γάρ marks the reason that the disciples should take up the cross in preparation for martyrdom. The rel. pron. ὅς with the particle of contingency ἐάν and the subjunc. (θέλῃ 3rd sg. pres. act. subjunc. of θέλω, "desire") functions like the prot. of a cond. sentence (pres. general; BDAG 56b–57c I.b.; BDF §380.1). Ψυχή, -ῆς, ἡ, "*life, soul" (BDAG 1098d–1100a 1.b.). Most EVV assume the former sense, "life," here. Αὐτοῦ may be subj., poss., or (if ψυχή means "soul" here) partitive. Σῶσαι (aor. act. inf. of σῴζω, "save, rescue") is a complementary inf. Ἀπολέσει (3rd sg. fut. act. indic. of ἀπόλλυμι, "destroy, *lose." The antecedent of αὐτήν is ψυχή. Ὅς δ' ἄν is identical in sense to ὅς ἐάν but adds δέ, which here has an adversative sense. Ἀπολέσῃ 3rd sg. aor. act. subjunc. of ἀπόλλυμι). Ἕνεκεν functions as a prep. mng. "because of, for the sake of" (BDAG 334c–d 1). The longer form ἐμοῦ is common of the obj. of prep. and cannot be assumed to be emphatic. Εὑρήσει 3rd sg. fut. act. indic. of εὑρίσκω, "find, discover, *obtain" (BDAG 411b–12c 3).

16:26 The interr. pron. τί ("what?") introduces a question. Τί (nom./acc. sg. neut.) serves as the dir. obj., which is possible for pass. vbs. that take two dir. obj. (dbl. acc. of pers.-thing) in the act. voice. Γάρ is common in questions, but Eng. idiom normally leaves it untranslated (BDAG 189a–90a 1.f.; NIV). Ὠφεληθήσεται (3rd sg. fut. pass. indic. of ὠφελέω, "receive help, be benefited" [pass.]) is delib. fut. (W 570–cognitive). Ἄνθρωπος is anar. because it is indef. Ἐάν plus the subjunc. (κερδήσῃ 3rd sg. aor. act. subjunc. of κερδαίνω, "gain") marks the prot. (which in this case stands after the apod.) of a 3rd-class cond. sentence that makes no assumption regarding the fulfillment of the condition. Κόσμος, -ου, ὁ, "world (as scene of earthly joys and possessions)" (BDAG 561b–63a 7.a.). Ὅλος, -η, -ον, "whole, entire" (BDAG 704a–c 1.b.β.). Δέ is adversative. Although ψυχή in 16:25 prob. means "life," most EVV assume a difference sense here: "soul" (BDAG 1098d–1100a 2.d.). Ζημιωθῇ (3rd sg. aor. pass. subjunc. of ζημιόω, "lose, forfeit") is the second vb. in a compound prot. and is also governed by ἐάν. The disjunctive ἤ ("or") introduces a second but related question. On τί, see 16:26a. Δώσει (3rd sg. fut. act. indic. of δίδωμι) is delib. fut. Ἄνθρωπος, 16:26a. Ἀντάλλαγμα, -ατος, τό, "something given in exchange, ransom" (BDAG 86d). The gen. τῆς ψυχῆς (16:26a) is influenced by the ἀντί pref. The prep. uses the gen. exclusively for its obj. The cstr. means: "in exchange for his soul."

16:27 Γάρ introduces the reason that forfeiting one's life to follow Jesus is wise. Μέλλει (3rd sg. pres. act. indic. of μέλλω, "be about to, be destined to") with the pres. inf. (ἔρχεσθαι pres. mid. inf. of dep. ἔρχομαι) denotes an action is certain to occur because of a divine decree: "will most certainly come" (BDAG 627c–28c 2.a.). Ὁ υἱὸς τοῦ ἀνθρώπου, 8:20. Ἐν τῇ δόξῃ identifies the state in which Jesus will come (BDAG

326c–30b 2.b.). Τοῦ πατρός may be gen. of source ("glory bestowed on him by his father") or *gen. of poss. ("in his Father's glory [which he shares];" NIV). Αὐτοῦ is gen. of rel. and the ref. is "the Son of Man." Μετά with the gen. (τῶν ἀγγέλων) expresses accompaniment: "together with his angels." Αὐτοῦ is prob. a gen. of poss. or authority, denoting that the angels serve him and are commanded by him. Τότε prob. means "at that time." Ἀποδώσει (3rd sg. fut. act. indic. of ἀποδίδωμι, "pay, reward") is predictive fut., referring to eschatological judgment. Ἑκάστῳ is dat. of indir. obj. Κατά with the acc. (τὴν πρᾶξιν acc. sg. fem. of πρᾶξις, -εως, ἡ, "deed, performance, activity;" BDAG 859d–60b) is marker of norm of similarity: "according to" (BDAG 512 5.a.β.). See Metzger 34. Αὐτοῦ is subj. gen. See Proverbs 24:12.

16:28 Ἀμὴν λέγω ὑμῖν, 5:18. Ὅτι introduces dir. discourse. Εἰσίν 3rd pl. pres. indic. of εἰμί, "there are" (impers.). Τινες is indef. pron. and limits the statement to a portion of the group. Τῶν ἑστώτων (gen. pl. masc. of pf. act. ptc. of ἵστημι, "stand" [intrans.]") is subst. and partitive. The pf. tense of this vb. functions like the pres. tense (BDAG 482a–83b C.1.). The adv. ὧδε ("here") modifies the ptc. Οἵτινες functions as the simple rel. pron. (BDAG 729d–30b 3). The dbl. neg. οὐ μή with the subjunc. (γεύσωνται 3rd pl. aor. mid. subjunc. of dep. γεύομαι, "taste, *experience") expresses emphatic negation: "(they) certainly will not experience. . . ." Θανάτου is gen. of dir. obj. Ἕως with the particle of contingency ἄν and the aor. subjunc. (ἴδωσιν 3rd pl. aor. act. subjunc. of ὁράω) denotes that the initiation of an event (death of some of those pres.) is dependent on the named circumstance (view of the coming of the Son of Man). See BDAG 422d–24c 1.a.β. Τὸν υἱὸν τοῦ ἀνθρώπου, 8:20. Ἐρχόμενον (acc. sg. masc. of pres. mid. ptc. of dep. ἔρχομαι) is pred. ptc. Ἐν with the dat. (τῇ βασιλείᾳ) may express accompaniment ("along with his kingdom;" BDAG 326c–30b 5.a.β.) or a *state or condition ("as king;" BDAG 326c–30b 7; G 341; F 636, 640). Since the cstr. is used with a vb. of motion, the phrase could also mark the goal ("coming to establish his kingdom;" BDAG 326c–30b 3).

FOR FURTHER STUDY

87. Crucifixion and Cross-Bearing

Cook, J. G. *Crucifixion in the Mediterranean World.* WUNT 327; Tübingen: Mohr Siebeck, 2014.

Fletcher, D. R. "Condemned to Die: The Logion on Cross-Bearing: What Does It Mean?" *Int* 18 (1964): 156–64.

Green, M. P. "The Meaning of Cross-Bearing." *BSac* 140 (1983): 117–33.

Griffiths, J. G. "The Disciple's Cross." *NTS* 16 (1970): 358–64.

Tanner, P. A. "The Cost of Discipleship: Losing One's Life for Jesus's Sake." *JETS* 56 (2013): 43–61.

HOMILETICAL SUGGESTIONS

The Demands of Discipleship (16:24–28)

1. Discipleship requires submission to Christ and self-denial
2. Discipleship requires a willingness to die in faithfulness to Christ
3. Discipleship requires following Jesus's example
4. Discipleship requires living today in light of final judgment

3. Jesus's Transfiguration (17:1–8)

17:1 Καί signals a close connection between this paragraph and the preceding paragraph and perhaps esp. 16:28. The phrase μεθ' ἡμέρας ἕξ prob. means six days after Jesus made the promise in 16:28 that some of his disciples would soon see him come as king. Παραλαμβάνει (3rd sg. pres. act. indic. of παραλαμβάνω, "take along") is historical pres. The historical pres. prob. emphasizes the singling out of this group of three, since it constitutes fulfillment of the promise to "some of you standing here" (16:28). Although a single def. art. (τόν) precedes three names joined by καί (Πέτρον καὶ Ἰάκωβον καὶ Ἰωάννην), it modifies only the first. This is not an example of the Granville Sharp cstr., since it does not apply to proper names (W 271–72). All names in Gk. are def. whether or not they are art. (W 245–47). Τὸν ἀδελφόν is acc. of simple appos., modifying Ἰωάννην. Αὐτοῦ is gen. of relationship and its referent is John. Ἀναφέρει (3rd sg. pres. act. indic. of ἀναφέρω, "bring or lead up") is historical pres. Εἰς ὄρος ὑψηλόν, 4:8. Κατ' ἰδίαν, 14:13.

17:2 Μετεμορφώθη 3rd sg. aor. pass. indic. of μεταμορφόω, "change in outward appearance" (pass.). Ἔμπροσθεν, "in front of" (BDAG 325a–c 1.b.). Ἔλαμψεν 3rd sg. aor. act. indic. of λάμπω, "shine, gleam." Αὐτοῦ is partitive gen. (modifying τὸ πρόσωπον). Ὡς is comp.: "like." Ἥλιος, -ου, ὁ, "sun." The def. art. is monadic. The shift from καί to δέ is prob. significant. Δέ is prob. adversative and contrasts the brilliance of Jesus's face with the luminosity of his glory when filtered by his garments. Αὐτοῦ is gen. of poss. but refers specifically to the garments (τὰ ἱμάτια) that Jesus was wearing at the moment. Ἐγένετο (3rd sg. 2nd aor. mid. indic. of dep. γίνομαι) refers to "becoming" rather than mere "being." Jesus's garments did not always have this appearance, but they became as bright as the light on this occasion. Although the adj. λευκός, -ή, -όν, often refers to the color white, it here means "bright, shining, gleaming" (BDAG 593b–c 1). Ὡς is comp. Both this and the previous comp. are intended to demonstrate the intensity of Jesus's glory. The def. art. (τό) modifying φῶς is either anaphoric (referring to the light of the sun mentioned in the previous clause), the *"familiar" art. (referring simply to the light that illuminates the earth [daylight]; 5:14), or generic (referring to light in general). See Metzger 34.

17:3 The καὶ ἰδού cstr. prompts attention to something extraordinary (BDAG 468b–d 1.b.β.). Ὤφθη (3rd sg. aor. pass. indic. of ὁράω, "be seen, appear" [pass.]) is unusual since one would expect a pl. vb. with the compound subj. (Μωϋσῆς [Moses] καὶ Ἠλίας [Elijah]). The awkwardness is heightened by the use of the pl. ptc. συλλαλοῦντες, which also takes "Moses and Elijah" as the subj. This is apparently a solecism. Not surprisingly, a number of scribes adjusted the vb. to the pl. number (C L W). The position of the indir. obj. αὐτοῖς may indicate that it is emphatic. Συλλαλοῦντες (nom. pl. masc. of pres. act. ptc. of συλλαλέω, "converse") may be *attrib. ("Moses and Elijah, who were conversing") or attendant circumstance (NLT). Μετ' αὐτοῦ with this particular vb. expresses interchange of action rather than mere association or accompaniment. **17:4** Ἀποκριθείς (nom. sg. masc. of aor. pass. ptc. of dep. ἀποκρίνομαι, "answer, reply") is pleonastic (most EVV). Δέ is adversative and implies that Peter's response was not appropriate to the situation. Κύριε is voc. of simple address. Καλόν is a pred. adj., and its position may be slightly emphatic. However, the pred. adj. often precedes forms of εἰμί in Matthew, so emphasis is doubtful. Ἐστίν 3rd sg. pres. indic. of εἰμί. The inf. phrase ἡμᾶς ὧδε εἶναι serves as the subj. of the vb. (W 600–601). Ἡμᾶς is acc. subj. of the inf. Ὧδε is adv. of place: "here." Εἶναι pres. inf. of εἰμί. The particle εἰ with the indic. vb. (θέλεις 2nd sg. pres. act. indic. of θέλω, "want, desire") marks the prot. of a 1st-class cond. sentence that assumes the fulfillment of the prot. Ποιήσω 1st sg. fut. act. indic. of ποιέω, "make, build." See Metzger 34–35. Σκηνή, -ῆς, ἡ, "temporary dwelling, hut (made from brush)." The dat. pron. and nouns σοί, Μωϋσεῖ, and Ἠλίᾳ are dat. of indir. obj. Each instance of the number μίαν is acc. of simple appos., modifying τρεῖς σκηνάς.

17:5 Ἔτι is an adv. expressing the continuance of an action in the past (BDAG 400a–c 1.a.β.). Αὐτοῦ λαλοῦντος (gen. sg. masc. of pres. act. ptc. of λαλέω) is gen. abs. and temp.: "While he was still speaking." Καί ἰδού, 17:3. Νεφέλη, -ης, ἡ, "cloud." Φωτεινός, -ή, -όν, "shining, radiant." Ἐπεσκίασεν 3rd sg. aor. act. indic. of ἐπισκιάζω, "overshadow, cover." The ref. to Moses in combination with νεφέλη, ἐπισκιάζω, and σκηνή recalls Exodus 40:35. The antecedent of αὐτούς is unclear. It certainly includes Jesus, Moses, and Elijah, and possibly (but not prob.) Peter, James, and John. The combination of καὶ ἰδού and the absence of a vb. suggest that φωνή is a nom. of exclamation (W 59–60). Ἐκ with the gen. (τῆς νεφέλης) locates the source of the voice: "from within the cloud." Due to the absence of a vb., λέγουσα (nom. sg. fem. of pres. act. ptc. of λέγω) is likely adj. Μου (modifying υἱός) is gen. of relationship. Ὁ ἀγαπητός is in the second attrib. position, which emphasizes both the noun and the adj. (W 306–7; R 777). Εὐδόκησα 1st sg. aor. act. indic. of εὐδοκέω, "take delight, be pleased." The vb. normally uses ἐν with the dat. (ᾧ) to mark the pers. obj. of delight. The rel. pron. ᾧ refers to υἱός. Ἀκούετε (2nd pl. pres. act. impv. of ἀκούω, "listen to") is prob. ingr.-prog. Αὐτοῦ is gen. of dir. obj., which is common with the vb. ἀκούω (BDAG 37c–38d 4).

17:6 Ἀκούσαντες (nom. pl. masc. of aor. act. ptc. of ἀκούω) is temp. (most EVV). The def. art. οἱ modifying μαθηταί is the art. of previous ref., referring to the disciples named in 17:1. Ἔπεσαν 3rd pl. 2nd aor. act. indic. of πίπτω, "fall." With the prep. phrase ἐπὶ πρόσωπον, the vb. πίπτω means "to throw oneself to the ground as a sign of devotion" (BDAG 815a–16a 1.b.α.). Αὐτῶν is partitive gen. Ἐφοβήθησαν 3rd pl. aor. pass. indic. of φοβέω, "be afraid" (pass.). Σφόδρα is an adv. of intensity or extremity: "extremely."

17:7 Προσῆλθεν 3rd sg. 2nd aor. act. indic. of dep. προσέρχομαι, "go toward, approach." Ἁψάμενος (nom. sg. masc. of aor. mid. ptc. of ἅπτω, "touch" [mid.]) is prob. ptc. of attendant circumstance (most EVV). Αὐτῶν is gen. of dir. obj., which is common with the mid. form of ἅπτω (BDAG 126a–d 2). Ἐγέρθητε (2nd pl. aor. pass. impv. of ἐγείρω) prob. expresses urgency: "Get up right away" (BDAG 271c–72c 13). All other occurrences of the impv. form of the vb. ἐγείρω in Matthew are in the pres. tense. (9:5; 10:8; 26:46). Φοβεῖσθε (2nd pl. pres. pass. impv. of φοβέω). The use of μή and the pres impv. in a prohibition calls for the cessation of an action already in progress: "Stop being afraid."

17:8 Ἐπάραντες (nom. pl. masc. of aor. act. ptc. of ἐπαίρω, "lift up") is prob. temp. (most EVV). Δέ marks the next development in the narrative. When τοὺς ὀφθαλμούς is the dir. obj. of forms of ἐπαίρω, the cstr. means "to look up(ward)." The cstr. is an idiom, which is not to be interpreted lit. Αὐτῶν is partitive gen. Εἶδον 3rd pl. aor. act. indic. of ὁράω. The combination εἰ μή means "except." The cstr. αὐτὸν Ἰησοῦν μόνον is capable of several interpretations. The pron. αὐτόν may serve as a second dir. obj. of the vb. If so, Ἰησοῦν is acc. of simple appos. (LEB; G 345). Alternatively, αὐτόν may be functioning as an *intensive adj. in the pred. position: "Jesus himself" (NASB; BDAG 152c–54a 1.a.α.).

FOR FURTHER STUDY

88. Jesus's Transfiguration

Bucur, B. G. "Matt 17:1–9 as a Vision of a Vision: A Neglected Strand in the Patristic Reception of the Transfiguration Account." *Neot* 44 (2010): 15–30.

Liefeld, W. L. "Theological Motifs in the Transfiguration Narrative." Pages 162–79 in *New Dimensions in New Testament Study*. Edited by R. N. Longenecker and M. C. Tenney. Grand Rapids: Zondervan, 1974.

Penner, J. A. "Revelation and Discipleship in Matthew's Transfiguration Account." *BSac* 152 (1995): 201–10.

Puigi Tàrrech, A. "The Glory on the Mountain: The Episode of the Transfiguration of Jesus." *NTS* 58 (2012): 151–72.

Quarles, C. *A Theology of Matthew: Jesus Revealed as Deliverer, King, and Incarnate Creator*. Phillipsburg, NJ: P&R, 2013.

Schreiner, T. "2 Peter 1:16–21." Pages 311–24 in *1, 2 Peter, Jude*. New American Commentary 37. Nashville: B&H, 2003.

HOMILETICAL SUGGESTIONS

Jesus Unveiled (17:1–8)

1. Jesus is the the prophet like Moses (Deut 18:15–19)
   a. Jesus's transfiguration is like Moses's experience in remarkable ways (Exod 24:12–18)
      1. Six days (Exod 24:16)
      2. A high mountain (Exod 24:13)
      3. The glory of the Lord (Exod 24:17)
      4. The voice from the cloud (Exod 24:16)
      5. Witnesses were afraid (Exod 34:30)

b. God's people must listen to and obey Jesus as the prophet like Moses (Deut 18:15, 18)

2. Jesus is the God of Moses

   a. Although Moses reflected the glory of God, Jesus radiates the glory of God (Exod 34:29–35; Matt 17:2)

   b. Although Moses's glory could be concealed by garments, Jesus's glory penetrates his garments (Exod 34:33, 35; Matt 17:2)

   c. Although Moses is God's servant, Jesus is God's Son (Matt 17:5)

   d. Although Moses is a mere human being, Jesus is described as a heavenly being

     1. Jesus is described as the figure in Daniel 10:1–11:2

     2. Jesus is described as Yahweh in Habakkuk 3:3–4

4. The Coming of Elijah (17:9–13)

17:9 Καταβαινόντων (gen. pl. masc. of pres. act. ptc. of καταβαίνω, "come down, descend") is gen. abs. and temp.: "As they were coming down." Αὐτῶν refers to Jesus and the three disciples. Ἐνετείλατο 3rd sg. aor. mid. indic. of ἐντέλλω, "command" (mid.). Αὐτοῖς refers to the three disciples (17:1). Λέγων (nom. sg. masc. of pres. act. ptc. of λέγω) is pleonastic. Εἴπητε (2nd pl. 2nd aor. act. subjunc. of λέγω) may prohibit the action as a whole and thus have an ingr. force (W 723–24). However, Matthew always uses the aor. tense for the impv. (twelve occurrences) and subjunc. forms (twenty-two occurrences) of λέγω, so it is probable that no special nuance for the aor. was intended: "Do not tell. . . ." Ὅραμα, -ατος, τό, "sight." Although most EVV tr. the noun as "vision," this tr. is confusing since the Eng. noun "vision" in religious contexts often refers to visionary experiences. However, the Gk. term often refers to something actually seen with one's eyes, and the context suggests that is the sense here. Thus the NIV's "what you have seen" is preferable to "vision" (CSB; ESV; LEB). The acc. of dir. obj. is often used with λέγω to identify the content of speech (BDAG 588a–90c 1.a.α.). The cstr. ἕως οὗ with a neg. (μηδενί) means "until, before." Ὁ υἱὸς τοῦ ἀνθρώπου, 8:20. Ἐκ νεκρῶν expresses separation: "from among the dead." Since ἐγείρω is capable of expressing several different mngs., the prep. phrase clarifies that it is a ref. to resurrection. Ἐγερθῇ 3rd sg. aor. pass. subjunc. of ἐγείρω, "be raised" (pass.).

17:10 Ἐπηρώτησαν 3rd pl. aor. act. indic. of ἐπερωτάω, "ask (a question)." Αὐτόν refers to Jesus. Λέγοντες (nom. pl. masc. of pres. act. ptc. of λέγω) is pleonastic. Τί is an interr. pron. and introduces a question. Οὖν is often used in questions introduced by τί and the combination means, "So, why . . . ?" or "Why then?" In this context the οὖν indicates that the question regarding Elijah was prompted by his appearance at Jesus's transfiguration. The def. art. (οἱ) modifying γραμματεῖς ("scribes") is generic. Λέγουσιν (3rd pl. pres. act. indic. of λέγω) is either customary or gnomic pres. and indicates that this is the established position of the scribes. Ὅτι introduces dir. discourse. Δεῖ 3rd sg. pres. act. indic. of δέω, "be necessary" (impers.). Ἐλθεῖν (aor. act. inf. of dep. ἔρχομαι) is a complementary inf. The acc. neut. adj. πρῶτον is here used as a temp. adv. and means "first," i.e., before the coming of the Messiah (NLT). See Malachi 4:4–5.

17:11 Ὁ δὲ ἀποκριθεὶς εἶπεν, 4:4. Μέν introduces a concessive clause that stands in sharp contrast with a second clause introduced by δέ: "Even though Elijah is coming . . . , nevertheless. . . ." Ἔρχεται (3rd sg. pres. mid. indic. of dep. ἔρχομαι) is futuristic pres. and prob. emphasizes the certainty that Elijah will come (W 535–37; NIV; LEB; NLT). Ἀποκαταστήσει (3rd sg. fut. act. indic. of ἀποκαθίστημι, "restore") is predictive fut. The fut. tense may indicate that Jesus expected Elijah to appear again before his parousia (G 347). Several commentators argue that the fut. tense is merely influenced by the wording of Malachi 4:4–5 and does not suggest that Jesus expected another appearance of Elijah before his return (H 2.499; Luz 2.400; D&A 2.714–15). Πάντα is subst.: "all things" (neut.).

17:12 Λέγω δὲ ὑμῖν ὅτι, 5:22. The temp. adv. ἤδη implies completion of an action at a prior point in time (BDAG 434c–d, 1.b.). Ἦλθεν 3rd sg. 2nd aor. act. indic. of dep. ἔρχομαι. Καί is prob. used here to emphasize a fact as surprising or unexpected: "and yet" (BDAG 494a–96c 1.b.η.). Ἐπέγνωσαν 3rd pl. 2nd aor. act. indic. of ἐπιγινώσκω, "recognize." Αὐτόν refers to Elijah. After a neg. clause, the adversative force of ἀλλά is heightened: "on the contrary" (BDAG 44c–45d 1.a.). Ἐποίησαν 3rd pl. aor. act. indic. of ποιέω, "do, treat (in a particular manner)." Ἐν αὐτῷ is a substitute for the simple dat. of disadvantage (BDAG 839b–42a 4.b.; BDAG 326c–30b 8). Ὅσα (ὅσος, -η, -ον, "how much") is here a shortened form of πάντα ὅσα and means "everything that, whatever" (BDAG 729a–c 2). Ἠθέλησαν 3rd pl. aor. act. indic. of θέλω, "want, desire." Οὕτως is retrospective and refers to the manner in which Elijah was treated. Καί is either *adjunctive (most EVV) or ascensive. Ὁ υἱὸς τοῦ ἀνθρώπου, 8:20. Μέλλει (3rd sg. pres. act. indic. of μέλλω, "be about to" or *"be destined to" [BDAG 627d–28c 1.c.α., 2.a.; ESV; D&A 2.716]). Πάσχειν (pres. act. inf. of πάσχω, "suffer") is a complementary inf. Ὑπ᾽ αὐτῶν expresses agency (BDAG 1035d–36d A.b.; 785a–86a 3.a.β.).

17:13 Τότε, "at that time." Συνῆκαν 3rd pl. aor. act. indic. of συνίημι, "understand." Ὅτι is recitative and shows the content of their knowledge. Περί with the gen. (Ἰωάννου) expresses ref.: "about." Τοῦ βαπτιστοῦ (Βαπτιστής, -οῦ, ὁ, "baptizer") is gen. of simple appos., modifying Ἰωάννου. Αὐτοῖς refers to the disciples.

FOR FURTHER STUDY

89. The Coming of Elijah

Allison, D. C., Jr. "Elijah Must Come First." *JBL* 103 (1984): 256–58.

Faierstein, M. M. "Why Do the Scribes Say That Elijah Must Come First?" *JBL* 100 (1981): 75–86.

Fitzmyer, J. A. "More About Elijah Coming First." *JBL* 104 (1985): 295–96.

Taylor, J. "The Coming of Elijah, Mt 17:10–13 and Mk 9:11–13: The Development of the Texts." *Revue Biblique* 98 (1991): 107–19.

HOMILETICAL SUGGESTIONS

A Secret Hard to Keep (17:9–13)

1. Jesus's transfiguration was a prophecy that must be kept secret until its fulfillment (Dan 12:4, 9)
2. John the Baptist was the Messiah's forerunner, fulfilling the prophecy about Elijah's coming (Mal 4:5–6)
3. Jesus is the Son of Man and the Suffering Servant who will atone for the sins of God's people (Daniel 7; Isaiah 53)

5. The Exorcism of the Demon-Possessed Boy (17:14–18)

17:14 Ἐλθόντων (gen. pl. masc. of 2nd aor. act. ptc. of dep. ἔρχομαι) is gen. abs. and temp. "When they (Jesus and the disciples) came to the crowd" (most EVV) . Προσῆλθεν 3rd sg. 2nd aor. act. indic. of dep. προσέρχομαι, "approach." Αὐτῷ is dat. of dir. obj. Γονυπετῶν (nom. sg. masc. of pres. act. ptc. of γονυπετέω, "kneel before") is attendant circumstance (most EVV). Αὐτῷ and αὐτόν both refer to Jesus.

17:15 Λέγων (nom. sg. masc. of pres. act. ptc. of λέγω) is attendant circumstance (most EVV). Κύριε is voc. of simple address. Ἐλέησον (2nd sg. aor. act. impv. of ἐλεέω, "have mercy") prob. expresses urgency. On κύριε, ἐλέησον, see 15:22. Μου (modifying τὸν υἱόν) is gen. of relationship. Ὅτι introduces the reason for the appeal. Σεληνιάζεται (3rd sg. pres. mid. indic. of dep. σεληνιάζομαι, "experience seizures") is iter. pres.; the seizures were episodic but occurred again and again. Κακῶς is an adv. expressing intensity of a neg. nature: "badly, severely." Πάσχει (3rd sg. pres. act. indic. of πάσχω, "suffer") is prob. prog. since he suffered from injuries incurred during his episodic seizures. Πολλάκις is an adv., expressing repetition: "many times, often, frequently." The adv. demonstrates that the vb. πίπτει (3rd sg. pres. act. indic. of πίπτω) is iter. pres. The def. art. τό that modifies πῦρ and ὕδωρ is generic.

17:16 Προσήνεγκα 1st sg. aor. act. indic. of προσφέρω, "bring." Καί is prob. used here to emphasize a fact as surprising or unexpected: "and yet" (BDAG 494a–96c 1.b.η.). The father expected the disciples to be able to heal his son. Ἠδυνήθησαν 3rd pl. aor. pass. indic. of δύναμαι, "be able." Αὐτόν is dir. obj. of the inf. θεραπεῦσαι (aor. act. inf. of θεραπεύω, "heal;" complementary) and refers to the son (17:15).

17:17 Ἀποκριθείς (nom. sg. masc. of aor. pass. ptc. of dep. ἀποκρίνομαι, "answer") is pleonastic. Δέ prob. marks a new development in the narrative. With the interjection ὦ, γενεά (γενεά, -ᾶς, ἡ, "generation") is voc. of emphatic address, expressing intense emotion (W 68–69). Ἄπιστος, -ον, "unbelieving, without faith." Διεστραμμένη (voc. sg. fem. of pf. pass. ptc. of διαστρέφω, "perverted, depraved" [pass.]) is adj. Ἕως ("until") with the interr. temp. art. πότε ("when?") means "how much longer?" Μεθ' ὑμῶν expresses association. Ἔσομαι (1st sg. fut. indic. of εἰμί) is delib. fut., posing a rhetorical question. Ἀνέξομαι (1st sg. fut. mid. indic. of ἀνέχω, "tolerate, put up with") is delib. fut. Ὑμῶν is gen. of dir. obj. Φέρετε (2nd pl. pres. act. impv. of φέρω) prob. issues a simple command without any emphasis on the continuation of the action. The aor. impv. of this vb. is rare and appears only once (out of eleven total impv. forms) in the NT. Μοι is dat. of indir. obj. Αὐτόν refers to the son. Ὧδε, "here."

17:18 Ἐπετίμησεν 3rd sg. aor. act. indic. of ἐπιτιμάω, "rebuke." Αὐτῷ is dat. of dir. obj. and may refer to the son (if masc.; G 351; F 661) or to the *demon (if neut.; most EVV; H 2.504). Although the shift in referent from αὐτῷ to αὐτοῦ might seem awkward if the former refers to the demon and the latter to the boy, such shifts in referent occur elsewhere in Matthew (17:9). Since the demon was not previously mentioned in the narrative, the pron. (if neut.) is prospective and anticipates the explicit ref. to the demon in the next clause. This view is supported by the recognition that in other accounts of his exorcisms, Jesus consistently rebuked demons rather than the victims that they possessed. Ἐξῆλθεν 3rd sg. 2nd aor. act. indic. of dep. ἐξέρχομαι, "go out." Ἀπ' αὐτοῦ expresses separation: "away from him." Ἐθεραπεύθη 3rd sg. aor. pass. indic. of θεραπεύω, "heal." Παῖς, παιδός, ὁ or ἡ, may mean "slave," "child (in the sense of one's son or daughter)," or "child (with regard to age rather than relationship)" and refer to one under the age of puberty. The ref. to the referent as a son rules out the first option. The absence of a gen. of rel. with the noun παῖς strongly implies the 3rd option (most EVV: "boy"). On ἀπὸ τῆς ὥρας ἐκείνης, see 15:28.

6. The Disciples' Small Faith (17:19–21)

17:19 Τότε prob. means "after that" but refers to a time only shortly after the previously recorded event. Προσελθόντες (nom. pl. masc. of 2nd aor. act. ptc. of dep. προσέρχομαι, "approach") is prob. ptc. of attendant circumstance (most EVV). Τῷ Ἰησοῦ is dat. of dir. obj. Κατ' ἰδίαν, 14:13. Διὰ τί, "why?" Ἡμεῖς is mildly emphatic and contrasts the disciples' inability with Jesus's effectiveness. Ἠδυνήθημεν 1st pl. aor. pass. indic. of dep. δύναμαι, "be able." Ἐκβαλεῖν (2nd aor. act. inf. of ἐκβάλλω, "throw out, cast out") is a complementary inf. Αὐτό refers to δαιμόνιον (also neut.).

17:20 Ὁ serves as a substitute for the pers. pron. Δέ introduces the next development in the narrative. Λέγει is historical pres. Αὐτοῖς refers to the disciples. Διά with the acc. (τὴν ὀλιγοπιστίαν acc. sg. fem. of ὀλιγοπιστία, -ας, ἡ, "weak or small faith") expresses cause. See Metzger 35. Ὑμῶν is subj. gen. Ἀμὴν γὰρ λέγω ὑμῖν, 5:18. Ἐάν with the subjunc. (ἔχητε 2nd pl. pres. act. subjunc. of ἔχω) marks the prot. of a 3rd-class cond. sentence, which makes no assumption regarding the fulfillment of the prot. Ὡς is comp. and refers to a comp. in size since it appears in the context of a ref. to ὀλιγοπιστία. Κόκκος, -ου, ὁ, "kernel, grain." Σίναπι, -εως, τό, "mustard plant." Σινάπεως may a gen. of source ("seed from a mustard plant"), gen. of product ("seed that produces a mustard plant"), or a simple *descriptive gen. ("seed of the mustard variety"). Ἐρεῖτε (2nd pl. fut. act. indic. of λέγω) is pred. fut. The proximate dem. pron. τούτῳ modifying τῷ ὄρει implies that Jesus was referring to a particular mountain within view of the group, prob. the Mount of Transfiguration, a particularly huge mountain (17:1). Μετάβα (2nd sg. aor. act. impv. of μεταβαίνω, "move") may express urgency. However, seven of the eight impv. forms of μεταβαίνω in the NT are in the aor. tense. Ἔνθεν is an adv., marking an orig. location: "from here." Ἐκεῖ is used to indicate a location relatively distant from the speaker: "over there" (BDAG 301c–d 2). Μεταβήσεται (3rd sg. 2nd fut. mid.

indic. of μεταβαίνω) is pred. fut., used to express a promise. Ἀδυνατήσει (3rd sg. fut. act. indic. of ἀδυνατέω, "be impossible") is pred. fut., used to express a promise. Ὑμῖν is dat. of ref.: "for you, as far as you are concerned."

17:21 This verse does not appear in the earliest uncials, several important minuscules, or several early versions. Common scribal errors do not explain its omission. Thus the verse was most likely absent from Matthew orig. but added to some mss. in the late second century to assimilate this Gospel to Mark 9:29. For this reason the ESV does not mention the verse; and the NIV and CSB mention it only in a footnote. See Metzger 35.

7. Jesus Predicts His Death and Resurrection (17:22–23)

17:22 Συστρεφομένων (gen. pl. masc. of pres. mid./pass. ptc. of συστρέφω, "gather") is gen. abs. The ptc. is either *refl. mid. ("when they gathered themselves") or pass. ("when they were gathered"). See Metzger 35. Δέ prob. introduces the next development in the narrative. Αὐτῶν refers to Jesus and his disciples. Αὐτοῖς refers to the disciples. Μέλλει (3rd sg. pres. act. indic. of μέλλω, "be about to, be destined to") may either express imminence (ESV; CSB; H 2.507) or *inevitability (BDAG 627c–28c 2; G 354; D&A 2.716; cf. 16:27). Ὁ υἱὸς τοῦ ἀνθρώπου, 8:20. Παραδίδοσθαι (pres. pass. inf. of παραδίδωμι, "hand over") is a complementary inf. and prob. divine pass. (H 2.507–8; D&A 2.734). France argues that the vb. means "betray," in which case the agent must be human rather than divine (F 663 n. 3). If this is a ref. to a divine act, it supports the emphasis on inevitability (due to divine ordination) often implied by the vb. μέλλω. The prep. phrase εἰς χεῖρας ἀνθρώπων (partitive gen.) seems to confirm the divine pass. The Son of Man is given over by God to human hands. Otherwise one would expect a ref. to the hands of the chief priest and elders, authorities, or the like.

17:23 Ἀποκτενοῦσιν (3rd pl. fut. act. indic. of ἀποκτείνω, "kill") is pred. fut. Αὐτόν refers to the Son of Man. Τῇ τρίτῃ ἡμέρᾳ is dat. of time: "on the third day." Ἐγερθήσεται (3rd sg. fut. pass. indic. of ἐγείρω, "raise [from the dead]") is pred. fut. and divine pass. (most EVV). Καί prob. introduces a result. Ἐλυπήθησαν 3rd pl. aor. pass. indic. of λυπέω, "be sad" (pass.). Σφόδρα is an adv. expressing intensity: "very, extremely" (BDAG 980a).

FOR FURTHER STUDY

90. The Exorcism of the Demon-Possessed Boy

Spencer, F. F. "Faith on Edge: The Difficult Case of the Spirit-Seized Boy in Mark 9:14–29." *RevExp* 107 (2010): 419–24.

Sterling, G. E. "Jesus as Exorcist: An Analysis of Matthew 17:14–20; Mark 9:14–29; Luke 9:37–43a." *CBQ* 55 (1993): 467–93.

Wilkinson, J. "The Case of the Epileptic Boy." *ExpTim* 79 (1967): 39–42.

HOMILETICAL SUGGESTIONS

The Power of Jesus (17:14–23)

1. Jesus has the power to cast out demons
2. Jesus has the power to accomplish the impossible
3. Jesus has the power to foresee the future

8. *Jesus's Payment of the Temple Tax (17:24–27)*

17:24 Δέ is a marker linking narrative segments (BDAG 213a–d 2). Ἐλθόντων (gen. pl. masc. of aor. act. ptc. of dep. ἔρχομαι) is gen. abs. and temp.: "When they came." Αὐτῶν refers to Jesus and his disciples. Προσῆλθον 3rd pl. 2nd aor. act. indic. of dep. προσέρχομαι, "come toward, approach." The def. art. οἱ indicates that the ptc. λαμβάνοντες (nom. pl. masc. of pres. act. ptc. of λαμβάνω) is subst.: "The ones who receive." Δίδραχμον, -ου, τό, "double drachma coin." Ὑμῶν (modifying ὁ διδάσκαλος) is prob. subj. gen. ("your teacher" = "the one who teaches you"). The use of the neg. οὐ anticipates a positive reply to the question. Thus the collectors assume that Jesus does pay the tax. Τελεῖ (3rd sg. pres. act. indic. of τελέω, "pay") is customary pres.

17:25 Λέγει (3rd sg. pres. act. indic. of λέγω) is historical pres. Ναί, "yes." Ἐλθόντα (acc. sg. masc. of aor. act. ptc. of dep. ἔρχομαι) is temp. (contemp.), and the acc. case shows that Peter (the referent of αὐτόν) is the subj. of the ptc. Προέφθασεν 3rd sg. aor. act. indic. of προφθάνω, "anticipate." Λέγων (nom. sg. masc. of pres. act. ptc. of λέγω) is ptc. of means: "Jesus anticipated him by saying" (Jesus spoke to Peter before Peter had opportunity to bring the matter up to him). Τί is the interr. pron., which in this case means "what?" rather than "why?" Σοι is ethical dat. (dat. of opinion). Δοκεῖ 3rd sg. pres. act. indic. of δοκέω, "seem." Σίμων is voc. of simple address. The def. art. οἱ (modifying βασιλεῖς) is generic. Τῆς γῆς is either gen. of subord. ("who rule over the earth") or *descriptive gen. ("earthly kings;" CSB). The combination of the ἀπό with the interr. pron. τίνων raises the question of source: "from whom?" Λαμβάνουσιν (3rd pl. pres. act. indic. of λαμβάνω) is either gnomic or customary pres. Τέλος, -ους, τό, "tax." Κῆνσος, -ου, ὁ, "poll-tax." The two ἀπό phrases are appos. and clarify the earlier phrase ἀπὸ τίνων. Αὐτῶν refers to the earthly kings and is gen. of relationship. Ἀλλότριος, -ία, -ον, "strange, belonging to anothers." The art. adj. ἀλλοτρίων is subst. and means "strangers" or "foreigners" (BDAG 47c–48a 1.b.β.).

17:26 Δέ introduces the next development within a narrative section. Εἰπόντος (gen. sg. masc. of aor. act. ptc. of λέγω) is gen. abs. and temp. (antecedent). The subj. of the ptc. is Simon. See Metzger 35–36. Ἀπὸ τῶν ἀλλοτρίων, 17:25. Ἔφη 3rd sg. aor. (or impf.) act. indic. of φημί, "state, say." Αὐτῷ refers to Simon. Ἄρα is an inferential particle ("so then, consequently") but is strengthened by the emphatic particle γε. The emphatic inference may be expressed by a paraphrase: "Then it is necessary to conclude that . . ." or "as a result" (H 2.512). Ἐλεύθερος, -έρα, -ον, "free (from obligation)" (BDAG 316d–317a 2). Εἰσίν 3rd pl. pres. indic. of εἰμί. The def. art. οἱ (modifying υἱοί) is anaphoric and refers to the sons discussed in 17:25.

17:27 Δέ is adversative (most EVV) and contrasts the lack of obligation with the compliance to the request. Ἵνα with the subjunc. (σκανδαλίσωμεν 1st pl. aor. act. subjunc. of σκανδαλίζω, "offend, cause offense") expresses purpose. Αὐτούς refers to those collecting the tax (17:24). Πορευθείς (nom. sg. masc. of aor. pass. ptc. of dep. πορεύομαι, "go, proceed") is prob. ptc. of attendant circumstance and assumes an impv. force due to its connection with the following imperatives: "Go!" In this context the prep. εἰς (with θάλασσαν) prob. means "to" rather than "into" (most EVV). However, the prep. phrase may modify the vb. that follows it (βάλε), in which case it means "into" (BDAG 12a a). Βάλε (2nd sg. 2nd aor. act. impv. of βάλλω). Ἄγκιστρον, -ου, τό, "fishhook." The art. ptc. ἀναβάντα (acc. sg. masc. of 2nd aor. act. ptc. of ἀναβαίνω, "come up") is adj., modifying ἰχθύν. Ἰχθύς, -ύος, ὁ, "fish." Πρῶτον may be acc. sg. masc. or acc. sg. neut. It may function adj. and modify ἰχθύν (most EVV). However, since acc. sg. neut. forms of adj. are often used adv., πρῶτον may modify ἀναβάντα: "the fish that comes up first." Ἆρον 2nd sg. 2nd aor. act. impv. of αἴρω, "take, pull up." Ἀνοίξας (nom. sg. masc. of aor. act. ptc. of ἀνοίγω, "open up") is prob. *temp. ("when you open;" most EVV), cond. ("if you open"), or attendant circumstance ("Open!" NIV). Αὐτοῦ refers to the fish and is partitive gen., modifying τὸ στόμα. Εὑρήσεις (2nd sg. fut. act. indic. of εὑρίσκω, "find, discover") is *predictive (most EVV) or impv. fut. Στατήρ, -ῆρος, ὁ, "stater, a silver coin worth four drachmas." Ἐκεῖνον is the remote dem. pron. and refers to the stater (though grammatically it could refer to the fish). Λαβών (nom. sg. masc. of 2nd aor. act. ptc. of λαμβάνω) is prob. ptc. of attendant circumstance (most EVV). Δός 2nd sg. aor. act. impv. of δίδωμι. The series of aor. impv. prob. stresses urgency. Αὐτοῖς refers to those collecting the tax (17:24). Ἀντί with the gen. (ἐμοῦ καὶ σοῦ) often expresses substitution or replacement. Here, however, it has a weakened sense—"on behalf of"—and is roughly equivalent to ὑπέρ (BDAG 87d–88b 3; D&A 2.747). Gundry argues that the prep. retains its stronger sense and refers to the redemptive nature of the tax (G 357; F 665; Exod 30:11–16).

FOR FURTHER STUDY

91. Payment of the Temple Tax

    Garland, D. E. "Matthew's Understanding of the Temple Tax (Matt 17:24–27)." *SBLSP* 26 (1987): 190–209.

    Mandell, S. "Who Paid the Temple Tax When the Jews Were Under Roman Rule?" *HTR* 77 (1984): 223–32.

92. The Coin in the Fish's Mouth

    Derrett, J. D. M. "Peter's Penny: Fresh Light on Matthew 17:24–7." *NovT* 6 (1963): 1–15.

    Harrison, J. R. "Modern Scholarship and the 'Nature' Miracles: A Defense of Their Historicity and Affirmation of Jesus's Deity." *RTR* 72 (2013): 86–102.

HOMILETICAL SUGGESTIONS

Children of the King (17:24–27)

1. Jesus's disciples are sons of the heavenly King, with all the privileges of sonship
2. Jesus's disciples should avoid giving unnecessary offense to others even if that means forfeiting their rights and privileges
3. Jesus's disciples should be confident in Jesus's ability to provide for their needs

B. FOURTH DISCOURSE: INSTRUCTIONS ABOUT LIFE
IN THE KINGDOM (18:1–35)

1. Greatness in the Kingdom (18:1–5)

18:1 Ἐν with the dat. τῇ ὥρᾳ may mark a period of time ("during that hour"), but here marks a point in time ("at that time"; BDAG 1102c–3c 3). The dem. pron. ἐκείνη refers to a point in time ascertainable from the context, i.e., immediately after Jesus's description of his disciples as the sons of the heavenly King (BDAG 301 b.β.). Nolland argues that the cstr. is not temp. but merely "marks thematic continuity in a section" (731). Προσῆλθον 3rd pl. 2nd aor. act. indic. of dep. προσέρχομαι. Λέγοντες (nom. pl. masc. of pres. act. ptc. of λέγω) is attendant circumstance (CSB; NIV). Τίς is the interr. pron. and the masc. gender indicates that it is pers.: "who?" The inferential particle ἄρα indicates that the question was prompted by the preceding discussion. The distinction between sons of the heavenly King and mere subjects makes the disciples wonder if there will be further distinctions in rank. Μείζων is nom. sg. masc. comp. of μέγας, μεγάλη, μέγα, "great." This is an example of the substitution of the comp. for the superl.: "greatest" (W 299–33; most EVV). Ἐστίν (3rd sg. pres. indic. of εἰμί) seems to assume the pres. aspect of the kingdom and suggests that the disciples did not see it as completely futuristic (H 2.516). However, some see this as an example of the futuristic pres. (D&A 2.756; cf. BDF §323). On τῇ βασιλείᾳ τῶν οὐρανῶν, see 3:2.

18:2 Προσκαλεσάμενος (nom. sg. masc. of aor. mid. ptc. of προσκαλέω, "summon") is a refl. mid.: "call to oneself." The ptc. likely expresses attendant circumstance (CSB; NIV). Παιδίον, -ου, τό is the dimin. form of παῖς ("child"). It normally refers to pre-pubescent children and most often to infants and toddlers (BDAG 749c–50a, 1.b.). Ἔστησεν (3rd sg. aor. act. indic. of ἵστημι) is transitive and causative ("caused to stand, set;" BDAG 482a–83b A.1.). Αὐτό (acc. sg. neut. of αὐτός) does not depersonalize or demean the child (as an "it"). The neut. gender of the pron. is normal since the noun παιδίον is neut. The prep. ἐν with the subst. use of the dat. sg. neut. adj. μέσῳ (μέσος, -η, -ον, "middle") means "in the midst/middle." Αὐτῶν is prob. best categorized as partitive.

18:3 Ἀμὴν λέγω ὑμῖν, 5:18. The particle of contingency ἐάν with the subjunc. vbs. στραφῆτε (2nd pl. 2nd aor. pass. subjunc. of στρέφω, "turn" [pass.]) and γένησθε (2nd pl. 2nd aor. mid. subjunc. of dep. γίνομαι) forms the prot. of a third-class cond. state-ment. It simply states a condition and makes no assumption about the fulfillment of the prot. Ἐάν with μή means "unless" (BDAG 267c–68a 1.c.β.). Ὡς is comp.: "like." Τὰ παιδία, 18:2. The dbl. neg. οὐ μή with the subjunc. (εἰσέλθητε 2nd pl. aor. act. sub-junc. of dep. εἰσέρχομαι) is emphatic negation: "You absolutely will not enter!" Τὴν βασιλείαν τῶν οὐρανῶν, 3:2.

18:4 Οὖν introduces an inference or conclusion from the preceding statement. Ὅστις combines the rel. pron. and the indef. pron. and means "anyone who" or "whoever" (BDAG 729 1.c.). Ταπεινώσει 3rd sg. fut. act. indic. of ταπεινόω, "humble." The use of the fut. may imply that none of the disciples had yet humbled themselves in this man-ner. The refl. pron. ἑαυτόν emphasizes the refl. nature of the action more strongly and explicitly than the refl. mid. Ὡς is comp. Τὸ παιδίον, 18:2. The near dem. pron. τοῦτο indicates that Jesus was referring specifically to the child in 18:2. The dem. pron. οὗτός is emphatic (BDAG 740b–41d 1.a.ε.) and means "this person (and no other)." Ἐστιν ὁ μείζων ἐν τῇ βασιλείᾳ τῶν οὐρανῶν, 18:1.

18:5 Although most EVV tr. ὅς ἐάν as if it were the equivalent of ὅστις ("whoever"), the combination here more closely resembles the sense of a cond. sentence of the fut. more vivid or pres. general type (BDAG 56b–57c I.b.; BDF §380): "if someone. . . ." Δέξηται 3rd sg. aor. mid. subjunc. of dep. δέχομαι, "welcome, receive" (BDAG 221b–c 3). Παιδίον, 18:2. Τοιοῦτος, -αύτη, -οῦτον, is a correlative adj. that highlights similarity to the noun it modifies: "like this one." The prep. phrase ἐπὶ τῷ ὀνόματί may refer to verbally calling out someone's name while performing an action (BDAG 711c–14c 1.d.γ.) or to acting as another's representative (N 733; F 679). The longer form and prob. the position of ἐμέ suggest that it is emphatic (BDAG 275a–c). Δέχεται (3rd sg. pres. mid. indic. of dep. δέχομαι, "welcome") is prob. gnomic.

FOR FURTHER STUDY

93. Greatest in the Kingdom

Oepke, A. *TDNT* 5.636–54.
Wenham, D. "A Note on Mark 9:33–42, Matt 18:1–6, Luke 9:46–50." *JSNT* 14 (1982): 113–18.

HOMILETICAL SUGGESTIONS

The Path to Greatness (18:1–5)

1. Childlike humility is essential to entering the kingdom
2. Childlike humility is essential to greatness in the kingdom
3. Kindness to children shows devotion to Jesus

2. The Dangers of Harming Other Believers (18:6–9)

18:6 Ὃς δ᾽ ἄν is the ὅς ἐάν cstr. with the postpositive δέ inserted. The δ᾽ ἄν is a result of elision (BDF §17). The ὅς ἐάν cstr. with the subjunc. (σκανδαλίσῃ 3rd sg. aor. act. subjunc. of σκανδαλίζω, "cause to sin, bring to a downfall") is often equivalent to the prot. of a cond. statement: "if someone causes . . . to sin" (BDAG 56b–57c I.b.; BDF §380). BDAG notes that the spiritual downfall may consist of immorality, unbelief, or acceptance of false teaching (926a–b, 1). On the phrase ἕνα τῶν μικρῶν τούτων, see 10:42. Τῶν marks the ptc. πιστευόντων (gen. pl. masc. of pres. act. ptc. of πιστεύω, "believe") as adj. and is tr. like a rel. pron.: "who believe." The prep. phrase εἰς ἐμέ identifies the obj. of the faith. The longer form of the 1st pers. sg. pron. is normal with most prep. and not emphatic. Συμφέρει (3rd sg. pres. act. indic. of συμφέρω, "to be advantageous, better for") is gnomic pres. Αὐτῷ is dat. of advantage. Ἵνα with the subjunc. vbs. κρεμασθῇ (3rd sg. aor. pass. subjunc. of κρεμάννυμι, "hang") and καταποντισθῇ (3rd sg. aor. pass. subjunc. of καταποντίζω, "sink/drown in the sea") is equivalent to a complementary inf. (BDAG 475c–77b 2.b.). Μύλος, -ου, ὁ, "millstone (used to crush and grind grain)." Ὀνικός, -ή, -όν, "associated with a donkey." Here the adj. distinguishes the massive millstone driven by the power of a donkey with the much smaller and lighter millstone powered by the hands of women. Περί is loc.: "around." Τράχηλος, -ου, ὁ, "neck." Αὐτοῦ is partitive gen. Πέλαγος, -ους, τό, "open sea (far from the shore), the depths (of the sea)." Τῆς θαλάσσης is partitive gen. The def. art. may be the well-known art. and refer to the Sea of Galilee or the Mediterranean Sea. However, gen. modifiers tend to mimic the head noun with regard to articularity (Apollonius's Canon; W 239–40), so the presence of the art. with the gen. is prob. not significant.

18:7 Οὐαί is an interjection denoting intense pain or displeasure: "woe!" (BDAG 734b–d 1.a.). Τῷ κόσμῳ is dat. of disadvantage. When the dat. follows οὐαί the cstr. functions like the pronouncement of a curse. The ἀπό is causal and marks the reason for the pronouncement of the woe. Σκάνδαλον, -ου, τό, "enticement to spiritual downfall, temptation" (18:6). Ἀνάγκη, -ας, ἡ, "necessity, inevitability." The copula ἐστίν is implied. Γάρ is causal. Ἐλθεῖν (2nd aor. act. inf. of dep. ἔρχομαι) is complementary. Τὰ σκάνδαλα is acc. subj. of the inf. Πλήν is an adv. used as an adversative conj.: "nevertheless" (BDAG 826c–d 1.b.). Δι' οὗ (δία with the gen. sg. masc. rel. pron.) identifies the pers. agent through whom the temptation comes. If the prep. denotes intermediate agency (as it often does; BDAG 223d–26a 4.a.), it may imply that another (Satan) is the ultimate source of the temptation.

18:8 Εἰ with the indic. (σκανδαλίζει 3rd sg. pres. act. indic. of σκανδαλίζω, 18:6) marks the prot. of a 1st-class cond. sentence that assumes the fulfillment of the prot. for the sake of argument. However, in Koine Gk. the cstr. is sometimes a virtual equivalent to ἐάν with the subjunc. (third-class condition) and refers to a purely hypothetical situation (BDF §372.3). See 5:29. Δέ is adversative and states an alternative to suffering the woe warned in 18:7. Σου (both occurrences) is partitive gen. Ἔκκοψον (2nd sg. aor. act. impv. of ἐκκόπτω, "cut off, sever") expresses urgency: "cut off (right away)." Αὐτόν (acc. sg. masc.) refers to hand (fem.) and foot (masc.) but appears in the masc. gender since πούς is the nearer referent. Βάλε (2nd sg. 2nd aor. act. impv. of βάλλω) expresses urgency. Ἀπό with the gen. (σοῦ) indicates separation: "away from you." Καλόν is an example of the use of the positive adj. for the comp. Καλόν ἐστιν is equivalent to συμφέρει (5:29, 30): "it is better." Σοί is dat. of advantage. Εἰσελθεῖν (2nd aor. act. inf. of dep. εἰσέρχομαι) is complementary. The def. art. τήν modifying ζωήν is *par excellence* and refers to life of the ultimate quality (W 222–23). Κυλλός, -ή, -όν, "deformed." Χωλός, -ή, -όν, "lame." The ἤ serves as a disjunctive particle ("or") in all instances in this verse except one. The ἤ before δύο χεῖρας is comp. (BDAG 432b–33b 2.b.β.) and means "rather than." Ἔχοντα (acc. sg. masc. of pres. act. ptc. of ἔχω) is either attendant circumstance (most EVV) or concessive: "despite having both hands and both feet." Βληθῆναι (aor. pass. inf. of βάλλω) is a complementary inf. and divine pass. The adj. αἰώνιον (modifying πῦρ) is in the second attrib. position, which places emphasis on both the noun and the adj. (W 306–7; R 777).

18:9 Εἰ . . . σου σκανδαλίζει σε, 18:8. Ἔξελε (2nd sg. 2nd aor. act. impv. of ἐξαιρέω, "remove, tear out;" BDAG 344a 1) expresses urgency. Αὐτόν refers to the eye. Καὶ βάλε ἀπὸ σοῦ· καλόν σοί ἐστιν, 18:8. Μονόφθαλμος, -ον, "one-eyed." Εἰς τὴν ζωὴν εἰσελθεῖν, 18:8. Ἤ is comp.: "rather than." Ἔχοντα βληθῆναι, 18:8. Γέεννα, -ης, ἡ, "Gehenna." The def. art. is prob. either *par excellence* or well-known. Τοῦ πυρός is either *attributive gen. ("fiery Gehenna;" LEB) or attributed gen. ("fire of hell" or "hellfire;" most EVV). Compare the sim. use of this gen. phrase in 13:42, 50.

FOR FURTHER STUDY

94. Salvation and Protection of the Little Ones

Agouridēs, S. "'Little Ones' in Matthew." *BT* 35 (1984): 329–34.
Wilson, G. T. "Conditions for Entering the Kingdom According to St Matthew." *PRS* 5 (1978): 40–51.

HOMILETICAL SUGGESTIONS

Stepping Stones or Stumbling Blocks: The Responsibility of Mature Believers (18:6–9)

1. Causing spiritual harm to another disciple will result in severe punishment:
   a. A punishment worse than death by drowning
   b. A punishment of eternal fire in Gehenna
2. Avoiding causing spiritual harm to a another disciple is worth enormous sacrifice:
   a. The sacrifice of one's hand
   b. The sacrifice of one's foot
   c. The sacrifice of one's eye

3. The Father's Love for Believers (18:10–14)

18:10 Ὁρᾶτε (2nd pl. pres. act. impv. of ὁράω) is ingr.-prog. When followed by μή and the aor. subjunc. (καταφρονήσητε 2nd pl. aor. act. subjunc. of καταφρονέω, "despise, treat with contempt"), the vb. ὁράω means to take measures to avoid an action: "beware, make sure that you do not" (BDAG 720c–21b B.2.). The cstr. is an intensification of the prohibition. Ἑνός is gen. of dir. obj. Μικρός, -ά, -όν, "small, little." Τῶν μικρῶν is subst. The near dem. pron. τούτων is retrospective and refers to "the little ones who believe in me" (18:6). Λέγω γὰρ ὑμῖν ὅτι, 5:20. Αὐτῶν (modifying οἱ ἄγγελοι) refers to the little ones and is prob. obj. gen.: "the angels who guard/represent/protect them." The pl. οὐρανοῖς refers to the abode of God. Διά with the subst. adj. παντός is temp. The phrase is a shortened form of διὰ παντὸς χρόνου. Διά functions as a marker of extension in time: "throughout the entire time, constantly." The adv. prep. phrase demonstrates that βλέπουσι (3rd pl. pres. act. indic. of βλέπω) is prog. pres. Τοῦ πατρός is partitive gen. Μου is gen. of relationship. The def. art. τοῦ followed by the prep. phrase ἐν οὐρανοῖς either functions like a rel. pron. ("who is in heaven;" LEB; ESV) or indicates that the prep. phrase is functioning like an adj. in the second pred. position ("heavenly;" NIV; cf. CSB).

18:11 This verse is absent from the earliest uncials, important minuscules, several early versions, and texts used by Origen and Eusebius. Scribes prob. inserted the verse from Luke 19:10. The verse is omitted by the NIV, CSB, ESV, LEB, and NLT. Although the UBS⁵ used a B rating for the omission of the verse, Metzger wrote that "there can be little doubt" that the words were a later scribal insertion (Metzger 36).

18:12 Τί is the interr. pron. and introduces a question. Although the neut. sg. form of the pron. sometimes means "why," when used with the vb. δοκεῖ (3rd sg. pres. act. indic. of δοκέω, "seem" [impers.]) it means "what?" (BDAG 254d–55c 2.b.α.). Ὑμῖν is ethical dat. (dat. of opinion; W 146–47). Ἐάν with the subjunc. (γένηταί 3rd sg. aor. mid. subjunc. of dep. γίνομαι) forms the prot. of a third-class cond. statement and introduces a hypothetical condition. The indef. pron. τινι is functioning adj. (BDAG 1007d–9a 2.b.α.): "some, a certain." Ἀνθρώπῳ is dat. of poss. (W 149–51): "belonging to a certain man." Ἑκατόν (indecl.), "one hundred." Πρόβατον, -ου, τό, "sheep." Πλανηθῇ (3rd sg. aor. pass. subjunc. of πλανάω, "go astray" [pass.] or poss. "be led astray" [N 743]) is governed by the ἐάν and forms the second half of the prot. After a number, ἐκ phrases often serve as substitutes for the partitive gen. (BDAG 295a–98b 4.a.α.). Thus ἕν ἐξ αὐτῶν means "one of them" rather than indicating that one separated "away from" or "out of" the fold. The neg. οὐχί assumes a positive answer to the question that it introduces. The neg. applies to both indic. vbs. (and the ptc. of attendant circumstance). Ἀφήσει (3rd sg. fut. act. indic. of ἀφίημι, "leave") is delib. fut. The def. art. τά is anaphoric and refers to those from the one hundred mentioned earlier who remained in the flock. Ἐνενήκοντα (indecl.), "ninety." Ἐννέα (indecl.), "nine." Πορευθείς (nom. sg. masc. of aor. pass. ptc. of dep. πορεύομαι, "go") is prob. attendant circumstance (CSB; LEB). Ζητεῖ (3rd sg. pres. act. indic. of ζητέω, "search") is prog. pres.: "keep on searching." The shift from the delib. fut. to the pres. was required by the author's desire to emphasize the continual nature of the search. The def. art. τό indicates that the ptc. πλανώμενον (acc. sg. neut. of pres. pass. ptc. of πλανάω) is subst. The use of the pres. tense prob. implies that the sheep continues to wander farther and farther from the fold. Cf. the use of the pf. tense in 18:13.

18:13 Ἐάν with the subjunc. (γένηται 3rd. sg. aor. mid. subjunc. of dep. γίνομαι, "occur, come about" [BDAG 196d–99d, 4.ε.]) forms the prot. of a 3rd-class cond. statement that introduces a hypothetical scenario. Εὑρεῖν (2nd aor. act. inf. of εὑρίσκω, "find") is epex. and identifies the action that occurred and is being emphasized in this cstr. Αὐτό refers to the lost sheep. Ἀμὴν λέγω ὑμῖν, 5:18. Ὅτι is recitative. Χαίρει (3rd sg. pres. act. indic. of χαίρω, "rejoice, be joyful") is either *gnomic (since such rejoicing is normal human nature) or prog. Ἐπί with the dat. (αὐτῷ) is causal: "because of it" (BDAG 363a–67c 6.c.). Μᾶλλον is the comp. adv. expressing greater degree: "more." The preceding comp. adv. shows that ἤ is likewise comp.: "than." Ἐπί is causal. Τοῖς ἐνενήκοντα ἐννέα, 18:12. Τοῖς functions like a rel. pron. preceding the adj. ptc. πεπλανημένοις (dat. pl. neut. of pf. pass. ptc. of πλανάω, "go astray").

18:14 Οὕτως is comp. adv. of manner: "in the same way." Ἐστίν 3rd sg. pres. indic. of εἰμί. The use of the prep. ἔμπροσθεν modifying θέλημα is unusual. One expected the subj. gen. instead. BDAG (325b–c 1.b.δ.) notes that the prep. is sometimes a "reverential way" to distance God from what happens. For God to want the destruction of one of the little ones who believe in Jesus was unthinkable, and the Gk. cstr. avoids directly associating such an idea with God even in the context of a denial. France (684) suggests that the prep. phrase reflects the Sem. idiom "pleasing in the eyes of" (BDF §214). When modifying πατρός, ὑμῶν is clearly gen. of relationship. See Metzger 36. Τοῦ ἐν οὐρανοῖς, 18:10. The ἵνα clause is a substitute for the complementary inf. (BDAG 475c–77b 2.c.α.). Ἀπόληται 3rd sg. aor. mid. subjunc. of ἀπόλλυμι, "perish" (pass.). Τῶν μικρῶν (modifying ἓν) is partitive. The dem. pron. τούτων is retrospective and points to the little ones who believe in Jesus (18:6).

FOR FURTHER STUDY

95. *The Parable of the Lost Sheep*

> Bishop, E. F. F. "Parable of the Lost or Wandering Sheep." *Australian Theological Review* 44 (1962): 44–57.

96. *The Angels of the Little Ones*

> Bucur, B. G. "Matt 18:10 in Early Christology and Pneumatology: A Contribution to the Study of Matthean Wirkungsgeschichte." *NovT* 49 (2007): 209–31.
> Koskenniemi, E. "Forgotten Guardians and Matthew 18:10." *TynBul* 61 (2010): 119–29.

HOMILETICAL SUGGESTIONS

God's Love for the "Little Ones" (18:10–14)

1. Disciples should not look down on other believers
2. God gives special privileges to all believers
3. God rejoices in the restoration of straying believers

4. Addressing a Disciple's Sin (18:15–20)

18:15 Δέ marks the transition to a new section of Jesus's discourse. Ἐάν with the subjunc. (ἁμαρτήσῃ 3rd sg. aor. act. subjunc. of ἁμαρτάνω) marks the prot. of a 3rd-class cond. sentence, which makes no assumption regarding the fulfillment of the prot. The phrase εἰς σέ is not in the oldest uncials or some early versions. It is prob. a scribal insertion. Thus Jesus's statement pertains to church discipline rather than settling pers. disputes. See Metzger 36. With ἀδελφός, σου is gen. of relationship. Ὕπαγε (2nd sg. pres. act. impv. of ὑπάγω, "go") is prob. ingr.-prog. When a second impv. follows ὑπάγω in the NT, a conj. between the two is almost always absent (BDAG 1028a–c 2.a.). This may imply that the two impv. were not intended to refer to two separate and distinct actions but that the impv. form of ὑπάγω merely emphasized the urgency of fulfilling the second impv. Ἔλεγξον (2nd sg. aor. act. impv. of ἐλέγχω, "reprove, show someone his wrong") expresses urgency. Μεταξύ with the gen. (σοῦ) is a marker of reciprocal relation ("between") that identifies the parties involved in the discussion. Αὐτοῦ refers to the sinning brother. The adj. μόνου ("alone") excludes other parties from this initial confrontation. Ἐάν with the subjunc. (ἀκούσῃ 3rd sg. aor. act. subjunc. of ἀκούω) marks the prot. of a 3rd-class cond. statement, which makes no assumption regarding the fulfillment of the prot. Engaging in the process of church discipline does not guarantee the repentance of the sinner. Σου is gen. of dir. obj. Ἐκέρδησας 2nd sg. aor. act. indic. of κερδαίνω, "gain, win over."

18:16 Ἐάν . . . ἀκούσῃ, 18:15. Παράλαβε (2nd sg. 2nd aor. act. impv. of παραλαμβάνω, "take along") expresses urgency. Μετά with the gen. (σοῦ) expresses accompaniment: "with you" (BDAG 636b–38b 2.a.β.). When followed by numbers (ἕνα ἢ δύο), the adv. ἔτι means "in addition to what was previously mentioned," thus "one or two more." Ἵνα plus the subjunc. (σταθῇ 3rd sg. aor. pass. subjunc. of ἵστημι, "be established" [pass.]) expresses purpose. Ἐπί serves as a marker of perspective mng. "on the basis of" (BDAG 363a–67c 8). Στόματος appears to be an example of metonymy, in which an instr. represents that which it produces (mouth = testimony; D&A 2.784). Μάρτυς, μάρτυρος, ὁ, "witness." Μαρτύρων is partitive gen. The anar. sg. attrib. πᾶν (modifying ῥῆμα) means "every (single)" and emphasizes the individual matters addressed in the discipline process. Although ῥῆμα normally means "word," it here means "matter, event" (BDAG 905a–c 2; H 2.533).

18:17 Δέ is prob. adversative. Ἐάν with the subjunc. (παρακούσῃ 3rd sg. aor. act. subjunc. of παρακούω, "ignore, refuse to listen;" BDAG 767d–68b 2) marks the prot. of a 3rd-class cond. statement that makes no assumption regarding the fulfillment of the prot. Αὐτῶν is gen. of dir. obj. Εἰπέ (2nd sg. 2nd aor. act. impv. of λέγω), see 4:3. Τῇ ἐκκλησίᾳ is dat. of indir. obj. The καί preceding τῆς ἐκκλησίας is either *ascensive ("even;" NIV; ESV) or adjunctive ("also;" LEB). Ἔστω 3rd sg. pres. impv. of εἰμί: "he must be." Σοι is ethical dat. ("as far as you are concerned;" "in your view;" W 146–47). Although some tr. render the cstr. as if it focused on the treatment of the sinner (NIV; NLT; BDAG 1106d–7a b), the grammar suggests that the concern here is one's opinion or estimation of the sinner. Ὥσπερ is a marker of similarity between states: "like." The unrepentant sinner should be regarded as possessing the same spiritual condition as the Gentile and traitorous and dishonest tax collector. Ἐθνικός, -ή, -όν, "Gentile, pagan." Τελώνης, -ου, ὁ, "tax collector."

18:18 Ἀμὴν λέγω ὑμῖν, 5:18. Ὅσα (acc. pl. neut. of ὅσος, -η, -ον: "as many as, whatever") is made more general by the addition of ἐάν: "Everything . . . ever" (BDAG 729a–c 2). Δήσητε 2nd pl. aor. act. subjunc. of δέω: "everything you ever bind. . . ." The subjunc. is required by the particle of contingency ἐάν. Ἔσται (3rd sg. fut. indic. of εἰμί) δεδεμένα (nom. pl. neut. of pf. pass. ptc. of δέω) is fut. pf. periph.: "will have already been bound." Οὐρανῷ refers to the abode of God even though it is sg. Cf. the use of the pl. in the parallel passage (16:19). Λύσητε 2nd pl. aor. act. subjunc. of λύω. Ἔσται (3rd sg. fut. indic. of εἰμί) λελυμένα (nom. pl. neut. of pf. pass. ptc. of λύω) is fut. pf. periph.: "will have already been loosed." The use of ὅσα ἐάν rather than ὅ ἐάν (16:19) suggests that the authority of the other disciples is at least as comprehensive as Peter's.

18:19 Πάλιν ("again") indicates that this declaration is related to the topic of the previous statement (BDAG 752b–53a 3). [Ἀμὴν] λέγω ὑμῖν, 5:18. See Metzger 37. The πάλιν is a discourse marker indicating that this statement is related to the previous one (BDAG 752b–53a 3). The authority of the disciples in binding and loosing is related to their effectiveness in prayer. Ὅτι is recitative. Ἐάν with the subjunc. (συμφωνήσωσιν 3rd pl. aor. act. subjunc. of συμφωνέω, "agree") marks the prot. of a 3rd-class cond. sentence, which makes no assumption regarding the fulfillment of the prot. When the prep. ἐκ follows a number, the prep. phrase is normally a simple substitution for the partitive gen. (BDAG 295d–98b 4.a.α.; BDF §164). Thus ἐξ ὑμῶν (following δύο) means "two of you." Περί when used with vbs. of speech identifies the topic of discussion: "about" (BDAG 797c–98d 1.a.). When anar. and sg., the attrib. adj. παντός often emphasizes each individual item of a category: "every single matter" or *"any matter." Πρᾶγμα, -ατος, τό refers to a matter or concern of any kind. Thus BDAG recommends translating περὶ παντὸς πράγματος "about anything at all" (BDAG 858d–59b 3). Although BDAG (56b–57c I.b.) and BDF (§367) state that the rel. pron. followed by ἐάν with the subjunc. is virtually equivalent to the prot. of a cond. sentence, the cstr. οὗ ἐὰν αἰτήσωνται seems to be a clear exception. Rather than forming a 2nd prot. ("if two agree" and "if they ask"), the presence of another prot. and the absence of a conj. between that prot. and the rel. clause suggests that the ἐάν merely adds an element of contingency to the rel. pron.: "(about anything at all) that you pray for" (cf. NIV; ESV; LEB; CSB; NLT). This is likely true as well in other sentences that lack another prot. Γενήσεται (3rd sg. fut. mid. indic. of dep. γίνομαι, "happen, be done;" BDAG 196d–199d 4.b.) is predictive fut. and expresses a promise. Αὐτοῖς is dat. of advantage. Παρά with the gen. (τοῦ πατρός) marks the point of origination or source: "from" (BDAG 756b–58c 3.a.β.). Μου is gen. of relationship. Τοῦ causes the prep. phrase ἐν οὐρανοῖς to function like an attrib. adj. or rel. clause: "heavenly Father, Father who is in heaven."

18:20 The gen. of place (W 124–25) of the rel. pron. (οὗ) functions as an adv. of place: "where" (BDAG 732d–34b 1.a.α.). Γάρ marks a reason for the assurance of answered prayer in 18:19. Εἰσιν (3rd pl. pres. indic. of εἰμί) συνηγμένοι (nom. pl. masc. of pf. mid. ptc. of συνάγω, "be gathered" [pass.]; BDAG 962b–63a 1.b.) is pf. periph. The phrase εἰς τὸ ὄνομα may be an idiom mng. "in deference to" or "while thinking of," in which case it would denote that Jesus is the reason and focus for the gathering: "so that I am the reason for their assembling" (BDAG 711c–14c 1.d.γ.). Kupp sees the phrase as representing "the allegiance, or identity marker, of this particular group" (*Emmanuel*, 189–92). The cstr. implies a high Christology. Others suggest that the prep. phrase means "as his representatives" (F 698). The poss. pron. ἐμόν is more emphatic than the use of the poss. gen. Ἐκεῖ, "there" refers to the place just mentioned, the place where Jesus's disciples are gathered. Ἐν μέσῳ αὐτῶν ("in their midst") is equivalent to μετά with the gen. Thus Jesus's statement is a fulfillment of the Immanuel promise in 1:23.

FOR FURTHER STUDY

97. Binding and Loosing

Basser, H. W. "Derrett's 'Binding' Reopened." *JBL* 104 (1985): 297–300.

Derrett, J. D. M. "Binding and Loosing (Matt 16:19, Matt 18:18, John 20:23)." *JBL* 102 (1983): 112–17.

Duling, D. C. "Binding and Loosing: Matthew 16:19; Matthew 18:18; John 20:23." *Forum* 3/4 (1987): 3–31.

Powell, M. A. "Binding and Loosing: A Paradigm for Ethical Discernment from the Gospel of Matthew." *Currents in Theology and Mission* 30 (2003): 438–45.

98. Church Discipline

Doriani, D. M. "Forgiveness: Jesus's Plan for Healing and Reconciliation in the Church (Matthew 18:15–35)." *SBJT* 13 (2009): 22–32.

Gibbs, J. A., and J. Kloha. "Following Matthew 18: Interpreting Matthew 18:15–20 in Its Context." *Concordia Journal* 29 (2003): 6–25.

Haines, S. M. "Southern Baptist Church Discipline, 1880–1939." *Baptist History and Heritage* 20 (1985): 14–27.

Laney, J. C. "The Biblical Practice of Church Discipline." *BSac* 143 (1986): 353–64.

Merkle, B. L. "The Meaning of Ἐκκλησία in Matthew 16:18 and 18:17." *BSac* 167 (2010): 281–91.

99. Jesus's Presence with His People

Kupp, D. D. *Matthew's Emmanuel: Divine Presence and God's People in the First Gospel.* SNTSMS 90. Cambridge: Cambridge University Press, 1996.

HOMILETICAL SUGGESTIONS

Church Discipline (18:15–20)

1. The grounds for church discipline: sin of a member
2. The process of church discipline: one on one, two or three witnesses, presentation to church
3. The aftermath of church discipline: repentance or regarded as unregenerate
4. The authority in church discipline: God guides the church's decision
5. The unity in church discipline: agreement among God's people ensures God's blessing

5. The Disciple's Obligation to Forgive Others (18:21–35)

18:21 Τότε prob. means "afterward." Προσελθών (nom. sg. masc. of 2nd aor. act. ptc. of dep. προσέρχομαι) is ptc. of attendant circumstance (most EVV). Κύριε is simple voc. Ποσάκις is an adv., referring to a number of occurrences and is often used to introduce questions (BDAG 855d–56a): "how many times?" Ἁμαρτήσει (3rd sg. fut. act. indic. of ἁμαρτάνω, "sin") and ἀφήσω (1st sg. fut. act. indic. of ἀφίημι, "forgive") are delib. fut. The question is "volitional" and concerns what one ought to do (W 570). Εἰς is used in a hostile sense to identify the victim of one's actions (BDAG 288d–93c 4.c.α.): "against me." Ἕως is used to mark the upper limit: "as many as, no more than" (BDAG 422d–24c 5). Ἑπτάκις, "seven times."

18:22 Λέγει is historical pres. and prob. gives special emphasis to this statement (Runge 125–44). Αὐτῷ refers to Peter. Ἀλλά is strongly adversative and contrasts

Jesus's rejection of the answer Peter expected with the correct answer. Ἕως, 18:21. Ἑβδομηκοντάκις, "seventy." The cstr. ἑβδομηκοντάκις ἑπτά may mean *"seventy-seven times" (Gen 4:24; most EVV) or be an abbreviated form of the expression ἑβδομηκοντάκις ἑπτάκις, "seventy times seven times" (BDAG 269c–d; BDF §248, 2).

18:23 Διὰ τοῦτο ("because of this") indicates that the truth illustrated by the parable is a result or necessary conclusion of Jesus's teaching in 18:22. Ὡμοιώθη (3rd sg. aor. pass. indic. of ὁμοιόω, "be like" [pass.]) is gnomic aor. Ἡ βασιλεία τῶν οὐρανῶν, 3:1. The dat. ἀνθρώπῳ identifies the standard of comp. (BDAG 707b–c). Βασιλεῖ is dat. of simple appos.: "a man, a king." Although BDAG labels the cstr. pleonastic (BDAG 81a–82c 4.a.), the cstr. identifies this king as a human and earthly kind (who in the parable represents the divine heavenly King). Ὅς introduces a rel. clause that describes the king. Ἠθέλησεν 3rd sg. aor. act. indic. of θέλω, "want." Συνᾶραι (aor. act. inf. of συναίρω, "settle, close out [an account]") is a complementary inf. Λόγος, -ου, ὁ, "account" (BDAG 598a–601d 2.a.). Μετά with the gen. (τῶν δούλων) expresses pers. association, established in this case through business transaction (BDAG 636b–38b 2.c.α.). Αὐτοῦ refers to the king and the gen. expresses poss. and authority.

18:24 Δέ introduces a new development in the narrative. Ἀρξαμένου (gen. sg. masc. of aor. mid. ptc. of ἄρχω, "begin" [mid.]) is gen. abs. and temp.: "when he began." Συναίρειν (pres. act. inf. of συναίρω, "settle") is a complementary inf. Προσηνέχθη 3rd sg. aor. pass. indic. of προσφέρω, "bring to (someone)." Αὐτῷ is dat. of indir. obj. Ὀφειλέτης, -ου, ὁ, "debtor, one who owes money." Τάλαντον, -ου, τό, "talent," a coin worth about six thousand days wages. Μύριοι, -αι, -α, "ten thousand," the highest number that can be expressed in Gk. in a single word and thus often used to refer to an incalculable number (BDAG 661b–c): "a zillion talents." Ταλάντων is obj. gen.: "a debtor who owed a thousand talents." If μυρίων is interpreted lit., the average Jewish day laborer would have to work approximately 200 thousand years to repay such a debt.

18:25 Ἔχοντος (gen. sg. masc. of pres. act. ptc. of ἔχω) is gen. abs. Although most gen. abs. ptc. are temp., this one appears to be causal: "Since he did not have. . . ." Δέ prob. introduces the next development in the narrative. Ἀποδοῦναι (aor. act. inf. of ἀποδίδωμι, "repay, pay back") is inf. of purpose: "he did not have (enough money) so that he could repay." Ἐκέλευσεν 3rd sg. aor. act. indic. of κελεύω, "command." Πραθῆναι (aor. pass. inf. of πιπράσκω, "sell") is inf. of indir. discourse (W 603–5). The pers. pron. αὐτόν is acc. subj. of the inf. (not dir. obj. of ἐκέκευσεν). The αὐτόν begins a list of four acc. subj. of inf. joined by καί (καὶ τὴν γυναῖκα καὶ τὰ τέκνα καὶ πάντα ὅσα ἔχει). The separation of the final three acc. from αὐτόν in word order may be due to the desire to avoid creating too great a distance between the vb. and inf. or may place emphasis on the debtor. The combination of the subst. adj. πάντα ("everything") and the correlative ὅσα that compares the number of objects seems to stress complete liquidation of the man's possessions: "every last thing that he had." Ἔχει (3rd sg. pres. act. indic. of ἔχω) is the pres. retained in indir. discourse (W 537–39) and should be tr. as past tense in Eng. idiom. Ἀποδοθῆναι (aor. pass. inf. of ἀποδίδωμι) is inf. of indir. discourse. The implied subj. of the inf. is "lord."

18:26 Πεσών (nom. sg. masc. of aor. act. ptc. of πίπτω, "fall") is ptc. of attendant circumstance. Οὖν is inferential and shows that the slave's actions are a response to the king's order. Προσεκύνει (3rd sg. impf. act. indic. of προσκυνέω, "bow down before") is ingr. (LEB): "he began bowing before him." Αὐτῷ is dat. of dir. obj. Λέγων is prob. attendant circumstance (NIV; CSB; NLT). See Metzger 37. Μακροθύμησον (2nd sg. aor. act. impv. of μακροθυμέω, "be patient") expresses urgency. After vbs. of emotion, ἐπί with the dat. (ἐμοί) may identify the basis for or *object of one's feelings (BDAG 363a–67c 6.c.; BDAG 612c–d 2): "be patient with me." When καί joins an indic. vb. (ἀποδώσω 1st sg. fut. act. indic. of ἀποδίδωμι, "repay") to an impv. vb. (μακροθύμησον), it often introduces the result that will follow fulfillment of the impv. (BDAG 494a–96c 1.b.ζ.). Πάντα is acc. of dir. obj. Σοι is indir. obj.

18:27 Δέ introduces a new development in the narrative. Σπλαγχνισθείς (nom. sg. masc. of aor. pass. ptc. of of dep. σπλαγχνίζομαι, "have sympathy, feel pity for") is either *causal (ESV; LEB) or attendant circumstance (NIV; CSB). Τοῦ δούλου is gen. of subord. The dem. pron. ἐκείνου emphasizes that this slave was the one previously mentioned (and described as owing an outrageous sum and offering promises that he could not possibly keep). Ἀπέλυσεν 3rd sg. aor. act. indic. of ἀπολύω, "release, set free." Αὐτόν refers to the slave. Δάνειον, -ου, τό, "loan." Ἀφῆκεν 3rd sg. aor. act. indic. of ἀφίημι, "forgive." Αὐτῷ is dat. of indir. obj.

18:28 Ἐξελθών (nom. sg. masc. of aor. act. ptc. of dep. ἐξέρχομαι, "go out") is either temp. (NIV; ESV; NLT) or attendant circumstance (CSB; LEB). Δέ signals a new development in the narrative. On ὁ δοῦλος ἐκεῖνος, see 18:27. Εὗρεν 3rd sg. 2nd aor. act. indic. of εὑρίσκω, "find, discover." When modifying a number (ἕνα), the gen. (τῶν συνδούλων) is clearly partitive. Σύνδουλος, -ου, ὁ, "fellow slave." The gen. αὐτοῦ indicates the slaves' association with one another. Apparently, the gen. of relationship is functioning like the dat. obj. of the prep σύν, which is prefixed to the vb. Ὅς introduces a rel. clause that describes the fellow slave. Ὤφειλεν (3rd sg. impf. act. indic. of ὀφείλω, "owe") is prog. and stresses simultaneity. Αὐτῷ (referring to the forgiven slave) is dat. of indir. obj. Ἑκατόν, "one hundred." Δηνάριον, -ου, τό, "denarius, average daily wage for a worker." Κρατήσας (nom. sg. masc. of aor. act. ptc. of κρατέω, "seize, grab") is attendant circumstance (CSB; NIV; NLT). Ἔπνιγεν (3rd sg. impf. act. indic. of πνίγω, "choke, strangle") is ingr. (CSB; NIV; ESV; LEB). Λέγων is attendant circumstance (CSB; NIV; ESV; LEB). Ἀπόδος (2nd sg. aor. act. impv. of ἀποδίδωμι, "repay") expresses urgency. The slave does not demand gradual repayment but complete repayment immediately. When used with the indef. pron. (τι) εἰ simply enhances the indefiniteness of the pron. ("whatever") rather than marking the prot. of a cond. sentence (BDAG 277b–79b 7; BDF §376). Some interpreters assert that the cstr. retains its orig. cond. force: "if . . . something" (N 758). Ὀφείλεις 2nd sg. pres. act. indic. of ὀφείλω.

18:29 Πεσὼν οὖν, 18:26. Ὁ σύνδουλος αὐτοῦ, 18:28. See Metzger 37. Παρεκάλει (3rd sg. impf. act. indic. of παρακαλέω, "beg") is ingr. (CSB; LEB). Λέγων is pleonastic. Μακροθύμησον ἐπ᾽ ἐμοί, καὶ ἀποδώσω σοι, 18:26.

18:30 Δέ is prob. adversative since it introduces a sentence that is contrary to expectation. The def. art. ὁ functions like the 3rd pers. pron.: "he." Ἤθελεν (3rd sg. impf. act. indic. of θέλω) is prog. The slave persisted in his refusal despite his fellow slave's continuing pleas. Ἀλλά is strongly adversative (CSB: "instead"). Ἀπελθών (nom. sg. masc. of aor. act. ptc. of dep. ἀπέρχομαι, "depart") is attendant circumstance (most EVV). Ἔβαλεν 3rd sg. 2nd aor. act. indic. of βάλλω. Φυλακή, -ῆς, ἡ, "prison." Ἔως ("until") followed by the aor. subjunc. (ἀποδῷ 3rd sg. aor. act. subjunc. of ἀποδίδωμι, "repay") indicates that the commencement of an action (in this case release from prison) is dependent on circumstances (repayment of the debt). See BDAG 422d–24c 1.a.β. The def. art. τό shows that the independent ptc. ὀφειλόμενον (acc. sg. neut. of pres. pass. ptc. of ὀφείλω) is subst.

18:31 Οὖν shows that the actions of the fellow servants are a response to the behavior of the servant described in vv. 28–30. Ἰδόντες (nom. pl. masc. of 2nd aor. act. ptc. of ὁράω, "see") is either *temp. (most EVV) or causal. However, the inferential particle clearly indicates that the actions of the servant were the cause of the fellow servants' emotional response and report to the king. Σύνδουλος, -ου, ὁ, "fellow servant." Αὐτοῦ, 18:28. The def. art. τά with the independent ptc. γενόμενα (acc. pl. neut. of 2nd aor. mid. ptc. of dep. γίνομαι, "happen") shows that the ptc. is subst.: "the things that happened." Ἐλυπήθησαν 3rd pl. aor. pass. indic. of λυπέω, "be sad or grieved" (pass.), (BDAG 604c–d 2). Σφόδρα, "extremely, very." When used with vbs. of emotion, the adv. "deeply" is a helpful tr. (CSB). Ἐλθόντες (nom. pl. masc. of 2nd aor. act. ptc. of dep. ἔρχομαι) is ptc. of attendant circumstance (most EVV). Διεσάφησαν 3rd pl. aor. act. indic. of διασαφέω, "report (the details)" (BDAG 236 2). Τῷ κυρίῳ is indir. obj. The refl. pron. ἑαυτῶν stands in the place of the poss. pron. (BDAG 268b–69b 3). This usage may be emphatic ("their own lord;" compare 8:22; 21:8; 25:1) and indicate that these servants had a loyalty to the king that the other servant lacked.

18:32 Τότε means "then" and indicates that the king immediately reacted to the report. Προσκαλεσάμενος (nom. sg. masc. of aor. mid. ptc. of προσκαλέω, "summon") is ptc. of *attendant circumstance (most EVV) or temp. (CSB). Αὐτόν refers to the unforgiving slave. Λέγει is historical pres. and emphasizes the content of the king's declaration. Δοῦλε πονηρέ is voc. of simple address. The adj. πᾶσαν with a sg. art. noun (τὴν ὀφειλήν) that is modified by a dem. pron. (ἐκείνην) focuses on wholeness or entirety: "that entire debt." The remote dem. pron. is retrospective and points specifically to the enormous debt described in 18:24. Ἀφῆκά 1st sg. aor. act. indic. of ἀφίημι, "forgive." Σοι is indir. obj. Ἐπεί functions as a causal conj.: "since, because" (BDAG 360b–c 2). Παρεκάλεσας 2nd sg. aor. act. indic. of παρακαλέω, "strongly urge, implore" (BDAG 764a–765d 3).

18:33 The neg. particle οὐκ introduces a question that anticipates an affirmative response. Ἔδει (3rd sg. impf. act. indic. of δέω, "be necessary" [impers.]) here expresses what should be rather than what must be (obligation rather than necessity; BDAG 213d–14c 2.b.). Καί is adjunctive: "also." Σέ is acc. subj. of the inf. Ἐλεῆσαι (aor. act. inf. of ἐλεέω, "show mercy") is a complementary inf. The def. art. τὸν (modifying σύνδουλον) is anaphoric and refers to the fellow slave in 18:28. On the gen. (σου) following forms of σύνδουλος, see 18:28. Ὡς is comp.: "like, as." Κἀγώ is a product of the crasis of καί and ἐγώ. The καί is adjunctive (LEB). Σέ may be slightly emphatic due to its position. Ἡλέησα 1st. sg. aor. act. indic. of ἐλεέω, "show mercy."

18:34 Ὀργισθείς (nom. sg. masc. of aor. pass. ptc. of ὀργίζω, "be angry") expresses *manner (NIV; ESV; W 627–28) or cause (LEB; CSB), or attendant circumstance (CSB). Παρέδωκεν 3rd sg. aor. act. indic. of παραδίδωμι, "hand over." Βασανιστής, -οῦ, ὁ, "torturer, jailer." The temp. conj. ἕως with the gen. neut. rel. pron. οὗ means "until." The slave would be released from the torturers' custody when the debt was fully repaid and not before. Ἀποδῷ 3rd sg. aor. act. subjunc. of ἀποδίδωμι, "repay." Matthew shifts between the aor. indic. and aor. subjunc. after ἕως οὗ with no apparent difference in mng. (1:25; 13:33; 14:22; 17:9). When the neut. sg. πᾶν is used with the art. ptc. (τὸ ὀφειλόμενον acc. sg. neut. of pres. mid. ptc. of ὀφείλω, "owe"), it has the sense "everything that you owe."

18:35 Οὕτως is a comp. adv. "in the same way." Καί is adjunctive. The adj. ὁ οὐράνοις is in the 2nd attrib. position, which places equal emphasis on the noun and the adj. The cstr. ὁ πατήρ μου ὁ οὐράνιος is equivalent to ὁ πατήρ μου ὁ ἐν τοῖς οὐρανοῖς (16:17). Ποιήσει 3rd sg. fut. act. indic. of ποιέω. Ὑμῖν is dat. of indir. obj. The particle of contingency ἐάν followed by μή with the subjunc. (ἀφῆτε 2nd pl. aor. act. subjunc. of ἀφίημι) means "unless" (BDAG 267b–68a 1.c.β.). The use of the subst. adj. ἕκαστος ("each one") focuses on the individual and emphasizes that forgiveness is a pers. (and not merely corporate) responsibility of Jesus's disciples. The grammar implies the presence of the partitive gen. ὑμῶν after ἕκαστος (BDAG 298b–c b): "each one of you." Matthew's mind evidently shifted back and forth from "each" and "you" (pl.) as the assumed subj. of the sentence. This explains the use of the 2nd pers. pl. vb. (though "each" is technically the subj.) and the awkward transition from "his (3rd sg.) brother" to "your (2nd pl.) hearts." The inconsistency in person and number is unusual for Matthew and technically constitutes two different solecisms. Contrast 18:19, in which the subj. "two of you" takes the expected 3rd pers. pl. vb. Ἀπό with the gen. (τῶν καρδιῶν) indicates the source of the forgiveness. Ὑμῶν is partitive gen. See Metzger 37.

FOR FURTHER STUDY

100. The Parable of the Talents

Buckley, T. W. *Seventy Times Seven: Sin, Judgment, and Forgiveness in Matthew.* Collegeville, MN: Liturgical Press, 1991.

de Boer, M. C. "Ten Thousand Talents: Matthew's Interpretation and Redaction of the Parable of the Unforgiving Servant (Matt 18:23–35)." *CBQ* 50 (1988): 214–32.

Scott, B. B. "The King's Accounting: Matthew 18:23–34." *JBL* 104 (1985): 429–42.

HOMILETICAL SUGGESTIONS

Experiencing and Expressing God's Forgiveness (18:21–35)

1. Jesus's disciples should express radical forgiveness to others

2. God forgave our enormous spiritual debt
3. We are obligated to forgive the spiritual debts of others
   a. To refuse to forgive is wicked
   b. To refuse to forgive expresses lack of gratitude for God's forgiveness
4. Refusal to forgive will result in severe and eternal punishment, since those who are truly forgiven will be forgiving

C. JOURNEY THROUGH JUDEA (19:1–20:34)

1. Jesus's Teaching on Marriage, Divorce, and Celibacy (19:1–12)

19:1 Καὶ ἐγένετο ὅτε ἐτέλεσεν ὁ Ἰησοῦς τοὺς λόγους τούτους, 7:28. Μετῆρεν 3rd sg. 2nd aor. act. indic. of μεταίρω, "go away" (BDAG 639a). Ἀπό expresses separation. Ἦλθεν 3rd sg. 2nd aor. act. indic. of dep. ἔρχομαι. Ὅριον, -ου, τό, "district (pl.)." Τῆς Ἰουδαίας is gen. of appos. Πέραν is an improper prep. mng. "across." The phrase πέραν τοῦ Ἰορδάνου prob. functions as an indecl. proper name for the region on the eastern side of the Jordan River (Perea; BDAG 796d–97a b.γ.; contrary to N 764). If so, "Judea" is used in a broad regional sense (F 709).

19:2 Ἠκολούθησαν 3rd pl. aor. act. indic. of ἀκολουθέω, "follow." Αὐτῷ refers to Jesus (19:1) and is dat. of dir. obj. Ἐθεράπευσεν 3rd sg. aor. act. indic. of θεραπεύω, "heal." Αὐτούς refers to the many crowds (ὄχλοι πολλοί). Ἐκεῖ, "there."

19:3 Προσῆλθον 3rd pl. 2nd aor. act. indic. of dep. προσέρχομαι, "approach, come to." Αὐτῷ refers to Jesus and is dat. of dir. obj. Πειράζοντες (nom. pl. masc. of pres. act. ptc. of πειράζω, "tempt, test") is ptc. of *purpose (CSB; NIV; LEB) or attendant circumstance (ESV; NLT). Attendant circumstance ptc. avoids the sense of monotony created by a series of one indic. vb. after another by alternating from ptc. to indic. or vice versa. Thus a series of even two attendant circumstance ptc. in a row would be unusual. Αὐτόν refers to Jesus. Λέγοντες (nom. pl. masc. of pres. act. ptc. of λέγω) is ptc. of attendant circumstance (CSB; NIV; LEB) or means (ESV; NLT). Although one can make a good case that λέγοντες is ptc. of means, normal Matthean style supports the ptc. of attendant circumstance. Εἰ functions as an interr. particle, introducing either a dir. (BDAG 277b–79b 4; BDF §440; R 916; most EVV) or indir. question (LEB). Ἔξεστιν 3rd sg. pres. indic. of ἔξειμι, "it is authorized, permitted" (impers.). This vb. is typically followed by a dat. (ἀνθρώπῳ) rather than the expected acc. subj. of the inf. Ἀπολῦσαι (aor. act. inf. of ἀπολύω, "divorce;" BDAG 117d–18b 5) is complementary. Τὴν γυναῖκα is dir. obj. of the inf. The gen. of relationship αὐτοῦ confirms that γυνή means "wife." Κατά with the acc. marks the reason for the action of the inf. (BDAG 511a–13d 5.a.δ.). The πᾶσαν with an anar. sg. noun (αἰτίαν) may mean "every" or "any" (BDAG 782b–84c 2.a.). In this case the difference between the two tr. is significant. The tr. "any" may imply that the Pharisees were questioning if even a single issue was an acceptable ground for divorce (perhaps because of familiarity with Jesus's strict view). The tr. *"every" would imply that the Pharisees asked whether Jesus saw "any and every" issue as an excuse for divorce (D&A 3.9; N 768 n. 7; H 2.547; F 711 n. 2). The Mishnah demonstrates that many Pharisees were lax in their view of marriage and affirmed a host of grounds for divorce as legitimate. The ESV, LEB, and CSB seem to imply the former view. The NIV and NLT clearly express the latter view.

19:4 Δέ introduces a new development in the dialogue. The def. art. ὁ functions like a rel. pron. (αὐτός). Ἀποκριθείς (nom. sg. masc. of aor. pass. ptc. of dep. ἀποκρίνομαι, "answer") is pleonastic. However, it does clarify the main vb. (εἶπεν 3rd sg. aor. act. indic. of λέγω) and the combination may be tr. "he said in response." The neg. οὐκ introduces a question that anticipates a positive reply. Ἀνέγνωτε 2nd pl. aor. act. indic.

of ἀναγινώσκω, "read." Ὅτι is recitative and introduces the content read. The art. ptc. κτίσας (nom. sg. masc. of aor. act. ptc. of κτίζω, "create") is subst.: "the One who created, the Creator." See Metzger 38. The prep. phrase ἀπ᾽ ἀρχῆς is temp. and marks the beginning point of an action that continued for some time thereafter: "from the beginning on." The cstr. seems to imply that God's creative work continues through procreation. The prep. phrase modifies the main vb. ἐποίησεν (3rd sg. aor. act. indic. of ποιέω, "make"), and its position may indicate that it is emphatic. Despite their position, ἄρσεν (ἄρσην, -εν, "male") and θῆλυ (θῆλυς, -εια, -υ, "female") are closely related to αὐτούς. The cstr. is an example of the dbl. acc. of object-complement in which the complement is a compound.: "he made them to be male and female." The quotation from Genesis 1:27 strictly follows the LXX. See Beale and Carson 58c–59c.

19:5 The conj. καί may indicate that ὁ κτίσας is the subj. of εἶπεν, which is the second vb. in a compound sentence (F 771; N 771). However, some see Jesus as the subj. of εἶπεν (Luz 2.489). Ἕνεκα functions as a prep. marking the cause or reason. The dem. pron. τούτου is retrospective and refers to the divine creation of male and female: "because of this." Καταλείψει (3rd sg. fut. act. indic. of καταλείπω, "leave behind") is either *gnomic (NLT; F 771), predictive (CSB; NIV), or impv. (ESV). The choice between these options is difficult, as the variety of tr. demonstrates. Of these options, the impv. interpretation seems least likely. First, the Heb. text of Genesis 2:24 uses the impf. Second, the context assumes that God (not humans) actually established a one-flesh union between husband and wife by his divine pronouncement. Thus 19:6b fits better with the gnomic view than the issuing of a mere command dependent on human obedience (N 771 n. 19). Third, since the later discussion distinguishes divine permission from divine command, one would have expected a vb. other than εἶπεν to introduce the quotation if it were a divine command. The anar. ἄνθρωπος is indef.: "a man." The art. πατέρα and μητέρα are an example of the substitution of the art. for the poss. pron. (W 215–16). Κολληθήσεται (3rd sg. fut. pass. indic. of κολλάω, "be joined, join oneself to" [pass.]) is either gnomic, predictive, or impv. (see καταλείψει). This is prob. a divine pass. (19:6). Τῇ γυναικὶ is prob. dat. of association. The pron. αὐτοῦ is gen. of relationship and confirms that γυνή means "wife." Ἔσονται (3rd pl. fut. indic. of εἰμί) is either gnomic, predictive, or impv. After forms of εἰμί, εἰς phrases function as substitutes for the pred. nom. (BDAG 288d–91c 8.a.β.) due to the influence of Sem. grammar. However, the εἰς phrase gives the vb. a slightly different nuance: "become" rather than merely "be" (BDAG 282d–86b 6). The def. art. οἱ shows that the independent adj. δύο is subst.: "the two (persons)." Σάρξ, σαρκός, ἡ, "(physical) body" (BDAG 914d–16b, 2). See Beale and Carson 59c–60c.

19:6 Ὥστε introduces an independent clause that states the result of the immediately preceding discussion in 19:4–5 (BDAG 1107a–c 1.a.). Οὐκέτι, "no longer." Εἰσίν 3rd pl. pres. indic. of εἰμί. Ἀλλά is strongly adversative, contrasting the apparent individuality of the couple with the unity established by the divine pronouncement. Σάρξ, 195. The inferential particle οὖν introduces the practical implication of the unity of the husband and wife established by God. The neut. gender of the rel. pron. ὅ precludes σάρξ (fem.) from serving as its antecedent. Thus, the antecedent is likely the divine act of joining the husband and wife. This is esp. likely since κολλάω and συζεύγνυμι are synonymous. The position of the rel. clause prob. denotes emphasis. The identification of ὁ θεός as the subj. of συνέζευξεν (3rd sg. aor. act. indic. of συζεύγνυμι, "join") suggests that κολληθήσεται (19:5) is a divine pass. The anar. ἄνθρωπος is indef. and part of a contrast between a created human being and the divine Creator. Χωριζέτω (3rd sg. pres. act. impv. of χωρίζω, "separate, divide") is a general precept with abiding force: "A human must not separate" (W 724–25).

19:7 Λέγουσιν (3rd pl. pres. act. indic. of λέγω) is historical pres. and the implied subj. is "the Pharisees." Αὐτῷ refers to Jesus. Οὖν introduces a question as prompted by the preceding statement (BDAG 736b–737b, 1.c.). The interr. pron. τί probes the motive for an action: "why?" The combination means "if what you are saying is correct, then why . . . ?" and implies that Jesus's statement contradicts Moses's command. Ἐνετείλατο 3rd sg. aor. mid. indic. of ἐντέλλω, "command" (mid.) (BDAG 339b–c). Δοῦναι (aor. act. inf. of δίδωμι) and ἀπολῦσαι (aor. act. inf. of ἀπολύω, "divorce") are inf. of indir. discourse. See Metzger 38. Βιβλίον, -ου, τό, is dimin. of βίβλος and refers to a brief document: "writ, certificate" (BDAG 176c–d 1). Ἀποστάσιον, -ου, τό is a legal technical term for the relinquishment of one's property incl. slaves or one's wife. The gen. is attrib.: "divorce certificate."

19:8 Λέγει is historical pres. Αὐτοῖς refers to the Pharisees. Ὅτι introduces a dir. quotation. The prep. πρός marks a point of ref., which here forms the basis or cause of the action: "in light of, because" (BDAG 873d–75c 3.e.α.). Σκληροκαρδία, -ας, ἡ, "hard-heartedness, stubbornness." Ὑμῶν is attributed gen. in that the head noun describes a characteristic of the gen. modifier. Ἐπέτρεψεν 3rd sg. aor. act. indic. of ἐπιτρέπω, "permit." Jesus's statement is a correction of the Pharisees' claim that Moses "commanded" divorce. The dat. of pers. ὑμῖν functions like the acc. subj. of the inf. Ἀπολῦσαι (aor. act. inf. of ἀπολύω, "divorce"). The gen. of relationship ὑμῶν confirms that τὰς γυναῖκας means "wives" rather than merely "women." On ἀπ᾽ ἀρχῆς, see 19:4. The repetition of this prep. phrase indicates its importance for Jesus's view of marriage. God's purpose for marriage is best illustrated by his statements before the fall and the corruption of humanity. Δέ is adversative and contrasts the legislation prompted by humanity's spiritual corruption with God's orig. purpose in creation. Γέγονεν 3rd sg. pf. act. indic. of dep. γίνομαι, "be." Οὕτως, "like this," in which a comp. is made to what precedes (Moses's permission to divorce due to humanity's hard-heartedness). See BDAG 741d–42c 1.b.

19:9 Λέγω δὲ ὑμῖν ὅτι, 5:22. The rel. pron. (ὅς) with the particle of contingency ἄν and the subjunc. (ἀπολύσῃ 3rd sg. aor. act. subjunc. of ἀπολύω, "divorce") functions like the prot. of a 3rd-class cond. sentence: "if someone divorced." Τὴν γυναῖκα αὐτοῦ, 19:8. Ἐπί with the dat. (πορνείᾳ) marks the basis for an action: "on the basis (grounds) of sexual immorality" (BDAG 363a–67c 6.a.). See Metzger 38. Γαμήσῃ (3rd sg. aor. act. subjunc. of γαμέω, "marry") also forms part of the prot. The adj. ἄλλην is subst. and the fem. gender shows that the ref. is to "another woman." Μοιχᾶται (3rd sg. pres. pass. indic. of μοιχάω, "commit adultery" [pass.]) is *gnomic (Quarles, *Sermon*, 134) or prog. pres. If gnomic, a prohibited second marriage may be only initially adulterous (the first sexual act in the illegitimate marriage is adulterous). If the vb. is prog. pres., all sexual acts in the unauthorized second marriage are adulterous.

19:10 Λέγουσιν is historical pres. Asyndeton is common with vbs. of speech (BDF §462). See Metzger 39. Αὐτῷ refers to Jesus. Εἰ with the indic. (ἐστίν) forms the prot. of a first-class cond. sentence that assumes the fulfillment of the prot. for the sake of argument. Οὕτως, "like this," in which a comp. is made to what precedes (refusal of permission to divorce except on grounds of marital infidelity). See BDAG 741d–42c 1.b. Αἰτία, -ας, ἡ, "case, circumstance, relationship" (BDAG 31a–b 2). Μετά with the gen. (τῆς γυναικός) is a marker of close association (BDAG 636b–38b 2.a.): "the relationship of a man with his wife." The placement of the neg. οὐ seems to indicate that it negates the vb. it immediately precedes (συμφέρει 3rd sg. pres. act. indic. of συμφέρω, "be helpful, advantageous, beneficial") rather than the complementary inf. γαμῆσαι (aor. act. inf. of γαμέω, "marry"): "it is not advantageous to marry."

19:11 The def. art. ὁ functions as a pers. pron.: "he." Δέ marks a new development in the discourse. It prob. should not be regarded as adversative since the statement agrees with but qualifies the disciples' statement. Αὐτοῖς refers to Jesus's disciples. The οὐ negates the subst. adj. πάντες rather than the vb.: "not everyone (only some)." Χωροῦσιν 3rd pl. pres. act. indic. of χωρέω, "accept, understand" (BDAG 1094 3. b.β.). Λόγος, -ου, ὁ, "statement, declaration" (BDAG 598d–601d 1.a.γ.). The dem. pron. τοῦτον is prob. prospective. Thus τὸν λόγον [τοῦτον] likely refers primarily to the saying regarding eunuchs in 19:12 (N 777 [though see the ref. to the disciples' statement as well]). However, it may be retrospective and refer to the disciples' statement that it is better not to marry at all in 19:10 (H 2.549–50; F 723; Carson 474). Λόγον means "saying." See Metzger 39. Ἀλλά is adversative and contrasts those who do not understand with those who do. The rel. pron. οἷς is dat. of indir. obj. Δέδοται (3rd sg. pf. pass. indic. of δίδωμι) is divine pass. The clause is an ellipsis. The clause means "but the one to whom the ability to accept it has been given does accept it."

19:12 Γάρ introduces the reason that singleness is better for some people. Εἰσίν is impers.: "there are . . . ." Εὐνοῦχος, -ου, ὁ, "a male who lacks sexual desire (because of castration)" (BDAG 409d). Οἵτινες (ὅστις) serves as a simple substitute for the rel. pron. (BDAG 729d–30b 3; most EVV). Ἐκ marks the source: "out of." Κοιλία, -ας, ἡ, "womb." Μητρός is partitive gen. Ἐγεννήθησαν 3rd pl. aor. pass. indic. of γεννάω, "give birth (when referring to the mother's role)" (BDAG 193c–94a 2). Οὕτως, "like this," referring to a state denoted in the preceding context: "as a eunuch." Εὐνουχίσθησαν 3rd pl. aor. pass. indic. of εὐνουχίζω, "castrate, emasculate" (BDAG 409c). Ὑπό with the gen. (τῶν ἀνθρώπων) expresses ultimate agency. Εὐνούχισαν 3rd pl. aor. act. indic. of εὐνουχίζω. In this occurrence the vb. should be taken figuratively (BDAG 409c; N 781; F 725): "choose celibacy." Ἑαυτούς is a refl. pron. that indicates that the individuals make themselves eunuchs, i.e., this is a voluntary choice. Διά with the acc. expresses cause. Τὴν βασιλείαν τῶν οὐρανῶν, 3:2. The art. independent ptc. δυνάμενος (nom. sg. masc. of pres. mid. ptc. of dep. δύναμαι, "be able") is subst.: "The one who is able." Χωρεῖν (pres. act. inf. of χωρέω, "accept") is a complementary inf. Χωρείτω (3rd sg. pres. act. impv. of χωρέω) is a general precept: "(he) must accept."

FOR FURTHER STUDY

101. Jesus's Teaching on Divorce and Remarriage

Blomberg, C. L. "Marriage, Divorce, Remarriage, and Celibacy: An Exegesis of Matthew 19:3–12." *TJ* 11 (1990): 161–96.

Bockmuehl, M. N. A. "Matthew 5:32, 19:9 in the Light of Pre-Rabbinic Halakhah." *NTS* 35 (1989): 291–95.

Fitzmyer, J. A. "Matthean Divorce Texts and Some New Palestinian Evidence." *TS* 37 (1976): 197–226.

Guenther, A. R. "The Exception Phrases: Except Πορνεία, Including Πορνεία or Excluding Πορνεία? (Matthew 5:32; 19:9)." *TynBul* 53 (2002): 83–96.

Holmes, M. W. "The Text of the Matthean Divorce Passages: A Comment on the Appeal to Harmonization in Textual Decisions." *JBL* 109 (1990): 651–64.

Instone-Brewer, D. *Divorce and Remarriage in the Bible: The Social and Literary Context.* Grand Rapids: Eerdmans, 2002.

Keener, C. S. *And Marries Another: Divorce and Remarriage in the Teaching of the New Testament.* Peabody, MA: Hendrickson, 1991.

Loader, W. R. G. "Did Adultery Mandate Divorce? A Reassessment of Jesus's Divorce Logia." *NTS* 61 (2015): 67–78.

Porter, S. E., and P. Buchanan. "On the Logical Structure of Matt 19:9." *JETS* 34 (1991): 335–39.

Wenham, G. J., W. A. Heth, and C. S Keener. *Remarriage After Divorce in Today's Church: Three Views.* Grand Rapids: Zondervan, 2006.

Witherington, B. "Matthew 5:32 and 19:9—Exception or Exceptional Situation? *NTS* 31 (1985): 571–76.

HOMILETICAL SUGGESTIONS

The Master's Teaching on Marriage (19:3–12)

1. Jesus rejected the Pharisees' casual view of marriage
2. Jesus taught that marriage was instituted by God in creation
3. Jesus taught that marriage consisted of a union of one man and one woman
4. Jesus taught that human beings do not have the authority to destroy a marital union
5. Jesus taught that divorce was permitted (not commanded) in the OT law because of the sinner's hardness of heart
6. Jesus transforms the sinful hearts of his disciples so that divorce should not be necessary for Jesus's followers (15:19; 5:8)
7. Jesus permitted victims of marital unfaithfulness to divorce
8. Jesus urged those whom he empowered to be celibate to remain single for the sake of the kingdom

2. *Jesus Blesses the Children (19:13–15)*

19:13 Τότε, "after that." Προσηνέχθησαν 3rd pl. aor. pass. indic. of προσφέρω, "bring to (someone)." Αὐτῷ refers to Jesus. Ἵνα with the subjunc. ἐπιθῇ (3rd sg. aor. act.

subjunc. of ἐπιτίθημι, "place, lay") and προσεύξηται (3rd sg. aor. mid. subjunc. of dep. προσεύχομαι, "pray") expresses purpose. The def. art. τάς (modifying χεῖρας) functions like a substitute for the poss. pron (or more precisely the partitive gen.; W 215–16). Αὐτοῖς refers to the children. Ἐπετίμησαν 3rd pl. aor. act. indic. of ἐπιτιμάω, "rebuke." Αὐτοῖς may refer either to the *children or to the unnamed agents who brought them to Jesus. However, Jesus's defense of the children in 19:14 suggests that they had been the target of the disciples' rebuke.

19:14 Δέ marks the next development in the narrative. Ἄφετε (2nd pl. aor. act. impv. of ἀφίημι, "permit") expresses urgency. The prohibition with the pres. impv. (κωλύετε 2nd pl. pres. act. impv. of κωλύω, "forbid, prohibit, prevent") calls for the cessation of an action already in progress (W 724). Αὐτά refers to the "little children." The neut. gender of the pron. does not depersonalize the children but is required by the neut. gender of παιδία. Ἐλθεῖν (2nd aor. act. inf. of dep. ἔρχομαι) is complementary, at least to κωλύετε and prob. ἄφετε as well. The prep. πρός takes the longer form ἐμέ as its obj. except after vbs. of motion, in which case it takes the enclitic form με (3:14; 11:28). Γάρ is causal. The position of τῶν τοιούτων prob. expresses emphasis. The gen. case expresses poss.: "belongs to such persons." The art. independent adj. τοιούτων is subst. "such persons" and identifies a group with certain characteristics (BDAG 1009c–10a c.α.). Ἐστίν (3rd sg. pres. indic. of εἰμί) is prob. gnomic. Ἡ βασιλεία τῶν οὐρανῶν, 3:2.

19:15 Ἐπιθείς (nom. sg. masc. of aor. act. ptc. of ἐπιτίθημι, "put, place [on]") is attendant circumstance (ESV; LEB) or temp. (NIV; CSB). The decision is difficult, but the prominence of the act of laying hands on the children in the narrative better supports the attendant circumstance classification. Αὐτοῖς refers to the children and is dat. of place or position. Ἐπορεύθη 3rd sg. aor. pass. indic. of dep. πορεύομαι, "proceed, go, travel." Ἐκεῖθεν, "from there."

FOR FURTHER STUDY

102. Jesus's Blessing on the Children

Derrett, J. D. M. "Why Jesus Blessed the Children (Mk 10:13–16 Par)." *NovT* 25 (1983): 1–18.

Robbins, V. K. "Pronouncement Stories and Jesus's Blessing of Children." *SBLSP* 21 (1982): 407–30.

HOMILETICAL SUGGESTIONS

Jesus Loves the Little Children (19:13–15)

1. Parents should seek Jesus's blessing for their children
2. Children should be encouraged to honor Jesus
3. Children are a model of the humility and dependence that should characterize Jesus's disciples

3. The Requirement for Eternal Life (19:16–26)

19:16 Ἰδού calls attention to an unusual event. The subst. εἷς functions like the indef. pron. τις (BDAG 291c–93c 3): "someone." Προσελθών (nom. sg. masc. of 2nd aor. act. ptc. of dep. προσέρχομαι, "approach") is attendant circumstance (most EVV). Αὐτῷ refers to Jesus. Διδάσκαλε is voc. of simple address. The interr. pron. τί ("what?") functions as an adj. (1006d–7d, 1.b.). See Metzger 39. Ἀγαθόν is subst.: "good thing/ deed." Ποιήσω (1st sg. fut. act. indic. of ποιέω) is delib. fut., posing a question about what one must do (volitional; W 570). Ἵνα with the subjunc. (σχῶ 1st sg. aor. act. subjunc. of ἔχω) expresses purpose.

19:17 Ὁ δὲ εἶπεν αὐτῷ, 19:11. The neut. interr. pron. τί questions the reason (BDAG 1006d–7d 2): "why?" Ἐρωτᾷς 2nd sg. pres. act. indic. of ἐρωτάω, "ask (a question)?" Περί with the gen. (τοῦ ἀγαθοῦ) identifies the topic of the question (BDAG 797c–98d 1.b.). Εἷς is subst.: "one person/being." Ἐστίν (3rd sg. pres. indic. of εἰμί) is gnomic. The art. and independent adj. ἀγαθός is subst.: "the good person." The def. art. may be *par excellence* in addition to serving as a subst. The statement echoes the language of the Shema (Deut 6:4; N 790; H 2.557). See Metzger 39–40. Δέ is prob. adversative since it follows Jesus's assertion that only one person is truly good. Εἰ with the indic. (θέλεις 2nd sg. pres. act. indic. of θέλω, "want") marks the prot. of a first-class cond. sentence that assumes the fulfillment of the prot. for the sake of argument. The def. art. τήν (modifying ζωήν) is prob. *par excellence*. Εἰσελθεῖν (2nd aor. act. inf. of dep. εἰσέρχομαι, "enter") is complementary. Τήρησον (2nd sg. aor. act. impv. of τηρέω, "keep, obey") expresses urgency. The def. art. τάς modifying ἐντολάς ("command-ments") is the well-known art. and refers to the commandments of the OT.

19:18 Λέγει is historical pres. Αὐτῷ refers to Jesus. The interr. pron. ποῖος, -α, -ον, may mean "of what kind?," but more likely serves as a substitute for the adj. use of the interr. pron. τίς (BDAG 843 2.b.α.): "which (commandments)?" The def. art. τό stands before an entire series of clauses and refers to the series or list (BDAG 686a–89c 2.h.α.). The vbs. used in the prohibitions are 2nd sg. fut. act. indic. and the fut. tense is impv. Φονεύσεις (φονεύω, "murder, commit homicide"). Μοιχεύσεις (μοιχεύω, "commit adultery"). Κλέψεις (κλέπτω, "steal"). Ψευδομαρτυρήσεις (ψευδομαρτυρέω, "give false testimony"). The commandments were arranged into four prohibitions followed by two (positive) commandments. See Beale and Carson 61b–62d.

19:19 Τίμα (2nd sg. pres. act. impv. of τιμάω, "honor") is a general precept. Among the impv. fut. vbs., this sole use of the pres. impv. stands out. However, Matthew's grammatical forms are consistent with the LXX. Ἀγαπήσεις (2nd sg. fut. act. indic. of ἀγαπάω, "love") is impv. fut. Πλησίον, "neighbor" (subst.). Σου is gen. of relationship. Ὡς is comp.: "in the same way, like." Σεαυτόν is the 2nd pers. reflex. pron.: "yourself." See Beale and Carson 61b–62d.

19:20 Λέγει is historical pres. Αὐτῷ refers to Jesus. Νεανίσκος, -ου, ὁ, "young man" (BDAG 667b 1). The near dem. pron. ταῦτα refers to the commandments that Jesus just quoted. The use of the neut. pron. to refer to the commandments confirms that the pron. τό in 19:19 may refer to commandments as well even though ἐντολή ("com-mandment") is fem. Ἐφύλαξα 1st sg. aor. act. indic. of φυλάσσω, "keep, observe" (a commandment or law; BDAG 1068b–d 5.a.). See Metzger 40. Τί, "what?" Ἔτι is an adv. expressing continuation: "still, even now." Ὑστερῶ (1st sg. pres. act. indic. of ὑστερέω, "lack, be in need of.") is prog. pres.

19:21 Ἔφη 3rd sg. aor. (or impf.) act. indic. of φημί, "say." Αὐτῷ refers to the young man. Εἰ with the indic. (θέλεις 2nd sg. pres. act. indic. of θέλω, "want") marks the prot. of a first-class cond. sentence that assumes the fulfillment of the prot. for the sake of argument. Τέλειος, -α, -ον, "perfect (in a moral sense; BDAG 995c–96b 4.a.)." See F 734 for the view that the term merely means "mature." Εἶναι (pres. act. inf. of εἰμί) is complementary. Ὕπαγε (2nd sg. pres. act. impv. of ὑπάγω, "go") is ingr.-prog. When a second impv. follows ὑπάγω in the NT, a conj. between the two is almost always absent (BDAG 1028a–c 2.a.). This may imply that the two impv. were not intended to refer to two separate and distinct actions but that the impv. form of ὑπάγω merely emphasized the urgency of fulfilling the second impv. Thus, ὕπαγε functions much like the interjection δεῦρο. Πώλησον (2nd sg. aor. act. impv. of πωλέω, "sell") expresses urgency. Σου is poss. gen. The def. art. τά indicates that the independent ptc. ὑπάρχοντα (acc. pl. neut. of pres. act. ptc. of ὑπάρχω, "belong") is subst.: "belongings, possessions" (BDAG 1029c–30a 1). Δός (2nd sg. aor. act. impv. of δίδωμι, "give") expresses urgency. Πτωχός, -ή, -όν, "poor, beggarly." When καί stands between an impv. and an indic. (ἕξεις 2nd sg. fut. [predictive] act. indic. of ἔχω), it normally introduces the result of obeying the impv. (BDAG 494a–96c 1.b.ζ.). Θησαυρός, -οῦ, ὁ, "treasure" (BDAG 456c–d 2.b.α.). The pl. οὐρανοῖς refers to heaven, the abode of God. Δεῦρο is an adv. that functions as an interjection: "Come!" (BDAG 220b 1). Ἀκολούθει (2nd sg. pres. act. impv. of ἀκολουθέω, "follow") is ingr.-prog. Μοι is dat. of dir. obj.

19:22 Ἀκούσας (nom. sg. masc. of aor. act. ptc. of ἀκούω, "hear") is temp. (most EVV). Δέ introduces the next development in the narrative. Νεανίσκος, -ου, ὁ "young man." Λόγος, -ου, ὁ, "statement." Ἀπῆλθεν 3rd sg. 2nd aor. act. indic. of dep. ἀπέρχομαι, "go away." Λυπούμενος (nom. sg. masc. of pres. mid. ptc. of λυπέω, "be sad" [pass.]; BDAG 604c–d 2.b.) is ptc. of manner. Γάρ introduces the reason for the man's sorrow. The cstr. ἦν (3rd sg. impf. indic. of εἰμί) and ἔχων (nom. sg. masc. of pres. act. ptc.) is periph. impf. (W 647–48). Κτῆμα, -ατος, τό, "possession" (BDAG 572b 1).

19:23 Δέ marks the next development in the narrative. Ἀμήν is an asseverative particle that introduces a solemn declaration. Ὅτι introduces a dir. quotation: "I assure you that, I solemnly tell you that." Πλούσιος, -ία, -ιον, "rich, wealthy." The subst. use of the adj. is anar. because it is indefin.: "a rich person." Δυσκόλως, "hardly, with difficulty." Εἰσελεύσεται 3rd sg. fut. mid. indic. of dep. εἰσέρχομαι, "enter." The fut. tense is *predictive (since entrance into the kingdom normally follows eschatological judgment) or gnomic. Τὴν βασιλείαν τῶν οὐρανῶν, 3:2.

19:24 Πάλιν indicates that this declaration is closely related to the topic of the previous statement (BDAG 752b–53a, 3). Δέ marks the next development in the dialogue. This statement is thus not a mere repetition of the preceding one but intensifies the earlier declaration. Even without ἀμήν, λέγω ὑμῖν is emphatically assertive (BDAG 588a–90c 2.d.). Εὔκοπος, -ον, "easy." Εὐκοπώτερον is nom. sg. neut. comp.: "easier." Ἐστίν (3rd sg. pres. indic. of εἰμί) is gnomic pres. Κάμηλον (κάμηλος, -ου, ὁ, "camel") is acc. subj. of the inf. (διελθεῖν 2nd aor. act. inf. of dep. διέρχομαι, "pass through [an obstacle]"). See Metzger 40. Διά reinforces the prep. prefixed to the vb. and portrays its object as an obstacle (BDAG 244b–d 3). Τρυπήμα, -ατος, τό, "hole (bored in an object)." Ῥαφίς, -ίδος, ἡ, "(sewing) needle."After the use of the comp. adj, ἤ is clearly comp. ("than") rather than disjunctive ("or"). Πλούσιον (19:23) is subst., indef., and acc. subj. of the complementary inf. εἰσελθεῖν (2nd aor. act. inf. of dep. εἰσέρχομαι, "enter"). Τὴν βασιλείαν τοῦ θεοῦ, 3:2.

19:25 Ἀκούσαντες (nom. pl. masc. of aor. act. ptc. of ἀκούω) is temp. (most EVV). Δέ marks the next development in the dialogue. Ἐξεπλήσσοντο (3rd pl. impf. pass. indic. of ἐκπλήσσω, "be amazed" [pass.]) is prog. impf. Σφόδρα (adv.) highly intensifies the vb.: "very (much)" (BDAG 980a). Λέγοντες (nom. pl. masc. of pres. act. ptc. of λέγω) is attendant circumstance (CSB; NIV; NLT). Τίς is the pers. interr. pron.: "who?" Ἄρα is an inferential particle used to show that a question was prompted by the preceding statement: "who then?" (BDAG 127b–d 1.a.). Δύναται 3rd sg. pres. mid. indic. of dep. δύναμαι, "be able." Σωθῆναι (aor. pass. inf. of σώζω, "save") is complementary.

19:26 Ἐμβλέψας (nom. sg. masc. of aor. act. ptc. of ἐμβλέπω, "look at [intently]") is attendant circumstance (most EVV). Δέ marks the next development in the dialogue. Παρά with the dat. (ἀνθρώποις) is a marker of pers. ref. (BDAG 756b–58b B.3.): "As far as human beings are concerned." The gloss in the NLT ("humanly speaking") captures the sense well. The neut. dem. pron. τοῦτο refers to the rich entering the kingdom (19:23, 24). Ἀδύνατος, -ον, "impossible." Ἐστίν (3rd sg. pres. indic. of εἰμί) is gnomic. Δέ is adversative and contrasts human impotence with divine omnipotence. Παρὰ θεῷ, "as far as God is concerned; if we are talking about God." The neut. subst. adj. πάντα means "everything." Δυνατός, -ή, -όν, "possible."

FOR FURTHER STUDY

103. The Camel and the Eye of the Needle

Best, E. "The Camel and the Needle's Eye: Mk 10:25." *ExpTim* 82 (1970): 83–89.
Derrett, J. D. M. "A Camel Through the Eye of a Needle." *NTS* 32 (1986): 465–70.

104. OT Law in Jesus's Teaching

Chandler, C. N. "'Love Your Neighbour as Yourself' (Leviticus 19:18b) in Early Jewish-Christian Exegetical Practice and Missional Formation." Pages 12–56 in *The Synoptic Gospels*. Vol. 1 of *"What Does the Scripture Say?": Studies in the Function of Scripture in Early Judaism and Christianity*. Edited by C. A. Evans and H. D. Zacharias. London: T&T Clark, 2012.
Fuller, R. H. "The Decalogue in the New Testament." *Int* 43 (1989): 243–55.

105. The Rich Young Ruler

Boer, H. R. "The Rich Young Ruler." *Reformed Journal* 26 (1976): 15–18.
Stanley, A. P. "The Rich Young Ruler and Salvation." *BSac* 163 (2006): 46–62.
Wenham, J. W. "Why Do You Ask Me About the Good: A Study of the Relation Between Text and Source Criticism." *NTS* 28 (1982): 116–25.

HOMILETICAL SUGGESTIONS

The Poorest Rich Man in the World (19:16–25)

1. Do not assume that you can earn eternal life through personal righteousness
2. Since only God is truly good, human beings are not capable of earning God's favor
3. Those who think they are keeping all the commandments fail to consider the full implications of those commandments
4. To earn salvation one must actually be perfect
5. Salvation requires following Jesus rather than trusting in oneself
6. Only God can conquer the selfishness and self-dependence of the rich

4. The Disciples' Sacrifice and Reward (19:27–30)

19:27 Τότε, "after that," with the similarity in topics suggesting close proximity in time. Ἀποκριθείς (nom. sg. masc. of aor. pass. ptc. of dep. ἀποκρίνομαι, "answer, reply") is pleonastic but clarifies that Peter's statement is a reply to Jesus's teaching in the preceding paragraph. Ἰδού is a particle that calls special attention to the statement it precedes. Ἡμεῖς is emphatic and implies that the twelve disciples have made greater sacrifices than others. Ἀφήκαμεν 1st pl. aor. act. indic. of ἀφίημι, "leave." The acc. neut. pl. subst. adj. πάντα means "everything." Ἠκολουθήσαμεν 1st pl. aor. pass. indic. of ἀκολουθέω, "follow." Σοι is dat. of dir. obj. The nom. sg. neut. interr. pron. τί means "what?" Ἄρα is inferential and indicates that the question flows from Jesus's preceding statements. Peter assumes that if refusal to give up one's riches excludes someone from the kingdom, sacrificing everything (the opposite of that refusal) would result in great reward. Ἔσται (3rd sg. fut. indic. of εἰμί) is predictive and refers to God's granting of eschatological reward. Ἡμῖν is dat. of advantage: "What will be (the benefit) to us?"

19:28 Δέ marks the next development in the dialogue. Ἀμὴν λέγω ὑμῖν ὅτι, 19:23. The repeated ὑμεῖς is clearly emphatic. The art. ptc. ἀκολουθήσαντες (nom. pl. masc. of aor. pass. ptc. of ἀκολουθέω, "follow") may be subst. and appos. ("You, the ones who followed me") or *adj. with the def. art. functioning like a rel. pron. ("You who followed me;" most EVV). Μοι is dat. of dir. obj. The prep. ἐν is a marker of a point in time. The def. art. τῇ modifying παλιγγενεσίᾳ is prob. the well-known art. and refers to an age highly anticipated by Jesus's followers. Παλιγγενεσία, -ας, ἡ, "renewal, new beginning." This important term refers to the renewal of creation during the Messiah's eschatological reign, thus CSB: "renewal of all things." Hagner (2.565) links the prep. phrase to the ptc. ἀκολουθήσαντες and regards it as a ref. to the new birth of the disciple: "those who follow me in personal regeneration." The temp. particle ὅταν ("whenever") does not portray the Messiah's reign as cond., but merely acknowledges uncertainty regarding the time of this reign (24:36). The subjunc. καθίσῃ (3rd sg. aor. act. subjunc. of καθίζω, "sit") is required by the particle of contingency with ὅταν. Ὁ υἱὸς τοῦ ἀνθρώπου, 8:20. Ἐπί with the gen. (θρόνου gen. sg. of θρόνος, -ου, ὁ, "throne") marks a location (BDAG 363a–67c 1.c.α.): "on." Δόξης is attrib. gen. (most EVV). Αὐτοῦ is gen. of poss. and refers to the Son of Man. Καθήσεσθε (2nd pl. fut. mid. [intrans.] indic.

of dep. κάθημαι, "sit") is predictive fut. and expresses a promise to be fulfilled in the eschatological era. Καί is *adjunctive (most EVV) or ascensive. The second ὑμεῖς is appos. and reminds the readers of the subj. of the sentence after the lengthy series of adj. and adv. clauses that followed the initial ὑμεῖς. Δώδεκα, "twelve." Κρίνοντες (nom. pl. masc. of pres. act. ptc. of κρίνω, "judge") is ptc. of *purpose or attendant circumstance: "sit on twelve thrones to judge." The def. art. τάς is the well-known art. Φυλή, -ῆς, ἡ, "tribe." Τοῦ Ἰσραήλ is partitive: "the twelve tribes that are part of Israel."

19:29 Πᾶς is subst. and pers.: "everyone." With πᾶς, ὅστις serves as a substitute for the rel. pron. ὅς (BDAG 729d–30b 1.b. and 3) Ἀφῆκεν 3rd sg. aor. act. indic. of ἀφίημι, "leave." Each occurrence of ἤ in this verse is disjunctive. Ἀγρός, -οῦ, ὁ, "(agricultural) field, farm." Ἔνεκεν functions as a prep. with the gen. to express a cause or reason. Ἑκατονταπλασίων, -ον, "a hundred times as much." Λήμψεται (3rd sg. fut. mid. indic. of λαμβάνω, "receive") and κληρονομήσει (3rd sg. fut. act. indic. of κληρονομέω, "inherit") are predictive fut. and express a promise. Since ζωήν is anar. and αἰώνιον modifies and follows it, the cstr. is an example of the fourth attrib. position (W 310–11). See Metzger 40.

19:30 Δέ is prob. adversative. Although the preceding verse might give the impression that one can calculate the degrees of reward that individuals will receive in eschatological judgment, this statement shows that divine judgment is often contrary to human expectations (F 746). The adj. πολλοί is attrib. and modifies the subst. adj. πρῶτοι: "many last ones, many (of those considered to be) last." Ἔσονται (3rd pl. fut. mid. indic. of εἰμί) is predictive and refers to eschatological judgment. Ἔσχατοι is a pred. adj. The second ἔσχατοι is subst. and serves as the subj. of a sentence in which the copula is merely implied, a cstr. common in Koine Gk. (BDF §127–28). Since the second clause is an inversion of the first, the adj. πολλοί is prob. implied in the second clause. The second πρῶτοι is a pred. adj.: "and many (considered to be) last will be first." This verse is best seen as the beginning of the parable of the day laborers that immediately follows (N 802).

FOR FURTHER STUDY

106. Παλιγγενεσία

    Burnett, F. W. "Παλιγγενεσία in Matt 19:28: A Window on the Matthean Community." *JSNT* 17 (1983): 60–72.

    _____. "Philo on Immortality: A Thematic Study of Philo's Concept of παλιγγενεσία." *CBQ* 46 (1984): 447–70.

    Derrett, J. D. M. "Palingenesia (Matthew 19:28)." *JSNT* 20 (1984): 51–58.

    Marshall, I. H. "The Hope of a New Age: The Kingdom of God in the New Testament." *Themelios* 11 (1985): 5–15.

    Sim, D. C. "The Meaning of παλιγγενεσία in Matthew 19.28." *JSNT* 50 (1993): 3–12.

HOMILETICAL SUGGESTIONS

A New World Is Coming (19:27–30)

1. Jesus promised a new creation, a perfect and eternal heaven and earth untainted by the effects of sin
2. Jesus promised that he would rule with all power and authority over people of every nation, tribe, and language
3. Jesus promised that his disciples would judge the people of national Israel
4. Jesus promised unimaginable reward to those who had made enormous sacrifices for his sake

5. *The Parable of the Day Laborers (20:1–16)*

20:1 Ὅμοιος, -οία, -οιον, "like, sim. to." Γάρ is causal and indicates that this parable illustrates the truth in 19:30 (D&A 3.71). Ἐστίν (3rd sg. pres. indic. of εἰμί) is gnomic. Ἡ βασιλεία τῶν οὐρανῶν, 3:2. Ἀνθρώπῳ is dat. after certain adj. (W 174). Οἰκοδεσπότῃ (dat. sg. masc. of οἰκοδεσπότης, -ου, ὁ, "master of the house") is dat. of appos. The cstr. ἀνθρώπῳ οἰκοδεσπότῃ prob. stresses the humanity of the authority figure in a manner that hinted that he represents the divine Master in the parable. Ὅστις serves as a substitute for the rel. pron. ὅς (BDAG 729d–30b 3). Ἐξῆλθεν 3rd sg. 2nd aor. act. indic. of dep. ἐξέρχομαι, "go out." Ἅμα functions as a prep. with a temp. adv. (πρωΐ) to denote simultaneity: "together with the dawn" (N 806) or "early in the morning" (BDAG 49b–c 2.b.; 892a–b). Μισθώσασθαι (aor. mid. inf. of μισθόω, "hire [for oneself]") is inf. of purpose. Ἐργάτης, -ου, ὁ, "laborer" (BDAG 390b 1.a.). Εἰς with the acc. (ἀμπελῶνα) serves as a substitute for the dat. of advantage and means "for his vineyard" (BDAG 288d–293c 4.g.). Ἀμπελών, -ῶνος, ὁ, "vineyard." Αὐτοῦ is gen. of poss.

20:2 Συμφωνήσας (nom. sg. masc. of aor. act. ptc. of συμφωνέω, "agree") is *temp. ("after he agreed;" CSB; LEB; ESV) or attendant circumstance (NIV; NLT). Δέ marks the next development in the narrative. Μετά with the gen. expresses the association of the employer and employees and emphasizes that the agreement was mutual (BDAG 636b–38b A.2.d.). Ἐργατῶν, 20:1. Ἐκ with a gen. noun referring to money serves as a periphrasis for the gen. of price (BDAG 295d–298b 4.b.; W 122; N 806 n. 145). Δηνάριον, -ου, τό, "denarius," the average wage for a day's work. On the purchasing power of a denarius, see N 806–7.The acc. τὴν ἡμέραν is distributive, which may be considered a subcategory of the acc. of extent of time (W 201–3; N 806 n. 145): "per day" (BDF §161). Ἀπέστειλεν 3rd sg. 2nd aor. act. indic. of ἀποστέλλω, "send." Αὐτούς refers to the laborers. Ἀμπελῶνα αὐτοῦ, 20:1.

20:3 Ἐξελθών (nom. sg. masc. of 2nd aor. act. ptc. of dep. ἐξέρχομαι) is *attendant circumstance (NIV) or temp. (CSB). The prep. περί indicates that the temp. ref. (τρίτην ὥραν) is an approximation (BDAG 797c–98d 2.b.). Τρίτος, -η, -ον, "third." The 3rd hour refers to the third hour after sunrise, typically around 9 a.m. Εἶδεν 3rd sg. 2nd aor. act. indic. of ὁράω, "see." The adj. ἄλλους is subst. and refers to other laborers. Ἑστῶτας (acc. pl. masc. of pf. act. ptc. of ἵστημι, "stand") is pred. ptc. The pf. tense narrows the sense of the lexeme rather than serving the normal functions of the pf.

(BDAG 482a–83b C.2.b.). Ἐν with the dat. marks the location. Ἀγορά, -ᾶς, ἡ, "market place." Ἀργός, -ή, -όν, "unemployed."

20:4 Ἐκείνοις refers to the unemployed laborers. The use of the remote dem. pron. merely distinguishes these laborers from those hired at daybreak. Ὑπάγετε (2nd pl. pres. act. impv. of ὑπάγω, "go") is ingr.-prog. Καί is adjunctive and ὑμεῖς is mildly emphatic (N 808). Εἰς τὸν ἀμπελῶνα, 20:1. The def. art. refers to the specific vineyard owned by the master. The combination of the rel. pron. ὅ with the particle of contingency ἐάν clearly functions as an equivalent to ὅ τι ("whatever") rather than like the prot. of a cond. sentence (most EVV; contrary to BDAG 56b–57c I.b.; BDF §380). The particle ἐάν required the subjunc. (ᾖ 3rd sg. pres. subjunc. of εἰμί). Δίκαιος, -αία, -ον, "just, fair." Δώσω (1st sg. fut. act. indic. of δίδωμι) is predictive and expresses a promise. Ὑμῖν is dat. of indir. obj.

20:5 The def. art. οἱ functions like a pers. pron.: "they." Δέ marks the next development in the narrative. Ἀπῆλθον 3rd pl. 2nd aor. act. indic. of dep. ἀπέρχομαι, "go away, depart." Πάλιν denotes repetition: "again." Ἐξελθών, 20:3. Περί, 20:3. Ἕκτος, -η, -ον, "sixth." Ἔνατος, -η, -ον, "ninth." The sixth and ninth hours refer to noon and 3:00 p.m. respectively. Ἐποίησεν 3rd sg. aor. act. indic. of ποιέω, "do." Ὡσαύτως, "likewise, in the same way."

20:6 Περί, 20:3. Δέ marks the next development in the narrative. Ἑνδέκατος, -η, -ον, "eleventh." The art. and independent adj. ἑνδεκάτην is subst.: "the eleventh hour." When time is calculated in hours, the number of hours are usually divisible by three and correspond to the Roman watch system that consisted of eight periods of three hours each, like the third, sixth, and ninth hours mentioned earlier in the parable. Reference to the eleventh hour is unusually precise and is obviously significant (D&A 3.72–73). Ἐξελθών, 20:3. Εὗρεν 3rd sg. 2nd aor. act. indic. of εὑρίσκω, "find, discover." The shift from ὁράω to εὑρίσκω is prob. more than merely stylistic. It likely implies the master's surprise (also indicated by his question) at an accidental discovery rather than that he was searching for additional workers. Note that the structure fits the description in BDAG 411b–12c 1.c.α. The adj. ἄλλους is subst. and refers to "other laborers." Ἑστῶτας, 20:3. Λέγει is historical pres. and prob. emphasizes the statement that it introduces. Τί, "why?" Ὧδε, "here." Ἑστήκατε (2nd pl. pf. act. indic. of ἵστημι, "stand"). On the significance of the tense, see BDAG 482a–83b B and C. The adj. ὅλην is a slight exaggeration since one hour of daylight remained. Τὴν ἡμέραν is acc. of extent of time: "all day long." Ἀργοί, 20:3.

20:7 Λέγουσιν is historical pres. Αὐτῷ refers to the master. Ὅτι offers a reason in response to the question "why?" in 20:6. Ἐμισθώσατο 3rd sg. aor. mid. indic. of μισθόω, "hire (for oneself)." Λέγει is historical pres. Αὐτοῖς refers to the laborers still not employed at the eleventh hour. Ὑπάγετε καὶ ὑμεῖς εἰς τὸν ἀμπελῶνα, 20:4. Hagner views the καί as ascensive (2.571), but it is prob. adjunctive (most EVV).

20:8 Ὀψία, -ας, ἡ, "evening." Δέ marks the next development in the narrative. Γενομένης (gen. sg. fem. of aor. mid. ptc. of dep. γίνομαι, "happen") is gen. abs. and temp.: "when it was evening." Λέγει is historical pres. Ἀμπελῶνος (20:1) is gen. of subord. Ἐπίτροπος, -ου, ὁ, "manager, foreman." Αὐτοῦ is gen. of authority. Κάλεσον (2nd sg.

aor. act. impv. of καλέω) expresses urgency. The def. art. τούς is anaphoric and refers to all of the workers previously mentioned in the parable. Ἐργάτης, -ου, ὁ, "laborer." Ἀπόδος (2nd sg. aor. act. impv. of ἀποδίδωμι, "pay" [BDAG 109d–10b 2]) expresses urgency. Αὐτοῖς refers to the workers and is dat. of indir. obj. Μισθός, -οῦ, ὁ, "wage." Ἀρξάμενος (nom. sg. masc. of aor. mid. ptc. of ἄρχω, "begin" [mid.]) is ptc. of means (if one limits ptc. of manner to those expressing emotion, per W 627–30): "by beginning." The prep. series ἀπό . . . ἕως (BDAG 105a–7b 2.c.β.; 422d–24c, 4) is used to mark order in a series by identifying the starting point and ending point: "starting from the last and continuing up to the first." The subst. adj. τῶν ἐσχάτων and τῶν πρώτων mean the last and the first workers to be hired.

20:9 Ἐλθόντες (nom. pl. masc. of 2nd aor. act. ptc. of dep. ἔρχομαι) is temp. (most EVV): "when (they) came." The prep. phrase περὶ τὴν ἑνδεκάτην ὥραν (20:6) is adj. and subst. The phrase "those around the eleventh hour" is short for "the ones that were hired around the eleventh hour." Ἔλαβον 3rd pl. 2nd aor. act. indic. of λαμβάνω, "receive." Ἀνά is distributive even though the number one is merely implied (BDAG 57d–58a 3): "a denarius apiece." Δηνάριον, 20:2.

20:10 Ἐλθόντες, 20:9. The art. and independent adj. πρῶτοι is subst. ("the first ones") and means "the first workers to be hired." Ἐνόμισαν 3rd pl. aor. act. indic. of νομίζω, "think." Ὅτι introduces the content of their thought expressed as an indir. quotation. Πλεῖον is the acc. sg. neut. comp. form of the adj. πολύς and means "more (in quantity)." Λήμψονται (3rd pl. fut. mid. indic. of λαμβάνω) is predictive, though in this case the prediction is incorrect. Καί prob. has an adversative nuance ("yet") since it introduces a statement contrary to expectations (BDAG 494a–96c 1.b.η.). Ἔλαβον [τὸ] ἀνὰ δηνάριον, 20:9. If the art. is orig., it is likely anaphoric and points back to the sim. agreement with the workers hired earlier (BDF §266.2; N 810). See Metzger 41. Καί is either *ascensive ("even they;" H 2.571) or adjunctive ("they also;" most EVV). Αὐτοί is emphatic.

20:11 Λαβόντες (nom. pl. masc. of 2nd aor. act. ptc. of λαμβάνω) is temp.: "When they received it." Δέ marks the next development in the narrative. Ἐγόγγυζον (3rd pl. impf. act. indic. of γογγύζω, "grumble") is inceptive: "they started grumbling." Κατά with the gen. (τοῦ οἰκοδεσπότου, 20:1) expresses opposition: "against the master of the estate" (BDAG 511a–13d 2.b.β.).

20:12 Λέγοντες (nom. pl. masc. of pres. act. ptc. of λέγω) is pleonastic and introduces the content of the grumbling. The dem. pron. οὗτοι indicates that the subst. adj. ἔσχατοι refers to the laborers just mentioned in 20:9. The subst. adj. refers to the last workers to be hired. The adj. μίαν refers to quantity and emphasizes one and no more: "a single, (only) one" (BDAG 291c–93c 1.a.α.). Ἐποίησαν 3rd pl. aor. act. indic. of ποιέω, "work" (BDAG 839b–42a 6). Since this clause expresses an action contrary to the expectations raised by the preceding clause, the conj. καί is slightly adversative: "and yet, in spite of this, nevertheless" (BDAG 494a–96c 1.b.δ.). The combination of the adj. ἴσος, -η, -ον with ποιέω (ἐποίησας 2nd sg. aor. act. indic. of ποιέω) means to make equal or treat equally (BDAG 480d–81a). Ἡμῖν is dat. after a certain adj. (W 174–75) and establishes a point of comp. Αὐτούς refers to the workers hired at the eleventh hour and serves as dir. obj.: "you treated them as equal to us" (BDAG 480d–81a). The art. ptc. βαστάσασι (dat. pl. masc. of aor. act. ptc. of βαστάζω, "bear, carry [a burden]" [BDAG 171b–d 2.b.β.]) may be appos., but more likely serves as a rel. clause: "who carried the burden" (most EVV). Βάρος, -ους, τό, "burden, weight." Τῆς ἡμέρας may be gen. of extent of time ("all day long"; NLT), appos. (CSB; ESV), or may modify the following noun (NIV). The cstr. is likely gen. of extent of time and thus modifies the vb. with the compound obj. Καύσων, -ωνος, ὁ, "burning heat." Several commentators suggest that the terms refers to a scorching east wind (G 398). If τῆς ἡμέρας modifies merely καύσωνα, the gen. prob. expresses source.

20:13 The def. art. ὁ functions as a substitute for the pers. pron. and serves as the subj. of the clause. Δέ marks the next development in the dialogue. Ἀποκριθείς (nom. sg. masc. of aor. pass. ptc. of dep. ἀποκρίνομαι, "answer" [pass.]) is pleonastic but clarifies that Jesus's statement was a reply to the laborers' protest. The adj. ἑνί is subst. Αὐτῶν is partitive. Ἑταῖρος, -ου, ὁ, "friend," is polite form of address to a stranger (BDAG 398c–d). Ἑταῖρε is voc. of simple address. Ἀδικῶ (1st sg. pres. act. indic. of ἀδικέω, "treat unfairly, cheat" (BDAG 20a–c 1.c.). The use of the neg. οὐχί to introduce the question anticipates a positive response. Δηναρίου (20:2) is gen. of price/value (W 122). Συνεφώνησας 2nd sg. aor. act. indic. of συνφωνέω, "agree." Μοι is dat. of association (W 159–60).

20:14 Ἆρον (2nd sg. 2nd aor. act. impv. of αἴρω, "take") expresses urgency. Σός, σή, σόν, "your" (2nd sg. poss. adj.). The art. adj. is subst.: "what is yours, what belongs to you" (BDAG 934b b.β.). Ὕπαγε (2nd sg. pres. act. impv. of ὑπάγω, "go [away]") is ingr.-prog. Θέλω 1st sg. pres. act. indic. of θέλω, "I want." Δέ is adversative and contrasts the laborer's expectations with the master's desire. The dem. pron. τούτω shows that the subst. adj. τῷ ἐσχάτῳ refers to a particular worker hired at the eleventh hour. The subst. is the indir. obj. of the inf. δοῦναι. Δοῦναι (aor. act. inf. of δίδωμι) is a complementary inf. The comp. particle ὡς compares the quantity or amount given to each individual. Καί is adjunctive. Σοί is indir. obj. of the inf. The comp. clause is short for "as I also gave to you."

20:15 The particle ἤ introduces an alternative: "or" (BDAG 432b–33b 1.d.β.). See Metzger 41. The neg. οὐκ introduces a question that anticipates a positive response. Ἔξεστιν 3rd sg. pres. indic. of ἔξεστιν, "it is right" (impers.). Μοι is dat. of ref. and after ἔξεστιν functions like the acc. subj. of the inf. The rel. clause ὅ (acc. sg. neut. of ὅς) θέλω (1st sg. pres. act. indic. of θέλω): "what I want." Ποιῆσαι (aor. act. inf. of ποιέω) is complementary. Ἐν marks the *instr. or location (BDAG 323a–b b). The art. adj. ἐμοῖς (ἐμός, -ή, -όν, "my," [1st sg. poss. pron.]) is subst. and either means *"my money (denarii)" or "my premises." The particle ἤ again introduces an alternative. Σου (modifying ὀφθαλμός) is partitive gen. Πονηρός ("evil") often means "envious, jealous" when describing the eye (BDAG 744a–c 1). Ἐστίν 3rd sg. pres. indic. of εἰμί. Ὅτι is causal. Ἐγώ is emphatic. When contrasted with the πονηρός ὀφθαλμός, the adj. ἀγαθός prob. means "kind, benevolent" (BDAG 3b–4b 2.a.α.). Εἰμί 1st sg. pres. indic. of εἰμί.

20:16 Οὕτως is an adv. that highlights the similarity between the truth in the clause it introduces and the preceding parable (BDAG 741d–42c 1.b.). Ἔσονται (3rd pl. fut.

indic. of εἰμί) is *predictive (anticipating eschatological judgment) or gnomic. This verbal form is implied in the second clause, which lacks an explicit copula. Οἱ ἔσχατοι and οἱ πρῶτοι are art. and independent, thus functioning as subst. The anar. adj. πρῶτοι and ἔσχατοι are pred. adj. See Metzger 41.

FOR FURTHER STUDY

107. The Parable of the Day Laborers

Caneday, A. B. "The Parable of the Generous Vineyard Owner (Matthew 20:1–16)." *SBJT* 13 (2009): 34–50.

Elliott, J. H. "Matthew 20:1–15: A Parable of Invidious Comparison and Evil Eye Accusation." *BTB* 22 (1992): 52–65.

Heinemann, H. "The Conception of Reward in Matt 20:1–16." *JJS* 1 (1949): 85–89.

Mitton, C. L. "Expounding the Parables: The Workers in the Vineyard (Matthew 20:1–16)." *ExpTim* 77 (1966): 307–11.

Naizer, E. R. "The Parable of the Labourers in the Vineyard (Matthew 20:1–16): Analyzing the Text Through Discourse Prominence." *UBS Journal* 6 (2009): 9–30.

Nelavala, S. "21st September: Proper 20—Matthew 20:1–16." *ExpTim* 119 (2008): 550–51.

Nelson, D. A. "Exposition of Matthew 20:1–16." *Int* 29 (1975): 288–92.

HOMILETICAL SUGGESTIONS

God's Judgment: Both Fair and Kind (20:1–16)

1. God is always just in his judgment and will at the very least give people what they deserve for their behavior
2. God will be amazingly kind to many and will give them far better than they deserve
3. God remains righteous even when he defies human standards of fairness

6. *Jesus Predicts His Crucifixion and Resurrection (20:17–19)*

20:17 Ἀναβαίνων (nom. sg. masc. of pres. act. ptc. of ἀναβαίνω, "go up") is *temp. (most EVV) or attendant circumstance (NIV). Παρέλαβεν 3rd sg. 2nd aor. act. indic. of παραλαμβάνω, "take along." Whether τοὺς δώδεκα is subst. (thus without μαθητάς) or attrib. (modifying μαθητάς), the mng. is the same. See Metzger 41–42. The prep. κατά with the acc. sg. fem. form of ἴδιος, -ία, -ον (ἰδίαν) forms an adv. phrase mng., "privately, by themselves" (BDAG 466c–67d 5). Ἐν with τῇ ὁδῷ is loc.: "on the road." Αὐτοῖς refers to the twelve disciples.

20:18 The presentative particle ἰδού draws attention to what follows: "Look!" Ἀναβαίνομεν 1st pl. pres. act. indic. of ἀναβαίνω, "go up." Ὁ υἱὸς τοῦ ἀνθρώπου, 8:20. Παραδοθήσεται (3rd sg. fut. pass. indic. of παραδίδωμι, "hand over") is predictive. Ἀρχιερεῦσιν and γραμματεῦσιν are dat. of indir. obj. Κατακρινοῦσιν (3rd pl. fut. act. indic. of κατακρίνω, "condemn") is predictive. Αὐτόν refers to the Son of Man. Although grammars generally classify θανάτῳ as an instr. dat. (BDF §195.2; R 535), "death" clearly identifies the goal or outcome of the sentencing rather than the instr. or means. Some ancient scribes evidently believed that the dat. expressed purpose or result, since Sinaiticus replaced the dat. with εἰς θάνατον.

20:19 Παραδώσουσιν (3rd pl. fut. act. indic. of παραδίδωμι, "hand over") is predictive. Αὐτόν refers to Jesus. Τοῖς ἔθνεσιν is dat. of indir. obj. Εἰς with the art. series of inf. (ἐμπαῖξαι aor. act. inf. of ἐμπαίζω, "ridicule;" μαστιγῶσαι aor. act. inf. of μαστιγόω, "scourge;" σταυρῶσαι aor. act. inf. of σταυρόω, "crucify") expresses purpose (W 590–92). Τῇ τρίτῃ ἡμέρᾳ is dat. of point in time: "on the third day." Since the ancients calculated time inclusively, this referred to any part of a first day, an entire day, and any part of a 3rd day. Ἐγερθήσεται (3rd sg. fut. pass. indic. of ἐγείρω, "raise, resurrect") is predictive.

FOR FURTHER STUDY

108. Crucifixion in the Roman World

Caneday, A. B. "'Anyone Hung upon a Pole Is Under God's Curse': Deuteronomy 21:22–23 in Old and New Covenant Contexts." *SBJT* 18 (2014): 121–36.

Chapman, D., and E. J. Schnabel. *The Trial and Crucifixion of Jesus: Texts and Commentary.* WUNT 344. Tübingen: Mohr Siebeck, 2015.

Cook, J. G. "Crucifixion as Spectacle in Roman Campania." *NovT* 54 (2012): 68–100.

_____. *Crucifixion in the Mediterranean World.* WUNT 327. Tübingen: Mohr Siebeck, 2014.

_____. "Roman Crucifixions: From the Second Punic War to Constantine." *ZNW* 104 (2013): 1–32.

Hengel, M. *Crucifixion in the Ancient World and the Folly of the Message of the Cross.* Philadelphia: Fortress, 1977.

HOMILETICAL SUGGESTIONS

The Road to the Cross (20:17–19)

1. Jesus boldly marched to Jerusalem even though he knew the destiny that awaited him there
2. Jesus gave a detailed prophecy of the events that awaited him in Jerusalem and his prophecy was fulfilled in every detail
3. Jesus is the Son of Man from Daniel 7:
   a. He came from heaven
   b. He will be worshipped by all the peoples of the earth
   c. He will reign as King at the Father's right hand forever

7. The Selfish Aspirations of Two Disciples (20:20–23)

20:20 Τότε, "after that." Προσῆλθεν 3rd sg. 2nd aor. act. indic. of dep. προσέρχομαι, "approach." Αὐτῷ is dat. of dir. obj. Τῶν υἱῶν is gen. of relationship. Ζεβεδαίου is gen. of relationship. Μετά denotes accompaniment. Αὐτῆς is gen. of relationship. Προσκυνοῦσα (nom. sg. fem. of pres. act. ptc. of προσκυνέω, "worship") and αἰτοῦσά (nom. sg. fem. of pres. act. ptc. of αἰτέω, "ask for") are ptc. of purpose: "approached him to worship and to ask" (most EVV). The enclitic τι is the indef. pron.: "something." Ἀπό identifies the source and αὐτοῦ refers to Jesus.

20:21 The def. art. ὁ functions as a pers. pron.: "he." Δέ marks the next development in the narrative. Αὐτῇ refers to the mother of 20:20. Τί is the interr. pron.: "what?" Θέλεις 2nd sg. pres. act. indic. of θέλω. Λέγει is historical pres. and the implied subj. is the mother. Αὐτῷ refers to Jesus. Εἰπέ (2nd sg. 2nd aor. act. impv. of λέγω, "speak" = "command"), see 4:3. Ἵνα is the marker of the obj. (BDAG 475c–77b 2.a.δ.). Καθίσωσιν 3rd pl. aor. act. subjunc. of καθίζω, "sit." Μου is gen. of relationship. The two instances of εἷς are nom. of simple appos. Ἐκ marks the location. The pl. number of δεξιῶν and εὐωνύμων (εὐώνυμος, -ον, "left") is unexpected but is normal with ἐκ. Both occurrences of σου with the ἐκ phrases are partitive gen. On the cstr., see 27:38. Ἐν marks the location. Σου (modifying τῇ βασιλείᾳ) is poss. or subj. gen.

20:22 Ἀποκριθείς (nom. sg. masc. of aor. pass. ptc. of dep. ἀποκρίνομαι, "answer" [pass.]) is pleonastic but clarifies that Jesus's statement is made in response to the mother's request. Δέ marks the next development in the dialogue. Οἴδατε 2nd pl. pf. (used as pres.) act. indic. of οἶδα, "know." Τί is the interr. pron.: "what?" Αἰτεῖσθε 2nd pl. pres. mid. indic. of αἰτέω, "ask" (BDAG 30b–d notes that the act. and mid. forms are used interchangeably with no real difference in mng.). Δύνασθε 2nd pl. pres. mid. indic. of dep. δύναμαι. The reply that follows shows that the vb. expresses a question rather than an affirmation. Πιεῖν (2nd aor. act. inf. of πίνω, "drink") is complementary. Ποτήριον, -ου, τό, "cup." The rel. pron. modifies ποτήριον and serves as the dir. obj. of the inf. πίνειν (pres. act. inf. [complementary] of πίνω). See Metzger 42. Ἐγώ is emphatic. Μέλλω 1st sg. pres. act. indic. of μέλλω, "be about to, be destined to." With the pres. inf., μέλλω either expresses inevitability or imminence (BDAG 627c–28c). Λέγουσιν is historical pres. Αὐτῷ refers to Jesus. Δυνάμεθα (1st pl. pres. mid. indic. of dep. δύναμαι) seems to be a more emphatic reply to the question than a simple yes (ναί).

20:23 Λέγει is historical pres. Αὐτοῖς refers to James and John. The μέν . . . δέ cstr. establishes a strong contrast. The μέν introduces a concessive clause and the δέ is adversative (BDAG 629d–30c 1.a.α.). Τὸ ποτήριον, 20:22. Μου first appears to be poss. gen., but 20:22 shows that it is actually subj. gen: "the cup that I will drink." Πίεσθε (2nd pl. fut. mid. indic. of πίνω, "call") is predictive. The art. inf. καθίσαι (aor. act. inf. of καθίζω, "sit") serves as the subj. of the sentence. Ἐκ δεξιῶν . . . καὶ ἐξ εὐωνύμων, 20:21. Μου is partitive gen. Ἐστίν 3rd sg. pres. indic. of εἰμί. Ἐμός, -ή, -όν is 1st sg. poss. pron.: "my, mine." Τοῦτο may be a scribal addition since it is absent from the earliest uncials, several early versions, and numerous citations in the early church fathers. Furthermore, witnesses that do contain it position it differently in the clause. The dem. pron. does not appear in the Marcan parallel so its inclusion here is not a result of harmonization. If orig. and positioned as it is in the UBS[5], the pron. is either a *nom. of simple appos. or acc. of dir. obj. of the inf. If τοῦτο is acc., the art. inf. τὸ καθίσαι functions like a pendant nom. Δοῦναι (aor. act. inf. of δίδωμι) is epex. (W 607). The conj. ἀλλά either has the rare mng. "except" (BDF §448.8) or the sentence has been shortened from οὐκ ἐμόν . . . ἀλλὰ τοῦ πατρός, ὅς δώσει οἷς ἡτοίμασται ὑπ' αὐτοῦ: "not mine . . . but the Father's, who will give to the ones for whom it has been prepared by him" (BDAG 44c–45d 1.a.). Most EVV assume an implied ἐστίν in the clause: "but it is for those for whom it was prepared" (cf. N 821). The rel. pron. οἷς is the dat. of advantage or indir. obj. of ἡτοίμασται (3rd sg. pf. pass. indic. of ἑτοιμάζω, "prepare"). Ὑπό is used with pass. vbs. to mark ultimate agency. Μου is gen. of relationship. See Metzger 42.

8. The Importance of Service (20:24–28)

20:24 Ἀκούσαντες (nom. pl. masc. of aor. act. ptc. of ἀκούω) is temp. (most EVV). The art. and independent adj. δέκα ("ten") is subst.: "the ten (other) disciples." Ἠγανάκτησαν 3rd pl. aor. act. indic. of ἀγανακτέω, "be indignant, angry." Περί is used with vbs. of emotion to identify the persons on whom the emotion is focused (NIV; ESV; CSB; cf. BDAG 797c–98d 1.c.).

20:25 Δέ introduces the next development in the narrative. Προσκαλεσάμενος (nom. sg. masc. of aor. mid. ptc. of προσκαλέω, "summon [to oneself]") is attendant circumstance (most EVV) or temp. Αὐτούς prob. refers to the twelve disciples rather than merely the ten. Οἴδατε (2nd pl. pf. act. indic. of οἶδα) is pf. with a pres. force (W 579–80). Ὅτι introduces the content of the disciples' knowledge. The art. and independent ptc. ἄρχοντες (nom. pl. masc. of pres. act. ptc. of ἄρχω, "rule") is subst.: "those who rule." Τῶν ἐθνῶν is gen. of dir. obj. (W 131–34), which is common with vbs. expressing authority. Κατακυριεύουσιν (3rd pl. pres. act. indic. of κατακυριεύω, "have mastery over, subjugate") is prob. gnomic pres. Αὐτῶν refers to the Gentile subjects of the rulers and is gen. of dir. obj. The art. and independent adj. μεγάλοι (μέγας, μεγάλη, μέγα, "great") is subst.: "The great ones." Κατεξουσιάζουσιν (3rd pl. pres. act. indic. of κατεξουσιάζω, "exercise authority, tyrannize") (BDAG 531a). Αὐτῶν is gen. of dir. obj. Both of the vbs. are pejorative (F 760 n. 15–16).

20:26 Οὕτως establishes a comp. with the oppressive secular authorities described in 20:25. Ἔσται (3rd sg. fut. indic. of εἰμί) is impv. fut. (CSB; ESV; LEB; W 569–70; H 2.581; F 755). Matthew uses the fut. indic. for categorical injunctions more frequently than the other evangelists (BDF §362). See Metzger 42. Ἐν ὑμῖν either means *"among you" (BDAG 326c–30b 1.d.; most EVV) or is a substitute for the dat. of ref. ("with you;" NIV). Ἀλλά is adversative and contrasts the prohibition of the preceding clause with the positive command in this clause. Although BDAG and BDF state that the combination of ὅς with the particle of contingency ἐάν and the subjunc. (θέλῃ 3rd sg. pres. act. subjunc. of θέλω) functions like the prot. of a cond. sentence, several clear exceptions exist in Matthew, and these cast doubt on the cond. view. The particle of contingency prob. makes the rel. pron. more indef. Thus most EVV tr. the clause "whoever wants" rather than "if someone wants." The prep. phrase ἐν ὑμῖν ("among you") may qualify the ὅς ἐάν and show that it refers to any member of the group of disciples (N 823). More likely, it modifies the adj. μέγας and defines the environment in which some wish to display their greatness (most EVV). Γενέσθαι (2nd aor. mid. inf. of dep. γίνομαι) is complementary. In this context γίνομαι prob. means "become"

(CSB; NIV) rather than merely "be" (ESV; NLT). Ἔσται (3rd sg. fut. indic. of εἰμί) is impv. fut. Ὑμῶν is obj. gen. ("your servant" refers to one who serves you), poss. gen., or gen. of authority.

20:27 καὶ ὅς ἂν (equivalent to ἐάν) θέλῃ ἐν ὑμῖν εἶναι πρῶτος ἔσται ὑμῶν δοῦλος, 20:26. **20:28** Ὥσπερ highlights similarity with what precedes: "just as" (BDAG 1106d–7a 1.b.). Ὁ υἱὸς τοῦ ἀνθρώπου, 8:20. Ἦλθεν 3rd sg. 2nd aor. act. indic. of dep. ἔρχομαι. Διακονηθῆναι (aor. pass. inf. of διακονέω, "serve") expresses purpose. Ἀλλά is strongly adversative and contrasts two opposites. Διακονῆσαι (aor. act. inf. of διακονέω) and δοῦναι (aor. act. inf. of δίδωμι) are inf. of purpose. The καί is prob. merely a coordinating conj. ("and"), but some commentators view it as epex. ("that is") so that Jesus's self-sacrifice is the means of his service to others (D&A 3.94–95; H 2.582). Τὴν ψυχήν means "life" rather than "soul" (BDAG 1098d–100a 1.b.). Αὐτοῦ refers to Jesus and is either poss. gen. or partitive gen. The two acc. nouns ψυχήν and λύτρον (λύτρον, -ου, τό, "ransom, price necessary to obtain release") are dbl. acc. of object-complement (W 182–89, esp. 185). The prep. ἀντί with the gen. (πολλῶν) emphasizes substitution—the ransom is offered as a substitute for the prisoner (Harris 52; H 2.583). BDAG suggests that the idea of substitution may have developed into intervention "on behalf of, for the sake of," in which ἀντί is the equivalent of ὑπέρ (BDAG 87d–88b 3). See Metzger 43.

FOR FURTHER STUDY

109. Jesus's Messianic Mission

Carter, W. "Jesus's 'I Have Come' Statements in Matthew's Gospel." *CBQ* 60 (1998): 44–62.

Edwards, J. C. "Pre-Nicene Receptions of Mark 10:45/Matt. 20:28 with Phil. 2:6–8." *JTS* 61 (2010): 194–99.

Wilcox, M. "On the Ransom-Saying in Mark 10:45c, Matt 20:28c." Pages 173–86 in *Geschichte—Tradition—Reflexion: Festschriften für Martin Hengel zum 70. Geburtstag.* Edited by H. Cancik, H. Lichtenberger, and P. Schäfer. Tübingen: Mohr Siebeck, 1996.

HOMILETICAL SUGGESTIONS

Celebrity or Servant? (20:20–28)

1. Jesus's disciples are sometimes characterized by selfish ambitions
2. Jesus's disciples should renounce selfish ambitions
   a. The ways of the kingdom are different from the ways of the world
   b. Jesus set the supreme example of service and self-sacrifice
3. Entrance into the kingdom is not a reward that we earn but is based on the ransom Jesus paid

9. Jesus Gives Sight to Two Blind Men (20:29–34)

20:29 Ἐκπορευομένων (gen. pl. masc. of pres. mid. ptc. of dep. ἐκπορεύομαι, "go [from]") is gen. abs. and temp.: "as they were going from Jericho." Αὐτῶν refers to Jesus and the disciples. Ἀπό expresses separation. Ἰεριχώ ("Jericho") is indecl. but must be gen. since it is the obj. of the prep. ἀπό. Ἠκολούθησεν 3rd sg. aor. act. indic. of ἀκολουθέω, "follow." Αὐτῷ refers to Jesus and is dat. of dir. obj. ὄχλος. Since the attrib. adj. πολύς is sg., it clearly refers to the size of the crowd rather than the number of crowds: "a huge crowd" (BDAG 847c–50a 2.a.).

20:30 Ἰδού is a presentative particle that calls attention to something unusual or enlivens a narrative (BDAG 468b–d). Τυφλός, -ή, -όν, "blind." Καθήμενοι (nom. pl. masc. of pres. mid. ptc. of dep. κάθημαι, "sit") is attrib. ("two blind men who were sitting") or attendant circumstance (most EVV). Παρά expresses proximity in location: "near, beside" (BDAG 756a–58b B.1.a.). Ἀκούσαντες (nom. pl. masc. of aor. act. ptc. of ἀκούω, "hear") is temp. (most EVV) or causal. Ὅτι introduces the content of the announcement that they heard. Παράγει (3rd sg. pres. act. indic. of παράγω, "pass by") is pres. retained in indir. discourse (W 537–39, esp. 539). Ἔκραξαν 3rd pl. aor. act. indic. of κράζω, "call out loudly, yell." Λέγοντες (nom. pl. masc. of pres. act. ptc. of λέγω) is pleonastic. Ἐλέησον (2nd sg. aor. act. impv. of ἐλεέω, "show mercy to, have mercy on"). Κύριε is voc. of simple address. Eng. readers may be surprised that υἱός is nom. rather than voc. However, the nom. is often used in appos. to the voc. (W 57; BDF §147). Υἱὸς Δαυίδ, 1:1. See Metzger 43.

20:31 Δέ marks the next development in the narrative and is left untranslated by most EVV. Ἐπετίμησεν 3rd sg. aor. act. indic. of ἐπιτιμάω, "rebuke." Αὐτοῖς refers to the blind men. Ἵνα introduces either a purpose clause (LEB) or *the prohibition spoken by the crowd in their rebuke (most EVV; BDAG 384d 1; 475c–77b, 2.a.δ.). Σιωπήσωσιν (3rd pl. aor. act. subjunc. of σιωπάω, "be quiet") is an indir. quotation since it is 3rd pers. The def. art. οἱ functions as a pers. pron. and subj.: "they." Δέ is clearly adversative, contrasting the order of the crowd with the blind men's opposite response. The sg. neut. comp. adj. μεῖζον serves as an adv.: "more (loudly)" (BDAG 623c–24d 3). Ἔκραξαν 3rd pl. aor. act. indic. of κράζω, "call out, yell." Λέγοντες· ἐλέησον ἡμᾶς, κύριε, υἱὸς Δαυίδ, 20:30. See Metzger 44.

20:32 Στάς (nom. sg. masc. of aor. act. ptc. of ἵστημι, "stand still" [BDAG 482a–83b B.1.]) is attendant circumstance (most EVV). Ἐφώνησεν 3rd sg. aor. act. indic. of φωνέω, "summon" (with acc.). Αὐτούς refers to the blind men and the acc. case helps determine the nuance of the vb. (BDAG 1071b–72c 3). Εἶπεν is not redundant since the quotation is different from the preceding summons. The interr. pron. τί means "what?" Θέλετε 2nd pl. pres. act. indic. of θέλω. Ποιήσω (1st sg. aor. act. subjunc. of ποιέω) functions like a complementary inf. (W 476, though the absence of ἵνα is unusual). Ὑμῖν is dat. of indir. obj.

20:33 Λέγουσιν is historical pres. Αὐτῷ refers to Jesus and is dat. of indir. obj. Κύριε is voc. of simple appos. Although it is possible that ἵνα with the subjunc. ἀνοιγῶσιν functions like an impv. (ESV; CSB; W 476–77; BDAG 475c–77b 2.g.), the reply to Jesus's question prob. assumes a portion of that question, and thus the vb. θέλομεν is implied. Consequently, ἵνα ἀνοιγῶσιν (3rd pl. aor. pass. subjunc. of ἀνοίγω, "open") functions like a complementary inf. (NIV; LEB; W 476; BDAG 475c–77b): "We want our eyes opened." Note though that the form is identical to the 3rd pl. pres. act. subjunc. form, in which case the vb. would be intrans.: "We want our eyes to open." Ἡμῶν is partitive gen.

20:34 Σπλαγχνισθείς (nom. sg. masc. of aor. pass. ptc. of dep. σπλαγχνίζομαι, "feel pity") is either *causal (CSB) or attendant circumstance (NIV). Δέ introduces the next development in the narrative. Ἥψατο 3rd sg. aor. mid. indic. of ἅπτω, "touch (mid.)." Ὄμμα, -ατος, τό, "eye." Αὐτῶν is partitive gen. and refers to the two blind men. Εὐθέως, "immediately." Ἀνέβλεψαν 3rd pl. aor. act. indic. of ἀναβλέπω, "see again, regain sight." Ἠκολούθησαν 3rd pl. aor. act. indic. of ἀκολουθέω, "follow." Αὐτῷ refers to Jesus and is dat. of dir. obj.

FOR FURTHER STUDY

110. Jesus as Son of David, Healer, and Exorcist

Baxter, W. S. "Healing and the 'Son of David': Matthew's Warrant." *NovT* 48 1 (2006): 36–50.

Kelly, C. "The Messiah: Whose Son Is He? Another Look at the Son of David and Son of God Titles in Matthew." *Trinity Seminary Review* 26 (2005): 17–28.

Kingsbury, J. D. "The Title 'Son of David' in Matthew's Gospel." *JBL* 95 (1976): 591–602.

Loader, W. R. G. "Son of David, Blindness, Possession, and Duality in Matthew." *CBQ* 44 (1982): 570–85.

Novakovic, L. *Messiah, the Healer of the Sick: A Study of Jesus as the Son of David in the Gospel of Matthew.* WUNT 170. Tübingen: Mohr Siebeck, 2003.

Van Egmond, R. "The Messianic 'Son of David' in Matthew." *Journal of Greco-Roman Christianity and Judaism* 3 (2006): 41–71.

HOMILETICAL SUGGESTIONS

I Was Blind but Now I See! (20:29–34)

1. Jesus had compassion on those that others viewed as a nuisance
2. The men were physically blind but spiritually insightful:
   a. They addressed Jesus as the Messiah (Son of David)
   b. They called Jesus Lord
   c. They petitioned Jesus as OT saints prayed to the God of Israel ("Lord, have mercy on us.")
3. Jesus fulfilled the prophecy of Isaiah 35:5: "The eyes of the blind will be opened"
4. Those who experience Jesus's love and power will follow him

IV. Jerusalem Ministry (21:1–28:20)

A. FINAL MINISTRY IN JERUSALEM (21:1–22:46)

1. *The Triumphal Entry (21:1–11)*

21:1 Ὅτε introduces a temp. clause ("when"). Although BDAG (1012d–13a 2) suggests that the ὅτε-τότε cstr. implies that the event introduced by τότε follows that of the preceding temp. clause, the τότε expresses a close temp. proximity between the two events that approaches simultaneity: "when . . . , at that time" (cf. 13:26). Ἤγγισαν 3rd pl. aor. act. indic. of ἐγγίζω, "come near." With ἐγγίζω, the prep. εἰς means "toward" rather than "into." The implication is that they had not yet entered Ἱεροσόλυμα. However, with ἦλθον (3rd pl. 2nd aor. act. indic. of dep. ἔρχομαι), the prep. εἰς does express entrance. With τὸ ὄρος τῶν ἐλαιῶν, the prep. εἰς means "on, in" and identifies the location of Bethphage. The sentence is a good illustration of the variety of mngs. that a single prep. can express even in consecutive usages. Ἀπέστειλεν 3rd sg. 2nd aor. act. indic. of ἀποστέλλω, "send (to accomplish a task)."

21:2 Λέγων is pleonastic and introduces the content of Jesus's commission. Πορεύεσθε 2nd pl. pres. mid. impv. of dep. πορεύομαι. The tense of the command prob. carries no special mng. since vbs. of motion are typically in the pres. tense in nonindicative moods. Κώμη, -ης, ἡ, "village." The def. art. τήν indicates that the prep. phrase κατέναντι ὑμῶν is adj. Κατέναντι is an improper prep. mng. "opposite" (BDAG 530d–31a 2). This may either refer to the opposite side of the Mount of Olives, the opposite side of the valley at the foot of the mountain, or the opposite side of the road (N 834). Εὐθέως prob. means "immediately upon entering the village." Εὑρήσετε (2nd pl. fut. act. indic. of εὑρίσκω, "find, discover") is predictive fut. Ὄνος, -ου, ὁ and ἡ, "donkey." Δεδεμένην (acc. sg. fem. of pf. pass. ptc. of δέω, "tie up") is pred. ptc. The fem. gender of the ptc. and the pron. αὐτῆς indicate that the donkey is female. Πῶλος, -ου, ὁ, "colt, foal." Λύσαντες (nom. pl. masc. of aor. act. ptc. of λύω, "loosen, release") is attendant circumstance and assumes the impv. force of the main vb. (most EVV). Ἀγάγετε (2nd pl. aor. act. impv. of ἄγω, "lead") may express urgency. Μοι is dat. of indir. obj.

21:3 Ἐάν with the subjunc. εἴπῃ (3rd sg. 2nd aor. act. subjunc. of λέγω) forms the prot. of a third-class cond. sentence that makes no assumption about the fulfillment of the prot. Ἐρεῖτε (2nd pl. fut. act. indic. of λέγω) is impv. Ὅτι is recitative. Due to its pl. number, αὐτῶν refers to the donkey and foal rather than the potential objector. Εὐθύς "immediately" expresses the potential objector's lack of any hesitancy in releasing the pair to the master. Ἀποστελεῖ (3rd sg. fut. act. indic. of ἀποστέλλω) is predictive.

21:4 Τοῦτο refers to the fulfillment of Jesus's instructions from 21:2–3. Γέγονεν ἵνα πληρωθῇ τὸ ῥηθὲν διὰ τοῦ προφήτου λέγοντος, 1:22. This is the ninth of the ten formula quotations. See Metzger 44.

21:5 The verse is a quotation of Zechariah 9:9 that differs in several ways from the LXX, perhaps under the influence of Isaiah 62:11. However, the similarities to the LXX are sufficient to suggest that Matthew was familiar with the LXX rdg. (N 835). Zechariah 9:9 has interesting parallels with the messianic prophecy in Genesis 49:10 (N 834). See Beale and Carson 63b–65b. Εἴπατε 2nd pl. 2nd aor. act. impv. of λέγω. Θυγάτηρ, -τρός, ἡ, "daughter." Σιών is gen. of relationship. Zion (Jerusalem) is personified as a parent. Ἰδού prompts attention to an unusual and important statement. Σου is gen. of subord. Ἔρχεται is prob. futuristic pres. and stresses the immediacy and certainty of the king's coming (W 535–37). Πραῢς, πραεῖα, πραῢ, "meek, humble." Καί may be a coordinating conj. or explicative ("namely") and introduces an explanation or example of the ascription of meekness (BDAG 494a–96c 1.c.). Ἐπιβεβηκώς (nom. sg. masc. of pf. act. ptc. of ἐπιβαίνω, "mount, ride"). The vb. prob. refers to mounting the animal, and the pf. tense is extensive-intensive. He has mounted the animal and now sits on it as he rides. The καί may be *explicative again (ESV; NLT). If so, ὄνος identifies the species of the animal and πῶλος identifies its age. However, since v. 7 distinguishes the two animals, the king may have mounted first one animal and then the other in turn (NIV; LEB). Υἱὸν ὑποζυγίου indicates that the foal is male and the offspring of a donkey (ὑποζύγιον, -ου, τό, "pack animal, donkey").

21:6 Πορευθέντες (nom. pl. masc. of aor. pass. ptc. of dep. πορεύομαι) and ποιήσαντες (nom. pl. masc. of aor. act. ptc. of ποιέω) are attendant circumstance (most EVV). The series of two attendant circumstance ptc. is unusual. Καθώς is an intensive comp. adv. that indicates that the disciples did precisely as Jesus commanded. Συνέταξεν 3rd sg. aor. act. indic. of συντάσσω, "order, give an order."

21:7 Ἤγαγον 3rd pl. 2nd aor. act. indic. of ἄγω, "lead." Ὄνον καὶ τὸν πῶλον, 21:2. Ἐπέθηκαν 3rd pl. aor. act. indic. of ἐπιτίθημι, "lay, put upon." Αὐτῶν refers to the donkey and foal. Ἐπεκάθισεν 3rd sg. aor. act. indic. of ἐπικαθίζω, "sit on." Ἐπάνω, "on top of." Αὐτῶν refers to τὰ ἱμάτια (G 410) and not the donkey and foal, per the law of the nearest referent. Notice that garments remain the focus of v. 8 as well. Most EVV leave the antecedent of the pron. ambiguous. However, the NIV specifies the correct referent: "place their cloaks on them for Jesus to sit on." Some scholars argue that the pron. is a generalizing pl. that refers to the animals viewed collectively but that Jesus rode only the foal (Turner, *Grammatical Insights*, 69; H 2.595). Soares Prabhu (*Formula Quotations*, 151) has provided convincing arguments against this view.

21:8 Δέ marks the next development in the narrative. Πλεῖστος, the superl. form of πόλυς, is attrib. and elative: "very large crowd" (BDAG 847c–50a c.a.; CSB; NIV; LEB). The ESV and NLT treat the adj. as superl. and trans. the noun ὄχλος as if it were partitive. However, there appears to be no basis for this since this passage employs neither μέρος nor the partitive gen. Ἔστρωσαν 3rd pl. 2nd aor. act. indic. of στρωννύω, "spread." On placing one's garments for a king to walk on, see 2 Kings 9:13. The refl. pron. ἑαυτῶν serves as a marker of poss. (BDAG 268b–69b 3). Ἔκοπτον (3rd pl. impf. act. indic. of κόπτω, "cut") is either prog. (most EVV) or inceptive. Κλάδος, -ου, ὁ, "branch." Ἀπό expresses separation: "cut branches off of the trees." Δένδρον, -ου, τό, "tree." Ἐστρώννυον (3rd pl. impf. act. indic. of στρωννύω) is either *prog. (most EVV) or inceptive.

21:9 The art. ptc. προάγοντες (nom. pl. masc. of pres. act. ptc. of προάγω, "preceding, go in front of") and ἀκολουθοῦντες (nom. pl. masc. of pres. act. ptc. of ἀκολουθέω, "follow, go behind") are attrib. and function like rel. clauses describing the crowds: "the crowds that were proceeding in front of him and behind him." Ἔκραζον (3rd pl. impf. act. indic. of κράζω, "shout") is prog. (most EVV) or inceptive. Λέγοντες is pleonastic and introduces the content of the shouts. The shout of the crowd merges elements of Psalm 118:25–26; 148:1; Job 16:19. See Beale and Carson 65b–66d. Ὡσαννά is an indecl. transliteration of a Heb. phrase used in a shout of praise: "hosanna." The dat. τῷ υἱῷ identifies the one to whom the praise is directed. Δαυίδ (indecl.) is a gen. of relationship. The anar. ptc. εὐλογημένος (nom. sg. masc. of pres. mid. ptc. of εὐλογέω, "bless") functions as a pred. adj.: "is blessed." The position of the ptc. prob. denotes emphasis. The art. and independent ptc. ἐρχόμενος (nom. sg. masc. of pres. mid. ptc. of dep. ἔρχομαι) is subst. and functions as the subj. The prep. phrase ἐν ὀνόματι followed by the gen. (κυρίου) prob. means "as the Lord's representative, commissioned and sent by the Lord" (BDAG 711c–14c 1.d.). Τοῖς ὑψίστοις (ὕψιστος, -η, -ον, "highest) means "highest heights/heavens" (BDAG 1045b–c 1).

21:10 Εἰσελθόντος (gen. sg. masc. of 2nd aor. act. ptc. of dep. εἰσέρχομαι) is gen. abs. and temp. Ἐσείσθη 3rd sg. aor. pass. indic. of σείω, "be stirred, agitated" (pass.) (BDAG 918c–d b; D&A 3.127). Πᾶσα (sg. with an art. noun [ἡ πόλις]) means "the whole, entire" (BDAG 782b–84c 4.b.). Λέγουσα is either a ptc. of result or *attendant circumstance (most EVV).

21:11 Ἔλεγον (3rd pl. impf. act. indic. of λέγω) is prob. prog.: "they kept saying". Ἰησοῦς is nom. of simple appos., modifying ὁ προφήτης. The def. art. ὁ with the prep. phrase ἀπὸ Ναζαρέθ nominalizes the phrase: "the prophet Jesus, the one from Nazareth." Τῆς Γαλιλαίας is partitive gen.

FOR FURTHER STUDY

111. The Triumphal Entry

Catchpole, D. R. "The 'Triumphal' Entry." Pages 319–34 in *Jesus and the Politics of His Day*. Edited by E. Bammel and C. F. D. Moule. Cambridge: Cambridge University Press, 1984.

Instone-Brewer, D. "The Two Asses of Zechariah 9:9 in Matthew 21." *TynBul* 54 (2003): 87–98.

Johnson, S. L. "The Triumphal Entry of Christ." *BSac* 124 (1967): 218–29.

Way, K. C. "Donkey Domain: Zechariah 9:9 and Lexical Semantics." *JBL* 129 (2010): 105–14.

HOMILETICAL SUGGESTIONS

Jesus: The Prophet-King (21:1–11)

1. Jesus fulfilled messianic prophecy (Isa 62:11; Zech 9:9)
2. Jesus was given a king's welcome
3. Jesus was praised and adored
4. Jesus was recognized as a prophet

2. The Cleansing of the Temple (21:12–17)

21:12 Εἰσῆλθεν 3rd sg. 2nd aor. act. indic. of dep. εἰσέρχομαι. See Metzger 44. Ἐξέβαλεν 3rd sg. 2nd aor. act. indic. of ἐκβάλλω. Πάντας modifies art. pl. subst. here and thus means "all" (BDAG 782–84c 1.b.β.). The art. τούς modifies both subst. ptc.: πωλοῦντας (acc. pl. masc. of pres. act. ptc. of πωλέω, "sell") and ἀγοράζοντας (acc. pl. masc. of pres. act. ptc. of ἀγοράζω, "buy"). Although the cstr. does not fit all the criteria of the Granville Sharp rule, since it is pl., the shared art. nevertheless seems to portrays those buying and selling as one entity—merchants (W 278–86; see subset e., "Both Groups Identical"). If "those buying" referred to all customers purchasing sacrificial animals, Jesus's action would likely have nearly cleared the temple. The "buying" prob. refers to merchants purchasing animals from vendors to resell to individual customers. Τράπεζα, -ης, ἡ, "table, counter (for business transactions)." Κολλυβιστής, -οῦ, ὁ, "money changers." The position of the phrase may express emphasis. Κατέστρεψεν 3rd sg. aor. act. indic. of καταστρέφω, "overturn, throw upside down." Τῶν πωλούντων (gen. pl. masc. of pres. act. ptc. of πωλέω) is subst. and poss. Περιστερά, -ᾶς, ἡ, "dove, pigeon."

21:13 Λέγει is historical pres. Γέγραπται (3rd sg. pf. pass. indic. of γράφω) is intensive (resultative) pf. and prob. expresses the abiding authority of the Scriptures (W 574–76). The quotation is a conflation of Isaiah 56:7 (first line) and Jeremiah 7:11 (second line). See Beale and Carson 67a–69c. Μου refers to Yahweh and is gen. of poss. Προσευχή, -ῆς, ἡ, "prayer." Προσευχῆς is gen. of purpose (W 100–101). Κληθήσεται (3rd sg. fut. pass. indic. of καλέω) may be predictive (most EVV; MT) or impv. (ESV). Δέ is adversative. Ὑμεῖς is emphatic. Ποιεῖτε (2nd pl. pres. act. indic. of ποιέω) is either *prog. (NIV; CSB), gnomic (ESV), or contextual perfective pres. (LEB; NLT; W 532–33). Αὐτὸν . . . σπήλαιον is dbl. acc. of object-complement. Σπήλαιον, -ου, τό, "cave (for refuge or hiding out)." Λῃστής, -οῦ, ὁ, "robber, bandit." Λῃστῶν is gen. of poss.

21:14 Προσῆλθον 3rd pl. 2nd aor. act. indic. of dep. προσέρχομαι. Τυφλοί and χωλοί are subst. adj. Χωλός, -ή, -όν, "crippled, lame." The blind and lame were restricted from entering the most hallowed sections of the temple complex (Lev 21:18–19; 2 Sam 5:8). Ἐθεράπευσεν 3rd sg. aor. act. indic. of θεραπεύω, "heal."

21:15 Ἰδόντες (nom. pl. masc. of 2nd aor. act. ptc. of ὁράω) is temp. (most EVV) or attendant circumstance (NLT). Δέ marks the next development in the narrative. Ἀρχιερεύς,

-έως, ὁ, "chief priest." Γραμματεύς, -έως, ὁ, "scribe, expert in the law." Θαυμάσιος, -α, -ον, "inspiring wonder or amazement." The art. and independent θαυμάσια is subst. and refers to awe-inspiring miraculous acts (Exod 3:20 [LXX]). The frequent association of such wonders with the unique expressions of Yahweh's power (cf. Pss 71:18; 76:15; 135:4 LXX) through the hand of Moses (Exod 3:20; Deut 34:12) during the Exodus (Ps 77:12) may hint at Jesus's deity or his identity as the prophet like Moses. In Matthew the term prob. refers to the miracles of 21:14 (D&A 3.140–41). Ἐποίησεν 3rd sg. aor. act. indic. of ποιέω. The art. ptc. κράζοντας (acc. pl. masc. of pres. act. ptc. of κράζω, "shout") is attrib. The def. art. may also modify λέγοντας, indicating that it is also attrib., or the ptc. may be *pleonastic and merely introduce the content of their shout (most EVV). Ὡσαννὰ τῷ υἱῷ Δαυίδ, 21:9. Ἠγανάκτησαν 3rd pl. aor. act. indic. of ἀγανακτέω, "be angry, indignant."

21:16 Εἶπαν 3rd pl. 2nd aor. act. indic. of λέγω. Ἀκούεις (2nd sg. pres. act. indic. of ἀκούω) is prog. The near dem. pron. οὗτοι refers to the children of 21:15. Λέγουσιν is prog. and indicates that the shouts of the children continue to the moment of this discussion. Δέ prob. merely introduces the next development in the dialogue. Λέγει is historical pres. Ναί is a particle of affirmation ("yes") that indicates that Jesus is aware of the children's praises and implies that he saw no reason to correct or rebuke them. Οὐδέποτε ("never") in a question gives the question the tone of an indictment. "Have you never read" implies that the pres. behavior of Jesus's opponents implies that they never read or somehow failed to understand the Psalm that Jesus quotes because their behavior is inconsistent with the truths revealed in that Psalm. Ἀνέγνωτε 2nd pl. 2nd aor. act. indic. of ἀναγινώσκω. Ὅτι is recitative. The biblical quotation is from Ps 8:3 and the portion quoted is identical to the LXX. See Beale and Carson 69c–70d. The prep. ἐκ prob. expresses source (most EVV). However, if the gen. στόματος is an example of metonymy ("mouth" is substituted for that which the mouth produces— utterances; BDAG 946d–47b 2; 18:16), then the ἐκ phrase may approximate the sense of a gen. of material. Νήπιος, -ία, -ιον, "infant." Θηλαζόντων (gen. pl. masc. of pres. act. ptc. of θηλάζω, "nurse, be fed at the breast") is subst. Νηπίων and θηλαζόντων are partitive gen. (most EVV) or gen. of source, depending on the nuance of στόμα. Κατηρτίσω (2nd sg. aor. mid. indic. of καταρτίζω, "prepare [for oneself]" [mid.]) is refl. Αἶνος, -ου, ὁ, "praise."

21:17 Καταλιπών (nom. sg. masc. of 2nd aor. act. ptc. of καταλείπω, "leave [behind]") is attendant circumstance (CSB; NIV) or temp. ("after he left"). Ἐξῆλθεν 3rd sg. 2nd aor. act. indic. of dep. ἐξέρχομαι, "exit." After a vb. with a prefixed ἐκ, the improper prep. ἔξω ("outside") emphasizes that Jesus proceeded beyond the boundaries of the city (τῆς πόλεως, referring to Jerusalem). Ηὐλίσθη 3rd sg. aor. pass. indic. of dep. αὐλίζομαι, "spend the night (in temporary sleeping arrangements)." Ἐκεῖ ("there") refers to Bethany.

FOR FURTHER STUDY

112. The Cleansing of the Temple

Bauckham, R. "Jesus's Demonstration in the Temple." Pages 72–89, 171–76 in *Law and Religion: Essays on the Place of the Law in Israel and Early Christianity*. Edited by B. Lindars. Cambridge: Clark, 1988.

Evans, C. A. "Jesus's Action in the Temple: Cleansing or Portent of Destruction?" *CBQ* 51 (1989): 237–70.

_____. "Jesus and the 'Cave of Robbers': Toward a Jewish Context for the Temple Action." *BBR* 3 (1993): 93–110.

_____. "A Note on Targum 2 Samuel 5:8 and Jesus's Ministry to the 'Maimed, Halt, and Blind." *Journal for the Study of the Pseudepigrapha* 15 (1997): 79–82.

Ham, C. A. *The Coming King and the Rejected Shepherd: Matthew's Reading of Zechariah's Messianic Hope*. Sheffield: Sheffield Phoenix, 2005.

Richards, E. R. "An Honor/Shame Argument for Two Temple Clearings." *TJ* 29 (2008): 19–43.

Roth, C. "The Cleansing of the Temple and Zechariah 14:21." *NovT* 4 (1960): 174–81.

HOMILETICAL SUGGESTIONS

Cleansing the House of Prayer (21:12–17)

1. Jesus fulfilled OT prophecy through the cleansing of the temple (Zech 14:20–21)
2. Jesus was angered by those who took advantage of the poor and neglected their spiritual needs (Lev 5:7; Jer 7:11)
3. Jesus accepted and healed those rejected from the temple (2 Sam 5:8)
4. Jesus accepted praise because God is worthy of praise (Ps 8:3)

3. The Destruction of the Fig Tree (21:18–22)

21:18 Πρωΐ is an adv. of time mng. "early in the morning." Δέ introduces a new pericope. Ἐπανάγων (nom. sg. masc. of pres. act. ptc. of ἐπανάγω, "return") is prob. temp. (most EVV). Ἐπείνασεν 3rd sg. aor. act. indic. of πεινάω, "be hungry."

21:19 On 21:19–31, see Metzger 44–46. Ἰδών (nom. sg. masc. of 2nd aor. act. ptc. of ὁράω) is *temp. or attendant circumstance. Συκῆ, -ῆς, ἡ, "fig tree." BDAG suggests that μίαν functions here as an indef. art. (291c–93c 3.b.). The prep. ἐπί does not mean "on" in this context since the tree would form a barrier to travel that would not likely be tolerated long. Instead, it serves as a marker of immediate proximity and indicates that the tree was close beside the road (BDAG 363a–67c 2.a.). The 2nd use of the prep ἐπί (modifying αὐτήν) also expresses close proximity: "he went up to it" (4.b.δ). Εὗρεν 3rd sg. 2nd aor. act indic. of εὑρίσκω, "find." Jesus's command and the clarification of the exception clause show that οὐδέν means "no fruit (figs) at all." Ἐν, "on" (BDAG 326c–30b 1.b.). Εἰ μή, "except." Φύλλον, -ου, τό, "leaf." Due to the lack of concord with φύλλα, the neut. sg. μόνον must be adv. and a marker of limitation: "only" (BDAG 658c–59c 2.a.). Λέγει is historical pres. Μηκέτι, "no longer, not from this point on." Ἐκ expresses source. Γένηται (3rd sg. 2nd aor. mid. subjunc. of dep. γίνομαι, "be produced" [BDAG 196d–99d 1]) is the prohibitive subjunc. (W 469) which has the force of an impv.: "Fruit must never again be produced by you." Εἰς marks duration of time (BDAG 288d–93c 2.b.) and with the obj. τὸν αἰῶνα means "forever." Ἐξηράνθη 3rd sg. aor. pass. indic. of ζηραίνω, "wither" (pass.) (BDAG 684d–85b 1.b.). Παραχρῆμα, "immediately."

21:20 Ἰδόντες (nom. pl. masc. of 2nd aor. act. ptc. of ὁράω) is temp. (most EVV). Ἐθαύμασαν 3rd pl. aor. act. indic. of θαυμάζω, "marvel, be astonished." Λέγοντες (nom. pl. masc. of pres. act. ptc. of λέγω) is attendant circumstance (most EVV). Πῶς may function as an interr. particle questioning the manner or way in which an action is performed ("how?"; most EVV) or as an exclamatory particle ("How [quickly]!"; Thayer 559c–560c, I.a.γ.). Παραχρῆμα ἐξηράνθη ἡ συκῆ, 21:19.

21:21 Ἀποκριθείς (nom. sg. masc. of aor. pass. ptc. of dep. ἀποκρίνομαι) is pleonastic but clarifies that Jesus's statement is a reply to the disciples. Δέ marks the next development in the dialogue. Ἀμὴν λέγω ὑμῖν, 5:18. Ἐάν with the subjunc. (ἔχητε 2nd pl. pres. act. subjunc. of ἔχω) and διακριθῆτε (2nd pl. aor. pass. subjunc. διακρίνω, "doubt") marks the prot. of a 3rd-class cond. statement that makes no assumption regarding the fulfillment of the prot. Οὐ μόνον . . . ἀλλὰ καί means "not only/merely . . . but also." The def. art. τό with the modifier serves as a substantiver (W 235) and refers to the act performed on the fig tree in 21:19. The gen. τῆς συκῆς is objective. Ποιήσετε (2nd pl. fut. act. indic. of ποιέω) is predictive (promissory). Κἄν results from a crasis of καί and ἄν. The particle of contingency indicates that this clause forms a second prot.: "if you say to this mountain." The dem. pron. τούτῳ suggests that Jesus was referring to a particular mountain within view. If it refers to the *Mount of Olives, it would hint at the fulfillment of Zech 14:4 (N 853; Evans 364; D&A 3.153 n. 30). If it refers to the Temple Mount, it would refer to the coming destruction of the temple (Telford 109–17). Εἴπητε 2nd pl. 2nd aor. act. subjunc. of λέγω. Ἄρθητι (2nd sg. aor. pass. impv. of αἴρω, "rise") and βλήθητι (2nd sg. aor. pass impv. of βάλλω) may express urgency. Γενήσεται (3rd sg. fut. mid. indic. of dep. γίνομαι) is predictive (promissory).

21:22 Καί may simply express continuation of Jesus's statement (CSB; ESV) or *may introduce a result: "and so" (BDAG 494a–96c 1.b.ζ.). Since uprooting a mountain and throwing it into the sea is a humanly impossible act, the promise regarding moving a mountain entails the assurance that God has the power to answer every prayer. Although most EVV tr. πάντα "whatever" or "anything," the subst. adj. is pl. ("all things/everything") and refers not to one but to many answered prayers (BDAG 782b–84c 1.d.β.). The correlative ὅσα with the particle of contingency ἄν makes the expression even more general (BDAG 729a–c 2). Αἰτήσητε 2nd pl. aor. act. subjunc. of αἰτέω. Ἐν marks the means by which the request is made. Πιστεύοντες (nom. pl. masc. of pres. act. ptc. of πιστεύω) is cond. (most EVV; W 632–33): "if you believe." Λήμψεσθε (2nd pl. fut. mid. indic. of λαμβάνω) is predictive (promissory).

FOR FURTHER STUDY

113. The Cursing of the Fig Tree

Derrett, J. D. M. "Moving Mountains and Uprooting Trees (Mk 11:22, Matt 17:20, 21:21, Lk 17:6)." *Bibbia e Oriente* 30 (1988): 231–44.

Scott, P. M. "Seasons of Grace? Christ's Cursing of a Fig Tree." Pages 188–206 in *Christology and Scripture: Interdisciplinary Perspectives.* Edited by A. T. Lincoln and A. Paddington. New York: T&T Clark, 2008.

Telford, W. R. *The Barren Temple and the Withered Tree. JSNTSup* 1. Sheffield: JSOT, 1980.

HOMILETICAL SUGGESTIONS

The Curse of the Fruitless (21:18–22)

1. Jesus can destroy by his mere command
2. Jesus will judge Israel for her spiritual fruitlessness
3. The prayers of Jesus's disciples will usher in the reign of Yahweh (Zech 14:4–9)

4. A Question Regarding Jesus's Authority (21:23–27)

21:23 Ἐλθόντος (gen. sg. masc. of 2nd aor. act. ptc. of dep. ἔρχομαι) is gen. abs., temp., and *antecedent (LEB) or contemp. (ESV; CSB; NLT): "after he entered the temple." Προσῆλθον 3rd pl. 2nd aor. act. indic. of dep. προσέρχομαι. Αὐτῷ, like αὐτοῦ, refers to Jesus. Διδάσκοντι (dat. sg. masc. of pres. act. ptc. of διδάσκω) is temp. and contemp.: "while he was teaching" (most EVV). Although Matthew uses the dat. abs. elsewhere (8:23), this ptc. does not fit the criteria since the dat. pron. is part of the independent clause. The art. τοῦ (modifying λαοῦ) is either *par excellence* or well-known and refers to the Israelites. Λέγοντες is attendant circumstance. The prep. ἐν (modifying ἐξουσίᾳ) serves as a marker of a means or instruction through which the action is performed: "by what authority" (BDAG 326c–30b 5.b.). Ποίᾳ may mark a question regarding class or kind ("what kind of authority?" [divine or human]) or simply serve as a substitute for the interr. pron. τίς. ("what authority?" BDAG 843d–44a 2.a.γ.; 22:36). Ταῦτα prob. refers primarily to acts such as the cleansing of the temple, but it may also include Jesus's supernatural acts, like miracles and exorcisms. Ποιεῖς is prog. pres. Ἔδωκεν 3rd sg. aor. act. indic. of δίδωμι. The near dem. pron. ταύτην indicates that the second question focuses on the authority mentioned in the preceding clause.

21:24 Ἀποκριθείς (nom. sg. masc. of aor. pass. ptc. of dep. ἀποκρίνομαι) is pleonastic but clarifies that Jesus's statement is a reply. Δέ marks the next development in the dialogue. Ἐρωτήσω (1st sg. fut. act. indic. of ἐρωτάω) is predictive. Κἀγώ results from crasis of καί and ἐγώ. Καί is adjunctive and ἐγώ is emphatic: "I . . . too." Λόγον means "question" (BDAG 598d–601d 1.b.β.). Ἐάν with the subjunc. (εἴπητε 2nd pl. aor. act. subjunc. of λέγω) forms the prot. of a 3rd-class cond. sentence that makes no assumption regarding the fulfillment of the prot. Ἐρῶ (1st sg. fut. act. indic. of λέγω) is predictive (promissory). Ἐν ποίᾳ ἐξουσίᾳ, 21:23.

21:25 Βάπτισμα, -ατος, τό, "baptism, immersion." Ἰωάννου is subj. gen.: "baptism per-formed by John." The interr. adv. πόθεν queries the source of John's baptism. Ἦν 3rd sg. impf. indic. of εἰμί. The prep. ἐξ expresses source. The disjunctive particle ἤ distinguishes two alternatives. The contrast of οὐρανοῦ and ἀνθρώπων suggests that "heaven" functions as a circumlocution for "God." The def. art. οἱ functions as a pers. pron. Διελογίζοντο (3rd pl. impf. mid. indic. of dep. διαλογίζομαι, "think, reflect, dis-cuss") is either *inceptive (LEB; H 2.609) or prog. BDAG suggests that the phrase ἐν ἑαυτοῖς indicates that διαλογίζομαι refers to internal reflection and that πρός with the acc. would have been used to refer to a group discussion (BDAG 232c–d 1). If the refl. pron. were sg., the prep. phrase would clearly describe an internal process. However, since it is pl. it may refer to group interaction. The pleonastic ptc. λέγοντες and the 1st pers. pl. forms of the vb. suggest that the group discussed the question and its potential implications (most EVV). Ἐάν with the subjunc. (εἴπωμεν) marks the prot. of a 3rd-class cond. statement. Ἐρεῖ 3rd sg. fut. act. indic. of λέγω Διὰ τί, "why." The inferential particle οὖν introduces the question to show that the views of the group did not result in appropriate action. The particle highlights the inconsistency between their convictions and their conduct. Ἐπιστεύσατε 2nd pl. aor. act. indic. of πιστεύω.

21:26 Ἐὰν δὲ εἴπωμεν, 21:25. Φοβούμεθα (1st pl. pres. pass. indic. of φοβέω) is prog. Γάρ introduces the reason for the fear of the crowds. Πάντες is subst. Ἔχω, "con-sider, view as" (BDAG 421a–22b 6). Ὡς προφήτην . . . τὸν Ἰωάννην is dbl. acc. of object-complement (W 181–89). The ὡς highlights the crowd's perspective regarding John's role (BDAG 1103d–6b 3.a.γ.).

21:27 Καί is resultative: "and so." Ἀποκριθέντες (nom. pl. masc. of aor. pass. ptc. of dep. ἀποκρίνομαι) is pleonastic but confirms that Jesus's statement is a reply. Ἔφη 3rd sg. aor. (or impf.) act. indic. of φημί. Although most EVV tr. καί as merely expressing continuation, it is prob. adjunctive and indicates that Jesus's reply is of the same eva-sive nature as that of the chief priests and elders. Αὐτός is emphatic. Οὐδέ, "neither, not . . . either," implies that Jesus's reply is sim. in kind to that of the Jewish leaders.

5. The Parable of the Two Sons (21:28–32)

21:28 Τί δοκεῖ with the dat. of pers. (ὑμῖν) is impers.: "what does it seem to you?" The anar. ἄνθρωπος is indef. so the introduction to the parable is equivalent to the use of the indef. pron. and ἄνθρωπος to introduce a parable (18:12). Εἶχεν (3rd sg. impf. act. indic. of ἔχω) is prog. The vb. ἔχω expresses close pers. relationship (BDAG 420a–22d 2.a.). Τέκνον, -ου, ό, "son" (BDAG 994b–95b 1.b.). Προσελθών (nom. sg. masc. of 2nd aor. act. ptc. of dep. προσέρχομαι) is attendant circumstance (most EVV). The art. adj. πρώτῳ is subst. Τέκνον is voc. of simple address. For ὕπαγε with a second impv. with asyndeton, see 5:24. The adv. of time σήμερον prob. expresses duration and hints than the father might give a different work assignment the next day. Ἐργάζου (2nd sg. pres. mid. impv. of dep. ἐργάζομαι, "work") is ingr.-prog. The def. art. τῷ implies poss.: "my vineyard" (W 215–16). Ἀμπελών, -ῶνος, ό, "vineyard."

21:29 The def. art. ό functions as a pers. pron. Ἀποκριθείς is pleonastic. Θέλω is prog. pres. The tr. "I do not want to" (CSB; LEB; BDAG 447c–48c 2) is preferable to "I will not" (NIV; ESV) since the latter tr. would seem to require the fut. form of ἐργάζομαι in this context. Δέ is adversative. Despite his lack of desire, the son still obeyed. Ὕστερος, -α, -ον, "late," is a positive adj. used as a comp. The neut. form is used adv.: "later." Μεταμεληθείς (nom. sg. masc. of aor. pass. ptc. of dep. μεταμέλομαι, "regret, change one's mind") is attendant circumstance (most EVV; BDAG 639c–d 2).

21:30 Προσελθών, 21:28. The art. adj. ἑτέρῳ is subst.: "the other son." Ὡσαύτως is an adv. expressing similarity/identity: "in a similar (on the same) way" (BDAG 1106c). ὁ δὲ ἀποκριθεὶς εἶπεν, 21:29. The pron. ἐγώ is emphatic and contrasts the second son's apparent eagerness to obey with the first son's initial refusal. The vb. θέλω may be implied. Alternatively, the pron. may be a shortened form of ἰδοὺ ἐγώ, which is used in the LXX as a formula of consent (H 2.613). The voc. of simple address κύριε ("sir") implies the son's respect for the father's authority and makes the contrast between his words and actions more offensive (D&A 3:168). Καί is concessive: "And yet" (BDAG 494a–96c 1.b.η.).

21:31 The interr. τίς introduces a question: "who?" The ἐκ phrase followed by a number (τῶν δύο, subst., "the two [sons]") is a substitute for the partitive gen. (BDAG 295d–298c 4.a.). Ἐποίησεν 3rd sg. aor. act. indic. of ποιέω. The def. art. τοῦ is previous ref. (21:28). Πατρός is subj. gen. Λέγουσιν is historical pres. The art. adj. πρῶτος is subst.: "the first (son in the parable)." Λέγει is historical pres. Ἀμὴν λέγω ὑμῖν, 5:18. Ὅτι is recitative. The def. art. modifying τελῶναι (τελώνης, -ου, ὁ, "tax collector") and πόρναι (πόρνη, -ης, ἡ, "prostitute") are generic. Since entrance into the kingdom is elsewhere associated with eschatological judgment (7:21–23), προάγουσιν (3rd pl. pres. act. indic. of προάγω, "go before, precede") is prob. futuristic (NLT) and expresses certainty (W 535–37). However, most EVV treat the vb. as prog. (NIV; CSB; LEB) and others treat it as gnomic (ESV). Τὴν βασιλείαν τοῦ θεοῦ, 3:2.

21:32 Γάρ is causal. The prep. ἐν prob. means "on" as part of the imagery of righteousness as a road or path on which one travels (BDAG 326c–30b 1.b.; cf. 5:25). Δικαιοσύνης is prob. gen. of appos., showing that righteousness is the characteristic symbolized by the (straight) road (BDAG 691a–92b 3.b.). Coming on the path of righteousness likely refers to being characterized by obedience to God's commands. Ἐπιστεύσατε 2nd pl. aor. act. indic. of πιστεύω. Δέ is adversative and contrasts the disbelief of one group with the belief of the other. Οἱ τελῶναι καὶ αἱ πόρναι, 21:31. Ἐπίστευσαν 3rd pl. aor. act. indic. of πιστεύω. Δέ is again adversative and contrasts the two different responses to John's ministry. Ὑμεῖς is emphatic. Ἰδόντες (nom. pl. masc. of 2nd aor. act. ptc. of ὁράω) is concessive (NIV; ESV): "although." Οὐδέ, "not even" (BDAG 734d–35a 3). See Metzger 46–47. Μετεμελήθητε 2nd pl. aor. pass. indic. of dep. μεταμέλομαι, "regret, change one's mind." D&A (3.171) suggest that the vb. here approaches the mng. of μετανοέω, "repent." Ὕστερον, 21:29. The inf. (πιστεῦσαι aor. act. inf. of πιστεύω) with the gen. art. (τοῦ) expresses purpose (LEB) or is epex. Although most tr. treat the inf. as a finite vb. coordinate with μετεμελήθητε, no syntactical category appears to justify this.

FOR FURTHER STUDY

114. The Parable of the Two Sons

Derrett, J. D. M. "The Parable of the Two Sons." *Studia Theologica* 25 (1971): 109–16.

Foster, P. "A Tale of Two Sons: But Which One Did the Far, Far Better Thing? A Study of Matt 21.28–32." *NTS* 47 (2001): 26–37.

Shae, G. S. "The Question on the Authority of Jesus." *NovT* 16 (1974): 1–29.

HOMILETICAL SUGGESTIONS

Promises, Promises (21:23–32)

1. John displayed God's authority by calling sinners to repentance
2. Jesus displayed God's authority by cleansing the temple and performing miracles
3. Tax collectors and prostitutes submitted to God's authority by repenting and believing
4. The chief priests and elders rejected God's authority by promising to obey but failing to keep that promise

6. The Parable of the Wicked Tenants (21:33–46)

21:33 Ἀκούσατε (2nd pl. aor. act. impv. of ἀκούω) prob. expresses urgency. The anar. ἄνθρωπος is indefinite (21:28). Ἦν is impers.: "there was." Οἰκοδεσπότης (-ου, ὁ, "master of the house, owner of an estate") is appos. (LEB). Ὅστις functions as a substitute for the simple rel. pron. (BDAG 729d–30b 3).: "who." Ἐφύτευσεν 3rd sg. aor. act. indic. of φυτεύω, "plant"). Ἀμπελών, -ῶνος, ὁ, "vineyard." Φραγμός, -οῦ, ὁ, "fence, protective wall." Αὐτῷ is loc. and indicates where the fence was placed. Περιέθηκεν 3rd sg. aor. act. indic. of περιτίθημι, "place around." Ὤρυξεν 3rd sg. aor. act. indic. of ὀρύσσω, "dig." Ἐν marks location and αὐτῷ refers to the vineyard. Ληνός, -οῦ, ἡ, "winepress." The vb. ᾠκοδόμησεν is 3rd sg. aor. act. indic. of οἰκοδομέω, "build, construct." Πύργος, -ου, ὁ, "lookout perch, watchtower." The description of the preparation and care for the vineyard contains clear allusions to the parable of the vineyard in Isaiah 5:1–7. See Beale and Carson 71b–73a. Ἐξέδετο 3rd sg. aor. mid. indic. of ἐκδίδωμι, "lease, rent out." Γεωργός, -οῦ, ὁ, "tenant farmer." Ἀπεδήμησεν 3rd sg. aor. act. indic. of ἀποδημέω, "go on a journey."

21:34 Ὅτε introduces a temp. clause. Ἤγγισεν 3rd sg. aor. act. indic. of ἐγγίζω, "draw near, approach." Τῶν καρπῶν is prob. gen. of product: "the season that produces fruit (during which fruit ripens and is harvested)." Ἀπέστειλεν 3rd sg. 2nd aor. act. indic. of ἀποστέλλω. Αὐτοῦ (modifying δούλους) may express poss. or authority. Λαβεῖν (2nd aor. act. inf. of λαμβάνω) expresses purpose. Αὐτοῦ (modifying καρπούς) is gen. of poss. and refers to the portion of the harvest that the owner of the vineyard was to receive as rent for the vineyard.

21:35 Λαβόντες (nom. pl. masc. of 2nd aor. act. ptc. of λαμβάνω) is attendant circumstance (most EVV). Οἱ γεωργοί, 21:33. The series of rel. pron. accompanied by μὲν ... δέ functions as dem. pron. (BDAG 725d–27d 2.b.): "one ... the other ... and the other. . . ." Ἔδειραν 3rd pl. aor. act. indic. of δέρω, "beat, punch, whip." Ἀπέκτειναν 3rd pl. aor. act. indic. of ἀκοκτείνω. Ἐλιθοβόλησαν 3rd pl. aor. act. indic. of λιθοβολέω, "throw stones at, execute by stoning."

21:36 Πάλιν expresses repetition (BDAG 752b–53a 2): "again." Ἀπέστειλεν, 21:34. Πλείονας (πολύς) is comp. (BDAG 847c–50a 1.b.α.) and refers to greater numbers (most EVV). Τῶν πρώτων is gen. of comp. Ἐποίησαν 3rd pl. aor. act. indic. of ποιέω. Ὡσαύτως, 21:30.

21:37 Ὕστερον, "later" (21:29). Δέ introduces a new development in the narrative that is unexpected. Ἀπέστειλεν, 21:34. Αὐτοῦ (modifying υἱόν) is gen. of relationship. Λέγων is attendant circumstance (CSB; NIV) or causal. Ἐντραπήσονται (3rd pl. fut. pass. indic. of ἐντρέπω, "respect" [pass.]) is predictive. Μου is gen. of relationship.

21:38 Δέ is prob. adversative and contrasts the action expected by the father with the tenant's brutality. Οἱ γεωργοί, 21:33. Ἰδόντες (nom. pl. masc. of 2nd aor. act. ptc. of ὁράω) is temp. (most EVV). The def. art. τόν (modifying υἱόν) is anaphoric. Ἐν ἑαυτοῖς, "among themselves," indicates inter-group communication. Κληρονόμος, -ου, ὁ, "heir." The def. art. is prob. monadic. Δεῦτε is a hortatory particle: "come on!" Ἀποκτείνωμεν (1st pl. pres. or aor. act. subjunc. of ἀποκτείνω) is hortatory: "let's kill!" Σχῶμεν (1st pl. aor. act. subjunc. of ἔχω) is hortatory ("let's take;" most EVV, though this is an unusual sense for the lexeme) or expresses possibility ("perhaps we may have"). Κληρονομία, -ας, ἡ, "inheritance." Αὐτοῦ is poss.

21:39 Καί may be resultative: "and so." Λαβόντες (nom. pl. masc. of 2nd aor. act. ptc. of λαμβάνω) is attendant circumstance (most EVV). See Metzger 47. Ἐξέβαλον 3rd pl. 2nd aor. act. indic. of ἐκβάλλω. The combination of ἐκβάλλω with the improper prep. ἔξω may recall the language of ritual expulsion in Lev 14:40. Ἀμπελῶνος, 21:33. Ἀπέκτειναν 3rd pl. aor. act. indic. of ἀποκτείνω.

21:40 Ὅταν adds the particle of contingency to the temp. particle to indicate that the time is uncertain: "whenever." Οὖν is inferential and anticipates the action that is a reasonable response to the tenants' behavior. Ἔλθῃ 3rd sg. 2nd aor. act. subjunc. of dep. ἔρχομαι. Τοῦ ἀμπελῶνος (21:33) is gen. of subord. The interr. pron. τί poses a question: "what?" Ποιήσει is delib. fut. Γεωργοῖς, 21:33. The remote dem. pron. ἐκείνοις may express contempt (BDAG 301d–2c a.γ.).

21:41 Λέγουσιν is historical pres. Although the adj. κακούς is anar., it is subst. and appos. to αὐτούς: "them, the bad men." The adv. κακῶς is part of a wordplay with κακούς and implies that the punishment was appropriate for the men's character. The NIV attempts to preserve the wordplay: "He will bring those wretches to a wretched end." Ἀπολέσει (3rd sg. fut. act. indic. of ἀπόλλυμι, "destroy") is predictive. Ἀμπελῶνα, 21:33. Ἐκδώσεται (3rd sg. fut. mid. indic. of ἐκδίδωμι, "lease, rent out." Γεωργοῖς, 21:33. Οἵτινες may serve as a substitute for the rel. pron. or it may generalize the ref. (compare BDAG 729d–30b 3 and 1 respectively) and indicate that the only condition for becoming a tenant is willingness to offer the fruits to the master. Ἀποδώσουσιν (3rd pl. fut. act. indic. of ἀποδίδωμι, "pay, repay") is predictive. Αὐτῶν (modifying καιροῖς) is gen. of product (21:34). The shift from the sg. καιρός (21:34) to the pl. indicates that the new tenants will maintain management of the vineyard for multiple seasons and with the evident satisfaction of the master.

21:42 Λέγει is historical pres. Οὐδέποτε, "never." Ἀνέγνωτε 2nd pl. 2nd aor. act. indic. of ἀναγινώσκω. The def. art. ταῖς modifying γραφαῖς is *par excellence* (W 222–23) and refers to the writings that surpass all others in value, or it is monadic and refers to the Scriptures as the only divinely inspired books (BDAG 206c–d 2.b.α.). The quotation is from Ps 118:22 and follows the LXX verbatim. See Beale and Carson 73a–74d. The anar. λίθον is prob. indef., but the rel. clause introduced by ὅν clearly identifies it. Ἀπεδοκίμασαν 3rd pl. aor. act. indic. of ἀποδοκιμάζω, "reject." The art. οἰκοδομοῦντες (nom. pl. masc. of pres. act. ptc. of οἰκοδομέω, "build) is subst.: "the builders." Οὗτος refers to λίθον: "this stone." Ἐγενήθη 3rd sg. aor. pass. indic. of dep. γίνομαι. The prep. εἰς is used with γίνομαι to mark the pred. nom. (BDAG 288d–91c 8.a.α): "became the head." Γωνίας (γωνία, -ας, ἡ, "corner") is partitive gen. Παρά with the gen. (κυρίου) marks the one who originates or directs: "caused by the Lord." Ἐγένετο 3rd sg. 2nd aor. mid. indic. of dep. γίνομαι. The dem. pron. αὕτη prob. refers to the head. Θαυμαστός, -ή, -όν, "awe-inspiring." Ὀφθαλμοῖς is an example of metonymy in which the organ of sight is substituted for the act of seeing: "sight, view." Ἡμῶν is a partitive gen. ("our eyes") but functions as a subj. gen. in the metonymy: "our sight."

21:43 Διὰ τοῦτο, "because of this." Λέγω ὑμῖν, 5:20. Ὅτι is recitative. Ἀρθήσεται (3rd sg. fut. pass. indic. of αἴρω) is pred. fut. and divine pass. The prep. ἀπό (ἀφ' ὑμῶν) emphasizes the separation already implied by the vb.: "taken away from you." Ἡ βασιλεία τοῦ θεοῦ, 3:2. Δοθήσεται (3rd sg. fut. pass. indic. of δίδωμι) is predictive fut. and divine pass. Ποιοῦντι (dat. sg. neut. of pres. act. ptc. of ποιέω) is attrib.: "a group of people who are producing." Αὐτῆς refers to "kingdom" and is prob. attrib. gen. and refers to fruit appropriate to the kingdom (NLT).

21:44 This verse is absent in several early witnesses. Some critics have suggested that the absence is from an accidental omission due to parablepsis related to homeoteleuton (αὐτῆς ends v. 43 and αὐτόν ends v. 44). However, the difference in case and gender between the two forms makes such confusion unlikely. An intentional omission due to theological motivations is unlikely, since an almost identical statement appears in Luke without significant variations in the ms. tradition suggesting that scribes were not troubled by the statement in the Lucan context. Some critics have suggested that early scribes added the verse to harmonize Matthew with Luke's form of the parable (see Luke 20:18). Yet subtle differences between Matthew and Luke (Matthew lacks Luke's πᾶς; uses the near dem. pron. τοῦτον rather than the remote dem. pron. ἐκεῖνον [which results in a change in the position of the pron.]; and does not immediately follow the OT quotation as does Luke) raise doubts that a scribe simply imported the verse from Luke. Due to this conflicting evidence, the C rating in the UBS[5] is justifiable. Nevertheless, the verse sits awkwardly in its pres. context in Matthew and this supports the committee's opinion that the verse is "an accretion to the text" (Metzger 47). The art. ptc. πεσών (nom. sg. masc. of 2nd aor. act. ptc. of πίπτω) is subst.: "the one who falls." The dem. pron. τοῦτον is anaphoric and points to the stone described in 21:42. Συνθλασθήσεται 3rd sg. fut. pass. indic. of συνθλάω, "break to pieces." The particle of contingency ἄν generalizes the rel. pron.: "on whomever, anyone." Πέσῃ 3rd sg. aor. act. subjunc. of πίπτω. Λικμήσει 3rd sg. fut. act. indic. of λικμάω, "crush" (BDAG 596b). Αὐτόν refers to the one on whom the stone falls. The verse likely alludes to Dan 2:34, 44.

21:45 Ἀκούσαντες (nom. pl. masc. of aor. act. ptc. of ἀκούω) is temp. (most EVV). Αὐτοῦ refers to Jesus and is subj. gen.: "the parable that he told." Ἔγνωσαν 3rd pl. 2nd aor. act. indic. of γινώσκω. Ὅτι marks the content of their knowledge. Λέγει is pres. retained in indir. discourse (W 537–38).

21:46 Ζητοῦντες (nom. pl. masc. of pres. act. ptc. of ζητέω) is concessive (most EVV): "Although they were seeking. . . ." Αὐτόν refers to Jesus and is dir. obj. of the inf. κρατῆσαι (aor. act. inf. [complementary] of κρατέω, "arrest"). Ἐφοβήθησαν 3rd pl. aor. pass. indic. of φοβέω, "fear, be afraid of" (pass.). Ἐπεί marks the reason (BDAG 360b–c 2) for their fear: "since, because." The prep. phrase εἰς προφήτην serves as a substitute for the pred. acc. (BDAG 288d–93c 8.b.). Εἶχον (3rd pl. impf. act. indic. of ἔχω, "consider . . . to be . . ." [BDAG 420a–22d 6]) is prog.

FOR FURTHER STUDY

115. The Parable of the Wicked Tenants

Evans, C. A. "Jesus's Parable of the Tenant Farmers in Light of Lease Agreements in Antiquity." *Journal for the Study of the Pseudepigrapha* 14 (1996): 65–83.

Hester, J. D. "Socio-Rhetorical Criticism and the Parable of the Tenants." *JSNT* 45 (1992): 27–57.

Horne, E. H. "The Parable of the Tenants as Indictment." *JSNT* 71 (1998): 111–16.

Newell, J. E., and R. R. Newell. "The Parable of the Wicked Tenants." *NovT* 14 (1972): 226–37.

Quarles, C. L. "The Use of the Gospel of Thomas in the Research on the Historical Jesus of John Dominic Crossan." *CBQ* 69 (2007): 517–36.

Snodgrass, K. *The Parable of the Wicked Tenants.* Tübingen: Mohr Siebeck, 1983.

————. "Recent Research on the Parable of the Wicked Tenants: An Assessment." *BBR* 8 (1998): 187–216.

Weren, W. J. C. "The Use of Isaiah 5,1–7 in the Parable of the Tenants (Mark 12,1–12; Matthew 21,33–46)." *Bib* 79 (1998): 1–26.

HOMILETICAL SUGGESTIONS

The Cost of Rejecting Jesus (21:33–46)

1. Israel covenanted with God to produce the fruits of righteousness
2. Israel refused to offer God the righteousness that they had promised
3. God sent prophets to call Israel to repentance
4. Israel persecuted and martyred God's prophets
5. God sent his Son Jesus to Israel
6. Israel rejected and killed Jesus
7. God would severely punish Israel for its rejection of Jesus

8. God would transfer the blessings of Israel to a new chosen people, the disciples of Jesus

7. *The Parable of the Wedding Feast (22:1–14)*

22:1 Ἀποκριθείς (nom. sg. masc. of aor. pass. ptc. of dep. ἀποκρίνομαι) is pleonastic. Πάλιν marks repetition and reminds readers that Jesus had just told other parables (21:28–32, 33–44). Ἐν παραβολαῖς is instr.: "he spoke through parables." Αὐτοῖς refers to the chief priests and Pharisees (21:43). Λέγων is pleonastic.

22:2 Ὡμοιώθη 3rd sg. aor. pass. indic. of ὁμοιόω, "be like." The use of the aor. tense may indicate that the parable describes pres. aspects of the kingdom (Carson *NTS* 277–82). Ἡ βασιλεία τῶν οὐρανῶν, 3:2. The dat. of dir. obj. ἀνθρώπῳ marks the standard of comp. Βασιλεῖ is dat. of simple appos.: "a human being, a king." The cstr. refers to a human king who in the parable represents the heavenly King. Ὅστις functions as a substitute for the simple rel. pron. (BDAG 729d–30b 3). Ἐποίησεν 3rd sg. aor. act. indic. of ποιέω, "prepare" (BDAG 839b–42a 2.f.). Nolland notes that the vb. is causative (885). Γάμος, -ου, ὁ, "wedding celebration." The sg. and pl. of this noun were often used interchangeably. Although BDAG claims that Josephus (*Ant.* 14 §§467–68) used the pl. form for the wedding feast and the sg. for the wedding ceremony (188c–89a 1), the distinction was not preserved elsewhere in Josephus and is doubtful even in this example. Τῷ υἱῷ is dat. of indir. obj. or advantage. Αὐτοῦ refers to the king and is a gen. of relationship.

22:3 Ἀπέστειλεν 3rd sg. aor. act. indic. of ἀποστέλλω. Καλέσαι (aor. act. inf. of καλέω) is a complementary inf. The art. and independent ptc. κεκλημένους (acc. pl. masc. of pf. pass. ptc. of καλέω) is subst. D&A note that the pf. pass. ptc. of καλέω is a technical term for the people of God in other contexts (3.199). Thus the form may hint that those who reject the invitation represent apostate Israel. With καλέω, the εἰς phrase identifies the event to which one is invited. Τοὺς γάμους, 22:2. Ἤθελον (3rd pl. impf. act. indic. of θέλω) is prog. and implies sustained unwillingness to a prolonged or multiple appeals (Hagner suggests the impf. is iter. in a sim. understanding [2.628]). Ἐλθεῖν (2nd aor. act. inf. of dep. ἔρχομαι) is complementary.

22:4 Πάλιν ἀπέστειλεν ἄλλους δούλους, 21:36. Λέγων is attendant circumstance (NIV; CSB) or means. Εἴπατε (2nd pl. 2nd aor. act. impv. of λέγω), see 4:3. Κεκλημένοις (dat. pl. masc. of pf. pass. ptc. of καλέω) is subst. Ἰδού calls attention to the announcement. Ἄριστον, -οῦ, τό, "(noon) meal" (BDAG 131c 2). Μου is gen. of source. Ἡτοίμακα (1st sg. pf. act. indic. of ἑτοιμάζω, "prepare") is extensive: "I have finished preparing my meal." Ταῦρος, -ου, ὁ, "bull." Μου is poss. Σιτιστός, -ή, -όν, "fattened." The subst. adj. means "fattened cattle" (BDAG 925b). Τεθυμένα (nom. pl. neut. of pf. pass. ptc. of θύω, "kill, slaughter") is prob. adj. with an implied copulative. Thus this clause mirrors the next one. Πάντα is subst.: "everything." Ἕτοιμος, -η, -ον, "ready, prepared." Δεῦτε is an exhortatory particle: "Come on!" Γάμους, 22:2.

22:5 The def. art. οἱ functions as a pers. pron.: "they." Δέ is prob. adversative. The generous invitation did not receive the expected response. Ἀμελήσαντες (nom. pl. masc. of aor. act. ptc. of ἀμελέω, "neglect, ignore") is attendant circumstance (BDAG 52c).

Ἀπῆλθον 3rd pl. 2nd aor. act. indic. of dep. ἀπέρχομαι, "go away." In combination with the rel. pron. ὅς, the μὲν . . . δέ cstr. marks items in a series (BDAG 629d–630c 1.c.): "one went to his own field; another went to his business." Ἀγρός, -οῦ, ὁ, "field." The poss. adj. ἴδιον clarifies that the invited guest ignores the summons in order to work his own land, not the land of the king. Sometimes ἴδιος is a simple substitute for αὐτοῦ (BDF §286). Ἐμπορία, -ας, ἡ, "business." Αὐτοῦ is poss.

22:6 Δέ marks a new development in the narrative. The subst. adj. λοιποί refers to the rest of the invitees who remained after the others departed (BDAG 602b–3a 2.b.). Κρατήσαντες (nom. pl. masc. of aor. act. ptc. of κρατέω, "seize") is prob. attendant circumstance (most EVV). Ὕβρισαν 3rd pl. aor. act. indic. of ὑβρίζω, "mistreat, abuse." Ἀπέκτειναν 3rd pl. aor. act. indic. of ἀποκτείνω, "kill."

22:7 Δέ marks a new development in the narrative. Ὠργίσθη 3rd sg. aor. pass. indic. of ὀργίζω, "be angry" (pass.). Πέμψας (nom. sg. masc. of aor. act. ptc. of πέμπω, "send") is attendant circumstance (most EVV). Στράτευμα, -ατος, τό, "army." Ἀπώλεσεν 3rd sg. aor. act. indic. of ἀπόλλυμι, "destroy." Φονεύς, -έως, ὁ, "murderer." The remote dem. adj. ἐκείνους expresses contempt (BDAG 301d–2c a.γ.). Αὐτῶν refers to the murderers and is poss. referring to the city in which they resided. Ἐνέπρησεν 3rd sg. aor. act. indic. of ἐμπίμπρημι, "set on fire, burn."

22:8 Τότε, "after that." Λέγει is historical pres. Μὲν . . . δέ establishes a stark contrast. Γάμος, 22:2. Ἕτοιμος, 22:4. The art. and independent ptc. κεκλημένοι (nom. pl. masc. of pf. pass. ptc. of καλέω, "invite") is subst. Ἦσαν 3rd pl. impf. indic. of εἰμί. Ἄξιος, -ία, -ον, "worthy, fit, deserving."

22:9 The particle οὖν draws an inference from the preceding statement. Since the first invitees were unworthy, others will be invited. Πορεύεσθε 2nd pl. pres. mid. impv. of dep. πορεύομαι, "travel." The use of the pres. tense is prob. not significant, since vbs. of movement and travel strongly prefer the pres. tense in nonindicative forms. Διέξοδος, -ου, ἡ, "intersection, exit ways (from the city)." The combination of the correlative ὅσους with the particle of contingency ἐάν generalizes the sense and includes any person and any number of persons: "all those who." Εὕρητε 2nd pl. 2nd aor. act. subjunc. of εὑρίσκω. Καλέσατε (2nd pl. aor. act. impv. of καλέω) prob. expresses urgency. Γάμους, 22:2.

22:10 Ἐξελθόντες (nom. pl. masc. of 2nd aor. act. ptc. of dep. ἐξέρχομαι) is prob. attendant circumstance (most EVV). The remote dem. adj. ἐκεῖνοι distinguishes these slaves from the group first sent out. Συνήγαγον 3rd pl. 2nd aor. act. indic. of συνάγω, "gather." Εὗρον 3rd pl. 2nd aor. act. indic. of εὑρίσκω. The τε καί cstr. (BDAG 993b–d 2.c.a.) closely relates opposites: "not only . . . but also." Πονηρούς and ἀγαθούς are subst. even though they are anar. Ἐπλήσθη 3rd sg. aor. pass. indic. of πίμπλημι, "fill." Γάμος, 22:2. Here the noun may refer to the venue for the wedding ("wedding hall") rather than the wedding itself. Several early scribes assumed this and substituted the term νυμφῶν for clarification. See Metzger 47. Ἀνακειμένων (gen. pl. masc. of pres. mid. ptc. of dep. ἀνάκειμαι, "recline [at the table], dine") is subst. and gen. of content, identifying that which fills the wedding banquet.

22:11 Εἰσελθών (nom. sg. masc. of 2nd aor. act. ptc. of dep. εἰσέρχομαι) is temp. (most EVV). Θεάσασθαι (aor. mid. inf. of dep. θεάομαι, "see" [BDAG 445c–46a 2]) expresses purpose. Ἀνακειμένους (acc. pl. masc. of pres. mid. ptc. of dep. ἀνάκειμαι, 22:10) is subst. Εἶδεν 3rd sg. 2nd aor. act. indic. of ὁράω. Ἐνδεδυμένον (acc. sg. masc. of pf. mid. ptc. of ἐνδύω, "wear" [mid.]) is pred.: "a man who was not wearing." Ἔνδυμα, -ατος, τό, "garment, clothes." Γάμου (22:2) is attrib.: "wedding garments."

22:12 Καί is resultative: "so." Λέγει is historical pres. Ἑταῖρος, -ου, ὁ, "friend," form of polite address to someone whose name is not known by the speaker (BDAG 398c–d). The interr. particle πῶς questions the means by which something was accomplished. Εἰσῆλθες 2nd sg. 2nd aor. act. indic. of dep. εἰσέρχομαι. Ἔχων (nom. sg. masc. of pres. act. ptc. of ἔχω) is concessive: "even though you do not have." Ἔνδυμα γάμου, 22:11. The def. art. ὁ functions as a rel. pron. Δέ is prob. adversative, since normally one would be obligated to reply to a query from the king. Ἐφιμώθη 3rd sg. aor. pass. indic. of φιμόω, "be silent" (pass.).

22:13 Τότε, "(immediately) after that." Δήσαντες (nom. pl. masc. of aor. act. ptc. of δέω, "bind, tie up") is attendant circumstance and assumes the force of the impv. Αὐτοῦ is partitive. Ἐκβάλετε 2nd pl. 2nd aor. act. impv. of ἐκβάλλω, "throw out." Ἐξώτερος, -α, -ον, "outside," is a comp. adj. used for the superl. (BDAG 355a–b 2): "outermost, farthest out." It is in the 2nd attrib. position. Ἔσται (3rd sg. fut. indic. of εἰμί) is predictive, and this indicates that the sentence by the king represents eschatological judgment. Ὁ κλαυθμὸς καὶ ὁ βρυγμὸς τῶν ὀδόντων, 8:12.

22:14 Γάρ identifies the reason for the exclusion and punishment of the man improperly attired. Εἰσίν 3rd pl. pres. indic. of εἰμί, is gnomic. Κλητός, -ή, -όν, "called, invited." Δέ is clearly adversative since it contrasts the characteristics of the many and the few, opposite concepts. Ἐκλεκτός, -ή, -όν, "chosen." The adj. πολλοί and ὀλίγοι are subst. Κλητοί and ἐκλεκτοί are pred. adj.

FOR FURTHER STUDY

116. Introduction to Parables

Carson, D. A. "The Homoios Word-Group as Introduction to Some Matthean Parables." *NTS* 31 (1985): 277–82.

117. The Parable of the Wedding Feast

Ballard, P. H. "Reasons for Refusing the Great Supper." *JTS* 23 (1972): 341–50.

Lemcio, E. E. "The Parables of the Great Supper and the Wedding Feast: History, Redaction and Canon." *Horizons in Biblical Theology* 8 (1986): 1–26.

Meyer, B. F. "Many (= All) Are Called, but Few (= Not All) Are Chosen." *NTS* 36 (1990): 89–97.

Sim, D. C. "The Man Without the Wedding Garment (Matthew 22:11–13)." *Heythrop Journal* 31 (1990): 165–78.

HOMILETICAL SUGGESTIONS

The Great Messianic Feast (22:1–14)

1. God will honor his Son Jesus with a great messianic feast (Rev 19:9)
2. God invited many Israelites to participate in this feast, but they refused because of worldly distractions
3. Some even rejected and murdered God's servants, the prophets, whom he sent to call sinners to repentance
4. God will harshly punish those who reject his gracious invitation through the destruction of Jerusalem and its inhabitants by the Roman army
5. God will offer salvation to others, including notorious sinners
6. Participation in the great messianic feast requires the "garment" of a transformed life
7. Those whose lives are not changed by Jesus will suffer eternal punishment

8. Paying Taxes to Caesar (22:15–22)

22:15 Τότε, "after that." Πορευθέντες (nom. pl. masc. of aor. pass. ptc. of dep. πορεύομαι) is attendant circumstance (most EVV). Συμβούλιον, -ου, τό, "council." Ἔλαβον 3rd pl. 2nd aor. act. indic. of λαμβάνω. The combination of the vb. λαμβάνω with συμβούλιον is synonymous with συμβουλεύω and is a phraseological Latinism mng. "form a plan, plot" (equivalent to the Latin *consilium capere*; BDAG 957b–c 3; BDF §5 3.b.). Ὅπως (with the subjunc.) serves as a conj. marking the purpose for an event. Παγιδεύσωσιν 3rd pl. aor. act. subjunc. of παγιδεύω, "entrap" (BDAG 747a–b). Ἐν (w. λόγῳ) marks the instr. Λόγῳ is likely a ref. to Jesus's own statement (most EVV), although Nolland argues it refers to the words of the Pharisees. Hagner (2.633) suggests that λόγος here means "something" and the prep. phrase means "on some matter."

22:16 Καί may be resultative: "and so." Ἀποστέλλουσιν is historical pres. Μετά with the gen. expresses accompaniment: "together with." The prep. prob. implies collaboration between the Pharisees and Herodians in the conspiracy against Jesus (BDAG 636b–38b 2.d.). Ἡρῳδιανοί, -ῶν, οἱ, "supporters of the Herodian dynasty." Λέγοντες (nom. pl. masc. of pres. act. ptc. of λέγω) is either attendant circumstance (most EVV) or a *purpose ptc.: "They sent their disciples . . . to say." Διδάσκαλε is voc. of simple address. Ἀληθής, -ές, ("true") means "honest, truthful." Εἶ 2nd sg. pres. indic. of εἰμί. Τοῦ θεοῦ is gen. of source ("way [of life] demanded by God;" H 2.635) or destination ("the way to God"). The phrase ἐν ἀληθείᾳ (lit. "in/with truth") means "truly" (BDAG 42b–43a 3). Διδάσκεις (2nd sg. pres. act. indic. of διδάσκω) and μέλει (3rd sg. pres. act. indic. of μέλω, "it is a concern" [impers.]) are prob. customary pres. Σοι is prob. ethical dat. Περὶ οὐδενός identifies the persons who are the focus of concern (or lack of it). The cstr. may best be rendered in Eng.: "You are not concerned about anyone." However, the statement does not deny Jesus's compassion for others but merely concern for whether they will affirm his views. Since denial of Jesus's partiality clarifies the statement "you are not concerned about anyone," apparently in order to avoid misinterpretation, γάρ is prob. explanatory

(BDAG 189a–90a 2; N 895) rather than causal. Βλέπεις is customary pres. Βλέπω εἰς πρόσωπον ("look into the face") refers to reading someone's facial expressions in order to gauge their emotional reaction. The phrase refers to tailoring one's speech in order to gain approval from others (BDAG 178d–79c 4). Most EVV tr. the cstr. as if it were equivalent to λαμβάνω πρόσωπον, an idiom referring to showing partiality or favoritism (BDAG 887c–88c 1.b.α.). Ἀνθρώπων is partitive gen.

22:17 Εἰπέ (2nd sg. 2nd aor. act. impv. of λέγω), see 4:3. Οὖν is inferential: "therefore (given your lack of concern for others' opinion/approval)." Τί is interr. pron.: "what?" Σοι is prob. ethical dat. Δοκεῖ 3rd sg. pres. act. indic. of δοκέω, "seem" (impers.) (BDAG 254c–55c 2.a.α.). The cstr. means "What does it seem to you?" or "What do you think?" Ἔξεστιν 3rd sg. pres. indic. of ἔξειμι, "it is right, proper." Δοῦναι (aor. act. inf. of δίδωμι) is complementary. Κῆνσος, -ου, ὁ, "tax." Καῖσαρ, -αρος, ὁ, "(Roman) emperor." The disjunctive particle ἤ marks opposite alternatives.

22:18 Δέ is prob. adversative (most EVV). Γνούς (nom. sg. masc. of 2nd aor. act. ptc. of γινώσκω) is prob. causal (LEB). Πονηρία, -ας, ἡ, "wickedness, sinfulness." Αὐτῶν is subj. gen. and refers to the disciples of the Pharisees and the Herodians. Τί is interr. pron.: "why?" Πειράζετε 2nd pl. pres. act. indic. of πειράζω, "test" (BDAG 792d–93d 3). The pres. tense may be prog. ("Why do you keep trying to entrap me?") since Matthew records previous attempts by the Jewish leaders to entrap Jesus (16:1; 19:3; 21:23–27). Ὑποκριταί is prob. an example of the use of the bare voc. without ὦ in emphatic or emotional address (W 68 n. 9). Ὑποκριτής, -οῦ, ὁ, "hypocrite, pretender."

22:19 Ἐπιδείξατε (2nd pl. aor. act. impv. of ἐπιδείκνυμι, "show") prob. expresses urgency. Νόμισμα, -ατος, τό, "coin (officially issued by the state)." Τοῦ κήνσου (22:17) is prob. gen. of destination: "coin used to pay the tax." The def. art. οἱ functions as a pers. pron. Προσήνεγκαν 3rd pl. 2nd aor. act. indic. of προσφέρω, "bring something to someone." Δηνάριον, -ου, τό, "denarius."

22:20 Λέγει is historical pres. The gen. interr. pron. τίνος ("whose") and the dem. pron. αὕτη modify both εἰκών and ἐπιγραφή. With εἰκών, -όνος, ἡ, "portrait." Ἐπιγραφή, "legend (inscription on a coin)."

22:21 Λέγουσιν is historical pres. Καίσαρος, 22:17. Τότε means "immediately after that." Λέγει is historical pres. Ἀπόδοτε (2nd pl. aor. act. impv. of ἀποδίδωμι, "pay [back]") expresses urgency. Οὖν is inferential. The picture and legend on the coin confirmed that the coin belonged to the emperor. The def. art. τά with the gen. Καίσαρος and τοῦ θεοῦ serves as a substantiver and the gen. is poss.: "the things that belong to Caesar/God." Καίσαρι and τῷ θεῷ are dat. of indir. obj.

22:22 Ἀκούσαντες (nom. pl. masc. of aor. act. ptc. of ἀκούω) is prob. temp. (most EVV): "When they heard." Ἐθαύμασαν 3rd pl. aor. act. indic. of θαυμάζω, "marvel." Ἀφέντες (nom. pl. masc. of aor. act. ptc. of ἀφίημι) is attendant circumstance (most EVV). Ἀπῆλθαν 3rd pl. 2nd aor. act. indic. of dep. ἀπέρχομαι, "go away, depart."

FOR FURTHER STUDY

118. Payment of Roman Taxes

Bruce, F. F. "Render to Caesar." Pages 249–63 in *Jesus and the Politics of His Day*. Edited by E. Bammel and C. F. D. Moule. Cambridge: Cambridge University Press, 1984.

Hart, H. J. "The Coin of 'Render unto Caesar' (a Note on Some Aspects of Mk 12:13–17; Matt 22:15–22; Lk 20:20–26)." Pages 241–48 in *Jesus and the Politics of His Day*. Edited by E. Bammel and C. F. D. Moule. Cambridge: Cambridge University Press, 1984.

Meier, J. P. "The Historical Jesus and the Historical Herodians." *JBL* 119 (2000): 740–46.

Owen-Ball, D. T. "Rabbinic Rhetoric and the Tribute Passage (Mt 22:15–22, Mk 12:13–17, Lk 20:20–26)." *NovT* 35 (1993): 1–14.

HOMILETICAL SUGGESTIONS

Duties to God and Government (22:15–22)

1. Jesus challenged the hypocrisy of the Pharisees:
   a. They pretended to affirm Jesus's truthfulness
   b. They pretended to accept the accuracy of Jesus's teaching
   c. They pretended to affirm Jesus's refusal to compromise to gain approval from others
   d. Yet they sought to trap him and manipulate their enemies to harm him
2. Jesus affirmed the duty to pay taxes to the emperor
3. Jesus taught the duty to submit one's life to the Creator

9. A Question Regarding Resurrection (22:23–33)

22:23 Ἐν marks a period of time during which an event occurred (BDAG 326c–30b 10.b.). The remote dem. pron. ἐκείνῃ is anaphoric and refers to the day during which the event recorded in the previous pericope occurred. Προσῆλθον 3rd pl. 2nd aor. act. indic. of dep. προσέρχομαι. Σαδδουκαῖος, -ου, ὁ, "Sadducee." See Metzger 48. Λέγοντες (nom. pl. masc. of pres. act. ptc. of λέγω) is attrib.: "who say. . . ." Εἶναι (pres. inf. of εἰμί) is inf. of indir. discourse (W 603–5). Ἀνάστασις, -εως, ἡ, "resurrection." Ἐπηρώτησαν 3rd pl. aor. act. indic. of ἐπερωτάω, "question."

22:24 Λέγοντες is pleonastic. Διδάσκαλε is voc. of simple address. The quotation from Moses conflates Deuteronomy 25:5 and Genesis 38:8 but is significantly different from the LXX. The introduction "Moses said" rather than "Moses wrote" may hint that the quotation is a loose paraphrase. See Beale and Carson 75a–77c. Ἐάν with the subjunc. (ἀποθάνῃ 3rd sg. aor. act. subjunc. of ἀποθνῄσκω, "die") marks the prot. of a third-class cond. sentence that makes no assumption about the fulfillment of the prot. Ἔχων expresses manner (in the broader sense of a state of the subj.): "without having children." The use of the pl. τέκνα is odd since the OT prescribed levirate marriage only for those who lacked even a single child. Ἐπιγαμβρεύσει (3rd sg. fut. act. indic. of ἐπιγαμβρεύω, "marry") and ἀναστήσει (3rd sg. fut. act. indic. of ἀνίστημι, "raise up") are impv. fut. France shows that ἐπιγαμβρεύω is not the normal vb. for marriage

but means specifically "fulfill the duty of an in-law" and thus is an apt term for the obligation of levirate marriage (835). The combination of ἀνίστημι and σπέρμα is an idiom mng. "conceive, procreate." Τῷ ἀδελφῷ is dat. of advantage: "for his brother."
22:25 Ἦσαν 3rd pl. impf. indic. of εἰμί. Παρά with the dat. (ἡμῖν) is prob. loc. and means "in our city" (BDAG 756b–58b B.1.b.β.). Ὁ πρῶτος is subst.: "the first brother." Γήμας (nom. sg. masc. of aor. act. ptc. of γαμέω, "marry") is attendant circumstance (most EVV) or *temp. (LEB): "(soon) after he married." Ἐτελεύτησεν 3rd sg. aor. act. indic. of τελευτάω, "die." Ἔχων (nom. sg. masc. of pres. act. ptc. of ἔχω) is causal: "since he did not have seed (offspring)." The vb. ἔχω refers to being in a close relationship with someone (BDAG 420a–22d 2.a.). Ἀφῆκεν 3rd sg. aor. act. indic. of ἀφίημι, "leave." Here the vb. means to leave behind and in the process entrust to another.
22:26 This sentence is heavily truncated. The adv. ὁμοίως signals the implied repetition of the entire preceding sentence except that ὁ δεύτερος καὶ ὁ τρίτος is substituted for ὁ πρῶτος. Ἕως serves as a marker of order in a series ("up to;" BDAG 422d–24c 4). The use of the pl. def. art. (τῶν) and the cardinal number ἑπτά indicates all seven brothers in succession shared the first brother's fate (CSB; NLT).
22:27 The adj. ὕστερον is used as a superl. (W 299–300) and the neut. serves as a temp. adv.: "last." Πάντων is partitive gen.: "last of all = finally." Ἀπέθανεν 3rd sg. 2nd aor. act. indic. of ἀποθνήσκω.
22:28 Ἐν marks a point in time: "at the resurrection." The def. art. τῇ modifying ἀναστάσει (22:23) is well-known and refers to the final general resurrection. Οὖν shows that the question explores an inference from the scenario just described. The interr. pron. τίνος is gen. of relationship: "whose?" Τῶν ἑπτά is partitive. Ἔσται is predictive and refers to the eschatological state. Πάντες is subst.: "All (of the brothers)." Γάρ is causal: "since." Ἔσχον 3rd pl. 2nd aor. act. indic. of ἔχω, "have in close relationship" (BDAG 420a–22d 2.a.). Hagner argues that the vb. indicates that the marriage had been consummated through a sexual act (2.641; cf. 1 Cor 5:1).
22:29 Ἀποκριθείς (nom. sg. masc. of aor. pass. ptc. of dep. ἀποκρίνομαι) is pleonastic. Πλανᾶσθε 2nd pl. pres. pass. indic. of πλανάω, "deceive." Εἰδότες (nom. pl. mac. of pf. [for aor.] act. ptc. of οἶδα) is causal (most EVV). The def. art. τάς modifying γραφάς is well-known or *par excellence*. Μηδέ is a neg. disjunctive: "nor." Τοῦ θεοῦ is gen. of poss. and refers to the power that belongs to God and that he exercises.
22:30 Γάρ is causal. Ἐν τῇ ἀναστάσει, 22:28. Οὔτε . . . οὔτε, "neither, nor" (BDAG 740a–b). Γαμοῦσιν (3rd pl. pres. act. indic. of γαμέω, "marry") and γαμίζονται (3rd pl. pres. pass. indic. of γαμίζω, "be given in marriage" [pass.]) are gnomic pres. Hagner translates the pres. tense vbs. as fut. tense since he recognizes that ἐν τῇ ἀναστάσει is temp. and refers to the general resurrection (2.638). France objects that the phrase "at the resurrection" refers to a state rather than a time so that it is equivalent to "in heaven." However, this explanation is not satisfactory. The tension between the temp. phrase and the pres. tense is immediately resolved when the vbs. are recognized as gnomic. The act. vb. likely refers to men and the pass. vb. to women (D&A 3.227; France 839). Ἀλλά is adversative. Ὡς is comp. Εἰσίν is gnomic. See Metzger 48.

22:31 Περί marks the topic of concern. Ἀναστάσεως, 22:31. Τῶν νεκρῶν is obj. gen. Οὐκ introduces a question that assumes a positive response: "Haven't you read?" Ἀνέγνωτε 2nd pl. 2nd aor. act. indic. of ἀναγινώσκω, "read." The art. ptc. ῥηθέν (acc. sg. neut. of aor. pass. ptc. of λέγω) is subst. and divine pass. (France 840). Ὑμῖν is dat. of indir. obj. and confirms that the divinely inspired Scriptures were intended to speak to the contemporary audience in addition to the orig. audience (D&A 3.230). Ὑπό with the gen. (τοῦ θεοῦ) expresses ultimate agency, confirms that the ptc. is a divine pass., and states that God is the ultimate author of the Pentateuch. Λέγοντος is pleonastic and introduces a quotation of Exod 3:6.

22:32 See Beale and Carson 77c–80a. The quotation is identical to the LXX except for the omission of ὁ θεὸς τοῦ πατρός σου and the addition of the def. art. before each occurrence of θεός. The omission might be theologically motivated, an intentional avoidance of the suggestion that the Pharisees were the seed of Abraham. One of the themes of this Gospel is that Jesus is the true Son of Abraham, the fulfillment of the Abrahamic covenant, and founder of the true Israel. The use of the pres. tense εἰμί is apparently critical to Jesus's argument. If the patriarchs had ceased to exist (as the annihilationist view of the Sadducees assumed), the impf. tense of the vb. would be expected ("I was the God of . . ."). See D&A 3.231–32; H 2.642. The def. art. modifying θεός in each occurrence is prob. monadic and implies monotheism. The adj. νεκρῶν and the ptc. ζώντων (gen. pl. masc. of pres. act. ptc. of ζάω) are subst. The gen. subst. modifying θέος may be regarded as expressing subord. or poss. but more likely means "worshipped by." Thus the God of the living does not mean that God is possessed by the living or rules over the living but that the living worship him. The statement that he is not the God of the dead may recall texts like Psalm 6:5; 30:9; 88:10–12; 115:17. See Metzger 48.

22:33 Καί is resultative: "and so." Ἀκούσαντες (nom. pl. masc. of aor. act. ptc. of ἀκούω) is temp. (most EVV). Ἐξεπλήσσοντο (3rd pl. impf. pass. indic. of ἐκπλήσσω, "be amazed" [pass.]) is prob. prog. and indicates a sustained emotional response. Ἐπί with the dat. (τῇ διδαχῇ) expresses the basis or reason for their amazement (BDAG 363a–367c 6). Αὐτοῦ is subj. gen. and refers to Jesus.

FOR FURTHER STUDY

119. The Debate with Sadducees Regarding Resurrection

Bolt, P. "What Were the Sadducees Reading? An Enquiry into the Literary Background of Mark 12:18–23." *TynBul* 45 (1994): 369–94.

Meier, J. P. "The Debate on the Resurrection of the Dead: An Incident from the Ministry of the Historical Jesus." *JSNT* 77 (2000): 3–24.

Trick, B. R. "Death, Covenants, and the Proof of Resurrection in Mark 12:18–27." *NovT* 49 3 (2007): 232–56.

Viviano, B. "Sadducees, Angels, and Resurrection (Acts 23:8–9)." *JBL* 111 3 (1992): 496–98.

HOMILETICAL SUGGESTIONS

Jesus's Defense of the Resurrection (22:23–33)

1. The Sadducees attempted to disprove the resurrection by arguing that it would require polyandry in eternity
2. Jesus showed that the argument was based on fallacious assumptions about resurrection life
3. Jesus showed that the view of the Sadducees was based on a superficial reading of Scripture

10. The Greatest Commandment (22:34–40)

22:34 Δέ marks a new development in the narrative. Ἀκούσαντες (nom. pl. masc. of aor. act. ptc. of ἀκούω) is temp. (most EVV). Ὅτι is recitative. Ἐφίμωσεν 3rd sg. aor. act. indic. of φιμόω, "silence, make someone be silent." Τοὺς Σαδδουκαίους, 22:23. Συνήχθησαν 3rd pl. aor. pass. (with act. force) indic. of συνάγω, "gather together." Ἐπί with the acc. marks location (BDAG 363a–67c 1.c.β.). Αὐτό serves as the identical adj. mng. "the same" (BDAG 152c–54a 3.b.). The art. adj. is subst., so the prep. phrase means "at the same place."

22:35 Ἐπηρώτησεν 3rd sg. aor. act. indic. of ἐπερωτάω, "question, pose a question." Ἐξ αὐτῶν functions as a partitive gen. Νομικός, -ή, -όν, "legal expert (subst.)." Νομικός is appos. See Metzger 48–49. Πειράζων (nom. sg. masc. of pres. act. ptc. of πειράζω, "entrap") expresses purpose (most EVV).

22:36 Διδάσκαλε is voc. of simple address. The interr. pron. ποία ("of what kind") is used as a substitute for τίς ("which, what?"): "which commandment?" (BDAG 843d–44a 2; N 910 n. 104). Μεγάλη is a positive adj. used in place of the superl. (most EVV; D&A 3.240): "the greatest commandment." The def. art. τῷ modifying νόμῳ is prob. *par excellence* and refers to the law of God.

22:37 The def. art. ὁ functions as a pers. pron. Ἔφη 3rd sg. aor. (or impf.) act. indic. of φημί, "say." Ἀγαπήσεις (2nd sg. fut. act. indic. of ἀγαπάω) is impv. fut. Κύριον is anar., prob. because it serves as a substitute for the proper name Yahweh. The def. art. τόν modifying θεόν is monadic. Σου identifies the worshipper of the deity (22:32). Ἐν marks the instr. Σου is partitive gen. The quotation here differs from the LXX by using ἐν rather than ἐκ in each prep. phrase and by using διανοίᾳ instead of δυνάμεως. See Beale and Carson 80b–82a.

22:38 The near dem. pron. αὕτη refers to the commandment in the preceding verse. Μεγάλη is a positive adj. used as a superl. The superl. use is supported by the monadic use of the art.: "the greatest commandment." Πρώτη refers to first in importance rather than first in time (BDAG 893d–94a 2.a.α.). Καί may be epex. (D&A 3.243) since "greatest" and "first in importance" are practically synonymous.

22:39 After the use of the adj. πρώτη to express importance, δευτέρα (δεύτερος, -α, -ον, "second") naturally means "second greatest" or "second most important." Ὅμοιος, -οία, -οιον, "like, sim." Αὐτῇ is dat. of comp. Ἀγαπήσεις (2nd sg. fut. act. indic. of ἀγαπάω) is impv. Πλησίον is an adj. used subst.: "neighbor, fellow human being." Σου is gen. of relationship. Ὡς is comp.: "like, in the same way that." Σεαυτόν is the 2nd pers. refl. pron. "yourself." The comp. clause is elliptical and means "in the same way that you love yourself." The commandment is a verbatim quotation of Leviticus 19:18 (LXX). See Beale and Carson 82a–c.

22:40 In connection with the vb. κρέμαται (3rd sg. pres. mid. indic. of κρεμάννυμι, "hang, depend"), the loc. use of the prep. ἐν means "on." The near dem. pron. ταύταις points to the two commandments discussed in the previous two verses. The adj. ὅλος modifies both ὁ νόμος and οἱ προφῆται, which are viewed as a single entity as is shown by the use of the sg. vb. The "Law and the Prophets" refers to the Old Testament.

FOR FURTHER STUDY

120. The Greatest Commandment

Foster, P. "Why Did Matthew Get the Shema Wrong? A Study of Matthew 22:37." *JBL* 122 (2003): 309–33.

Hultgren, A. J. "The Double Commandment of Love in Mt 22:34–40: Its Sources and Compositions." *CBQ* 36 (1974): 373–78.

Martin, B. L. "Matthew on Christ and the Law." *TS* 44 (1983): 53–70.

Park, E. C. "A Soteriological Reading of the Great Commandment Pericope in Matthew 22:34–40." *BR* 54 (2009): 61–78.

HOMILETICAL SUGGESTIONS

The Illegal Behavior of the Legal Expert (22:34–40)

1. All-consuming love for God is the greatest of the commandments
2. Love for others that supplants concern for self is the second great commandment
3. Fulfilling the essence of the law is more important than being an expert in the law

11. The Messiah's Sonship (22:41–46)

22:41 Συνηγμένων (gen. pl. masc. of pf. pass. [w. act. force] ptc. of συνάγω, "gather") is gen. abs. and temp.: "after the Pharisees gathered together." Ἐπηρώτησεν 3rd sg. aor. act. indic. of ἐπερωτάω, "question." Αὐτούς refers to the Pharisees.

22:42 Λέγων is pleonastic and and introduces Jesus's question. Τί δοκεῖ with dat., 22:17. Περί with the gen. (τοῦ χριστοῦ) marks the topic of opinion. The def. art. with χριστοῦ is monadic. The interr. pron. τίνος is gen. of relationship: "whose son?" Λέγουσιν is historical pres. Τοῦ Δαυίδ is gen. of relationship. The bare gen. is short for "David's son."

22:43 Λέγει is historical pres. The interr. particle πῶς ("in what way?") may mean "in what sense?" (BDAG 900d–901c 1.a.). However, the context suggests that Jesus did not so much seek to clarify the sense in which the Messiah is David's Lord as to clarify the sense in which he is David's son. Thus most EVV tr. πῶς "how?" so that the question demonstrates that the Messiah is not merely David's son but his Lord also. Οὖν is inferential. Ἐν prob. means "under the influence of" (BDAG 832c–836d 4) and πνεύματι refers not to David's spirit but to the Holy Spirit who inspired the Davidic Psalm (cf. Mark 12:36). Καλεῖ (3rd sg. pres. act. indic. of καλέω) is prob. prog. Jesus viewed David as still speaking under the influence of the Spirit through the Scriptures. Αὐτὸν κύριον is dbl. acc. of object-complement. Λέγων may be pleonastic (CSB), *causal (NIV; NLT), temp., or express means.

22:44 This verse is a quotation of Ps 110:1, which agrees completely with the LXX except for the use of ὑποκάτω instead of ὑποπόδιον and the use of the def. art. before κύριος. See Beale and Carson 82c–84b. Matthew's anar. κύριος suggests that the noun is functioning as a proper noun and a substitute for the divine name Yahweh (N 916). The def. art. and the gen. of subord. μου indicate that κυρίῳ serves as a title expressing authority. Τῷ κυρίῳ μου refers to one to whom David relates as a servant or slave. Κάθου (2nd sg. pres. mid. impv. of dep. κάθημαι) is ingr.-prog.: "Take a seat and remain seated." The prep. ἐκ is loc. but in this case expresses merely position and not direction: "at" (BDAG 491b–492b 2). The gen. pl. neut. δεξιῶν (δεξιός, -ά, -όν, "right") is subst. and refers to one's right side. Μου is partitive gen. Ἕως with the particle of contingency ἄν and the subjunc. (θῶ 1st sg. aor. act. subjunc. of τίθημι, "put, place") normally marks the termination of the action of the main clause. In this context, it appears to identify the goal at which the action of the main clause will culminate. The subjection of the Messiah's enemies does not bring an end to his enthronement but is the culmination of the enthronement. Ἐχθρός, -ά, -όν, "enemy (subst.)." Σου is prob. a gen. of relationship although it refers to a hostile relationship and expresses no family connection. Ὑποκάτω is an adv. used as a prep. with the gen.: "under." Σου (modifying ποδῶν) is partitive gen.

22:45 Εἰ with the indic. (καλεῖ) marks the prot. of a first-class cond. sentence that assumes the fulfillment of the prot. for the sake of argument. Οὖν is inferential and indicates that the question is drawn from the preceding statement (Ps 110:1). Αὐτὸν κύριον is dbl. acc. of object-complement. Πῶς ("how, in what way?") here means "in what sense?" (22:43). Αὐτοῦ is gen. of relationship.

22:46 Καί is prob. resultative. Ἐδύνατο (3rd sg. impf. mid. indic. of dep. δύναμαι) is prob. prog. Ἀποκριθῆναι (aor. pass. inf. of dep. ἀποκρίνομαι) is complementary. Ἐτόλμησεν 3rd sg. aor. act. indic. of τολμάω, "dare to." Τις is indef. pron.: "anyone." The ἀπό phrase marks the beginning of a time period. The dem. pron. ἐκείνης points to the specific day on which the preceding dialogue occurred. Ἐπερωτῆσαι (aor. act. inf. of ἐπερωτάω) is a complementary inf. The combination of οὐδὲ . . . οὐκέτι means "nor any longer" or "never . . . again" (BDAG 736b–737c 1).

FOR FURTHER STUDY

121. The Messiah as Son of David and Son of God

Bateman, H. W., IV. "Psalm 110:1 and the New Testament." *BSac* 149 (1992): 438–53.
Callan, T. "Psalm 110:1 and the Origin of the Expectation That Jesus Will Come Again." *CBQ* 44 (1982): 622–36.
Davis, B. C. "Is Psalm 110 a Messianic Psalm?" *BSac* 157 (2000): 160–73.

Kingsbury, J. D. "The Title 'Son of David' in Matthew's Gospel." *JBL* 95 (1976): 591–602.

Loader, W. R. G. "Christ at the Right Hand: Ps 110:1 in the New Testament." *NTS* 24 (1978): 199–217.

HOMILETICAL SUGGESTIONS

The Identity of the Messiah (22:41–46)

1. The Messiah is David's descendant
2. The Messiah is David's Lord

B. THE REBUKE OF THE PHARISEES AND ABANDONMENT
OF THE TEMPLE (23:1–39)

1. Jesus's Denunciation of the Scribes and Pharisees (23:1–7)

23:1 Τότε prob. signals a transition in the narrative and indicates that Jesus addressed the crowds and disciples soon after his dialogue with the Pharisees, perhaps on the same occasion. Ἐλάλησεν 3rd sg. aor. act. indic. of λαλέω.

23:2 Λέγων is pleonastic. Τῆς Μωϋσέως is prob. poss. The seat or chair of Moses prob. referred to the place where Moses sat when he received the law (the vb. tr. "stayed" in Deuteronomy 9:9 may mean "sat"). A replica of this seat may have been prominent in synagogues of the time. Καθέδρα, -ας, ἡ, "seat, chair." Ἐκάθισαν (3rd pl. aor. act. indic. of καθίζω, "sit") is gnomic. The use of the def. art. with Φαρισαῖοι shows that the categories "scribes" and "Pharisees" are not to be collapsed.

23:3 Πάντα is subst.: "everything." Οὖν indicates that the obligation to obey the scribes and Pharisees is an inference drawn from their position as Moses's representatives. The correlative ὅσα with the particle of contingency ἐάν and the subjunc. Εἴπωσιν (3rd pl. aor. act. subjunc. of λέγω) makes the expression more general and inclusive. Ποιήσατε (2nd pl. aor. act. impv. of ποιέω) may express urgency, but prob. expresses a simple command, since the next impv. (τηρεῖτε 2nd pl. pres. act. impv. of τηρέω, "fulfill, keep") is marked by a shift to the pres. tense. On the other hand, since τηρέω means "persist in obedience" (BDAG 1002a–d 3), the prog. nature of the pres. tense better suits the mng. of the lexeme. Κατά with the acc. (τὰ ἔργα) is used as a periphrasis to express similarity (BDAG 511a–13d 5.b.α.). Δέ is clearly adversative. Αὐτῶν is subj. gen. and refers to the scribes and Pharisees. Μή with the pres. impv. (ποιεῖτε) expresses a general prohibition rather than calling for the cessation of action (W 724–25). Γάρ is causal. Λέγουσιν and ποιοῦσιν (3rd pl. pres. act. indic. of λέγω and ποιέω respectively). The pres. tenses are prob. customary (W 521–22).

23:4 Δεσμεύουσιν (3rd pl. pres. act. indic. of δεσμεύω, "tie up [in a bundle]") is customary pres. Δέ introduces the next development in the discourse. Φορτίον, -ου, τό, "load, burden." Βαρύς, -εῖα, -ύ, "heavy, burdensome." Δυσβάστακτος, -ον, "difficult to carry." See Metzger 49. Ἐπιτιθέασιν (3rd pl. pres. act. indic. of ἐπιτίθημι, "put, place upon") is customary pres. Ὦμος, -ου, ὁ, "shoulder." The def. art. τῶν is generic. Ἀνθρώπων is partitive gen. Αὐτοί is emphatic. Δέ is adversative. Δάκτυλος, -ου, ὁ, "finger." The dat. δακτύλῳ is instr.: "with their finger." Αὐτῶν is partitive gen. Θέλουσιν (3rd pl. pres. act. indic. of θέλω) is customary pres. Κινῆσαι (aor. act. inf. of κινέω, "move, *remove"). Αὐτά refers to the heavy burdens.

23:5 Δέ marks a slight shift in topic. Αὐτῶν is subj. gen. Ποιοῦσιν (3rd pl. pres. act. indic. of ποιέω) is customary pres. Πρός with the art. inf. θεαθῆναι (aor. pass. inf. of dep. θεάομαι, "see, look at") expresses purpose. The def. art. τοῖς (with ἀνθρώποις) is generic. The dat. case of ἀνθρώποις expresses pers. agency (W 163–66). Πλατύνουσιν (3rd pl. pres. act. indic. of πλατύνω, "enlarge." Γάρ is causal and introduces the evidence that confirms Jesus's accusation. Φυλακτήριον, -ου, τό, "phylactery (leather box containing Scripture passages and worn on the forearm and forehead)." Αὐτῶν is poss.

gen. Μεγαλύνουσιν (3rd pl. pres. act. indic. of μεγαλύνω, "enlarge, elongate") is customary pres. Κράσπεδον, -ου, τό, "tassel (on four corners of a male Israelite's outer garment per Num 15:37–41; Deut 22:12)."

23:6 Φιλοῦσιν (3rd pl. pres. act. indic. of φιλέω) is customary pres. Πρωτοκλισία, -ας, ἡ, "place of honor." The prep. ἐν may be temp. ("during the dinners") or *loc. ("at the dinners;" most EVV). Δεῖπνον, -ου, τό, "dinner, supper." Πρωτοκαθεδρία, -ας, ἡ, "seat of honor." Ἐν is loc.

23:7 Ἀσπασμός, -οῦ, ὁ, "greeting." Ἐν marks a location. Ἀγορά, -ᾶς, ἡ, "market place." Καλεῖσθαι (pres. pass. inf. of καλέω) is a complementary inf. The pres. tense is prob. iter. Ὑπό with the gen. (τῶν ἀνθρώπων) expresses ultimate agency. Ῥαββί is a transliteration of a Heb. form of address mng. "my lord" that was used in first-century Palestine as an honorary title for teachers of the law: "rabbi." See Metzger 49.

2. Jesus's Prohibition of Practices Encouraged by the Scribes and Pharisees (23:8–12)

23:8 Ὑμεῖς is emphatic. Δέ is adversative. Μή with the aor. subjunc. κληθῆτε (2nd pl. aor. pass. subjunc. of καλέω) expresses a general prohibition that forbids an action as a whole (W 723–24). Ῥαββί, 23:7. Γάρ is causal. Ἐστίν is gnomic pres. Ὑμῶν is objective gen. Ὑμεῖς is emphatic. Ἀδελφοί is pred. nom. Ἐστέ is gnomic pres.

23:9 Πατέρα is prob. the acc. of complement in an implied dbl. acc. of object-complement, since καλέω often is accompanied by such a cstr.: "Do not call anyone your father. . . ." Μή with the aor. subjunc. (καλέσητε 2nd pl. aor. act. subjunc. of καλέω) expresses prohibition of an action as a whole (W 723–24). Ὑμῶν is gen. of relationship. See Metzger 49. Γάρ is causal. Ἐστίν is gnomic pres. Ὑμῶν is gen. of relationship. The art. adj. οὐράνιος may be subst. and in appos. to ὁ πατήρ ("your father, the heavenly One") or in the *2nd attrib. position: "your heavenly Father" (ESV; LEB).

23:10 Κληθῆτε, 23:8. Καθηγητής, -οῦ, ὁ, "instructor." Ὅτι is causal. Ὑμῶν is obj. gen. Ὁ Χριστός is in appos. to καθηγητής.

23:11 The art. adj. μείζων (nom. sg. masc. superl. of μέγας) is subst.: "the greatest." Ὑμῶν is partitive. Ἔσται is impv. fut. Ὑμῶν is obj. gen. Διάκονος, -ου, ὁ, "servant."

23:12 Ὅστις, "any person, whoever." Ὑψώσει (3rd sg. fut. act. indic. of ὑψόω, "exalt") may be an example of the substitution of the fut. indic. for the conative pres.: "Anyone who tries to exalt." Ἑαυτόν is the 3rd sg. refl. pron.: "himself." Ταπεινωθήσεται (3rd sg. fut. pass. indic. of ταπεινόω, "humble") is either *predictive (referring to eschatological exaltation) or gnomic. Ταπεινώσει (3rd sg. fut. act. indic. of ταπεινόω) may be an example of the substitution of the fut. indic. for the conative pres.: "whoever tries to humble himself." Ὑψωθήσεται (3rd sg. fut. pass. indic. of ὑψόω) is either *predictive or gnomic.

FOR FURTHER STUDY

122. Denunciation of Scribes and Pharisees

Mason, S. "Pharisaic Dominance before 70 CE and the Gospels' Hypocrisy Charge (Matt 23:2–3)." *HTR* 83 (1990): 363–81.

Powell, M. A. "Do and Keep What Moses Says (Matthew 23:2–7)." *JBL* 114 (1995): 419–35.

Rabbinowitz, N. S. "Matthew 23:2–4: Does Jesus Recognize the Authority of the Pharisees and Does He Endorse Their Halakhah?" *JETS* 46 (2003): 423–47.

123. The Seat of Moses

Newport, K. G. C. "A Note on the 'Seat of Moses.'" *Andrews University Seminary Studies* 28 (1990): 53–58.

Renov, I. "The Seat of Moses." *Israel Exploration Journal* 5 (1955): 262–67.

124. Phylacteries

Tigay, J. H. "On the Term Phylacteries (Matt 23:5)." *HTR* 72 (1979): 45–53.

Vermès, G. "Pre-Mishnaic Jewish Worship and the Phylacteries from the Dead Sea." *Vetus Testamentum* 9 (1959): 65–72.

HOMILETICAL SUGGESTIONS

When Spiritual Leaders Are Hypocrites (23:1–12)

1. Do not let the hypocrisy of the leader discourage you from believing and obeying the biblical truths that they taught (1–3)
2. Refuse to follow the poor example of hypocritical spiritual leaders (4–7):
   a. Do not impose unbiblical standards on others (4)
   b. Do not make a show of your piety (5)
   c. Do not pursue self-aggrandizement (6–7)
3. Seek to honor God and humble yourself (8–12)

3. Woes Against the Scribes and Pharisees (23:13–33)

23:13 Οὐαί is an interjection that pronounces doom or disaster on a person or thing (BDAG 734b–d 1.a.). Ὑμῖν is dat. of indir. obj. Γραμματεῖς and Φαρισαῖοι are voc. of simple address, appos. to ὑμῖν, and further identify the persons against whom the woe is pronounced. Ὑποκριτής, -οῦ, ὁ, "hypocrite." Ὑποκριταί is voc. of emotional address. Ὅτι is causal and states the reason that Jesus pronounced woe on these groups. Κλείετε (2nd pl. pres. act. indic. of κλείω, "shut, lock") is *gnomic or prog. pres. Τὴν βασιλείαν τῶν οὐρανῶν, 3:2. Ἔμπροσθεν means "immediately in front of" (BDAG 325a–c 1.b.γ.) and in Eng. idiom may be tr. "in the faces of." Ὑμεῖς is emphatic. Γάρ is causal. Εἰσέρχεσθε (2nd pl. pres. mid. indic. of dep. εἰσέρχομαι) is *gnomic or prog. pres. The art. ptc. εἰσερχομένους (acc. pl. masc. of pres. mid. ptc. of dep. εἰσέρχομαι) is subst. and the pres. tense is conative: "those who are trying to enter." Ἀφίετε (2nd pl. pres. act. indic. of ἀφίημι, "permit") is *gnomic or prog. pres. Εἰσελθεῖν (2nd aor. act. inf. of dep. εἰσέρχομαι) is a complementary inf. The vbs. are likely gnomic since they are part of a broad characterization of the scribes and Pharisees. See Metzger 50.

23:14 This verse does not appear in the oldest mss. or many ancient versions. The mss. that do contain it disagree on its placement. Some place it between vv. 12 and 13. Others place it between vv. 13 and 14. It is prob. an interpolation based on Mark 12:40 or Luke 20:47.

23:15 Οὐαὶ ὑμῖν, γραμματεῖς καὶ Φαρισαῖοι ὑποκριταί, ὅτι, 23:13. Περιάγετε (2nd pl. pres. act. indic. of περιάγω, "travel across") is gnomic pres. The art. adj. ξηράν (ξηρός, -ά, -όν, "dry") means "dry land" (BDAG 685a–b 1). Ποιῆσαι (aor. act. inf. of ποιέω) is inf. of purpose. Προσήλυτος, -ου, ὁ, "convert (from paganism to Judaism)." Ὅταν with the aor. subjunc. γένηται means "whenever it happens (he makes a convert)." Ποιεῖτε (2nd pl. pres. act. indic. of ποιέω) is gnomic. Αὐτὸν υἱόν is dbl. acc. of object-complement. Υἱός refers to a person who is worthy of a particular fate, which is expressed by the gen. case (BDAG 1024b–27b 2.c.β.). Γέεννα, -ης, ἡ, "Gehenna, hell." Διπλότερον is sg. neut. comp. adj. of διπλοῦς, -ῆ, -οῦν, "double" and serves as an adv. "twice as much." Ὑμῶν is gen. of comp.

23:16 Οὐαὶ ὑμῖν, 23:13. Ὁδηγός, -οῦ, ὁ, "guide, leader." Ὁδηγοί is voc. of emotional address. The art. ptc. λέγοντες (voc. sg. masc. of pres. act. ptc. of λέγω) is attrib.: "who say." Ὅς plus ἄν and the subjunc. (ὀμόσῃ 3rd sg. aor. act. subjunc. of ὀμνύω, "swear") functions like the prot. of a cond. sentence (BDAG 56b–57d I.b.β.; BDF §380, 1): "if anyone swears" (cf. NIV; ESV). Ἐν with the dat. (τῷ ναῷ) marks the obj. by which one swears rather than the location in which the swearing occurred. Οὐδέν ἐστιν (lit. "it is nothing") means that the oath is not valid or binding. Ὅς δ᾽ ἂν ὀμόσῃ has the same mng. as earlier in the verse, except that δέ has been added. Δέ is adversative and contrasts the nonbinding oath with the binding oath. Ἐν marks the obj. by which one swears. Ξρυσός, -οῦ, ὁ, "gold." The def. art. τοῦ (modifying ναοῦ) is monadic. The gen. ναοῦ is *partitive ("gold that is part of the temple") or source ("gold from the temple"). Ὀφείλει (3rd sg. pres. act. indic. of ὀφείλω, "be obligated [to fulfill his vow];" BDAG 743b–c 2.b.α.) is gnomic.

23:17 Μωροί and τυφλοί are voc. of emotional address. Γάρ marks the basis for Jesus's charge that the scribes and Pharisees are foolish and blind. Although the interr. pron. τίς is masc., it should be tr. "what" or "which" since it refers to the masc. nouns "gold" and "temple." Μείζων is nom. sg. masc. comp. of μέγας, μεγάλη, μέγα: "greater." Ξρυσός, 23:16. The art. ptc. ἁγιάσας (nom. sg. masc. of aor. act. ptc. of ἁγιάζω, "sanctify, consecrate") is attrib.: "the sanctuary that consecrates."

23:18 The conj. καί introduces a second ruling declared by the scribes and Pharisees as part of a sequence begun in 23:16. Ὅς ἂν ὀμόσῃ ἐν, 23:16. Θυσιαστήριον, -ου, τό, "altar." The art. is monadic, indicating that the cstr. refers to the altar in the Jerusalem temple. Οὐδέν ἐστιν, 23:16. Ὅς δ᾽ ἂν ὀμόσῃ ἐν, 23:16. Δῶρον, -ου, τό, "gift." The def. art. τῷ indicates that the prep. phrase ἐπάνω αὐτοῦ ("on it;" BDAG 359b–c 1.b.) is adj. Ὀφείλει, 23:16.

23:19 See Metzger 50. Τυφλοί is voc. of emotional address. Since the question proposes two options, the interr. pron. τί is best tr. "which?" Γάρ identifies the evidence supporting the charge of blindness. Μεῖζον is nom. sg. neut. comp. of μέγας, μεγάλη, μέγα. Δῶρον, -ου, τό, "gift." The disjunctive ἤ marks an alternative. Θυσιαστήριον, 23:18. The art. ptc. ἁγιάζον (nom. sg. neut. of pres. act. ptc. of ἁγιάζω, "sanctify, consecrate") is attrib.: "the altar that sanctifies."

23:20 Οὖν is inferential and draws a conclusion from the principle that the altar is greater because it sanctifies the gift placed on it. The art. ptc. ὀμόσας (nom. sg. masc.

of aor. act. ptc. of ὀμνύω, "swear") is subst. With the vb. ὀμνύω, the prep. ἐν marks the object by which someone swears. Θυσιαστηρίῳ, 23:18. Ὀμνύει (3rd sg. pres. act. indic. of ὀμνύω) is gnomic pres. The def. art. τοῖς with the prep. phrase ἐπάνω αὐτοῦ serves as a substantiver: "all that is on it." Αὐτῷ and αὐτοῦ refer to the altar.

23:21 Ὁ ὀμόσας ἐν . . . ὀμνύει, 23:21. The art. ptc. κατοικοῦντι (dat. sg. masc. of pres. act. ptc. of κατοικέω, "inhabit, dwell in") is subst. and pers.: "the One who dwells in it."

23:22 Ὁ ὀμόσας ἐν . . . ὀμνύει, 23:21. The def. art. τοῦ (modifying θεοῦ) is monadic. The art. ptc. καθημένῳ (dat. sg. masc. of pres. mid. ptc. of dep. κάθημαι, "sit") is subst.: "the One who sits." The adv. ἐπάνω serves as an improper prep. with the gen. (αὐτοῦ) and means "on" (BDAG 359b–c 1.b.).

23:23 Οὐαὶ ὑμῖν, γραμματεῖς καὶ Φαρισαῖοι ὑποκριταί, ὅτι, 23:13. Ἀποδεκατοῦτε (2nd pl. pres. act. indic. of ἀποδεκατόω, "tithe, give a tenth") is customary pres. Ἡδύοσμον, -ου, τό, "mint." Ἄνηθον, -ου, τό, "dill." Κύμινον, -ου, τό, "cumin." The series of seasonings appears to end with that of least value (BDAG 575b). Καί prob. has a slightly adversative sense—"and yet"—since it is part of a contrast between the groups' attention to minutiae of rabbinic law and their neglect of more important matters. Ἀφήκατε (2nd pl. aor. act. indic. of ἀφίημι, "neglect, omit" [BDAG 156b–57b 3.b.]) is prob. gnomic. However, a rationale for the shift from the pres. to the aor. is admittedly evasive. Most EVV tr. the aor. tense as if it were pf. (NIV; ESV; CSB) but some (LEB; NLT) tr. it like a customary pres. Βαρύς, -εῖα, -ύ, "heavy, important." Βαρύτερα is comp. and subst. However, this is likely an example of the substitution of the comp. for the superl.: "the most important matters." This is likely, since the dem. pron. used to refer to acts of tithing and important matters of the law are pl. The def. art. τοῦ (with νόμου) is prob. either monadic or *par excellence*. Τὴν κρίσιν, τὸ ἔλεος, and τὴν πίστιν are acc. of simple appos. that identify the matters of the law that are more important than the tithing of seasonings. The near dem. pron. ταῦτα refers to the nearer referents: justice, mercy, and faithfulness. Ἔδει (3rd sg. impf. act. indic. of δέω, "be necessary") is prob. prog. and refers to a continual necessity due to an ongoing obligation to God. This vb. does not appear in the aor. tense, perhaps because the lexeme generally refers to an ongoing state. Ποιῆσαι (aor. act. inf. of ποιέω) is complementary. Κἀκεῖνα is the result of crasis of the conj. καί and the remote dem. pron. The remote dem. pron ἐκεῖνα refers to the acts of tithing the individual seasonings. Ἀφιέναι (pres. act. inf. of ἀφίημι, "neglect") is a second complementary inf. Thus Jesus spoke of two necessities, obeying the most important elements of the law and refusing the neglect the least important elements. See Metzger 50.

23:24 Ὁδηγοὶ τυφλοί, 23:16. Here the noun may be voc. of emotional address (most EVV) or pred. nom. with an implied copulative: "you are blind guides." This latter option prevents the verse from being an incomplete sentence. However, an incomplete sentence may be expected in emotional address. The art. ptc. διϋλίζοντες (nom. pl. masc. of pres. act. ptc. of διϋλίζω, "strain out, filter out [a liquid, like wine]") is attrib. Κώνωψ, -ωπος, ὁ, "gnat, mosquito (or possibly larvae)." Κάμηλος, -ου, ὁ, "camel." Δέ is adversative. Καταπίνοντες (nom. pl. masc. of pres. act. ptc. of καταπίνω, "swallow up, gulp down") is a second attrib. ptc. and shares the def. art. modifying the first attrib. ptc.: "who strain out . . . and gulp down. . . ."

23:25 Οὐαὶ ὑμῖν, γραμματεῖς καὶ Φαρισαῖοι ὑποκριταί, ὅτι, 23:13. Καθαρίζετε (2nd pl. pres. act. indic. of καθαρίζω, "[ritually] cleanse, purify" [BDAG 488c–89b 3.b.α.]") is customary pres. The adv. ἔξωθεν functions as an adj. The art. and independent position indicate that it is subst.: "the outside" (BDAG 354d–55a 3). The def. art. τοῦ and τῆς are generic. Ποτήριον, -ου, τό, "cup." The gen. ποτηρίου is partitive. Παροψίς, -ίδος, ἡ, "dish, plate." Δέ is adversative. Like ἔξωθεν, ἔσωθεν ("inside") is an adv. that is often used adjectivally. In this clause, the adv. is anar. and that suggests that it functions as a true adv. Γέμουσιν 3rd pl. pres. act. indic. of γέμω, "be full of." With the vb. γέμω, the bare gen. or an ἐκ phrase is used to identify the content that fills the object or person. Ἁρπαγή, -ῆς, ἡ, "robbery, stolen property." Under the influence of Luke 11:39, most EVV treat the noun as a ref. to greed. BDAG suggests that the noun refers to that which has been stolen (133c–34a 2), which would imply that the wine in the ritually purified cup had been stolen from someone else. Ἀκρασία, -ας, ἡ, "self-indulgence, lack of self-control." See Metzger 50. The NLT apparently assumes that the scribes and Pharisees are the intended subj. of the vb. γέμουσιν and thus incorrectly translates the vb. as 2nd pl.: "inside you are filthy." The use of the 3rd pers. vb. by Matthew clearly indicates that "cup" and "dish" are the subj. of the clause. Luke 11:39 shows that the inside of the cup is filled with greed and immorality. However, the text implies that the scribes and Pharisees are filled with corruption as they gulp down the contaminated contents of the cup.

23:26 Φαρισαῖε τυφλέ is voc. of emotional address. The shift from the voc. pl. to the voc. sg. makes the command more dir. and pers., thus more intense. Καθάρισον (2nd sg. aor. act. impv. of καθαρίζω, "purify") expresses urgency. The neut. sg. form of the adj. πρῶτος (πρῶτον) is used adverbially. It may refer to being first in a sequence or first in importance. Here the two senses are mingled. The purification of the contents of the cup precedes that of the outside of the cup because it is the more important step. Ἐντός is an adv. ("inside") that is used adjectivally. The art. and independent form of the adj. indicates that it is subst.: "the inside." Τοῦ ποτηρίου, 23:25. Ἵνα with the subjunc. (γένηται 3rd sg. aor. mid. subjunc. of dep. γίνομαι) expresses result. Καί is adjunctive: "also" (most EVV). Ἐκτός is an adv. ("outside") that is used adjectivally. The art. and independent form of the adj. indicates that it is subst.: "the outside." Αὐτοῦ refers to the cup and is partitive gen. See Metzger 50.

23:27 Οὐαὶ ὑμῖν, γραμματεῖς καὶ Φαρισαῖοι ὑποκριταί, ὅτι 23:13. Παρομοιάζετε (2nd pl. pres. act. indic. of παρομοιάζω, "be [very] sim. to") is customary pres. The prep. prefixed to the vb. intensifies it. Τάφος, -ου, ὁ, "tomb." Κεκονιαμένοις (dat. pl. masc. of pf. pass. ptc. of κονιάω, "whitewash, cover with white plaster") is attrib.: "tombs that have been whitewashed." Οἵτινες functions as a simple rel. pron. (BDAG 729d–30b 3). Μέν . . . δέ marks a strong contrast. Ἔξωθεν, "outside, on the outside." Φαίνονται (3rd pl. pres. mid. indic. of φαίνω, "appear [to be]"[with act. sense]) is gnomic. Ὡραῖος, -α, -ον, "attractive, beautiful." Ἔσωθεν, "inside." Δέ is adversative and highlights the contrast between the outer appearance and inner contents. Γέμουσιν (3rd pl. pres. act.

indic. of γέμω, "be full of") is gnomic. With γέμω, the gen. (ὀστέων gen. pl. of ὀστέον, -ου, "bone, skeletal remains") identifies the content that fills an object. Νεκρῶν is partitive gen. With an anar. sg. subst., the adj. πάσης emphasizes individual components of a category: "every single unclean thing." Ἀκαθαρσία, -ας, ἡ, "something causing ritual defilement; an unclean thing."

23:28 Οὕτως is a comp. adv.: "similarly." Καί is adjunctive. Ὑμεῖς is emphatic. Ἔξωθεν, "outside, on the outside." Μὲν . . . δέ establishes a strong contrast between two clauses, the first of which is concessive. Φαίνεσθε (2nd pl. pres. mid. indic. of φαίνω, "appear [to be]"[with act. sense]) is gnomic. Τοῖς ἀνθρώποις is ethical dat. The adj. δίκαιοι is a pred. adj. Ἔσωθεν, "inside, inwardly." Ἐστέ 2nd pl. pres. indic. of εἰμί. Μεστός, -ή, -όν, "full of." Ὑποκρίσεως and ἀνομίας are gen. after certain adj.

23:29 Οὐαὶ ὑμῖν, γραμματεῖς καὶ Φαρισαῖοι ὑποκριταί, ὅτι, 23:13. Οἰκοδομεῖτε (2nd pl. pres. act. indic. of οἰκοδομέω, "build, construct") is customary pres. Τάφος, -ου, ὁ, "tomb." The def. art. τῶν is the well-known art. The prophets are the OT prophets familiar to Jesus's audience. Προφητῶν identifies those interred in the tombs and could be considered poss. or obj. gen. Κοσμεῖτε (2nd pl. pres. act. indic. of κοσμέω, "decorate, beautify;" BDAG 560b–d 2.a.β.) is customary pres. Μνημεῖον, -ου, τό, "grave." Τῶν is the well-known art. The gen. δικαίων identifies those buried in the graves and could be considered poss. or obj. gen.

23:30 Λέγετε is customary pres. Εἰ with the indic. in the prot. and ἄν with the indic. in the apod. are hallmarks of a second-class (contrary to fact) cond. sentence. Normally the use of the impf. vb. in the prot. and apod. expresses pres. contrary-to-fact condition and the use of the aor. vb. in the prot. and apod. expresses past contrary-to-fact condition. However, since εἰμί lacks an aor. form, the impf. vb. must serve in both pres. and past contrary-to-fact cond. sentences. Here the context indicates that the sentence is a past contrary-to-fact cond. statement: "If we had been. . . , we would not have been . . . ." Ἤμεθα 1st pl. impf. mid. indic. of εἰμί. The first occurrence of the vb. in this verse has the sense "be alive (in a particular time period)" (BDAG 282d–86b 4). The second occurrence has the more common sense "be." Ἐν marks a time period during which an action occurs (BDAG 329c–30b 10). Τῶν πατέρων identifies those who lived during these days and is thus subj. gen. Ἡμῶν is gen. of relationship. Κοινωνός, -οῦ, ὁ, "partner, sharer." With κοινωνός, the gen. (αὐτῶν) or dat. modifier identifies those with whom the person partners. The prep. marks the activity in which the partners participate together. Αἷμα, -ατος, τό, "blood." Αἷμα is a metonymy for "murder," an act of wrongfully shedding the blood of a victim. See the use of φονεύω in 23:31 and the ref. to shedding blood in 23:35. At the lit. level, τῶν προφητῶν is partitive gen. However, in the metonymy, the gen. phrase is objective. The def. art. is the well-known art.

23:31 Ὥστε introduces an independent clause that is result of the preceding statement: "Therefore, as a result." Μαρτυρεῖτε (2nd pl. pres. act. indic. of μαρτυρέω, "testify") is prog. pres. Ἑαυτοῖς is 3rd pers. refl. pron., which serves as a 2nd pers. refl. pron. (BDAG 268b–69c 1.b.) and is dat. of disadvantage: "against yourselves" (most EVV). Ὅτι is recitative and introduces the content of the testimony. Φονευσάντων (gen. pl.

masc. of aor. act. ptc. of φονεύω, "murder") is subst. and gen. of relationship: "sons of those who murdered." The def. art. τούς (modifying προφήτας) is the well-known art. **23:32** Καί is prob. resultative: "and so." Ύμεῖς is emphatic. Πληρώσατε (2nd pl. aor. act. impv. of πληρόω, "fill up") expresses urgency. The use of the impv. is unexpected and prompted some scribes to emend the vb. to a fut. (e.g., B) or aor. (e.g., D) indic. The impv. is permissive (impv. of toleration), expressing irony or biting sarcasm: "Go ahead and fill up. . . ." (W 488–89; R 948). Μέτρον, -ου, τό, "measure, measuring instr." Πατέρων is subj. gen.: "the measure that your fathers partially filled." Ύμῶν is gen. of relationship.

23:33 Ὄφις, -εως, ὁ, "snake." Ὄφεις is voc. of emotional address. Γέννημα, -ατος, τό, "offspring." Γεννήματα is voc. of emotional address. Ἔχιδνα, -ης, ἡ, "(poisonous) snake." Ἐχιδνῶν is gen. of source. Πῶς is used in a dir. question with the subjunc. (φύγητε 2nd pl. aor. act. subjunc. of φεύγω, "flee, escape") to deny implicitly the possibility of an action (BDAG 900d–901c 1.a.ε.): "How can you possibly escape?" Ἀπό expresses separation. Γέεννα, -ης, ἡ, "Gehenna, hell." Γεέννης is gen. of destination (most EVV): "judgment that sentences you to hell."

FOR FURTHER STUDY

125. Woes to Scribes and Pharisees

Allison, D. C., Jr. "Matt 23:39 = Luke 13:35b as a Conditional Prophecy." *JSNT* 18 (1983): 75–84.

Baarda, T. "The Reading 'Who Wished to Enter' in Coptic Tradition: Matt 23.23, Luke 11.52, and 'Thomas' 39." *NTS* 52 (2006): 583–91.

Batey, R A. "Jesus and the Theatre." *NTS* 30 (1984): 563–74.

Campbell, D. K. "NT Scholars' Use of OT Lament Terminology and Its Theological and Interdisciplinary Implications." *BBR* 21 (2011): 213–25.

Derrett, J. D. M. "Receptacles and Tombs (Mt 23:24–30)." *ZNW* 77 (1986): 255–66.

Flowers, H. J. "Matthew 23:15." *ExpTim* 73 (1961): 67–69.

Hoad, J. "On Matthew 23:15." *ExpTim* 73 (1962): 211–12.

Hood, J. B. "Matthew 23–25: The Extent of Jesus's Fifth Discourse." *JBL* 128 (2009): 527–43.

Hultgren, A. J. *Jesus and His Adversaries: The Form and Function of the Conflict Stories in the Synoptic Tradition.* Minneapolis: Augsburg, 1979.

Keener, C. S. "'Brood of Vipers' (Matthew 3.7; 12.34; 23.33)." *JSNT* 28 (2005): 3–11.

Knowles, M. P. "Serpents, Scribes, and Pharisees." *JBL* 133 (2014): 165–78.

Köstenberger, A. J., and D. A. Croteau. "'Will a Man Rob God?' (Malachi 3:8): A Study of Tithing in the Old and New Testaments." *BBR* 16 (2006): 53–77.

Lachs, S. T. "On Matthew 23:27–28." *HTR* 68 (1975): 385–88.

Maccoby, H. "The Washing of Cups." *JSNT* 14 (1982): 3–15.

Neusner, J. "First Cleanse the Inside: The 'Halakhic' Background of a Controversy-Saying." *NTS* 22 (1976): 486–95.

Saldarini, A. J. "Delegitimation of Leaders in Matthew 23." *CBQ* 54 (1992): 659–80.

_____. "Understanding Matthew's Vitriol." *BR* 13 (1997): 32.

Sanders, E. P. "Judaism and the Grand 'Christian' Abstractions: Love, Mercy, and Grace." *Int* 39 (1985): 357–72.

Scharen, H. "Gehenna in the Synoptics." *BSac* 149 (1992): 324–37.

Simmonds, A. R. "'Woe to You, Hypocrites!': Re-Reading Matthew 23:13–36." *BSac* 166 (2009): 336–49.

HOMILETICAL SUGGESTIONS

Woe or Whoa? Will We Repent Before Judgment Falls? (23:1–33)

1. Jesus pronounced judgment on hypocrites who say one thing but do another (23:2–3)
2. Jesus pronounced judgment on legalists who make obeying God burdensome and oppressive (23:4)
3. Jesus pronounced judgment on showmen who parade their piety to impress others (23:5)
4. Jesus pronounced judgment on egotists who crave the spotlight (23:6–12)
5. Jesus pronounced judgment on false teachers who condemn others by their very efforts to save them (23:13–14)
6. Jesus pronounced judgment on liars who play word games to justify their deception (23:16–22)
7. Jesus pronounced judgment on interpreters who focus on minutiae and neglect what is most important (23:23–24)
8. Jesus pronounced judgment on ritualists who focus on ritual purity and neglect spiritual purity (23:25–28)
9. Jesus pronounced judgment on judges who feel morally superior to others, when they are really worse (23:29–33)

4. Persecution of Jesus's Representatives by the Scribes and Pharisees (23:34–36)

23:34 Διὰ τοῦτο, "because of this." Τοῦτο is retrospective and refers to the preceding discussion, prob. particularly the coming judgment of the scribes and Pharisees. Ἰδού ("look!") calls attention to the statement it introduces (BDAG 468b–d 1.b.δ.). Ἐγώ is emphatic. Ἀποστέλλω (1st sg. pres. act. indic. of ἀποστέλλω, "send [on a mission or with a message]") is prog. pres. Σοφός, -ή, -όν, "wise." Although anar., σοφούς is subst.: "wise men, sages." Both occurrences of the prep. phrase ἐξ αὐτῶν are substitutes for the partitive gen. and function as subst. that serve as dir. obj. (BDAG 295d–98b 4.a.γ.). Ἀποκτενεῖτε (2nd pl. fut. act. indic. of ἀποκτείνω, "kill"), σταυρώσετε (2nd pl. fut. act. indic. of σταυρόω, "crucify"), μαστιγώσετε (2nd pl. fut. act. indic. of μαστιγόω, "flog, whip"), and διώξετε (2nd pl. fut. act. indic. of διώκω, "pursue, persecute") are pred. fut. The prep. series ἀπό . . . εἰς in which the obj. of the preps. is the same lemma means "from one . . . to another. . . ."

23:35 Ὅπως with the subjunc. ἔλθῃ (3rd sg. 2nd aor. act. subjunc. of dep. ἔρχομαι) expresses purpose. The prep. ἐπί with the acc. (ὑμᾶς) marks the persons to or against whom an action is performed (BDAG 363a–67c 14.b.β.). Πᾶν with an anar. sg. noun (αἷμα, 23:30) emphasizes the individual members of a category (BDAG 782b–84c 1.a.α.): "every (single) drop of blood." The attrib. adj. δίκαιον describes the blood as righteous because its source is a righteous person. Ἐκχυννόμενον (nom. sg. neut.

of pres. pass. ptc. of ἐκχύννω, "pour out") is attrib.: "that was poured out." Ἄβελ, which as a Sem. name does not inflect, is partitive gen. or gen. of source. The art. adj. δικαίου is prob. *attrib. ("righteous Abel;" most EVV). Alternatively, it may be subst. and appos. ("the righteous person"), thus balancing this cstr. with the appos. phrase modifying Ζαχαρίου. The prep. series ἀπὸ . . . ἕως marks the beginning and end of a series of events (BDAG 105a–7b 2.c.β.). Ζαχαρίου is partitive gen. or gen. of source. Υἱοῦ is gen. of simple appos. Βαραχίου is gen. of relationship. The rel. pron. ὅν introduces a description of Zachariah. Ἐφονεύσατε 2nd pl. aor. act. indic. of φονεύω, "murder." Μεταξύ, "between, in the middle of" (with the gen.). Ναός, -οῦ, ὁ, "temple." Θυσιαστήριον, -ου, τό, "altar."

23:36 Ἀμὴν λέγω ὑμῖν, 5:18. Ἥξει (3rd sg. fut. act. indic. of ἥκω, "come, occur") is predictive fut. The near dem. pron. ταῦτα is retrospective and refers to the judgment that the scribes and Pharisees will face for their sin and hypocrisy. Γενεά, -ᾶς, ἡ, "generation [in the sense of all those living at a specific time]." The near dem. pron. ταύτην indicates that Jesus is referring to the lifetime of his contemporaries.

FOR FURTHER STUDY

126. The Coming Persecution by the Scribes and Pharisees

Boring, M. E. "Christian Prophecy and Matthew 23:34–36: A Text Exegesis." *SBLSP* 11 (1977): 117–26.

Byron, J. "Abel's Blood and the Ongoing Cry for Vengeance." *CBQ* 73 (2011): 743–56.

Gallagher, E. L. "The Blood from Abel to Zechariah in the History of Interpretation." *NTS* 60 (2014): 121–38.

Grant, F. C. "The Son of Barachiah." *Anglican Theological Review* 4 (1921): 70–74.

North, J. L. "Reactions in Early Christianity to Some References to the Hebrew Prophets in Matthew's Gospel." *NTS* 54 (2008): 254–74.

Peels, H. G. L. "The Blood 'from Abel to Zechariah' (Matthew 23,35; Luke 11,50f.) and the Canon of the Old Testament." *ZNW* 113 (2001): 583–601.

Rieske, S. M. "What Is the Meaning of 'This Generation' in Matthew 23:36." *BSac* 165 (2008): 209–26.

HOMILETICAL SUGGESTIONS

Enough! (23:34–36)

1. Jesus graciously sent his representatives to call Israel to repentance
2. Israel refused to repent and severely persecuted Jesus's followers
3. God will judge Israel for its rejection and persecution of the prophets and disciples
4. God's judgment will fall before Jesus's contemporaries had died

5. Jesus's Lament over Jerusalem (23:37–39)

23:37 Ἰερουσαλήμ is voc. of emotional address. The repetition of the voc. intensifies the expression of emotion. The art. ptc. ἀποκτείνουσα (voc. sg. fem. of pres. act. ptc. of ἀποκτείνω, "kill") is *subst. and appos. (ESV) or attrib. (CSB; LEB). Due to the coordinating conj. καί, the def. art. modifying ἀποκτείνουσα modifies λιθοβολοῦσα as well. Thus λιθοβολοῦσα (voc. sg. fem. of pres. act. ptc. of λιθοβολέω, "stone [to death]") is *subst. and appos. or attrib. The art. and independent ptc. ἀπεσταλμένους (acc. pl. masc. of pf. pass. ptc. of ἀποστέλλω, "send") is subst. Ποσάκις ("how often") is an exclamation rather than a question (BDAG 855c–d). Ἠθέλησα 1st sg. aor. act. indic. of θέλω. Ἐπισυναγαγεῖν (aor. act. inf. of ἐπισυνάγω, "gather") is a complementary inf. Σου (modifying τὰ τέκνα) is gen. of relationship. The combination of the rel. pron. (ὅν) and τρόπον (τρόπος, -ου, ὁ, "way, manner") means "in the way that" or "just as" (BDAG 1016d–17b 1). Ὄρνις, -ιθος, ἡ, "hen." Ἐπισυνάγει (3rd sg. pres. act. indic. of ἐπισυνάγω, "gather") is gnomic. Νοσσίον, -ου, τό, "young (of a bird)." Αὐτῆς is gen. of relationship. Ὑπό with the gen. (τὰς πτέρυγας) marks location: "under." Πτέρυξ, -υγος, ἡ, "wing." Καί is adversative: "and yet." Ἠθελήσατε 2nd pl. aor. act. indic. of θέλω, "want, be willing."

23:38 Ἰδού, 23:34. Ἀφίεται (3rd sg. pres. pass. indic. of ἀφίημι, "leave, abandon") is divine pass. Ὑμῶν (modifying ὁ οἶκος) is poss. The temple is the house of humans rather than the house of God. Ἔρημος, -ον, "deserted." See Metzger 50–51.

23:39 Λέγω γὰρ ὑμῖν, 5:20. The dbl. neg. οὐ μή with the subjunc. Ἴδητε (2nd pl. 2nd aor. act. subjunc. of ὁράω) is emphatic negation: "you certainly will not see me." The position of με may indicate slight emphasis. The prep. series ἀπό . . . ἕως establishes the starting point and ending point of a time period: "from . . . until. . . ." Ἄρτι, "now" (BDAG 136a–b 3). The particle of contingency ἄν normally appears with subjunc. vbs. in temp. clauses (BDAG 56b–57c I.c.). Εἴπητε 2nd pl. 2nd aor. act. subjunc. of λέγω. The next clause states the content of their anticipated proclamation, a quotation of Ps 118:26. Εὐλογημένος (nom. sg. masc. of pres. pass. ptc. of εὐλογέω, "bless") functions as a pred. adj. Although BDAG (407d–8c 2.a.) suggests that the blessing refers to the word of blessing with which one person greets another, more likely the ptc. is a divine pass. and refers to God's bestowal of his favor (CSB). The art. ptc. ἐρχόμενος (nom. sg. masc. of pres. mid. ptc. of dep. ἔρχομαι) is subst.: "the one who is coming." The phrase ἐν ὀνόματι prob. means "as a commissioned representative of." Κυρίου is gen. of poss. and refers to Yahweh (Ps 118:26).

FOR FURTHER STUDY

127. Jesus's Lament over Jerusalem

> Blevins, C. D. "Under My Wings: Jesus's Motherly Love: Matthew 23:37–39." *Review & Expositor* 104 (2007): 365–74.
> Carter, W. "Matthew 23:37–39." *Int* 54 (2000): 66–68.

HOMILETICAL SUGGESTIONS

Countdown to Judgment (23:37–39)

1. The people of Jerusalem had rejected and murdered the prophets sent to them
2. Jesus longed to protect them from the punishment they deserved by suffering it in their place

3. The people of Jerusalem rejected Jesus and refused to accept his protection
4. God abandoned the Jerusalem temple as a precursor to the city's coming judgment
5. Jesus would abandon Jerusalem and not return until the city honored him as King

C. FIFTH DISCOURSE: THE FALL OF JERUSALEM
AND THE COMING KINGDOM (24:1–25:46)

1. Introduction to the Olivet Discourse (24:1–3)

24:1 Ἐξελθών (nom. sg. masc. of 2nd aor. act. ptc. of dep. ἐξέρχομαι, "exit, go out of") is *attendant circumstance (most EVV) or temp. (LEB). Ἀπό expresses separation: "away from the temple (courts)." Ἐπορεύετο (3rd sg. impf. mid. indic. of dep. πορεύομαι, "walk") is prog. Προσῆλθον 3rd pl. aor. act. indic. of dep. προσέρχομαι. Ἐπιδεῖξαι (aor. act. inf. of ἐπιδείκνυμι, "show, point out") is inf. of purpose. This purpose is unexpected since Jesus had obviously seen the buildings of the temple before. Perhaps the disciples were simply drawing his attention to the "impressive profile" of the temple from a particular vantage point (N 958) or pointing out the buildings as a gentle correction to Jesus's statement that the temple was desolate (23:38). Αὐτῷ is indir. obj. and refers to Jesus. Οἰκοδομή, -ῆς, ἡ, "building." The def. art. τοῦ (modifying ἱεροῦ) is monadic, referring to the one true temple. The gen. ἱεροῦ is partitive.

24:2 Δέ is prob. adversative and marks a correction of the disciples' misunderstanding. The def. art. ὁ functions as a pers. pron. Ἀποκριθείς (nom. sg. masc. of aor. pass. ptc. of dep. ἀποκρίνομαι) is pleonastic. Αὐτοῖς refers to the disciples. The neg. οὐ assumes an affirmative reply to the question. Βλέπετε (2nd pl. pres. act. indic. of βλέπω) is prog. The near dem. pron. ταῦτα prob. refers to all the structures that were part of the temple complex. Ἀμὴν λέγω ὑμῖν, 5:18. The dbl. neg. οὐ μή with the subjunc. ἀφεθῇ (3rd sg. aor. pass. subjunc. of ἀφίημι, "leave in place") is emphatic negation: "Absolutely no stone will be left in place. . . ." The rel. pron. ὅς introduces a description of λίθος. Καταλυθήσεται (3rd sg. fut. pass. indic. of καταλύω, "destroy, demolish") is predictive fut. Both vbs. are likely divine pass. (N 959).

24:3 Καθημένου (gen. sg. masc. of pres. mid. ptc. of dep. κάθημαι, "sit") is gen. abs. and temp.: "While he was sitting." Δέ introduces the next development in the narrative. Αὐτοῦ refers to Jesus. Ἐπί w. gen., "on." Ἐλαία, -ας, ἡ, "olive tree." Ἐλαιῶν is prob. gen. of appos., in which the gen. serves to name a particular mountain (W 95–100; cf. Luke 19:29). Προσῆλθον 3rd pl. 2nd aor. act. indic. of dep. προσέρχομαι, "approach." Αὐτῷ is dat. of dir. obj. (after certain vbs.). Κατά with the acc. expresses isolation or separateness (BDAG 511a–13d 1.c.) and with the obj. ἰδίαν means "privately" (BDAG 466c–67d 5). Λέγοντες (nom. pl. masc. of pres. act. ptc. of λέγω) is attendant circumstance (most EVV) or purpose. Εἰπέ (2nd sg. 2nd aor. act. impv. of λέγω), see 4:3. Ἡμῖν is dat. of indir. obj. The near dem. pron. ταῦτα refers to the demolition of the temple (24:2). Ἔσται (3rd sg. fut. indic. of εἰμί) is predictive. The 2nd pers. poss. pron. σῆς is used in place of the subj. gen. Παρουσία, -ας, ἡ, "coming, arrival (of a god or king)." The use of the sg. art. noun σημεῖον with two gen. modifiers παρουσίας and συντελείας both sharing the same def. art. suggests that the disciples assumed a single sign would announce both events and thus that the parousia and the end of the age would be concurrent (H 2.688; France 894). Note that this is not an example of the Granville Sharp rule (contrary to H), since it applies strictly to pers. nouns. Συντελεία,

-ας, ἡ, "completion, consummation, end" (BDAG 974d–75a). Τοῦ αἰῶνος is prob. obj. gen.

2. The Initial Birth Pains Preceding the End (24:4–8)

24:4 Ἀποκριθείς (nom. sg. masc. of aor. pass. ptc. of dep. ἀποκρίνομαι) is pleonastic. Βλέπετε (2nd pl. pres. act. impv. of βλέπω) is ingr.-prog. Βλέπω followed by μή with the aor. subjunc. (πλανήσῃ 3rd sg. aor. act. subjunc. of πλανάω, "mislead, deceive") means to watch out for or beware of something (BDAG 178d–79c 5). In this cstr. μή has the sense "lest" (BDAG 646 2.a.β.).

24:5 Πολλοί is subst.: "many people." Γάρ is causal and states the reason to beware. Ἐλεύσονται (3rd pl. fut. mid. indic. of dep. ἔρχομαι) is predictive. The phrase ἐπὶ τῷ ὀνόματί μου prob. means "mentioning or using my name" (BDAG 711c–14c 1.d.ε.; N 961). Alternatively, it may mean "assuming another's office," thus claiming the messianic role of Jesus (H 2.690). Λέγοντες may be ptc. of *means or attendant circumstance. Ἐγώ is emphatic. The def. art. ὁ (modifying χριστός) is monadic or well-known. Πολλούς is subst. Πλανήσουσιν (3rd pl. fut. act. indic. of πλανάω, "mislead, deceive") is predictive.

24:6 Μελλήσετε (2nd pl. fut. act. indic. of μέλλω, "will certainly") is predictive fut. and may stress either the imminence or *certainty of the fut. action (BDAG 627c–28c). Ἀκούειν (pres. act. inf. of ἀκούω) is complementary. Πόλεμος, -ου, ὁ, "war." Ἀκοή, -ῆς, ἡ, "report, rumor." Πολέμων is obj. gen. (the wars are reported by others) or gen. of ref. ("reports about wars"). Ὁρᾶτε (2nd pl. pres. act. impv. of ὁράω) is ingr.-prog. Like βλέπω (24:4), ὁράω with μή means to be alert to and avoid a danger (BDAG 719b–20b B.2.). Θροεῖσθε (2nd pl. pres. pass. impv. of θροέω, "be disturbed, panic") expresses a general precept. Δεῖ 3rd sg. (impers.) pres. act. indic. of δέω, "it is necessary." Γάρ is causal and introduces the reason to avoid panic. Γενέσθαι (2nd aor. mid. inf. of dep. γίνομαι, "happen") is complementary. The cstr. is elliptical and implies the acc. subj. of the inf. πολέμους or ταῦτα. See Metzger 51. Οὔπω, "not yet." Τέλος, -ους, τό, "end." The shift from συντελεία in v. 3 to τέλος in vv. 6, 13, and 14 may simply express the richness of Matthew's vocabulary or may indicate a *distinction in events. Some commentators view τέλος as a ref. to the *"end" or destruction of the temple (F 903, 909) rather than the end of the age but others (N 963) see the distinction as overly subtle. Both terms appear in Dan 9:27 (to which Jesus alludes in 24:15), in which they have distinct references: τέλος refers to the end of the week or seven, at which time sacrifice and drink offering are suspended; συντελεία refers to the end of the desolation.

24:7 Ἐγερθήσεται (3rd sg. fut. pass. indic. of ἐγείρω, "rise up against" [pass.]; BDAG 271c–72c 11). Γάρ is causal. Ἐπί is a marker of hostile action (BDAG 363a–67c 12.b.). Ἔσονται (3rd pl. fut. indic. of εἰμί) is predictive. Λιμός, -οῦ, ὁ, "famine." Σεισμός, -οῦ, ὁ, "earthquake." See Metzger 51. Κατά with the acc. (τόπους) is distributive and refers to various places serially: "from place to place; in one place after another."

24:8 The dem. pron. ταῦτα is retrospective and refers to the difficulties Jesus mentioned in 24:4–7. Ὠδίν, -ῖνος, ἡ, "birth pain, labor pain." Ὠδίνων is partitive gen.

HOMILETICAL SUGGESTIONS

The Beginning of the End (24:4–8)

1. Birth pains are initially mild but grow in intensity and increase in frequency. The difficulties that precede the end will likewise grow in intensity and increase in frequency. The initial contractions that will ultimately lead to the end include:
   a. The rise of false Messiahs
   b. Wars between nations
   c. Famines and natural disasters
2. These first birth pains alert disciples to prepare for the future without being alarmed

3. The Final Birth Pains Preceding the End (24:9–14)

24:9 Τότε prob. means "after that" and introduces a second phase in the prelude to the destruction of the temple that follows the "beginning of birth pains." However, it may mean "at that time" and portray the events of this paragraph as part of the beginning of birth pains (N 965; H 2.694; F 900 n. 26). Determining whether the uses of τότε in this discourse are sequential ("after that") or contemp. ("at that time") has a significant impact on interpretation of this discourse, and the questions are difficult. Παραδώσουσιν (3rd pl. fut. act. indic. of παραδίδωμι, "hand over") and ἀποκτενοῦσιν (3rd pl. fut. act. indic. of ἀποκτείνω, "kill") are predictive fut. Εἰς with the acc. (θλῖψιν) marks the goal (BDAG 288d–93c 4.a.: "for persecution, to be persecuted"). The repetition of ὑμᾶς may place emphasis on it. Jesus's disciples will be the focus of the persecution. Ἔσεσθε (2nd pl. fut. indic. of εἰμί) and μισούμενοι (nom. pl. masc. of pres. pass. ptc. of μισέω, "hate") is fut. periph. cstr. that prob. emphasizes the prog. and enduring nature of the hatred (W 648–49). With the pass. ptc., the prep. ὑπό with the gen. (πάντων τῶν ἐθνῶν) identifies the ultimate agents. Διά with the acc. (τὸ ὄνομά) identifies the cause.

24:10 Τότε may mean "at that time" (F 904) or *"after that," indicating that the actions of v. 10 are a response to the prior events described in v. 11 (N 965). Σκανδαλισθήσονται (3rd pl. fut. pass. indic. of σκανδαλίζω, "fall away" [pass.]; BDAG 926a–b 1.a.), παραδώσουσιν (3rd pl. fut. act. indic. of παραδίδωμι, "hand over, betray"), and μισήσουσιν (3rd pl. fut. act. indic. of μισέω, "hate") are predictive fut. Πολλοί is subst.: "many (of those who are persecuted)." The repetition of the reciprocal pron. ἀλλήλους is prob. emphatic and highlights the horror of professing disciples turning against one another.

24:11 Ψευδοπροφήτης, -ου, ὁ, "false prophet." Ἐγερθήσονται (3rd pl. fut. pass. indic. of ἐγείρω, "appear" [pass.]; BDAG 271c–72c 12) and πλανήσουσιν (3rd pl. fut. act. indic. of πλανάω, "deceive, lead astray") are predictive fut. Πολλούς is subst.: "many people."

24:12 Διά with the acc. sg. neut. def. art. and inf. (πληθυνθῆναι aor. pass. inf. of πληθύνω, "grow, increase" [pass.]; BDAG 826a–b 1.b.) expresses cause (W 596–97). Ἀνομία, -ας, ἡ, "lawlessness." The def. art. τήν with ἀνομίαν is abstract (W 226–27).

Ἀνομίαν is acc. subj. of the inf. Ψυγήσεται (3rd sg. fut. pass. indic. of ψύχω, "grow cold" [pass.]; BDAG 1100c) is predictive fut. The def. art. τῶν marks the adj. πολλῶν as subst. The adj. may be an example of the use of the positive adj. for the comp. (NIV; W 297, 597): "the love of most people." The gen. πολλῶν is subj.

24:13 Δέ is adversative and contrasts those who succumb to the pressures of persecution with those who remain faithful. The art. and independent ptc. ὑπομείνας (nom. sg. masc. of aor. act. ptc. of ὑπομένω, "endure") is subst. Εἰς with the acc. (τέλος) expresses extension in time up to a goal: "to the end" (BDAG 289d–91c 2.a.α.). Τέλος, 24:6. The phrase εἰς τέλος does not necessarily refer to the end of the temple or the end of the age but may merely mean "to the very last" (10:22; F 907). The dem. pron. οὗτος is subst., appos., and particularly emphatic (BDAG 740b–41c 1.a.ε.; LEB). Σωθήσεται (3rd sg. fut. pass. indic. of σῴζω) is predictive fut. and divine pass. The vb. may refer to physical deliverance ("will be saved" CSB) rather than spiritual salvation.

24:14 Κηρυχθήσεται (3rd sg. fut. pass. indic. of κηρύσσω, "preach") is predictive fut. Τῆς βασιλείας is prob. gen. of ref. (NLT). The prep. ἐν prob. expresses extension: "throughout" (BDAG 326c–30b 3; ESV; NLT). Οἰκουμένη, -ης, ἡ, "inhabited world, Roman empire." Εἰς marks the purpose or *intended use (most EVV; BDAG 288d–93c 4.d.). Μαρτύριον, -ου, τό, "testimony." The phrase πᾶσιν τοῖς ἔθνεσιν is practically synonymous with ἐν ὅλῃ οἰκουμένῃ and creates emphasis (N 967). Τότε may mean "at that time" or *"after that." If the latter, Jesus did not necessarily promise that the end would occur immediately after the completion of worldwide gospel proclamation. Ἥξει (3rd sg. fut. act. indic. of ἥκω, "come to pass, occur") is pred. fut. Τὸ τέλος, 24:6.

HOMILETICAL SUGGESTIONS

The Final Countdown (24:9–14)

The final birth pains are most intense and frequent. The intensity and frequency of signs increases before the end.

1. Persecution will intensify to the point that believers are martyred
2. Hatred will be unleashed against the followers of Jesus
3. Alleged disciples will renounce Jesus and become bitter informants against true disciples
4. False prophets will mislead many followers
5. Lawlessness will increase
6. Christians' love will grow cold
7. True believers will persevere and proclaim the gospel to the ends of the earth

4. The Desolation of the Temple and the Disciple's Escape (24:15–22)

24:15 Οὖν is inferential and introduces the appropriate response to the preceding warnings and looks beyond 24:14 to 24:9–13. Others see the οὖν as adversative (N 969). Ὅταν with the subjunc. (ἴδητε) does not mark the action itself as cond. or merely possible. It merely indicates that the time of the event is unknown (at least to the disciples). The phrase τὸ βδέλυγμα τῆς ἐρημώσεως is drawn from Daniel 9:27, although the LXX uses the pl. form of the gen. modifier. Βδέλυγμα, -ατος, τό, "detestable thing, abomination." The term prob. refers to something that pollutes or defiles the temple (BDAG 172a–b). Ἐρήμωσις, -εως, ἡ, "devastation, destruction, desolation" (BDAG 392b). See the closely related adj. ἔρημος in 23:38. The art. and independent ptc. ῥηθέν (acc. sg. neut. of 2nd aor. pass. ptc. of λέγω) is subst. and a divine pass.: "what was spoken (by God)." Διά with the gen. (Δανιήλ) marks the intermediate agent through whom God spoke. The def. art. τοῦ with προφήτου marks the prophet as well-known and the cstr. is appos. Ἑστός (acc. sg. neut. of pf. act. ptc. of ἵστημι, "stand") is a pred. ptc. The pf. tense is equivalent in sense to the pres. (BDAG 482a–83b C.2.b.). Although τόπῳ is anar., the adj. ἁγίῳ and the context (24:2) confirm that it refers to the holy place, the inner sanctum of the temple. The art. and independent ptc. ἀναγινώσκων (nom. sg. masc. of pres. act. ptc. of ἀναγινώσκω, "read") is subst. ("the reader") and a parenthetic nominative (W 53–54). Νοείτω (3rd sg. pres. act. impv. of νοέω, "understand") is ingr.-prog.

24:16 Τότε, "at that time." The def. art. οἱ serves as a substantiver with the prep. phrase ἐν τῇ Ἰουδαίᾳ: "those who are in Judea" (W 231–35, esp. 235). Φευγέτωσαν (3rd pl. pres. act. impv. of φεύγω, "flee, escape") is ingr.-prog. The def. art. with ὄρη is prob. the well-known art. and prob. refers to the Transjordanian Mountains of the Decapolis. The city of Pella is located in the foothills of these mountains (Eusebius, *History* 3.5.3).

24:17 The def. art. ὁ with the prep. phrase ἐπὶ τοῦ δώματος functions as a substantiver (W 231–35, esp. 235): "The person on the roof." Δῶμα, -ατος, τό, "(flat) roof." Μή with the aor. impv. (καταβάτω 3rd sg. aor. act. impv. of καταβαίνω, "go down, descend") prohibits the action as a whole. The inf. ἆραι (aor. act. inf. of αἴρω, "take away, remove") expresses purpose. The def. art. τά functions as a substantiver with the prep. phrase ἐκ τῆς οἰκίας. Αὐτοῦ is gen. of poss.

24:18 The def. art. ὁ with the prep. phrase ἐν τῷ ἀγρῷ serves as a substantiver: "the person in the field." Ἀγρός, -οῦ, ὁ, "(agricultural) field." Μή with the aor. impv. (ἐπιστρεψάτω 3rd sg. aor. act. impv. of ἐπιστρέφω, "turn around, go back") forbids the action as a whole (W 723 n. 27). Ὀπίσω, "back." Ἆραι, 24:17. Αὐτοῦ (modifying τὸ ἱμάτιον) is gen. of poss.

24:19 Οὐαί ("woe;" BDAG 734b–d) seems to express pity rather than the displeasure and disgust that it expressed in the denunciation of the Pharisees in Matthew 23. Δέ may be adversative and indicate that pregnant or nursing mothers cannot flee with the same haste demanded of others. The art. and independent ptc. ἐχούσαις (dat. pl. fem. of pres. act. ptc. of ἔχω) and θηλαζούσαις (dat. pl. fem. of pres. act. ptc. of θηλάζω, "nurse [an infant], breast-feed") are subst.: "to the women who are pregnant or breast-feeding." Ἔχω plus ἐν γαστρί (γαστήρ, -τρός, ἡ, "womb") is an expression mng. "be pregnant." Ἐν marks a period of time during which something occurs. The remote dem. pron. ἐκείναις refers to the days during which the flight must occur.

24:20 Προσεύχεσθε (2nd pl. pres. mid. impv. of dep. προσεύχομαι, "pray") is ingr.-prog. Δέ marks the next development in the discourse. With the vb. προσεύχομαι, ἵνα marks the objective of the prayer (BDAG 475c–77b 2.a.γ.) and functions like an inf. of indir. discourse (most EVV). Γένηται 3rd sg. aor. mid. subjunc. of dep. γίνομαι. Φυγή, -ῆς, ἡ, "flight." Ὑμῶν is subj. gen. Χειμών, -ῶνος, ὁ, "winter." Χειμῶνος is gen. of time, identifying the period of time during which an action occurs (W 123–24): "during the winter." Μηδέ, "nor." Σαββάτῳ is dat. of time mark the point of time at which an action occurs (W 155–57, esp. 157): "on the sabbath."

24:21 Γάρ identifies the reason to pray as 24:20 commanded. Ἔσται is predictive fut. Τότε means "at that time." Θλῖψις, -εως, ἡ, "affliction, tribulation." Μεγάλη may be an example of the use of a positive adj. for the elative ("very severe") or *superl. ("most severe") since the rel. clause that follows indicates that this tribulation is unrivaled in its severity. When μέγας is used to express intensity of unpleasant events, adj. like "severe" better communicate the sense of the adj. in Eng. idiom. Οἵα (οἷος, -α, -ον) is a rel. pron., expressing similarity to something or class: "of such a kind as." Γέγονεν (3rd sg. pf. act. indic. of dep. γίνομαι) is extensive. The prep. series ἀπό . . . ἕως establishes the beginning and end of a period of time: from . . . until. . . ." Κόσμου is subj. gen. The art. adv. νῦν functions as a subst.: "the pres. time" (BDAG 681b–82b 1.a.β.). Οὐδέ, "nor." The dbl. neg. οὐ μή with the subjunc. γένηται (3rd sg. aor. mid. subjunc. of dep. γίνομαι) is emphatic negation that denies the possibility of an occurrence: "nor can ever occur."

24:22 Εἰ with the aor. indic. (ἐκολοβώθησαν 3rd pl. aor. pass. indic. of κολοβόω, "shorten") in the prot. and ἄν with the aor. indic. (ἐσώθη 3rd sg. aor. pass. indic. of σῴζω) in the apod. form a second-class cond. sentence that assumes the untruth of the condition and result: "If the days were not shortened, no human being would be saved." The phrase αἱ ἡμέραι ἐκεῖναι matches ἐκείναις ταῖς ἡμέραις in 24:19 and thus likely refers to the events described in 24:15–19. Some commentators argue that the phrase refers to the entire period of "great distress" that includes the fall of Jerusalem but extends far beyond it to include the whole inter-advent period (Carson 564; Blomberg 359–60). Σῴζω refers to physical deliverance from death rather than spiritual salvation (H 2.703). Σάρξ, "human being" (BDAG 914d–16b 3.a.). Both vbs. are divine pass. (N 976). Δέ is adversative and contrasts the potential of God failing to act with God's gracious intervention. Διά with the acc. identifies the motivation for God's action: "for the sake of." Ἐκλεκτός, -ή, -όν, "chosen." The art. and independent adj. ἐκλεκτούς is subst.: "the chosen ones." Κολοβωθήσονται (3rd pl. fut. pass. indic. of κολοβόω, "shorten") is predictive fut. and divine pass.

HOMILETICAL SUGGESTIONS

From Desecration to Desolation (24:15–22)

1. The destruction of the temple will be preceded by an act of desecration
2. This desecration is the signal for believers to flee from Jerusalem
3. This flight is urgent and must not be delayed
4. This flight will impose hardship on those who undertake it

5. The suffering associated with the temple's destruction will be unparalleled in human history
6. God will graciously shorten the period of suffering for the sake of Jesus's followers

5. Distinguishing the Return of the True Messiah from the Rise of False Messiahs (24:23–28)

24:23 Τότε may mean "after that" and locate the messianic claims that follow in the period after the flight from Jerusalem (N 978). *Alternatively, it may mean "at that time" and refer to messianic claims at the approximate time of the desecration of the temple and the destruction of the city. Thus, Jesus was warning against believing false promises of miraculous deliverance from the messianic claimants that would not prove true. Ἐάν with the subjunc. (εἴπῃ 3rd sg. 2nd aor. act. subjunc. of λέγω) marks the prot. of a third-class cond. statement that makes no assumption regarding the fulfill-ment of the prot. Τις prob. has the nuance "anyone." Regardless of the identity of the speaker, one who claims that the Messiah has returned during this season should not be believed. Ἰδού is a prompter of attention: "Look!" (BDAG 468b–d 1). The repeated adv. of place ὧδε . . . ὧδε is sometimes treated as the equivalent to ὧδε . . . ἐκεῖ ("here . . . there;" BDAG 1101b–d 1.b.; NIV; ESV; NLT). However, this tr. seems to imply a single speaker whose opinion changes from a claim that the Messiah is in his presence to a claim that the Messiah is at a greater distance. Instead, the disjunctive particle ἤ prob. contrasts the claims of two different speakers, in which both claim that the Messiah is near them. Thus "here . . . over here" (CSB; LEB) is prob. more accurate. The def. art. ὁ modifying χριστός is monadic and refers to the single "anointed one" whose coming was promised in the OT. Μή with the aor. subjunc. (πιστεύσητε 2nd pl. aor. act. subjunc. of πιστεύω) prohibits the action as a whole: "Do not believe it at all."
24:24 Γάρ introduces the reason for Jesus's prohibition. Ἐγερθήσονται (3rd pl. fut. pass. indic. of ἐγείρω, "appear" [BDAG 271c–72c 11]) is predictive fut. Ψευδόχριστος, -ου, ὁ, "false or bogus Messiah." Ψευδοπροφήτης, -ου, ὁ, "false or bogus prophet." Δώσουσιν (3rd pl. fut. act. indic. of δίδωμι, "produce" [BDAG 242a–43c 4]) is predictive fut. Τέρας, -ατος, τό, "amazing feat, wonder." The distinction between "signs" and "won-ders" is sometimes blurred. Σημεῖα may have symbolic significance. Τέρατα simply astound through the display of supernatural power. Ὥστε with the inf. (πλανῆσαι aor. act. inf. of πλανάω) expresses result. Although BDAG (1107b–c 2.a.β.) states that the cstr. here expresses actual result, the prot. εἰ δυνατόν, indicates that the result is merely intended (telic rather than ecbatic; Carson 565). Since the prot. εἰ δυνατόν merely implies a copulative and since the apod. consists of an inf. rather than an indic. vb., which might be accompanied by ἄν, the form alone cannot indicate whether the con-dition belongs to the first or second class. However, since 24:22 indicates that concern for the elect prompted God to shorten the days of severe suffering, the context implies that the elect are under divine protection and thereby protected from deception by false Messiahs and prophets as well. Thus the cstr. is likely a second-class cond. that assumes that it is not possible for the elect to be deceived (KJ21; H 2.706; Turner,

Matthew 578). Καί is ascensive ("even;" D&A 3.352). The art. adj. ἐκλεκτούς (24:22) is subst.

24:25 Ἰδού calls attention to the fact that Jesus forewarned his followers (BDAG 468b–d 1). Προείρηκα (1st sg. pf. act. indic. of προλέγω, "tell beforehand, alert in advance") is consummative pf.

24:26 Οὖν is inferential and introduces a conclusion based on Jesus's warning. Ἐάν with the subjunc. (εἴπωσιν 3rd pl. aor. act. subjunc. of λέγω) forms the prot. of a 3rd-class cond. statement. Ἰδού, 24:23. Μή with the aor. subjunc. ἐξέλθητε (2nd pl. 2nd aor. act. subjunc. of dep. ἐξέρχομαι) and πιστεύσητε (2nd pl. aor. act. subjunc. of πιστεύω) express prohibition of action as a whole: "Do not go out at all" and "Do not believe them at all." Ταμεῖον, -ου, τό, "inner room."

24:27 Γάρ is causal. Ὥσπερ . . . οὕτως ("just as . . . so too") mark the prot. and apod. of a comp. statement. Ἀστραπή, -ῆς, ἡ, "lightning." Ἐξέρχεται (3rd sg. pres. mid. indic. of dep. ἐξέρχομαι) is gnomic pres. Ἀπό with the gen. (ἀνατολῶν) marks the place at which movement begins. Ἀνατολή, -ῆς, ἡ, "rising, *east" (2:1). Φαίνεται (3rd sg. pres. mid. indic. of φαίνω, "shine, flash" [with act. sense]) is gnomic pres. Ἕως is used to identify the place that is the ultimate destination of movement (BDAG 422d–24c 3.a.). Δυσμή, -ῆς, ἡ, "west" (pl.). Ἔσται is pred. fut. Παρουσία, 24:3. Τοῦ υἱοῦ τοῦ ἀνθρώπου, 9:6.

24:28 The particle of place ὅπου combined with the particle of contingency ἐάν means "wherever" or "whenever." However, the particle of place in the next clause confirms that the mng. "wherever" is intended. The subjunc. vb. (ἦ 3rd sg. pres. subjunc. of εἰμί) is required by the particle of contingency. Πτῶμα, -ατος, τό, "corpse, human remains." Ἐκεῖ, "there." Συναχθήσονται (3rd pl. fut. pass. indic. of συνάγω, "gather") is gnomic fut. Ἀετός, -οῦ, ὁ, "eagle, *vulture" (N 981).

HOMILETICAL SUGGESTIONS

Counterfeit Christs (24:23–28)

1. If someone has to tell you about it, Christ has not returned
2. If someone attempts to use miracles to convince you, Christ has not returned
3. If his location is distant or secret, Christ has not returned
4. If his glory is not displayed for all the world to see, Christ has not returned

6. The Coming of the Son of Man (24:29–31)

24:29 Δέ marks the next development in the narrative. The topic shifts from the period of intense tribulation to the period that immediately follows it. Εὐθέως, "immediately." Μετά with the acc. referring to an event (τὴν θλῖψιν, 24:21) is temp.: "after the tribulation." Τῶν ἡμερῶν ἐκείνων is gen. of time: "that occurs during those days." The remote dem. pron. ἐκείνων is retrospective (24:19). The rest of the verse is a conflation and rewording of several OT texts (esp. Isa 13:10; 34:4). Ἥλιος, -ου, ὁ, "sun." Σκοτισθήσεται (3rd sg. fut. pass. indic. of σκοτίζω, "grow dark, darken") is predictive fut. and prob. divine pass., although the vb. is always pass. in the LXX, NT, and early Christian literature. Σελήνη, -ης, ἡ, "moon." The def. art. modifying ἥλιος and σελήνη are monadic. Δώσει (3rd sg. fut. act. indic. of δίδωμι) is predictive fut. Φέγγος, -ους, τό, "light, radiance, glow." Αὐτῆς is gen. of source. Ἀστήρ, -έρος, ὁ, "star." Πεσοῦνται (3rd pl. fut. mid. indic. of πίπτω, "fall") is predictive fut. Ἀπό with the gen. (τοῦ οὐρανοῦ) expresses separation and marks the orig. position from which the stars will fall. Δύναμις, -εως, ἡ, "(military) force." BDAG suggests that the term portrays the heavenly bodies as armies (262b–63c, 4). Τῶν οὐρανῶν may be partitive or *attrib. gen. (CSB; NIV). Σαλευθήσονται (3rd pl. fut. pass. indic. of σαλεύω, "shake") is pred. fut. and prob. divine pass.

24:30 Τότε, "at that time." Φανήσεται (3rd sg. fut. pass. indic. of φαίνω, "appear" [with act. sense]; BDAG 1046d–47d 2.a.) is predictive fut. Σημεῖον, -ου, τό, "sign." Τοῦ υἱοῦ τοῦ ἀνθρώπου (9:6) may be gen. of appos., source, or obj. gen. ("the sign that symbolizes the Son of Man"). Although the term σημεῖον was used in the question in 24:3, the difference in modifiers (τῆς σῆς παρουσίας vs. τοῦ υἱοῦ τοῦ ἀνθρώπου) may indicate that Jesus was referring to a different sign. The sg. οὐρανῷ prob. means "sky." This description may suggest that the phenomena in 24:29 constitute the sign (N 983). Hagner dismisses that possibility based on the assumption that the τότε that begins the verse must mean "after that" (2.713). Τότε prob. means "next in sequence." Κόψονται (3rd pl. fut. mid. indic. of κόπτω, "beat oneself, mourn" [mid.]; BDAG 559b–c 2) is predictive fut. Φυλή, -ῆς, ἡ, "*tribe, nation" (BDAG 1069). Τῆς γῆς may refer to the entire earth (N 984) or to *"the land (of Israel)." Since the ref. is an allusion to Zech 12:10–14, which refers to the house of David and inhabitants of Jerusalem, incl. the clans of David, Nathan, Levi, Shimei and all the rest of the clans, the phrase likely refers to the tribes of the land of Israel. ὄψονται (3rd pl. fut. mid. indic. of ὁράω, "see, perceive, witness") is predictive fut. Τὸν υἱὸν τοῦ ἀνθρώπου, 9:6. The description of the Son of Man is derived from Dan 7:14. Ἐρχόμενον (acc. sg. masc. of pres. mid. ptc. of dep. ἔρχομαι) is a pred. ptc. Ἐπί with the gen. (τῶν νεφελῶν) marks the position of the Son of Man. Τοῦ οὐρανοῦ is either attrib. gen. ("heavenly clouds") or *gen. of source ("clouds from heaven"). Μετά with the gen. (δυνάμεως καὶ δόξης πολλῆς) marks attendant circumstance: "with power and great glory" (BDAG 636b–38b 3.b.). See Beale and Carson 86b–90a.

24:31 Ἀποστελεῖ (3rd sg. fut. act. indic. of ἀποστέλλω) is predictive fut. The gen. pron. αὐτοῦ that modifies τοὺς ἀγγέλους and is likely a gen. of authority, indicating that the angels are ruled by him. Μετά with the gen. (σάλπιγγος) marks an accompanying phenomenon (BDAG 636b–38b 3.b.) or an object that serves as equipment (3.c.) distinct from the means. Thus the Son of Man does not blast the trumpet as a signal that sends out his angels. Instead, either the trumpet is the equipment that the angels will later use to gather the elect (CSB) or a *trumpet blast (some early mss. make this interpretation explicit by adding φωνῆς; most EVV; see Metzger 51) that is the Son of Man's signal to prepare the elect for their gathering by the angels (Isa 27:13; N 985). Σάλπιγξ, -ιγγος, ἡ, "trumpet, *trumpet blast." If σάλπιγξ refers to a trumpet blast, the adj. μεγάλης means "loud." Ἐπισυνάξουσιν (3rd pl. fut. act. indic. of ἐπισυνάγω, "gather") is predictive fut. Τοὺς ἐκλεκτούς, 24:22. The gen. αὐτοῦ refers to the Son of Man and is either gen. of authority or subj. gen. (the Son of Man chose them). Τέσσαρες, "four."

Ἄνεμος, -ου, ὁ, "wind." The expression "four winds" (τεσσάρων ἀνέμων) prob. refers to the four directions or points of the compass (Zech 2:10 LXX; 1 Chr 9:24 LXX). The ἀπό . . . ἕως prep. series defines the outer limits of the area from which the chosen ones are gathered (BDAG 105a–7b 2.a.). Ἄκρον, -ου, τό, "outer limit, end." Οὐρανῶν and αὐτῶν (which refers to "heavens") are partitive gen.: "from one end of heaven to the other." The phrase about gathering the chosen ones from one end of heaven to the other is derived from Deut 30:4 (LXX), which refers to the regathering of the exiles.

7. The Parable of the Fig Tree (24:32–35)

24:32 Δέ marks the next development in the discourse. Ἀπό with the gen. (συκῆς) expresses source. The def. art. τῆς (modifying συκῆς) is generic (W 227–28). Μάθετε (2nd pl. 2nd aor. act. impv. of μανθάνω, "learn") expresses urgency. Ὅταν ("whenever") combined with ἤδη ("already") prob. means "as soon as" (most EVV). Κλάδος, -ου, ὁ, "branch." Αὐτῆς is partitive gen. The particle of contingency that is a component of ὅταν requires the subjunc. (γένηται 3rd sg. aor. mid. subjunc. of dep. γίνομαι). Ἁπαλός, -ή, -όν, "tender." Φύλλον, -ου, τό, "leaf." Ἐκφύῃ (3rd sg. pres. act. subjunc. of ἐκφύω, "sprout") is prob. prog. The NLT treats the pres. tense as ingr. but this is not a normal category for the pres. Γινώσκετε (2nd pl. pres. act. indic. of γινώσκω) is gnomic pres. Ὅτι is recitative and introduces the content of knowledge. Ἐγγύς, "near (in time)" (BDAG 271a–c 2.a.). Θέρος, -ους, τό, "summer."

24:33 Οὕτως ("in the same way") means based on the observation of indicators as in the preceding parable. Καί is adjunctive and implies that the adv. οὕτως refers to what precedes (BDAG 740b–41d 1.b.). Ὑμεῖς is emphatic. Ὅταν, "whenever." The subjunc. form ἴδητε (2nd pl. 2nd aor. act. subjunc. of ὁράω) is required by the particle of contingency that is a component of ὅταν. The near dem. pron. ταῦτα refers to the matters discussed in 24:4–28, which serve as an indicator that the events of 24:29–31 are near. Γινώσκετε ὅτι ἐγγύς, 24:32. The subj. of ἐστίν may be pers. ("he," referring to the Son of Man; most EVV; N 988; H 2.715) or impers. ("it," referring to the climactic event described in 24:29–31). The prep. phrase ἐπὶ θύραις (θύρα, -ας, ἡ, "door, gate") is loc. and appos. The phrase is an expression for very close proximity that likely leads to a dir. encounter (BDAG 462a–b 1.a. and b.α.; cf. Jas 5:9).

24:34 Ἀμὴν λέγω ὑμῖν ὅτι, 5:18. The dbl. neg. οὐ μή with the subjunc. (παρέλθῃ 3rd sg. aor. act. subjunc. of dep. παρέρχομαι, "pass away, disappear;" BDAG 775d–76c 3) Γενεά, -ᾶς, ἡ, "generation, contemporaries." The near dem. αὕτη indicates that Jesus is referring to *his own contemporaries or to the generation contemporary with the signs leading to the coming of the Son of Man (or both). Ἕως with the particle of contingency ἄν and the subjunc. (γένηται) implies the indefinite time of the events. The near dem. pron. ταῦτα may refer to all of the events described in the preceding verses incl. indicators and the coming of the Son of Man (24:3–31; France 929–30). However, many scholars argue that the phrase "all these things" excludes the events of 24:29–31 (N 987; H 2.715), assuming that it retains the same sense that it bore in 24:33.

24:35 Ὁ οὐρανὸς καὶ ἡ γῆ is a merism that refers to the entire universe. Παρελεύσεται (3rd sg. fut. mid. indic. of dep. παρέρχομαι, "pass away, disappear") is predictive fut.

Δέ is adversative and contrasts the permanence of Jesus's words with the transience of the universe. Μου is subj. gen. and indicates that the words were spoken by Jesus. The dbl. neg. οὐ μή with the subjunc. (παρέλθωσιν 3rd pl. aor. act. subjunc. of dep. παρέρχομαι) is emphatic negation and adamantly denies that Jesus's predictions will fail.

HOMILETICAL SUGGESTIONS

The King Assumes His Throne (24:29–35)

1. Christ will take his throne immediately after the destruction of the temple (24:29a)
2. Christ will take his throne after the upheaval of the cosmos (24:29b)
3. Christ will take his throne after those who crucified him mourn for their sin (24:30)
4. Christ will take his throne when he restores the exiled people of God (24:31)
5. Christ will take his throne before his contemporaries die out (24:34)
6. Christ will take his throne undoubtedly and most certainly (24:35)

8. The Time and Circumstances of the Parousia (24:36–41)

24:36 Περὶ δέ with the gen. (τῆς ἡμέρας ἐκείνης καὶ ὥρας) prob. marks a major shift in topic in the discourse (France 936–37; H 2.716; N 990). Δέ marks the next development in the discourse and the περί phrase announces the new topic. Thus the cstr. here has a sim. function to Paul's rhetorical usage. Some see here a major divide in the discourse, in which Jesus turns from addressing the first question from 24:3 to response to the second question (esp. France 936–37). For arguments against this position, see Carson 570, 552–55. BDAG suggests that the prep. phrase merely modifies the clause that follows it (BDAG 797c–98d 1.h.). Οἶδεν 3rd sg. pf. (used for pres.) act. indic. of οἶδα. The οὐδὲ . . . οὐδέ cstr. means "not even . . . and not even" (BDAG 734d–35a 3). The gen. phrase τῶν οὐρανῶν modifying οἱ ἄγγελοι is prob. attrib. and the phrase is roughly equivalent to ἄγγελοι ἐν τῷ οὐρανῷ (22:30). See Metzger 51–52. Εἰ μή ("except") marks an exception to the seemingly all-inclusive οὐδείς. After εἰ μή, the adj. μόνος is pleonastic (BDAG 658c–59c 1.a.γ.). The adj. serves to emphasize that the Father is the sole exception.

24:37 Γάρ is causal and introduces confirmation of the statement that no person except the Father knows the time of the Parousia. Ὥσπερ marks the prot. of a comp. and οὕτως marks the apod.: "just as . . . even so" (BDAG 1106d–7a). Although rare when modifying nouns, τοῦ Νῶε is best understood as gen. of time and refers to the days during which Noah lived. Ἔσται (3rd sg. fut. indic. of εἰμί) is predictive fut. Ἡ παρουσία, 24:3. Τοῦ υἱοῦ is subj. gen. Τοῦ υἱοῦ τοῦ ἀνθρώπου, 9:6.

24:38 Ὡς marks the prot. and οὕτως (24:39) marks the apod. of a comp. Γάρ introduces the basis for the statement in 24:37. The indic. ἦσαν (3rd pl. impf. indic. of εἰμί) combines with the nom. pl. masc. of the pres. act. ptc. τρώγοντες (τρώγω, "eat [noisily];" BDAG 1019b), πίνοντες, γαμοῦντες (γαμέω, "marry [a wife]"), and γαμίζοντες (γαμίζω, "give [one's daughter] in marriage") to form the impf. periph. cstr. The impf. is prog. (H 2.719): "they kept on eating and drinking. . . ." The two uses of the conj. καί join the ptc. in two closely related pairs. Ἐν marks a period of time. See Metzger 52. The def. art. ταῖς shows that the prep. phrase πρὸ τοῦ κατακλυσμοῦ is adj. Κατακλυσμός, -οῦ, ὁ, "flood." Ἄχρι is used as a prep. with the gen.: "until." The phrase ἄχρι ἧς ἡμέρας means "until the day when" (BDAG 160c–61a 1.a.α.). Εἰσῆλθεν 3rd sg. 2nd aor. act. indic. of dep. εἰσέρχομαι. Κιβωτός, -οῦ, ἡ, "ark, barge."

24:39 Καί shows that this clause continues the prot. of the comp. begun in 24:38. Ἔγνωσαν 3rd pl. 2nd aor. act. indic. of γινώσκω, "understand" (BDAG 199d–201b 3.b.). Ἦλθεν 3rd sg. 2nd aor. act. indic. of dep. ἔρχομαι. Κατακλυσμός, 24:38. Ἦρεν 3rd sg. 2nd aor. act. indic. of αἴρω, "take away, sweep away" (BDAG 28b–29a 3). Ἅπας, -ασα, -αν was orig. an intensive form of πᾶς, but the NT does not appear to distinguish the two adj. (BDAG 98c; BDF §275). The form is not likely intensive here since Noah and his family are not included. Οὕτως, 24:38. Ἔσται [καὶ] ἡ παρουσία τοῦ υἱοῦ τοῦ ἀνθρώπου, 24:37.

24:40 Τότε, "at that time." Ἔσονται (3rd pl. fut. indic. of εἰμί) is predictive fut. Ἀγρός, -οῦ, ὁ, "(agricultural) field." Παραλαμβάνεται (3rd sg. pres. pass. indic. of παραλαμβάνω, "take [away]" [BDAG 767d–768b 1]) and ἀφίεται (3rd sg. pres. pass. indic. of ἀφίημι, "leave behind") are prob. futuristic pres. (N 994) and stress the certainty of the action (W 535–37). Although the masc. gender of the subst. εἷς is often generic, the shift to the fem. μία in 24:41 indicates that it is gender specific: "one man." The distinction between tasks (farming and grinding flour) supports this specificity.

24:41 Ἀλήθουσαι (nom. pl. fem. of pres. act. ptc. of ἀλήθω, "grind [flour];" [BDAG 43d–44a]) may be cond. or *temp.: "while two women are grinding flour." Since Luke's parallel (17:35) uses a fut. periph. cstr., most EVV versions assume that the ptc. clause here was intended to be an independent clause. BDF (§418.2) protests that "the ptcp. is not good Greek" based on a sim. assumption. Μύλος, -ου, ὁ, "(hand) mill." The fem. μία matches the fem. gender of the ptc. (cf. 24:40). Παραλαμβάνεται and ἀφίεται, 24:40.

9. The Command to Be Prepared (24:42–44)

24:42 Οὖν is inferential and introduces the proper response to the preceding teaching (H 2.720). Γρηγορεῖτε (2nd pl. pres. act. impv. of γρηγορέω, "be alert, vigilant;" [BDAG 208]) is ingr.-prog. Ὅτι is causal. Οἴδατε 2nd pl. pf. (for pres.) act. indic. of οἶδα. Ποίᾳ ἡμέρᾳ is dat. of time (W 155–57). See Metzger 52. Ἔρχεται (3rd sg. pres. mid. indic. of dep. ἔρχομαι) is futuristic pres. and prob. emphasizes the certainty of the Lord's coming (W 535–36).

24:43 Δέ is prob. adversative and contrasts a scenario in which the time of an arrival is unknown with another in which the time is known. The dem. pron. ἐκεῖνο is prospective and it refers to the statement introduced by ὅτι. Γινώσκετε (2nd pl. pres. act. impv. of γινώσκω) is ingr.-prog. Ὅτι introduces the content of knowledge. Εἰ with the indic. vb. in a secondary tense forms the prot. of a second-class cond. sentence. The use of the aor. vb. (as opposed to the impf.) ᾔδει (3rd sg. pluperf. [for aor.] act. indic.

of οἶδα) expresses a past contrary-to-fact condition: "If he had known" (W 694–96). Οἰκοδεσπότης, -ου, ὁ, "master of the house, homeowner." Ποίᾳ φυλακῇ is dat. of time and refers to a point or period of time at which an action occurs. Φυλακή, -ῆς, ἡ, "watch, one of four three-hour periods of the night" (BDAG 1067c–68b 4.). Κλέπτης, -ου, ὁ, "thief, burglar." Ἔρχεται 3rd sg. pres. mid. indic. of dep. ἔρχομαι. The indic. vb. in a secondary tense (ἐγρηγόρησεν 3rd sg. aor. act. indic. of γρηγορέω, "keep watch") with ἄν marks the apod. of the 2nd-class cond. statement. Εἴασεν 3rd sg. aor. act. indic. of ἐάω, "allow, permit." Διορυχθῆναι (aor. pass. inf. of διορύσσω, "break through") is a complementary inf.

24:44 Διὰ τοῦτο is causal and the following ὅτι clause suggests that it is primarily prospective and refers to the unknown time of the Son of Man's coming. Καί is adjunctive. Ὑμεῖς is emphatic. Γίνεσθε (2nd pl. pres. mid. impv. of dep. γίνομαι) is ingr.-prog. (W 721–22). Ἕτοιμος, -η, -ον, "ready, prepared." Ὅτι is causal. The rel. clause ᾗ οὐ δοκεῖτε (2nd pl. pres. act. indic. of δοκέω, "think, suppose, expect") modifies ὥρᾳ (a dat. of time): "in an hour in which you are not expecting it." Ὁ υἱὸς τοῦ ἀνθρώπου, 9:6. Ἔρχεται (3rd sg. pres. mid. indic. of dep. ἔρχομαι) is futuristic pres. and stresses the certainty of the Son of Man's coming.

10. The Wise and the Foolish Servants (24:45–51)

24:45 The interr. pron. τίς introduces a question. The inferential particle ἄρα indicates that the question is prompted by the immediately preceding discussion about preparedness. Φρόνιμος, -ον, "wise." The rel. pron. ὅν introduces a further description of the slave. Κατέστησεν 3rd sg. aor. act. indic. of καθίστημι, "appoint, put in charge" (BDAG 492c–d 2.a.). Ἐπί expresses power or authority over something (BDAG 363a–67c 9.a.). Οἰκετεία, -ας, ἡ, "group of slaves for a household." Αὐτοῦ is gen. of poss. The gen. art. τοῦ with the inf. (δοῦναι aor. act. inf. of δίδωμι) expresses purpose. Τροφή, -ῆς, ἡ, "nourishment, food." Ἐν with the obj. καιρῷ is temp. and refers to the appropriate point in time: Καιρός refers to a moment that is esp. appropriate (BDAG 497c–98d 1.b.).

24:46 Μακάριος (BDAG 610d–11c 1.a.) has the sense "fortunate" and refers primarily to temp. and material circumstances. Although BDAG treats this occurrence as a ref. to divine favor (2.a.), this confuses the lit. mng. of the parable with its allegorical ref. The dem. pron. ἐκεῖνος is retrospective and confirms that the slave is the one spoken of in the preceding verse. The rel. pron. ὅν introduces a further description of the servant. Ἐλθών (nom. sg. masc. of 2nd aor. act. ptc. of dep. ἔρχομαι) is temp.: "when he comes" (most EVV). Αὐτοῦ is gen. of subord. Εὑρήσει 3rd sg. fut. act. indic. of εὑρίσκω, "find." Οὕτως, "thus, so," is retrospective and refers to the description of the slave's action in 24:45. Ποιοῦντα (acc. sg. masc. of pres. act. ptc. of ποιέω) is pred. ptc.

24:47 Ἀμὴν λέγω ὑμῖν, 5:18. Ὅτι is recitative and introduces Jesus's declaration. Ἐπί with the dat. (πᾶσιν τοῖς ὑπάρχουσιν) has the same sense as the prep. with the gen. in 24:45 and expresses authority over something (BDAG 363a–67c 9.b.). The art. and independent ptc. ὑπάρχουσιν (dat. pl. neut. of pres. act. ptc. of ὑπάρχω, "be at one's disposal") is subst.: "possessions" (BDAG 1029d–30a 1). Αὐτοῦ is poss. gen. Καταστήσει (3rd sg. fut. act. indic. of καθίστημι, "appoint, give authority over") is predictive fut.

24:48 Δέ is adversative and contrasts the conduct of the foolish slave with that of the wise slave. Ἐάν is followed by a series of four subjunc. vbs. (εἴπῃ, ἄρξηται, ἐσθίῃ, and πίνῃ), which together form the prot. of a third-class cond. statement that makes no implication regarding the fulfillment of the condition. Εἴπῃ 3rd sg. 2nd aor. act. subjunc. of λέγω. The dem. pron. ἐκεῖνος prob. refers to the same servant as 24:45. However, Jesus now imagines that he manifests a different character than in 24:45. With λέγω, the phrase ἐν τῇ καρδίᾳ αὐτοῦ means to "think to oneself" (BDAG 508b–9c 1.b.β.). Χρονίζει (3rd sg. pres. act. indic. of χρονίζω, "delay, linger;" [BDAG 1092a]) is prog. pres. Μου is gen. of subord.

24:49 Καί coordinates the vb. ἄρξηται with εἴπῃ in 24:48 and indicates that both vbs. are part of the prot. of the cond. sentence. Ἄρξηται 3rd sg. aor. mid. subjunc. of ἄρχω, "begin" [mid.]. Τύπτειν (pres. act. inf. of τύπτω, "beat") is a complementary inf. Σύνδουλος, -ου, ὁ, "fellow slave." Αὐτοῦ is gen. of association (W 128–30). Δέ is adversative and contrasts his harsh treatment of his peers with his own self-indulgence. The subjunc. vbs. ἐσθίῃ (3rd sg. pres. act. subjunc. of ἐσθίω, "eat") and πίνῃ (3rd sg. pres. act. subjunc. of πίνω, "drink") are also part of the prot. introduced by ἐάν in 24:48. Μετά with the gen. (τῶν μεθυόντων) is associative and identifies the ones in whose company an action is performed (BDAG 636b–38b A.2.b.). The art. and independent ptc. μεθυόντων (gen. pl. masc. of pres. act. ptc. of μεθύω, "be intoxicated, drunk") is subst.: "the drunks" (BDAG 626a).

24:50 Ἥξει (3rd sg. fut. act. indic. of ἥκω, "come") is predictive fut. Τοῦ δούλου is gen. of subord. The remote dem. pron. ἐκείνου may express disdain (BDAG 301d–2c a.γ.). The two ἐν phrases (ἐν ἡμέρᾳ and ἐν ὥρᾳ) followed by the rel. pron. ᾗ means "on/in the day/hour on/in which." Προσδοκᾷ (3rd sg. pres. act. indic. of προσδοκάω, "expect, anticipate") and γινώσκει (3rd sg. pres. act. indic. of γινώσκω, "know, realize") are prog. pres.

24:51 Διχοτομήσει (3rd sg. fut. act. indic. of διχοτομέω, "cut in two, dismember;" BDAG 253a) is predictive fut. Μέρος, -ους, τό, "share, place" (BDAG 633b–34a 2). Αὐτοῦ is either gen. of destination or poss. Μετά with the gen. (τῶν ὑποκριτῶν): "among, in the company of" (BDAG 636b–38b, A.1.). Θήσει (3rd sg. fut. act. indic. of τίθημι, "arrange, ordain;" BDAG 1003b–4b 1.b.ζ.). Ἐκεῖ, "there." Ἔσται ὁ κλαυθμὸς καὶ ὁ βρυγμὸς τῶν ὀδόντων, 13:42.

FOR FURTHER STUDY

128. The Olivet Discourse

Beasley-Murray, G. R. *Jesus and the Last Days: The Interpretation of the Olivet Discourse*. Peabody, MA: Hendrickson, 1993.

Berry, C. E. "The Destruction of Jerusalem and the Coming of the Son: Evangelical Interpretations of the Olivet Discourse in Luke." *SBJT* 16 3 (2012): 62–74.

Cooper, B. "Adaptive Eschatological Inference from the Gospel of Matthew." *JSNT* 33 (2010): 59–80.

Evans, C. A. "Predictions of the Destruction of the Herodian Temple in the Pseudepigrapha, Qumran Scrolls, and Related Texts." *Journal for the Study of the Pseudepigrapha* 10 (1992): 89–147.

Friedrichsen, T. A. "A Note on Και Διχοτομησει Αυτον (Luke 12:46 and the Parallel in Matthew 24:51)." *CBQ* 63 (2001): 258–64.

Gibbs, J. A. *Jerusalem and Parousia: Jesus's Eschatological Discourse in Matthew's Gospel*. St. Louis: Concordia Academic, 2000.

Glancy, J. A. "Slaves and Slavery in the Matthean Parables." *JBL* 119 (2000): 67–90.

Ham, C. "Reading Zechariah and Matthew's Olivet Discourse." Pages 85–97 in *The Gospel of Matthew*. Vol. 2 of *Biblical Interpretation in Early Christian Gospels*. Edited by T. R. Hatina. New York: T&T Clark, 2008.

Kirchhevel, G. D. "He That Cometh in Mark 1:7 and Matt 24:30." *BBR* 4 (1994): 105–11.

Martín, G. "Procedural Register in the Olivet Discourse: A Functional Linguistic Approach to Mark 13." *Bib* 90 (2009): 457–83.

Pate, C. M. "Revelation 6: An Early Interpretation of the Olivet Discourse." *CTR* 8 (2011): 45–55.

Sim, D. C. "The Dissection of the Wicked Servant in Matthew 24:51." *Hervormde Teologiese Studies* 58 (2002): 172–84.

Stanton, G. N. "'Pray That Your Flight May Not Be in Winter or on a Sabbath' (Matthew 24:20)." *JSNT* 37 (1989): 17–30.

Taylor, J. "'The Love of Many Will Grow Cold': Matt 24:9–13 and the Neronian Persecution." *Revue Biblique* 96 (1989): 352–57.

Toussaint, S. D. "A Critique of the Preterist View of the Olivet Discourse." *BSac* 161 (2004): 469–90.

Walvoord, J. F. "Christ's Olivet Discourse on the End of the Age." *BSac* 128 (1971): 109–16.

Wenham, D. *The Rediscovery of Jesus's Eschatological Discourse*. Sheffield: JSOT, 1984.

Wilson, A. I. *When Will These Things Happen? A Study of Jesus as Judge in Matthew 21–25*. Carlisle: Paternoster, 2004.

Wong, E. K. "The Matthaean Understanding of the Sabbath: A Response to G. N. Stanton." *JSNT* 44 (1991): 3–18.

Wright, N. T. *Jesus and the Victory of God*. Minneapolis: Fortress, 1996.

HOMILETICAL SUGGESTIONS

The Glorious Return of the Son of God (24:36–51)

1. Only the Father knows the time of Jesus's glorious return
2. The wicked will be unprepared for the judgment that accompanies Jesus's glorious return
3. Unsuspecting people will be in the middle of normal daily activities at the time of Jesus's glorious return
4. Some will be saved, and some will be destroyed at the time of Jesus's glorious return
5. Believers should live in a state of constant preparedness for Jesus's glorious return
6. Believers should live every day as if it were the day of Jesus's glorious return

11. The Parable of the Ten Virgins (25:1–13)

25:1 Τότε prob. means "at that time" and prob. refers to the time of the master's coming mentioned at the climax of the preceding parable (D&A 3.394; N 1003). It highlights a distinction between the pres. manifestation of the kingdom (in which it is not too late to enter) and the consummation of the kingdom (at which time it will be too late to enter). The fut. tense of ὁμοιωθήσεται (3rd sg. fut. pass. indic. of ὁμοιόω, "be like" [pass.]) confirms that the parable illustrates the eschatological state of the kingdom (H 2.728). Ἡ βασιλεία τῶν οὐρανῶν, 3:2. Δέκα, "ten." Παρθένος, -ου, ἡ refers to a young woman who has not had sexual relations and is old enough to marry. In the context of wedding rituals, the term is comparable to "bridesmaid" (NLT) if one maintains the historic distinction between bridesmaids and matrons. Παρθένοις is dat. of dir. obj. Although αἵτινες could be a substitute for the simple rel. pron., BDAG suggests it indicates that persons belong to a certain class (729d–30b, 2.a.). Thus the rel. clause shows that Jesus was referring to the virgins who had a specific role in a wedding party. Λαβοῦσαι (nom. pl. fem. of 2nd aor. act. ptc. of λαμβάνω) is attendant circumstance (most EVV). Λαμπάς, -άδας, ἡ, "torch, lamp, *lantern" (esp. used to provide light outdoors)." On the specific mng. of the noun here, see N 1004–5 and D&A 3.395–96. The gen. of the refl. pron. (ἑαυτῶν) serves as a substitute for the poss. pron. (BDAG 268b–69b 3.a.) but may emphasize poss. more strongly (cf. 8:22; 21:8). The word choice emphasizes that the lamps and oil for the wedding procession were supplied by the girls rather than the hosts of the wedding. This highlights the girls' responsibility in preparing for the groom's arrival. Ἐξῆλθον 3rd pl. 2nd aor. act. indic. of dep. ἐξέρχομαι. Εἰς expresses purpose. Ὑπάντησις, -εως, ἡ, "meeting." Νυμφίος, -ου, ὁ, "groom (in a wedding)." Τοῦ νυμφίου is obj. gen. See Metzger 52–53.

25:2 Πέντε, "five." Δέ marks the next development in the story. The prep. ἐκ phrase (ἐξ αὐτῶν) serves as a substitute for the partitive gen. Ἦσαν 3rd pl. impf. indic. of εἰμί. Μωρός, -ά, -όν, "foolish, stupid." Φρόνιμος, -ον, "wise, prudent."

25:3 Γάρ marks the reason for the preceding description of each group. The art. and independent adj. μωραί is subst.: "the foolish virgins." Λαβοῦσαι (nom. pl. fem. of 2nd aor. act. ptc. of λαμβάνω) may be temp. (CSB; ESV; LEB) or *concessive (NIV). Τὰς λαμπάδας, 25:3. Αὐτῶν is poss. gen. Ἔλαβον 3rd pl. 2nd aor. act. indic. of λαμβάνω. Μετά with the gen. (ἑαυτῶν) is a marker of placement. On the use of the refl. pron. ἑαυτῶν in place of the pers. pron., see 25:1. This phrase may be short for *μετὰ τῶν λαμπάδων ἑαυτῶν (N 1005) and thus anticipate 25:4 or may mean "with them" and strengthen the sense of λαμβάνω. Ἔλαιον, -ου, τό, "(olive) oil."

25:4 Δέ is adversative (most EVV) and contrasts the wise with the foolish. The art. and independent adj. φρόνιμοι is subst.: "the wise virgins." Ἔλαβον ἔλαιον, 25:3. Ἐν marks location. Ἀγγεῖον, -ου, τό, "container." Μετά with the gen. (τῶν λαμπάδων) is a marker of placement. Ἑαυτῶν, 25:1.

25:5 Δέ prob. marks the next development in the story. Χρονίζοντος (gen. sg. masc. of pres. act. ptc. of χρονίζω, "delay, be later than expected") is gen. abs. and temp. Τοῦ νυμφίου, 25:1. Ἐνύσταξαν 3rd pl. aor. act. indic. of νυστάζω, "become drowsy." Πᾶσαι is subst.: "they all, all of them." Ἐκάθευδον (3rd pl. impf. act. indic. of καθεύδω, "sleep") is ingr. ("they fell asleep;" most EVV). See the same pair of vbs. and sequence of tense in 2 Sam 4:6.

25:6 Δέ prob. marks the next development of the narrative. Μέσης functions as an adj.: "mid-, in the middle of." Νυκτός is gen. of time: "at midnight" (W 122–24). Since the gen. of time normally refers to kind of time as opposed to the dat. of time, which refers to a specific point in time (W 122–23), the phrase "in the middle of the night" may best capture the idea (N 1007; H 2.729; cf. D&A 3.398). Κραυγή, -ῆς, ἡ, "shout." Γέγονεν (3rd sg. pf. act. indic. of dep. γίνομαι) is an aoristic (dramatic) pf. that highlights the action (Carson 576; Moule 14, 202; BDF §343.3; W 578–79). Ἰδού is a marker of strong emphasis: "here is . . . !" (BDAG 468b–d 2). The interjection introduces the content of the shout. Ὁ νυμφίος (25:1) is pred. nom. Ἐξέρχεσθε (2nd pl. pres. mid. impv. of dep. ἐξέρχομαι) is ingr.-prog. Εἰς ἀπάντησιν, 25:1.

25:7 Τότε, "at that time/moment." The particle prob. emphasizes the immediacy of the response to the cry. Ἠγέρθησαν 3rd pl. aor. pass. indic. of ἐγείρω, "wake up" [pass.]. Παρθένοι, 25:1. The dem. pron. ἐκεῖναι limits the phrase πᾶσαι αἱ παρθένοι to those mentioned earlier in the parable. Ἐκόσμησαν 3rd pl. aor. act. indic. of κοσμέω, "trim (a lamp)" (BDAG 560b–d 1). Τὰς λαμπάδας ἑαυτῶν, 25:1. The refl. pron. appears to emphasize that each virgin was responsible for trimming her own lamp.

25:8 Δέ marks a new development. Αἱ μωραί, 25:3. Ταῖς φρονίμοις, 25:4. Εἶπαν 3rd pl. aor. act. indic. of λέγω. Δότε (2nd pl. aor. act. impv. of δίδωμι) expresses urgency. Ἐκ marks the source. Τοῦ ἐλαίου, 25:3. Ὑμῶν is poss. gen. Ὅτι marks the reason for the desperate request. Αἱ λαμπάδες, 25:1. Ἡμῶν is poss. gen. Σβέννυνται (3rd pl. pres. pass. indic. of σβέννυμι, "go out, be extinguished") is futuristic pres. ("Our lamps are about to go out") or *prog. ("Our lamps are going out;" N 1007; H 2.729).

25:9 Ἀπεκρίθησαν 3rd pl. aor. pass. indic. of dep. ἀποκρίνομαι. Δέ is adversative (most EVV). Αἱ φρόνιμοι, 25:4. Λέγουσαι (nom. pl. fem. of pres. act. ptc. of λέγω) is pleonastic (CSB; NIV) or a ptc. of means (ESV). The combination of μήποτε with οὐ μή appears only here in the NT and only rarely elsewhere in early Christian literature (Didache 4:10). Here, as in the Didache, μήποτε is an expression of negated purpose: "lest, for fear that, *since otherwise." The dbl. neg. οὐ μή with the subjunc. expresses emphatic negation: "there surely will not be enough." Ἀρκέσῃ 3rd sg. aor. act. subjunc. of ἀρκέω, "be enough" (BDAG 131d–32a). Ἡμῖν and ὑμῖν are dat. of indir. obj. Πορεύεσθε (2nd pl. pres. mid. impv. of dep. πορεύομαι) is ingr.-prog. Μᾶλλον, "instead" (BDAG 613d–14c 3.a.β.). Πρός marks the direction of movement: "to the sellers" (BDAG 873d–75c 3.a.α.). Πωλοῦντας (acc. pl. masc. of pres. act. ptc. of πωλέω, "sell") is subst.: "the sellers, the ones who sell." Ἀγοράσατε (2nd pl. aor. act. impv. of ἀγοράζω, "buy") may express urgency or *reflect the brief nature of the financial transaction. Ἑαυταῖς is dat. of indir. obj.

25:10 Ἀπερχομένων (gen. pl. fem. of pres. mid. ptc. of dep. ἀπέρχομαι) is gen. abs., temp., and contemp. Αὐτῶν refers to the five foolish virgins. Ἀγοράσαι (aor. act. inf. of ἀγοράζω, "buy") expresses purpose. Ἦλθεν 3rd sg. 2nd aor. act. indic. of dep. ἔρχομαι. Νυμφίος, 25:1. Ἕτοιμος, -η, -ον, "prepared, ready." The art. and independent ἕτοιμοι is subst.: "the virgins who were prepared." The adj. recalls the command in 24:44:

"Be ready!" (N 1008). Εἰσῆλθον 3rd pl. 2nd aor. act. indic. of dep. εἰσέρχομαι. Μετά with the gen. (αὐτοῦ) expresses accompaniment: "together with him." Εἰς marks the location that was entered. Γάμος, -ου, ὁ, "wedding celebration." The pl. (τοὺς γάμους) is often used to refer to the banquet. Ἐκλείσθη 3rd sg. aor. pass. indic. of κλείω, "close, lock." Θύρα, -ας, ἡ, "door."

25:11 The acc. sg. neut. form of the comp. adj. ὕστερον functions as an adv: "later." Δέ marks a new development. Ἔρχονται (3rd pl. pres. mid. indic. of dep. ἔρχομαι) is historical pres. and marks a point of emphasis in the parable (N 1009). Καί is prob. adjunctive: "also" (CSB; NIV). Λοιπαί is attrib.: "the rest of." Παρθένοι, 25:1. Λέγουσαι (nom. pl. fem. of pres. act. ptc. of λέγω) is attendant circumstance (CSB; NIV). Κύριε is formally voc. of simple address (due to the absence of ὦ; W 67–69), but the repetition of the address intensifies the appeal. Ἄνοιξον (2nd sg. aor. act. impv. of ἀνοίγω) expresses urgency.

25:12 The def. art. ὁ functions as a pers. pron. Δέ is prob. adversative (most EVV). Ἀποκριθείς (nom. sg. masc. of aor. pass. ptc. of dep. ἀποκρίνομαι) is pleonastic but clarifies that the statement is a reply. Εἶπεν 3rd sg. 2nd aor. act. indic. of λέγω. Ἀμὴν λέγω ὑμῖν, 5:18. Οἶδα 1st sg. pf. (for pres.) act. indic. of οἶδα.

25:13 Οὖν is inferential and introduces the practical application of the parable. Γρηγορεῖτε (2nd pl. pres. act. impv. of γρηγορέω, "be alert, vigilant") is ingr.-prog. Ὅτι is causal. Οἴδατε (2nd pl. pf. [for pres.] act. indic. of οἶδα) is prog. After οὐκ, οὐδέ means "nor." See Metzger 53.

FOR FURTHER STUDY

129. The Parable of the Ten Virgins

Argyle, A. W. "Wedding Customs at the Time of Jesus." *ExpTim* 86 (1975): 214–15.

Donfried, K. P. "Allegory of the Ten Virgins (Matt 25:1–13) as a Summary of Matthean Theology." *JBL* 93 (1974): 415–28.

Waller, E. "Mt 25:1–13: The Parable of the Ten Virgins." *Proceedings* 1 (1981): 85–109.

Walvoord, J. F. "Christ's Olivet Discourse on the End of the Age: The Parable of the Ten Virgins." *BSac* 129 (1972): 99–105.

Young, R. D. "Matthew 25:1–13." *Int* 54 (2000): 419–22.

HOMILETICAL SUGGESTIONS

Here Comes the Bridegroom! (25:1–13)

1. We must be prepared for Jesus's return even if it is later than we expect (25:1–8)

2. We can prepare ourselves for Jesus's return but others cannot prepare us (25:9)

3. If we wait too late to prepare, we will be excluded from the kingdom (25:10–13)

12. The Parable of the Talents (25:14–30)

25:14 Ὥσπερ marks the prot. of a comp. The sentence contains an anacoluthon and the apod. must be supplied. The apod. is prob. sim. to the one in 24:37: οὕτως ἔσται ἡ παρουσία τοῦ υἱοῦ τοῦ ἀνθρώπου. Γάρ is causal and introduces another reason to be vigilant as commanded in 25:13. Ἀποδημῶν (nom. sg. masc. of pres. act. ptc. of ἀποδημέω, "go on a journey") is attrib.: "who was going on a journey." The pres. tense is futuristic: "about to go on a journey" (N 1013; H 2.734). Ἐκάλεσεν 3rd sg. aor. act. indic. of καλέω. The attrib. adj. ἰδίους emphasizes the man's ownership of the slaves more strongly than the poss. pron. would (BDAG 466c–67d 1.a., 2). Perhaps the adj. indicates the unusual nature of the master's action (N 1014). Παρέδωκεν 3rd sg. aor. act. indic. of παραδίδωμι, "entrust" (BDAG 761c–63b 1.a.). The use of παραδίδωμι rather than δίδωμι makes it clear that the money still belonged to the master. Αὐτοῖς refers to the slaves. The art. and independent ptc. ὑπάρχοντα (acc. pl. neut. of pres. act. ptc. of ὑπάρχω, "be at one's disposal") is subst.: "possessions" (BDAG 1029c–30a 1). Αὐτοῦ refers to the slaveowner and is gen. of poss.

25:15 The three occurrences of the rel. pron. ᾧ function as dem. pron.: "to this one . . . to the other . . . to the other." The μὲν . . . δὲ . . . δέ cstr. does not emphasize contrast, but demarcates the elements of a series (BDAG 629d–30c 1.c.). Ἔδωκεν 3rd sg. aor. act. indic. of δίδωμι. Πέντε, "five." Τάλαντον, -ου, τό, "talent (coin of high value)." Κατά marks the standard according to which the money was assigned. Ἰδίαν emphasizes that the assignment was made according to the owner's assessment of each person and his ability: "each person's" (BDAG 466c–67d 1.b.). Δύναμιν, "ability, capability" (BDAG 262b–63d 2). Ἀπεδήμησεν 3rd sg. aor. act. indic. of ἀποδημέω, "go on a journey." Despite the verse division in Eng. tr., εὐθέως ("immediately") begins the next sentence. See Metzger 53.

25:16 Πορευθείς (nom. sg. masc. of aor. pass. ptc. of dep. πορεύομαι) is attendant circumstance (most EVV). The art. and independent ptc. λαβών (nom. sg. masc. of aor. act. ptc. of λαμβάνω) is subst.: "the one who received five talents." Ἠργάσατο 3rd sg. aor. mid. indic. of dep. ἐργάζομαι, "work, do business" (BDAG 389b–90a 1). Ἐν marks the instr. or resources with which he transacted business and αὐτοῖς (neut.) refers to the five talents. Ἐκέρδησεν 3rd sg. aor. act. indic. of κερδαίνω, "gain." The adj. ἄλλα ("more;" BDAG 46d–47b 3) is subst. and the neut. gender confirms that it refers to the talents: "five more talents" (25:20). Πέντε, "five."

25:17 Ὡσαύτως "in the same way" (by investing wisely like the slave with five talents). Ὁ τὰ δύο is short for ὁ τὰ δύο λαβών (cf. 25:16). Ἐκέρδησεν ἄλλα, 21:16.

25:18 Δέ is adversative and contrasts the behavior of this slave with that of the other two. Ὁ λαβών, 25:16. Ἀπελθών (nom. sg. masc. of 2nd aor. act. ptc. of dep. ἀπέρχομαι) is attendant circumstance (most EVV). Ὤρυξεν 3rd sg. aor. act. indic. of ὀρύσσω, "dig (a hole in)." Γῆν means "ground, soil" (BDAG 196a–c 6.a.). Ἔκρυψεν 3rd sg. aor. act. indic. of κρύπτω, "hide." Ἀργύριον, -ου, τό, "silver (money)." The def. art. τοῦ is monadic (6:24) and κυρίου is poss. gen. Αὐτοῦ is gen. of subord.

25:19 Δέ marks the next development in the narrative. Μετά marks a point in time that precedes the action of the vb.: "after" (BDAG 636b–38b B.2.a.). When the adj.

πολύς modifies a noun that expresses time (χρόνον), it means "long, a lengthy period of" (BDAG 847c–50a 2.a.α.). Ἔρχεται (3rd sg. pres. mid. indic. of dep. ἔρχομαι) and συναίρει (3rd sg. pres. act. indic. of συναίρω, "settle [in the sense of bringing a financial matter to completion]") are historical pres. Levinsohn suggests that the historical pres. serves to "reactivate" the master of the slaves and to indicate he has a role to play (207). The vbs. may be foregrounded to highlight the symbolism of the parable, in which the master represents the Lord, who will come and settle accounts with human beings in eschatological judgment. Δούλων is gen. of subord. The dem. pron. ἐκείνων is anaphoric and refers to the slaves mentioned in the preceding context. Λόγον, "account" (BDAG 598d–601d 2.b.). Μετά with the gen. (αὐτῶν) expresses mutual influence or interchange of action between two parties (BDAG 636b–38b 2.c.α.).

25:20 Προσελθών (nom. sg. masc. of 2nd aor. act. ptc. of dep. προσέρχομαι, "go forward, approach") is attendant circumstance (most EVV). Ὁ τὰ πέντε τάλαντα λαβών, 25:16. Προσήνεγκεν 3rd sg. aor. act. indic. of προσφέρω, "offer, pres." Ἄλλα πέντε τάλαντα, 25:16. Λέγων (nom. sg. masc. of pres. act. ptc. of λέγω) is attendant circumstance. Κύριε is voc. of simple address. Παρέδωκας 2nd sg. aor. act. indic. of παραδίδωμι, "entrust." Ἴδε (2nd sg. aor. act. impv. of ὁράω, "look") may express urgency (or excitement). Ἐκέρδησα 1st sg. aor. act. indic. of κερδαίνω, "gain."

25:21 Ἔφη 3rd sg. aor. (or impf.) act. indic. of φημί, "say." Αὐτῷ may be slightly emphatic due to its position. Αὐτοῦ is gen. of subord. The adv. εὖ is used as an interjection that commends someone for his service or performance (BDAG 401d–2a 2): "Well done! Great job!" Δοῦλε ἀγαθὲ καὶ πιστέ is voc. of simple address: "good and trustworthy slave." With the acc. obj. (ὀλίγα), ἐπί prob. expresses ref.: "with regard to a few things." With the gen. object (πολλῶν), ἐπί expresses authority over something. BDAG suggests that there is no significant difference in mng. between the two cstr. here (363a–67c, 9.a. and c.), but the differences in the adj. πιστός and the vb. καθίστημι suggest that the shift in the case of the obj. of the prep. signals a difference in mng. Note that BDAG elsewhere (820d–21c, 1.a.α.) treats ἐπί with πιστός as equivalent to ἐν and tr. it "in connection with." Ἧς 2nd sg. impf. indic. of εἰμί. Καταστήσω (1st sg. fut. act. indic. of καθίστημι, "put in charge") is predictive (promissory). Εἴσελθε 2nd sg. 2nd aor. act. impv. of dep. εἰσέρχομαι, "enter." All seven instances of the impv. form of this vb. (Matt 6:6; 7:13; 25:21, 23; Mark 13:15; Acts 9:6) are in the aor. tense. Thus the tense is prob. due more to the nature of the lexeme than a desire to express urgency. Χαρά, -ᾶς, ἡ, "joy, gladness." Since the vb. εἰσέρχομαι does not often refer to experiencing emotion, some scholars suggest that χαρά refers to a festive dinner or banquet (BDAG 1077a–c 2.c.). However, εἰσέρχομαι may mean "experience" or "share in," which fits this context well (BDAG 293d–94c 2; NIV; CSB). Τοῦ κυρίου may be subj. gen., in which case the ref. is to the *master's joy that he feels and the slave will share (NIV; CSB) or is gen. of source, referring to the joy that the master grants. Σου is gen. of subord. The master refers to himself in the 3rd pers.

25:22 Προσελθών, 25:20. Καί is adjunctive and highlights the similarity between this slave's approach and the previous slave's. Ὁ τὰ δύο τάλαντα is short for ὁ . . . λαβών, 25:18. Κύριε, . . . τάλαντά μοι παρέδωκας ἴδε ἄλλα . . . τάλαντα ἐκέρδησα, 25:20.

25:23 Ἔφη αὐτῷ ὁ κύριος αὐτοῦ· εὖ, δοῦλε ἀγαθὲ καὶ πιστέ, ἐπὶ ὀλίγα ἦς πιστός, ἐπὶ πολλῶν σε καταστήσω· εἴσελθε εἰς τὴν χαρὰν τοῦ κυρίου σου, 25:21.

25:24 Δέ marks the next development in the narrative. Προσελθών, 25:20. Καί is adjunctive and highlights that this slave approached the master like the previous two slaves did. However, his similarity to them ends there, since his statement is in stark contrast to theirs. Ὁ τὸ ἓν τάλαντον λαβών (25:18) now becomes ὁ . . . εἰληφώς (nom. sg. masc. of pf. act. ptc. of λαμβάνω). The purpose of the tense shift is unclear. Κύριε is voc. of simple address. Ἔγνων 1st sg. 2nd. aor. act. indic. of γινώσκω. In an error uncharacteristic of the tr., the LEB treats this vb. as a causal ptc. Σε is the dir. obj. of the vb. ἔγνων, which initially creates doubts that ὅτι is recitative. Not surprisingly, some mss. (D Θ) and tr. (NIV) that treat the ὅτι as recitative omit σε. The ὅτι is prob. recitative and marks a second object of knowledge, in which the object from the preceding clause becomes the subj. of the ὅτι clause (BDAG 731d–32d 1.f.; CSB; LEB; ESV). The cstr. expresses that the slave knew the master personally, and that entailed knowledge of his demeanor and behavior patterns. Σκληρός, -ά, -όν, "harsh, cruel," is attrib.: "you are a cruel man." Εἶ 2nd sg. pres. indic. of εἰμί. Ἄνθρωπος is pred. nom. Θερίζων (nom. sg. masc. of pres. act. ptc. of θερίζω, "harvest") is attrib.: "who harvests." Ἔσπειρας 2nd sg. aor. act. indic. of σπείρω, "sow (seeds)." Συνάγων (nom. sg. masc. of pres. act. ptc. of συνάγω, "gather [crops]") is attrib.: "and who gathers." Ὅθεν, "from where, whence." Διεσκόρπισας 2nd sg. aor. act. indic. of διασκορπίζω, "scatter." The vb. prob. refers to scattering seed, but some scholars think that it refers to winnowing.

25:25 Φοβηθείς (nom. sg. masc. of aor. pass. ptc. of φοβέω, "be afraid" [pass.]) is *causal (LEB; NLT) or attendant circumstance (NIV; ESV; CSB). The tr. that regard the ptc. as attendant circumstance generally treat the καί as introducing a result (BDAG 494a–96c 1.b.ζ.). Ἀπελθών (nom. sg. masc. of 2nd aor. act. ptc. of dep. ἀπέρχομαι) is attendant circumstance (most EVV). Ἔκρυψα 1st sg. aor. act. indic. of κρύπτω. Τὸ τάλαντόν, 25:15. Σου is poss. gen. Γῇ, 25:18. Ἴδε (2nd sg. 2nd aor. act. impv. of ὁράω) calls attention to the talent. Ἔχεις (2nd sg. pres. act. indic. of ἔχω). The pres. tense is prob. prog.: "you (still) have what belongs to you," i.e., "I did not risk and lose your talent." The neut. art. 2nd pers. sg. poss. adj. (τὸ σόν) is subst. and means "what belongs to you."

25:26 Ἀποκριθείς (nom. sg. masc. of aor. pass. ptc. of dep. ἀποκρίνομαι) is pleonastic, but clarifies that the statement is a reply (most EVV). Αὐτοῦ is gen. of subord. Although the interjection ὦ is absent, the severity of the description of the slave and the punishment to which he was assigned suggests that the cstr. πονηρὲ δοῦλε καὶ ὀκνηρέ is voc. of emotional address. Ὀκνηρός, -ά, -όν, "idle, lazy" (BDAG 702a 1). Ἤδεις (2nd sg. pluperf. [for aor.] act. indic. of οἶδα) is prob. interr., as the punctuation in the UBS[5], NIV, and ESV suggest. If interrogatory, the question involves an indictment. The slave did not actually know what he thought he knew and the master's treatment of the other two slaves proves that the slave's opinion of the master was incorrect and unfair. The CSB and NLT treat the clause as cond., since the οὖν in the next verse implies that the steps in v. 27 are an inference based on the assumption in v. 26. Ὅτι is recitative and introduces the content of knowledge. Θερίζω (1st sg. pres. act. indic. of θερίζω, "harvest") is prob. customary pres. since it involves a characterization of the master. Ἔσπειρα 1st sg. aor. act. indic. of σπείρω, "sow (seeds)." Συνάγω (1st sg. pres. act. indic. of συνάγω, "gather [crops]") is prob. customary and involves a characterization of the master. Ὅθεν, "from where, whence." Διεσκόρπισα 1st sg. aor. act. indic. of διασκορπίζω, "scatter."

25:27 Οὖν is inferential and introduces a description of the behavior that would have been appropriate. Ἔδει (3rd sg. impf. act. indic. of δέω, "it is necessary" [impers.]) indicates that something that should have taken place did not occur (BDAG 213d–14c 2.d.). Σε is acc. subj. of the inf. Βαλεῖν (aor. act. inf. of βάλλω) is complementary. Τὰ ἀργύρια, 25:18. Μου is poss. gen. Τραπεζίτης, -ου, ὁ, "banker" (BDAG 1013d). Καί is resultative: "so, and then." Ἐλθών (nom. sg. masc. of 2nd aor. act. ptc. of dep. ἔρχομαι) is temp. and contemp. Ἐγώ is emphatic. Ἐκομισάμην 1st sg. aor. mid. indic. of κομίζω, "get back, recover" [mid.] (BDAG 557c–d 2). The use of a secondary tense and the particle of contingency ἄν presents this clause as the apod. of a second-class cond. statement, in which both the prot. and apod. are contrary to fact. Although the preceding clause lacks the particle εἰ, ἔδει expresses the necessity of an action that did not occur and thus functions like the prot. of a second-class cond. Thus the last clause means "so when I came I would have recovered what belonged to me." The art. and independent poss. adj. ἐμόν is subst.: "what is mine, my property" (BDAG 323a–b b). Σύν with the impers. dat. obj. (τόκῳ) means: "with" (BDAG 961c–62b 3.a.α.). Τόκος, -ου, ὁ, "interest (on money lent)."

25:28 Ἄρατε (2nd pl. aor. act. impv. of αἴρω, "take away" [BDAG 28c–29a 3]) may express urgency but the nature of the lexical idea prompts preference for the aor. in commands. The command was apparently issued to other slaves. Οὖν is inferential and shows that the treatment of the slave is a response to his failure to fulfill his duty. Ἀπό with the gen. (αὐτοῦ) expresses separation and clarifies the mng. of ἄρατε. Τὸ τάλαντον, 25:15. Δότε (2nd pl. aor. act. impv. of δίδωμι) may express urgency. The art. and independent ptc. ἔχοντι (dat. sg. masc. of pres. act. ptc. of ἔχω) is subst.: "the one who has." The def. art. τὰ modifying δέκα τάλαντα is anaphoric and refers to the ten talents presented to the master by the first slave. The ref. confirms that the reward mentioned in 25:21 involved permitting the faithful slave to keep both what the master orig. entrusted to him and the additional amount that the investment earned.

25:29 Γάρ introduces the reason for the master's response to the wicked slave and reward of the faithful slaves. Nolland refers to this use as "explanatory" (1019) but this label is best reserved for the use of γάρ as a marker of clarification (BDAG 189a–90a 2). The art. and independent adj. παντί is subst. and pers. (masc.) and ἔχοντι (dat. sg. masc. of pres. act. ptc. of ἔχω) is attrib.: "to everyone who has (something)." Δοθήσεται (3rd sg. fut. pass. indic. of δίδωμι) and περισσευθήσεται (3rd sg. fut. pass. indic. of περισσεύω, "cause to have an abundance") are predictive. At the lit. level, the unnamed agent is the master. Δέ is adversative and contrasts the fate of the faithful slaves and the unfaithful slave. Τοῦ μὴ ἔχοντος (gen. sg. masc. of pres. act. ptc. of ἔχω) is subst. and gen. of separation (most EVV). Καί is ascensive ("even") and stresses the full extent of the wicked slave's impoverishment. The rel. pron. ὅ is acc. sg. neut. and serves as the dir. obj. of ἔχει (2nd sg. pres. act. indic. of ἔχω): "what he has." Ἀρθήσεται (3rd sg. fut. pass. indic. of αἴρω, "take away") is pred. and the master is the unnamed agent. Ἀπ᾽ αὐτοῦ, 25:28.

25:30 Ἀχρεῖος, -ον, "worthless, of no profit to the owner" (BDAG 160b 1). Ἐκβάλετε 2nd pl. 2nd aor. act. impv. of ἐκβάλλω, "throw out." The nature of the lexeme prob. prompted use of the aor. The only use of the pres. impv. of ἐκβάλλω in the NT is in Matt 10:18, in which the pres. tense is iter. Εἰς τὸ σκότος τὸ ἐξώτερον· ἐκεῖ ἔσται ὁ κλαυθμὸς καὶ ὁ βρυγμὸς τῶν ὀδόντων, 8:12.

FOR FURTHER STUDY

130. The Parable of the Talents

Brisson, E. C. "Matthew 25:14–30." *Int* 56 (2002): 307–10.

Chenoweth, B. "Identifying the Talents: Contextual Clues for the Interpretation of the Parable of the Talents (Matthew 25:14–30)." *TynBul* 56 (2005): 61–72.

Dipboye, C. "Matthew 25:14–30—to Survive or to Serve?" *RevExp* 92 (1995): 507–12.

Naegele, J. "Translation of *Talanton* 'Talent.'" *BT* 37 (1986): 441–43.

Ukpong, J. S. "The Parable of the Talents (Matt 25:14–30): Commendation or Critique of Exploitation? A Social-Historical and Theological Reading." *Neot* 46 (2012): 190–207.

Walvoord, J. F. "Christ's Olivet Discourse on the End of the Age: The Parable of the Talents." *BSac* 129 (1972): 206–10.

HOMILETICAL SUGGESTIONS

It Will Soon Be Payday! (25:14–30)

1. The Lord has entrusted great responsibilities to his disciples that they must fulfill before his return (25:14)
2. These responsibilities are consistent with the gifts and abilities of each disciple (25:15)
3. The disciples should use the time until the Lord returns to prepare for his coming by fulfilling their responsibilities (25:16–18)
4. The Lord will return to determine whether we fulfilled our responsibilities, even though this may take longer than some expect (25:19)
5. The Lord is both a gracious and harsh judge: gracious to the faithful and harsh to the negligent (25:21, 26–28)
   a. Those who fulfill the responsibilities that the Lord entrusts to them will be richly rewarded (25:21–22, 28)
   b. Those who neglect the responsibilities that the Lord entrusts to them will be eternally punished (25:30)

13. Judgment of the Nations (25:31–46)

25:31 Δέ marks the next development in the discourse. BDAG incorrectly lists this occurrence of ὅταν as an instance in which the particle "pert. to an action that is conditional, possible, and, in many instances, repeated," approximating the sense of ἐάν

(BDAG 730d–31c 1, esp. 1.a.β.). The particle indicates that the timing of the action is unknown (cf. 24:36), but not that the action itself is cond. or merely possible. Both Jesus and Matthew clearly viewed the Parousia of the Son of Man as certain. Ἐλθῃ 3rd sg. 2nd aor. act. subjunc. of dep. ἔρχομαι. Ὁ υἱὸς τοῦ ἀνθρώπου, 9:6. Ἐν marks a state or condition (BDAG 326c–30b 2.a.): "clothed in, surrounded by his glory." Αὐτοῦ may be gen. of *source, producer, or poss. If source, the glory emanates from the Son of Man. The adj. πάντες suggests that all angelic beings attend the Son of Man. Consequently, some scribes added the adj. ἅγιοι to exclude fallen angels. Μετά with the gen. (αὐτοῦ) indicates accompaniment (BDAG 636b–638b 2.a.α.). Τότε means "(immediately) after that." Καθίσει (3rd sg. fut. act. indic. of καθίζω) is predictive fut. Ἐπί with the gen. (θρόνου) marks location above and in contact with an object: "on." Δόξης is attrib. gen.: "glorious throne." Αὐτοῦ is poss. gen. The Son of Man is no intruder or usurper. The throne is reserved for him, and he alone is to occupy it.

25:32 Συναχθήσονται (3rd pl. fut. pass. indic. of συνάγω) is predictive fut. The agent(s) of the pass. vb. is unnamed. Since the angels gather (ἐπισυνάγω) the elect in 24:31 and are mentioned in 25:31, perhaps they gather the nations as well. Ἔμπροσθεν with the gen. (αὐτοῦ) means "in the presence of" and is often used to describe appearance before a judge for verdict and sentencing (BDAG 325a–c 1.b.β.). The adj. πάντα modifying τὰ ἔθνη portrays a throng of enormous size. Ἀφορίσει (3rd sg. fut. act. indic. of ἀφορίζω, "separate") is predictive fut. Αὐτούς may refer to the nations, but the use of the masc. rather than the neut. form suggests that the referent is the many individuals that constitute the various nations (N 1025, though N reaches this conclusion based on context rather than grammar). Ἀπό expresses separation. The comp. particle ὥσπερ indicates that the separation of individual nations by the Son of Man is analogous to that performed by the shepherd. Ποιμήν, -ένος, ὁ, "shepherd." The def. art. ὁ modifying ποιμήν may be *generic (W 227–31) or anaphoric. If anaphoric, the ref. is likely to be the shepherd of Ezekiel 34:17, 20, in which case the Son of Man is compared to Yahweh. Ἀφορίζει (3rd sg. pres. act. indic. of ἀφορίζω) is gnomic. Πρόβατον, -ου, τό, "sheep." Ἀπό expresses separation. Ἔριφος, -ου, ὁ, "goat."

25:33 Μὲν . . . δέ marks an emphatic contrast in which μέν is concessive and δέ adversative (BDAG 629d–30c 1.a.). Στήσει (3rd sg. fut. act. indic. of ἵστημι, "place") is predictive fut. Τὰ πρόβατα, 25:32. Ἐκ marks a location (BDAG 295d–98b 2). When pl. and in the independent position, the adj. δεξιός means "right side" (BDAG 217c–18a 1.a.). Αὐτοῦ refers to the Son of Man and is partitive gen. Τὰ ἐρίφια, 25:32. Ἐξ marks a location and the pl. independent form of εὐώνυμος means "left side."

25:34 Τότε means "after that [the division of the nations]." Ἐρεῖ (3rd sg. fut. act. indic. of λέγω) is pred. fut. ὁ βασιλεύς refers to the Son of Man, a royal figure in Daniel 7. The def. art. ὁ modifying βασιλεύς is par excellence. The def. art. τοῖς is a substantiver: "those on his right side. Ἐκ δεξιῶν αὐτοῦ, 25:33. Δεῦτε is a hortatory particle: "Come on!" The art. and independent ptc. εὐλογημένοι (voc. pl. masc. of pf. pass. ptc. of εὐλογέω, "bless") is subst.: "you who have been blessed." The pf. ptc. seems to be resultative (most EVV) and describe the ongoing state brought about by a divine blessing on the heirs of the kingdom that was granted earlier. Nolland, however, argues that the pf. is futuristic since the LXX frequently uses the pf. to describe future blessing (1027). Τοῦ πατρός identifies the agent who performed the blessing. Μου is gen. of relationship. Κληρονομήσατε (2nd pl. aor. act. impv. of κληρονομέω, "inherit") expresses urgency, esp. since the aor. impv. is combined with δεῦτε. Ἡτοιμασμένην (acc. sg. fem. of pf. pass. ptc. of ἑτοιμάζω, "prepare") is attrib.: "the kingdom that has been prepared." Ὑμῖν is indir. obj. of the ptc. Ἀπό marks the time at which an action begins: "since" (BDAG 105a–7b 2.b.). Καταβολή, -ῆς, ἡ, "founding, beginning." Κόσμου is prob. obj. gen. The phrase ἀπὸ καταβολῆς κόσμου means "since (God's) act of founding the world." The fact that the kingdom was prepared for these specific nations at creation shows that their inheritance of the kingdom was not based on their actions. This suggests that the reasons stated for their inheritance in 25:35 are evidence that they have been blessed by God rather than the basis for that blessing.

25:35 Γάρ marks the evidences (D&A 3.427) that confirm that these nations are among those previously blessed by God and for whom he prepared the kingdom from the foundation of the world. Ἐπείνασα 1st sg. aor. act. indic. of πεινάω, "be hungry." Ἐδώκατε 2nd pl. aor. act. indic. of δίδωμι. Μοι is dat. of indir. obj. Φαγεῖν (aor. act. inf. of ἐσθίω, "eat") is inf. of purpose. If a dir. obj. of ἐδώκατε had been explicit, the inf. would have been epex. (John 4:32). Ἐδίψησα 1st sg. aor. act. indic. of διψάω, "be thirsty." Ἐποτίσατε 2nd pl. aor. act. indic. of ποτίζω, "give a drink." Με is acc. of dir. obj. in an implied dbl. acc. of pers.-thing. Ξένος, -η, -ον, "foreign, foreigner" (subst.). Ἤμην 1st sg. impf. indic. of εἰμί. Συνηγάγετε 2nd pl. aor. act. indic. of συνάγω, "invite as a guest" (BDAG 962b–63a 4). On this sense, see Judg 19:15, 18 (LXX) and N 1030.

25:36 The pred. adj. γυμνός implies the copulative ἤμην. Γυμνός, -ή, -όν, "poorly clothed" (BDAG 208b–d 2). Περιεβάλετε 2nd pl. aor. act. indic. of περιβάλλω, "clothe, provide clothes for" (BDAG 799b–d 2.e.). Ἠσθένησα 1st sg. aor. act. indic. of ἀσθενέω, "be sick." Ἐπεσκέψασθε 2nd pl. aor. mid. indic. of dep. ἐπισκέπτομαι, "visit, take care of." Φυλακή, -ῆς, ἡ, "prison" (BDAG 1067c–68a 3). Ἤμην, 25:35. Ἤλθατε 2nd pl. 2nd aor. act. indic. of dep. ἔρχομαι. The prep. πρός is typically used with the acc. of pers. after ἔρχομαι to identify the person to whom the subj. is coming (BDAG 393c–95b 1.a.β.): "to."

25:37 Τότε, "after that," introduces the next event in the sequence. Ἀποκριθήσονται (3rd pl. fut. pass. indic. of dep. ἀποκρίνομαι, "answer" [pass.]) is predictive fut. The art. and independent adj. δίκαιοι is subst. and the masc. gender indicates that it is pers.: "the righteous people." Λέγοντες (nom. sg. masc. of pres. act. ptc. of λέγω) is pleo-nastic. Κύριε is voc. of simple address. The interr. adv. of time πότε introduces a dir. question: "when?" The πότε modifies all of the indic. vbs. in the verse and indicates that they are interrogatory indic. The position of σε may express emphasis. Εἴδομεν 1st pl. aor. act. indic. of ὁράω. Πεινῶντα (acc. sg. masc. of pres. act. ptc. of πεινάω, "be hungry") is pred. ptc. and identifies the state of the king when the righteous saw him. Ἐθρέψαμεν 1st pl. aor. act. indic. of τρέφω, "feed." Διψῶντα (acc. sg. masc. of pres. act. ptc. of διψάω, "be thirsty") is pred. ptc. Ἐποτίσαμεν 1st pl. aor. act. indic. of ποτίζω, "give a drink."

25:38 Δέ seems to serve merely to break up the series of questions into brief sections. Πότε δέ σε εἴδομεν, 25:37. Ξένον, 25:35. Συνηγάγομεν 1st pl. 2nd aor. act. indic. of συνάγω, "gather." Γυμνόν, 25:36. Περιεβάλομεν 1st pl. aor. act. indic. of περιβάλλω, "clothe, provide clothes for."

25:39 Δέ, 25:38. Πότε σε εἴδομεν, 25:37. Ἀσθενοῦντα (acc. sg. masc. of pres. act. ptc. of ἀσθενέω, "be sick") is pred. ptc. (see 25:37). Φυλακῇ, 25:36. Ἤλθομεν 1st pl. 2nd aor. act. indic. of dep. ἔρχομαι. Πρός, 25:36.

25:40 Ἀποκριθείς (nom. sg. masc. of aor. pass. ptc. of dep. ἀποκρίνομαι) is pleonastic but clarifies that the statement is a reply to the question of the righteous ones. Ὁ βασιλεύς ἐρεῖ, 25:34. Αὐτοῖς refers to the righteous people. Ἀμὴν λέγω ὑμῖν, 5:18. Ἐπί with the acc. (ὅσον) serves as a marker of measure: "to the extent" (BDAG 363a–67c 13). The correlative of extent ὅσος may express *time (NLT; BDAG 729a–c 1.b.) or quantity (NIV; CSB; BDAG 729a–c 2). Since the statement is a reply to questions introduced by πότε, the temp. use of ὅσος is most likely. Ἐποιήσατε 2nd pl. aor. act. indic. of ποιέω. Ποιέω encompasses all of the benevolent actions listed in 25:35–36. The near dem. pron. τούτων prob. implies that the "brothers" are pres. and visible to both the king and the righteous. Τῶν ἀδελφῶν is partitive gen. Μου is gen. of relationship. Ἐλάχιστος, -ίστη, -ον, "least," superl. form of μίκρος. Nolland suggests that the adj. may recall the uses of the positive adj. in 10:42; 18:6, 10, 14 (1032). Τῶν ἐλαχίστων is attrib. and in the 2nd attrib. position that places emphasis on both the noun and the adj. while making the adj. climactic (W 306–7; R 777). Ἐμοί is emphatic (BDAG 275a–c). Kindness to the brother of lowest standing was service to the king himself, who was "the greatest" in dramatic contrast to "the least."

25:41 Τότε ἐρεῖ, 25:34. Καί is adjunctive. Ἐξ εὐωνύμων, 25:33. The def. art. τοῖς with the prep. phrase is a substantiver: "the ones on his right side." Πορεύεσθε (2nd pl. pres. mid. impv. of dep. πορεύομαι, "go") is prob. ingr.-prog. The aor. impv. of this vb. (like most vbs. of motion) is relatively rare (only four out of twenty-seven total occurrences; Matt 8:9; Luke 7:8; Acts 9:11; 28:26). Ἀπό expresses separation: "away from." Mss. that include the def. art. with the ptc. κατηραμένοι (nom. or *voc. pl. masc. of pf. pass. ptc. of dep. καταράομαι, "be cursed" [pass.]) regard the ptc. as subst.: "you who are cursed, you cursed ones" (most EVV). If anar., the ptc. could be interpreted as adv. and causal: "since you have been cursed." However, the subst. interpretation is more likely (with or without the art.), since it results in greater symmetry with the king's pronouncement in 25:34. Τὸ αἰώνιον is in the 2nd attrib. position and emphasizes both the noun and adj. but presents the adj. as climactic. The art. ptc. ἡτοιμασμένον (acc. sg. neut. of pf. pass. ptc. of ἑτοιμάζω, "prepare") is attrib. and best tr. as a rel. clause in which the def. art. functions like a rel. pron. Based on the form of 25:34, one expects the indir. obj. ὑμῖν. The substitution of τῷ διαβόλῳ καὶ τοῖς ἀγγέλοις αὐτοῦ implies that although God prepared the kingdom at creation for the righteous whom he blessed, he did not prepare hell for the cursed ones, but for the devil and his angels. Διάβολος, -ον, "devil" (subst.). The def. art. is monadic. It was likely the description of demons as the devil's angels that prompted scribes to insert the adj. ἅγιοι in 25:31.

25:42 See 25:35.

25:43 See 25:35b–36. Ἀσθενής, -ές, "sick."
25:44 See 25:37. Αὐτοί is emphatic. Ἀσθενῇ, 25:43. Διηκονήσαμεν 1st pl. aor. act. indic. of διακονέω, "serve, help."
25:45 See 25:40. Hagner rightly argues that the omission of the phrase τῶν ἀδελφῶν μου is simply an abridgment and does not indicate a change in mng. from the phrase in 25:40 (746). The shorter form that appears here was prob. the basis for the deletion of τῶν ἀδελφῶν μου and is not evidence (contrary to D&A 3.428 n. 53) that the phrase in 25:40 was a scribal addition supporting a later Christian application to disciples.
25:46 Ἀπελεύσονται (3rd pl. fut. mid. indic. of dep. ἀπέρχομαι, "go away, depart") is predictive fut. The near dem. pron. οὗτοι is subst. and refers to the cursed ones. Κόλασις, -εως, ἡ, "torture, punishment." Δέ is strongly adversative and contrasts the two very different destinies of the righteous and the cursed. Οἱ δίκαιοι is subst.: "the righteous ones." The vb. ἀπελεύσονται from the preceding clause is implied.

FOR FURTHER STUDY

131. Judgment of the Nations

Grindheim, S. "Ignorance Is Bliss: Attitudinal Aspects of the Judgment according to Works in Matthew 25:31–46." *NovT* 50 (2008): 313–31.

Ladd, G. E. "The Parable of the Sheep and the Goats in Recent Interpretation." Pages 191–99 in *New Dimensions in New Testament Study*. Edited by R. N. Longenecker and M. C. Tenney. Grand Rapids: Zondervan, 1974.

Pond, E. W. "The Background and Timing of the Judgment of the Sheep and Goats." *BSac* 159 (2002): 201–20.

————. "Who Are the Sheep and Goats in Matthew 25:31–46?" *BSac* 159 (2002): 288–301.

Weber, K. "The Image of Sheep and Goats in Matthew 25:31–46." *CBQ* 59 (1997): 657–78.

HOMILETICAL SUGGESTIONS

One Left Turn to Destruction (25:31–46)

1. When the Son of Man returns, he will judge all people of all nations (25:31–33)
2. Those who have displayed allegiance to Jesus by kindnesses to his disciples will enter his kingdom (25:34–40)
   a. God has graciously blessed the heirs of the kingdom
   b. God has prepared his kingdom for his heirs since creation
3. Those who rejected Jesus by ignoring the needs of his disciples will be eternally punished (25:41–46)
4. People show how they respond to Jesus by their treatment of his disciples (25:40, 46)

D. JESUS'S PASSION (26:1–27:66)

Matthew 26–27 constitutes a new section of the Gospel that may be subdivided into six subsections that are demarcated using a framing device. See N 1042–43.

1. The Conspiracy Against Jesus (26:1–5)

26:1 Καὶ ἐγένετο ὅτε ἐτέλεσεν ὁ Ἰησοῦς πάντας τοὺς λόγους τούτους is important for understanding the structure of the Gospel. Similar markers appear at the end of each of the five major discourses (7:28; 11:1; 13:53; 19:1; 26:1). The cstr. here is identical to 7:28 and 19:1 except for the addition of the adj. πάντας. The adj. suggests that the cstr. here marks the conclusion of all the major discourses (H 2.754; N 1044). Now that the instruction contained in the discourses is complete, Jesus announces that his death is imminent.

26:2 Οἴδατε 2nd pl. pf. [for pres.] act. indic. of οἶδα. The pres. time rather than prog. aspect is prominent. Ὅτι marks the content of the knowledge. Μετά with the acc. is a temp. marker: "after two days." Πάσχα, τό, "Passover festival" (indecl.). The preceding temp. phrase confirms that γίνεται (3rd sg. pres. mid. indic. of dep. γίνομαι) is futuristic pres. and highlights the immediacy and certainty of the occurrence. Ὁ υἱὸς τοῦ ἀνθρώπου, 9:6. Παραδίδοται (3rd sg. pres. pass. indic. of παραδίδωμι, "hand over") is futuristic pres. (most EVV) and emphasizes immediacy and certainty of the action. Εἰς with the def. art. τό and inf. (σταυρωθῆναι aor. pass. inf. of σταυρόω, "crucify") expresses purpose.

26:3 Τότε prob. means "at that time." The plotting of the Jewish leaders was concurrent with Jesus's statement. Συνήχθησαν 3rd pl. aor. pass. indic. of συνάγω, "gather." Οἱ ἀρχιερεῖς καὶ οἱ πρεσβύτεροι τοῦ λαοῦ, 21:23. Αὐλή, -ῆς, ἡ, "courtyard, *palace" (BDAG 150c 2.b.; most EVV). Τοῦ ἀρχιερέως is gen. of poss. The art. ptc. λεγομένου (gen. sg. masc. of pres. pass. ptc. of λέγω) is either *attrib. (most EVV) and thus to be tr. as a rel. clause (who was called) or subst. and appos. ("the one called;" NLT).

26:4 Συνεβουλεύσαντο 3rd pl. aor. mid. indic. of συμβουλεύω, "plot [mid.]" (BDAG 957a 2). Ἵνα with the subjunc. (κρατήσωσιν 3rd pl. aor. act. subjunc. of κρατέω, "arrest;" BDAG 564c–65a 3.a.) and ἀποκτείνωσιν (3rd pl. aor. act. subjunc. of ἀποκτείνω) marks purpose. Δόλος, -ου, ὁ, "cunning" (BDAG 256c–d). Δόλῳ is dat. of means.

26:5 Ἔλεγον (3rd sg. impf. act. indic. of λέγω) is prob. iter. and indicates that, during the meeting, they repeatedly refused to consider action during the Passover festival. Δέ is prob. adversative and highlights that the scheme of the leaders was contrary to Jesus's prophecy in 26:2. The neg. μή is used in the abbreviated quotation since a hortatory subjunc. is implied (BDAG 644d–46d 1.c.ζ.): "Let's not arrest him at the festival." Ἐν with the dat. (τῇ ἑορτῇ) is marker of a period of time during which an event occurs (BDAG 326c–30b 10.a.). Ἵνα with the subjunc. (γένηται 3rd sg. 2nd aor. mid. subjunc. of dep. γίνομαι) expresses purpose. Θόρυβος, -ου, ὁ, "uproar, riot" (BDAG 458b–c 3.b.). Ἐν, "among." Λαῷ refers to common Jewish people in contrast with the Jewish leaders (BDAG 586c–87a 2.a.).

FOR FURTHER READING

132. The Trial and Execution of Jesus

Brown, R. *The Death of the Messiah: From Gethsemane to the Grave (A Commentary on the Passion Narratives in the Four Gospels).* New York: Doubleday, 1994.

HOMILETICAL SUGGESTIONS

The Murderous Plot (26:1–5)

1. Jesus's execution came after his teaching ministry was completed
2. Jesus's execution occurred during Passover to show that he died as our sacrifice
3. Jesus's execution was plotted by deceptive men
4. Jesus's execution was orchestrated by men who feared the crowds when they should have feared God

2. The Anointing at Bethany (26:6–13)

26:6 Δέ marks the next development in the narrative. Τοῦ Ἰησοῦ γενομένου (gen. sg. masc. of aor. mid. ptc. of dep. γίνομαι) is gen. abs. and temp.: "when Jesus was in Bethany." Σίμωνος is gen. of poss. Λεπρός, -ά, -όν, "with a bad skin disease." Τοῦ λεπροῦ is subst. and gen. of simple appos.: "the person with a bad skin disease, the leper." The context suggests that Simon had been healed, so the more appropriate tr. is "former leper" (cf. NLT).

26:7 Προσῆλθεν 3rd sg. aor. act. indic. of dep. προσέρχομαι. Αὐτῷ is dat. of dir. obj. Ἔχουσα (nom. sg. fem. of pres. act. ptc. of ἔχω) is attrib.: "a woman who had." Ἀλάβαστρος, -ου, ὁ, "vase [for holding perfume or ointment]." Such vessels were often made of alabaster, but the word was also used for vases made of other materials, much like the reed of a modern flute may be made of synthetic material rather than actual reed. Μύρον, -ου, τό, "perfume, aromatic ointment." Βαρυτίμος, -ον, "very expensive, valuable." Κατέχεεν 3rd sg. aor. act. indic. of καταχέω, "pour." Αὐτοῦ is partitive gen. Ἀνακειμένου (gen. sg. masc. of pres. mid. ptc. of dep. ἀνάκειμαι, "recline [at the table to eat]" is gen. abs. and temp.: "while he was reclining."

26:8 Ἰδόντες (nom. pl. masc. of aor. act. ptc. of ὁράω) is temp. (most EVV). Δέ prob. marks the next development in the narrative. Ἠγανάκτησαν 3rd pl. aor. act. indic. of ἀγανακτέω, "be angry [in response to a perceived wrong]." Λέγοντες (nom. pl. masc. of pres. act. ptc. of λέγω) is *attendant circumstance (most EVV) or ptc. of result. Εἰς with the interr. pron. τί questions the purpose of an action: "What is the purpose of; why?" Ἀπώλεια, -ας, ἡ, "waste" (BDAG 127a–b 1). The use of the noun suggests that the question is a rhetorical indictment, since the action would not have been a waste if it had a meaningful purpose. The near dem. pron. αὕτη clarifies that the ref. is to the action just performed.

26:9 The impf. vb. ἐδύνατο (3rd sg. impf. mid. indic. of dep. δύναμαι, "be able") indicates that the action of the following inf. was previously possible but is no longer. Thus the vb. is best tr. "could" (BDF §358). Γάρ introduces the reason for the accusatory question. Τοῦτο refers to the perfume (μύρον) and is acc. subj. of the inf. Πραθῆναι (aor. pass. inf. of πιπράσκω, "sell") is complementary. The adj. πολλοῦ is subst. and gen. of price (W 122): "for much money." A second acc. subj. of the inf. ("this money") is implied (NIV; NLT). Δοθῆναι (aor. pass. inf. of δίδωμι) is complementary. Πτωχοῖς (dat. pl. masc. of πτωχός, -ή, -όν, "poor") is subst. and indir. obj. of the inf.

26:10 Δέ marks the next development in the dialogue. Γνούς (nom. sg. masc. of aor. act. ptc. of γινώσκω) is causal (most EVV) or attendant circumstance. Αὐτοῖς refers to the disciples who criticized the apparent waste. The interr. pron. τί queries the reason for the behavior. Κόπος, -ου, ὁ, "trouble" (BDAG 558d–59a 1). The use of the pl. may be intensive and indicate that they caused multiple problems for the woman. Παρέχετε 2nd pl. pres. act. indic. of παρέχω, "cause" (BDAG 776c–77a 3.a.). Γάρ introduces the reason for Jesus's own indicting question. Ἠργάσατο 3rd sg. aor. mid. indic. of dep. ἐργάζομαι. With the vb. ἐργάζομαι, the prep. εἰς marks the indir. obj. to whom the action is done (BDAG 389b–90a 2.a.).

26:11 Γάρ marks the first reason that the woman's action should be considered good. Nolland appears to view all three γάρ clauses as parallel (1054). However, it is more likely that the last two γάρ clauses are subord. to the first. Τοὺς πτωχούς, 26:9. Ἔχετε (2nd pl. pres. act. indic. of ἔχω) is gnomic. Μετά expresses accompaniment. The refl. pron. ἑαυτῶν is used in place of the 2nd pl. pron. It may be emphatic and function like a combination of the pers. pron. and the intensive use of αὐτός (BDAG 268b–69b 1.b.). Ἐμέ is emphatic both by form and position. Δέ is adversative and contrasts the positive (what the disciples do have) with the neg. (what they do not have). Ἔχετε (2nd pl. pres. act. indic. of ἔχω) is futuristic pres. (NIV; ESV; NLT) or *gnomic (CSB; LEB).

26:12 Γάρ introduces a second reason for a positive appraisal of the woman's action. Βαλοῦσα (nom. sg. fem. of aor. act. ptc. of βάλλω, "pour" [BDAG 163b–64a 3.b.) is *temp. (NIV; LEB) or means (CSB; NLT). Αὕτη identifies the woman as the subj. of both the ptc. and the main vb. Τὸ μύρον, 26:7. The shift from ἐπὶ τῆς κεφαλῆς to ἐπὶ τοῦ σώματός may be necessary merely to highlight the significance of the act (since the entire body was anointed at burial; N 1055 n. 47) or to indicate that the perfume applied to the head ran down to his body also. Some early scribes removed the apparent discrepancy by conforming the phrase in 26:7 to the one here. Μου is partitive. The inf. phrase πρὸς τὸ ἐνταφιάσαι με is in a position that prob. expresses emphasis. Πρός plus the def. art. τό and the inf. ἐνταφιάσαι (aor. act. inf. of ἐνταφιάζω, "prepare for burial" [BDAG 339b)) expresses purpose (W 590–92, 611) of the vb. ἐποίσεν and με is the dir. obj. of the inf.: "in order to prepare me for burial." Ἐποίησεν 3rd sg. aor. act. indic. of ποιέω.

26:13 Ἀμὴν λέγω ὑμῖν, 5:18. The combination of the particle of place ὅπου and particle of contingency ἐάν means "wherever, anywhere" (BDAG 717b–c 1.a.δ.). The particle of contingency requires the subjunc. vb. (κηρυχθῇ 3rd sg. aor. pass. subjunc. of κυρύσσω, "preach, proclaim"). Τὸ εὐαγγέλιον with the dem. pron. τοῦτο is short for τοῦτο τὸ εὐαγγέλιον τῆς βασιλείας (24:14). Ἐν ὅλῳ τῷ κόσμῳ is equivalent to ἐν ὅλῃ τῇ οἰκουμένῃ and thus reinforces the allusion to 24:14. Λαληθήσεται (3rd sg. fut. pass.

indic. of λαλέω) is predictive fut. Καί is adjunctive. The rel. clause ὃ ἐποίησεν (3rd sg. aor. act. indic. of ποιέω) αὕτη serves as the subj. of the vb. λαληθήσεται. Εἰς marks the purpose of the action. Μνημόσυνον, -ου, τό, "memory." Αὐτῆς is obj. gen.: "in memory of her" which means "in order to memorialize her."

FOR FURTHER STUDY

133. The Anointing at Bethany

Barton, S. C. "Mark as Narrative: The Story of the Anointing Woman (Mk 14:3–9)." *ExpTim* 102 (1991): 230–35.

Corley, K. E. "The Anointing of Jesus in the Synoptic Tradition: An Argument for Authenticity." *Journal for the Study of the Historical Jesus* 1 (2003): 61–72.

Daube, D. "Anointing at Bethany and Jesus's Burial." *Anglican Theological Review* 32 (1950): 186–99.

Farkasfalvy, D. "The Meaning of the Word Εὐαγγέλιον in the Story of the Anointment at Bethany: The Anointing at Bethany: Mar 14:3–9 / Mt 26:6–13 / Jn 12:1–8." Pages 241–49 in *"Perché stessero con lui": Scritti in onore di Klemens Stock SJ, nel suo 75° compleanno*. Edited by L. de Santos and S. Grasso. Rome: Gregorian and Biblical Press, 2010.

Legault, A. "Application of the Form-Critique Method to the Anointings in Galilee and Bethany (Matt 26:6–13, Mk 14:3–9, John 12:1–8)." *CBQ* 16 (1954): 131–45.

HOMILETICAL SUGGESTIONS

A Disciple's Gift (26:6–13)

1. The woman's gift was extravagant: how will you express love for Christ? (26:6–9)
2. The woman's gift was appropriate: how did it picture the gospel of Christ? (26:10–12)
   a. The poverty in Israel showed that people were sinners who needed a Savior (cf. Deut 15:4–5; 15:11; Matt 26:11)
   b. The perfume on Jesus showed that he was about to die as a sacrifice for sinners (26:12, 28)
3. The woman's gift was historic: how will others remember your service to Christ? (26:13)

3. Judas's Act of Treachery (26:14–16)

26:14 Τότε, "after that." On the flexibility of τότε in Matthew, see N 1058 and Levinsohn 94–97. Πορευθείς (nom. sg. masc. of aor. pass. ptc. of dep. πορεύομαι) is attendant circumstance (most EVV). Εἷς is subst. Τῶν δώδεκα is partitive gen. The art. ptc. λεγόμενος (nom. sg. masc. of pres. pass. ptc. of λέγω, "be named" [pass.] [BDAG 588a–590c 4]) is *subst. and appos. (CSB; NIV; LEB) or attrib. (ESV). Ἰσκαριώτης (nom. sg. masc.) is appos. to Ἰούδας and prob. means "men from Kerioth" (BDAG 480d). See Metzger 53. The prep. phrase πρὸς τοὺς ἀρχιερεῖς modifies the ptc. despite its distance from it (most EVV).

26:15 Τί, "what thing (amount of money)." Θέλετε 2nd pl. pres. act. indic. of θέλω. Μοι is indir. obj. of the inf. δοῦναι (aor. act. inf. of δίδωμι), and the inf. is complementary. Κἀγώ is the result of crasis of καί and ἐγώ. The καί is prob. resultative: "so" (BDAG 494a–496c 1.b.ζ.). However, most EVV tr. it as if it were cond.: "if I." Yet this tr. confuses the nature of the transaction. The betrayal is not the condition for the payment. The payment is the condition for the betrayal. Ὑμῖν is in a position that may be emphatic. Παραδώσω 1st sg. fut. act. indic. of παραδίδωμι, "hand over, betray." Δέ marks the next development in the narrative. The def. art. οἱ functions as a pers. pron. and the subj. of the vb.: "they." Ἔστησαν 3rd pl. aor. act. indic. of ἵστημι, "pay" (BDAG 482a–83b A.6.b.). Τριάκοντα, "thirty." Ἀργύριον, -ου, τό, "silver money." This last clause is an allusion to Zech 11:12.

26:16 Ἀπό marks the starting point in a process. Τότε, "that time." Ἐζήτει (3rd sg. impf. act. indic. of ζητέω, "seek, look for." Εὐκαιρία, -ας, ἡ, "favorable opportunity" (BDAG 407a). Ἵνα with the subjunc. (παραδῷ 3rd sg. aor. act. subjunc. of παραδίδωμι, "hand over, betray") expresses purpose.

FOR FURTHER STUDY

134. Judas's Betrayal of Jesus

Carlson, R. P. "From Villain to Tragic Figure: The Characterization of Judas in Matthew." *CurrTM* 37 (2010): 472–78.

Klassen, W. "Judas and Jesus: A Message on a Drinking Vessel of the Second Temple Period." Pages 503–20 in *Jesus and Archaeology*. Edited by J. H. Charlesworth. Grand Rapids: Eerdmans, 2006.

_____. *Judas: Betrayer or Friend of Jesus?* Minneapolis: Fortress, 1996.

HOMILETICAL SUGGESTIONS

The Traitor's Deal (26:14–16)

1. Judas betrayed Jesus voluntarily (26:14)
2. Judas betrayed Jesus greedily (26:15)
3. Judas betrayed Jesus sneakily (26:16)

4. Preparation for the Passover (26:17–19)

26:17 Δέ marks the next development in the narrative. The art. adj. πρώτη is subst. and an ellipsis for τῇ πρώτῃ ἡμέρᾳ (BDAG 892c–94a, 1.a.α.). The dat. marks a point in time: "on the first day." Ἄζυμος, -ον, "unleavened." The art. neut. pl. form of the adj. refers to the Festival of Unleavened Bread, which technically began on the day after Passover but was often used less formally to refer to Passover and the Festival of Unleavened Bread combined (BDAG 23a; Jos. *Ant.* 14 §21). Τῶν ἀζύμων is partitive gen. Προσῆλθον 3rd pl. 2nd aor. act. indic. of dep. προσέρχομαι. Λέγοντες (nom. pl. masc. of pres. act. ptc. of λέγω) is *attendant circumstance (most EVV) or purpose. Θέλεις 2nd sg. pres. act. indic. of θέλω. Although θέλω is often followed by the complementary inf. or substitutions for the complementary inf. (ὅτι or ἵνα clauses), it is occasionally followed by a delib. subjunc. (ἑτοιμάσωμεν 1st pl. aor. act. subjunc. of ἑτοιμάζω, "prepare") that confirms that the indic. θέλω is interrogatory: "Where do you want us to prepare?" (BDAG 447c–48c 1). Σοι is indir. obj. of ἑτοιμάσωμεν (BDAG 400c–401a 1). Φαγεῖν (aor. act. inf. of ἐσθίω, "eat") is a *complementary or purpose inf. Τὸ πάσχα, 26:2.

26:18 Δέ marks a shift in speaker and the next development in the dialogue. The def. art. ὁ functions as a pers. pron. and the subj. of εἶπεν. Ὑπάγετε (2nd pl. pres. act. impv. of ὑπάγω, "go") is ingr.-prog. Δεῖνα, ὁ, ἡ, τό, "such and such a person." This is Matthew's short ref. to the host identified in Mark 14:13–14. Εἴπατε (2nd pl. 2nd aor. act. impv. of λέγω) does not seem to express any special urgency (see 4:3). Λέγει is prob. not a true historical pres. here. The disciples are relaying Jesus's message as his representatives so it is as if the teacher were speaking at the moment. The gen. μου is not easily classified. The cstr. ὁ καιρός μου means "the time of my death" (H 2.765). The adv. ἐγγύς means "near in time, imminent" (BDAG 271a–c 2.a.). Ἐστίν 3rd sg. pres. indic. of εἰμί. Πρός with the acc. (σέ) prob. expresses proximity rather than accompaniment (BDAG 873d–75c 3.g.) and thus is distinct from μετά, suggesting the tr. "at your house" (NIV; ESV; NLT). The prep. does not seem to imply that this host actually participated in the Passover meal with Jesus and his disciples. Ποιῶ (1st sg. pres. act. indic. of ποιέω, "observe, celebrate [a festival or feast]" [BDAG 839b–42a 2.f.]) is voluntative ("I want to celebrate") or *futuristic (NIV; ESV; NLT), emphasizing immediacy. Τὸ πάσχα, 26:2. Μετά with the gen. (τῶν μαθητῶν) marks the company with which an experience is shared (BDAG 636b–38b 2.b.).

26:19 Καί is prob. resultative: "so" (NIV; CSB; NLT). Ἐποίησαν 3rd pl. aor. act. indic. of ποιέω. Though most EVV treat ὡς here as a comp. particle ("as"), it may simply mark the obj. of the clause and thus function like a rel. pron. (BDAG 1103d–6b 1.b.β.): "they did what he commanded." Συνέταξεν 3rd sg. aor. act. indic. of συντάσσω, "order, direct." Αὐτοῖς is dat. of dir. obj. Ἡτοίμασαν 3rd pl. aor. act. indic. of ἑτοιμάζω, "prepare." Τὸ πάσχα, 26:2.

5. The Celebration of the Last Supper: Identifying the Betrayer (26:20–25)

26:20 Δέ marks the next development in the narrative. The gen. abs. ὀψίας δὲ γενομένης is temp. and contemp. (8:16): "when evening came." Ἀνέκειτο (3rd sg. impf. mid. indic. of dep. ἀνάκειμαι, "recline [to eat]") is prog. Μετά with the gen. (τῶν δώδεκα) identifies the fellow participants in the meal (26:18). See Metzger 53.

26:21 Ἐσθιόντων (gen. pl. masc. of pres. act. ptc. of ἐσθίω) αὐτῶν is gen. abs., temp., and contemp.: "while they were eating." Ἀμὴν λέγω ὑμῖν, 5:18. Ὅτι introduces a dir. quotation. Εἷς is subst.: "one person." The ἐκ phrase (ἐξ ὑμῶν) serves as a substitute for the partitive gen.: "one of you." Παραδώσει 3rd sg. fut. act. indic. of παραδίδωμι, "betray."

26:22 Λυπούμενοι (nom. pl. masc. of pres. pass. ptc. of λυπέω, "be sad, grieve" [pass.]) is *attendant circumstance (NIV; ESV) or causal. Σφόδρα intensifies the ptc.: "very sad." Ἤρξαντο 3rd pl. aor. mid. indic. of ἄρχω, "begin" [mid.]. Λέγειν (pres. act. inf. of λέγω) is complementary. Αὐτῷ refers to Jesus and is dat. of indir. obj. Although the implied subj. of ἤρξαντο is pl., the subst. εἷς is appos. to the implied subj. The adj. ἕκαστος is distributive ("each one, one after another") and thus imparts plurality to the subst. (BDAG 298b–c b; cf. 18:35). Although the neg. μή introduces a question that anticipates a neg. reply, the marker μήτι does so more emphatically (BDAG 649c–d): "Surely I am not the one, am I?" Ἐγώ is emphatic. Although κύριε is not accompanied by the interjection ὦ, it is voc. of emotional address (due to the ptc. λυπούμενοι).

26:23 Δέ marks a shift in speaker and the next development in the dialogue. The def. art. ὁ functions as a pers. pron. and the subj. of the vb. Ἀποκριθείς (nom. sg. masc. of aor. pass. ptc. of dep. ἀποκρίνομαι) is pleonastic but clarifies that Jesus's statement is a reply to the preceding question (26:22). The art. and independent ptc. ἐμβάψας (nom. sg. masc. of aor. act. ptc. of ἐμβάπτω, "dip") is subst. If the aor. were immediate past/dramatic, "the one who just now dipped," the identity of the betrayer would be clear. However, this use of the aor. is mainly reserved for the indic. mood (W 564–65), and it appears that the group did not immediately discern the identity of the betrayer. Μετά with the gen. (ἐμοῦ) means "together with" and seems to indicate simultaneity. The art. χεῖρα means "his hand" (most EVV). Τρύβλιον, -ου, τό, "bowl." Since the betrayer had his hand in the same bowl and apparently at the same time as Jesus, he was likely sitting in close proximity to Jesus. The appos. οὗτος is emphatic (BDAG 740b–41d 1.a.ε.). Παραδώσει (3rd sg. fut. act. indic. of παραδίδωμι, "betray") is predictive fut.

26:24 The μέν . . . δέ cstr. expresses a strong contrast. Ὁ υἱὸς τοῦ ἀνθρώπου, 9:6. Ὑπάγει (3rd sg. pres. act. indic. of ὑπάγω, "go away, *die" [BDAG 1028a–c 3]) is futuristic pres., stressing immediacy and certainty. Καθώς is the intensive comp. particle ("just as") and indicates that Jesus's death perfectly matches the biblical predictions. Γέγραπται (3rd sg. pf. pass. indic. of γράφω) is prob. resultative (W 574–76): "it is/stands written." Περὶ αὐτοῦ, "about him." The interjection οὐαί pronounces woe or calamity in an expression of severe displeasure and echoes Jesus's renunciation of the hypocrites in chapter 23 (BDAG 734b–d 1.a.). The use of the remote dem. pron. ἐκείνῳ to describe someone in Jesus's immediate presence implies relational distance. Δία with the gen. (οὗ) expresses agency: "by whom." Παραδίδοται (3rd sg. pres. pass. indic. of παραδίδωμι, "betray") is prob. prog. and hints that the treachery has already begun. The positive adj. καλόν functions as a comp. (W 297–98): "better." The secondary tense (ἦν 3rd sg. impf. indic. of εἰμί) marks the apod. of a second-class cond. sentence (past contrary to fact) that assumes an untruth for the sake of argument (despite the absence of ἄν). Normally the past contrary to fact cond. sentence uses the aor. in both the prot. and apod. but this was not possible here since εἰμί is defective in the aor. The placement of the apod. before the prot. emphasizes the apod. Αὐτῷ is prob. dat. of ref. Εἰ with the indic. in a secondary tense (ἐγεννήθη 3rd sg. aor. pass. indic. of γεννάω, "be born" [pass.]) forms the prot. of the cond. sentence. Ἐκεῖνος may express contempt.

26:25 Ἀποκριθείς, 26:23. Δέ marks a shift in speakers and new development in the dialogue. The art. ptc. παραδιδούς (nom. sg. masc. of pres. act. ptc. of παραδίδωμι) is subst.: "the one who was betraying him." Μήτι ἐγώ εἰμι, 26:22. The shift from the voc. κύριε in 26:22 to ῥαββί is significant and prob. contrasts true discipleship with false discipleship (H 2.767–68). Λέγει is historical pres. and likely highlights the importance of Jesus's statement (N 1068). Σύ is emphatic. Εἶπας 2nd sg. 2nd aor. act. indic. of λέγω. The statement "you said it" is implicitly affirmative and confirms Judas' guilt (H 2.768; N 1068).

HOMILETICAL SUGGESTIONS

A Fool's Bargain (26:14–25)

1. Judas thought his betrayal was secret, but it was known to Jesus (26:14–16, 23)
2. Judas thought his betrayal was profitable, but it was costly (26:15, 24)
3. Judas thought that Jesus was a rabbi, but he is Lord (26:22, 25)

6. The Celebration of the Last Supper: New Significance (26:26–30)

26:26 Δέ marks the next development in the narrative. Ἐσθιόντων (gen. pl. masc. of pres. act. ptc. of ἐσθίω, "eat") αὐτῶν is gen. abs., temp. and contemp.: "while they were eating." Λαβών (nom. sg. masc. of aor. act. ptc. of λαμβάνω) is attendant circumstance (most EVV). The placement of the subj. (ὁ Ἰησοῦς) and asyndeton may help identify this ptc. as attendant circumstance. Εὐλογήσας (nom. sg. masc. of aor. act. ptc. of εὐλογέω, "bless") is *temp. and antecedent (NIV; ESV; LEB; "after he blessed [it]") or attendant circumstance (CSB; NLT; but note both tr. treat the ptc. as temp. in 26:27). Ἔκλασεν 3rd sg. aor. act. indic. of κλάω, "break (a loaf of bread), tear (flatbread)." Δούς (nom. sg. masc. of aor. act. ptc. of δίδωμι) is temp. and contemp. (LEB?) since the offering of the bread must coincide with the command to take it. Λάβετε (2nd pl. 2nd aor. act. impv. of λαμβάνω) and φάγετε (2nd pl. 2nd aor. act. impv. of ἐσθίω) prob. express urgency: "Take (now) and eat (now)." Only one of the twelve impv. forms of λαμβάνω is in the pres. tense (2 John 10), and that is in a prohibition that calls for cessation of an action. Thus the aor. seems to be the default tense for the impv. of λαμβάνω. Nevertheless, seven of the twelve impv. forms of ἐσθίω are in the pres. tense. The near dem. pron. τοῦτο refers to the bread. Ἐστίν (3rd sg. pres. indic. of εἰμί) means "represent, symbolize" (BDAG 282c–86b 2.c.α.; H 2.772), a sense common in the parables (13:19–23, 37–39). Μου is partitive.

26:27 Λαβών (26:26) is attendant circumstance (thus paralleling the use in 26:26; most EVV) or temp. and antecedent (LEB). Ποτήριον, -ου, τό, "cup." See Metzger 54. Εὐχαριστήσας (26:26) is temp. and antecedent (paralleling 26:26; most EVV). Ἔδωκεν 3rd sg. aor. act. indic. of δίδωμι. Αὐτοῖς refers to the disciples and is indir. obj. Λέγων (26:26) is attendant circumstance. Πίετε (2nd pl. 2nd aor. act. impv. of πίνω, "drink") prob. expresses urgency: "drink (now)." With πίνω, the prep. ἐκ identifies the obj. from which one drinks (BDAG 295d–98b 1.a.). Αὐτοῦ refers to the cup. The subst. πάντες (BDAG 782b–84c 1.d.α.) is an ellipsis for πάντες ὑμεῖς (23:8; 26:31).

26:28 Γάρ introduces the reason for the command. Τοῦτο refers to the content of the cup. Ἐστίν, 26:26. Μου is partitive. Διαθήκη, -ης, ἡ, "covenant" (BDAG 228a–29a 2). The def. art. τῆς is *par excellence* or well-known and indicates that the ref. is to the new covenant promised by the prophets (Jer 31:31–34; Ezek 36:24–27). Διαθήκης is best categorized as a gen. of product since the phrase refers to the sacrificial blood that initiates the covenant (cf. Exod 24:8). See Metzger 54. The art. ptc. ἐκχυννόμενον (nom. sg. neut. of pres. pass. ptc. of ἐκχύννω, "pour out" [BDAG 312c–d 1.a.) is attrib. and best tr. as a rel. clause. Περί with the gen. (πολλῶν) identifies those in whose interest or to whose advantage an action is performed (BDAG 797c–98d 1.f.). The adj. πολλῶν is subst. and the masc. pers. and generic: "many people." Εἰς marks the purpose and result. Ἄφεσις, -έσεως, ἡ, "pardon, cancellation, forgiveness" (BDAG 155b–c 2). Ἁμαρτιῶν is obj. gen.

26:29 Λέγω δὲ ὑμῖν, 5:22. Οὐ μή with the subjunc. (πίω 1st sg. 2nd aor. act. subjunc. of πίνω, "drink") is emphatic negation: "I absolutely will not drink." Ἀπό . . . ἕως marks the beginning and end of a period of time. Ἄρτι, "now" (BDAG 136a–b 3). Ἐκ here marks the substance one drinks (John 4:13) rather than the container from which one drinks (26:27). The dem. pron. τούτου clarifies that Jesus is referring specifically to the wine of the Passover celebration. Γένημα, -ατος, τό, "produce, fruit" (BDAG 193a–b). Ἄμπελος, -ου, ἡ, "grapevine." Τῆς ἀμπέλου is gen. of source. The phrase ἡμέρας ἐκείνης recalls 24:36. Ὅταν, "whenever," is esp. appropriate since the day is known only to the Father. Αὐτό refers to the fruit. Μετά with the gen. (ὑμῶν) identifies the company with which one participates in an action. Καινός, -ή, -όν, "new" (BDAG 496d–97b 2). The adj. καινόν may function as an adj. modifying αὐτό (most EVV; France 995). However, since it is acc. sg. neut., it may also function as an adv.: "in a new way" N 1085). Some commentators attempt to interpret it as both adj. and adv. at the time time (H 2.774) but this is unlikely. After a ref. to the new covenant (26:28), the adv. sense seems most likely, though the focus may be temp. rather than manner: "in a new era" (H 2.774: "in the new setting of eschatological fulfillment"). BDAG notes that the adj. is often "eschatological" (496d–97b 3.b.). Thus καινόν may clarify the mng. of ἡμέρας ἐκείνης. Τοῦ πατρός (modifying βασιλείᾳ) is subj. gen. or poss. gen. Μου is gen. of relationship. **26:30** Ὑμνήσαντες (nom. pl. masc. of aor. act. indic. of ὑμνέω, "sing a hymn" [intrans.] [BDAG 1027c–d b]) is temp. and antecedent (most EVV). Ἐξῆλθον 3rd pl. 2nd aor. act. indic. of dep. ἐξέρχομαι. Τὸ ὄρος τῶν ἐλαιῶν, 24:3.

FOR FURTHER STUDY

135. The Last Supper

Beaty, J. M. "Was the Last Supper a Passover Seder?" Pages 66–89 in *Passover, Pentecost and Parousia: Studies in Celebration of the Life and Ministry of R. Hollis Gause*. Edited by S. J. Land, R. D. Moore, and J. C. Thomas. Dorset, UK: Deo, 2010.

Ham, C. "The Last Supper in Matthew." *BBR* 10 (2000): 53–69.

Marcus, J. "Passover and Last Supper Revisited." *NTS* 59 (2013): 303–24.

Routledge, R. L. "Passover and Last Supper." *TynBul* 53 (2002): 203–21.

Smith, B. D. "The Chronology of the Last Supper." *WTJ* 53 (1991): 29–45.

HOMILETICAL SUGGESTIONS

The Last Supper (26:26–30)

1. The Supper is symbolic, not sacramental
2. The bread symbolizes Jesus's body given as an atoning sacrifice
3. The cup represents Jesus's blood poured out as a covenant-initiating sacrifice
4. The promise anticipates Jesus's return, which will bring about a new creation
5. The gospel prompts celebration and singing

7. The Prophecy of Abandonment and Denial (26:31–35)

26:31 Τότε, "after that," marks the beginning of a new pericope. Λέγει is historical pres. and highlights the statement that it introduces. Ὑμεῖς is emphatic, and the adj. πάντες stresses that no one in the group is excluded. Σκανδαλισθήσεσθε (2nd pl. fut. pass. indic. of σκανδαλίζω, "be repelled by, fall into sin, *fall away [pass. followed by ἐν]") is predictive fut. The context suggests that the falling away entails abandonment and denial of Jesus. After the pass. voice of σκανδαλίζω, ἐν may mark the person who repels the subj. (BDAG 926a–b 1.b.) or mark express cause (most EVV). Ἐν is marker of a period of time. The near dem. pron. ταύτῃ modifying τῇ νυκτί refers to the night that had already begun. Γάρ marks the basis for Jesus's prediction. Γέγραπται (3rd sg. pf. pass. indic. of γράφω) is resultative: "it stands written" (W 574–76). It introduces a quotation of Zech 13:7 that differs from the LXX in several ways (Beale and Carson 91a–93a, esp. 92b–c). Πατάξω (1st sg. fut. act. indic. of πατάσσω, "strike, hit") is predictive fut. Ποιμήν, -ένος, ὁ, "shepherd." Διασκορπισθήσονται (3rd pl. fut. pass. indic. of διασκορπίζω, "scatter") is predictive fut. Πρόβατον, -ου, τό, "sheep." Τῆς ποίμνης is poss. gen.

26:32 Δέ is adversative and contrasts the mistreatment of the shepherd and scattering of his sheep with his resurrection and regathering of his disciples. Μετὰ τό with the inf. (ἐγερθῆναι aor. pass. inf. of ἐγείρω) is temp. and expresses antecedent time: "after I am raised." Με is acc. subj. of the inf. Προάξω (1st sg. fut. act. indic. of προάγω, "lead") is predictive fut. Since leading the flock was a primary function of the shepherd, this sentence identifies Jesus as the shepherd and his disciples (ὑμᾶς) as the sheep in 26:31.

26:33 Ἀποκριθείς (nom. sg. masc. of aor. pass. ptc. of dep. ἀποκρίνομαι) is pleonastic but clarifies that Peter's words are a reply to Jesus's prophecy. Δέ is adversative. Εἰ with the indic. (σκανδαλισθήσονται 3rd pl. fut. pass. indic. of σκανδαλίζω, 26:32) forms the prot. of a first-class cond. sentence that assumes fulfillment of the prot. Πάντες is subst.: "all (your other disciples)." On ἐν with σκανδαλίζω, see 26:32. Ἐγώ is emphatic. Οὐδέποτε, "not ever, never." Σκανδαλισθήσομαι (1st sg. fut. pass. indic. of σκανδαλίζω).

26:34 Ἔφη 3rd sg. aor. (or impf.) act. indic. of φημί, "say." Ἀμὴν λέγω, 5:18. Ὅτι is recitative. Ἐν ταύτῃ τῇ νυκτί, 26:31. Πρίν with the anar. inf. (φωνῆσαι aor. act. inf. of φωνέω, "sound out at a high vol., crow [of a rooster]") expresses subsequent time (W 596, 609): "before the rooster crows." Ἀλέκτωρ, -ορος, ὁ, "rooster." Ἀλέκτορα is acc. subj. of the inf. Τρίς, "three times," modifies the main vb. that follows it rather than the inf. that precedes it. Ἀπαρνήσῃ (2nd sg. fut. mid. indic. of dep. ἀπαρνέομαι, "deny" [BDAG 97c–d 1]).

26:35 Λέγει is historical pres. and highlights Peter's statement. Κἄν is the result of crasis of καί and ἄν. The καί is ascensive and ἄν expresses contingency: "even if." Δέῃ (3rd sg. pres. act. subjunc. of δέω, "it is necessary" [impers.]) expresses condition. Με is acc. subj. of the inf. (ἀποθανεῖν aor. act. inf. of ἀποθνῄσκω). The inf. is complementary. Σύν identifies the person with whom one shares an experience (BDAG 961c–62b 1.b.β.). The dbl. neg. οὐ μή with the fut. indic. (ἀπαρνήσομαι 1st sg. fut. mid. indic. of dep. ἀρνέομαι, "deny") expresses emphatic negation just as it does with the subjunc. (BDAG 644d–46d 4.b.). Ὁμοίως, "likewise, similarly." Εἶπαν 3rd pl. 2nd aor. act indic. of λέγω.

FOR FURTHER STUDY

136. Jesus as Zechariah's Shepherd

Foster, P. "The Use of Zechariah in Matthew's Gospel." Pages 65–85 in *The Book of Zechariah and Its Influence: Papers of the Oxford-Leiden Conference*. Edited by C. M. Tuckett. Aldershot, UK: Ashgate, 2003.

Menken, M. J. "Striking the Shepherd: Early Christian Versions and Interpretations of Zechariah 13,7." *Bib* 92 (2011): 39–59.

Moss, C. M. *The Zechariah Tradition and the Gospel of Matthew*. Berlin: de Gruyter, 2008.

Nolland, J. "The King as Shepherd: The Role of Deutero-Zechariah in Matthew." Pages 133–46 in *The Gospel of Matthew*. Vol. 2 of *Biblical Interpretation in Early Christian Gospels*. Edited by T. R. Hatina. London: T&T Clark, 2008.

HOMILETICAL SUGGESTIONS

The Smitten Shepherd (26:31–35)

1. Jesus predicted that his disciples would abandon him despite their protests (26:31, 33–35)
2. Jesus's abandonment by his disciples shows he is the Shepherd of Zechariah 13:7:
   a. He will be pierced by the residents of Jerusalem (Zech 12:10)
   b. He will be identified as Yahweh (Zech 12:10)
   c. His death will cause great mourning in Jerusalem (Zech 12:10–14)
   d. His death will result in the washing away of sin (Zech 13:1–2)
3. Jesus will regather his scattered disciples after his resurrection and exaltation (26:32; 28:7, 16)

8. Gethsemane (26:36–46)

26:36 Τότε, "after that," introduces the next pericope. Ἔρχεται is historical pres. and highlights Jesus's entrance into Gethsemane. Μετά with the gen. expresses accompaniment. Αὐτῶν refers to the disciples. Χωρίον, -ου, τό, "place, field." Λεγόμενον (acc. sg. neut. of pres. pass. ptc. of λέγω) is attrib. and best tr. as a rel. clause. Γεθσημανί, "olive press," refers to an olive orchard located on the Mount of Olives (BDAG 191a–c). Λέγει is historical pres. and highlights Jesus's command to his disciples. Καθίσατε (2nd pl. aor. act. impv. of καθίζω, "sit") may express urgency. Αὐτοῦ is the neut. gen. of αὐτός, which serves as a deitic (pointing) adv. to identify a position relatively close or far (BDAG 154a). Since it is contrasted with ἐκεῖ ("there"), it refers to a position relatively close and thus means "here." Ἕως functions as a prep. with the gen. sg. neut. rel. pron. (οὗ) and a subjunc. vb. (προσεύξωμαι 1st sg. aor. mid. subjunc. of dep. προσεύχομαι), expressing contemporaneousness (BDAG 422d–24c 2.c.): "while I go there and pray." Ἀπελθών (nom. sg. masc. of 2nd aor. act. ptc. of dep. ἀπέρχομαι) is attendant circumstance (most EVV).

26:37 Παραλαβών (nom. sg. masc. of 2nd aor. act. ptc. of παραλαμβάνω, "take along") is prob. temp. and contemp. ("as he took along. . . . ;" poss. CSB; ESV) or attendant circumstance (NIV; NLT). Ζεβεδαίου is gen. of relationship. Ἤρξατο 3rd sg. aor. mid. indic. of ἄρχω, "begin" (mid.). Λυπεῖσθαι (pres. pass. inf. of λυπέω, "be sad, grieve" [pass.]) and ἀδημονεῖν (pres. act. inf. of ἀδημονέω, "be anxious, distressed") are complementary inf.

26:38 Τότε, "after that," introduces the next major development in the pericope. Λέγει is historical pres. and highlights Jesus's statement. Αὐτοῖς refers to Peter, James, and John. Περίλυπος, -ον, "very sad, deeply grieved" (BDAG 802c–d). Unlike earlier usages in Matthew, ψυχή refers to the seat of emotions (BDAG 1098d–1100a 2.c.): "soul." Ἕως with the gen. (θανάτου) is a marker of degree that identifies the highest limit: "to the point of death." This clause (περίλυπος . . . θανάτου) is an allusion to Pss 41:6, 12; 42:5 (LXX). Μείνατε (2nd pl. aor. act. impv. of μένω) prob. expresses urgency. Ὧδε, "here." Γρηγορεῖτε (2nd pl. pres. act. impv. of γρηγορέω, "be watchful") is ingr.-prog. Μετά with the gen. expresses accompaniment: "together with."

26:39 Προελθών (nom. sg. masc. of 2nd aor. act. ptc. of dep. προέρχομαι, "go forward") is attendant circumstance (NLT) or temp. and contemp.: "when he went forward." The acc. sg. neut. adj. μικρόν functions adv. and means "a short distance." Ἔπεσεν 3rd sg. 2nd aor. act. indic. of πίπτω. The phrase ἐπὶ πρόσωπον αὐτοῦ, lit. "on his face," clarifies that the vb. πίπτω refers to intentionally prostrating oneself facedown on the ground (BDAG 815a–16a 1.b.α.). Προσευχόμενος (nom. sg. masc. of pres. mid. ptc. of dep. προσεύχομαι) is *attendant circumstance (most EVV) or ptc. of purpose: "to pray." Λέγων is pleonastic and introduces the content of Jesus's prayer. Although the interjection ὦ is absent, the context confirms that πάτερ is voc. of emotional address. Μου is gen. of relationship. Εἰ with the indic. (ἐστίν) forms the prot. of a first-class cond. statement that assumes the fulfillment of the prot. for the sake of argument. Παρελθάτω (3rd sg. 2nd aor. act. impv. of dep. παρέρχομαι, "pass by, pass over (without causing harm)" (BDAG 775d–76b 5). This vb. was used to describe the Lord passing over the homes of the Hebrews during the Passover (Exod 12:23 LXX). Ἀπό prob. expresses separation rather than source: "away from me." The def. art. τό is prob. anaphoric and refers either to the cup that referred to a destiny of suffering known from the OT (Isa 51:17, 22; Lam 4:21; Pss 10:6; 74:9; "the cup of wrath," H 2.783) or *the cup at the Last Supper that symbolized Jesus's shed blood (N 1084, 1099). The near dem. pron. τοῦτο implies that the suffering is imminent.

Πλήν is used as an adversative conj. that adds an important qualification: "and yet, nevertheless" (BDAG 826c–d 1.b.). The comp. particle ὡς serves as a marker of the subj. (BDAG 1103d–6b 1.b.β.) of the implied vb. γενηθήτω (26:42). Ἐγώ and σύ are emphatic. The vb. θέλεις is implied after σύ. See Metzger 54.

26:40 Ἔρχεται, εὑρίσκει, and λέγει are historical pres. Καθεύδοντας (acc. pl. masc. of pres. act. ptc. of καθεύδω, "sleep") is attrib., modifying αὐτούς: "he found them sleeping." Although Jesus addressed his words only to Peter, he used the 2nd pl. vb. (ἰσχύσατε 2nd pl. aor. act. indic. of ἰσχύω, "be able"), suggesting that he held Peter primarily responsible for the behavior of the group. Οὕτως is inferential and indicates that the question was prompted by what precedes (a description of the disciples' sleep): "so" (BDAG 741d–42c 1.b.). The use of the neg. οὐκ anticipates a positive response. The disciples had the ability but had not used it. Γρηγορῆσαι (aor. act. inf. of γρηγορέω, "be watchful") is complementary. Μετ᾽ ἐμοῦ, 26:38.

26:41 Γρηγορεῖτε, 26:38. Προσεύχεσθε 2nd pl. pres. mid. impv. of dep. προσεύχομαι. The conj. ἵνα may be used to mark the objective or petition of a prayer (BDAG 475c–77b 2.a.γ.; ESV; LEB) but more likely expresses the purpose of the prayer (BDAG 475c–77b 1.a.; NIV; CSB; NLT). Εἰσέλθητε 2nd pl. 2nd aor. act. subjunc. of dep. εἰσέρχομαι. Πειρασμός, -οῦ, ὁ, "temptation." The μέν . . . δέ cstr. emphasizes a contrast. The def. art. τό and ἡ prob. function as substitutes for the poss. pron. Thus τὸ πνεῦμα is a ref. to the spirit of the disciple rather than the Holy Spirit. Πρόθυμος, -ον, "willing, eager." Ἀσθενής, -ές, "weak" (BDAG 142d–43a 2.a.).

26:42 Πάλιν signals the repetition of an action, but ἐκ δευτέρου clarifies that this is the first repetition: "a second time." Δεύτερος, -α, -ον, "second (in a series)" (BDAG 220d–21a 2). The prep. ἐκ denotes temp. sequence (BDAG 295d–98b 5.b.β.). Ἀπελθών (nom. sg. masc. of aor. act. ptc. of dep. ἀπέρχομαι) is attendant circumstance (most EVV). Προσηύξατο 3rd sg. aor. mid. indic. of dep. προσεύχομαι. Λέγων is pleonastic and introduces the content of the prayer. Πάτερ μου, εἰ οὐ δύναται, 26:39. The subst. dem. pron. τοῦτο refers to "this cup" (26:39). Παρελθεῖν (2nd aor. act. inf. of dep. παρέρχομαι, 26:39) is complementary. The combination of the particle of contingency ἐάν and the neg. particle μή means "unless" (BDAG 267b–68a 1.c.β.). Αὐτό refers to the cup. Πίω 1st sg. 2nd aor. act. subjunc. of πίνω. Γενηθήτω τὸ θέλημά σου, 6:10.

26:43 Ἐλθών (nom. sg. masc. of aor. act. ptc. of dep. ἔρχομαι) is attendant circumstance (most EVV). Εὗρεν 3rd sg. 2nd aor. act. indic. of εὑρίσκω. Αὐτοὺς καθεύδοντας, 26:40. Ἦσαν 3rd pl. impf. indic. of εἰμί. Γάρ introduces the reason they slept. Αὐτῶν is partitive gen. Βεβαρημένοι (nom. pl. masc. of pf. pass. ptc. of βαρέω, "be weighed down, be heavy" [BDAG 166d a]) is (with ἦσαν) pluperf. periph. (W 648–49): "their eyes had been weighed down, had become heavy."

26:44 Ἀφείς (nom. sg. masc. of aor. act. ptc. of ἀφίημι) is *temp. and antecedent ("after he left") or attendant circumstance (NIV). Ἀπελθὼν προσηύξατο, 26:42. Πάλιν signals the repetition of an action, but ἐκ τρίτου clarifies that this is the second repetition: "a third time." The prep. ἐκ denotes temp. sequence (BDAG 295d–98b 5.b.β.). Τρίτος, -η, -ον, "third" (BDAG 1016b–c 1.b.). The attrib. position of αὐτόν shows that it is functioning as the identical adj: "the same" (BDAG 152c–54a, 3.a.). Λόγος can refer to a variety of different kinds of speech, but in this context it clearly refers to a prayer (BDAG 598d–601d 1.a.β.). Εἰπών is pleonastic.

26:45 Τότε, "after that." Ἔρχεται πρὸς τοὺς μαθητὰς καὶ λέγει αὐτοῖς is sim. to 26:40 except that now all three disciples, rather than merely Peter, are addressed. Καθεύδετε (2nd pl. pres. act. indic. or impv. of καθεύδω, "sleep") and ἀναπαύεσθε (2nd pl. pres. mid. indic. or impv. of ἀναπαύω, "rest" [mid.]) are difficult to classify with confidence. If indic., the vbs. are either *interrogatory ("Are you still sleeping?;" cf. NIV; LEB; CSB) or exclamatory ("You are still sleeping!"). If impv., the vbs. are either part of a sarcastic indictment ("Go ahead and sleep!;" NLT; France 1007–8), a command to postpone sleep until later (ESV), or genuine permission to sleep (H 2.784–85). On the range of possibilities, see BDAG 602b–3b 3.a.α. and N 1105. Λοιπός, -ή, -όν, "remaining." The acc. sg. neut. λοιπόν is adv. and may mean "in the fut., in the meantime, *still." The statement and command that immediately follow prevents viewing the two vbs. as sincere commands. Ἰδού calls attention to what follows. Ἤγγικεν (3rd sg. pf. act. indic. of ἐγγίζω, "draw near, come close") is resultative: "the hour is near." Ὁ υἱὸς τοῦ ἀνθρώπου, 9:6. Παραδίδοται (3rd sg. pres. pass. indic. of παραδίδωμι, "hand over") is prog. Ἁμαρτωλῶν is partitive gen.

26:46 Ἐγείρεσθε 2nd pl. pres. mid. impv. of ἐγείρω, "wake up, get up." The pres. tense is default since nineteen of the twenty impv. forms of ἐγείρω in the NT are pres. Ἄγωμεν (1st pl. pres. act. subjunc. of ἄγω, "go" [BDAG 16b–17a 5]) is hortatory: "Let's go!" Ἰδοὺ ἤγγικεν, 26:45. The art. and independent ptc. παραδιδούς (nom. sg. masc. of pres. act. ptc. of παραδίδωμι, "hand over, betray") is subst.: "the one who is betraying me, my betrayer."

FOR FURTHER STUDY

137. Gethsemane

Brown, R. E. *The Death of the Messiah: From Gethsemane to the Grave (A Commentary on the Passion Narratives in the Four Gospels).* New York: Doubleday, 1994.

Huizenga, L. A. "Obedience unto Death: The Matthean Gethsemane and Arrest Sequence and the Aqedah." *CBQ* 71 (2009): 507–26.

Quarles, C. L. "Was Jesus an Open Theist? A Brief Examination of Greg Boyd's Exegesis of Jesus's Prayer in Gethsemane." *SBJT* 8 (2004): 102–11.

HOMILETICAL SUGGESTIONS

Dark Gethsemane (26:36–46)

1. Jesus's struggle displays his humanity (26:38)
2. Jesus's supplication displays his identity ("my Father," 26:39)
3. Jesus's submission displays his humility (26:42–44), as he wished to escape the cross:
   a. Only if salvation were possible without his death
   b. Only if this were the Father's desire
4. Jesus's stamina displays his dependency (26:40–41, 43–46)

9. Jesus's Arrest (26:47–56)

26:47 Αὐτοῦ λαλοῦντος (gen. sg. masc. of pres. act. ptc. of λαλέω) is gen. abs., temp. and contemp. The adv. ἔτι emphasizes the contemp. nature of the action: "while he was still speaking." Ἰδού calls special attention to Judas's arrival, which fulfills Jesus's prophecy. Τῶν δώδεκα is partitive gen. The vb. ἦλθεν is sg. despite the compound subj., since the focus is on Judas. The first instance of μετά (modifying αὐτοῦ) expresses accompaniment. The second instance of μετά (modifying μαχαιρῶν καὶ ξύλων) marks concrete obj. that serve as equipment (BDAG 636b–38b 3.c.): "equipped or armed with." Μάχαιρα, -ης, ἡ, "short sword, dagger" (BDAG 622a–b 1). Ξύλον, -ου, τό, "(wooden) club" (BDAG 685b–86a 2.a.β.). With the vb. of motion ἔρχομαι, the prep. ἀπό marks the starting point from which Judas and the crowd moved. Τῶν ἀρχιερέων καὶ πρεσβυτέρων τοῦ λαοῦ, 21:23.

26:48 Δέ prob. marks the next development in the narrative. The art. and independent ptc. (παραδιδούς nom. sg. masc. of pres. act. ptc. of παραδίδωμι, "hand over, betray") is subst.: "his betrayer." Ἔδωκεν 3rd sg. aor. act. indic. of δίδωμι. Σημεῖον, "signal" (BDAG 920b–21b 1). Λέγων may be pleonastic (most EVV) or *ptc. of means. The particle of contingency ἄν with the rel. pron. ὅν means "whomever." Φιλήσω 1st sg. aor. act. subjunc. of φιλέω, "greet with a kiss." Although BDAG (1056c–57a 2) sees the kiss as a special indication of affection, the context suggests that φιλέω is here a mere synonym for καταφιλέω (26:49) and no special affection is necessarily implied (NLT). Αὐτός is pred. nom.: "it is he." Κρατήσατε (2nd pl. aor. act. impv. of κρατέω, "arrest" [BDAG 564c–65a 3.a.]) may express urgency.

26:49 The adv. εὐθέως implies that Judas gave his instructions immediately before he approached Jesus rather than when the group was assembled in the presence of the Jewish leaders. Προσελθών (nom. sg. masc. of aor. act. ptc. of dep. προσέρχομαι) is prob. attendant circumstance (most EVV). Χαῖρε (2nd sg. pres. act. impv. of χαίρω) is a formalized greeting equivalent to the modern Eng. "Hello!" Ῥαββί is an honorary title that disciples used for outstanding teachers of the law (BDAG 902a). Κατεφίλησεν 3rd sg. aor. act. indic. of καταφιλέω, "greet with a traditional kiss" (BDAG 529c).

26:50 Ἑταῖρος, -ου, ὁ, "companion, *fellow" (BDAG 398c–d). In the two previous occurrences in Matthew, the noun was used by the authority figure in rebukes (20:13; 22:12). Jesus does not elsewhere use the term of his own disciples, so the term may imply his rejection of Judas here. Ἑταῖρε is voc. of simple address. The mng. of the clause ἐφ᾽ ὅ πάρει is still disputed. Hagner describes the clause as "extremely difficult" (2.789). Scholars (cf. D&A 3.509–10) have suggested that the clause is the result of textual corruption or an aposiopesis (intentional fragment). The cstr. may be *interr. (CSB), in which case ἐπί with the acc. (ὅ) prob. expresses purpose (BDAG 363a–67c 11) and the rel. pron. functions as an interr. pron. (BDAG 725d–27d 1.i.β.; "for what purpose, why?"; D&A 3.509 n. 26 [on the basis of the church fathers]; T 49) or as a substitute for the dem. pron. ("for this purpose;" "for this kiss" D&A 3.510). Πάρει (3rd sg. pres. indic. of πάρειμι, "be present") sometimes has the sense of the pf. (though pres.): "have come." The cstr. may instead be elliptical and impv. (NIV; ESV; LEB; NLT; N 1110), in which case the rel. pron. retains its normal sense

(BDAG 725d–27d 1.b.α.): "(Do that) for which you came." Hagner (2.789) and Brown (1385–88) see the clause as an exclamation and rebuke: "For this you have come!" Τότε, "at that moment." Προσελθόντες (nom. pl. masc. of 2nd aor. act. ptc. of dep. προσέρχομαι) is attendant circumstance (most EVV). Ἐπέβαλον 3rd pl. 2nd aor. act. indic. of ἐπιβάλλω, "put on." With τὰς χεῖρας ἐπί and a pers. obj. (Ἰησοῦν), the vb. means "seize violently." Ἐκράτησαν 3rd pl. aor. act. indic. of κρατέω, "arrest."

26:51 Ἰδού calls attention to what follows. The def. art. τῶν makes the prep. phrase μετὰ Ἰησοῦ subst. The gen. is partitive: "one of the men with Jesus." Ἐκτείνας (nom. sg. masc. of aor. act. ptc. of ἐκτείνω, "stretch out") is attendant circumstance (most EVV). Ἀπέσπασεν 3rd sg. aor. act. indic. of ἀποσπάω, "pull out, draw (a sword)" (BDAG 120a–b 1). Μάχαιραν, 26:47. Πατάξας (nom. sg. masc. of aor. act. ptc. of πατάσσω, "strike" [BDAG 786a–b 1.b.]) is attendant circumstance (most EVV). Τοῦ ἀρχιερέως is gen. of poss. or authority. Ἀφεῖλεν 3rd sg. 2nd aor. act. indic. of ἀφαιρέω, "detach by force, cut off" (BDAG 154b–c 1). Αὐτοῦ is partitive. Ὠτίον, -ου, τό, "ear," is the dimin. form of οὖς but identical in mng. to the more common noun in this period (BDAG 1107c).

26:52 Τότε, "after that." Λέγει is historical pres. and highlights the statement that it introduces. Ἀπόστρεψον (2nd sg. aor. act. impv. of ἀποστρέφω, "return, put back") prob. expresses urgency: "Put your sword back right away!" Μάχαιραν, 26:47. Σου is poss. Αὐτῆς refers to the sword. Γάρ introduces the reason for the preceding command. The art. and independent ptc. λαβόντες (nom. pl. masc. of 2nd aor. act. ptc. of λαμβάνω, "draw [a sword]" [BDAG 583b–85a 1]) is subst.: "everyone who draws a sword." Ἐν (modifying μαχαίρῃ) marks the instr.: "by the sword." Ἀπολοῦνται (3rd pl. fut. mid. indic. of ἀπόλλυμι, "die" [BDAG 115d–16c 1.b.α.]) is gnomic pres. and states a general principle.

26:53 The particle ἤ is used to introduce a rhetorical question (BDAG 432a–32b 1.d.α.). Δοκεῖς (2nd sg. pres. act. indic. of δοκέω, "suppose") is interr. Ὅτι introduces the content of thought. Παρακαλέσαι (aor. act. inf. of παρακαλέω, "call someone for help" [BDAG 764d–65d 1.c.]) is complementary. Καί is resultative. Παραστήσει (3rd sg. fut. act. indic. of παρίστημι, "put at someone's disposal") is predictive fut. Ἄρτι, "now." Πλείω is acc. pl. neut. comp. of πολύς and is adv.: "more than" (BDAG 847c–50a 2.b.β.). Λεγιών, -ῶνος, ἡ, "legion," referred to a group of approximately 6,000 soldiers plus 6,000 auxiliary troops (BDAG 587d–88a). The gen. ἀγγέλων identifies the soldiers who compose these legions.

26:54 Πῶς, "how?" Οὖν is used in a rhetorical question to show a consequence of the preceding discussion: "how then (if angels rescue Jesus)?" Πληρωθῶσιν (3rd pl. aor. pass. subjunc. of πληρόω, "fulfill") expresses possibility: "How is it possible for the Scriptures to be fulfilled?" The def. art. modifying γραφαί is *par excellence*. Ὅτι is causal: "since." Οὕτως, "in this way." Δεῖ 3rd sg. pres. act. indic. of δέω, "be necessary" (impers.). Γενέσθαι (aor. mid. inf. of dep. γίνομαι) is complementary.

26:55 Ἐν is a marker of a period of time. The comp. clause ὡς ἐπὶ λῃστήν is elliptical: "like you were coming against a thief." Ἐπί may specify direction (BDAG 363a–67c 2.b.α.) or *opposition (12.b.). Ἐξήλθατε 2nd pl. aor. act. indic. of dep. ἐξέρχομαι. Μετὰ μαχαιρῶν καὶ ξύλων, 26:47. Συλλαβεῖν (aor. act. inf. of συλλαμβάνω, "arrest" [BDAG 955d–56a 1.a.]) expresses purpose. Κατά with the acc. ἡμέραν is distributive: "daily, every day" (BDAG 511a–13d 2.c.). Ἐκαθεζόμην (1st sg. impf. mid. indic. of dep. καθέζομαι, "sit") is prog. Διδάσκων (nom. sg. masc. of pres. act. ptc. of διδάσκω) may be *temp. ("while I was teaching"), purpose, or attendant circumstance. Ἐκρατήσατε 2nd pl. aor. act. indic. of κρατέω, "arrest."

26:56 Τοῦτο δὲ ὅλον γέγονεν ἵνα, 1:22. Πληρωθῶσιν 3rd pl. aor. pass. subjunc. of πληρόω, "fulfill." Τῶν προφητῶν is gen. of producer or subj. gen.: "the writings by the prophets." Τότε, "at that time." Ἀφέντες (nom. pl. masc. of aor. act. ptc. of ἀφίημι, "leave behind, desert") is attendant circumstance (most EVV). Ἔφυγον 3rd pl. 2nd aor. act. indic. of φεύγω, "flee, escape."

FOR FURTHER STUDY

138. Jesus's Arrest

Brown, R. E. *The Death of the Messiah: From Gethsemane to the Grave (A Commentary on the Passion Narratives in the Four Gospels)*. New York: Doubleday, 1994.

Gosling, F. A. "O Judas! What Have You Done?" *EvQ* 71 (1999): 117–25.

Huizenga, L. A. "Obedience unto Death: The Matthean Gethsemane and Arrest Sequence and the Aqedah." *CBQ* 71 (2009): 507–26.

Klassen, W. "The Authenticity of Judas' Participation in the Arrest of Jesus." Pages 389–410 in *Authenticating the Activities of Jesus*. Edited by C. A. Evans. Leiden: Brill, 1999.

Suggit, J. N. "Comrade Judas: Matthew 26:50." *Journal of Theology for Southern Africa* 63 (1988): 56–58.

Taylor, J. E. "The Garden of Gethsemane: Not the Place of Jesus's Arrest." *Biblical Archaeology Review* 21 (1995): 26.

HOMILETICAL SUGGESTIONS

Under the Cover of Night (26:47–56)

1. Jesus's arrest showed the Jewish leaders' hostility (26:47, 55)
2. Jesus's arrest showed Judas' treachery (26:48–49)
3. Jesus's arrest showed Peter's loyalty (26:51)
4. Jesus's arrest showed Jesus's purity (26:51–54):
   a. Jesus would not use human violence to escape the cross (26:52)
   b. Jesus would not exercise divine prerogatives to escape the cross (26:53)
   c. Jesus would not defy OT prophecies to escape the cross (26:54)
5. Jesus's arrest showed the Scriptures' reliability (26:56)

10. Trial by Sanhedrin (26:57–68)

26:57 Δέ marks the next development in the narrative. The art. and independent ptc. κρατήσαντες (nom. pl. masc. of aor. act. ptc. of κρατέω, "arrest") is subst. Ἀπήγαγον 3rd pl. 2nd aor. act. indic. of ἀπάγω, "lead away." Τὸν ἀρχιερέα is acc. of simple appos. identifying Καϊάφαν. The marker of location ὅπου refers to the place where Caiaphas was, apparently his palace. Οἱ πρεσβύτεροι, 15:2. Συνήχθησαν 3rd pl. aor. pass. indic. of συνάγω, "be gathered" [pass.].

26:58 Δέ marks the next development in the narrative. Ἠκολούθει (3rd sg. impf. act. indic. of ἀκολουθέω) is prog. and emphasizes simultaneity (W 543–44; CSB; NLT). Since Matthew earlier used the ἀπό . . . ἕως prep. series to identify the beginning and ending points of movement (24:31), one naturally suspects the same sense here. However, the ἀπό apparently expresses separation ("from far away") rather than beginning point (most EVV). Μακρόθεν is an adv. that orig. meant "from far away" but the use of the ἀπό of separation became necessary when the θεν suffix lost its separative force (BDAG 612b–c; BDF §104; R 300). Ἕως with the gen. is an improper prep. used to mark a limit reached: "as far as" (BDAG 422d–24c 3.a.). Αὐλή, -ῆς, ἡ, "courtyard." Τοῦ ἀρχιερέως is poss. gen. Εἰσελθών (nom. sg. masc. of aor. act. ptc. of dep. εἰσέρχομαι) is *attendant circumstance (most EVV) or temp. and antecedent. Ἔσω, "inside," refers to a position with an area, in this case, Caiaphas' courtyard. "Inside" should not be confused with "indoors." Peter was still outside (26:69). Ἐκάθητο (3rd sg. impf. mid. indic. of dep. κάθημαι, "sit") is prob. ingr.: "he began sitting, took a seat." Μετά with the gen. expresses accompaniment. Ὑπηρέτης, -ου, ὁ, "assistant, attendant" (BDAG 1035b–c). Ἰδεῖν (aor. act. inf. of ὁράω) expresses purpose. Τέλος, -ους, τό, "outcome" (BDAG 998a–99b 3).

26:59 Δέ marks the next development in the narrative. The pl. οἱ ἀρχιερεῖς prob. refers to the high priests, living former high priests, and those qualified to serve as fut. high priests (BDAG 139a–b 2.a.). Τὸ συνέδριον, 5:22. Ἐζήτουν (3rd pl. impf. act. indic. of ζητέω) is prog.: "they kept seeking." Ψευδομαρτυρία, -ας, ἡ, "false testimony." Κατά with the gen. (τοῦ Ἰησοῦ) denotes opposition: "against Jesus" (BDAG 511a–13d 2.b.β.). Ὅπως with the subjunc. (θανατώσωσιν 3rd pl. aor. act. subjunc. of θανατόω, "put to death, execute" (BDAG 443d–44a 1).

26:60 Εὗρον 3rd pl. 2nd aor. act. indic. of εὑρίσκω. Προσελθόντων (gen. pl. masc. of 2nd aor. act. ptc. of dep. προσέρχομαι) is concessive: "even though many false witnesses came forward" (most EVV). Ψευδόμαρτυς, -υρος, ὁ, "false witness." Δέ is adversative. Ὕστερον, "later, *finally" (BDAG 1044b–c 2.b.β.). Προσελθόντες (nom. pl. masc. of 2nd aor. act. ptc. of dep. προσέρχομαι) is attendant circumstance. Δύο is subst.: "two (false)witnesses."

26:61 The dem. pron. οὗτος is subst.: "this man." Ἔφη (3rd sg. aor. [or impf.] act. indic. of φημί, "state") introduces a statement presented as a dir. quotation. Καταλῦσαι (aor. act. inf. of καταλύω, "destroy") is complementary. Ναός, -οῦ, ὁ, "temple." Τοῦ θεοῦ is poss. gen. Διά marks a period of time within which an action is performed (BDAG 223d–26a 2.b.): "within three days." Οἰκοδομῆσαι (aor. act. inf. of οἰκοδομέω, "build") is complementary.

26:62 Ἀναστάς (nom. sg. masc. of aor. act. ptc. of ἀνίστημι, "stand up") is attendant circumstance (most EVV). Οὐδέν may be subst., in which case one may adjust the punctuation of the UBS[5] and form two questions of οὐδὲν . . . καταμαρτυροῦσιν. The first question is then οὐδὲν ἀποκρίνῃ: "Are you not going to answer?" (cf. NIV; ESV; LEB; NLT; N 1128). Ἀποκρίνῃ (2nd sg. pres. mid. indic. of dep. ἀποκρίνομαι) is interr. Τί οὗτοί σου καταμαρτυροῦσιν (3rd pl. pres. act. indic of καταμαρτυρέω, "testify against") then forms a second question: *"Why are these testifying against you?" or "What are these men testifying against you?" (depending on the sense of the interr. τί). Thayer (τίς, 624d–25d 1.e.α.) suggests that the second question is a "condensed expression" for τί τοῦτο ἐστιν, ὃ οὗτοι σου καταμαρτυροῦσιν. The punctuation of the UBS⁵ may be best sustained if οὐδέν (acc. sg. neut.) functions adv.: "in no way" (BDAG 735a–d 2.b.γ.): "Are you not answering in any way what these are testifying against you?" (cf. CSB). Alternatively, BDF suggests that τί is short for Mark's ὅ τι, which introduces a rel. clause "that which" (§298.4).

26:63 Δέ is prob. adversative. Ἐσιώπα 1st sg. impf. act. indic. of σιωπάω, "be silent, say nothing." Ἐξορκίζω 1st sg. pres. act. indic. of ἐξορκίζω, "put under oath." Κατά marks that by which one swears (BDAG 511a–13d A.2.a.). The adj. ptc. ζῶντος (gen. sg. masc. of pres. act. ptc. of ζάω) is in the second attrib. position and places emphasis on both the noun and ptc. while presenting the ptc. as climactic. Ἵνα is a marker of objective and serves as a substitute for the complementary inf. (BDAG 475c–77b 2.a.δ.). The subjunc. (εἴπῃς 2nd sg. aor. act. subjunc. of λέγω) is normal after ἵνα. In indir. questions, the particle εἰ frequently has the sense "whether" (BDAG 277b–79b 5.b.α.). Σύ is emphatic. Εἶ 2nd sg. pres. indic. of εἰμί. Ὁ υἱός is nom. of simple appos. to ὁ χριστός. Τοῦ θεοῦ is gen. of relationship.

26:64 Λέγει is historical pres. and highlights Jesus's statement. Σὺ εἶπας is implicitly affirmative (26:25). The emphatic σύ suggests the sense "You said that, not I." Thus Jesus treated the question as the high priest's admission of Jesus's identity but did not explicitly affirm this identity. It is best read as a "qualified affirmative" that indicates that Jesus would define the titles in the question differently than the high priest (France 1026). The adversative πλήν ("only, nevertheless;" BDAG 826c–d 1.b.) contrasts the preceding evasive response with a frank admission. Λέγω ὑμῖν emphasizes the statement it introduces. Ἀπό marks the temp. starting point for an action (BDAG 105a–7b 2.b.α.). Ἄρτι, "now, the pres. time" (BDAG 136a–b 3). Thus the phrase means "from now on." CSB and NLT suggest the mng. "in the future," but this sense is unsubstantiated and seems redundant, since it adds nothing to the fut. vb. The prep. phrase suggests that the predictive ὄψεσθε (2nd pl. fut. mid. indic. of ὁράω) is either prog. or *iter. and refers to a sequence of future revelations of the Son of Man's enthronement (France 1028; D&A 3.530–31). Alternatively, the prep. phrase may modify the ptc. rather than the indic. vb. (Luke 22:69; cf. H 2.800), but Matthew's word order makes this unlikely. Another possibility, the simplest of the solutions, is that later scribes and modern editors misunderstood Matthew and that he intended the single adv. ἀπαρτί rather than the temp. prep. phrase: "certainly" (BDAG 97d; BDF §12.3; D&A 3.530–31). However, this word is rare in the NT. The only other potential occurrences are Rev 14:13 (depending on text critical decisions) and perhaps John 13:19. Furthermore, Matthew used ἀπ' ἄρτι elsewhere in 23:39 and 26:29. Jesus's statement combines allusions to Daniel 7:13 and Psalm 110:1. Τὸν υἱὸν τοῦ ἀνθρώπου, 9:6. Καθήμενον (acc. sg. masc. of pres. mid. ptc. of dep. κάθημαι, "sit") is pred. ptc. Ἐκ marks a position and the pl. δεξιῶν refers to the right side (BDAG 217c–18a 1.a.). Τῆς δυνάμεως is partitive gen., and the noun serves as a reverent substitution for the divine name (BDAG 262b–63c 1.a.). Ἐρχόμενον (acc. sg. masc. of pres. mid. ptc. of dep. ἔρχομαι) is pred. ptc. Ἐπί with the gen. (τῶν νεφελῶν) marks position on a surface: "on the clouds" (BDAG 363a–67c 1.a.). Τοῦ οὐρανοῦ is prob. attrib. and refers to the nature of the clouds: "heavenly, in heaven."

26:65 Τότε, "at that moment." Διέρρηξεν 3rd sg. aor. act. indic. of διαρήγνυμι, "tear (garments as a sign of grief)." Λέγων is attendant circumstance (most EVV). Ἐβλασφήμησεν 3rd sg. aor. act. indic. of βλασφημέω, "blaspheme, defame (God)" (BDAG 178a–d b). The neut. sg. interr. pron. τί means "why?" Χρεία, -ας, ἡ, "need." Μαρτύς, -οῦ, ὁ, "witness." Μαρτύρων is obj. gen.: "need of witnesses." Ἴδε (2nd sg. 2nd aor. act. impv. of ὁράω) functions as an interjection since no conj. links it to the following impv. and since the sg. is used in addressing a group (BDAG 466a–c 4.a.): "Pay attention!" Νῦν demonstrates that ἠκούσατε (2nd pl. aor. act. indic. of ἀκούω) is immediate past/dramatic aor. (W 564–65). Βλασφημία, -ας, ἡ, "blasphemy."

26:66 Τί, "what?" With the dat. of pers. (ὑμῖν), δοκεῖ (3rd sg. pres. act. indic. of δοκέω) means "think" (BDAG 254c–55c 2.b.α.): "What do you think?" Δέ marks the next development in the dialogue and a shift in speaker. The def. art. οἱ functions as a pers. pron. and the subj. Ἀποκριθέντες (nom. pl. masc. of aor. pass. ptc. of dep. ἀποκρίνομαι) is pleonastic. Ἔνοχος, -ον, denotes punishment deserved: "deserving of" (BDAG 338d–39a 2.b.α.). Θανάτου is obj. gen.

26:67 Τότε, "after that." Ἐνέπτυσαν 3rd pl. aor. act. indic. of ἐμπτύω, "spit on" (BDAG 325c–d). Εἰς indicates movement directed at a surface: "on his face" (BDAG 288d–91c 1.a.γ.). Ἐκολάφισαν 3rd pl. aor. act. indic. of κολαφίζω, "beat with fist" (BDAG 555c–d 1). Δέ prob. introduces a new development in the narrative and suggests that a period should be placed after αὐτόν rather than a comma (NIV; ESV; NLT). The def. art. οἱ functions as a pers. pron. and subj. Ἐράπισαν 3rd pl. aor. act. indic. of ῥαπίζω, "slap."

26:68 Λέγοντες is attendant circumstance (most EVV). Προφήτευσον (2nd sg. aor. act. impv. of προφητεύω) expresses urgency. Despite the absence of the particle ὦ, the context shows that χριστέ is voc. of emotional address. The art. and independent ptc. παίσας (nom. sg. masc. of aor. act. ptc. of παίω, "strike, hit") is subst.: "Who is the one who struck you?"

FOR FURTHER STUDY

139. Caiaphas

Bond, H. K. *Caiaphas: Friend of Rome and Judge of Jesus*. Louisville: Westminster John Knox, 2004.

Evans, C. A. "Excavating Caiaphas, Pilate, and Simon of Cyrene: Assessing the Literary and Archaeological Evidence." Pages 323–40 in *Jesus and Archaeology*. Edited by J. H. Charlesworth. Grand Rapids: Eerdmans, 2006.

Horbury, W. "The 'Caiaphas' Ossuaries and Joseph Caiaphas." *Palestine Exploration Quarterly* 126 (1994): 32–48.

Reinhartz, A. *Caiaphas the High Priest*. Studies on Personalities of the New Testament. Columbia: University of South Carolina, 2011.

140. The Charge of Blasphemy

Bock, D. L. *Blasphemy and Exaltation in Judaism: The Charge Against Jesus in Mark 14:53–65.* Grand Rapids: Baker, 2000.

_____. "Blasphemy and the Jewish Examination of Jesus." *BBR* 17 (2007): 53–114.
Brown, R. E. *The Death of the Messiah: From Gethsemane to the Grave (A Commentary on the Passion Narratives in the Four Gospels).* New York: Doubleday, 1994.
Catchpole, D. R. "The Answer of Jesus to Caiaphas: Matt 26:64." *NTS* 17 (1971): 213–26.
_____. "You Have Heard His Blasphemy." *TynBul* 16 (1965): 10–18.
Evans, C. A. "In What Sense Blasphemy? Jesus Before Caiaphas in Mark 14:61–64." *SBLSP* 30 (1991): 215–34.

141. The Historicity of Jesus's Trial Before the Sanhedrin

Catchpole, D. R. "The Problem of the Historicity of the Sanhedrin Trial." Pages 47–65 in *The Trial of Jesus: Cambridge Studies in Honour of C. F. D. Moule.* Edited by E. Bammel. Naperville, IL: Alec R. Allenson, 1970.
Instone-Brewer, D. "Jesus of Nazareth's Trial in the Uncensored Talmud." *TynBul* 62 (2011): 269–94.

HOMILETICAL SUGGESTIONS

Miscarriage of Justice (26:57–68)

1. Jesus's innocence
   a. Crooked judges sought to condemn Jesus with false testimony
   b. The testimony of the witnesses did not concur, so no charges would be made
2. Jesus's silence
   Jesus refused to defend himself because of his intention to go to the cross
3. Jesus's confession
   Jesus confessed his identity as
   a. Messiah
   b. Son of God
   c. The One the Jewish leaders would see enthroned as King in heaven
4. Jesus's condemnation
   The high priest and Sanhedrin found Jesus guilty of blasphemy and sentenced him to death
5. Jesus's suffering
   The leaders unleashed their hostility against Jesus

11. Peter's Three Denials (26:69–75)

26:69 Δέ marks the next development in the narrative. Ἐκάθητο (3rd sg. impf. mid. indic. of dep. κάθημαι) is prog. and emphasizes simultaneity (W 543–44): "meanwhile Peter was still sitting" (cf. NLT). The def. art. τῇ is anaphoric and refers to 26:58. Αὐλή, -ῆς, ἡ, "courtyard." Προσῆλθεν 3rd sg. 2nd aor. act. indic. of dep. προσέρχομαι. The adj. μία stresses the singularity of the noun, since the use of the sg. noun already indicates that only one is in view. Perhaps the singularity is emphasized because the testimony of a single individual was not sufficient to indict Peter (Deut 19:15). Παιδίσκη, -ης, ἡ, "female slave" (BDAG 750c–51a). Λέγουσα is attendant circumstance. Καί is adjunctive. Σύ is emphatic. Ἦσθα 2nd sg. impf. indic. of εἰμί. Μετά with the gen. (Ἰησοῦ) marks close association (BDAG 636b–38b 2.a.γ.): "with Jesus." Γαλιλαῖος, -α, -ον, "Galilean, inhabitant of Galilee" (subst.). Γαλιλαίου is gen. of simple appos.

26:70 Δέ marks the next development in the dialogue and a shift in speakers. The def. art. ὁ functions as a pers. pron. and subj. Ἠρνήσατο 3rd sg. aor. mid. indic. of dep. ἀρνέομαι, "deny." Ἔμπροσθεν, "in the presence of, in front of." Πάντων is subst. Λέγων is pleonastic.

26:71 Δέ introduces the next development in the narrative. Ἐξελθόντα (acc. sg. masc. of 2nd aor. act. ptc. of dep. ἐξέρχομαι) is temp. and contemp.: "when he went out." Πυλών, -ῶνος, ὁ, "entrance, gate." This prob. refers to the gate of the courtyard. Now that he has been spotted, Peter is seeking to exit. Εἶδεν 3rd sg. 2nd aor. act. indic. of ὁράω. Ἄλλη is subst. Λέγει is historical pres. and highlights the second accusation, which constituted sufficient evidence for an indictment. The def. art. τοῖς indicates that the adv. ἐκεῖ is functioning as a subst.: "to those who were there (at the entrance)." See Metzger 54. Ἦν 3rd sg. impf. indic. of εἰμί. Μετὰ Ἰησοῦ, 26:69. Ναζωραῖος, -ου, ὁ, "Nazarene, inhabitant of Nazareth" (2:23). Τοῦ Ναζωραίου is gen. of simple appos.

26:72 Ἠρνήσατο, 26:70. Μετά with the gen. (ὅρκου) marks an attendant circumstance (BDAG 636a–638b 3.b.): "with an oath." Ὅτι is recitative.

26:73 Μετὰ μικρόν is temp.: "after a little while." Δέ marks the next development in the narrative. Προσελθόντες (nom. sg. masc. of 2nd aor. act. ptc. of dep. προσέρχομαι) is attendant circumstance. The art. and independent ptc. ἑστῶτες (nom. pl. masc. of pf. act. ptc. of ἵστημι) is subst. Although most EVV treat the ptc. as if it were pres., the pf. ptc. is best tr. like a pluperf. vb., since it is rel. to an aor. main vb.: "those who had been standing there." The subst. refers to the group present earlier when the second slave girl made her charge. Ἀληθῶς, "truly, really." Καί is adjunctive. Σύ is emphatic. Ἐξ αὐτῶν is partitive: "one of them." Καί is *ascensive (CSB; LEB) or adjunctive. Γάρ introduces evidence to support the preceding assertion. Λαλιά, -ᾶς, ἡ, "way of speaking, dialect, accent" (BDAG 583a–b 2.a.). Σου is subj. gen. Δῆλος, -η, -ον, "evident, obvious." Ποιεῖ (3rd sg. pres. act. indic. of ποιέω) is prog.

26:74 Τότε, "after that." Ἤρξατο 3rd sg. aor. mid. indic. of ἄρχω, "begin" (mid.). Καταθεματίζειν (pres. act. inf. of καταθεματίζω, "curse") and ὀμνύειν (pres. act. inf. of ὀμνύω, "swear, take an oath") are complementary inf. Ὅτι is recitative. Ἀλέκτωρ, -ορος, ὁ, "rooster." Ἐφώνησεν 3rd sg. aor. act. indic. of φωνέω, "crow."

26:75 Ἐμνήσθη 3rd sg. aor. pass. indic. of dep. μιμνήσκομαι, "remember." Τοῦ ῥήματος is gen. of dir. obj. Ἰησοῦ is subj. gen. Εἰρηκότος (gen. sg. masc. of pf. act. ptc. of λέγω) is attrib. and tr. like a pluperf., since the pf. ptc. is antecedent to the aor. main vb.: "Jesus's word that he had spoken previously." The ptc. refers to the statement in 26:34. Ὅτι is recitative. Πρίν . . . με, 26:34. Ἐξελθών (nom. sg. masc. of 2nd aor. act. ptc. of dep. ἐξέρχομαι) is attendant circumstance (most EVV). Ἔκλαυσεν 3rd sg. aor. act. indic. of κλαίω, "cry, weep." The adv. πικρῶς intensifies a vb. with neg. connotations: "intensely, bitterly" (BDAG 813a–b).

FOR FURTHER STUDY

142. Peter's Denial of Jesus

Brown, R. E. *The Death of the Messiah: From Gethsemane to the Grave (A Commentary on the Passion Narratives in the Four Gospels)*. New York: Doubleday, 1994.

Gerhardsson, B. "Confession and Denial before Men: Observations on Matt 26:57–27:2." *JSNT* 13 (1981): 46–66.

Watt, J. M. "Of Gutturals and Galileans: The Two Slurs of Matthew 26:73." Pages 107–20 in *Diglossia and Other Topics in New Testament Linguistics*. Edited by S. E. Porter. Sheffield, Sheffield Academic Press, 2000.

HOMILETICAL SUGGESTIONS

Broken Man, Broken Promises (26:69–75)

1. Peter was overconfident in his ability to follow Christ to death (26:33, 35)
2. Peter slept when he needed to pray for strength (26:40)
3. Peter denied the Lord three times just as Jesus predicted (26:69–74)
4. Peter was broken by his failure to fulfill his commitment to Jesus (26:75)

12. The Plot to Use Roman Authority to Execute Jesus (27:1–2)

27:1 Δέ marks the next development in the narrative. Πρωΐας (πρωΐα, -ας, ἡ, "[early] morning") γενομένης (gen. sg. fem. of aor. mid. ptc. of dep. γίνομαι) is gen. abs., temp., and contemp.: "when it was morning." Συμβούλιον, -ου, τό, "consultation." Ἔλαβον 3rd pl. 2nd aor. act. indic. of λαμβάνω. Συμβούλιον combined with a form of λαμβάνω is a Latinism (equivalent to consilium capere) mng. "plan, plot" (BDAG 957b–c 3; BDF §5, 3b). See 12:14; 22:15; 27:7; 28:12. The art. λαοῦ refers to the Israelites and the gen. is partitive or gen. of subord. Κατά with the gen. (τοῦ Ἰησοῦ) expresses the hostile intention of the plot (BDAG 511a–13d 2.b.β.): "against Jesus." Ὥστε with the inf. (θανατῶσαι aor. act. inf. of θανατόω, "execute, put to death") expresses purpose (BDAG 1107a–c 2.b.). Αὐτόν refers to Jesus and is dir. obj. of the inf.

27:2 Καί may be resultative (NIV): "so." Δήσαντες (nom. pl. masc. of aor. act. ptc. of δέω, "tie up") is *attendant circumstance (NIV; ESV) or temp. (CSB; LEB). Ἀπήγαγον 3rd pl. 2nd aor. act. indic. of ἀπάγω, "lead away." Παρέδωκαν 3rd pl. aor. act. indic. of παραδίδωμι, "hand over." Πιλάτῳ is dat. of indir. obj. On the var. Πιλάτω, see Metzger 54. Τῷ ἡγεμόνι (ἡγεμών, -όνος, ὁ, "governor, top administrator of a Roman province") is dat. of simple appos.

13. Judas's Remorse and Death (27:3–10)

27:3 Τότε appears to introduce a new unit of narrative closely related to the previous unit but with a "modified cast." One participant (Judas) was featured earlier in the passion narrative and others were active in the current episode (chief priests and elders). See Levinsohn 96–97. Ἰδών (nom. sg. masc. of 2nd aor. act. ptc. of ὁράω) is temp. (most EVV). The art. ptc. παραδιδούς (nom. sg. masc. of pres. act. ptc. of παραδίδωμι, "betray") is subst. and appos.: "the one who betrayed him." After vbs. of sense perception (like ὁράω), ὅτι serves as a marker of content (BDAG 731d–32d 1.b.). Κατεκρίθη 3rd sg. aor. pass. indic. of κατακρίνω, "condemn, pronounce guilty, sentence (to death)." Μεταμεληθείς (nom. sg. masc. of aor. pass. ptc. of dep. μεταμέλομαι, "have extreme regret, be very sorry;" BDAG 639c–d 1) is attendant circumstance (most EVV). Ἔστρεψεν 3rd sg. aor. act. indic. of στρέφω, "bring back, return" (BDAG 948c–49a 2.). The def. art. τά is anaphoric (26:15). Τριάκοντα ἀργύρια (26:15).

27:4 Λέγων is attendant circumstance (most EVV). Ἥμαρτον 1st sg. 2nd aor. act. indic. of ἁμαρτάνω, "sin." Παραδούς (nom. sg. masc. of 2nd aor. act. ptc. of παραδίδωμι, "betray") is either ptc. of means (CSB; ESV; LEB) or *cause (NIV; NLT). Αἷμα may be an example of metonymy in which "blood" as essential to physical life refers to the entire person (NLT). However, translating the term as "man" (NLT) obscures the apparent allusion to Deuteronomy 27:25, which indicates that Judas was cursed for receiving a gift to condemn an innocent person to death. Ἀθῷος, -ον, "innocent." See Metzger 55. Δέ marks a shift in speaker in a dialogue. The def. art. οἱ functions as a pers. pron. and serves as the subj. of the clause. Τί, "what?" Πρός with the acc. (ἡμᾶς) marks ref. or concern (BDAG 873d–75c 3.e.γ.). The elliptical expression means "What is that to us?" or "How does that concern us?" Σύ is emphatic and reinforces the expression of disinterest by the chief priests and elders. Ὄψη (2nd sg. fut. mid. indic. of ὁράω) may be predictive or *impv. fut. (most EVV). If predictive, the statement would mean that Judas will eventually see that Jesus deserved the penalty he would suffer. However, the phrase is prob. a Latinism (*tu videris*) and impv. (BDF §362; N 1151). The impv. fut. is more common in Matthew than in other NT writers.

27:5 Καί is prob. resultative (NIV; CSB). Ῥίψας (nom. sg. masc. of aor. act. ptc. of ῥίπτω, "throw, throw down") is *attendant circumstance (CSB; NIV; NLT) or temp. and antecedent. Τὰ ἀργύρια, 26:15. In some contexts, ναός refers to the sanctuary rather than the entire temple complex (27:51). However, the term sometimes refers to the entire temple precinct incl. outer courts (BDAG 665d–66c 1.b.). Since Judas was not permitted to enter the sanctuary, he likely threw the money into it from the Court of Israel. Ἀνεχώρησεν 3rd sg. aor. act. indic. of ἀναχωρέω, "depart, go away." Since ἀναχωρέω and ἀπέρχομαι are synonyms, it is unlikely that ἀπελθών is attendant circumstance (contrary to most EVV). More likely, the ptc. is temp. and antecedent. The ptc. emphasizes that Judas' suicide occurred after his departure from the temple. Ἀπήγξατο 3rd sg. aor. mid. (refl.) indic. of ἀπάγχω, "hang oneself" (BDAG 95c).

27:6 Δέ marks the next development in the narrative. Λαβόντες (nom. pl. masc. of 2nd aor. act. ptc. of λαμβάνω) is attendant circumstance (most EVV). Τὰ ἀργύρια, 26:15. Ἔξεστιν, "it is permitted" (impers.). Βαλεῖν (2nd aor. act. inf. of βάλλω) is a complementary inf. Αὐτά refers to the silver coins. Κορβανᾶς, -ᾶ, ὁ, "temple treasury." Ἐπεί marks a reason (BDAG 360b–c). Τιμή, -ῆς, ἡ, "price." The gen. αἵματος identifies that for which the price is paid. The noun αἷμα is metonymy for the act of shedding another's blood, execution.

27:7 Δέ marks the next development in the narrative. On the Latinism συμβούλιον λαβόντες, see 27:1. Λαβόντες (nom. pl. masc. of 2nd aor. act. ptc. of λαμβάνω) is either *attendant circumstance (CSB; ESV) or temp. and antecedent (LEB; NLT). Ἠγόρασαν

3rd pl. aor. act. indic. of ἀγοράζω, "buy." Ἐκ with the gen. (αὐτῶν referring to the silver coins) is a substitute for the gen. of price (BDAG 295d–98b 4.b.). Ἀγρός, -οῦ, ὁ, "field." Κεραμεύς, -έως, ὁ, "potter." The gen. κεραμέως is poss. Εἰς marks the purpose that the field would serve. Ταφή, -ῆς, ἡ, "burial, *burial ground" (BDAG 991d–92b 2). The art. and independent adj. ξένοις (ξένος, -η, -ον, "foreign") is subst.: "stranger, alien, foreigner" (BDAG 684a–c 2.a.) and is dat. of advantage.

27:8 Διό marks an inference from what precedes: "for this reason." Ἐκλήθη 3rd sg. aor. pass. indic. of καλέω. Ἀγρός, 27:7. Ἕως functions as a prep. with the gen. art. and an adv. of time (BDAG 422d–24c 1.b.α.). Σήμερον, "today, this very day."

27:9 Τότε, "at that time." Ἐπληρώθη (3rd sg. aor. pass. indic. of πληρόω, "fulfill") is divine pass. The art. and independent ptc. ῥηθέν (nom. sg. neut. of 2nd aor. pass. ptc. of λέγω) is subst. and divine pass. Διά with the gen. (Ἰερεμίου) marks the intermediate agent. Τοῦ προφήτου is gen. of simple appos. See Metzger 55 and F 1037. Λέγοντος is pleonastic. The citation is a conflation of Zechariah 11:13; Jeremiah 18:2; 19:1–13; 32:7–9; and Exodus 9:12. See Beale and Carson 95a–97a. Ἔλαβον 1st sg. or *3rd pl. 2nd aor. act. indic. of λαμβάνω. Τὰ τριάκοντα ἀργύρια, 26:15. Τὴν τιμήν (27:6) is acc. of simple appos. The art. and independent ptc. τετιμημένου (gen. sg. masc. of pf. mid. or *pass. ptc. of τιμάω, "set a price, value") is subst. and the gen. identifies the person or thing for whom/which a price is paid. The ptc. may refer to a *person (Jesus) or to the field. Ἐτιμήσαντο 3rd pl. aor. mid. indic. of τιμάω, "value, set a price." Some EVV view the ptc. and the rel. clause as unnecessarily redundant and tr. only one or the other (NIV; NLT). Most EVV also treat the prep. phrase ἀπὸ υἱῶν Ἰσραήλ as identifying the agents who performed the action. However, this is unlikely since ἐτιμήσαντο is mid. rather than pass. and it is doubtful that the prep. phrase modifies the pass. ptc. that is more remote. The cstr. prob. means "from among the sons of Israel" (F 1037 n. 7).

27:10 Ἔδωκαν 3rd pl. aor. act. indic. of δίδωμι. See Metzger 55. Αὐτά refers to the silver coins. Εἰς marks the use or end for which the money was given (BDAG 288d–93c 4.d.). Τὸν ἀγρὸν τοῦ κεραμέως, 27:7. Καθά, "just as" (BDAG 487c–d; BDF §453). Συνέταξεν 3rd sg. aor. act. indic. of συντάσσω, "order, direct."

FOR FURTHER STUDY

143. Judas's Death

Conard, A. "The Fate of Judas: Matthew 27:3–10." *Toronto Journal of Theology* 7 (1991): 158–68.

Oropeza, B. J. "Judas' Death and Final Destiny in the Gospels and Earliest Christian Writings." *Neot* 44 (2010): 342–61.

Upton, J. A. "The Potter's Field and the Death of Judas." *Concordia Journal* 8 (1982): 213–19.

Van de Water, R. "The Punishment of the Wicked Priest and the Death of Judas." *Dead Sea Discoveries* 10 (2003): 395–419.

144. Pontius Pilate

Bond, H. K. *Pontius Pilate in History and Interpretation*. SNTSMS 100. Cambridge: Cambridge University Press, 1998.

Taylor, J. E. "Pontius Pilate and the Imperial Cult in Roman Judaea." *NTS* 52 4 (2006): 555–82.

HOMILETICAL SUGGESTIONS

The Ominous Threat of Judgment (27:1–10)

1. The chief priests were wicked shepherds who did not have compassion on dying sheep (27:3–5; Zech 11:4–5)
2. The valuing of the Shepherd at thirty pieces of silver shows that the people have rejected the Shepherd (26:15; Zech 11:12)
3. The casting of the thirty pieces of silver into the sanctuary signals that God has withdrawn his favor and annulled his covenant with the people (27:5–7; Zech 11:8–14)
4. The "field of the potter" and the ref. to "innocent blood" warn that God would shatter the city of Jerusalem like one shatters a potter's jar (27:6, 9–10; Jer 19:1–13)

14. Jesus Before Pilate (27:11–14)

27:11 Δέ marks the next development in the narrative. Ἐστάθη 3rd sg. aor. pass. (intrans.) indic. of ἵστημι, "stand." Ἔμπροσθεν, "before, in the presence of." The prep. is often used to describe an appearance before a judge (BDAG 325a–c 1.b.β.). Ἡγεμών, 27:2. Ἐπηρώτησεν 3rd sg. aor. act. indic. of ἐπερωτάω, "interrogate" (BDAG 362a–b 1.b.). Λέγων is pleonastic. Σύ is emphatic and may imply a mocking tone to the question. The def. art. is prob. monadic: "the one true king." Τῶν Ἰουδαίων is gen. of subord. Δέ marks the next development in the dialogue and indicates a shift in speakers. Ἔφη 3rd sg. aor. (or impf.) act. indic. of φημί, "say." Σύ is emphatic. The cstr. σὺ λέγεις implies Jesus acceptance of the title (26:25; H 2.818).

27:12 Ἐν τῷ with the inf. (κατηγορεῖσθαι pres. pass. inf. of κατηγορέω, "bring charges against") indicates contemp. time: "while he was being charged (with crimes)." Αὐτόν is acc. subj. of the inf. Ὑπό with the gen. (τῶν ἀρχιερέων καὶ πρεσβυτέρων) marks the agents who perform the action of the pass. inf. The position of οὐδέν may indicate emphasis. Ἀπεκρίνατο 3rd sg. aor. mid. indic. of dep. ἀποκρίνομαι.

27:13 Τότε, "then, at that time." Λέγει is historical pres. and highlights the statement that it introduces. The neg. οὐκ implies an affirmative reply to the question: "Don't you hear?" The correlative pron. πόσα (πόσος) is interr. and pertains to quantity: "How many things?" (BDAG 855d–56a 2.b.α.). With the vb. καταμαρτυροῦσιν (3rd pl. pres. act. indic. of καταμαρτυρέω, "testify against"). The prefixed prep. κατά functions to express hostile speech (BDAG 511a–13d A.2.b.β.), and the gen. σου functions like the obj. of this prep. Thus the gen. expresses hostile intention directed against someone: "against you."

27:14 Ἀπεκρίθη 3rd sg. aor. pass. indic. of dep. ἀποκρίνομαι. Αὐτῷ is dat. of indir. obj. The prep. πρός with the acc. (ἕν ῥῆμα) expresses ref.: "with ref. to a single charge" (BDAG 873d–75c 3.e.α.). Οὐδέ, "not even." In the context of a legal interrogation, ῥῆμα likely means "charge" rather than merely "word" (H 2.819). For three different tr. options, see N 1163–64 n. 336. Ὥστε with the inf. (θαυμάζειν pres. act. inf. of θαυμάζω, "amaze") expresses result. Τὸν ἡγεμόνα (27:2) is acc. subj. of the inf. Λίαν is an adv., expressing high degree: "very" (2:16; 4:8; 8:28).

15. Jesus or Barabbas (27:15–23)

27:15 Δέ marks the next development in the narrative. Κατά with the acc. (ἑορτήν) is distributive (BDAG 511a–13d 2.c.).: "at each feast/festival." Ἑορτή, -ῆς, ἡ, "festival, celebration." Εἰώθει (3rd sg. pluperf. act. indic. of εἴωθα, "be accustomed") serves like an aor.: "was accustomed." Ὁ ἡγεμών, 27:2. Ἀπολύειν (pres. act. inf. of ἀπολύω, "release") is a complementary inf. Although ἕνα may be attrib., modifying δέσμιον, the placement of the dat. of indir. obj. τῷ ὄχλῳ suggests that ἕνα is subst. ("one person") and δέσμιον (δέσμιος, -ου, ὁ, "prisoner") is acc. of simple appos. Ἤθελον (3rd pl. impf. act. indic. of θέλω) is prog.

27:16 Δέ marks the next development in the narrative. Εἶχον (3rd pl. impf. act. indic. of ἔχω) is prob. prog. and emphasizes simultaneity (W 543–44) with the festival and Pilate's related custom, as the τότε ("at that time") confirms. Δέσμιον, 27:15. Ἐπίσημος, -ον, "well-known, *notorious" (BDAG 378b 2). Λεγόμενον (acc. sg. masc. of pres. pass. ptc. of λέγω) is attrib. Although the ms. evidence for the inclusion of Ἰησοῦν is weak, the committee of the UBS[5] included it in the text based on scribal probability (Metzger 56). See also N 1164, 1168–69. Βαραββᾶν is a common Aram. patronymic name mng. "son of Abba."

27:17 Οὖν is inferential: "so." Συνηγμένων (gen. pl. masc. of pf. pass. [poss. with act. force] ptc. of συνάγω, "gather") αὐτῶν is gen. abs., temp. and antecedent: "after they had been gathered." Τίνα is interr.: "whom?" Θέλετε 2nd pl. pres. act. indic. of θέλω. The aor. subjunc. ἀπολύσω (1st sg. aor. act. subjunc. of ἀπολύω, "release") serves in place of the complementary inf. or ἵνα with the subjunc. Ὑμῖν is dat. of dir. obj. On the var. Ἰησοῦν τόν, 27:16. Βαραββᾶν, 27:16. The disjunctive ἤ distinguishes two options. The art. ptc. λεγόμενον (acc. sg. masc. of pres. pass. ptc. of λέγω) is attrib.

27:18 Γάρ introduces the reason for Pilate's offer. Ἤδει 3rd sg. pluperf (for aor.) act. indic. of οἶδα. Ὅτι marks the content of the knowledge. Διά with the acc. (φθόνον) identifies the cause or motive. Φθόνος, -ου, ὁ, "envy, jealousy." Παρέδωκαν 3rd pl. aor. act. indic. of παραδίδωμι, "hand over."

27:19 Δέ marks the next development in the narrative. Καθημένου (gen. sg. masc. of pres. mid. ptc. of dep. κάθημαι, "sit") αὐτοῦ is gen. abs., temp., and contemp.: "while he was sitting." Βῆμα, -ατος, τό, "judicial bench, judgment seat." Ἀπέστειλεν 3rd sg. 2nd aor. act. indic. of ἀποστέλλω, "send (a representative with a message)." Αὐτοῦ is gen. of relationship and confirms that γυνή means "wife." Λέγουσα (nom. sg. fem. of pres. act. ptc. of λέγω) introduces the content of the message spoken by the wife. The elliptical clause (which omits a copulative) μηδὲν σοὶ καὶ τῷ δικαίῳ ἐκείνῳ is difficult even though its sense is clear. The closest parallel is the statement of the demon-possessed men in 8:29. The two dat. are prob. dat. of association (W 159), so the command urges Pilate to have no association with Jesus whatsoever. The independent and art.

adj. δικαίῳ is subst.: "that righteous man." Γάρ introduces the reason behind the appeal. Ἔπαθον 1st sg. 2nd aor. act. indic. of πάσχω, "suffer." Σήμερον, "today." Κατά with the acc. (ὄναρ) is a temp. indicator expressing simultaneity (1:20): "during a dream" (BDAG 511a–13d 2.a.). Δία with the acc. (αὐτόν) is causal: "because of him."

27:20 Δέ marks a new development in the narrative. Ἔπεισαν 3rd pl. aor. act. indic. of πείθω, "persuade." Ἵνα with the subjunc. (αἰτήσωνται 3rd pl. aor. mid. subjunc. of αἰτέω, "ask" [BDAG 30b–d for the lack of distinction with the act.]; and ἀπολέσωσιν 3rd pl. aor. act. subjunc. of ἀπόλλυμι, "destroy") functions like a complementary inf. (BDF §392). Δέ is adversative and contrasts the intended fates of Barabbas and Jesus.

27:21 Ἀποκριθείς (nom. sg. masc. of aor. pass. ptc. of dep. ἀποκρίνομαι, "answer") is pleonastic but confirms that Pilate's statement is a reply. Ὁ ἡγεμών, 27:2. Τίνα θέλετε ἀπὸ τῶν δύο ἀπολύσω ὑμῖν, 27:17. The phrase ἀπὸ τῶν δύο is a substitute for the partitive gen: "Which of the two?" (BDAG 105a–7c 1.f.). The def. art. οἱ serves in place of a pers. pron. and as the subj. of the sentence.

27:22 Λέγει is historical pres. and highlights the statement that follows. Οὖν is inferential and indicates that the question is prompted by the preceding statement. Ποιήσω (1st sg. fut. act. indic. or *aor. act. subjunc. of ποιέω) is delib. (W 570, 466–67). With the dbl. acc., the vb. ποιέω means to do something to someone (839b–42a, 4.a.). The art. ptc. λεγόμενον (acc. sg. masc. of pres. pass. ptc. of λέγω) may be subst. (and thus appos.; LEB) or *attrib. (most EVV). Λέγουσιν is historical pres. and highlights the crowds' response to Pilate's question. Σταυρωθήτω (3rd sg. aor. pass. impv. of σταυρόω, "crucify") prob. expresses urgency (note the use of the pres. impv. in Luke 23:21). See W 720.

27:23 Δέ marks the next development in the dialogue and a shift in speaker. The def. art. ὁ functions like a pers. pron. and as the subj. Ἔφη 3rd sg. aor. (or impf.) act. indic. of φημί, "say." Γάρ prob. has the sense "why?" here at the beginning of a question (BDAG 189a–90a 1.f.). Τί functions as an interr. adj. (BDAG 1006d–7d 1.b.) and the adj. κακόν is subst.: "What evil thing?" Ἐποίησεν 3rd sg. aor. act. indic. of ποιέω. Δέ marks the next development in the dialogue and a shift in speaker. The def. art. οἱ functions like a pers. pron. Περισσῶς, "intensely, even more loudly." Ἔκραζον (3rd pl. impf. act. indic. of κράζω, "cry out, shout") is either prog. (CSB) or *ingr. (LEB) and indicates a new intensity to the cries. Λέγοντες is pleonastic. Σταυρωθήτω, 27:22.

16. Pilate Capitulates to the Crowd (27:24–26)

27:24 Δέ marks the next development in the narrative. Ἰδών (nom. sg. masc. of aor. act. ptc. of ὁράω) is temp. and contemp.: "when Pilate saw" (most EVV). After a vb. of perception, ὅτι marks what was observed. Ὠφελεῖ (3rd sg. pres. act. indic. of ὠφελέω, "accomplish") and γίνεται (3rd sg. pres. mid. indic. of dep. γίνομαι) are pres., retained in indir. discourse, a usage common after vbs. of perception as well as speech (W 537–39). Ἀλλά is adversative and μᾶλλον serves as a marker of an alternative, thus reinforcing the adversative: "but instead." Θόρυβος, -ου, ὁ, "turmoil, uproar." Λαβών (nom. sg. masc. of 2nd aor. act. ptc. of λαμβάνω) is attendant circumstance (most EVV). Ἀπενίψατο (3rd sg. aor. mid. indic. of ἀπονίπτω, "wash") is refl.: "he washed his own hands." Ἀπέναντι functions as a prep. with the gen. (τοῦ ὄχλου) and indicates that Pilate and the crowd were facing each other: "opposite the crowd" (BDAG 101b–c 1.b.α.). Λέγων is either temp. ("as he said") or attendant circumstance. Ἀθῷος, -ον, "innocent." Ἀπό expresses separation (BDAG 105a–7b 1.b.). Τούτου is prob. subst. and partitive gen.: "the blood of this man" (most EVV). See Metzger 56–57. Ὑμεῖς is emphatic. Ὄψεσθε (2nd pl. fut. mid. indic. of ὁράω) is impv. fut. The dismissive command and the ref. to innocence and blood echo 27:4. Pilate has unwittingly turned the chief priests' and elders' own words against them.

27:25 Ἀποκριθείς (nom. sg. masc. of aor. pass. ptc. of ἀποκρίνω) is pleonastic but confirms that the following statement is in reply to Pilate. Αὐτοῦ is partitive gen. Both uses of ἐπί refer to conditions, in this case blood guilt, that come upon people (BDAG 363a–67c 14.b.β.). Ἡμῶν is gen. of relationship.

27:26 Τότε introduces the conclusion that fulfills the objective for one of the participant's (Pilate) involvement in the narrative (Levinsohn 96). Ἀπέλυσεν 3rd sg. aor. act. indic. of ἀπολύω, "release." Δέ is adversative and contrasts the fates of Barabbas and Jesus. Φραγελλώσας (nom. sg. masc. of aor. act. ptc. of φραγελλόω, "scourge, flog" (BDAG 1064c–d) is either temp. and antecedent (CSB; LEB) or attendant circumstance (NIV). Παρέδωκεν 3rd sg. aor. act. indic. of παραδίδωμι, "hand over." Ἵνα with the subjunc. (σταυρωθῇ 3rd sg. aor. pass. subjunc. of σταυρόω, "crucify") expresses purpose.

FOR FURTHER STUDY

145. Barabbas

> Maclean, J. K. B. "Barabbas, the Scapegoat Ritual, and the Development of the Passion Narrative." *HTR* 100 (2007): 309–34.
>
> Merritt, R. L. "Jesus Barabbas and the Paschal Pardon." *JBL* 104 (1985): 57–68.
>
> Moses, R. E. "Jesus Barabbas, a Nominal Messiah? Text and History in Matthew 27.16–17." *NTS* 58 (2012): 43–56.

146. Pontius Pilate and Caesar

> On Pilate, see For Further Study 144.
>
> McGing, B. C. "Pontius Pilate and the Sources." *CBQ* 53 (1991): 416–38.
>
> Messner, B. E. "'No Friend of Caesar': Jesus, Pilate, Sejanus, and Tiberius." *Stone-Campbell Journal* 11 (2008): 47–57.

147. The Blood-Curse of the Crowd

> Cargal, T. B. "'His Blood Be upon Us and upon Our Children': A Matthean Double Entendre." *NTS* 37 (1991): 101–12.
>
> Hamilton, C. S. "'His Blood Be upon Us': Innocent Blood and the Death of Jesus in Matthew." *CBQ* 70 (2008): 82–100.

HOMILETICAL SUGGESTIONS

Miscarriage of Justice (27:11–26)

1. An innocent defendant: the Roman trial confirmed Jesus's innocence (27:18, 23)
2. A crooked judge: the Roman trial displays Pilate's culpability (27:19, 24)
3. A criminal prosecutor: the Roman trial emphasizes the people's responsibility for Jesus's death (27:25)

17. Jesus Mocked by Roman Soldiers (27:27–37)

27:27 Τότε introduces a new unit of narrative with a different cast—the Roman soldiers. Στρατιώτης, -ου, ὁ, "soldier." The gen. τοῦ ἡγεμόνος (27:2) expresses authority and is the inverse of the gen. of subord.: "under the governor's authority." Παραλαβόντες (nom. pl. masc. of aor. act. ptc. of παραλαμβάνω, "take") is attendant circumstance (most EVV). Πραιτώριον, -ου, τό, "praetorium" (referring to either Herod's palace or *fortress, Antonia; BDAG 859b–c). Συνήγαγον 3rd pl. 2nd aor. act. indic. of συνάγω, "gather." Ἐπί is used with the acc. (αὐτόν) to express close proximity (BDAG 363a–367c 4.b.δ.): "up close to him." Σπεῖρα, -ας, ἡ, "(Roman) cohort," consisting of a tenth of a legion, approximately six hundred men.

27:28 Ἐκδύσαντες (nom. pl. masc. of aor. act. ptc. of ἐκδύω, "strip [one's garments]") is attendant circumstance (most EVV). See Metzger 57. Χλαμύς, -ύδος, ἡ, "military cloak." Κόκκινος, -η, -ον, "red, scarlet." Περιέθηκαν 3rd pl. aor. act. indic. of περιτίθημι, "drape around."

27:29 Πλέξαντες (nom. pl. masc. of aor. act. ptc. of πλέκω, "weave, plait") is attendant circumstance (most EVV). Στέφανος, -ου, ὁ, "wreath, crown." Ἐκ marks the material out of which an object is made (BDAG 295d–98b 3.h.). Ἄκανθα, -ης, ἡ, "thorn plant." Ἐπέθηκαν 3rd pl. aor. act. indic. of ἐπιτίθημι, "place, put." Κάλαμος, -ου, ὁ, "staff." The sg. and art. adj. δεξιᾷ refers to the right hand. Αὐτοῦ is partitive gen. Γονυπετήσαντες (nom. pl. masc. of aor. act. ptc. of γονυπετέω, "kneel") is attendant circumstance (most EVV). Ἔμπροσθεν, "before, in front of." Ἐνέπαιξαν 3rd pl. aor. act. indic. of ἐμπαίζω, "ridicule, mock." See Metzger 57. Αὐτῷ is dat. of dir. obj. Λέγοντες is attendant circumstance (NIV), pleonastic (CSB), or *ptc. of means: "they ridiculed him by saying." Χαῖρε (2nd sg. pres. act. impv. of χαίρω, "be joyful") was the common greeting in Gk. equivalent to "hello" in modern American Eng. The greeting was not reserved for royalty or dignitaries as the Eng. tr. "Hail!" (most EVV) may suggest (cf. 26:49; 28:9). Βασιλεῦ is voc. of dir. address. Τῶν Ἰουδαίων is gen. of subord., identifying the Jews as the subjects of the king.

27:30 Ἐμπτύσαντες (nom. pl. masc. of aor. act. ptc. of ἐμπτύω, "spit on") is attendant circumstance (most EVV). The dir. obj. of the vb. ἐμπτύω is normally identified by the dat. case or the use of the prep. εἰς. Ἔλαβον 3rd pl. 2nd aor. act. indic. of λαμβάνω. Κάλαμον, 27:29. Ἔτυπτον (3rd pl. impf. act. indic. of τύπτω, "beat, strike") is *iter. (NIV "again and again;" LEB "repeatedly") or prog. (CSB "kept").

27:31 Ὅτε "when" indicates that the completion of one action led immediately to the next. Ἐνέπαιξαν 3rd pl. aor. act. indic. of ἐμπαίζω, "ridicule, mock." The aor. tense is prob. consummative and stresses cessation of the action (W 559–60): "when they finished mocking him" (most EVV tr. the aor. as an Eng. pf. to express the notion of cessation; NLT: "when they were finally tired of mocking him"). Ἐξέδυσαν 3rd pl. aor. act. indic. of ἐκδύω, "strip (one's garments)". The dbl. acc. αὐτὸν τὴν χλαμύδα (27:28) is dbl. acc. of pers.-thing. Ἐνέδυσαν 3rd pl. aor. act. indic. of ἐνδύω, "dress, clothe." Αὐτὸν τὰ ἱμάτια is dbl. acc. of pers.-thing. Ἀπήγαγον 3rd pl. 2nd aor. act. indic. of ἀπάγω, "lead away." Εἰς τό with the inf. (σταυρῶσαι aor. act. inf. of σταυρόω, "crucify") expresses purpose: "in order to crucify him."

27:32 Δέ marks the next development in the narrative. Ἐξερχόμενοι (nom. pl. masc. of pres. mid. ptc. of dep. ἐξέρχομαι, "go out, exit") is temp. and contemp.: "as they were going out (of the praetorium)." Εὗρον 3rd pl. 2nd aor. act. indic. of εὑρίσκω, "find." Κυρηναῖος, -ου, ὁ, "Cyrenian." Either the noun is appos. or it functions as an adj. (BDAG 575d–76a). Cyrene was in North Africa, in the location of modern Libya. Ὀνόματι is prob. dat. of ref. The dat. of this noun commonly means "named, by name." Due to the absence of a conj. with two independent clauses, a period should prob. follow Σίμωνα rather than a comma. Τοῦτον is subst. and refers to Simon. Ἠγγάρευσαν 3rd pl. aor. act. indic. of ἀγγαρεύω, "force into service." Ἵνα with the subjunc. (ἄρῃ 3rd sg. aor. act. subjunc. of αἴρω, "pick up, carry") expresses purpose. Σταυρός, -οῦ, ὁ, "cross." Αὐτοῦ may be poss. gen. or an obj. gen., referring to the cross on which Jesus will be crucified.

27:33 Ἐλθόντες (nom. pl. masc. of 2nd aor. act. ptc. of dep. ἔρχομαι) is temp. and contemp.: "when they came" (CSB; ESV; LEB). Λεγόμενον (acc. sg. masc. of pres. pass. ptc. of λέγω) is attrib.: "a place that is called." Γολγοθᾶ, ἡ, is an Aram. place name mng. "Skull Place." Ἔστιν λεγόμενος (nom. sg. masc. of pres. pass. ptc. of λέγω) is pres. periph. If so, the shift from the neut. rel. pron. to the masc. ptc. is a solecism. Κρανίον, -ου, τό, "skull."

27:34 Ἔδωκαν 3rd pl. aor. act. indic. of δίδωμι, "give." Πιεῖν (2nd aor. act. inf. of πίνω, "drink") is inf. of purpose. Οἶνος, -ου, ὁ, "wine." Οἶνον is dir. obj. of ἔδωκαν. Μετά is a marker of close association (BDAG 636b–38b 2.e.). Χολή, -ῆς, ἡ, "bitter substance." Μεμιγμένον (acc. sg. masc. of pf. pass. ptc. of μίγνυμι, "mix, blend") is attrib.: "that had been mixed with a bitter substance." Γευσάμενος (nom. sg. masc. of aor. mid. ptc. of dep. γεύομαι, "taste") is temp. and contemp.: "when he tasted it" (most EVV). Ἠθέλησεν 3rd sg. aor. act. indic. of θέλω. Πιεῖν (2nd. aor. act. inf. of πίνω) is a complementary inf.

27:35 Δέ marks the next development in the narrative. Σταυρώσαντες (nom. pl. masc. of aor. act. ptc. of σταυρόω, "crucify") is temp. and antecedent: "after they crucified him" (most EVV). Διεμερίσαντο 3rd pl. aor. mid. indic. of διαμερίζω, "distribute (objects to persons)." The distribution of the garments implies that Jesus was stripped again before the crucifixion. Βάλλοντες (nom. pl. masc. of pres. act. ptc. of βάλλω, "throw, cast") is ptc. of means: "by casting lots." Κλῆρος, -ου, ὁ, "lot (a marked object such as a pebble or stick tossed in order to make decisions by chance)." See Metzger 57. The text alludes to Psalm 22:18 (Carson and Beale 97d).

27:36 Καθήμενοι (nom. pl. masc. of pres. mid. ptc. of dep. καθήμαι, "sit") is treated as attendant circumstance in most EVV. However, use of the pres. ptc. for attendant circumstance is rare. More likely, the ptc. is temp. and contemp.: "while they were sitting (to cast their lots)." Ἐτήρουν (3rd pl. impf. act. indic. of τηρέω, "guard") is prog. and emphasizes simultaneity (W 543–44) thus strengthening the suspicion that the ptc. is temp.

27:37 Ἐπέθηκαν 3rd pl. aor. act. indic. of ἐπιτίθημι, "place, put." Ἐπάνω with the gen. (τῆς κεφαλῆς) means "above, over." Αἰτία, -ας, ἡ, "legal charge (for which one is punished)." Γεγραμμένην (acc. sg. fem. of pf. pass. ptc. of γράφω, "write") is attrib. ὁ βασιλεύς is nom. of simple appos. Τῶν Ἰουδαίων is gen. of subord.

18. Jesus Taunted on the Cross (27:38–44)

27:38 Τότε introduces a new narrative section with a new cast (Levinsohn 96). Σταυροῦνται (3rd pl. pres. act. indic. of σταυρόω, "crucify") is historical pres. and highlighted for significance. Λῃστης, -ου, ὁ, "robber, bandit." The εἷς . . . καὶ εἷς . . . cstr. means "one . . . and the other . . ." (BDAG 291c–93c 5.a.). Ἐκ with the pl. neut. subst. adj. δεξιῶν means "on the right side" (BDAG 217c–18a 1.a.). Similarly, ἐξ εὐωνύμων, "on the left side."

27:39 Δέ marks a new development in the narrative. The art. and independent ptc. παραπορευόμενοι (nom. pl. masc. of pres. mid. ptc. of dep. παραπορεύομαι, "pass by") is subst.: "those who were passing by." Ἐβλασφήμουν (3rd pl. impf. act. indic. of βλασφημέω, "verbally abuse, insult") is prog. Κινοῦντες (nom. pl. masc. of pres. act. ptc. of κινέω, "move back and forth, shake [one's head in scorn]") is prob. ptc. of means: "by shaking their heads and saying."

27:40 Λέγοντες is prob. ptc. of means. The passersby insulted Jesus by both their action and their speech. The def. art. ὁ modifies both καταλύων (nom. sg. masc. of pres. act. ptc. of καταλύω, "destroy, raze") and οἰκοδομῶν (nom. sg. masc. of pres. act. ptc. of οἰκοδομέω, "build") and marks them as subst. Ναός, -οῦ, ὁ, "temple." Ἐν marks the period of time within which an action occurs: "within three days." Σῶσον (2nd sg. aor. act. impv. of σῴζω, "save, rescue") expresses urgency. Σεαυτοῦ is 2nd pers. sg. refl. pron., "yourself." See Metzger 58. If the καί is not deemed orig., the cond. clause begins a new sentence (most EVV). Εἰ with the indic. (εἶ) marks the prot. of a first-class cond. statement that assumes the fulfillment of the prot. for the sake of argument. Κατάβηθι (2nd sg. aor. act. impv. of καταβαίνω, "come down") expresses urgency. Ἀπό expresses separation. Σταυρός, -οῦ, ὁ, "cross."

27:41 Ὁμοίως, "similarly." Καί is adjunctive (ESV; LEB). Ἐμπαίζοντες (nom. pl. masc. of pres. act. ptc. of ἐμπαίζω, "ridicule, insult") is attendant circumstance (most EVV). Μετά marks fellow participants in the action and not merely the company within which the action takes place (most EVV; esp. NIV). Ἔλεγον (3rd pl. impf. act. indic. of λέγω) is prog. or iter.

27:42 Ἔσωσεν 3rd sg. aor. act. indic. of σῴζω. Δύναται 3rd sg. pres. mid. indic. of dep. δύναμαι. Σῶσαι (aor. act. inf. of σῴζω) is complementary. Although a few witnesses make the next clause (Βασιλεὺς Ἰσραήλ ἐστιν) a condition by adding εἰ (Metzger 58), the statement is likely either a question (NLT) or a *declaration made in jest (most EVV). Καταβάτω (3rd sg. 2nd aor. act. impv. of καταβαίνω) expresses urgency and this is confirmed by the adv. νῦν. Ἀπό expresses separation: "come down off of the cross." Σταυρός, -οῦ, ὁ, "cross." Πιστεύσομεν (1st pl. fut. act. indic. of πιστεύω) is promissory rather than merely predictive. The combination of the impv. and the fut. indic. establishes an implicitly cond. sentence: "He must come down off of the cross and (if he does) we will believe." In combination with πιστεύω, ἐπί marks the obj. of one's faith.

27:43 The first half of this verse. is a paraphrase of Ps 22:9 (Carson and Beale 98a). Πέποιθεν 3rd sg. pf. (with pres. mng.) act. indic. of πείθω, "depend on, trust in" (BDAG 791c–92c 2.a.). Ἐπί identifies the object of trust and dependence. Ῥυσάσθω (3rd sg. aor. mid. impv. of dep. ῥύομαι, "rescue") expresses urgency as is confirmed by the adv. νῦν. Εἰ with the indic. (θέλει 3rd sg. pres. act. indic. of θέλω) marks the prot. of a first-class cond. sentence that assumes the fulfillment of the prot. for the sake of argument. The LEB understandably regards the αὐτόν as the dir. obj. of ῥυσάσθω and treats θέλει as implying a complementary inf. ("if he wants to [rescue him]"). However, this overlooks the allusion to Psalm 22:9, in which the clause θέλει αὐτόν means "desire/take pleasure in him" (most EVV). Γάρ introduces the reason that one may assume that God took pleasure in Jesus. Ὅτι introduces a dir. quotation. The position of θεοῦ may be emphatic.

27:44 Δέ marks the next development in the narrative. Τὸ αὐτό is the adv. use of the identical adj. and means "in the same way" (BDAG 152c–54a 3.b.). Καί is adjunctive. Λῃσταί, 27:44. The art. ptc. συσταυρωθέντες (nom. pl. masc. of aor. pass. ptc. of συσταυρόω, "crucify together with") is attrib. Ὠνείδιζον (3rd pl. impf. act. indic. of ὀνειδίζω, "mock, heap insults") is prog.

FOR FURTHER STUDY

148. Jesus's Mockery and Torture by the Roman Soldiers

Burrows, M. "The Fortress Antonia and the Praetorium." *Biblical Archaeologist* 1 (1938): 17–19.

Chapman, D. W. *Ancient Jewish and Christian Perceptions of Crucifixion.* WUNT 244. Tübingen: Mohr Siebeck, 2008.

Cook, J. G. *Crucifixion in the Mediterranean World.* WUNT 327. Tübingen: Mohr Siebeck, 2014.

Donaldson, T. L. "The Mockers and the Son of God (Matthew 27:37–44): Two Characters in Matthew's Story of Jesus." *JSNT* 41 (1991): 3–18.

Hengel, M. *Crucifixion in the Ancient World and the Folly of the Message of the Cross.* Philadelphia: Fortress, 1977.

Schmidt, T. E. "Mark 15:16–32: The Crucifixion Narrative and the Roman Triumphal Procession." *NTS* 41 (1995): 1–18.

Taylor, J. E. "Golgotha: A Reconsideration of the Evidence for the Sites of Jesus's Crucifixion and Burial." *NTS* 44 (1998): 180–203.

HOMILETICAL SUGGESTIONS

Making a Bad Joke of the Good News (27:27–44)
1. Sinners mocked Jesus's claim to be King (27:27–31, 42)
2. Sinners mocked Jesus's claim to be the Son of God (27:40, 43–44)
3. Sinners mocked Jesus's claim to be the Savior (27:40, 42)

19. The Final Hours of the Crucifixion (27:45–54)

27:45 Δέ marks the next development in the narrative. The ἀπό . . . ἕως cstr. establishes a temp. beginning and ending point in order to define a period of time. Ἕκτος, -η, -ον, "sixth." Σκότος, -ους, τό, "darkness." Ἐγένετο 3rd sg. 2nd aor. mid. indic. of dep. γίνομαι, "come about" (BDAG 196d–99d, 3.a.). Ἐπί with the acc. prob. refers to movement from one place to another (BDAG 363a–67c 4.b.β.): "across, over." Τὴν γῆν may refer either to the entire earth or to the *land (of Israel) (2:6, 20; 4:15; 10:15; 27:51; most EVV; H 2.843; France 1075; *Gos. Pet.* 15), particularly in the vicinity of Jerusalem. Ἔνατος, -η, -ον, "ninth." The sixth and ninth hours refer to the beginning and end of the third watch of the day, which extended from noon to 3 p.m.

27:46 Περί indicates that the temp. phrase is an approximation. Ἐνάτην, 27:45. Ἀνεβόησεν 3rd sg. aor. act. indic. of ἀναβοάω, "cry out." The prefixed prep. seems to intensify the sense of the vb. This is confirmed by the dat. of manner (or instr.) φωνῇ μεγάλῃ. Λέγων is pleonastic and introduces the content of the shout. Ηλι ηλι λεμα σαβαχθανι is the transliteration of an Aram. paraphrase of Ps 22:2 (Carson and Beale 99c–d). Τοῦτ' ἔστιν introduces the Gk. tr. of the paraphrase and means "that is, that means" (BDAG 740b–41d 1.b.ε.; BDF §§12.3; 17; 132.2; R 705). The context and repetition suggests that θεέ should be regarded as voc. of emotional address. Μου may be regarded as gen. of subord. but more specifically identifies the worshipper of the Deity. Ἱνατί, "for what purpose? why?" Ἐγκατέλιπες 2nd sg. 2nd aor. act. indic. of ἐγκαταλείπω, "forsake, abandon, desert."

27:47 Δέ marks the next development. Ἑστηκότων (gen. pl. masc. of pf. (for pres.) act. ptc. of ἵστημι, "stand") is subst. and partitive: "some of the people who were standing." Ἀκούσαντες (nom. pl. masc. of aor. act. ptc. of ἀκούω) is prob. temp. and contemp. (most EVV). Ἔλεγον (3rd pl. impf. act. indic. of λέγω) is prog. and emphasizes simultaneity with the temp. ptc. Ὅτι is recitative. Ἠλίας, -ου, ὁ, "Elijah." Φωνεῖ 3rd sg. pres. act. indic. of φωνέω, "call, summon."

27:48 Εὐθέως, "immediately." Δραμών (nom. sg. masc. of 2nd aor. act. ptc. of τρέχω, "run") is attendant circumstance. Ἐκ with the gen. after a number is a substitute for the partitive gen. Λαβών (nom. sg. masc. of 2nd aor. act. ptc. of λαμβάνω) is attendant circumstance (most EVV) or ptc. of means. Σπόγγος, -ου, ὁ, "sponge." Πλήσας (nom. sg. masc. of aor. act. ptc. of πίμπλημι, "fill with") is attendant circumstance (most EVV) or *ptc. of means. The τε coordinates the two preceding ptc. (BDAG 993b–d

2.a.). Ὄξος, -ους, τό, "sour wine, vinegar." Περιθείς (nom. sg. masc. of aor. act. ptc. of περιτίθημι, "put on, wrap around") is attendant circumstance (most EVV) or *ptc. of means. Κάλαμος, -ου, ὁ, "stalk, staff." Ἐπότιζεν (3rd sg. impf. act. indic. of ποτίζω, "give a drink to") is prob. conative (NIV; CSB). The conative impf. implies that Jesus refused to drink or was unable to drink.

27:49 Δέ is prob. adversative (most EVV). Ἔλεγον (3rd pl. impf. act. indic. of λέγω) prob. expresses simultaneity and indicates that the bystanders were protesting the person's action as he performed it. Ἄφες (2nd sg. aor. act. impv. of ἀφίημι, "let, leave") is often combined with the 1st pers. subjunc. (ἴδωμεν 1st pl. aor. act. subjunc. of ὁράω) in a *request for permission (BDAG 156b–57b, 5.b.; CSB; 7:4). However, most EVV treat ἄφες as a separate command mng. "Leave him alone!" or "Wait!" (N 1209 supports the tr. "Wait!;" cf. F 1073 n. 3). The sense "leave him alone" is doubtful here, since Matthew does not elsewhere use an impv. form of ἀφίημι in the sense "leave" without a stated dir. obj. (cf. 5:24, 40; 8:22; 15:14). After an indir. question, εἰ often has the sense "whether (or not)" (BDAG 277b–79b 5.a.). Ἠλίας, Elijah (27:47). Σώσων (nom. sg. masc. of aor. act. ptc. of σῴζω) is ptc. of purpose. On the lengthy var. found in several early mss., see Metzger 59.

27:50 Δέ marks the next development. Πάλιν and the repetition of φωνῇ μεγάλῃ from 27:46 may hint that the cry was the same utterance as earlier. Κράξας (nom. sg. masc. of aor. act. ptc. of κράζω, "cry out") is *temp. and antecedent (NIV) or attendant circumstance (most EVV). Ἀφῆκεν (3rd sg. aor. act. indic. of ἀφίημι) means "release, give up, emit" (BDAG 156b–57b 1.b.). Although the expression ἀφῆκεν τὸ πνεῦμα is often assumed to be the equivalent of the idiom ἀφῆκεν τὴν ψυχήν, mng. "give up one's soul," Matthew's expression is not elsewhere used to speak of mere physical death.

27:51 The series of καί conjunctions closely connects the events of vv. 51–52 with Jesus's death. They are prob. to be viewed as simultaneous rather than sequential. Ἰδού calls attention to extraordinary events. Καταπέτασμα, -ατος, τό, "curtain, veil." Ναός, -οῦ, ὁ, "temple." Ἐσχίσθη (3rd sg. aor. pass. indic. of σχίζω, "split") is divine pass. Ἀπό . . . ἕως establishes a range of movement: "from . . . to." The adv. ἄνωθεν ("from above") functions as a subst. and the obj. of the prep. Similarly, the adv. κάτω ("down") is subst. For the use of ἀπό with adv., see 26:58; 27:55. Εἰς marks the result: "into two pieces, resulting in two pieces." Ἡ γῆ prob. means "ground" or "land" and refers to Jerusalem and its vicinity. Ἐσείσθη (3rd sg. aor. pass. indic. of σείω, "shake") is divine pass. Πέτρα, -ας, ἡ, "rock." Ἐσχίσθησαν (3rd pl. aor. pass. indic. of σχίζω, "split") is divine pass.

27:52 Μνημεῖον, -ου, τό, "grave, tomb." Ἀνεῴχθησαν (3rd pl. aor. pass. indic. of ἀνοίγω, "open") is divine pass. The expression appears to be drawn from Ezek 37:12. Κεκοιμημένων (gen. pl. masc. of pf. pass. [with act. force] ptc. of κοιμάω, "sleep") is attrib. The art. adj. ἁγίων is subst.: "the saints." Ἠγέρθησαν (3rd pl. aor. pass. indic. of ἐγείρω, "raise") is divine pass.

27:53 Ἐξελθόντες (nom. pl. masc. of aor. act. ptc. of dep. ἐξέρχομαι, "exit") is prob. temp. and antecedent. Μνημεῖον, -ου, τό, "grave, tomb." The prep. phrase μετὰ τὴν ἔγερσιν αὐτοῦ modifies the following vb. rather than the preceding ptc. (see NIV mg.;

H 2.850). In addition to 27:53, Matthew uses μετά with the acc. to express temp. priority nine times (1:12; 17:1; 24:29; 25:19; 26:2, 32, 33; 27:62, 63). Except for Matthew 27:62, in which the prep. phrase functions as a pred. adj. with εἰμί, the prep. phrase always precedes the vb. or vbs. which it modifies. Ἔγερσις, -εως, ἡ, "resurrection." Αὐτοῦ may be subj. (referring to Jesus's resurrection of the saints) or *obj. gen. (referring to Jesus's own resurrection). Εἰσῆλθον 3rd pl. 2nd aor. act. indic. of dep. εἰσέρχομαι, "enter." Ἐνεφανίσθησαν 3rd pl. aor. pass. indic. of ἐμφανίζω, "appear, become visible." On the orig. rdg. of the text and correct punctuation, see Quarles, ΜΕΤΑ ΤΗΝ ΕΓΕΡΣΙΝ ΑΥΤΟΥ.

27:54 Δέ marks the next development in the narrative. Ἐκατόνταρχος, -ου, ὁ, "centurion, commander of a hundred soldiers" (see BDAG 298d–99a for a discussion of the different spellings). Τηροῦντες (nom. pl. masc. of pres. act. ptc. of τηρέω, "guard") is subst. Ἰδόντες (nom. pl. masc. of aor. act. ptc. of ὁράω) is temp. and contemp. (most EVV) or *causal. Σεισμός, -οῦ, ὁ, "earthquake." Τὰ γενόμενα (acc. pl. neut. of 2nd aor. mid. ptc. of dep. γίνομαι, "happen, come about") is subst.: "the things that happened." Ἐφοβήθησαν 3rd pl. aor. pass. indic. of φοβέω, "be afraid" [pass.]. Σφόδρα, "very." Λέγοντες is attendant circumstance. Ἀληθῶς, "truly, really." Ἦν 3rd sg. impf. indic. of εἰμί.

FOR FURTHER STUDY

149. Jesus's Death and the Accompanying Signs

Forbes, G. "Darkness over All the Land: Theological Imagery in the Crucifixion Scene." *RTR* 66 (2007): 83–96.

Gurtner, D. M. "Interpreting Apocalyptic Symbolism in the Gospel of Matthew." *BBR* 22 (2012): 525–45.

————. *The Torn Veil: Matthew's Exposition of the Death of Jesus*. SNTSMS 139. Cambridge: Cambridge University Press, 2007.

Quarles, C. L. "ΜΕΤΑ ΤΗΝ ΕΓΕΡΣΙΝ ΑΥΤΟΥ: A Scribal Interpolation in Matthew 27:53?" *TC: A Journal of Biblical Textual Criticism* 20 (2015): 1–15.

Senior, D. "The Death of Jesus and the Resurrection of the Holy Ones." *CBQ* 38 (1976): 312–29.

Witherup, R. D. "The Death of Jesus and the Raising of the Saints: Matthew 27:51–54 in Context." *SBLSP* 26 (1987): 574–85.

HOMILETICAL SUGGESTIONS

The Death of God's Son (27:45–56)

1. The darkness shows God's judgment on sinners because of their murder of his Son (27:45; Amos 8:7–10)
2. The torn veil threatens God's destruction of the temple because of the death of his Son (27:51)
3. The opening of the tombs and the resurrection of the dead shows the inauguration of the new covenant by the death of his Son (27:52–53; Ezek 37:1–14)

4. The phenomena surrounding Jesus's death confirmed his identity as the Son of God (27:54)

20. The Female Disciples at the Crucifixion (27:55–56)

27:55 Δέ marks a new development. Ἦσαν 3rd pl. impf. indic. of εἰμί. Ἀπό expresses separation and the phrase modifies the following inf. Μακρόθεν, "from far away, from a distance," functions as a subst. For Matthew's use of ἀπό with adv., see 26:58; 27:51. Θεωροῦσαι (nom. pl. fem. of pres. act. ptc. of θεωρέω, "see, observe") may be attendant circumstance (most EVV). However, the cstr. is prob. periph. The adv. ἐκεῖ in no way diminishes the possibility, though Nolland (1233) prefers to call the cstr. "quasi-periphrastic" due to the ἐκεῖ (cf. 27:61). Αἵτινες (ὅστις) serves in place of the simple rel. pron. (BDAG 729d–30b 3). Ἠκολούθησαν 3rd pl. aor. act. indic. of ἀκολουθέω, "follow." Τῷ Ἰησοῦ is dat. of dir. obj. Διακονοῦσαι (nom. pl. fem. of pres. act. ptc. of διακονέω, "serve") expresses *purpose (NIV) or attendant circumstance (CSB). Αὐτῷ is dat. of dir. obj.

27:56 Ἐν expresses presence in a group. Μαγδαληνή, -ῆς, ἡ, "woman from Magdala." The placement of the gen. of relationship τοῦ Ἰακώβου καὶ Ἰωσήφ between the def. art. and μήτηρ shows that Mary was the mother of both James and Joseph. Μήτηρ is nom. of simple appos.

21. The Burial of Jesus (27:57–61)

27:57 Δέ marks a new development. Ὀψία, -ας, ἡ, "evening." Γενομένης (gen. sg. fem. of 2nd aor. mid. ptc. of dep. γίνομαι) is gen. abs. The gen. abs. expresses contemp. time: "when evening came." Ἦλθεν 3rd sg. 2nd aor. act. indic. of dep. ἔρχομαι. Πλούσιος, -ία, -ιον, "rich, wealthy." Ἀπό with the gen. (Ἀριμαθαίας) marks orig.: "from Arimathea." Τοὔνομα is the result of crasis of τὸ ὄνομα (BDF §18). The acc. sg. form is adv.: "named, by name, namely." After the rel. pron. ὅς, καί is adjunctive and αὐτός is emphatic. The cstr. may be tr. "also himself" or even "likewise" (Thayer 85b–87b, I.1.). Ἐμαθητεύθη 3rd sg. aor. pass. indic. of μαθητεύω, "be or become a disciple." After the intrans. use of μαθητεύω, the dat. (τῷ Ἰησοῦ) identifies the teacher to whom the disciple submitted.

27:58 Προσελθών (nom. sg. masc. of 2nd aor. act. ptc. of dep. προσέρχομαι, "approach") is attendant circumstance (most EVV). Ἠτήσατο 3rd sg. aor. mid. indic. of αἰτέω, "ask" (without significant distinction between act. and mid. voices; BDAG 30b–d). Τὸ σῶμα here means "corpse." Τότε, "at that time." Ἐκέλευσεν 3rd sg. aor. act. indic. of κελεύω, "order, command." Ἀποδοθῆναι (aor. pass. inf. of ἀποδίδωμι, "give up, yield") is inf. of indir. discourse (W 603–5). The implied subj. of the inf. is τὸ σῶμα.

27:59 Λαβών (nom. sg. masc. of 2nd aor. act. ptc. of λαμβάνω) is attendant circumstance. Ἐνετύλιξεν 3rd sg. aor. act. indic. of ἐντυλίσσω, "wrap (up)." Σινδών, -όνος, ἡ, "linen cloth." Σινδόνι is dat. of material (W 169–70). Καθαρός, -ά, -όν, "pure, clean." Although the adj. could refer to fabrics that did not mix two different fibers, here it likely means "clean" (most EVV), since mixing fibers in fabric was forbidden to the Jews (Lev 19:19).

27:60 Ἔθηκεν 3rd sg. aor. act. indic. of τίθημι, "put, place." Καινός, -ή, -όν, "new,
*unused." Μνημείῳ, 27:52. Ἐλατόμησεν 3rd sg. aor. act. indic. of λατομέω, "hewn,
cut." Πέτρᾳ, 27:52. Προσκυλίσας (nom. sg. masc. of aor. act. ptc. of προσκυλίζω, "roll
[up]") is attendant circumstance (most EVV) or temp. (CSB). Θύρα, -ας, ἡ, "door."
Θύρᾳ seems to be an example of the rare local dat. but may also be regarded as indir.
obj.: "to the door." Ἀπῆλθεν 3rd sg. 2nd aor. act. indic. of dep. ἀπέρχομαι.
27:61 On the impf. periph. cstr. with ἐκεῖ, see 27:55. Καθήμεναι, nom. pl. fem. of pres.
mid. ptc. of dep. κάθημαι. Ἀπέναντι, "opposite, directly across from." Τάφος, -ου, ὁ,
"grave, tomb" is used interchangeably with μνημεῖον by Matthew (cf. 27:60).

22. The Attempt to Secure the Tomb (27:62–66)

27:62 Δέ marks a new development. The def. art. τῇ shows that the adv. ἐπαύριον
("tomorrow") is serving as a subst. adj. The fem. gender was used because of an
implied ἡμέρα (BDAG 360a). The cstr. is a dat. of time, indicating point in time. Ἥτις
is a substitute for the simple rel. pron. Μετά with the acc. is used temp. ("after") and
only here follows the vb. in Matthew. See 27:53. Παρασκευή, -ῆς, ἡ, "preparation,
usually referring to Friday as the day of preparation for the Sabbath" (BDAG 771b).
Συνήχθησαν 3rd pl. aor. pass. (with act. force) indic. of συνάγω, "gather." The use of
the prep. πρός with a pers. obj. (Πιλᾶτον) to describe the location to which the leaders
gathered is usual. Πρός is used elsewhere with the συναγ- word group (Mark 1:33) but
not with a pers. object. However, the context does not support interpreting the prep. as
an expression of hostility.
27:63 Λέγοντες is attendant circumstance (most EVV). Κύριε is voc. of simple address.
Ἐμνήσθημεν 1st pl. aor. pass. indic. of dep. μιμνήσκομαι, "remember." Ὅτι marks the
content remembered. Πλάνος, -ον, "deceitful," is used subst.: "deceiver, imposter"
(BDAG 822c–d). Ἔτι, "still," expresses continuance. However, with the impf. (and
the pres. ptc. with an aor. vb. assumes the nuance of the impf.), the adv. generally
means continuance to a point in the past at which time the action ceased. Ζῶν (nom.
sg. masc. of pres. act. ptc. of ζάω, "live") is temp. and contemp. as implied by the adv.
ἔτι. Ἐγείρομαι 1st sg. pres. pass. indic. of ἐγείρω, "raise (from the dead)" is divine pass.
and futuristic pres. and emphasizes certainty.
27:64 The inferential οὖν shows that the request was prompted by Jesus's prediction. Κέλευσον (2nd sg. aor. act. impv. of κελεύω, "order, command") prob. expresses
urgency. Ἀσφαλισθῆναι (aor. pass. inf. of ἀσφαλίζω, "make secure [to prevent theft]")
is inf. of indir. discourse. Τὸν τάφον, 27:61. Μήποτε with the subjunc. (κλέψωσιν 3rd
pl. aor. act. subjunc. of κλέπτω, "steal" and εἴπωσιν 3rd pl. aor. act. subjunc. of λέγω)
expresses a negated purpose: "so that . . . do not steal." Ἐλθόντες (nom. pl. masc. of
2nd aor. act. ptc. of dep. ἔρχομαι) is attendant circumstance (most EVV). Ἠγέρθη (3rd
sg. aor. pass. indic. of ἐγείρω, "raise [from the dead]") is divine pass. Καί is resultative. Ἔσται 3rd sg. fut. indic. of εἰμί. Πλάνη, -ης, ἡ, "deception." Χείρων, -ον, "worse,"
comp. of κακός.
27:65 Ἔφη 3rd sg. aor. (or impf.) act. indic. of φημί, "say." Ἔχετε (2nd pl. pres. act.
indic. [or impv.] of ἔχω) may be declarative indic. ("you [already] have;" cf. CSB;

LEB; ESV; F 1094) or a *permissive impv. ("you may have;" cf. BDAG 563b; NIV; H 2.863). The classification determines whether the custodia prob. consisted of *Roman soldiers or the temple guard. Κουστωδία, -ας, ἡ, "guard (composed of soldiers)." Ὑπάγετε 2nd pl. pres. act. impv. of ὑπάγω, "go." Ἀσφαλίσασθε 2nd pl. aor. mid. impv. of ἀσφαλίζω, "make secure." If an intensive mid., the vb. would emphasize that the Jewish leaders were responsible for securing the tomb, which would support viewing ἔχετε as an indic. However, the mid. is consistently used for the act. (BDAG 147b–c). The rel. adv. ὡς functions as a comp. particle mng. "like, as." BDAG suggests the trans. "make it as secure as you know how," and most EVV adopt this or a sim. tr. However, the normal sense for the cstr. would seem to be "make it secure like you know how to do"—an affirmation of the leaders' competence in supervising the securing of the tomb (cf. N 1239).

27:66 Δέ marks the next development in the narrative. The def. art. οἱ functions as a substitute for the pers. pron. and serves as subj. Πορευθέντες (nom. pl. masc. of aor. pass. ptc. of dep. πορεύομαι, "proceed, go") is attendant circumstance (most EVV). Ἠσφαλίσαντο 3rd pl. aor. mid. (for act.) indic. of ἀσφαλίζω, "make secure." Τὸν τάφον, 27:61. Σφραγίσαντες (nom. pl. masc. of aor. act. ptc. of σφραγίζω, "seal [with wax and signet to prevent unauthorized opening]") is ptc. of means (most EVV). The prep. μετὰ with the gen. (τῆς κουστωδίας, 27:65) marks the soldiers of the custodia as participants in the action. The placement of the prep. phrase prob. implies their participation in both securing and sealing the tomb.

FOR FURTHER STUDY

150. Jesus's Burial

Dijkhuizen, P. "Buried Shamefully: Historical Reconstruction of Jesus's Burial and Tomb." *Neot* 45 (2011): 115–29.

Evans, C. A. *Jesus and the Ossuaries: What Jewish Burial Practices Reveal About the Beginning of Christianity.* Waco, TX: Baylor University Press, 2003.

_____. "Jewish Burial Traditions and the Resurrection of Jesus." *Journal for the Study of the Historical Jesus* 3 (2005): 233–48.

O'Collins, G., and D. Kendall. "Did Joseph of Arimathea Exist?" *Bib* 75 (1994): 235–41.

HOMILETICAL SUGGESTIONS

Reasons to Believe the Resurrection of Jesus (27:55–66)

1. The need for a tomb was well-established (so Jesus was not merely unconscious)
   a. The trained executioner confirmed Jesus's death (so he was not merely unconscious)
   b. The women who had followed Jesus confirmed his identity (so no one was crucified in Jesus's place) (27:55–56)
2. The location of the tomb was well-known (so the empty tomb was not a case of mistaken identity)

      a. Its location was well known to Joseph, the owner

      b. Its location was well known to the two Marys

3. The entrance to the tomb was well secured (so Jesus's disciples did not steal the corpse)

      a. The tomb was guarded by a Roman watch

      b. The tomb was sealed by imperial authority

      c. The tomb was supervised by the chief priests and Pharisees

E. JESUS'S RESURRECTION (28:1–20)

1. Discovery of the Empty Tomb (28:1–7)

28:1 Δέ marks the next development in the narrative. The adv. ὀψέ functions as a prep. with the gen. mng. "after" (N 1245; H 2.868). Σαββάτων refers to a single Sabbath despite the pl. form (BDAG 909b–10a 1.b.β.). Although this usage of the pl. for the sg. when referring to this and other festivals is puzzling, it is found elsewhere in the NT as well as in the LXX, Philo, Josephus, and pagan Gk. writers (BDF §141.3; R 408). The art. ptc. ἐπιφωσκούσῃ (dat. sg. fem. of pres. act. ptc. of ἐπιφώσκω, "become daylight") is subst. and the dat. of time indicates a point in time: "at daybreak, dawn." Εἰς also marks a temp. phrase and means "on" (BDAG 288d–91c 2.a.β.). Μίαν serves as a substitute for the ordinal number, is subst., and is short for μίαν ἡμέραν, "the first day." The second occurrence of σαββάτων means "week" (BDAG 909b–10a 2.b.). ῏Ηλθεν 3rd sg. 2nd aor. act. indic. of dep. ἔρχομαι. Θεωρῆσαι (aor. act. inf. of θεωρέω) is inf. of purpose. The def. art. τόν is anaphoric and refers to the tomb in which Jesus was buried (27:61) and which the women previously visited. Τάφον, 27:61.

28:2 Ἰδού prompts attention to an extraordinary event. Σεισμός, -οῦ, ὁ, "earthquake." Ἐγένετο 3rd sg. 2nd aor. mid. indic. of dep. γίνομαι, "occur, happen." Γάρ is causal (cf. esp. CSB) and implies that the earthquake was the result of the angel's activity (N 1247). Καταβάς (nom. sg. masc. of aor. act. ptc. of καταβαίνω, "descend, come down") is attendant circumstance (most EVV). Προσελθών (nom. sg. masc. of 2nd aor. act. ptc. of dep. προσέρχομαι) is attendant circumstance (most EVV). Ἀπεκύλισεν 3rd sg. aor. act. indic. of ἀποκυλίω, "roll away." Ἐκάθητο (3rd sg. impf. mid. indic. of dep. κάθημαι) is prog. and stresses simultaneity. The angel was still sitting on the stone when the women approached. Ἐπάνω with gen. (αὐτοῦ), "on."

28:3 Δέ marks the next development in the narrative. ῏Ην 3rd sg. impf. indic. of εἰμί. Εἰδέα, -ας, ἡ, "appearance." The normal spelling of the noun is ἰδέα (BDAG 279b), but replacement of the vowel with the diphthong has numerous parallels in ancient texts (BDF §23). Ἀστραπή, -ῆς, ἡ, "lightning." ῎Ενδυμα, -ατος, τό, "garment, clothing." Λευκός, -ή, -όν, "white." Ὡς may function with the adj. to express meeting a standard of comp. ("as white as snow"), but see comment on 27:65. Χιών, -όνος, ἡ, "snow."

28:4 Δέ marks a new development in the narrative. Ἀπό is causal (BDAG 105a–7b 5.a.). Φόβος, -ου, ὁ, "fear." Αὐτοῦ is obj. gen. Ἐσείσθησαν 3rd pl. aor. pass. indic. of σείω, "be shaken, tremble" (pass.). The art. and independent ptc. τηροῦντες (nom. pl. masc. of pres. act. ptc. of τηρέω, "guard") is subst.: "the guards." Ἐγενήθησαν 3rd pl. 2nd aor. pass. indic. of dep. γίνομαι.

28:5 Δέ marks a new development in the narrative. Ἀποκριθείς (nom. sg. masc. of aor. pass. ptc. of dep. ἀποκρίνομαι) is pleonastic. The use of the pres. impv. φοβεῖσθε (2nd pl. pres. mid. impv. of φοβέω) in the prohibition prob. calls for the cessation of an action already in progress. Ὑμεῖς is emphatic (H 2.868; D&A 3.667). The soldiers had good reason to fear the angel, but the women did not (N 1248). Γάρ introduces the reason that the women need not fear the angel. Ὅτι identifies the content of the angel's knowledge. The art. ptc. ἐσταυρωμένον (acc. sg. masc. of pf. pass. ptc. of σταυρόω, "crucify") is attrib.: "Jesus, who has been crucified." Ζητεῖτε 2nd pl. pres. act. indic. of ζητέω.

28:6 Ἐγέρθη 3rd sg. aor. pass. indic. of ἐγείρω. Γάρ identifies the reason for Jesus's absence. The intensive comp. particle καθώς stresses that Jesus's predictions were fulfilled in complete detail. Δεῦτε, "Come!" Ἴδετε (2nd pl. 2nd aor. act. impv. of ὁράω) expresses urgency. Ἔκειτο (3rd sg. impf. mid. indic. of dep. κεῖμαι, "lie, recline") is prog. Nolland (1250 n. 26) suggests that the form is pass. ("he was laid") based on Mark 16:6, but this is unlikely due to Matthew's shift from the aor. to the impf.

28:7 Ταχύς, -εῖα, -ύ, "quick, swift." The acc. sg. neut. adj. ταχύ functions adverbially: "quickly." Πορευθεῖσαι (nom. pl. fem. of aor. pass. ptc. of dep. πορεύομαι) is attendant circumstance and assumes an impv. force due to the connection to εἴπατε. Εἴπατε (2nd sg. 2nd aor. act. impv. of λέγω), see 4:3. Ὅτι introduces dir. discourse (recitative). Ἠγέρθη 3rd sg. aor. pass. indic. of ἐγείρω. Ἀπό expresses separation. The art. adj. (τῶν νεκρῶν) is subst. Ἰδού prompts attention to an important declaration. Προάγει (3rd sg. pres. act. indic. of προάγω) is prob. fut. pres. Ὄψεσθε (2nd pl. fut. mid. indic. of ὁράω) is predictive fut. The repeated usage of ἰδού is unusual and signals the importance of the entire statement and the identity of the speaker.

2. The Women Encounter Jesus (28:8–10)

28:8 Ἀπελθοῦσαι (nom. pl. fem. of 2nd aor. act. ptc. of dep. ἀπέρχομαι) is attendant circumstance (most EVV). Ταχύ, 28:7. Μνημεῖον, -ου, τό, "grave, tomb." Μετά marks the emotions that accompany an action (BDAG 636b–38b 3.a.). Φόβος, -ου, ὁ, "fear." Ἔδραμον 3rd pl. 2nd aor. act. indic. of τρέχω, "run." Ἀπαγγεῖλαι (aor. act. inf. of ἀπαγγέλλω, "report, announce") expresses purpose.

28:9 Ἰδού calls attention to an extraordinary event. Ὑπήντησεν 3rd sg. aor. act. indic. of ὑπαντάω, "meet (as friends)." Λέγων is attendant circumstance (most EVV). Χαίρετε (2nd pl. pres. act. impv. of χαίρω, "be joyful") is the common Gk. greeting and equivalent to the modern Eng. "hello" (BDAG 1074b–75c 2.a.; F 1102). Δέ marks a new development. The def. art. αἱ functions like a pers. pron. and serves as the subj. of the sentence. Προσελθοῦσαι (nom. pl. fem. of aor. 2nd act. ptc. of dep. προσέρχομαι) is attendant circumstance (most EVV). Ἐκράτησαν 3rd pl. aor. act. indic. of κρατέω, "grab, take hold of." Προσεκύνησαν 3rd pl. aor. act. indic. of προσκυνέω, "worship."

28:10 Τότε appears to introduce the conclusion of the narrative section (Levinsohn 96–97). Λέγει is historical pres. and emphasizes the statement that it introduces. Μὴ φοβεῖσθε, 28:5. Ὑπάγετε 2nd pl. pres. act. impv. of ὑπάγω. Ἀπαγγείλατε (2nd pl. aor. act. impv. of ἀπαγγέλω, "report, announce") expresses urgency. Ἵνα with the subjunc. ἀπέλθωσιν (3rd pl. 2nd aor. act. subjunc. of ἀπέρχομαι) expresses urgency. Κἀκεῖ is the result of crasis of καί and ἐκεῖ: "and there." Ὄψονται (3rd pl. fut. mid. indic. of ὁράω) is predictive fut.

3. The Attempted Cover-up (28:11–15)

28:11 Πορευομένων (gen. pl. fem. of pres. mid. ptc. of dep. πορεύομαι) αὐτῶν is gen. abs., temp. and contemp. After the gen. abs., ἰδού introduces a new element of the narrative and highlights its importance. Κουστωδία, -ας, ἡ, "guard (composed of soldiers)." Τῆς κουστωδίας is partitive gen. Ἐλθόντες (nom. pl. masc. of 2nd aor. act. ptc. of dep. ἔρχομαι) is attendant circumstance (most EVV). Ἀπήγγειλαν 3rd pl. aor. act. indic. of ἀπαγγέλω, "report, announce." Ἅπας, -ασα, -αν, is an intensive form of πᾶς and prob. indicates that the soldiers did not omit a single significant detail. The art. ptc. γενόμενα (acc. pl. neut. of 2nd. aor. mid. ptc. of dep. γίνομαι) is subst.

28:12 Συναχθέντες (nom. pl. masc. of aor. pass. ptc. of συνάγω) is temp. and antecedent (most EVV). Τε coordinates the two ptc. and indicates that they are nonsequential (BDAG 993b–d 2.a.). Συμβούλιον, -ου, τό, "council." The cstr. συμβούλιον λαμβάνειν means "plot, form a plan" (27:1). Λαβόντες (nom. pl. masc. of 2nd aor. act. ptc. of λαμβάνω) is temp. and antecedent. Ἀργύριον, -ου, τό, "silver (coin)." Ἱκανός, -ή, -όν, "enough," here refers to a large amount (BDAG 472b–c 3.b.). Ἔδωκαν 3rd pl. aor. act. indic. of δίδωμι. Στρατιώτης, -ου, ὁ, "soldier."

28:13 Λέγοντες is attendant circumstance (most EVV). Εἴπατε (2nd pl. 2nd aor. act. impv. of λέγω) is prob. ingr. and urges the soldiers to revise their account. Ὅτι introduces a dir. quotation. Νυκτός is gen. of time which stresses "kind of time." The implication may be that the darkness made the theft possible and/or the late hour explained the soldiers' struggle to remain awake and vigilant. Ἐλθόντες (nom. pl. masc. of 2nd aor. act. ptc. of dep. ἔρχομαι) is attendant circumstance. Ἔκλεψαν 3rd pl. aor. act. indic. of κλέπτω, "steal." Ἡμῶν κοιμωμένων (gen. pl. masc. of pres. pass. [for act.] ptc. of κοιμάω, "sleep") is gen. abs., temp. and contemp.

28:14 Ἐάν with the subjunc. ἀκουσθῇ (3rd sg. aor. pass. subjunc. of ἀκούω) forms the prot. of a 3rd-class cond. statement that makes no assumption about the fulfillment of the prot. The use of the 3rd-class condition rather than the first may suggest that the leaders were minimizing the risks of the deception. Ἐπί serves as a marker of the authority before whom a legal proceeding is conducted (BDAG 363a–67c 10). This cstr. suggests that the soldiers who guarded the tomb were Roman rather than part of the temple guard. It is unlikely that a formal legal complaint against the temple guard for falling asleep on duty would have been brought before the Roman ruler. Ἡγεμών, -όνος, ὁ, "governor, prefect." Ἡμεῖς is emphatic. Πείσομεν (1st pl. fut. act. indic. of πείθω, "persuade") is promissory. Ἀμέριμνος, -ον, "free from worry or concern." Ποιήσομεν (1st pl. fut. act. indic. of ποιέω) is promissory.

28:15 The def. art. οἱ functions as a pers. pron. and the subj. Λαβόντες (nom. pl. masc. of 2nd aor. act. ptc. of λαμβάνω) is attendant circumstance. Τὰ ἀργύρια, 28:12. Ἐποίησαν 3rd pl. aor. act. indic. of ποιέω. Ὡς is comp.: "as." Ἐδιδάχθησαν 3rd pl. aor. pass. indic. of διδάσκω. Διεφημίσθη (3rd sg. aor. pass. indic. of διαφημίζω, "spread widely, disseminate") is ingr. The marker of continuance μέχρι τῆς σήμερον (BDAG 644b–d 2.a.) shows that this began an action that continued for a long period. Σήμερον (adv. of time), "today," is used adj. The fem. def. art. τῆς implies ἡμέρας whether or not the noun was explicit in the orig. text.

FOR FURTHER STUDY

151. Discovery of the Empty Tomb

Boyarin, D. "'After the Sabbath' (Matt. 28:1): Once More into the Crux." *JTS* 52 (2001): 678–88.

Grayston, K. "The Translation of Matthew 28:17." *JSNT* 21 (1984): 105–9.

van der Horst, P. W. "Once More: The Translation of οἱ δέ in Matthew 28:17." *JSNT* 27 (1986): 27–30.

McKay, K. L. "The Use of *hoi de* in Matthew 28:17." *JSNT* 24 (1985): 71–72.

O'Collins, G. "Mary Magdalene as Major Witness to Jesus's Resurrection." *TS* 48 (1987): 631–46.

Waters, K. L., Sr. "Matthew 28:1–6 as Temporally Conflated Text: Temporal-Spatial Collapse in the Gospel of Matthew." *ExpTim* 116 (2005): 295–301.

Winger, M. "When Did the Women Visit the Tomb?" *NTS* 40 (1994): 284–88.

HOMILETICAL SUGGESTIONS

He Is Risen Indeed! (28:1–15)

1. Jesus's resurrection was supported by the empty tomb
2. Jesus's resurrection was attested by the promise of an angel
3. Jesus's resurrection was proven by his appearance to his followers
4. Jesus's resurrection was challenged by a contradictory story concocted by his opponents

4. The Great Commission (28:16–20)

28:16 Ἕνδεκα, "eleven." Ἐπορεύθησαν 3rd pl. aor. pass. indic. of dep. πορεύομαι. The gen. rel. pron. οὗ serves as an adv. of place (BDAG 732d–33a 1.b) and marks a destination: "where, to which." Ἐτάξατο 3rd sg. aor. mid. (for act.) indic. of τάσσω, "order, determine."

28:17 Ἰδόντες (nom. pl. masc. of 2nd aor. act. ptc. of ὁράω) is temp. and contemp.: "when they saw him." Προσεκύνησαν 3rd pl. aor. act. indic. of προσκυνέω, "worship." Δέ is adversative. The def. art. οἱ functions like an indef. pron. In combination with δέ it introduces a second group that is a part or subgroup of the larger group mentioned just before it (BDAG 686a–89c 1.b.; N 1262; McKay, "*Hoi de*," 71–72; van der Horst, "Once More," 27–30). Ἐδίστασαν 3rd pl. aor. act. indic. of διστάζω, "doubt, hesitate in doubt."

28:18 Προσελθών (nom. sg. masc. of 2nd aor. act. ptc. of dep. προσέρχομαι) is attendant circumstance. Ἐλάλησεν 3rd sg. aor. act. indic. of λαλέω. Λέγων is pleonastic. Ἐδόθη (3rd sg. aor. pass. indic. of δίδωμι) is divine pass. For support of an allusion to Dan 7:14, see F 1112–13.

28:19 Οὖν is inferential and indicates that Jesus's command is grounded in his absolute authority. Πορευθέντες (nom. pl. masc. of aor. pass. ptc. of dep. πορεύομαι) is attendant circumstance and assumes an impv. force since it modifies an impv. Μαθητεύσατε (2nd pl. aor. act. impv. of μαθητεύω) expresses urgency. Βαπτίζοντες (nom. pl. masc. of pres. act. ptc. of βαπτίζω, "immerse, baptize") is ptc. of *means (F 1115) or attendant circumstance (H 2.887: "supplementary imperatives"). Αὐτούς refers to the implied dir. obj. of the main vb. The precise mng. of the phrase εἰς τὸ ὄνομα is difficult to determine. The phrase prob. refers to calling out the name and dedicating to the one who bears the name (BDAG 711c–14d 1.b.γ.). The use of the sg. τὸ ὄνομα with three gen. of poss. indicates that the Father, the Son, and the Holy Spirit share a single name. The phrase "the name" is prob. used in typical Jewish fashion to refer to the divine name Yahweh. Thus the cstr. affirms the deity and unity of the three persons and implies incipient trinitarian doctrine (cf. F 1118).

28:20 Διδάσκοντες (nom. pl. masc. of pres. act. ptc. of διδάσκω) is ptc. of *means (F 1115) or attendant circumstance (H 2.887: "supplementary imperatives"). Τηρεῖν (pres. act. inf. of τηρέω, "guard, keep") is inf. of indir. discourse ("teach them 'keep everything . . .'") or purpose. The use of the correlative pron. ὅσα rather than the simple rel. pron. emphasizes the importance of keeping every single one of Jesus's commands. Ἐνετειλάμην 1st sg. aor. mid. indic. of ἐντέλλω, "command." The cstr. πάντα ὅσα with the 1st sg. form of ἐντέλλω seems to allude to texts like Exod 23:22; 25:22; 29:35; 31:11; 34:11, in which Yahweh speaks, or texts like Deut 6:2; 11:8, 13, 22; 12:11, 14; 13:18; 15:5; 27:1, 10; 28:15; 30:2, in which Moses speaks. Since a promise of enduring presence immediately follows (cf. Exod 23:20–26; 29:42–46) and the one embodying the divine presence bears his name (28:19; Exod 23:21), the former group of texts provides the most probable background. Ἰδού prompts attention to an important statement and heightens the climactic nature of the final declaration of the Gospel. The expression ἐγὼ μεθ' ὑμῶν εἰμι mirrors the explanation of the name Ἐμμανουήλ in 1:23 (μεθ' ἡμῶν ὁ θεός) and thus asserts Jesus's deity. Συντέλεια, -ας, ἡ, "completion."

FOR FURTHER STUDY

152. Jesus's Final Commissioning of His Disciples

Hubbard, B. J. *Matthean Redaction of a Primitive Apostolic Commissioning.* Society of Biblical Literature Dissertation Series 19. Missoula, MT: Society of Biblical Literature, 1974.

Keesmaat, S. C., and B. J. Walsh. "Some Reflections on the Ascension." *Theology* 95 (1992): 193–200.

Meier, J. P. "Nations or Gentiles in Matthew 28:19?" *CBQ* 39 (1977): 94–102.

Reeves, K. H. "They Worshipped Him, and They Doubted: Matthew 28.17." *BT* 49 (1998): 344–49.

Schaberg, J. *The Father, the Son and the Holy Spirit: The Triadic Phrase in Matthew 28:19b.* Society of Biblical Literature Dissertation Series 61. Chico, CA: Scholars Press, 1982.

Ulrich, D. W. "The Missional Audience of the Gospel of Matthew." *CBQ* 69 (2007): 64–83.

Viviano, B. T. "The Trinity in the Old Testament: From Daniel 7:13–14 to Matt 28:19." *Theologische Zeitschrift* 54 (1998): 193–209.

HOMILETICAL SUGGESTIONS

Raised to Rule! (28:16–20)

1. Jesus's resurrection inspires worship
2. Jesus's resurrection displays his authority
3. Jesus's resurrection demands obedience to his commission
4. Jesus's resurrection guarantees his enduring presence

Exegetical Outline

I. Introduction (1:1–4:16)
  A. Genealogy, Birth, and Childhood of Jesus (1:1–2:23)
     1. Title (1:1)
     2. Genealogy (1:2–17)
     3. Jesus's Birth (1:18–25)
     4. The Visit of the Magi (2:1–12)
     5. The Flight to Egypt (2:13–15)
     6. The Slaughter of the Children of Bethlehem (2:16–18)
     7. Herod's Death and the Return to Israel (2:19–23)
  B. Preparation for Jesus's Ministry (3:1–4:16)
     1. The Beginning of John's Ministry (3:1–6)
     2. John's Message (3:7–12)
     3. Jesus's Baptism by John (3:13–17)
     4. Jesus's Temptation in the Wilderness (4:1–11)
     5. Beginning of Jesus's Galilean Ministry (4:12–16)
II. Galilean Ministry (4:17–16:20)
  A. First Stage of Jesus's Galilean Ministry (4:17–25)
     1. Calling of First Disciples (4:17–22)
     2. Jesus's Teaching and Healing in Galilee (4:23–25)
  B. First Discourse: Sermon on the Mount (5:1–7:29)
     1. Introduction (5:1–16)
        a. Setting (5:1–2)
        b. Beatitudes (5:3–12)
        c. Salt and Light (5:13–16)
     2. Body of the Sermon (5:17–7:12)
        a. Teaching About the Law (5:17–20)
        b. Six Antitheses (5:21–48)
           i. First Antithesis: Murder (5:21–26)
           ii. Second Antithesis: Adultery (5:27–30)
           iii. Third Antithesis: Divorce (5:31–32)
           iv. Fourth Antithesis: Oaths (5:33–37)
           v. Fifth Antithesis: Retaliation (5:38–42)

355

    5. The Parable of the Two Sons (21:28–32)

    6. Parable of the Wicked Tenants (21:33–46)

    7. Parable of the Wedding Feast (22:1–14)

    8. Paying Taxes to Caesar (22:15–22)

    9. Question regarding Resurrection (22:23–33)

   10. The Greatest Commandment (22:34–40)

   11. The Messiah's Sonship (22:41–46)

B. Rebuke of the Pharisees and Abandonment of the Temple (23:1–39)

    1. Jesus's Denunciation of the Scribes and Pharisees (23:1–7)

    2. Jesus's Prohibition of Practices Encouraged by the Scribes and Pharisees (23:8–12)

    3. Woes Against the Scribes and Pharisees (23:13–33)

    4. Persecution of Jesus's Representatives by the Scribes and Pharisees (23:34–36)

    5. Lament over Jerusalem (23:37–39)

C. Fifth Discourse: The Fall of Jerusalem and the Coming Kingdom (24:1–25:46)

    1. Introduction to Olivet Discourse (24:1–3)

    2. The Initial Birth-Pangs Preceding the End (24:4–8)

    3. The Final Birth-Pangs Preceding the End (24:9–14)

    4. The Desolation of the Temple and Disciple's Escape (24:15–22)

    5. Distinguishing the Return of the True Messiah from the Rise of False Messiahs (24:23–28)

    6. The Coming of the Son of Man (24:29–31)

    7. The Parable of the Fig Tree (24:32–35)

    8. The Time and Circumstances of the Parousia (24:36–41)

    9. Command to Be Prepared (24:42–44)

   10. The Wise and the Foolish Servants (24:45–51)

   11. Parable of the Ten Virgins (25:1–13)

   12. Parable of the Talents (25:14–30)

   13. Judgment of the Nations (25:31–46)

D. Jesus's Passion (26:1–27:66)

    1. The Conspiracy Against Jesus (26:1–5)

    2. The Anointing at Bethany (26:6–13)

    3. Judas' Act of Treachery (26:14–16)

    4. Preparation for the Passover (26:17–19)

    5. Celebration of the Last Supper: Identifying the Betrayer (26:20–25)

    6. Celebration of the Last Supper: New Significance (26:26–30)

    7. Prophecy of Abandonment and Denial (26:31–35)

    8. Gethsemane (26:36–46)

    9. Jesus's Arrest (26:47–56)

   10. Trial by Sanhedrin (26:57–68)

   11. Peter's Three Denials (26:69–75)

Grammar Index

Scripture Index